“Victim of History”: Cardinal Mindszenty

A Biography

MARGIT BALOGH

"Victim of History": Cardinal Mindszenty

A Biography

The Catholic University of America Press
WASHINGTON, D.C.

This book was produced under the auspices
of the Research Centre for the Humanities of the Hungarian Academy of Sciences
and with the support of the Pallas Athene Innovation and Geopolitical Foundation

Translated by Andrew T. Gane
Proofreading by Gabriella Herczegh, Judit Hézser and Ian Kemp-Potter

The paper used in this publication meets the minimum requirements of American National Standards for Information Science—Permanence of Paper for Printed Library Materials, ANSI Z.

∞

Cataloging-in-Publication Data available from the Library of Congress
ISBN 978-0-8132-3494-6

CONTENTS

ABBREVIATIONS

AANY	Archives of the Archdiocese of New York
AAS	Acta Apostolicae Sedis
ÁBTL	Állambiztonsági Szolgálatok Történeti Levéltára [Historical Archives of the Hungarian State Security]
AGS	Archivio Generale dei Scolopi (Rome)
AMAE AD	Archives du Ministères des Affaires étrangères (Paris) Archives diplomatiques
ÁVH	Államvédelmi Hatóság (1948–56) [State Protection Authority]
ÁVO	Magyar Államrendőrség Államvédelmi Osztálya (1946–48) [Hungarian State Police State Protection Department]
AVP RF	Arkhiv Vneshney Politiki Rossiyskoy Federatsii [Archive of Foreign Policy of the Russian Federation]
CDPP	Christian Democratic People's Party
CL	Central Leadership
cf.	confer [put it together]
cs.	csomó [fascicle]
d.	doboz [box]
DPP	Democratic People's Party
f.	fons
fol.	folio

FRL	Ferences Rendtartomány Levéltára [Archive of Franciscan province]
GARF	Gosudarstvennyi Arkhiv Rossiyskoy Federatsii [State Archive of the Russian Federation]
GR	General Records
GyPL	Egyházmegyei Levéltár, Győr – püspökségi levéltár [Diocesan Archive, Győr: Episcopal Archive]
HAS	Hungarian Academy of Sciences
HCP	Hungarian Communist Party
HSWP	Hungarian Socialist Workers' Party
HWPP	Hungarian Working People's Party
KALOT	Katolikus Agrárifjúsági Legényegyletek Országos Testülete [Catholic Agrarian Youth League]
KFL	Kalocsai Főegyházmegyei Levéltár [Kalocsa Diocesan Archive]
KÜM	Külügyminisztérium [Hungarian Ministry of Foreign Affairs]
l.	list [page]
LÜ PO	Legfőbb Ügyészség Politikai Osztály [Office of the Prosecutor General, Political Department]
Mm.	Mindszenty magánlevéltár [Mindszenty private archive]
MMAL	Magyarországi Mindszenty Alapítvány Levéltára, Mindszenty Archívum [Archives of the Hungarian Mindszenty Foundation, Mindszenty Archives]
MNL	Magyar Nemzeti Levéltár [National Archives of Hungary]
MNL ZML	Magyar Nemzeti Levéltár Zala Megyei Levéltára [National Archives of Hungary of Zala County Archives]
MNM	Magyar Nemzeti Múzeum [Hungarian National Museum]
NARA	National Archives and Records Administration, College Park, Maryland
n.d.	no date
n.p.	no page

NSC	National Security Council
op.	opis [unpublished inventory of a fond, a list of delo (file)]
ÖStA, AdR, BMfAA	Österreichisches Staatsarchiv (Wien), Archiv der Republik, Bundesministerium für Auswärtige Angelegenheiten
ő.e.	őrzési egység [archival unit]
PC	Political Committee
PIL	Politikatörténeti és Szakszervezeti Levéltár [Political Historical and Trade Union Archive]
PMKL	Piarista Rend Magyar Tartományának Központi Levéltára [Central Archive of the Hungarian Province of the Piarist Order]
PL	Prímási Levéltár [Primatial Archives]
PPL	Pécsi Püspöki levéltár [Episcopal Archives of Pécs]
RGANI	Rossiiskii Gosudarstvennyi Arkhiv Noveishei Istorii [Russian State Archive of Contemporary History]
RGASPI	Rossiiskii Gosudarstvennyi Arkhiv Sotsial'no-politicheskoi Istorii [Russian State Archive of Socio-Political History]
SZEK	Szombathelyi Egyházmegyei Könyvtár [Szombathely Diocesan Library]
SZEL AC	Szombathelyi Egyházmegyei Levéltár Acta Cancellariae [Szombathely Diocesan Archive Acta Cancellariae]
SZTTI	Szociális Testvérek Társasága Történeti Irattára [Historical Archive of the Sisters of Social Service]
t.	tétel [item]
TÜK	Titkos Ügykezelés [Classified Information Management]
VÉL	Veszprémi Érseki és Főkáptalani Levéltár [Veszprém Archbishop's and Principal Chapter's Archive]
ZML	Zala Megyei Levéltár [Zala County Archives]
ZMMPI	Zalaegerszegi Mária Magdolna Plébánia Irattára [Archive of the Parish Church of Mária Magdolna, Zalaegerszeg]

"I shall keep on fighting... until the coffin closes above me."

(József Mindszenty, Csorna, June 15, 1946)

INTRODUCTION

"Victim of history," "martyr from behind the Iron Curtain," "a stubborn old man," "the Hungarian Gandhi" – these are just some of the epithets which, depending on personal temperament and sympathies, people used to describe Cardinal Mindszenty, the head of the Catholic Church in Hungary at the time of the communist takeover in 1948. Which of these epithets is closest to reality? The nuanced explanation calls for a long book analyzing the complexity of the Soviet system in Eastern Europe, this is the monograph you are holding in your hand. By now Mindszenty has been forgotten in most countries but Hungary. At the time of his death in 1975, he was known all over the world as a symbol of the struggle of the Catholic Church against Communism. In the United States numerous schools and streets were named after Mindszenty and US presidents from Eisenhower to Nixon had to deal with the cardinal.

He held the post of archbishop of Esztergom (Hungary) – and the accompanying status of primate – from 1945 until 1974, but during this period of almost three decades he served barely four years in office. The political police (Államvédelmi Hatóság [ÁVH], in English: State Protection Authority) arrested him on December 26, 1948, and the Budapest People's Court subsequently sentenced him to life imprisonment. One of the accusations against Mindszenty, based on the Stalinist belief in conspiracies, was his attempt to re-establish Habsburg rule in Hungary by referring to the cardinal's legitimist leanings and his contacts with Otto von Habsburg. This political conflict between the Communist Party and the Catholic Church in Hungary also had a much lesser known aspect: it was closely related to a struggle for the interpretation of the role of Catholicism in Hungarian history. TIME Magazine made Mindszenty "Man of the Year" in 1949. One year later, in 1950, Hollywood produced the movie "Guilty of Treason" with Charles Bickford starring as Mindszenty. Made in the Cold War era, the film imaginatively portrayed the brutal abuse of prisoners held by the communist regime. Five years later, Alec Guinness played the role of the cardinal in Peter Glenville's movie "The Prisoner."

Mindszenty regained freedom during the 1956 revolution but only for several days. He was granted asylum by the US Embassy in Budapest from November 4, 1956 to September 28, 1971. When Pope Paul VI received the Hungarian foreign minister in 1971, he called Mindszenty "the victim of history". His last years were spent free at last, but far away from his homeland. Between 1971 and 1975 he traveled a lot, visited Hungarian minorities and also non-Hungarian Catholic organizations as well as persons who identified themselves with the anticommunist fight. He traveled throughout Western European countries and visited the United States, Canada, South America, Africa and Australia. His story got wide publicity in 1974, when his memoirs were published in Frankfurt. The book proved to be one of those works that cracked the monolithic communist ideological bloc with their messages.

During his life he launched and set in motion numerous initiatives, while also being compelled to find his place – and that of his church – in a world of frequent changes. In the 15 years he spent at the American diplomatic mission in Budapest enormous changes took place in the world while his personality remained frozen into the past. When in 1971 he left the US embassy in Budapest for Rome, both Eastern and Western media looked at him as a relic of the past: Mindszenty did not fit into the spirit of the *détente* and *Ostpolitik*. During the "second Cold War" of the 1980s Mindszenty could be of political use again as a symbol of the most likely never-ending struggle against "the empire of evil". On the 10th anniversary of Mindszenty's death in 1985 Ronald Reagan described him as "one of those rare human beings, who became a living symbol of courage and faith within his own lifetime." On May 3, 1991, Cardinal Mindszenty's ashes were brought to Hungary in a veritable march of triumph. The criminal proceedings launched against József Mindszenty in 1949 were proclaimed null and void by the Supreme Court of Hungary in March 2012. His beatification is in progress: On February 13, 2019 Pope Francis approved the resolution declaring that "Servant of God," Cardinal József Mindszenty, archbishop of Esztergom, late primate of Hungary, had cultivated the Christian virtues on a heroic level. Venerators of the cardinal are waiting eagerly for his beatification.

The exceptional life story left an indelible mark on 20th-century Hungarian history. Even today his name resonates and is a major buzzword: a plebeian conservative and rather nationalistic prelate, a man with a historical mission who was unwaveringly opposed to the Nazis and who regularly clashed with the dictatorships, becoming both one of the persecuted under communism and a principal victim of diplomatic efforts to placate communism. The appraisal of Mindszenty has varied from uncritical adulation to stigmatizing diabolization. Unsurprisingly, the latter template has its antithesis: the collective memory of the Hungarian émigré population and – in recent years – the domestic Catholic community has been dominated by the impression of a martyr leader, attributing to Mindszenty no less than a glorified life. His views have been integrated into the national ideology of conservative and right-wing intellectuals, while leftist and liberal intellectuals seek to add nuance to the one-sided and false perceptions of earlier periods. In the discourse on memory policy, the least divisive stance would be one that portrays Mindszenty as a contradictory actor in a very complex story rather than as the hero or anti-hero of a national drama. In this way he could be depicted as someone of impeccable morals who nevertheless committed grave errors, an exemplary albeit occasionally inconsistent figure.

Over the years many books have been published on Mindszenty. Other than in Hungarian, the greatest number of works have been published in German, English, French and Italian, and there are even works on Mindszenty in Arabic. The first wave of books on the Hungarian prelate came shortly after his show trial or in the ensuing years. Unsurprisingly, the works published in Hungary under Communism served the purpose of justifying the prosecution of Mindszenty. In contrast, publications abroad focused on the injustices of the court case brought against him. Hungarian political pamphlets portrayed Mindszenty as nothing other than an American stooge and a fascist cleric. This characterization did not change even after 1956. Except for some ideological-propagandist works, nothing was published about Mindszenty in Hungary for decades. It is only natural that the available analyses polemicize with each other on several issues. The "spirit of Helsinki," the East-West Conference for Security and Cooperation in Europe however, brought a fresh breeze into the world of academia, which was still subordinated to party political goals. In the 1980s the established "template" on Mindszenty underwent a degree of refinement, but Hungarian historians were still not in a position to break free from the schematic and one-dimensional portrayal of the past. It was only on the eve of the collapse of communism that some free-thinking historians could attempt to give a more nuanced picture. The real breakthrough has come only in recent years, thanks in large part to Ádám Somorjai's primary source publications, which focuses on the final third of Mindszenty's life: the period between 1956–1975.

This present work is based on research conducted over the past decade and a half. The contents comprise my findings and conclusions based on material drawn from thirty-eight archives in Hungary and twenty archives elsewhere. In Hungary, abundant archival sources are found at the National Archives of Hungary, the Esztergom Primatial Archives, and the Archives of the Diocese of Szombathely. In the United States, the principal relevant archives and libraries are the National Archives and Records Administration (NARA) and the various presidential libraries (the Truman, Eisenhower, Kennedy, Johnson and Nixon Libraries). With a view to reconstructing the background connections and contemporary perceptions, I also examined the diplomatic reports of various countries, in particular many of the reports submitted to their home governments by the Austrian, British, Czechoslovak, French, Italian, and United States ambassadors/envoys to Hungary and to the Holy See, as well as the reports of the special US presidential envoy to the Vatican. For several decades Hungary lay in the Soviet sphere of interest, and so an analysis of Russian sources is also crucial. Although accessibility to those sources has improved during the past two decades, progress still needs to be made in terms of the ease of research. A welcome development is the publication in Moscow of several primary document collections, which include documents about the situation of the Churches in Hungary, albeit few of these documents relate directly to Mindszenty.

Today there are only two groups of archives with relevant documents concerning the Mindszenty affair that remain to be researched. These are the Vatican's archives and the KGB archive(s). Of these, one of the most fascinating for future researchers will doubtless be the Archivio Storico della Seconda Sezione (dei Rapporti con gli Stati) della Segreteria di Stato [Historical Archive of the Second Section of the Secretariat of State], which contains the documents of the former Congregation of Extraordinary Ecclesiastical Affairs and the Council for the Public Affairs of the Church. The papers of Agostino Cardinal Casaroli, who influenced for decades the Vatican's policy towards the communist countries, have also been brought to this archive from Parma. Access to these documents is eagerly awaited by historians, because a selection of them have already been published by Giovanni Barberini in *La politica del dialogo: Le carte Casaroli sull'Ostpolitik vaticana* (The policy of dialogue: Casaroli's documents on the Vatican's Eastern policy), but there remain many sources to be researched. Further fact-finding will of course require work in other archives too: for example, in the currently inaccessible archive of Cardinal Franz König, archbishop of Vienna (from 1956 to 1985). When all these sources become accessible, we will gain a clearer picture of many historical events and developments that are still shrouded in mystery and it will be easier to fathom the motives of Vatican decision-makers.

As regards the research work, it is wise to recognize that results depend not only on the enthusiasm and diligence of the researcher but also on the funding opportunities. For this reason, I am sincerely indebted to the Hungarian Academy of Sciences for providing support and assistance towards obtaining funding for, among other things, this English translation, which is to be published in the United States. I also offer my sincere gratitude to the colleagues and friends who assisted me in my work.

*

My immodest aim is to portray the events realistically, to provide an interesting yet documented account of the life of József Mindszenty – one that reveals the personality of the man with all his doubts and with all his certainties. Bringing the reader closer to the person of Mindszenty is often a more difficult task than that of revealing the cleric or the politician. In his public role, Mindszenty seems never to have been driven by his own individual interest. In his person there was a complete fusion of the public and private interests. Even so, his human character as an individual determined the manner in which he sought to achieve public goals. My purpose in writing this book has been to illuminate the factors that lay behind the human struggles, to dispel the myths and the stereotypes, and to reveal the driving forces and true contours of events.

It is no simple task to identify the principal milestones in the life of a man who witnessed – and participated in – such a great number of momentous events. Possibly, an even greater challenge is how to distinguish the facts from the propaganda slogans and delusions. My portrait is of a pensive man who sometimes made mistakes, who struggled with everyday problems, and whose destiny was sealed by exceptional historical circumstances. The picture I draw is neither that of an unbending and infallible man nor that of a bigoted and obstinate prelate. There is no denying that József Mindszenty was a controversial and polarizing figure. As so often, the truth lies between the two extremes. Still, whether one accepts or rejects him, the moral example set by József Mindszenty through his implacable opposition to dictatorship must be acknowledged. Regardless of our perceptions of him, we recognize that the story of his life exceeds the confines of a private biography. Indeed, a survey of his life-story represents a good opportunity to ask ourselves what it meant to be a Christian (and not just a Catholic Christian) in 20th-century Hungary. In appraising his life, we may also seek to identify Christianity's message to the world today – a message that transcends ideological differences.

Budapest, May 1, 2021
The author

CHAPTER 1

SCHOOL PHOTOGRAPH (1911)

CHAPTER 1

Writer, Soldier or Priest?

CHILDHOOD – FASCINATED BY HEROES AND SAINTS

József Mindszenty was born as József Pehm in the village of Mindszent (Vas County, Hungary) on March 29, 1892. He changed his surname to Mindszenty in 1942. Mindszent (meaning All Saints) is an ancient Hungarian settlement that was first mentioned in 1314. The name of the village was taken from the former All Saints' Church in the parish. The village lies in the western part of Transdanubia; traveling by horse carriage it lay one hour from Vasvár and two hours from Zalaegerszeg. The present-day village still has just one street and a small baroque church. The number of inhabitants has fallen from around a thousand a century ago to barely four hundred today.

Family

József Pehm's parents, who were married in 1891, worked in viticulture and farming. János Pehm (1864–1946), József's father, was a highly respected burgher and a local magistrate who served, for four decades, as chairman of the local parish and of the Catholic school board. Subsequently – and until his death – he served as forest master. In 1733, an ancestor, András Pehm, had received a noble title from King Charles III of Hungary (Charles

VI, Holy Roman emperor) as a reward for valor shown against the Ottomans.[1] József Pehm's mother, Borbála Kovács (1875–1960), was orphaned as a child and married his father at the young age of seventeen. Her ancestors had been ennobled in 1663.[2] Ennoblement had not been accompanied automatically by a higher economic or occupational status. Indeed, the family's noble ancestors included a craftsman, a farmer, a head shepherd, and a farmer with four oxen. Other ancestors, however, had been learned men: a grand provost, a parish priest, a state official, a military officer, and a judge at the Hungarian Royal Court. Evidently, Austrians/Germans were also to be found among the father's ancestors (the surname 'Pehm' is an Austrian-Bavarian variant of 'Böhm,' meaning Bohemian), but József Pehm always proudly identified himself and his family as Hungarian.

János Pehm and Borbála Kovács had six children, with József being the firstborn. Two of his siblings lived to be adults, namely his sisters Anna and Teréz, both of whom were widowed at a young age. The two sisters kept in contact with József Mindszenty even during the decade and a half he spent at the US Legation. József's childhood years were a time of hard work. As was the norm among the rural population, he helped in the poultry yard, watched over the geese, took the cows to pasture, collected brushwood, chopped wood, laid the fire, sowed seeds, weeded the garden, harvested grapes, and picked fruit. In the time that remained he attended school. His stubbornness and persistence seem to have been inherited from his quiet and sensible mother, a determined woman who boldly faced difficulties and gave József a God-fearing, virtuous and loving upbringing.

While his mother nurtured the family at home, his father worked outdoors, cultivating a two-acre vineyard as well as ten hectares of cropland. József received from his father the first lessons in public life: organizing public works and road construction, giving support to the widows, orphans and domestic maids, protecting the crops, collecting taxes, managing

1. Prímási Levéltár [Primatial Archives] (hereafter: PL) Processus Josephi Card. Mindszenty (hereafter: Processus), V–700/32. 92. fol. The patent of nobility in Latin of András Pehm, secretary of the Locotenetial Council, Vienna, January 12, 1733 (facsimile).

2. "Sváb-e a hercegprímás?" [Is the Prince Primate Swabian?], *A Szív* [The Heart] 31, no. 33 (1946): 2; PL Processus, V–700/1. 119. fol. Minutes of interrogation of the suspect József Mindszenty, Budapest, January 11, 1949. In the document the surname *Pehm* is written in various forms: *Pehm*, *Péhm*, *Phem* and *Pem*.

municipal property and the property of the local ownership association, and dealing with loungers. József's father was a broadminded man of integrity who worked tirelessly and resolutely. He was a severe but just man who, uncharacteristically for a farmer, was well-read. He would often tell his son stories about glorious achievements of the past, wise statesmen, and heroes who had sacrificed their lives for the country. But he also told him of traitors and mutinous factions. Through the telling of bedtime stories, he familiarized his son with the lives and deeds of the Hunyadi brothers, Pál Kinizsi, and the Zrínyi family. József Mindszenty's Hungarian and Christian identity was rooted in his native village and in his family.

The Premonstratensian Student

József was barely 10 years old when his parents determined his fate. After five years at elementary school, they decided that József should continue his studies rather than work on the family's land. (As the firstborn son, he would generally have been expected to help his father on the land.) The resolve of the parents testifies to their ambitions for their son, but we also know that their decision was influenced by the village cantor and teacher, in whose opinion József was an intelligent boy. Furthermore, there were the examples in József's own family – the relatives who had risen to be provosts or high-ranking military officers and whose life-stories proved that ditching the agrarian life was not always an impossible dream. The decision to keep József in school imposed, however, a hefty burden on the parents. Tuition fees had to be paid – at least during the initial years and until he merited a scholarship. For the parents this meant more work and sacrifice. Their hopes for József seem to have wavered only once – on the unexpected death of their younger son, who had been expected to cultivate the family-owned land. Indeed, at that time Pehm senior considered removing József from grammar school, but his wife insisted that their son continue his education. In this way the task of cultivating the fields was left to József's sisters.

In 1903 a pubescent József Pehm embarked on his first major journey away from his native village, registering as a pupil at the Royal Catholic Grammar School in Szombathely. The school was run by the Premonstratensian Order. The boy from the dusty and muddy village was greatly impressed by Szombathely, a college town of some thirty thousand inhabitants, with paved roads, squares, parks, ancient churches, a marble cathedral, and a huge grammar school that looked more like a palace. József's years in Szombathely would greatly influence his spirit, his intellect and his chosen path in life.

In accordance with the contemporary custom, József took board and lodging with a Szombathely family. In his first year at grammar school, he had around eighty classmates; most of the boys came from intellectual, artisan or trading families. Having previously attended a rural elementary school with a single teacher and just one class, József must have found it difficult to adjust to life at an urban grammar school and to overcome his feelings of inferiority and his lack of city manners. It could not have been easy for him to make the grades. As his mother later recalled: "Once he asked me whether someone who went to school but who failed to make the grades would immediately be sent down. I told him that this would not happen [...] as the pupil would be given another chance to improve his grades, which, however, would require hard study, as there was no other way. [...] I also used to tell him to make sure he didn't fail, because when upper-class children failed, they would simply retake the test, but if a peasant boy failed, he would be laughed at and mocked."[3] In his memoirs, Mindszenty admitted that it had taken him several years to overcome his disadvantage and catch up with the better educated city boys.

The school report card of József Pehm reveals a hardworking and enthusiastic student without particular talent. In the lower grades, his results were merely average, and so there was no question of a tuition fee exemption. By the fifth grade, however, his results were good or excellent in all subjects other than Greek language, arithmetic and physical education (in these subjects, the result was "satisfactory"). In the sixth grade, he received good or excellent results in every subject. In Hungarian and in history, he received excellent results from the second grade onwards.[4] The strict academic approach of the grammar school suited József Pehm's natural inclination towards discipline, stamina and order. When his

3. Szociális Testvérek Társasága Történeti Irattára [Historical Archive of the Sisters of Social Service] (hereafter: SZTTTI) 1241/96. Conversation with the primate's mother, February 21, 1949.

4. Lajos Kuntár, "Mindszenty József szombathelyi diákévei", *Vasi Honismereti Közlemények* [Vas County's Publications of Homeland Knowledge] 19, no. 1 (1992): 7–16.

strength of will was tried and tested, the results were plain to see. On completion of the seventh grade, he and two other boys received the grammar school's highest award, a prize of one gold coin. By this time, he had become one of the best pupils in his class.[5] A year later, he spoke on behalf of his fellow school leavers at the school's graduation ceremony.

During the eight years of grammar school, more than a half of the original eighty classmates dropped out, and József Pehm was the only peasant farmer's son to complete his education. In his final year at school, József received excellent results in all subjects other than Physics, for which he received a good result. It was not difficult for him to answer the question of "what to do next": in line with parental expectations and owing to his reading and his studies, he felt a priestly calling.

IN A CASSOCK

In the fall of 1911, having completed his grammar school education, the young Pehm began his theological studies at the Szombathely Seminary. He made good progress at the seminary, receiving mostly "eminent" results.[6] Pehm grew to be loved by his tutors and superiors, who deepened his commitment to the priestly calling. He was convinced that there could be no greater happiness than to explain to the people the commandments, the virtues, and the corporal and spiritual works of mercy (the Beatitudes), and to dispense the sacraments.

Studies

The diligent student soon caught the attention of Count János Mikes, bishop of Szombathely. Mikes was greatly impressed by Pehm's fervor for the priesthood and the reverent manner with which he wore the cassock, the symbol of the priesthood and service to Christ. Therefore, when Pehm completed his first year at the seminary, Bishop Mikes expressed a wish to send him to the prestigious Collegium Pazmanianum (est. 1623) in

5. Kelemen Kárpáti, ed., *A Szombathelyi Kir. Katholikus Főgimnázium Értesítője 1909–1910* (Szombathely: Egyházmegyei Könyvnyomda, 1910), 68, 82.

6. István Mészáros, "Mindszenty és Vas megye", *Vasi Szemle* [Vas County Review] 49, no. 3 (1995): 323.

Vienna for the purpose of further study at the Faculty of Theology of the University of Vienna.[7]

József Pehm, however, chose not to avail himself of this opportunity. (It was only in 1947 – that is, almost four decades later – that he made his first visit to the Collegium Pazmanianum, as the archbishop of Esztergom. Ironically, he would spend his final years there, from 1971 to 1975.) Feelings of inferiority, against which he had struggled throughout his time at grammar school, still lurked within him, and the challenge of studying in Vienna seemed perhaps too great. Engaging in a little bit of mythmaking, some commentators have argued that his decision to stay in Hungary reflected a desire to serve as a village priest in place of an ecclesiastical career. At any rate, Pehm's decision surprised Mikes, who viewed the chance to study in Vienna as a privilege of the talented and as an opportunity to learn languages and acquire knowledge of the world – which would have benefited even a traditional priestly career.

Pehm thus remained at the Szombathely Seminary, where, since 1861, the Association of Saint Augustine had been offering the seminarians tuition in the Hungarian language and patriotism, while developing their intellectual knowledge and their verbal and written skills. Papers submitted anonymously to the contests of the school of religious literature were judged by a panel of students and teachers, with the accepted papers then being published in yearbooks entitled *Munkálatok* (Works). In his very first year as a seminarian, József Pehm authored eight treatises, a translation, a description of nature, and a poem. His treatises show that he was becoming increasingly well-read and discovering new ideals in life. The subjects touched upon included dogmatic theology, asceticism, homiletics, the history of literature, history, and social issues. For his critics, the most successful work was a biography of the legendary Irish liberation hero and political campaigner, Daniel O'Connell (1775–1847): "Although the author's handwriting is very difficult to read, we nevertheless enjoyed reading his work. He endears O.'s character to the reader. He presents him as a spokesman, a popular leader and a statesman. [...] The author deserves our appreciation and praise, and we ask him to enrichen our Association by writing similar works. [...] We also

7. Szombathelyi Egyházmegyei Levéltár Acta Cancellariae [Szombathely Diocesan Archive Acta Cancellariae] (hereafter: SZEL AC) 5305–07/1912. Bishop János Mikes's letter to the seminarian József Pehm, Szombathely, September 16, 1912.

request him not to commit further atrocities against the eyes of his critics and that he should write more legibly."[8] These words concluded the review. It is certainly true that József Pehm's rather spidery handwriting is barely legible. The chosen subject matter indicates how the young seminarian, who was barely 20 years of age, was looking for role models: in O'Connell he had found a charismatic figure, a hero of Irish constitutional nationalism and a campaigner for Irish liberation. The essay also reveals that, in the young Pehm's value system, nationalism was the synopsis of the religious idea, spirituality (faith and knowledge, morality and education), popular identity and human feeling.

It was during this period that József Pehm wrote his first and last poetic work. The poem *Indulóra* (To the March) is quite simply an agitation rhyme composed in adolescent fervor against the faith-denying movements of the era (liberalism, freemasonry, and social democracy – referred to in the poem as the "triple enemy") and popularizing a league founded to strengthen Catholic awareness and identity.[9] The poem received withering criticism, and the critics agreed to its publication "in the happy hope" that the author "shall refrain in the future from seeking to endear himself to us by means of such verses." At the time, no-one took exception to the nationalist and anti-Judaic view of history that is presented in the poem. In the world of ideas, it would seem that the young Pehm had already been affected by the new antisemitism of the turn of the century, which attributed liberalism, freemasonry and social democracy to "Jewish influence."

Pehm's translation skills were also rather weak, as noted by the critics of his submission *Aranyszájú Szent János magyarázatai Szent Péter apostol leveleihez* (Saint John Chrysostom's explanations of the Epistles of Saint Peter the Apostle): "The translated text is short, and the translation is not always in good Hungarian; there are some strange expressions and in several places he failed to give a faithful rendering of the text. The last two pages are completely unconnected to the translation, and it seems he wrote them merely with a view to writing something, so the two pages would not be empty."[10] Still, the critics praised his devotion to the matter and his zeal.

8. Szombathelyi Egyházmegyei Könyvtár [Szombathely Diocesan Library] (hereafter: SZEK). Works of the Saint Augustine Association, 1911–12. Critique of the 34th entry.

9. Ibid., 31st entry.

10. Ibid., 12th entry.

As a second-year seminarian, Pehm received praises for a paper entitled *A világ ura és az utópiák* (The master of this world and the utopias). He reviewed the literature published on utopia from classical antiquity until his own era, doing so – according to his critics – in an entertaining style. The main issue in Pehm's work is whether the world venerates Christ or Belial. This question would accompany him throughout his career. Indeed, he was to experience almost his whole life as a battle against the Antichrist and against Evil, made topically manifest by the attempts of Hitler and Stalin to achieve world dominion. As a third-year seminarian, he won an award for his article entitled *Szent Márton lelkipásztorkodásának korszerűsége* (The topicality of Saint Martin's pastoral work). According to his reviewers, Pehm offered an excellent analysis of religious, spiritual and cultural needs in the fourth century A.D. and of the coming together of the Gallic provinces and the teachings of Christ. The subject matters chosen by Pehm prove his attraction to the history of the early centuries and his enthusiasm, even as a young man, for the idea of being a warrior for Christ.

In the final two years of his studies in theology, World War I was already raging. Szombathely accommodated many of the war-wounded. Bread, lard and sugar vanished from local stores, and life for the town's inhabitants became increasingly difficult. The period also saw the arrival in the town of the hyenas of war – the speculative military operators, the smugglers and the usurers. The seminarians watched closely as the events unfolded: the war, they believed, revealed man's true nature. It turned everything upside down, thereby weakening people's faith and strengthening secularism and opposition to the Church. The task of a priest was to fight for those who were wavering, to act as a guardian to the weak, and to console the mourners. On completion of his studies, József Pehm had become convinced that a priest should offer guidance amid the social and ideological confusion, doing so by way of personal example and through preaching.

In his final examinations as a seminarian, József Pehm received an excellent result.[11] On June 12, 1915, he was ordained at Szombathely Cathedral by the diocesan bishop, Count János Mikes. Originally, Pehm had wanted to celebrate his first Mass at the same cathedral, far from his

11. SZEL AC 2567/1915. Ratings of the teachers and students of the Szombathely Seminary, June 8, 1915.

childhood acquaintances and relatives. His mother, however, insisted that he come to their village. And so, to the great pride and satisfaction of his parents, and in the presence of his relatives and the local villagers, he offered his first Mass in the church where he had been christened.

Curate, Catechist, and Counter-Revolutionary

Bishop Mikes assigned the young József Pehm to the village of Felsőpaty alongside the River Rába, where, as curate and catechist, he assisted the local parish priest, a man named Béla Geiszlinger (1876–1948). Pehm remained in this post until February 1, 1917.

His tasks required him to walk for several hours each day. As catechist, he had to visit all the local schools twice a week, and his parochial tasks included giving sermons, dispensing the sacraments, visiting the sick, and taking funerals. In addition, he tended to the spiritual needs of the mainly Russian, Italian, Romanian, and French-speaking men at the local prisoner-of-war camp. From the outset, he was considered a strict priest who rigorously adhered to and enforced church rules. On more than one occasion he shamed, with his sharp remarks, villagers who cursed or who failed to attend church services. In a clear sign of his detachment, the people of Felsőpaty used to say that when Pehm wanted to smile he would "go to the attic." Geiszlinger noted Pehm's combative approach and his lack of empathy for his parishioners, who "feared him, in spite of his young age, more than their parish priest."[12]

In 1916, during his curacy at Felsőpaty, József Pehm published his first scholarly work: *Az édesanya a vallás, társadalmi kérdés és költészet tükrében* (The mother as reflected in religion, social issues and poetry). The book, which bears witness to substantial knowledge of world literature and art history, was published in two editions in a single year, with all copies being sold. Years later, Pehm continued to receive congratulatory messages from readers of the book. The ideas contained in the book had been mulled over for some time. Indeed, Pehm had first written on the subject as part of an assignment at grammar school. Then, as a 20-year-old seminarian, he had

12. SZEK ős. XXVIII/alsó II. Emlékezések: Recollections of Károly Arany, former head of the Zalaegerszeg printers, sheet III/c.

submitted a 100-page essay on the topic in a contest run by the Saint Augustine Association, receiving a gold prize and a critical review in support of publication.[13]

On February 1, 1917, Bishop Mikes unexpectedly appointed József Pehm as religious education teacher at the Royal Hungarian State Grammar School in Zalaegerszeg.[14] At the time, Zalaegerszeg was a typical small town of government officials and artisans with a total population of barely 13,000. Albeit a county center and the "capital" of the Göcsej region, Zalaegerszeg was rather isolated from the vibrant heart of the nation and the cultural and economic centers, in part because there was no direct rail connection to Budapest. Catholics comprised a majority in its urban society, which tended to be inward-looking and insular. Moreover, the town's leaders were very conservative and mostly of gentry stock. The town had only few landmarks: the main church, county hall, the grammar school, the gendarme barracks, the cavalry barracks, and the Golden Lamb Hotel, the latter being the major local venue for cultural and community life. According to the census of 1920, the population comprised 10,744 Catholics, 1,657 Jews, 405 Calvinists, and 330 Lutherans. In addition, there were very small numbers of Greek Orthodox, Greek Catholics (Uniate), and Unitarians. For almost three decades, this "sleepy, dusty town" in western Hungary was the home of József Pehm. Zalaegerszeg was to play a profound and definitive role in his life, just as he too left an indelible mark on the town.

After his appointment, József Pehm took the secondary teaching examinations for religious instruction. In the seven subjects, he received good marks in five and excellent marks in two ("Ethics" and "Education and Teaching").[15] As some of the teaching staff had been drafted into military service, he was required not only to teach religious education but also – in the 1917–1918 school year – to serve as a form-master and teach Latin. Sometimes he would even cane the boys, a typical form of school discipline at the time. A former pupil evoked the atmosphere in his lessons as follows: "He brought military discipline to the pastoral care of children. He did not really understand the language of children, but rather aroused their

13. Mária Dobri, "'...szívélyesen üdvözöl barátod és híved...' Pehm (Mindszenty) József és Géfin Gyula barátságáról," *Vasi Szemle,* 49, no. 2 (1995): 275.

14. SZEL AC 209/1917. Dispositio.

15. SZEL AC 3219/1917. József Pehm's catechist exam.

fears by dint of his rather suggestive personality."[16] He disliked new things, prohibiting his pupils from going to movie theaters and discouraging them from reading color magazines and partaking in harmful behaviors. His pupils were required to study diligently. A critical pupil recalled the following: "He was cold and unapproachable towards all his pupils. He showed no interest in school outings, the traditional May Day picnics or other school events where direct contact with his pupils would have been possible. He never took part in such events. In his contact with non-Catholic pupils (e.g., when substituting for other teachers), he ignored them in an offensive manner. It was as though they were non-existent; he did not even notice them."[17]

The Religious Education teacher József Pehm got involved in urban public life: he was elected to the supervisory board of the credit union and to the municipal council. On public holidays he often gave celebratory speeches that were well received. Meanwhile world historical events were at a turning point. The war had destroyed not only Russian czarism but also the Austro-Hungarian Monarchy. The loss of the war and the radicalization of the various national groups had resulted in the break-up of the centuries-old Habsburg Empire. In Hungary the Autumn Rose Revolution was triumphant on October 31, 1918, and several weeks later a people's republic was proclaimed.

The winds of change soon reached the County of Zala, and when national elections were proclaimed for early 1919 the political parties began preparing for the coming skirmishes. At the time, the Christian Social People's Party, a party representing political Catholicism, formed the main opposition to the governing coalition of liberals, radicals and social democrats, which was led by Count Mihály Károlyi (1875–1955), the president of the Republic. It was in the Christian Social People's Party that József Pehm found his first opportunities to take on a role in public life and politics. Acting on behalf of the party, he spoke out in favor of the monarchy as the only legitimate form of government in Hungary in the media, at public and town hall meetings, and in the county assemblies.

16. Imre András, ed., *Kerkai Jenő emlékezete* (Budapest: Egyházszociológiai Intézet, 1995), 22–23.

17. Politikatörténeti és Szakszervezeti Levéltár [Political Historical and Trade Union Archive] (hereafter: PIL) 274. f. [fons] 7/249. 1. fol.

Pehm sensed the opportunities presented by mass communication and argued that journalism could be a most effective pastoral tool. At Christmas 1918, with a view to suppressing the "contagious ideas" of the leftists, he launched a conservative-legitimist weekly entitled *Zalamegyei Ujság* (Zala County Newspaper). Reflecting the political confusion of the period, only a few editions of the newspaper were published initially. József Pehm's career in public life was soon brought to a halt by the authorities: on March 9, 1919, he was detained in Szombathely on suspicion of counter-revolutionary incitement. He was placed under house arrest at the Bishop's Palace in the town. A pretext for his arrest was not really needed: Pehm had refused to sign the oath of allegiance to the republic; he had become involved in counter-revolutionary activities in western Hungary; and in a newspaper article he had cast doubt on the legitimacy of the transfer of the rights of royal patronage (of the apostolic king) to the new popular government.[18]

In a rather lenient manner, two police sergeants guarded the "dangerous enemy." On March 21, the government of the country in Budapest passed into the hands of the Revolutionary Councils Republic. Two months later, Pehm was transferred from Szombathely to Zalaegerszeg, where he was allowed to reside freely on condition that he refrain from agitation.[19] The leaders of the commune evidently had other matters on their mind and no time to bother about a priest. Pehm, however, proceeded to converse with "suspicious elements," and so, on May 20, he was branded an "incorrigible element" and deported from Zala County.[20] He was then required to appear daily before the workers' council in his native village, which the authorities

18. *Zalamegyei Ujság* 2, no. 9, February 22, 1919, in SZEL Mikes János püspök iratai [Documents of Bishop János Mikes] III.1. j. 3. d.

19. PL Mindszenty magánlevéltár [Mindszenty private archive] (hereafter: Mm.) 17. d. [doboz = box] Envelope "1943–45." Letter of Károly Briglevics, former prefect and government commissioner of Zala County to Márkus Erdős, "plenipotentiary political representative." Zalaegerszeg, May 15, 1919.

20. Concerning all of this, József Pehm himself made a statement at Zalaegerszeg Court: "I was interned in Szombathely already at the time of the Károlyi government. After the outbreak of communism, I was detained in the same place. On May 19, I was transferred to Zalaegerszeg, where I was freed by Márkus Erdős, but the next day he called me in again and interned me at my place of residence, Csehimindszent, instructing me that I should report to the workers' council there twice a day." Magyar Nemzeti Levéltár [National Archives of Hungary] (hereafter: MNL) Zala Megyei Levéltár [Zala County Archives] (hereafter: ZML) VII. 2. Papers of Zalaegerszeg Court, Criminal (Political) special bundles, 1920–44, 7. d. 991/1920. Minutes, Zalaegerszeg, June 2, 1920.

had designated as his permanent place of residence.[21] In this way Pehm spent the remaining days of the proletarian dictatorship at the parental home. Only after the passing of the revolutionary storm could he return to Zalaegerszeg on August 3.

His first church sermons after his return were fairly moderate in tone. For instance, on Saint Stephen's Day (August 20), he preached in a sermon about the need to reestablish social peace on the basis of Jesus' commandment to love. A few weeks later, however, Pehm's tone had changed and he spared no details: "Károlyi and his associates are guilty of the abominations of communism," "[we have seen] torrents of blood and the gallows," "the deluded poor are still poor, but the Jewish commissars have become loaded... with money."[22] Revolutions were the "monster offspring of liberalism and social democracy," while the press was the "source of all filth."[23] The young parish priest's memory of the revolutions could only be negative; for him there had been nothing uplifting in their drama. As József Pehm saw it, the bourgeois popular republic and the Bolshevik commune constituted an integral whole in terms of the harm caused, with millions of Hungarians being pushed into minority status by the Treaty of Trianon. He could not accept that the departure and – in a symbolic sense – burial of the historical elite meant that there had been no alternative in the fall of 1918.

Pehm applauded heartily when a national army led by Miklós Horthy de Nagybánya, one-time rear admiral of the Austro-Hungarian navy, marched into Budapest on November 16, 1919. At Pehm's parish church in Zalaegerszeg, Horthy, the country's elected regent, was portrayed as the man who would restore the nation's self-esteem and serve as a model for all Hungarians. Meanwhile Horthy's army became an object of pride and a signal of hope for the fulfillment of revisionist desires. Yet, just as Pehm had become disillusioned with the "red baron," Mihály Károlyi, so also he rapidly distanced himself from Regent Miklós Horthy. He considered the former to have destroyed the monarchy and the latter to have betrayed the anointed king.

21. MNL Vas Megyei Levéltára [Vas County Archives] 3129/D/1919. Vas County Directory to Csehimindszent Village Council. Szombathely, May 24, 1919. See György Feiszt, "Mindszenty a direktórium túsza," *Vasi Honismereti Közlemények* 19, no. 1 (1992): 18.

22. PL Mm. 32. d. Draft sermons: Pacsa, November 14, 1919.

23. *Zalamegyei Ujság*3, no. 100, August 15, 1920, 2. For the original text, see PL Mm. 33. d. Draft sermons: "The fall of the commune, 1920, town hall."

CHAPTER 2

THE ABBOT-PRIEST JÓZSEF PEHM, 1927

CHAPTER 2

The Parish Priest of Zalaegerszeg

QUALIS REX, TALIS GREX
AS THE PRIEST, SO ALSO HIS FLOCK

The years between Hungary's defeat in the war, the loss of territory in the Treaty of Trianon, and the subsequent political consolidation (1918–1921) were characterized by transition. The reorganization of the Hungarian state and the restoration of domestic order gathered pace with the national assembly elections of late January 1920. The next milestone was the signing of the peace treaty on June 4, 1920. The first tasks of the national assembly were to determine the form of government and to establish the powers of the head of state. A republic was rejected by all political parties, as this form of government was inseparably linked with the bad memory of the revolutions. Instead, citing legal continuity, the political parties declared their support for the monarchy. They disagreed, however, over who should be king: the legitimists insisted on Charles IV, but the supporters of a freely elected king argued that, in his statement made at Eckartsau on November 13, 1918, Charles had recognized the right of the Hungarian nation to determine its form of government, whereby the House of Habsburg had lost its right of succession.

As the peace conference had also prohibited a Habsburg restoration, the political parties agreed upon the election of a temporary head of state.

Among the various candidates, Miklós Horthy (1868–1957) received the support of the majority. At the time of the Republic of the Councils, Horthy – a Calvinist and former Austro-Hungarian vice-admiral – had served as minister of war in the counter-revolutionary government. He had then been appointed as commander-in-chief of the counter-revolutionary army. On March 1, 1920, the national assembly duly elected Horthy as Hungary's regent. He was to remain head of state until October 16, 1944. His attitudes and approach as regent were characterized by conservatism, anti-communism and nationalism. He proved able to rise above party political interests and sustain a balance of power between the large landowners, the wealthy (upper-) middle class, and the historical middle class. He was suited to this role on account of his experience, his political flexibility, his knowledge of languages, and his masculine appearance. When necessary, he was also rather adept at making paternalistic utterances. Although he never achieved brilliance as a politician, Horthy has nevertheless come to symbolize the quarter-century between 1920 and 1944.

The former ruler, Charles IV, went into exile in Switzerland. From there he made two attempts to regain the royal throne of Hungary. His first bid came at Easter in 1921, when – even to the surprise of his legitimist followers in Hungary – he arrived at Bishop János Mikes's palace in Szombathely and then traveled by car to the Royal Palace in Buda, where he demanded that Horthy relinquish power. The latter, however, managed to persuade the former king that the successor states would regard a Habsburg restoration as a *casus belli*, and that a war would result in Hungary's complete destruction. Charles returned to Switzerland, having largely accepted Horthy's line of argument.

In the ensuing domestic political storm, Horthy dismissed the prime minister, Count Pál Teleki (1879–1941), whose support at the time of the attempted royal coup had been half-hearted. On April 14, 1921, Horthy appointed Count István Bethlen (1874–1946) as Teleki's successor. The Transylvanian aristocrat Bethlen had become a key political player in the years following 1918. As prime minister, he proved to be a realist politician. He constructed an enduring system of government, yielding no ground to those who demanded greater democracy or a dictatorship. His term as prime minister (1921–1931) saw the consolidation of the rule of law, Hungary's (re)integration into the international community, the introduction of a new currency (the pengő in 1926), rapid economic growth, and significant progress in the social policy field. In view of these developments, the decade between 1921 and 1931 is known by historians as the Bethlen consolidation.

God's Caretaker

Shortly after József Pehm's return to Zalaegerszeg, the post of municipal parish priest became vacant. On August 20, 1919, the parish council unanimously decided to offer the parish to József Pehm, the religious education teacher. The diocesan bishop, Count János Mikes, was delighted to meet the parish's request: he felt a strong connection with the young priest on account of their shared experience of detention and persecution during the Republic of the Councils. On October 1, 1919, Bishop Mikes appointed József Pehm as parish priest of Zalaegerszeg. In terms of the number of parishioners it was a major parish, but the bishop was confident that Pehm was up to the task even though he lacked experience on account of his youth. (Mikes too had been appointed parish priest at the age of 25.) If, on hearing of the many conflicts, Mikes subsequently wondered whether he had given Pehm excessive power prematurely, he must have kept quiet about his doubts. Indeed, for as long as the bishop remained in office – and even after his retirement – he proved to be a staunch supporter of his priest. Evidently, on appointing Pehm as parish priest of Zalaegerszeg, Bishop Mikes had no inkling of the extraordinary career he was helping to set in motion.

The parish of Zalaegerszeg is one of county's oldest parishes with church register books dating back to 1703. Around 1919, the parish comprised the town of Zalaegerszeg and six neighboring villages with a total population of 15,000. József Pehm began his service to his parishioners in the period of transition that began with Hungary's defeat in World War I and was to end with the political stabilization in the aftermath of the Trianon shock and the crushing of the revolution. He served first as curate in the parish and then, from 1921, as the parish priest.

József Pehm set about his new task with great energy and enthusiasm. The outside world saw nothing (or barely anything) of his inner struggle to convince people that he was not just a "lucky peasant priest" who had happened to be in the right place at the right time. The faithful saw before them a strong and purposeful priest. From the very outset he did what he considered to be right for a man in holy orders. He had grown up thinking that a priest should be shown respect by his parishioners: in the village the priest was to be the "Authority," the man who stood, by virtue of the consecration, in the service of the church's divinely ordained vocation – to bear witness to Christ, the mediator of salvation. For Pehm, therefore, his task was to teach people about God and nurture them for a life lived in accordance with God's commandments.

Pehm fulfilled the customary tasks of a priest in exemplary fashion. He accompanied the faithful from the crib to the grave. As the head of his parish, he carefully checked the accounts, drafting annual budgets on expenditures and revenues. The minutes of the parish council meetings testify to the care and diligence shown by Pehm. Barely a year went by without some maintenance or construction work or an acquisition. Such projects were funded by donations or sometimes even loans.

Pehm's superior, Bishop János Mikes, was satisfied with the work of the new parish priest. On July 1, 1921, Mikes appointed Pehm as archdeacon,[1] indicating once again his confidence in the priest. In this post, Pehm assumed a responsibility for the coordination of the pastoral work of several parish churches, thereby increasing his influence. Three years later, in 1924, he received the title of abbot of Pornó named after Saint Margaret of Antioch.[2] The Abbey of Pornó, which had closed by the eighteenth century, was one of a number of titular abbot titles given by diocesan bishops to deserving secular priests in recognition of their work. As a sign of the title, the abbots could use pontifical insignia; they could hold masses in the same way as bishops; and they had the right to wear a pectoral cross and an episcopal ring even when attending civil functions. Pehm's inauguration as an abbot was attended by notables from throughout Zala County and the city. As the press reported, "the bishop arrived in the town on a four-in-hand

1. Zalaegerszegi Mária Magdolna Plébánia Irattára [Archive of the Parish Church of Mária Magdolna, Zalaegerszeg] (hereafter: ZMMPI). Filed documents 1920–23. Appointment certificate no. 2573/1921, Szombathely, May 22, 1921.

2. Veszprémi Érseki és Főkáptalani Levéltár [Veszprém Archbishop's and Principal Chapter's Archive] (hereafter: VÊL) I.1.41. 133. The appointment of József Pehm as abbot of Pornó, January 25, 1924.

(horse-drawn carriage) between lines of children and scouts on both sides and to the sound of bells ringing."[3] Thereafter and until 1944, József Pehm's title was "abbot-priest." When, in 1944, he was appointed bishop, he had to return his previous title to the bishop of Szombathely.

The Press Apostle

József Pehm showed an interest in everything – from world politics, to events at national, regional and local level, to the progress at school of his protégés. He was a true priest, but a lot more too. Events in his life led him to become "en passant" an agriculturist, an accountant, a newspaper editor and distributor, a builder, a teacher, a historian, and a warrior for the faith. One might say he was a "man of many dimensions."

Reflecting on his many dimensions, we can state that, after the provision of pastoral care, Pehm's next priority was the church's presence in municipal life. The relaunching of the *Zalamegyei Ujság* was a practical step towards achieving this goal, for the nearest newspaper publication of the "correct spirit," *Vasvármegye* (Vas County) was published in Szombathely (capital of Vas County) and was often delivered to places in the neighboring Zala County only after a couple of days' delay. The relaunch was subject to strict press controls on the part of the state. The material was subject to censure, and the prime minister had to be informed about the operations of the press organs in the past. According to Pehm's assessment the newspaper was "Christian and irredentist through and through."[4] The young parish priest soon proved his organizational capabilities. The owner of the newspaper was the Zala County Newspaper-publishing Company, which Pehm had founded. In 1920, with a view to reducing printing costs and securing market dominance, he established a printing company called the Zrínyi Printing and Book-Selling Company, of which he was company chairman until 1944. The newspaper was published on time for a period of twenty-five years, with the last edition appearing on November 3, 1944. At first it was a weekly newspaper, but

3. *Zalavármegye* [Zala County] 3, no. 37, March 28, 1924, title page; SZEL AC 91/1924. Minister of Culture Kuno Klebelsberg's transcript to Bishop János Mikes, Budapest, January 7, 1924.

4. MNL ZML IV.401c. 93/eln.–1922. József Pehm's letter to Prefect Béla Kolbenschlag, Zalaegerszeg, May 10, 1922.

soon it was being published four times a week and then, from September 1921, it was published daily apart from on Mondays. The *Zalamegyei Ujság* was the first daily newspaper in the history of Zala County to call itself "Christian politically." The newspaper undeniably played an increasingly important role in molding public opinion.

Edited and distributed by a small reliable team of people, the newspaper remained under József Pehm's control until the very end. In a sense it became his pulpit outside the church. Pehm viewed the non-Catholic press as his opponent, never underestimating the threat. Having examined the statistics, he appraised that the urban intelligentsia was interested in Christian newspapers, whereas "the villages are swimming in opinions excreted by the revolutionary press."[5] Years later he stated that the newspaper's main achievement had been to defend the Catholic faith and Catholic interests.

Favored topics of leading articles in the newspaper were critiques of the revolutions, the post-war dismemberment of the Kingdom of Hungary, peaceful revisionism, and – especially – public life events in the county. Even so, the church pulpit remained his real terrain. When, in January 1920, Pehm apparently saw a draft of the peace treaty for Hungary, the priest reflected in a dramatic sermon on the staggering reports about the dismemberment of the country.[6] He expressed not only bereavement but also anger. Yet he did not blame developments on Hungary's defeat in war or on the events that had led to this defeat. Rather, in Pehm's view, Trianon – the place where the peace treaty with defeated Hungary was signed – was punishment for liberalism, Marxism, cosmopolitanism, and all such evil machinations. The basis of his thinking was revisionism, as it was for almost all political schools of thought in Hungary at the time. Pehm's paragon or model was not an ethnically reconstituted Central Europe, but a strong Hungarian Christian kingdom – Saint Stephen's Hungary with its thousand years of history. He welded Catholicism to territorial integrity. A majority of Christian intellectuals in Hungary thought in similar terms at the time.

Pehm's newspaper watched vigilantly for signs of a revival in revolutionary spirit. Indeed, the *Zalamegyei Ujság* became the chief guardian of a

5. József Pehm, "Egy sajtóstatisztika," *Egyházi Lapok – Papok Közlönye* [Ecclesiastical Papers – Priests' Gazette] 46, no. 12 (1923): 128.

6. PL Mm. 32. d. Draft sermons, January 18, 1920. "Conclusion of Peace."

communist-free county. In this regard, it met the government's expectations. On the other hand, with its support for legitimism (a Habsburg restoration), it stood diametrically opposed to the regime of Miklós Horthy. The legitimists were demanding not merely the restoration of the monarchy but the return of Charles IV to the throne, who would be succeeded – after his death – by the first-born son Otto, who was entitled to the throne based on the Pragmatic Sanction of 1723 (the Hungarian Parliament voted for the Pragmatic Sanction in that year), which determined the indivisibility of the empire and the strict order of succession. The legitimist politicians were of the view that the return of the Habsburg king would bring with it the territorial integrity of the country. They argued that if Charles – the representative of legal continuity – were to sit on the throne and bear the crown of Saint Stephen, the founder of the state, this would create a legal basis for repossession of those parts of the country belonging to the Holy Crown that had been broken off. It was precisely this line of argument – so seductive to the Hungarian public – that convinced the Entente to prohibit the return of Charles IV to Hungary. The Entente would not countenance a Habsburg restoration, in view of the risk of territorial demands and the threat they posed to peace.

József Pehm and the other vocal Christian politicians in Zalaegerszeg were not *theoretical legitimists* who expected the national assembly to resolve the issue of the king at a suitable point in time. Rather, they were so-called *intransigent* (or *orthodox*) *legitimists* seeking a Habsburg restoration. It would seem that Pehm became an orthodox legitimist rather than simply a Royalist owing to the personal influence of his bishop, Count János Mikes. As a young priest, Mikes had been a confidant of Charles IV. In the post-war period, he had become a leader of the legitimist movement supporting the House of Habsburg's right to the throne. Pehm enjoyed the confidence of the legitimist elite (i.e., Bishop János Mikes and his circle of friends), but he "stuck out" among the legitimists who surrounded Bishop Mikes on account of his peasant background. All the others in the circle were aristocrats.

In the aftermath of Charles IV's second failed attempt to return (October 20, 1921), the national assembly announced the dethronement of the Habsburgs and the restoration of the nation's right to choose a king. The Hungarian government's position on the matter did not change even after the death of Charles IV (April 1, 1922). From this time onwards, the legitimist movements were considered unlawful. Even so, the *Zalamegyei Ujság* continued to give support to legitimist arguments, doing so in such a reckless manner that on April 14, 1922 the Bethlen government banned the newspaper in the very midst of an election campaign for the national assembly.[7] The stated reason for the ban was the newspaper's publication of a legitimist proclamation on the death of Charles IV in spite of a prime ministerial announcement that had warned mayors of the illegal nature of such a proclamation. József Pehm immediately appealed against the decision. His arguments were the same as those he often employed later on: Pehm immediately interpreted the violations of his interests as anti-Catholicism even though it was he who had broken the rules.

The prohibition was met with consternation among local legitimists. Political passions overflowed during a wine-filled municipal fest: one of the legitimists used a soda bottle to attack pro-government revelers, while the editor of the banned *Zalamegyei Ujság* used his fists.[8] The fate of the newspaper was resolved when the editor was replaced. After a forced break of several months Prime Minister István Bethlen revoked the ban, warning, however, that it would be automatically reinstated "if the newspaper returned to its former ways and once again sowed disobedience among the denominations."[9] The election campaign took place during the ban, and so the newspaper completely missed it.

Editions of the newspaper published prior to the ban (particularly those published in 1919) were characterized both by legitimism and by the virulent antisemitism of the "Christian" political line.[10] The editorial board was unable and unwilling to distance itself from the antisemitic Zeitgeist of the era. Instead, it followed the example set by the national dailies, which were exploiting the growing power of the Christian constituency and regularly addressing the "Jewish question" in their columns. The president of the Jew-

7. MNL ZML IV.401b. 15/biz.–1922. Telegram decree no. 59.661/1922 of the minister of interior on the prohibition of the publication and dissemination of the *Zalamegyei Ujság*.

8. *Zalavármegye* 1, no. 9, April 21, 1922, cover page.

9. MNL ZML IV.401c. 93/eln.–1922. Notification of the prefect, Béla Kolbenschlag, concerning the Prime Minister's decision No. 4856/1922. M. E., June 10, 1922.

10. Hanebrink, Paul A., *In defense of Christian Hungary: religion, nationalism, and antisemitism, 1890–1944* (Cornell University Press, 2006).

ish congregation in Zalaegerszeg protested the newspaper's antisemitism at the town council's first meeting in the post-revolutionary period, which was held on August 21, 1919.[11] In his response, József Pehm disputed his fellow councilor's assertions. Rather than attack the Jewish denomination the newspaper was, in Pehm's view, calling upon Hungarian Christians to construct a new Hungary based on Christian foundations. At the same time, he repeated the demand made in the newspaper article: the denomination and the nation should remove from their midst the "figures" that were spreading the infidel communist ideas. His message was synchronous with the propaganda of the Christian nationalist politicians and "defenders of the race." Such propaganda had drawn a connection between "red propaganda" and the press and had begun to take a stand against the "Jewish," "destructive" and "subversive" newspapers.

Leading articles in the *Zalamegyei Ujság* repeated the same goal in the emotive language of tabloid journalism, writing of the "Galician Jewish horde that seeks the destruction of the nation and is a blight on religion." The Jews were quite simply "a stinking ulcer," "an ugly mob," "the trash of the garbage tip," and "a hideous festering wound." They were responsible for the plague of discord that had struck the Hungarian nation.[12] Communists were described in similar terms: a parasitical "army of leaches" on the body of the nation, "a nest of rats" that "poured out the testicles onto this tired body that could no longer resist."[13] "If the newspaper's tone was sometimes sharp, my pen was driven at all times by the Christian national idea that had been humiliated to dust," Pehm explained, thereby acknowledging the exaggerations of the newspaper.[14]

József Pehm summarized his views on the opportunities presented by the press and the responsibility of the Catholic press in a brochure published in 1920 and entitled *Vigyázzatok az ujsággal!* (Beware of the newspaper!).[15] He thought in just two categories: the "good" Catholic and

11. MNL ZML V.1606. XXVI. The minutes of the meeting of the body of representatives of Zalaegerszeg on August 21, 1919.

12. *Zalamegyei Ujság* 2, no. 29, September 14, 1919, cover page; *Zalamegyei Ujság* 2, December 18, 1919, cover page.

13. *Zalamegyei Ujság* 2, no. 29, September 14, 1919.

14. *Zalamegyei Ujság* 2, no. 33, September 23, 1919, 2. In: MNL ZML IV.401b. 8/biz.–1919.

15. József Pehm, *Vigyázzatok az ujsággal!* (Zalaegerszeg: Zalaegerszegi Sajtóbizottság, n. d. [no date] [1920]).

the "bad" Jewish-liberal press. Since the end of the 19th century this black and white mentality had been typical of the Hungarian press movement, which had been influenced by ideas of Leo XIII.[16] Regarding the "bad" press, it was popular at the time to view the Republic of the Councils as the realization and fulfillment of the Jewish spirit. Pehm thought similarly, but his critique of the Jews was not rooted in an offensive or marginalizing racial-biological distinction but arose from his conviction that Hungary's future could only be built on a Christian-Catholic foundation. After World War I, Hungary's Jews were increasingly regarded as an alien population that threatened the legacy of St. Stephen, the country's Christian identity, and the leading economic role of the Hungarian constituent nation. Undoubtedly, there were few non-Jews among the people's commissars of the Republic of the Councils. Moreover, Hungarian Jews played a decisive role in domestic capitalism, in the intellectual professions, and especially in the press. It is little wonder that a provincial priest could see no further than the "sacristy curtain," which viewed the Jews as the killers of Christ and the enemy of the Catholic church. Consequently, he was bound to portray Jewry in pejorative terms. In 1949, Mindszenty himself acknowledged: "Today I would certainly use different words and not say what I did then with my young head."[17]

After the ban on its publication was lifted, the *Zalamegyei Ujság* toned down its antsemitic rhetoric. This was thanks in part to an initiative of Prime Minister Bethlen, who requested the editors of the Christian newspapers to refrain from publishing extreme articles and commentary on the "Jewish question."[18] In other areas too, the newspaper showed greater restraint after its relaunch. It continued to condemn social democracy but moderated its criticism of the governing party. The publication became a "normal" Hungarian local newspaper. Revisionist in tone, it reported on the intricacies of public life in Zalaegerszeg and Zala County and, in less detail, on national and international events. It covered the general meeting of the local Jewish congregation in the same

16. Tibor Klestenitz, *A katolikus sajtómozgalom Magyarországon 1896–1932* (Budapest: Complex Kiadó, 2013), 33–35.

17. PL Processus, V–700/1. 169. fol. Minutes of József Mindszenty's questioning by the people's prosecutor, January 21, 1949.

18. *Zalavármegye* 1, no. 56, August 13, 1922, 2.

way as it did scout camps or football matches held in the county. The newspaper's vigorous support for the monarchy subsided, and reports on the royal family were limited to the news column.

Thanks to Pehm, press polemics frequently disturbed the sleepy town's peace. Indeed, there was a constant battle of words between Pehm's newspaper, which opposed the government, and the pro-government *Zalavármegye* (Zala County) and its successor, the *Zalai Napló* (Zala Diary). The result was the break-up of the faithful of Zalaegerszeg into two opposing factions. On one occasion the *Zalai Napló*, referred sardonically to Pehm as "the Napoleon of Zala,"[19] in an allusion to the intellectual "autarchy" that he imposed upon believers and his tendency to brand anyone who failed to meet his "high standards" a bad Catholic.[20] The tensions did not abate. Rather, the disputes became so aggravated that the parties often ended up at a court of law.

The Good Pastor

Whenever József Pehm took his place in the pulpit, his somewhat round-shouldered figure underwent a transformation: authority and power, simplicity and humility emanated concurrently from him, regardless of the nature of the occasion. His manly firmness captivated people's attention. With his large, piercing eyes he seemed to peer into people's souls. He preached in a light but persuasive manner. In the use of his voice, he avoided gimmickry. Moreover, he rarely gesticulated. He prepared his sermons with great care; the line of thought was clear and concise. Often the language was a little antiquated, but mostly high-brow. The lush Hungarian style of Pehm's sermons appealed to people, as did his use of striking historical analogies and similes. He never sought to cut short what he had to say. As time passed, he became a highly experienced and talented preacher. Indeed, as primate he attracted large crowds even in Protestant regions of the country.

Pehm's sermons were not missionary proclamations. Rather, he would discuss specific issues and then address the tasks arising. For instance, he

19. Gábor Tarján, "*Mindszenty József 1917–1945*" (PhD dissertation, Faculty of Humanities, ELTE, 1981), 39 and 156.

20. *Zalai Napló* 1, no. 109, May 14, 1933, cover page.

spoke of Darwinism, examined humanity's social situation from ancient times until the modern era, reflected upon the women's issue, feminism, and the power of the press, doing so in conjunction with the customary topics – Jesus' actions as a witness, the Eucharist, love, mercy, sin and redemption, vanity, impatience, selfishness, sensuality, morality, faith and apologetics, the virtues and the Good Shepherd, martyrdom. He often spoke of the tasks of the affluent and their responsibility towards society. From the pulpit he frequently instructed and castigated the congregation. He lambasted the extremes of fashion, the squandering of resources and opportunities, the lack of generosity and empathy, the hedonism of the upper class, and unnecessary spending. He embraced the customary dress of Hungarian women: "It is not my intention to dress the world in a woolen cloth... but it runs against aesthetics for adult women, especially those who are not slim, to show their figures, which require concealing."[21] He also condemned in his sermons those who viewed church as a fashion show or mass as an opportunity for dating.

When, on March 25, 1924, József Pehm took his place in the pulpit for the first time as a benedicted abbot, he spoke to the congregation about change:

> ...until now I have been your shepherd; now I have become your father. The word abbot is derived from abbas meaning father. The father has troubles. Each of the abbot's insignia has profound significance. The ring, the cross, the crosier tell me of a difficult duty. The ring betroths me to my congregation, my future reckoning is connected in my hand. The cross signifies the burdens of life as a spiritual pastor. The crosier urges continuous protection of the flock, for it is surrounded by a thousand dangers and temptations. I watch over and I am concerned, and you should understand this not as being unfit but as natural.[22]

One of the people who congratulated him was struck, in a visionary way, by this particular attribute of the young abbot – one that stuck to him for longest: "...I feel that your soul, yes honored friend – however our fate

21. PL Mm. 33. d. Draft sermons: "Fashion. MK. July 30, 1920."

22. PL Mm. 31. d. Draft speeches and reflections: "Benediction as abbot, March 25, 1924."

shall unfold – will always serve this line, which we set as a goal together, the uncompromising and intransigent Christian line."[23]

Over time the parish priest Pehm found out when and how people living in the town were satisfying their religious obligations. It was jokingly said about him that he held in his head an account for every Zalaegerszeg inhabitant, with up-to-date information in the "debit" and "credit" columns. There is documentary evidence that he did indeed request and receive detailed data on Catholic taxpayers in the town and the county, their financial status, their tax base and tax conduct, investments and redemptions. If someone failed to attend Sunday mass, Pehm would seek to persuade him or her until the person concerned saw reason. If he heard about some immoral behavior going on in the town, he personally would take steps in the matter. When a local woman with four children ran away from her husband to Szombathely after 28 years of marriage, Pehm requested the chaplain there to take action: "Please persuade her to return to her husband and end the separation."[24] Pehm would not tolerate common-law marriages in Zalaegerszeg. He would keep on nagging the offenders until they gave in and had their relationship sanctified. He kept an eye on worshippers and ran checks on people who came to confess. He paid regular visits to families too, and single people. He took great care that, where possible, no-one should depart this life without receiving the sacraments. He even took an interest in the spiritual care of seasonal workers: he requested detailed data from the mayor about who was entering service, where and for how long. [25] Pehm was inclined to judge people's work based on religious fervor. He often expressed his dissatisfaction with the activities of members of his flock. "Nutty old women folk, they are deterred by hysterical reports,"[26] he said in condemnation when, in reaction to the Third Reich's annexation of Austria (1938), a third of those who had previously signed up, cancelled their participation in the 34th Eucharistic World Congress, which was to be held in Budapest in May 1938. More than

23. VÉL I.1.44.a. 1601/1944. A greeting from someone with an illegible signature, Budapest, February 18, 1924.

24. ZMMPI iktatott iratok (filed documents) 1928–30. 2093/1929. Letter of József Pehm to unnamed chaplain in Szombathely, Zalaegerszeg, July 3, 1929.

25. Ibid., Letter of József Pehm to the mayor and notary, n. p. [no place].

26. PL Mm. 43. d. József Pehm's diary, entry for May 25–30, 1938.

once Pehm sought to arrange for people he considered right for the job to be placed in influential positions and to remove those he considered incompetent.

As the parish priest, József Pehm automatically became the chairman of the local Roman Catholic congregation. The congregation's statute had been approved by the responsible diocesan bishop on January 27, 1917. The congregation functioned in such a way as to permeate all public and cultural life in the town, directed and overseen by the parish priest. The chairman of the congregation had broad powers: he presided over the general meeting, meetings of the congregational council and disciplinary committee, as well as various other committees. Additional tasks were implementing resolutions, supervising officials and requesting disciplinary proceedings against them when necessary, etc. Being a member of the congregational council afforded a degree of status; whoever was elected immediately became a member of the local Catholic elite. Yet an analysis of the functioning of the council reveals that its powers were more or less limited to giving approval; and there was no real autonomy. As chairman, Pehm expected members of the congregation to support the position of the congregation at all public forums,[27] and this position usually meant his stance. In effect, Pehm's will was realized both in the town and in the county via this council.

Pehm's perfectionist, relentless and consistent behavior rather overwhelmed the people around him. His authority was growing and he was determined to implement his will.

> He is just thirty-three years old, but he has already cleaved out of the public life in the Göcsej region significant political power. I do not want to touch upon his priestly vocation. If only he would stay in his church!... But in all areas he seeks to be the leading and directing force. Yet he is not called to this role. He is a man of inexperience. And political intolerance is his motivation. Whoever refuses to follow him and pay homage to his ideals, he regards as the enemy and treats him accordingly...[28]

27. ZMMPI jegyzőkönyvek 1930–40. 32. fol. Minutes of the meeting on June 22, 1930, of the body of representatives of Zalaegerszeg Roman Catholic Community.

28. Márton Szekeres, *Egy ujságiró kálváriája* (Budapest: Published by the author, n. d. [1927]), 12.

These hot-tempered lines were written by a defeated political adversary, but despite their bias they hit the nail on the head: the abbot-priest József Pehm was an influential figure – or, indeed, principal actor – in local public life, whose agility, methods, and religious intolerance split the local population. Even so, no one can deny that his efforts bore fruit. At a meeting of the congregational council on November 8, 1931, the following summary of progress in the congregation was heard:

> A decade and a half ago, five priests were working in the parish. Today, there are 15 priests with the retirees. [...] There are now several clubs. The current charity work is so great that the poor can rightly appreciate it; the places and times of church services of the branches have multiplied. [...] Rather than three schools, there are now seven. [...] Church attendance has increased. In 1930, the number of holy communions was 106,241. [...] In 1915, the number of communicants was 24,000 according to a surviving record. Even in 1922 the number was just 43,115. In 1921, 30.2 percent of the deceased aged over five were buried without the sacraments. In 1929, the figure had fallen to seven percent, because of a large increase in the number of confessions for the sick (2,465).[29]

In the 1930s, 3–8 percent of the deceased were buried without the sacraments. The lowest figure – 2.2 percent – was reached in 1943, when just five deceased persons were buried without the sacraments.[30] Pehm's exemplary work in the field of church organization was recognized not only by local people but also by senior ecclesiastical leaders and Catholic figures in public life. Zalaegerszeg was often cited as a "model parish" where church attendance had increased at a faster rate than in the diocese and country as a whole, and where there had been similar, above-average increases in the number of communicants and the number of people actively involved in the work of the congregation.

29. ZMMPI jegyzőkönyvek 1930–40. 155–156. fol. Minutes of the meeting on December 8, 1931, of the body of representatives of Zalaegerszeg Roman Catholic Community.

30. Állambiztonsági Szolgálatok Történeti Levéltára [Historical Archives of the Hungarian State Security] (hereafter: ÁBTL) 3.1.9. V–700/26. 98–99. fol. Report on religious life at Presbytery No. 1 in Zalaegerszeg.

One of Pehm's first appearances in public life occurred when, in the autumn of 1919, he added his name to the dramatic appeal of the Mayor of Zalaegerszeg: he initiated a relief operation, calling on his fellow councilors to take action to deal with poverty and with the mortal threat posed by the coming winter. At Pehm's suggestion, the rural population was also included in the operation to collect money, whereby the focus was placed on wealthy landowners and on the priests, teachers and notaries that made up the rural intelligentsia.[31] Pehm had begun to establish this relief system while he was still a Religious Education teacher. The system was used to support the continued study of the talented sons of peasant families with many children. Pehm collected and gave donations. Seminarians and needy students were given support worth 20–30 pengős. Each year he arranged lodgings in the town for 25 students, who stayed with honest tradesmen and widows who also benefited from the arrangement, as the students paid rent. Pehm's charity network went well beyond mere almsgiving: the inescapable duty of love was the motive. In 1936 he founded the County Catholic Caritas for the Assistance of Schoolchildren, and the membership fee of one pengő was used to buy footwear. As part of the so-called "bare-foot campaign," on average a thousand elementary school pupils were given shoes free of cost. In this way, Pehm's foundation supplemented similar campaigns run by the county authorities. The fostered students often came to him, and he brought the boys up in place of their absent fathers. He rarely praised the children; rather, he tended to criticize them. The students respected József Pehm as their benefactor, but they also feared him because he was so strict. Pehm's efforts to help the poor earned him many sincere supporters and sympathizers. The people he helped were forever grateful.

While Pehm was sensitive to the problems of the poor and lived his own life in a simple and puritanical fashion, he was adamant that people should show him the respect due to him as a priest. On one occasion, he was asked to take the customary annual mass for gendarmes, and a young policeman was sent to extend a formal verbal invitation. A disgruntled Pehm declined to receive him, arguing that the gendarme commander should send an officer

31. MNL ZML V.1606. XVI, 32–36. fol. Minutes of the general meeting of the Zalaegerszeg Body of Representatives on November 8, 1919; Zoltán Paksy, *Zalaegerszeg társadalma és politikai élete 1919–1939* (Zalaegerszeg: Millecentenáriumi Közalapítvány, 2011), 44–45.

rather than a non-commissioned officer to the abbot-priest of Zalaegerszeg when ordering a mass. While his religious instructors and chaplains used bicycles or motorbikes to get around, Pehm never did so. Pehm had horses and a coachman – it was reported in the newspapers when the horses were startled.[32] He did not tolerate mocking or disrespectful comments about the church. He denounced the director of the municipal hospital in Zalaegerszeg after the man described Jesus Christ as "the curly-haired fair Jewish kid."[33] Interestingly, the doctor in question was the Zalaegerszeg chairman of the governing party which Pehm so disdained. He publicly called a Catholic watchmaker a "vile ragman," because the watchmaker had awaited the Virgin Mary's Day procession with a cigarette in hand and a hat on his head. This outburst led to a court case against Pehm, who was accused of defamation. The court found Pehm guilty and ordered him to pay 200 crowns, but the court also condemned the watchmaker for causing offense to religion.[34]

If someone in his environment stumbled, Pehm rarely offered an opportunity for a new beginning. "I threw out, on grounds of stealing, three women employees, the coachman, the vintner, the farmer in Ságod and the servants."[35] He not only dismissed them; he also formally accused them of theft. The case was heard by the Royal Court of Zalaegerszeg. All of the accused claimed innocence, and one of them – a 68-year-old cook – complained that on her dismissal she had not received her wages for seven months. Pehm reacted to the statements of the accused with characteristic intransigence: "People who steal will also lie. [...] And yet for their spiritual salvation they should admit contritely to their deeds."[36] In the end, the

32. *Zalavármegye* 4, no. 137, October 25, 1925, 3.

33. SZEK ős. XXVIII/alsó II. Emlékezések: Recollections of the teacher Gyula Bucsis, n. d. 14. fol.

34. SZEL AC 2700/1923. Judgment of the Zalaegerszeg Royal District Court, Zalaegerszeg, November 7, 1922, and Judgment No. Bf.I. 437/6/1923 of the Zalaegerszeg Royal Court.

35. PL Mm. 43. d. József Pehm's diary: entry of April 18, 1940. (The coachman later took revenge for his dismissal by giving an interview with a reporter from the newspaper *Szabad Nép* [Free People]. Entitled *The True Face of the "Mighty Abbot,"* the article was published on December 12, 1948 and claimed that everyone in Zalaegerszeg hated the abbot. The coachman gave a very negative impression, claiming that Mindszenty had forced him to live in the stables in inhumane conditions and that he had been given very little to eat. At the same time, he had been required to work day and night. *Szabad Nép* 6, no. 287, December 12, 1948, 5.)

36. *Zalai Magyar Élet* [Hungarian Life in Zala County] 1, no. 212, December 5, 1940, cover page and 2.

court acquitted three of the defendants and sentenced four of them to seven days in jail. The cook's seven-day jail sentence was suspended for three years on probation.

The story of one of Pehm's former catechist priests is, however, a shining example of forgiveness and discernment. When, owing to a snow storm, the catechist failed to arrive in time for the mass, Pehm initially punished him. However, when the catechist spoke frankly about his problems, informing Pehm that he had not received his salary for over six months, Pehm showed him understanding. He revised the mass roster and within two days arranged for the Ministry of Culture and Religious Affairs to transfer the missing salary to the catechist. He then attended the carnival show put on by the catechist's students, even though the venue (the house of culture) could only be heated to around 10–12 degrees Celsius (50–54 degrees Fahrenheit) because of the outside cold. As the catechist later recalled:

> From that time onwards I always looked at him with respect, as I had done before, and I realized that Zalaegerszeg had a priest that was respected by everyone and loved and feared by very many. He was a resolute individual, who, if he said one thing, would then always say the next. He always kept his word whatever the circumstances, and he was an extremely austere, simple and prayerful soul.[37]

The following typifies the strictness he showed towards himself and towards his flock. A woman who had confessed and been absolved wished to receive the Eucharist, but the priest, József Pehm, denied her communion, passing silently in front of her.[38] The matter resulted in an investigation by the diocesan court, at which Pehm stated that the woman was unworthy to receive frequent Communion because he had seen her drunk in the company of male strangers. "I have no need for daily communicants who are always at the bar measuring out drinks," he exclaimed peremptorily. "[Such behavior] represents the compromising of devotion. I decided to

37. SZEK ős. XXVIII/alsó II. Emlékezések: Recollections of Antal Fonnyadt, parish priest of Rum. N. p., n. d.

38. SZEL AC 1263/1922. Report of Mrs. Antal Schnatter to the episcopal see. N. d.

pick up a broom..."[39] Pehm began his clean-up exercise on the woman whose lifestyle he regarded as blatantly frivolous. Still, the "cleansing" of frequent communicants was rejected by Pehm's diocesan bishop, because it violated the principles of the Code of Canon Law.[40]

Despite such warnings from his superiors, Pehm continued to exhibit a spirit of ruthlessness rather than of understanding in certain matters. We know, for instance, that Pehm had the main door to the church locked after the commencement of mass. In a literal interpretation of Canon 1262 of the 1917 Code of Canon Law, which mentions the separation of men and women in church, Pehm insisted on the implementation of the traditional seating pattern in church, with men sitting in pews on the right side (of the altar) and women in pews on the left side. Pehm's stance on this issue soon resulted in conflicts with his parishioners. When a devout churchgoer refused to move to another pew despite being ordered to do so, Pehm called the police and enforced his will with official assistance. The scandal was reported in the press and a complaint lodged with the bishop, who noted with resignation the following: "It would be a shame to argue with Pehm, for he cannot be persuaded."[41] Pehm's diary account of the same event mentions his disquiet but also makes excuses: "I was sorry that I had to arrange for the widow Mrs. Fangler to be removed from the men's pew by a policeman. This woman is annoyed with me. She seduced a curate and friend of mine. These clerical women are anti-clerical when it comes to me."[42]

If Pehm was heavy-handed in his treatment of the faithful, he was even more so in his own backyard, in the parish. Based on the recollections of his curates and catechists, the parish seems to have been organized along strict lines and in a more or less patriarchal fashion.

> He demanded exactness from them in every respect.[43] No one could go to the pulpit unprepared.[44] The chaplains who were assigned to him did not

39. Ibid., József Pehm's report to Bishop János Mikes, Zalaegerszeg, August 19, 1921.

40. Ibid., Letter of Bishop János Mikes to József Pehm, Szombathely, 1921.

41. Kalocsai Főegyházmegyei Levéltár [Kalocsa Diocesan Archive] (hereafter: KFL) I.1.c. Folder 4. Notebook, January 29, 1942.

42. PL Mm. 43. d. József Pehm's diary: entry of early January 1942.

43. SZEK ős. XXVIII/alsó II. Emlékezések: Recollections of Károly Arany, the former head of the Zalaegerszeg printing press, sheet XLV.

44. Ibid., Recollections of the parish priest of Rum, Antal Fonyadt. N. p., n. d.

like to be in Zalaegerszeg on account of his strictness, for, as they said, they had no free time and the abbot was always finding something for them to do. ...a chaplain that spent at least a year in Zalaegerszeg 'with the bishop of Zalaegerszeg' – as people throughout the county used to refer, among themselves, to József Mindszenty – would receive a more serious post from the diocesan bishop, because Mindszenty's teachings and Mindszenty's discipline were a guarantee for filling a vacant post as catechist in a higher school or as parish priest.[45] He gave the impression of being an extraordinary man with a broad perspective, who was interested in everything, from world politics, which was already in a state of turmoil, to municipal, diocesan and religious affairs.[46] His amazing capacity for work, which rarely let him retire to bed before the midnight hour. His exemplary life as a priest, his absolute promptness, his devotion to clerical work, including the long hours spent hearing confessions, his meticulous approach to office management, his fully prepared sermons, his various lectures, his inspection visits to our theology classes, set an excellent example to the young priests.[47]

For the smallest transgression, Pehm would discipline his curates and catechists – and even priests in the deanery. His frank manner of speech did not appeal to all; he had more than one adversary and coveter even at the bishop's hall on account of his curtness. At the same time, he was adept at dealing with embarrassing situations. When a young girl greeted Pehm with a poem and then fell to the floor with her bouquet of flowers landing at his feet, he jokingly asked her: "Little girl, you managed that very well. How long have you been practicing it?"[48] On another occasion he lamented the old pine trees that were to be felled. Still, his treatment of a novice priest taking his first mass was chilling. The parents of the novice "were living separately, and his elder sister was in a nonvalid mixed [marriage]" and so, by way of punishment, Pehm chose not to attend the celebratory

45. Ibid., Recollections of Károly Arany, sheet XLV.

46. Ibid., Recollections of the parish priest Ernő Bontó. N. p. July 19, 1989.

47. Ibid., Recollections of Honorary Canon István Holbert. Vasvár, June 14, 1989.

48. Lecture of the Salesian monk, János Szőke at the conference *Emlékezés és történelem* [Remembrance and History], Budapest, May 17, 2005.

lunch after the first mass. "I had to strike a wound," he wrote in his diary.[49] Pehm/Mindszenty's personality was one of such ambiguity and contradiction until his very death. He clung rigorously to his faith, to his office, and to all its trappings. And one might well say that he was insensitive and excessively strict. Yet we also know that he could be gentle, caring and merciful when faced with human frailty. In terms of character he was both a compassionate and gentle-spirited priest and an indefatigable and steel-willed *miles Christi* (soldier of Christ).

József Pehm made great efforts to encourage the development of Catholic associations, clubs and organizations. His tenure in Zalaegerszeg saw the establishment of many new parochial associations alongside the old ones. Most of them were devotional or cultural associations, operating on the basis of age group, occupation, social status or goals and purposes. For some 25 years, Pehm personally led the Catholic Men's League and the Ladies' Congregation. Both these bodies, whose members came from the local Catholic elite, aimed primarily to enliven religious life and deepen religious sentiment. Pehm's "favorite" was the Ladies' Congregation with its membership of trusted, legitimist upper-class women, who directed all the Catholic rallies and processions held in Zalaegerszeg. His second-favorite association was the National Association of Hungarian Women. When realizing his ideas, Pehm would often rely on the support of women and the women's associations. In 1931, Pehm became a board member of the local branch of the Hungarian Revisionist League and thus part of a "team" that included a Lutheran pastor, a chief rabbi, a prefect who belonged to the Governing Party, and other people with whom he would have been unlikely to cooperate on any other issue.[50] The other Catholic associations were run by chaplains or catechists under Pehm's guidance.

József Pehm initiated many county and municipal cultural events, including, for instance, the commemoration of Bishop Márton Padányi Biró, who had governed the Diocese of Veszprém between 1745 and 1762, to which Zalaegerszeg had belonged at the time. In preparation for the commemorative event, Pehm undertook substantial historical research, which ultimately led to the publication of a book and the discovery of an

49. PL Mm. 43. d. József Pehm's diary: entries of June 26 and 28, 1936.
50. *Zalavármegye* 10, no. 122, June 2, 1931.

exemplar. His five-hundred-page monograph was published in late 1934 under the title of *Padányi Biró Márton veszprémi püspök élete és kora* (The Life and Times of Márton Padányi Biró, the bishop of Veszprém).[51] This distinguished bishop of the eighteenth century had made great efforts, after the destruction of the Ottoman era, to rebuild the depleted and severely shaken Catholic Church. Pehm was enthralled by the figure of the bishop, an "iron-willed man and leader," a Catholic warrior and Royalist priest, a paragon of the Hungarian Baroque spirit, who after his initial successes found himself in confrontation with the pope and with the imperial ruler, for copies of his book, *Enchiridion de fide* (1750), an apologetic anti-Protestant work, were confiscated on orders from the monarch and on grounds of incitement to religious intolerance. Pehm, in his work, supported Márton Biró throughout. Indeed, he felt it was now his task to continue the work of rebuilding the church and defending the faith. Pehm's historical work was impressive. Even today its contents can be of use to historians and researchers. Pehm's acquaintances were quick to read the book and offer their congratulations to its author. Almost everyone noticed the character similarities between Bishop Márton Padányi Biró and József Pehm.

Abbot Pehm resided in the presbytery, a building that served several purposes. The ground floor housed a Catholic book shop as well as the printing facility and editorial and publishing offices of the *Zalamegyei Ujság* – all of which had been founded by József Pehm. In 1936, the catechists, who had been living in another house, moved to the presbytery, which in the meantime had been converted into a two-story building. This set-up lasted barely three years. The former tranquility of the presbytery, a building that some mockingly referred to as the "Pehminarium," was replaced by noise and disturbance, reflecting the increased number of functions. Even so, there were no real conflicts until Pehm received word that there had been claims that food at the presbytery was excessively expensive and poor in quality. It is true that Pehm spent very little on the meals, and the amount of food served at lunch would have been rather little for others even on Lenten days. When Pehm was told that people were mocking and disparaging of the food served at his presbytery, he took such great offense that –

51. József Pehm, *Padányi Biró Márton veszprémi püspök élete és kora* (Zalaegerszeg: Zrínyi Nyomdaipari Rt., 1934).

contrary to the wishes of the diocesan authority – he gave final notice to the "gluttonous" catechists, who were to leave the premises on September 1, 1940. Pehm was sure that they would soon realize that "my table was both cheaper and better."[52] From that time onwards, the catechists were not permitted to sit with Pehm at his dining-table; rather, they were required to take their meals in a kitchen-diner. As we shall see later on, the unilateral decision to end the catechists' stay at the presbytery became more than an internal issue. Indeed, in terms of its consequences, the decision explains in part why Pehm gave up his diocesan roles.

Abbot Pehm was the embodiment of discipline and the supreme guardian of morality. In the course of time the faithful gradually grew accustomed to him, even while they resented and grumbled about him. Those whose dislike of him did not disappear – especially the people he had humiliated and the couples he had forced to sit on different sides of the aisle – transferred their allegiance to Zalaegerszeg's second church, which had been established in the meantime and was being run by the Franciscans. Pehm knew everyone in the town, and his knowledge was more than one might have expected from a good shepherd. People trusted Pehm as the parish priest and were quick to share their problems with him. There was a close bond between the priest and his flock. In every street, Pehm had a "representative" among the women. These "house apostles" informed him of joys, sorrows, misery and negligence.

His successor as dean characterized József Pehm as follows: "A truly priestly life. Tough, but not only with others, rather also on himself. He has a great social sensitivity. He is a strict but loving father to his congregation."[53] Pehm was wracked by internal tensions, and he looked dissatisfied and impatient most of the time. For many he seemed to radiate a spirit of harshness and pride. He was a man of simple tastes bordering on the ascetic, and he was very harsh on himself as priest. He was not interested in appearances. People recognized him from afar, as he went about the town wearing an enormous faded hat with drooping edges, a rather worn coat, and a threadbare cassock. Even as an aged prelate, he wore modest clothing – generally his weekday or Sunday cassock. His integrity as priest, his

52. SZEL AC 1676/1940. From József Pehm to József Grősz, Zalaegerszeg, July 18, 1940.

53. ZMMPI esperesi iratok (decanal documents) 1942–57. From Archdeacon Imre Keszei to Bishop József Grősz, Zalalövő, January 5, 1943.

everyday efforts to strengthen religious and social life, his immense capacity for work and his accuracy were recognized even by his critics.

As time passed, he was affected by an illness that so often afflicts people who work too hard or who were forced as children to become independent prematurely: Graves' disease accompanied by hyperthyroidism. In consequence of the disease, the tolerance threshold of Pehm's nervous system decreased. By exercising self-control, he sought to hold his temper in check and avoid emotional outbursts. He barely let anyone get close to him and he trusted no-one. He had few trusted confidants. All this explains perhaps why he tended to be regarded as a cold, haughty and supercilious man. He could relax only among his closest staff. They were the only ones to hear him chat amiably and tell jokes and stories. Still, even his jokes were aimed at moral edification or the discernment of social truth. Those who were closest to him believed that his lack of knowledge of people meant that he struggled to select suitable employees and confidants.

On the Women's Issue

József Pehm/Mindszenty had experienced the stirring and purifying effect of creativity in 1934 when he was working on his book on Márton Padányi Biró. His urge for creativity was still strong, and over the years he had thought more about his book on the role of mothers, which had run to barely a hundred pages and had been published in two editions in 1916. Under the same title, *Az édesanya* (Mother), József Pehm published two more books in 1940 and 1942. Only the title is the same, for the two books – both substantial works – differ completely in terms of content. Their publication accorded with the Teleki government's policy and its so-called national policy service propaganda plan. The purpose of the latter was to promote the completion of works – literary works or applied artwork – that, among other things, "report on and propagate the idea of motherhood, the associated uplifting feelings, and a mother's beauty."[54]

The content of the books reflected Pehm's ideas about the family: in line with his Christian beliefs, he argued that the healthy development of the nation and society was dependent on the existence of strong and

54. MNL OL K29 1. cs., c. dosszié (folder), 34. fol.

healthy families. And the personality of the mother formed the center of the family and its moral foundation. Pehm modeled the person of the mother on his own mother, making out of her a paragon in the turmoil of world war. His mother was inseparable from the person of József Pehm/ Mindszenty. He protected her as he hung around his mother's skirt and took care of her when he was a school pupil and a seminarian. Later on, he sought to protect her everywhere. Even when he was in prison or taking refuge at the American Legation, he was with her in spirit. His mother remained a paragon or model for József Pehm throughout his life. In his childhood he had feared her, perhaps because she and he were too similar in terms of their nature. Then, in adulthood, he had respected and esteemed her. There are many stories telling of his love and devotion. Moreover, his books radiate the mother-son relationship.

The volume published in 1942 examines the role of the mother outside the family, from the perspective of the Virgin Mary and as reflected in the church, the homeland, and religious life. The work contains several anticommunist and anti-bolshevik sections, as well as a number of sentences that draw analogies between the war against the Soviet Union and the battles fought several centuries earlier against the infidel Turks and Tatars. In writing these paragraphs and sentences, Pehm was simply following the relevant Catholic teachings: as early as 1846, Pius IX had condemned communism in his encyclical *Qui pluribus*, subsequently comparing it on several occasions to "the plague." After 1945, both of Pehm's works were placed on the fourth list of "fascist, anti-democratic and anti-Soviet books"[55] whereby all known copies of the book had to be surrendered to the authorities by January 20, 1947. Pehm's *Az édesanya* (Mother) received an odd significance at the time of the show trial against him: Hungarian far-right émigrés considered nominating his book for a Nobel Prize in the field of literature. Their idea seems to have been to draw attention to the fate of the prince primate rather to the unquestionable literary values of his book: "even if it does not get a Nobel Prize, the noise made will be enough," they argued.[56]

55. SZEK ős. XXVIII/alsó I. Public document No. 1 of 1947 from the Szombathely Diocesan Authority, January 9, 1947.

56. Hoover Institution Archives (Stanford, California), Tibor Florian, Box 6. Alphabetical File, Mindszenty, József Cardinal documents circa 1949–75. Folder 1. Letter of Lajos Marschalkó to Tibor Flórián, n. p., n. d.

Published in three editions, the book – a continuation of the previous theme – necessarily begs the question: Why does a man in the prime of his youth write repeatedly about his mother, why does he place her on a pedestal, and why does he make out of her a sacred role model? It is a virtue to love one's parents, but here perhaps we are also talking about the Woman. The Virgin Mary and the mother: these are the two women that a consecrated priest may openly love and surround by a special reverence (worship must be reserved for God). Rather than suppress his instinctual desire for the other sex, which might have caused unhealthy compulsions, the young Pehm managed to transform its essence, raising it to a higher plane and ridding himself of desire by focusing on the love of a mother.

Pehm/Mindszenty's chosen topic also signals, however, that the author was interested in the ocean of problems facing society, including one of the most acute issues, that of women, which for him could be reduced, in most cases, to the issue of motherhood. Some of the women presented in his works are angel-like beings, while others are powerful demons. The commendable women were associated with the following notions: compliance, patience, subordination of the will. Such women were driven by intuition rather than reason, by their hearts rather than by their minds. Still, as Pehm wrote, the praise of women was to be undertaken in gingerly fashion, for a woman exposed to sin had the capacity to destroy the most beautiful diamond. The sin is none other than the beauty, the sensuality, and the physicality with which women enchant men. Pehm mentioned some examples of sinful women: the Circes, who were capable of turning men into swine, the Delilahs, who stole Samson's strength, and, of course, the Cleopatras, who stopped Antonius on the road to glory. The Soviet Bolshevik women comprised a special category of women's depravity. Pehm was critical of any sign of masculinization, and for him this covered attempts by women to achieve self-realization in the manner of men.

During this era, the responsibility expected from a woman began to transcend the family framework. In the nineteenth century, the issue of women's suffrage had arisen, albeit only among a narrow intellectual elite. Still, the traditional Christian ideal of the woman had remained largely unchanged, whereby the most-valued female attributes were sacrifice and self-denial. József Pehm/Mindszenty stuck with this formula: while men were characterized by creativity and intelligence, the essence of a woman's nature was her capacity to reproduce. For Pehm, the eternal feminine ideals of Christianity were: Mary and Martha, Mary Magdalene, Saint Paula, Saint Monica (Monica of Hippo), and Saint Elizabeth. Although beautiful and gentle, the most important feature of these perfect women was their willingness to make sacrifices, to exercise self-denial, and to live for others rather than themselves. For Pehm motherhood was the true vocation and ultimate destiny of a woman: "Marriage is the real path for women."[57]

József Mindszenty's Mother series did not contain his own eccentric doctrines. Rather, in the books he passed on the official Catholic teachings of the time to his readers on such subjects as the new ideologies, the family, women, vocation, marriage, childbearing, sexuality, abortion and divorce. When the first Mother book was published (1916), women were still unable to vote in Hungary. It was only in 1918, under Count Károlyi's republican government, that People's Law No. 1 introduced general, secret, equal and direct elections and granted women the right to vote. The year 1920 saw the election of Hungary's first female member of Parliament, Margit Slachta, a Missionary Sister whose subsequent fate came to be linked, in many respects, with that of József Mindszenty.

At the time Slachta was already a well-known figure in the women's movement and a spokesperson for "Christian feminism." József Pehm, who was just eight years younger than Slachta, had recently begun his priestly vocation and the attention of the young assistant priest had not been drawn to the issue of women's suffrage. Later on, Pehm simply ignored the issue. He did not address in detail the issue of women's education, but he argued in general terms for women not to become breadwinners. On the other hand, he sympathized with Slachta's idea that women should have career opportunities in occupations that were suited to them and that this would serve the public good. Pehm moved on from his own conservative attitudes – more on this later – and in 1929 he arranged for the School Sisters of Notre Dame to open a mission in Zalaegerszeg for the purpose of educating local girls.

57. József Pehm, *Az édesanya*, vol. 1 (Zalaegerszeg: Zrínyi Nyomdaipari Rt., 1940), 25.

Some of the villages within the parish lay 4–8 kilometers from its center and had a total population of 4,000. The distance of these parishioners from the presbytery made pastoral work among them rather inefficient. Moreover, the parish church, built in the eighteenth century, could no longer accommodate the congregation, which had rapidly grown in size over a period of 150 years. There had been an idea – even before Pehm's arrival – to build a second church in the parish, but nothing had come of these plans. Pehm decided to revisit these plans and update them. The first real impulse was a large donation received in 1921 from Countess Valéria Batthyány, the wife of Count Pál Batthyány, the former prefect of Zala County. The donation added 365,000 crowns to the church construction fund – a huge addition to the existing sum of just 10,000 crowns. The tireless Pehm set to work with great fervor on one of the largest projects of his life.

The Second Church in Zalaegerszeg

With a view to coordinating the construction of Zalaegerszeg's second church, in the spring of 1924 the parish established a Church Construction Committee with József Pehm as the committee's supervisor and executive chairman.[58] After many rumors, it was only on February 1, 1925 that the committee resolved, following a proposal by the Mayor of Zalaegerszeg, Mátyás Czobor, "to build the church in memory of Charles IV, the last apostolic martyr king of Hungary."[59] Even today the church is the only one in the world consecrated to the Habsburg ruler.

Pehm received the site of the new church – formerly a military training area – from the municipality at no cost. He then managed to acquire most of the building materials at discounted prices or for barter. The first prize in the design competition was won by Iván Kotsis, a professor at the technical university. His design – *Holy Trinity* – foresaw a classical Baroque church with simple lines and a capacity for 2,300 people. (Kotsis also designed the Regnum Marianum church in Budapest, which was built in

58. SZEL AC 1123/1924. Minutes of the meeting of the Zalaegerszeg Congregation on April 6, 1924; *Zalamegyei Ujság* 10, no. 224, September 25, 1927, 10–11.

59. SZEL AC 755/1925. Minutes of the caucus meeting of the Construction Committee of Zalaegerszeg Roman Catholic Church No. 2, February 1, 1925.

1931 and torn down in 1951.) Events then began to accelerate. The new church's foundation stone was laid at a ceremony on June 28, 1925, and construction work began a month later. In December decisions were taken concerning the finishing work. Then, on May 9, 1926, a ceremony was held to mark the erection of the cross, by which time the consecration of the church was already under preparation.

Abbot Pehm personally checked the cash books, and it was he who signed the contracts and who raised the necessary funds – the latter evidently being his most difficult task. The naming of the church – its unprecedented consecration to Charles IV – meant that the legitimists had a personal stake in its rapid construction and were willing to make donations to the building fund. Collections were made even on the American continent, with donations arriving from Hungarian émigrés with family ties to Zala County and from Catholic newspapers and magazines in the United States. Donations were also received from France, Austria, the Kingdom of Serbs, Croats and Slovenes, and Romania. (In the United States, one priest even exploited the name of Pehm to collect donations that were not then used for the stated purpose.)[60] By the time the church was consecrated, the sum of donations amounted to 1,276,861,000 crowns.[61] Even such generous pledges failed to meet the sum of expenditures. Consequently, in 1925 and 1926 the Parish of Zalaegerszeg levied a church tax on each local Catholic (each congregation member) equal in value to the amount of tax paid by the same person to the Hungarian state as its citizen (i.e., the church tax was 100% of the state tax). For some years subsequently a group of Zalaegerszeg Catholics protested against the levied tax, which had far exceeded the standard rate.[62] Their protests, however, were in vain, because at the time the *rate* of the church tax was not subject to any legal restrictions. Rather, the rate could be freely determined by a parish, subject to the approval of the diocesan bishop.

The church was ultimately built with unprecedented speed. Count János Mikes, bishop of Szombathely, consecrated the new church to King Charles IV at a major ceremony held on September 25, 1927. Pehm invited all the leading legitimists to the consecration, and almost all of them came. Until this ceremony, József Pehm had been known at best as Bishop Mikes's priest.

60. SZEL AC 2427/1931. Letter of József Pehm to Bishop János Mikes, December 22, 1931.
61. *Zalamegyei Ujság* 10, no. 224, September 25, 1927.
62. *Zalavármegye* 4, no. 124, October 10, 1925, 2; Szekeres, *Egy ujságiró kálváriája*, 28–36.

Now, however, he became a recognized and esteemed figure in his own right among legitimist circles. Pehm's joy was dampened somewhat by the actions of the prefect of Zala County, György Gyömörey, who disliked him intensely. Gyömörey barred Pehm from making a speech at the consecration and from giving the sermon at the holy mass. Pehm, who had been the driving force behind the construction project, never forgave Gyömörey for this snub.[63]

The new church was run by the Franciscan monks. It was not long before their relations with the abbot-priest deteriorated, and a financial dispute lay at the root of the conflict. During the construction of the church, the parish accumulated a huge debt, the security for which was the new church together with the monastery. The monks, however, sought independence. Moreover, they found it difficult to accommodate some of the demands made by Pehm, who wished to regulate every detail of the Franciscan monks' lives. The pent-up tensions exploded in a very public manner in 1931, when the Franciscan prior petitioned the general assembly of the municipal administrative committee on account of the parish's refusal to pay for the pews that had been made for the church. In his submission, the prior criticized Pehm, reproaching him for the harsh conditions and for letting the monks go without food or even starve. In his response, Abbot Pehm explained that he had declined to fund the pews because they had been ordered without the parish's (i.e., his) knowledge.[64] The dispute, which often descended into pettiness, was resolved only eleven years later when Zalaegerszeg's second parish – the Parish of the Sacred Heart of Jesus – was established on January 1, 1942. Subsequently, the new parish was responsible for maintaining the Charles IV church and the monastery.

Schools, Presbyteries, and Curations

The Charles IV church had barely been completed when József Pehm set out his goal of building a convent school where girls could be offered secondary and higher education. For the abbot-priest, the education of girls

63. MNL ZML IV.401b. 37/biz.–1929. Letter of Prefect György Gyömörey to József Pehm, March 9, 1929.

64. MNL OL P233 Ferences Rendtartomány Levéltára [Archive of Franciscan province] (hereafter: FRL), 6. cs. 1/a t. 416/1931. Letter of the prior, Alajos Erős to the lawyer László Árvay, April 18, 1931; Ibid., Letter of József Pehm to the provincial, Viktor Vinkovits, March 4, 1931.

was a particularly important field, as girls raised in the Catholic spirit would become the mothers of the future. Catholic families of strong faith would come to form a strong Catholic nation. Pehm was dreaming of a complex school system comprising three independent parts: elementary school for the under-10s, middle school (*polgári iskola*) for girls aged 10–14; and an elementary teacher training institute for girls aged 14–19. In this way, a six-year-old elementary school pupil could be transformed, by the age of nineteen, into a qualified elementary school teacher, thereby mitigating the shortage of teachers in rural areas of Zala County.

Support for Pehm's endeavors came in the form of the Bethlen government's policy on culture and education. Owing to the ban on rearmament laid down in the Treaty of Trianon, the Hungarian government allocated the available budgetary resources to education, culture and science, all of which were designated as strategic sectors. Even so, the dream could not have become reality without the enthusiastic support of Mátyás Czobor, mayor of Zalaegerszeg, and the approval of Bishop Mikes. The municipality of Zalaegerszeg turned out to be a partner of great significance: it contributed plots of land and construction materials and it also agreed to fund the cost of heating the new building. Moreover, the municipality also agreed to provide a local tax exemption to the School Sisters of Notre Dame, the Catholic order that was to run the school.[65] A large part of the investment funding was provided by Count Kuno Klebelsberg, the Hungarian minister of culture. It was he who laid the foundation stone of the school building, which had been designed by the architect Count István Csáky. This ceremony took place on June 17, 1928.[66] Unsurprisingly, József Pehm became the executive chairman of the Notre Dame Convent School Construction Committee.

In his creative fever, Abbot Pehm mixed party politics with the construction work. When construction of the school began, there were 139 construction workers living in the town, most of whom were jobless. All but nine of them were Social Democratic trade union members. Having

65. MNL ZML V.1606. XXIII, 78–81. fol. Minutes of the general assembly of the municipal council of Zalaegerszeg on 19 April 1926; SZEL AC 2868/1926. Letter of József Pehm to Bishop János Mikes, September 16, 1926; MNL ZML V.1606. XXV, 75–78. fol. Minutes of the general assembly of the municipal council of Zalaegerszeg on April 2, 1928.

66. Ibid., XXXII, 208–209. fol. Minutes of the ceremonial assembly of the municipal council of Zalaegerszeg on August 1, 1935.

refused to employ these men, Pehm brought in workers from elsewhere who had an allegiance to the Christian Social Party. The local workers then submitted a complaint to the municipal council. After several months of indecision, scandal and resignations, the council instructed the mayor to request the builder (Pehm) to employ some of the local trade unionist workers. The abbot-priest ignored the request and continued to bar the subcontractors from taking on Social Democratic workers. In the end, the firms had little choice but to employ local workers, because a wall built by the "guest workers" collapsed...[67]

The school construction project proceeded at a rapid pace, notwithstanding such skirmishes with the trade unions as well as the funding difficulties, construction disputes and the extreme cold of winter. On a daily average, 300 workers were employed on the project, and the number sometimes increased to as many as 600 workers. By August 1929 the nuns were able to move into the building, but it was not until October that the construction project was complete. The neo-Romanesque building consisted of five parts: a convent with space for 70 nuns; a 300-square-meter chapel with a height of 11 meters; boarding accommodation for 90 students; a convent school; a gymnasium/assembly hall with a stage, a movie projector, changing facilities and storeroom.[68] The whole school complex was one of the most modern in Hungary at the time, and the complex included the first elementary teacher training center and the first secondary school for girls in Zala County. The benediction and official opening of the complex took place on October 6, 1929. It was a particularly special occasion because, at the request of Abbot Pehm, Cardinal Jusztinián Serédi, prince primate of Hungary, conferred the benediction.[69]

After the construction of the convent, Abbot Pehm initiated several other smaller building projects, all of which provided work to construction workers at the time of the Great Depression. In 1930, he arranged for the construction of a stage – similar to the one in Budapest – in Zalaegerszeg's expanded Catholic House. In 1936 various extensions were made to the

67. Tarján, "*Mindszenty József 1917–1945*," 43.

68. ZMMPI esperesi iratok 1919–29. Report of the dean, József Pehm on the deanery, n. p. [1929].

69. PL Cat. D/c 3240/1929. József Pehm's letter of request to Jusztinián Serédi, August 27, 1929.

presbytery. Thereafter the ground floor of the building housed a bank, a clothes' shop and a shoe shop, while rooms on the second floor were let to elementary and high school catechists.[70] The municipal old people's home lacked sufficient capacity, and so Pehm arranged for the construction of an old people's shelter with thirty beds. It opened in Zalaegerszeg on May 1, 1938. Pehm showed through his actions that he was sensitive to people in poverty and distress. He wrote the following words in an appeal for donations: "As I walk around the town, I see that there are still around 15–20 old people aged over 70 who are living in almost animal-like conditions and that cannot stay in those circumstances."[71] Still, in the harsh language of the people of Zalaegerszeg, he noted that he had the old people on their knees praying throughout the day.[72] In 1939, he arranged for repairs to the Stations of the Cross and to a damaged mural in the chancel. In 1942, he oversaw the construction of an ice rink run by the parish, while in 1943 he arranged for two cemeteries to be revamped. The construction of a home for Catholic apprentices was to have been his final major building project. He obtained a site for the home as well as state funding, a loan and the building materials, but the project could not proceed because of the war. In order to operate the benefice and to fund the construction projects, Pehm frequently had no choice but to take out loans. Indeed, the parish even issued a promissory note. The security for the loans was not only real collateral but also Pehm's reputation as a public figure. He was often able to obtain benign support from the municipality, from the county, from government offices, and from patrons as well as parishioners.

In addition to the various building projects, another important aspect of József Pehm's work concerned efforts to (re)organize the parishes. He took on such tasks when he was appointed as the bishop's commissioner. This appointment was made after he had criticized Zala County's backwardness in the ecclesiastical and educational field at the diocesan synod in 1927. His criticism at the synod had been accompanied by a solution plan: the reorganization of the branch parishes and the creation

70. SZEL AC 1684/1936, 1986/1936, 2073/1936, 2454/1938. Documents about the rent contracts.

71. ZMMPI iktatott iratok 1940–42. József Pehm's draft letter to the minister of interior, n. p. [1940].

72. PL Mm. 17. d. Envelope "1943–45." József Pehm's biographical summary; Tivadar Artner, "A bíborosról, gyermekszemmel: Emlékezés Mindszenty Józsefre", *Vigilia* 58, no. 8 (1993): 588.

– where a benefice could provide the necessary funding – of new parishes, curations (curation = an independent ministry without the status of parish but having its own pastor and benefice) and "expositures" (expositure = a chaplaincy belonging to a parish center and with a local resident chaplain working under the direction of the parish), all of which would have at least 800 congregants.[73] His plan, which was inspired in part by the reform ideas postulated during the reign of Joseph II, won the support of the synod.

As the bishop's commissioner, Pehm drafted a map of the area showing the number of congregants, the location of the branches and the distances. Based on this map, he then designated the locations of the new centers. Owing to Pehm's tireless work as an organizer, sixteen new curations were established during the next decade and a half. In this way, by 1941, the total number of pastoral centers, parishes and curations in Zala County increased from 25 to 41, representing a 64 percent increase. Abbot Pehm, having obtained funding from local, county and national potentates and donations from bankers and aristocrats, succeeded in establishing five new Catholic places of worship. In addition, he acquired five vicarages by way of donations and bought or built nine further vicarages.[74] As a consequence of his reorganizing activity, oversized parishes disappeared, which resulted in shorter distances between parochial centers and branches and in a lower parishioner-to-priest ratio. The effect of these measures was an improvement in the quality of pastoral work. Pehm worked on the program of reorganization for a period of thirteen years; it was his favorite task in his life as a priest. The formation of the curations was not accomplished without resistance. Pehm summarized the downsides of his work as follows: "I struggled with the evil and ignorance within people, with the heathens, with the priests and with low-life Catholics; I fell into ditches and I hid in stooks during summer downpours; my path in snowstorms was cleared by snowplows and snow shovels. My ears and my legs froze; I slept through the winter in unheated rooms, I lived the miserable life of the backward people."[75]

73. SZEL Pehm József iratai, I. d. József Pehm, *Zala segélykiáltása: A plébániák szaporításának ügye a szombathelyi egyházmegye zalai részében* [Zala's cry for help: The issue of the multiplication of parishes in the Zala area of the Szombathely diocese], Zalaegerszeg: October 24, 1927.

74. *Zalamegyei Ujság* 23, no. 132, June 12, 1940, cover page; Gyula Perger, "Mindszenty (Pehm) József tevékenysége a szombathelyi egyházmegyében, különös tekintettel a zalai kuráciák megszervezésére", (PhD thesis, Pázmány Péter Katolikus Egyetem, Budapest, 2007), 191.

75. SZEL AC 1348/1941. József Pehm's note No. 1510/1941 to József Grősz, March 22, 1941.

In recognition of his work in this field, on February 20, 1937, Pope Pius XI awarded Pehm the title of papal prelate, following a proposal to this effect by József Grősz, apostolic governor of Szombathely.[76] Despite the organizational successes, the work was unexpectedly ended in 1941. Indeed, Abbot Pehm resigned from his post as bishop's commissioner in Zala County on March 22 (prior to this, he had also resigned from his post as dean and as bishop's advisor).[77] The backdrop to this decision appears to have been a rather acrimonious dispute with József Grősz, who was diocesan bishop at the time. The dispute had arisen over the lifestyle of a particular priest in the diocese. Grősz had shown greater understanding for the priest, while Pehm had proved relentlessly strict. Ultimately, this was the same personality who was to reveal himself so often in later years: a strict but extremely consistent man who was tough and self-assured and who never conceded an inch once he had made a decision. The friction between the diocesan bishop and his priest evidently left an indelible mark on both men. It certainly added an interesting facet to their relationship in later years when Pehm, who had been Grősz's subordinate, became, as prince primate and head of the Hungarian Catholic Bishops' Conference, his superior.

IN THE THICK OF PUBLIC LIFE

As parish priest of Zalaegerszeg and thus as one of the largest tax-payers in the area, Pehm immediately became a highly respected member of the county assembly and the municipal council. Pehm, a highly influential personality in the local political elite, belonged to a conservative group whose members had acquired considerable moral capital at the time of the revolutions and who represented both monarchism and Christian Socialism.[78]

In most countries around the world, political activity by priests was prohibited by the laws of the land or through a concordat with the Vatican. In Austria and Germany, however, such political activity was acceptable, while in Hungary it was common practice. For József Pehm it was natural

76. VÉL I.1.41. 134. Appointment of József Pehm as papal prelate, February 20, 1937.

77. SZEL AC 1348/1941. Letter of József Grősz to József Pehm, June 16, 1941.

78. Zoltán Paksy, "Kisvárosi elit: Zalaegerszeg város virilisei 1873–1939," in *Végvárból megyeszékhely: Tanulmányok Zalaegerszeg történetéből*, ed. András Molnár (Zalaegerszeg: Zala Megyei Levéltár, 2006), 169–94.

that a priest should play a political role. Even so, he himself never became a candidate for member of Parliament, even though his popularity meant that he could have obtained any one of the mandates in Zala County. Instead, Pehm chose to support a candidate who could most credibly represent Christian national values and those of legitimism, either in a coalition with the governing party or as a loyal member of the opposition. In 1919–1920, Pehm's views were closest to those of the Christian Social People's Party, but thereafter he drew closer to the Party of Christian National Unification, which János Csernoch, the prince primate, also supported.[79] Pehm's work diary from the period reveals an active involvement in party work. As an agitator for the Christian Social People's Party, he could be seen at public meetings throughout the county. He even arranged for the Catholic House in Zalaegerszeg to function as party headquarters for a while.[80] It was largely due to Pehm that Christian Democracy and legitimism remained the primary political current in Zala County throughout the Horthy era.

Legitimist Opposition to the Government

The legitimists of the period considered themselves to be the true patriots; they believed that they were continuing the purest and most beautiful of Hungary's historical traditions and that time would prove them right. As time passed, it became a generally accepted view that legitimism was unrelated

79. The origins of the Hungarian Christian Party date back to 1895, when the *Catholic People's Party* was formed under Count Nándor Zichy's leadership. The early years of the century saw the emergence of the Christian Socialist movement, which gave rise to the *National Christian Socialist Party*. At times these two branches of political Catholicism fused together, but at other times there was separation. Under "Christian Party" we mean the *Party of Christian National Unification* in 1919 and 1920 (the party was established in advance of the elections), the *Christian National Party* in 1920–22 (the legal successor of this party, the *Christian National Agrarian and Civic Party*, was formed in 1922 and remained in operation throughout 1923), the *Party of Christian National Unity* between 1922 and 1926 (the party did not join Bethlen's Unity Party), the *Christian Economic and Social Party* from 1926 (the party was led by Count János Zichy), and the *United Christian Party* from 1937 (the party was created through the merger of several parties). In 1943, the latter party was renamed the *Christian People's Party*.

80. PL Mm. 43. d. József Pehm's diary: the pages after the following heading "Keresztény Szociális Párt vezetősége, Zalaegerszeg" [Leadership of the Christian Social Party]; ZMMPI Pártok, egyesületek [Parties, associations] – Papers of the Christian Social Party, 1919; *Zalamegyei Ujság* 2, no. 30, September 23, 1919, 4, in MNL ZML IV.401b. 8/biz.–1919.

to party politics and that it was a universal national ideal. This meant that one could support it as the member of any party or movement. The political power of the ideal weakened, however, after Charles IV's unsuccessful attempt to reoccupy the throne. After the king's death, the idea faded away.

Pehm had been a legitimist since a young age, but his continuing support for legitimism was influenced by events. On the death of Charles IV, Pehm wavered in his view, for the existence of a crowned monarch became a thing of the past. "I was worried that an insistence on the pragmatic sanction would take us into the labyrinth of French royalism," he wrote years later,[81] referring to the decades after Napoleon when the restoration of the monarchy in 1830 led to a further revolution. It would have been difficult to portray the young son of Charles IV, Prince Otto, as the constitutional ruler and the embodiment of national unity. However, in the course of a pilgrimage in 1924, Pehm met in person with Prince Otto von Habsburg, who was twelve years old at the time and living in exile. Prince Otto left a profound impression on him. Thereafter Pehm wholly accepted the idea that the son of the deceased monarch had a real, albeit weaker, link with the country. Thus Hungary still had a lawful king, whose coronation was being prevented only by the circumstances at hand.[82] The principle of legal continuity and historical constitutionalism, manifest in an insistence on the rights of the legitimate king, could be upheld by means of such argumentation.

Owing to his support for legitimism, Pehm found himself in opposition to Regent Miklós Horthy, whom he could not accept as the constitutional head of state. Moreover, for Pehm, Horthy's Calvinist religion rendered him a heretic. From time to time Pehm voiced – if only symbolically – the antipathy he felt for Horthy. The first national scandal in this regard came in 1924 when Pehm opted not to hold a celebratory church service on the occasion of Horthy's fifty-sixth birthday (June 18, 1924). After this act of defiance, Pehm received an official note from the prefect instructing him to hold a celebratory mass on Horthy's name-day (December 6).[83] For

81. Magyarországi Mindszenty Alapítvány Levéltára, Mindszenty Archívum [Archives of the Hungarian Mindszenty Foundation, Mindszenty Archives] (hereafter: MMAL) József Mindszenty, "Egy különös sorsú nemzet" (unpublished manuscript, chapter 12).

82. SZEK ős. XXVIII/alsó II. Emlékezések: Recollections of Gyula Bucsis, n. d. 11. fol.

83. ZMMPI iktatott iratok 1924–27. Prefect Ferenc Tarányi's notification to József Pehm, November 25, 1924.

a good number of years, the monarchist Pehm, counting on the complicity of his bishop, acknowledged only halfheartedly the Regent's name-day and refrained from displaying the flag in church on that day. In the Catholic Church, there is no requirement to hold celebratory masses on national holidays, and so Abbot Pehm's custom of holding an ordinary mass may be viewed as an act of defiance vis-à-vis the Hungarian state.[84] Pehm's "boycotts" were particularly striking given that, from 1924 onwards, every Catholic church in Hungary was required, by virtue of an order issued by Prince Primate János Csernoch, to hold a requiem mass on the anniversary of the death of Charles IV (April 1). Government officials stayed away from these commemorative occasions, but the Hungarian state tolerated them, as it also did the holding of celebratory masses on the birthday of Prince Otto (November 20). Each year a mass was held on Otto's birthday at St. Stephen's Basilica in Budapest. The mass was pontificated by a different bishop each year, and the sermon was given by a prominent churchman. In 1933, when Otto reached the age of twenty-one years, the honor of giving the sermon fell to Abbot Pehm. He contrasted the fragmentation of the nation with the institution of the monarchy, emphasizing that "the light of the holy crown alone can break through the tears of the nation."[85] The provocative celebration of the prince's birthday was disturbed by protests and led to a parliamentary interpellation. In response, Ferenc Keresztes-Fischer, the minister of interior, issued a statement confirming that constitutionally Hungary remained a kingdom, but that the throne could not be occupied for the time being in view of the domestic and foreign political situation. Abbot Pehm experienced first-hand the controversy that could arise from a single act of political defiance.

Priest and (Party) Politics

While Pehm never renounced his legitimist convictions and his opposition in principle to the regime, the results of the political and economic

84. Tivadar Artner, "A bíborosról, gyerekszemmel," 589; *Zalavármegye* 2, no. 142, December 11, 1923, cover page.

85. *Nemzeti Újság* [National Newspaper] 15, no. 264, November 21, 1933, 4. For the transcript of the speech, see PL Mm. 32. d. Draft sermons: "At the Otto mass, Budapest, November 20."

consolidation prompted him to make a firm compromise. His parish church – as all others in Zala County – celebrated the tenth anniversary of Horthy's regency (March 1, 1930) with a Te Deum in thanksgiving praise.[86] On this occasion, Pehm had little choice but to comply, as the government apparatus had stressed the need to celebrate the anniversary. Indeed, a circular letter from the state secretary for interior affairs had specifically addressed the "small-minded" and "unconscionable" priests who were reluctant to hold services in thanksgiving. Even so, Pehm was noticeably absent from a ceremonial session of the county assembly held to mark Horthy's tenth anniversary as regent, and he chose not to attend a ceremonial session of the county assembly held on the twentieth anniversary (March 1, 1940).

Pehm's newspaper, the *Zalamegyei Ujság*, gradually shifted its stance from strong opposition to the government authorities to a kind of loyal opposition. In many respects this was a logical development, as the country's ecclesiastical elite constituted one of the legitimizing foundations of the Horthy regime and was rapidly becoming an integral part of the contemporary political and economic fabric. In the long term, a provincial priest could not relentlessly cross over the boundary of tolerable criticism and defy the regime in such spectacular fashion, especially since he was a member of both the county assembly and the municipal administrative committee. His speeches to the assembly and to the committee were debated by the newspapers on several occasions. When, in the county assembly, Pehm was told to be quiet after having protested vehemently against the decision of the Hungarian government to establish diplomatic relations with the Soviet Union (1934), a lively discussion arose in the press about the involvement of priests in politics. Some commentators argued that priests should exercise their religious, civic and public duties but should not politicize or even express their political preferences. If, however, a priest did become active in party politics, he should expect to be treated as a politician rather than as a priest. József Pehm's opinion could not have been more different. In the *Zalamegyei Ujság* he wrote, in a leading article entitled "Priest and Politics" (*Pap és politika*), about the connection between a priestly calling and an active role in politics:

86. MNL ZML IV.401b. 24/biz.–1930. Letter of József Pehm to the prefect, György Gyömörey, February 8, 1930.

> Political activity could only be separated from the priestly calling if religion and politics were separable... Yet religion is not mere theory; rather it is life and reality, which directs morality and thus also the nation, the family, the individual, the truth, the legal system, the economy, in a word, all of life. On the other hand, politics strongly interferes in the matters of religion and in the matters of the external organizations of religion, and so a counterbalance is required, the counter-intervention of religion in politics.[87]

According to the teachings of the popes and the Church, a priest could take part in the public discourse, but a church pulpit should never be used to make a political speech. Indeed, such conduct was prohibited under the rules of the Catholic Church. Where, then, was the boundary between politics and public life to be drawn? Was it permissible for Pehm to castigate his political opponents from the pulpit? Approaching the issue from Pehm's perspective, we have to acknowledge that he, as a deeply religious man, viewed the whole of human life as the fulfillment of God's will. Consequently, for Pehm, man must not withdraw from the world but must take an active part in it, as this too was ordained by God. Seen from this perspective, politics was a *means* for the church to exert influence on social and private life, as only a strong church could serve individuals and the community effectively. This conviction was the basis of and driving force for all of Abbot Pehm's practical work, for his political and public activities, and for his publishing and academic work.

At the general elections in 1926 and again in 1931, Baron István Kray, a legitimist, ran as the joint candidate of the Governing Party and the Christian Socialist camp for election in the Zalaegerszeg constituency. Pehm was less than enthusiastic in his support for Kray, a counselor at the Ministry of Public Welfare and Employment. Nevertheless, Pehm deferred to the will of his bishop and welcomed Kray when, on November 29, 1926, he came to Zalaegerszeg in order to introduce himself to local people. At the election, after a very close fight, Kray won the seat by a margin of 128 votes over his rival. In 1931, István Kray stood as a candidate with a pro-Christian program. He was reelected to represent Zalaegerszeg without an

87. *Zalamegyei Ujság* 9, no. 25, January 31, 1926, cover page.

opposing candidate. József Pehm could rely fully on István Kray as Zalaegerszeg's parliamentary representative and on the valuable political contacts who became accessible through (legitimist politician) Kray. Still, fate is inscrutable: codenamed *Magasházi*, Kray would later become one of the most reliable agents of the communist secret police with the task of observing and reporting on Prince Primate József Mindszenty.[88]

By this time, József Pehm was no longer merely one of a multitude of provincial priests. He had become the intellectual and ecclesiastical leader of Zalaegerszeg society, a man who corresponded with state secretaries and government ministers on a whole range of different issues. As time passed, his reputation and esteem outgrew the boundaries of the municipality and, indeed, of the county. By the 1930s, he was considered to be a definitive figure in the civic and political movements of western Hungary.

"In Zala County the Mood is Explosive"

The peaceful decade of the Bethlen administration was shaken by the world economic crisis, which erupted in 1929. There followed mass protests reminiscent of earlier revolutions, a partial suspension of the constitution, and drastic financial measures. The government of Count István Bethlen collapsed under the pressure. Bethlen was succeeded as prime minister by Count Gyula Károlyi (1871–1947), who formed a transitional government with the aim of managing the crisis through traditional means. His efforts, however, proved to be unsuccessful, as the challenges of the era required a new leadership style, new politicians and, above all, new principles and methods. The liberal-conservative administration of the 1920s was steadily replaced by a form of government that was authoritarian even while it preserved the formal constitutional order and the parliamentary system. The exercise of power became dictatorial in certain respects.

The "strong man" of the new regime was Gyula Gömbös de Jákfa (1886–1936), the former minister of defense, who, in the fall of 1932, took over the reins of government amid such heightened expectations. A legitimist,

88. ÁBTL 3.1.5. O–11.701. 152. fol. Appendix to the Proposal for Compromising Otto Habsburg, December 4, 1958.

however, could have only antipathy for the new prime minister, as he was the man who had earlier prevented the king's second attempt to return. Moreover Gömbös was a Lutheran. The new prime minister initiated structural changes to the system of government that were aimed at enabling the country to overcome the economic crisis, thereby preventing a possible leftist resurgence. Another factor in these developments was Gömbös's desire to accommodate the new type of politics that was unfolding in Europe at the time, namely the rise of authoritarian regimes in Austria and Italy.[89] Gömbös thus took steps to limit the traditional conservative forces of the governing party and its coalition partner, the Christian Party, while at the same stepping up efforts to build a modern right-wing political party that could appeal to the masses. Abbot Pehm joked in the *Zalamegyei Ujság* about Gömbös's methods: "To make a party – on paper – for the prime minister is not a great joke. Mussolini, however, first made his party and only then did he become prime minister..."[90] In the end, all this mocking and criticism proved justified, since the dictatorial aspects of government policy strengthened under Gömbös.

The Christian Party elite feared that this new government party (the Party of National Unity), the Independent Smallholders' Party (est. October 1930) and the Nazi-type parties on the far right – which were yet to become serious political contenders but whose voices could already be heard – would win over the Catholic masses and take them away from the Christian Party. In order to debate the political and social situation, thirteen leading churchmen, among them Abbot József Pehm, came together at a meeting held in Székesfehérvár on March 12, 1933. The major issue at the conference was whether to keep the traditional Christian Party or establish a new party. Several of those assembled urged the creation of a new political party that was expressly Catholic, provincial/rural and agrarian. The most sensible position was formulated by József Pehm, who admitted that the Christian Party was impotent while also underlining the dangers of experimenting with the establishment of a new party. Pehm also expressed opposition to the idea of dividing the party into a provincial/rural agrarian party and an

89. Jenő Gergely, *Gömbös Gyula: Vázlat egy politikai életrajzhoz* (Budapest: Elektra Kiadóház, 1999); József Vonyó, *Gömbös Gyula és a jobboldali radikalizmus: Tanulmányok* (Pécs: Pro Pannónia Kiadói Alapítvány, 2001); József Vonyó, *Gömbös Gyula* (Budapest: Napvilág Kiadó, 2014).

90. *Zalamegyei Ujság* 16, no. 179, August 10, 1933, cover page.

urban Christian socialist party in Budapest as this "would mean at most a double death."[91] Hence Pehm favored reforming the old party rather than establishing a new party. Subsequent developments proved the abbot-priest from Zalaegerszeg right. The Catholic Bishops' Conference insisted on the old party and the old politicians, and so it was not until the fall of 1944 that a new Christian party could be formed. The meeting in Székesfehérvár ended with an agreement that each participant would make a suggestion before the next meeting concerning who else should be invited to attend. In the end twenty-seven priests attended the next meeting held two months later. The resolutions made at the second meeting, which were then submitted to Esztergom, reflected in full Pehm's pro-reform stance outlined above. However, Prince Primate Jusztinián Serédi, acting in his capacity as the archbishop of Esztergom, received the resolutions without comment and promptly placed them on file. In this way an opportunity for the Christian Party to be reformed and make progress was lost.

In Zala County, however, Abbot Pehm refused to allow the Christian Party to stagnate. In October 1933 he attended, as county chairman of the party, a meeting in Nagykanizsa where those attending protested against Gömbös's plan for a one-party system (the Party of National Unity) and against the establishment of a personal dictatorship. "In Zala County the mood is explosive," wrote Pehm to his only confidant and friend, Gyula Géfin.[92] Abbot József Pehm's relationship with György Gyömörey, the pro-Gömbös Catholic prefect, took an irrevocable turn for the worse. The dispute between these two definitive personalities culminated in a spectacular press trial. In the end, however, the fate of Prefect György Gyömörey did not hinge on Abbot Pehm's dissatisfaction; rather Gyömörey's future course in life was sealed by domestic political developments. On March 4, 1935, Gyula Gömbös reshuffled his cabinet and made fundamental changes to his government, dismissing the old guards who had worked for the conservative Bethlen. Consequently, Bethlen's man in Zala County, György Gyömörey, who had been appointed as early as 1926, lost his post

91. PL Cat. D/c 1467/1933. 11. fol. Minutes on the clergy conference held in Székesfehérvár on March 13, 1933.

92. SZEL Géfin Gyula hagyatéka. Levelezések [Legacy of Gyula Géfin. Correspondence], VIII. Letter of József Pehm to Gyula Géfin. Zalaegerszeg, October 8, 1933. Published in Dobri, "...szívélyesen üdvözöl barátod és híved...," 279.

as prefect even while his achievements were recognized. He was the only prefect to be dismissed at that time. His "crime" seems to have been a failure to support, or to support sufficiently, Gömbös's policies.[93]

Gyömörey's successor as prefect was the one-time Christian Party member of Parliament, Tibor Tabódy, who was now a close supporter of Gömbös. The Catholic Tabódy was the second Prefect of Zala County whom – despite his pro-Gömbös stance – Pehm could just about bear; otherwise "he was a nightmare for all the prefects."[94] When Tabódy took office, Abbot Pehm agreed with the new prefect's plans for reform, which were designed to spur the county's economic and social development. Even so, Pehm emphasized that "The public in Zala County has always jealously guarded the essential integrity and inviolability of the ancient constitution and the tried and tested form of county self-government."[95] This thinly-veiled warning was a reminder that as the government's man, Tabódy would only enjoy the confidence of the people of Zala County for as long as he defended the autonomous rights of the county and was able to stop or at least slow down the efforts of the Gömbös government aimed at centralizing public administration.

The new prefect tried to reciprocate the trust placed in him: at the national elections in 1935 (March 31–April 4, 1935), he succeeded in helping the governing party candidate to victory. Pehm and the local Christian socialists had supported not the victor, but a Catholic "independent" candidate campaigning on the basis of a conservative, legitimist program. Their candidate, however, had failed to make it past the first round.[96] At these elections, the Christian Economic and Social Party, which had proved incapable of renewal, lost more than half of its 31 seats in the Parliament. Even so, with its fourteen successful candidates, the party came third

93. MNL OL K 148, 911. cs. 1935/11/1189; MNL OL K 27, Minutes of the Ministerial Meeting of 12 March 1935, Annex II. part, 111–112. Minister of Interior Miklós Vitéz Kozma's proposal to the Ministerial Council, March 7, 1935.

94. ÁBTL 3.2.4. K–384/2. 15. fol. "The Primate." Béla Kovrig's characterization of József Mindszenty, September 24, 1946.

95. MNL ZML IV.402. 550. Minutes of the County General Assembly of March 18, 1935; *Zalai Napló* 3, no. 64, March 19, 1935, 2.

96. Paksy, *Zalaegerszeg társadalma és politikai élete 1919–1939*, 102–05.

overall in the election.[97] Pehm had his own critical opinion of the whole election: in one of his letters he wrote of a political Sahara and of the Governing Party voters who had been bought for 1 pengő.[98]

The Christian Party subsequently proved incapable of overcoming this disastrous defeat. The erosion of its support base proved irrevocable, and the attempted reforms of the "young ones" petered out into nothing. The "veterans" then joined together to establish – on January 26, 1937 – the United Christian Party, a fusion of various groupings. Their efforts, however, were not accompanied by either a process of modernization or a generational change. In the meantime, the National Socialists had strengthened on the far right, while, on the left, a popular front movement was beginning to evolve in the form of the so-called March Front, which grouped together populist (*népi*) writers and rural researchers, leftist university students, and antifascist intellectuals.

Pehm identified ignorance and social dissatisfaction as the factors that explained the spread of National Socialism and the increasing fanaticism in the villages. In his view, some kind of cautious modernization was required, given the rigidness of the social structure. Therefore, in 1937, Pehm, who was, by this time, a papal prelate, invited the "young ones" to consultations in Zalaegerszeg, with the ultimate aim of revising his own reform proposals and establishing a new party – perhaps in cooperation with other political groups. Once again unity proved elusive, but the Prelate Pehm achieved recognition as the leading figure in attempts to renew Christian (party) politics.

József Pehm stretched out an arm to other organizations that had social and patriotic leanings. In a series of photographs published as a supplement to the August 1, 1937 issue of the *Nemzeti Újság* (National Newspaper) – after photographs of a football match, of the Hungarian pavilion at the Paris Exposition, and of "the heir to the throne, King Otto II" – we find a picture of József Pehm holding a mass at the flag dedication ceremony in Zala-

97. The governing party (Party of National Unity) received 908,000 votes, the Smallholders Party 402,000 votes, the Christian Party 180,000 votes, and the Social Democratic Party 132,000 votes.

98. SZEL Géfin Gyula hagyatéka. Levelezések [Legacy of Gyula Géfin. Correspondence], VIII. Letter of József Pehm to Gyula Géfin. Zalaegerszeg, June 18, 1935. Published in Dobri, "...szívélyesen üdvözöl barátod és híved...," 280.

egerszeg of the Front Soldier Association. The *Nemzeti Újság*, however, was read in the aulas of Esztergom, too. And so a few days later Prince Primate Jusztinián Serédi inquired of József Grősz, the apostolic governor of Szombathely, how was it that Pehm had consecrated the standard of the front soldiers when two years earlier the Bishops' Conference had banned the blessing of any flags other than those of Catholic churches, associations and schools.[99] Moreover, as the photograph showed, Abbot Pehm had stood at the altar wearing a miter and holding a crosier, which, however, was permitted only in exceptional liturgical acts. In his reply, Grősz emphasized that Pehm had not received authorization for such an act.[100] Abbot Pehm's patronage of the front soldiers typifies his intellectual orientation: he fostered from the pulpit the same patriotic spirit in support of which these organizations had been established. In his address to the soldiers standing before the altar, Pehm spoke of patriotism and of the power and infinite nature of faith in Christ, doing so in a manner that might seem overbearing today. On this occasion too, he stressed that where there was no faith, there could be no love of country; consequently, the unbeliever could not be a true Hungarian.

In 1936 Gyula Gömbös died, and he was succeeded as prime minister by Kálmán Darányi (1886–1939), the former minister of agriculture. In May 1938, Darányi stepped down, and the talented financial expert Béla Imrédy (1891–1946) became prime minister. (In 1946, Imrédy would be executed as a war criminal.) Since Imrédy's program was based on the papal social encyclical, Pehm heartily supported it. Moreover, Imrédy's term as prime minister saw the signing – in November 1938 – of the First Vienna Award, which returned to Hungary the southern part of Slovakia. It was this success that Pehm wished to honor when he proposed that Imrédy be made an honorary citizen of Zalaegerszeg. When making this proposal, Pehm evidently failed to consider the significance of the territorial gain in the process that led Hungarian foreign policy towards a deepening German orientation, and he also disregarded Imrédy's attempts to remove from government the fundamental elements of parliamentary democracy. Imrédy's marvelous revolution, which proclaimed "new Hungarian life on

99. SZEL AC 2207/1937. Letter of Prince Primate Jusztinián Serédi to József Grősz, apostolic governor, August 4, 1937.

100. Ibid., Reply of József Grősz to Prince Primate Jusztinián Serédi, August 19, 1937.

ancient Hungarian soil," was hardly at variance with Pehm's own thinking. Like many others, he too was mesmerized by the slogans that promised "spiritual reform," social measures, and "Christian solidarity." Pehm actively supported the Movement of Hungarian Life (Magyar Élet Mozgalom), thereby promoting the unity of right-wing forces in Zala County and adding to the chances of the joint candidates of the governing party and Christian Party in the upcoming national elections of 1939.

Sectarianism

The pre-Trianon Kingdom of Hungary had been a multinational and predominantly Catholic country. Catholics had made up 60 percent of the population and other denominations around 40 percent. In consequence of the border changes after World War I, this ratio had changed to 68:32. The religious diversity was naturally accompanied by sectarianism, elicited in the main by socio-economic and funding issues. A constant topic of discussion was whether financial support from the state was being allocated fairly. Further, Catholics and Protestants repeatedly accused each other of seeking to monopolize well-paid jobs and influential positions. Catholics complained of Protestant oppression, while Calvinists and Lutherans spoke of a silent but relentless counter-reformation. Sectarian controversy surrounding the division of posts, positions and jobs was particularly intense in traditional rural areas where everyone knew almost everyone.

In Zalaegerszeg Catholics accounted for 82 percent of total inhabitants, a higher rate than the national average. And the Catholic share of the population was even higher in Zala County as a whole. Pehm was not known for religious tolerance either in public life or in his private life. As parish priest he soon shattered the religious peace of the local community, and many instances of his religious intolerance were recorded. A memorable occasion in this respect was a ceremony in commemoration of heroes held on August 20, 1922. According to the official program, separate blessings in memory of the fallen were to be given by a Catholic priest (i.e., Pehm), a Lutheran pastor, and a Jewish rabbi. Both the Lutheran pastor and the rabbi arrived at the ceremony dressed in their religious vestments, but they were treated as unwelcome guests and were not given seats. This was the first occasion when the pro-government press mockingly referred to

József Pehm as the local "Atyaúristen" (Almighty God, meaning an omnipotent super-being), seeing in him the source of the unbecoming treatment of the Lutheran pastor and the rabbi. On another occasion, Pehm had local gendarmes remove Adventist and Baptist ministers from the town as they celebrated the Lord's Supper.[101]

Pehm linked the issue of religious unity with that of political unity, always giving precedence to Catholic interests. Sectarian differences intensified in Zala County when, on October 21, 1936, the minister of interior appointed Count Béla Teleki as prefect in place of Tibor Tabódy, who had unexpectedly passed away. A Calvinist prefect in a Catholic county! Feathers had already been ruffled a year earlier on the government's selection of a Calvinist as its local candidate in the national elections. And now it was compounding its earlier decision by appointing a member of a religious minority as prefect. Pehm sought to prevent the appointment before its official announcement, but his efforts were in vain: "If someone is suitable for office, then their religious affiliation cannot be an obstacle to their appointment. It could cause the greatest harm to the Christian and national camp [...] if appointments to posts were made on the basis of denominational percentage ratios," the minister of interior, who himself was a Catholic, stated firmly and irrevocably.[102] His opinion reflected the practice of the government, which emphasized a general allegiance to Christianity as against an affiliation with a particular denomination, whereby the government's aim was to prevent antagonisms from threatening political stability. Pehm, however, could not accept that the "undivided spirituality of the area" should be disregarded, as such a policy would not only result in religious apathy but also weaken the united front of Catholics against the Bolshevik "people's front." "With a Protestant prefect in Catholic Zala County the red peril will not be any smaller."[103] The response to his stubbornness was a mere invitation: if he came to Budapest, he should call in for a chat.[104] József Grősz, the apostolic administrator, also

101. Statement by Jenő Szigeti, an Adventist minister, November 23, 2010. (The incident involved Jenő Szigeti's father, who was also an Adventist minister.)

102. PL Mm. 21. d. "Teleki főispán" c. iratköteg [Bundle of documents entitled "Prefect Teleki"]. Letter of Minister of Interior Miklós Kozma to József Pehm, September 29, 1936.

103. Ibid., Letter of József Pehm to Miklós Kozma, October 5, 1936.

104. Ibid., Letter of Miklós Kozma to József Pehm, October 8, 1936.

asked Pehm to exercise discernment: "Count Teleki's personality and his Catholic wife were a sufficient guarantee that we will encounter understanding from a Catholic perspective, probably more understanding than we might be shown by however many Catholic prefects. [...] our smartest course of action is to eat this frog and put on a brave face."[105]

The disputes between the pro-Horthy and Calvinist prefect and the royalist and Catholic abbot-priest were an enduring feature of their terms in office. The priest failed to topple the prefect, who remained in office until October 27, 1944. This failure was not for lack of trying, as we know that Pehm attempted to persuade the Prime Minister's Office that Count Teleki was biased and unsuitable for office, arguing that the prefect had no experience of public administration; that he had rudely failed to attend a reception given by the diocesan bishop of Szombathely; that he was handing out jobs to Protestants with the result that 33 percent of the teachers at the state grammar school were Protestant; that he had appointed the son of a Lutheran pastor to work in an area with exclusively Catholic doctors, and that this man had, furthermore, professed to be German in 1941. And what was the much-maligned prefect's opinion of Pehm? "His personality – whether he was acting in a public or private capacity – virtually radiated absolute intransigence," Teleki wrote decades later, in 1957. Still, he expressed great respect for Pehm's (Mindszenty's) conduct after 1945.[106]

For Abbot Pehm, Christian unity meant in reality the victory of Catholicism rather than a dialogue leading to convergence. His intransigence and religious fundamentalism arose from his clerical conservatism. In this he was not alone, as conservatism was the defining character of the church's spirituality at the time. Until the Second Vatican Council (Vatican II), a faithful Catholic could attend a Protestant religious service for family reasons alone. Canon 1258 of the Code of Canon Law – in force from 1918 – stated that it was not lawful for a Catholic priest to cooperate with non-Catholics "*communicatio in sacris*," that is, in liturgical acts or rites. On January 6, 1928, Pope Pius XI issued the encyclical *Mortalium animos* on "true religious unity," which nipped in the bud the growing enthusiasm for ecumenism. Since 1919, however, Christian unity had

105. Ibid., Letter of József Grősz to József Pehm, September 21, 1936.

106. His words are quoted in Károly Maróthy-Meizler, *Az ismeretlen Mindszenty* (Buenos Aires: Editorial Pannonia, 1958), 138.

become a watchword in Hungarian politics, and the state expected the various denominations to join together in legitimizing its military and civilian ceremonies. As the "all-Christian image" of the Christian-national camp loosened, so the hard externals of the doctrinal differences returned.

József Pehm's "national anthem affair" was linked with this trend. In 1934, he was attacked in an article published by the pro-government *Zalai Napló* for having refused to sing the national anthem after a ceremonial mass held in commemoration of the Hungarian revolution and war of independence of 1848–49. Rather than sing the anthem with other members of the congregation, Pehm had left the church "in protest" and much to their consternation.[107] The journalist brusquely admonished Abbot Pehm: "You are not the Church's sole infallible voice; you are not God's sovereign envoy in Zala County." Then he questioned Pehm's patriotism and used "humiliating expressions in a strikingly crude manner" to describe his priestly vocation.[108] Pehm's response was swift, galvanizing his supporters to oppose a newspaper that was unacceptable "from a Catholic and moral standpoint." The case ended up in court. In the end, however, the court made no judgment on the matter, as the plaintiff journalist, unsure of a favorable outcome in the case, withdrew his suit and, indeed, apologized to Pehm.[109]

The issue that lay at the root of the press polemics of 1934–35 was whether or not the national anthem could be sung in a Catholic church. Dogmatic (doctrinal) grounds were cited by those opposed to the singing of a national anthem, which included the words "This nation has suffered for all sins of the past and the future." The Catholic view, they argued, was that a person could not suffer for the sins of the future, as God does not punish people in the present for the sins they may (or will) commit in the future, as this would mean they could freely sin subsequently. The more permissive viewpoint was that the lyrics of the national anthem were metaphoric and fell under poetic license. The controversy had been brought to a close by the Bishops' Conference: at a meeting on October 23, 1903, they had approved the national anthem from a doctrinal standpoint

107. *Zalai Napló* 2, no. 62, March 18, 1934, 1–2.

108. SZEL AC 668/1935. Judgment No. 2873/1934/11, Szombathely, April 10, 1935.

109. ÁBTL 3.1.9. V–700/40. 200. fol. Statement of Péter János Sylvester to the Szombathely Royal Court; MNL ZML IV. 401b. 2/biz.–1935. The lawyer Miklós Nyáry's letter to the prefect, Tibor Tabódy, July 25, 1935.

and consented to it being sung in Catholic churches, albeit only at the end of a mass.[110]

On making his irreverent exit, Abbot Pehm may have been driven by considerations similar to those cited by dogmatic opponents of the national anthem. Moreover, Ferenc Kölcsey, the author of the national anthem's lyrics, had been a Calvinist. Owing to his legitimist convictions, Pehm went beyond doctrinal anti-Protestantism. Indeed, one might say that he wished to adhere to the practice of the era of the counter-reformation with Márton Padányi Biró as his exemplar. His book on Padányi Biró had been inspired by apologetics, and it exhorted the reader towards a combative Catholic consciousness rather than defensive apologetics. In the specific case, Pehm requested and received a judgment from the diocesan office, which did not accord with his own opinion: according to the Bishops' Conference "when the national anthem is sung at the end of a church service, the priest conducting the church service should remain by the altar until the singing ends."[111] When, however, the same inquiry was made at the court, the office "glossed over" Pehm's conduct, stating – accurately – that the singing of the national anthem was not a church rite, and so various practices had developed: some priests remained at the altar while it was sung, while others exited the church.[112]

Sectarianism overlay the national anthem affair, and so, in view of the above, there was no chance that Abbot Pehm would make a gesture of any sort to the Protestants. In 1932, the priests of the Zalaegerszeg deanery protested in a letter to members of the national assembly – a letter written and signed by Pehm – against the general ban on the publishing of newspapers on Reformation Day (October 31). Other deans in the diocese were invited to join the protest.[113] The Protestant religious holiday, however,

110. Zoltán Kovács, "Hetyey Sámuel pécsi püspök (1897–1903)," in *Egyházi arcélek a pécsi egyházmegyéből* ed. Tamás Fedeles, Zoltán Kovács, and József Sümegi (Pécs: Fény Kft., 2009), 145–51.

111. ZMMPI esperesi iratok 1935–37. Letter of János Kappel, the episcopal secretary, to József Pehm, December 30, 1935.

112. SZEL AC 668/1935. Bishop János Mikes's transcript to Miklós Valkó, Council Chairman of the Royal Court, April 24, 1935.

113. ZMMPI esperesi iratok 1930–32. Letter to the representatives, Zalaegerszeg, June 14, 1932; SZEL AC 1603/1932. Minutes of the Spring 1932 meeting of the Zalaegerszeg Deanery, Zalahásházy, May 31, 1932.

had traditionally been recognized in Hungary; it would not have been possible to simply disregard it. When, however, a government decree made October 31 a national school holiday, Pehm called upon the county assembly to remind the government that it should not endanger national unity by adopting such measures. He then produced a report that showed, based on statistics going back several years, the sectarian breakdown of the various institutions of Zala County, of the administrative committee, of the gendarmerie, of the audit office, and of senior municipal officials. His demand was that the division of jobs between Catholics and Protestants should be adjusted to the county's Catholic-Protestant ratio (i.e., 93:7).

Some years later, when he was prince primate, Mindszenty left a parish supper held after a village confirmation ceremony because the local Calvinist minister had also been invited. Before he left, he gave the parish priest a choice: either the Calvinist minister would go or he, the primate, would do so. The parish priest said that, having invited the Calvinist minister to the supper, he could not now send him away. On hearing this, the prince primate turned around and went home. And yet, the next morning – by way of atonement – he sent the priest a red cincture symbolizing an award. The true great change came in the final years of his life, some years after the Second Vatican Council, when the primary consideration became whether his partner was a Hungarian or not a Hungarian, and a person's religious affiliation was of only secondary interest to him. On one occasion in the United States an elderly Calvinist minister greeted him, whereupon Mindszenty embraced him and said, "My dear Hungarian brother!"[114] This telling anecdote reveals a significant change in Mindszenty's personality. During the early part of his career, provincialism and his limited geographic milieu had kept him from becoming a supporter of a rapprochement between the Christian denominations. As time passed, however, his horizons broadened, particularly, it seems, after he identified Nazism as the common enemy: "Now with Christianity in general danger and while keeping our Catholic convictions and our interest in view, let us not be the ones to prevent social peace with the Protestant denominations and even the possibility of cooperation. There too there are people of good will and here too there

114. Országos Széchényi Könyvtár Kézirattár [National Széchényi Library] (hereafter: OSZK Kt.) 514. fond, 127. ő. e. [őrzési egység = archival unit] Papers of István Gereben: The Calvinist pastor Imre Bertalan greets József Mindszenty, New Brunswick, September 30, 1973.

are unreliable ones," he wrote as one of the tactical resolutions of a conference of priests that he convened in 1938.[115] Evidently, Christian unity and a deepening of religious life remained his guiding principles later on in life, but as archbishop of Esztergom he became more open-minded. Once he was in high office, a different ego – that of a national politician – came to the fore. It was a symbolical act, when on November 30, 1946, József Mindszenty consecrated László Bánáss as bishop at St. Anna's Church in Debrecen, a city where Catholics had been prohibited from building a church until 1715. In 1947 the denominations joined together to prevent religious instruction from becoming a voluntary subject in schools rather than a compulsory subject. Even so, the growing openness to the other denominations did not mean that József Mindszenty, as primate, accepted the necessity of establishing a political party that could oppose the communists and whose members would be both Catholics and Protestants. At the time, Mindszenty was still thinking in terms of a Catholic party, as will be described in greater detail in a subsequent chapter of this book.[116] All of this is hardly surprising: the Catholic Church found it difficult to accept the principle of freedom of religion, doing so only after the Second Vatican Council.

Against Nazism

On March 12, 1938, Germany annexed Austria; the western part of Hungary now lay in the immediate vicinity of Hitler's Germany. The far right in Hungary gained momentum. Arrow Cross insignia appeared in buttonholes or at least under the lapels. For the Christian Party, the most dangerous opponent was no longer the Smallholders' Party but the far-right radicals. The Hungarian Bishops' Conference was bewildered and indecisive. It could not reject out of hand the social program put forward by the National Socialists. In the fall of 1937, six months after Pope Pius XI issued the encyclical *Mit brennender Sorge* (With Burning Concern) condemning totalitarianism, National Socialism, racial theory and racist persecution, the Hungarian Bishops' Conference adopted a taciturn

115. PL Processus, V–700/48. 18. fol. Tactical decisions (italics in the original).

116. ÁBTL 3.1.9. V–103.458. 117. fol. Memorandum on Jenő Czettler's interrogation, January 15, 1951.

resolution on the need for priests to shun the Arrow Cross movement, but the bishops took no further measures for the time being. The bishops did not detect in the Arrow Cross movement the same ruthless methods as those employed by the Nazis in Germany, and so they limited their inquiry to an examination of whether or not the Arrow Cross was hostile towards religion and towards the Catholic Church. In a formal sense, Arrow Cross members – unlike their German Nazi counterparts – were not against religion or the Church. Indeed, some of them ostentatiously claimed to be "good Christians," one example being Ferenc Szálasi whose fervent Catholicism has been much dwelt upon.

The anti-clericalism of the era filled Pehm with anguish and concern. "Anti-clerical winds are blowing from Moscow and Berlin" were his prescient words, spoken from the pulpit of the church in Zalaegerszeg on March 15, 1937.[117] On countless occasions, he found a way to condemn – in the presence of Zalaegerszeg's Catholic elite – the anti-Christian Aryan supremacist teachings of the Nazis, doing so from the pulpit, in his capacity as parish chairman, or when speaking to the various Catholic associations.

Pehm requested and received permission from his bishop to read *Der Mythus des XX. Jahrhunderts* (The Myth of the Twentieth Century) by Alfred Rosenberg, the leader and soul of "the new German paganism."[118] Published in 1930, the work had been placed on the Vatican's list of banned books. Pehm used quotations from Rosenberg's book to prove, in simple and specific terms that could be understood by everyone, the dangers of the new ideology: "He treats the Church with the greatest loathing. The work of the Aryan Jesus was falsified by the Jewish Apostle Paul, it is claimed. The Pope is a demonic figure, a fraud, who prevents people from thinking for themselves and who proclaims demonic witchcraft. The clergy are like shamans." Pehm's conclusion was simple and clear: "From a national perspective, this ideology is harmful for every non-Germanic people. The deification of the Germanic race necessarily leads to contempt for, and the oppression of, the other races. Rosenberg indiscriminately executes every great man who was not born into the German race and he condemns all ideas that are not of Germanic

117. PL Mm. 33. d. Draft sermons: "Prelate's greeting, March 16, 1937."

118. SZEL AC 2202/1937. József Pehm's petition to József Grősz, apostolic governor, August 16, 1937; Ibid., Grősz's authorization, August 18, 1937.

origin."[119] Pehm drew an analogy between Nazism and Bolshevism, and he discounted the Nazis' anti-communism. In one of his sermons he explained that "the totalitarian state idea means that the state does not merely practice what it has done until now, but that it also seeks the ideological and moral transformation of all citizens. That is, it removes the right and mission of the family and of the Church, which have been received by both the one and the other on the basis of natural law or by way of a substantive provision from God. Neither can we diminish the family into a simple raven's nest, nor can the Church abandon – for the sake of Rosenberg, let's say – its warmth and its work stretching back two thousand years."[120]

Having read Rosenberg's book, József Pehm had no illusions about the ideology of Nazism. He saw clearly the Nazis' hostility towards the Church and the dangers of importing their ideas. Indeed, he recognized the mortal threat posed by National Socialism to Christianity as a whole. At the same time, however, he did not believe Nazism could be defeated by a "popular front" made up of Marxists and large landowners, the haute bourgeoisie and smallholder farmers. Rather, he was counting on the power and force of Christianity. The manifest weakness of the Christian Party prompted Prelate Pehm to once again invite to a conference – to be held in Budapest on Easter Tuesday, April 19, 1938 (i.e., just over a month before the holding of the 34th Eucharistic Congress in the city) – all those who were willing to think together about the role of Christian party politics and links with the Arrow Cross movement. The period leading up to the conference was a fateful one: six weeks prior to the conference, on March 13, 1938, Germany annexed Austria, an action that left western Hungary in the immediate vicinity of Hitler's Germany. In view of the speed of rearmament and the increase in tensions, a new world war seemed ever more likely.

The meeting was held behind closed doors and was completely confidential. It was not reported on in the newspapers, and even Prince Primate Serédi received no prior information and learned of the meeting from a complaint.[121] Those attending the meeting adopted a memorandum in which they concluded that ever since the *Anschluss* (Austria's annexation by

119. PL Mm. 33. d. Draft sermons: "1937. Ladies' Congregation, Men's League."
120. Ibid.
121. PL Cat. D/c–1496/1938. Drégelypalánk, April 22, 1938.

Germany), "mysterious hands" had been seeking to undermine people's trust in the old political parties and push the discontented masses towards the Arrow Cross movement. The attendees then committed themselves to a constitutional form of government that was national, social, Christian and "developmental in a modern sense," while also rejecting both Nazi neo-paganism and proletarian dictatorship. Opinions were divided over the practical steps that needed to be taken immediately. As before, Prelate Pehm's suggestion that a new party be established that would take the middle road between the Christian Party and the National Socialists was considered untimely. An attempt was made to maneuver between the governing party, which was drafting anti-Jewish legislation at the time, and the far-right opposition party. The drafters of the memorandum could not, therefore, simply ignore the "Jewish question," which they regarded as a social, economic and ideological problem rather than a racial issue. The memorandum mentions with pride Act XXV of 1920, which is generally known as the "numerus clausus" and was the first antisemitic law in the history of Hungarian law-making and the first to be adopted in Europe after World War I. The authors of the memorandum concluded that the imposition of partial restrictions on Jews in the social and economic fields lay in the interest of Christians. However, the restrictions should not be introduced in the "revolutionary" manner demanded and proclaimed by the far right. Rather, a managed economy and state-controlled cooperatives were the best means to achieve the goal. In view of its neutrality, the memorandum might be viewed as a shift towards the far right. Perhaps, however, its contents merely reflected the clumsiness of those seeking a new path and the lack of preparedness of the supporters of political Catholicism and the Christian Party. At the time, Hungary's political elite as a whole was seeking some kind of *modus vivendi* that would slow down the spread of Nazism in Hungary and block the expansion of German interests.

Once again, however, party political developments proved József Pehm right: the country lacked a modern and popular political party that could appeal to the masses. In 1938–39 the Christian Party became almost completely defunct, whereupon most of its members joined Count Pál Teleki's new government party, the Party of Hungarian Life. For most of his life the highly respected geographer and convinced Anglophile Teleki had been preoccupied by his academic work. In February 1939, however, he reluctantly agreed to serve as prime minister for the second time, having already been Hungarian prime minister for a period of nine months in 1920–21. At the elections in 1939, the governing party once again secured an absolute majority, while the Christian Party fared even worse than in 1935. (It should be noted, however, that two of its eight parliamentary representatives were from Zala County!) Abbot Pehm's influence in public life is underlined by the fact that a person esteemed by the public could be found who then unified the United Christian Party and governing party voters. The local dignitary Kristóf Thassy was chosen as the joint candidate with a rather subdued program. Thassy chose not to outbid his Arrow Cross opponent by making irresponsible promises. Further, he avoided any discussion of the "Jewish question" even though the issue had entered the government policy arena with Parliament's adoption in May of the first anti-Jewish legislation (the First Jewish Law). Despite the Arrow Cross's propaganda campaign, which was pursued with even greater intensity than in 1935, the unity of the conservative and Christian camp in Zalaegerszeg remained intact and the Christian Party candidate Kristóf Thassy won the election with the government's support. Meanwhile, Count Móric Esterházy, who had been prime minister in 1917 and was now included on the party's county list, also received a parliamentary seat.[122]

At the time, Pehm recognized that the reform-conservative policies of Count Pál Teleki provided the best chance of defending Hungarian national interests and defending the homeland. Indeed, among Teleki's first measures was an action banning the Arrow Cross Party. Associated with Teleki's name is the National Policy Service, which had been established in 1939 to monitor and avert the hostile propaganda that was appearing in Hungary and to develop a desirable public atmosphere and public attitude. A longstanding priority for Teleki was government policy towards the diasporic populations in western Hungary, that is to say, the national education of ethnic Germans who did not belong to the *Volksbund*, an organization that represented Third Reich interests. Responding to the lofty call of national defense, József Pehm joined those parish priests who were willing, when interacting with their congregations and the public, to support government interests, to shape public attitudes, to monitor and

122. Paksy, *Zalaegerszeg társadalma és politikai élete 1919–1939*, 112–25.

report on the public mood, and to counter malicious rumors. It was during this period that József Pehm came into close contact with such influential government officials as Béla Kovrig, the university professor who in 1944 elaborated a modern socio-economic program that was inspired by Christian Socialist and Christian Democratic values. According to Kovrig, Pehm "happily undertook the task of monitoring Arrow Cross machinations in Zala County, informing me of what he learned, offering guidance as to whom we should equip with anti-Arrow Cross leaflets; indeed, he himself was willing to produce such leaflets and disseminate them by way of his people."[123] The National Policy Service never became more than a rather inexact strategy for action. Indeed, after the suicide of Prime Minister Teleki on April 3, 1941 the scheme fell apart.

Pehm's hostility towards the Nazis is indisputable. In a symbolic move that followed much self-questioning, in the summer of 1942 Pehm (now aged 50) changed his German-sounding surname to Mindszenty. He did this at a time when, under the influence of German propaganda, many among Hungary's "Volksdeutschen" (ethnic Germans) were re-Germanizing their surnames.[124] The name designated by Abbot Pehm in his petition for a change of surname was derived from the name of his native village (Csehimindszent). However, instead of the simple letter "i" (Mindszenti), he requested Mindszenty with a "y" – which would normally have indicated noble ancestry but in Pehm's case seems to have reflected a degree of snobbery on his part. At the time (and in other periods too), surnames ending in "y" were highly popular, as they signified that one belonged (or aspired to belong) to the nobility, to the elite or – at least – to the middle class. The choice of such a surname was indicative, moreover, of a desire to accommodate society and meet contemporary social expectations. The new surname was recorded in the church baptismal register of Csehimindszent on August 29, 1942.

123. ÁBTL 3.2.4 K–384/2. 16. fol. Béla Kovrig's characterization of József Mindszenty, September 24, 1946.

124. Ministry of Public Administration and Justice, Authority Department, Registry Section, Petition No. 016944/1942 submitted by József Pehm to the minister of interior, July 20, 1942.

Hungary steadily drifted into war at Hitler's side. The initial successes of the revisionist policy served to further consolidate the regime. In accordance with the provisions of the First Vienna Award (November 2, 1938), Hungary re-annexed twelve thousand square kilometers of territory that had belonged to Czechoslovakia since the Treaty of Trianon. (Most of this territory had formed a part of Slovakia, which had been granted greater autonomy within Czechoslovakia after the Munich Agreement of September 1938, but the re-annexed territory also included a part of Czechoslovakia's Carpathian-Rus region.) Pehm welcomed enthusiastically the collapse of the Versailles system and expressed hopes of further territorial revision. "We need the whole of the Hungary of 1910," Pehm declared when Béla Imrédy, Hungary's prime minister at the time, was made an honorary citizen of Zalaegerszeg at a ceremony in the town. Pehm himself had proposed that Imrédy receive this honor in recognition of his role in securing the First Vienna Award. Subsequently, thankful for the return of the lost territories to Hungary, Pehm even forgave Horthy, hailing the regent and his government for the success of their revisionist endeavors.

In the spring of 1939, Hungarian forces marched into the residual part of the Carpathian-Rus region, and then, following the Second Vienna Award (August 30, 1940), Hungary re-annexed the northern part of Transylvania, which had belonged to Romania since the Treaty of Trianon. The return of the lost territories did not, however, satisfy Hungarian demands in full. Moreover, Germany's role as mediator meant that Hungary was now even more indebted to Hitler's Reich. This substantial "debt" was a bitter pill for Hungary to swallow. Germany required ever larger shipments of raw materials and foodstuffs, and meeting such demands had a detrimental effect on the domestic supply of goods in Hungary (bread and flour had to be rationed). The radicalized minority of the country's ethnic Germans could freely conspire, while radical new measures were taken to address the "Jewish question" (the Hungarian legislature adopted three new anti-Jewish laws: in 1938, 1939, and 1941). The head of the Arrow Cross, Ferenc Szálasi, was released from prison. Szálasi saw himself as a messianic figure who would bring salvation to the nation. Under his leadership the far right became a united force. In 1940, Hungary signed the Tripartite Pact, affiliating itself with the Axis, and soon the government of Prime Minister Pál Teleki was fulfilling all of Germany's demands.

Re-Annexation of the Mura Region

On December 12, 1940, Hungary and Yugoslavia signed a treaty of eternal friendship, but several months later Hitler contacted Regent Horthy, requesting that Hungary participate in the campaign against Yugoslavia in return for German recognition of the Hungarian leadership's territorial claim to a part of the Vojvodina region. It was obvious to Teleki that his idea of armed neutrality was falling apart. Further, he recognized that Hungary, by participating in the campaign, would violate the treaty of eternal friendship with Yugoslavia and become a henchman of the Nazi empire. Weighed down by his responsibility for the situation, he shot himself in the head on April 3, 1941, a day after the German army began marching against Yugoslavia. In his diary, Pehm recorded the news of Teleki's death and of the passage of German troops through Hungary towards Yugoslavia:

> April 3. German vehicles are chugging along the county's roads and through the town. It is a dizzying parade. In the morning hours we hear that Prime Minister Teleki has died suddenly and tragically. T[eleki] was an anglophile, like a good many Hungarians. A German offensive. A German hand is suspected. Only in the evening is a suicide reported. April 4. A painful Friday. Many penitents. Sitting in the confessional from six until 10.45, I feel the vibration caused by every single German military vehicle that passes through.[125]

It was, therefore, without Teleki that Hungary reached the final milestone in its territorial expansion. On April 11, 1941, concurrently with the German invasion of Serbia and the Syrmia (Szerémség) and Banat (Bánság) regions, the Hungarian army advanced into the Baranja (Baranya) and Bačka (Bácska) regions, which had been occupied by Serbian troops in 1918. In the ensuing days and weeks, the Mura region was also returned

125. PL Mm. 43. d. József Pehm's diary, entries from April 3 and 4, 1941.

to Hungary. This latter region, which consisted of the *Muravidék* area (Slovenian: *Prekmurje*) and the *Muraköz* area (Croatian: *Međimurje*), had constituted parts of Vas County and Zala County from the eleventh century until the end of World War I. In terms of its ecclesiastical administration, the *Muravidék* area (*Prekmurje*) had belonged to the Szombathely diocese (Hungary) until 1923, from which time it had been administered by the bishop of Maribor (Slovenia) – as apostolic governor – in line with an ecclesiastical legal settlement that reflected the territorial changes contained in the Treaty of Trianon. On April 16, 1941, Hungarian troops took possession of the *Muravidék* area with its majority Hungarian population. Euphoric celebrations took place in the major towns of the area, each of which had been decked out with Hungarian flags. The return of the area to Hungarian jurisdiction led József Pehm to action: in Alsólendva, the principal Hungarian town in the area, he and five other priests gave a mass at the Catholic church.[126]

In the *Muraköz* area (*Međimurje*), in what had once been the Csáktornya and Perlak districts of Zala County, the situation was more complicated.[127] The majority of people in this area were Catholic Croats. In an ecclesiastical administrative sense, these people had belonged to the Archdiocese of Zagreb ever since the thirteenth century, even though the area had formed a part of Hungary until the Treaty of Trianon. At the population census of 1910, 5,766 people in this area – from a total population of 90,387 and including most of the thousand-strong Jewish community – had self-identified as Hungarians. At the same census, 22,557 additional Hungarian speakers (i.e., Hungarian-speaking Croats, Slovenians, etc.) had been recorded. These figures show that the vast majority of people in the area (approx. 91% of the population) were Croats. Evidently, this population share was the consequence of events and trends in earlier centuries, including the Ottoman occupation and the failure of Hungarian assimilation (Magyarization) efforts. The situation was rendered even more complex by the fact that Croatia, which had declared independence from Yugoslavia on April 10, 1941, also laid claim to the area. In the end, the

126. *Zalamegyei Ujság* 14, no. 86, April 17, 1941, 2.

127. See László Göncz, *A muravidéki magyarság 1918–1941* (Lendva: Magyar Nemzetiségi Művelődési Intézet, 2001); László Göncz, *Felszabadulás vagy megszállás? A Mura mente 1941–1945* (Lendva: Magyar Nemzetiségi Művelődési Intézet, 2006), http://www.doksi.hu.

Croatian military administration remained in place until July 9, 1941, at which time the Royal Hungarian Army occupied the area.

It is a popular myth that the fate of the *Muraköz* area (whether it should belong to Croatia or to Hungary) was decided by a rather agile Abbot Pehm. Still, while his role should not be overstated, nor should it be underestimated. For we know that Pehm's old nemesis, the prefect, Count Béla Teleki, asked him to lead Hungarian propaganda efforts aimed at the re-annexation of the *Muraköz* area and that Pehm accepted this assignment without hesitation.[128] Just over a month earlier, Pehm had been complaining to the government about the prefect. Now, however, the two men saw eye to eye on the issue of the *Muraköz* area. Pehm, who had grown accustomed to endless work but had recently resigned from his church duties outside the parish, needed an outlet for his spare energy. The first half of 1941 thus brought a marked change in József Pehm's life. His priorities shifted from community-organizing work among local Catholics in Zala County to a new focus on the *Muraköz* area.

His diary entries from this period are full of his anxieties and complaints concerning the wrangling over the re-annexation. As part of the propaganda campaign, on April 27, 1941, Abbot Pehm held a Sunday field mass at Čakovec (Csáktornya) in the heart of the *Muraköz* region. The church service was a field mass because in this way it could be held without a permit from the competent ordinarius, the archbishop of Zagreb. Around four thousand Catholics from 103 villages and towns in the *Muraköz* area came to the field mass, holding village signs and the Hungarian tricolor. When the mass ended, the crowd chanted enthusiastically for the return of the *Muraköz* area to Hungary, which they were ready to defend even by force of arms. All of this was reported on in a telegram message drafted at the presbytery in Zalaegerszeg and sent to Horthy, Hitler, and Mussolini.[129]

Such well-staged and spectacular acts of propaganda were effective but not cheap. To raise funds, Pehm once again set about knocking on doors. Indeed, he launched a regular onslaught of requests and statements directed at the government. Hungary's official re-annexation of the *Muraköz* area was slow in coming, even though the Croatian administration was

128. PL Mm. 29. d. Confidential report no. 126/1942 of the Zalaegerszeg captain of the Royal Hungarian Police to the police chief, June 2, 1942.

129. Ibid. Letter of Abbot-Priest József Pehm to Regent Miklós Horthy, July 26, 1941.

crumbling and some Croatian officials had already departed voluntarily. In a renewed exertion of mass pressure, more than twelve thousand signatures were collected for a statement of loyalty to Hungary. A delegation then took the signatures to Zalaegerszeg, requesting that they be forwarded to the regent, Miklós Horthy. In a solemn speech, József Pehm welcomed this delegation. After his words of inspiration, the county assembly sent a telegram of gratitude to Horthy.[130] A further initiative was a march held in Prelog (Perlak) on May 11, 1941. As many as twelve thousand people attended the march, with mounted soldiers, floral carriages, and music. The crowds expressed their support for Hungary, for the Hungarian army, and for Horthy, demanding that the *Muraköz* area be placed under Hungarian administration. According to the recollections of local people, however, the crowds were compelled to take part in the pro-Hungarian marches; their participation was neither voluntary nor enthusiastic. The uncertainty of the *Muraköz* area's fate elicited an ambiguous response among local inhabitants. With a view to their own survival, they sought to accommodate the expectations of both Hungarian and Croatian government apparatuses.

In Hungarian government circles, such mass protests were looked upon less and less favorably. Pehm's ardor was fading, too. Still, seeking progress in the matter, he chose to conceal his reservations for the time being. He thus requested an audience with Regent Horthy, who, after all, had ordered – on April 11 – the military advance to proceed all the way to "the thousand-year old southern border." Miklós Horthy received the abbot-priest of Zalaegerszeg on May 16, 1941, who then wryly noted his impressions in his diary: "...I went to see the Regent, because I did not want people to say he had not done [anything] for the Muraköz area. Well, H[orthy] was not interested in this matter; he spoke rather about futuristic art instead. [...] His answer to the spiritual conflicts: what I say, I do not swear to, others will have their say in this matter; but when the Hungarian army goes into an area, it does not usually depart from there. He looked with boredom at the pictures from Perlak (of May 11). It is difficult to negotiate here! I won't

130. MNL ZML IV.402. 663. Minutes of the County Assembly on May 8, 1941. See also László Göncz, "Álmaink álma Alsólendva és a Muraköz: Mindszenty (Pehm) József erőfeszítései a Mura mente visszacsatolásáért," in *Zalai Múzeum*, vol. 21 (Zalaegerszeg: Göcseji Múzeum, 2013), 45–58.

be coming here again soon!"[131] The next day (May 17), the prime minister and the minister of foreign affairs instructed the Prefect of Zala County to refrain from any further efforts. "We say no," Pehm "replied" in his diary. The official report was more zestful. It stated that Horthy had ended his meeting with Pehm by instructing him in confidence that "Muraköz's affiliation must be resolved by societal means, it cannot belong to someone else rather than to Hungary, and so [we must] keep on working [towards this goal]."[132] The "societal means" meant the "spontaneous" articulation and manifestation of a demand by the masses, which could then serve, metaphorically, as an arsenal of munitions for the government, as it sought to preserve and promote its revisionist foreign policy interests. All of this explains Pehm's self-confidence and the willingness of government ministers – and even the head of government – to meet with this small-town priest, who was otherwise known only in ecclesiastical and legitimist circles. He successfully broadened his network of contacts to include several senior members of the government in power.

The early summer was full of tensions and unexpected developments. The government had to weigh up many domestic and foreign policy considerations before it came to a decision on the future of the Muraköz area. The nub of the dilemma was whether to renounce Hungary's claim to the area with a view to strengthening Croatia, which had good relations with the Axis powers, or whether to insist on Hungary's right to re-annex the area, which had been an integral part of the historical Kingdom of Hungary in spite of the very modest ethnic Hungarian population share. For the sake of a lasting friendship with Croatia and for economic and military reasons, the Hungarian government opted to acknowledge Croatia's claim to the Muraköz area. In doing so, it abandoned the idea that the area formed an integral part of Hungary. When the government's position became public knowledge, people in Zala County and throughout the country took to the streets: "The municipalities are putting up bill-boards with a message for the government, ambitious political speakers are holding mass protests, and opposition politicians are stirring up the

131. PL Mm. 43. d. József Pehm's diary, entry of May 16, 1941.

132. Ibid., 29. d. Confidential report of the Zalaegerszeg captain of the Royal Hungarian Police to the police chief, June 2, 1942.

poison."[133] On May 25, 1941, a delegation of eight people from the Muraköz area traveled to Budapest to meet with Horthy. However, instead of being received by the Regent himself, they were redirected to Prime Minister László Bárdossy, who proceeded to annoy the delegation by stating that "There are no Hungarians in the Muraköz area."[134] Abbot Pehm then requested a meeting with Minister of Interior Ferenc Keresztes-Fischer. At the meeting, which took place on May 28, Pehm held the minister "under siege" for almost an hour seeking to persuade him that Croatian influence was not such a relevant factor in Muraköz and that the area rightfully belonged to Hungary. In response, Keresztes-Fischer pledged merely that the government would not act precipitously.

On another occasion, József Pehm met with Prime Minister László Bárdossy. Based on what we know from the sources, this meeting was rather tense and fell well short of expectations. Bárdossy had been greatly irritated by the accusations of treason made against his person and the government. Moreover he had been informed by his advisors that Abbot Pehm had fostered and nurtured such accusations. Pehm denied having been involved: "When confronted with the voice, lecturing and accusations of his grace, Mr. B[árdossy], I did not remain silent, and having rejected these accusations, I stood up and departed."[135] Reports of these events soon spread, with a growing distortion of the truth and adding to the number of Pehm's admirers. A year later, even the prelate referred back to this meeting, noting how Bárdossy had even offered him the post of prime minister "but I did not seek it."[136] Out of irritation Bárdossy may well have said: "If you can do it better, take my place." As time passed, Pehm seems to have given increasing credence to the words he heard at the meeting and to have used them to nurture his own ambitions.

On June 22, 1941, Germany launched its attack on the Soviet Union, but even this major event of the war only temporarily eclipsed the news from the *Muraköz* area. In Zala County, immense propaganda efforts were still

133. MNL OL K64–1941–67/a–390. Report of Ferenc Marosy, Hungarian legate in Zagreb, to Prime Minister László Bárdossy on preparations for the Hungarian–Croatian border negotiations, June 19, 1941.

134. PL Mm. 43. d. József Pehm's diary, entry of May 25, 1941.

135. Ibid., 29. d. Letter of József Pehm to unknown recipient, June 18, 1941.

136. OSZK Kt. 107/83. fond, 25. ő. e. Letter of József Pehm to Mrs. Jenő Udvardy, September 10, 1942.

being made, promoting the re-attachment of the *Muraköz* area to Hungary. On June 27, 1941, at the behest of József Pehm, the administrative committee of Vas County called on the government to take possession of the *Muraköz* area, in both a *de facto* and legal sense.[137] On July 5, at the request of 116 members of the administrative committee, an extraordinary meeting of the county assembly was held to discuss the issue. In a persuasive speech grounded in history, Abbot Pehm underlined the importance of Hungary's territorial integrity and gave his support to the patriotic but unrealistic (irredentist) political goal of restoring the country's historical borders. Finally, he motioned as follows: "Let the military and civil administration move into the ancient territory of the county!"[138] Pehm's stance on the issue (i.e., "we want it all back") was understandable in view of the winning mood engendered by the re-annexations. Indeed, Hungary's territorial gains had strengthened the belief that the resurrection of St. Stephen's Hungary (the restoration of the pre-1526 borders) was not merely an impossible dream. In elated mood, the Zala County administrative committee demanded the *de facto* re-annexation of the area. It even adopted a resolution stating that "it adheres under all circumstances and uncompromisingly to the part [of the county] that has been torn from its body and from its soul [...] It considers the Muraköz area to be an integral part of the county, which it will never renounce."[139] The text of the resolution was then forwarded to the Regent, to the prime minister, to the speakers of both houses of Parliament, and to the minister of interior and the minister of defense. In essence, the resolution of the county assembly merely gave emphasis to something that Bárdossy had already achieved in Rome in the meantime, namely the return of the *Muraköz* area to Hungary.

Several factors resulted in Hungary's decision, which ran completely counter to Croatia's stance on the issue: pressure from the Hungarian army (which was keeping order in the *Muraköz* area), a process of bargaining between the Hungarian prime minister and Mussolini, and Hitler and Mussolini's ongoing political game in which they simultaneously encouraged both Croatians and Hungarians to seize more territory. Additional factors were the public's craving for the restoration of the

137. *Zalamegyei Ujság* 24, no. 151, July 5, 1941, cover page.

138. MNL ZML IV.402. 665. Minutes of the County Assembly on July 5, 1941.

139. Ibid.

historical borders of Hungary and a series of patriotic acts that Pehm, among others, seems to have instigated. Pressure from Hungarian society and from the local population in the *Muraköz* area inspired government policy makers, who might otherwise have been more cautious, to take a riskier course of action. All these factors led to the decision to install a Hungarian military administration in the *Muraköz* area on July 9, 1941. This administration was replaced by a civil one on August 29. Some months later, on December 16, the Hungarian Parliament adopted Act XX on the re-annexation of the *Muraköz* area to Hungary.

For Full Integration

Following re-annexation, Hungarian laws went into force in the re-annexed area, and local officials, teachers and administrators swore an oath of allegiance to the Hungarian state. Numerous tasks awaited the social committee led by Pehm. Public health and public security were in an alarming state: "There are many shirkers, slackers, communists, and Arrow Cross men... Their roads are in a poor state of repair and are neglected... Tax morale is zero.... The schools are in an indescribably filthy and shabby state."[140] Pehm mentioned a whole series of measures in every strategically important field – interior, defense, commerce, industry, finance, and education. He emphasized the invaluable role of learning, of elementary school teachers, and of the clergy in reinstalling a sense of belonging to Hungary. The reshaping of consciousness was facilitated by the replacement of the public administrative apparatus, a process which Pehm himself significantly influenced.

The Zala County authorities assisted in multiple ways the integration of the re-annexed areas. At the behest of three committee members (Pehm being one of them), Zala County undertook to fund the education at military cadet school of two youths from the re-annexed areas, with boys from families with many children being given preference over others. The county assembly then set up a foundation for this specific purpose. At Pehm's behest the county assembly voted for an annual grant of 3,500 pengős, beginning

140. PL Mm. 29. d. Letter of József Pehm to Sándor Brand, County Deputy-Lieutenant, July 18, 1941.

in 1941, to be awarded to thirteen students from the re-annexed area who were studying at grammar schools in the county.[141] In 1942, József Pehm received 2,000 pengős from the county support fund to be spent on "the support of impoverished families in the southern areas that have been returned to the county."[142] Until 1941 Pehm had provided board and lodging to twelve students each year. After the re-annexation of the *Muraköz* area, this figure quickly increased to 35–37 students on average.[143] The figure had risen to 43 by 1943, by which time 30,000 pengős were needed to look after so many students.[144] Pehm continued this charity work even as bishop: 12–15 students were given free meals at the Bishop's Palace in Veszprém. This form of support was given mostly to the sons of poor families with many children and especially to those who were preparing for the priestly vocation.

Abbot Pehm was very keen on fostering the Hungarian language, but he was also aware that it would be impossible to make Hungarian the language of public administration in the *Muraköz* area. He recommended instead a practice that had been in place under the Dual Monarchy: the use of the local *Muraköz* "language" (i.e., a dialect of Croatian rather than literary Croatian). Accordingly, public officials were to learn this dialect as soon as possible and by 1942 at the latest.[145] The short-term consequence of this proposal was not only that one dialect of Croatian was given preference over another, but also that a wall was raised between Croatian and fellow Croatian. This latter development favored Hungary's minorities policy in the long term.

After the introduction of a civilian administration Abbot Pehm set about providing Hungarian priests to the faithful in the *Muraköz* area. He took this measure, having noticed that a majority of the local Croatian priests were hostile to the Hungarian state. The import of Hungarian priests was the short-term solution, but in the long run the aim was to reorganize the ecclesiastical administration of the area. This, however,

141. MNL ZML IV.402. 674. Minutes of the County Assembly on December 11, 1941.

142. PL Mm. 28. d. Coupon sent by Deputy-Lieutenant Sándor Brand to József Pehm, May 5, 1942.

143. VÉL I.1.44.a. 3225/1945. József Mindszenty: Curriculum vitae.

144. PL Mm. 29. d. Statement on assistance given to students from the Međimurje (Muraköz), June 4, 1943.

145. MNL ZML IV.402. 677. Minutes of the County Assembly on February 12, 1942.

would be no easy task, as the 22 parishes in the *Muraköz* area still belonged, in an ecclesiastical sense, to the Archdiocese of Zagreb, which was headed at the time by Cardinal Alojzije Viktor Stepinac. (Like Pehm, Stepinac would later be imprisoned by the postwar communist regime.) A special feature of the situation was that Cardinal Stepinac needed the permission of the Hungarian authorities in order to come to the *Muraköz* area and preside over confirmation services. The only way around this was for the Holy See to appoint a vicarius for the *Muraköz* area, who would be a consecrated bishop and therefore able to substitute for the cardinal at such services. Moreover, the Franciscan friars of Čakovec belonged to the Franciscan Province of Croatia, and so the Hungarian Franciscan provincial had no jurisdiction over their friary.

In the course of history there had already been several failed attempts to detach the *Muraköz* area from the Archdiocese of Zagreb. Hungary's political re-annexation of the area once again raised the possibility of a change in the area's ecclesiastical administration. The means to achieve this aim were to be the same as those used successfully to accomplish the political territorial changes: the exertion of pressure through the dispatch of delegations and letters. Abbot Pehm struggled alone to link the ecclesiastical restructuring of the area – and, in the longer term, its re-Catholicization – to the broader "correction" in its ethnic composition (i.e., the reversal of a centuries-old process of Croatization). In the fall of 1941, Prince Primate Jusztinián Serédi proposed to the Holy See that the *Muraköz* area be placed under the jurisdiction of the bishop of Szombathely. Pehm, however, was of the view that the archbishop was acting too slowly. He made a complaint but received only an annoyed response.[146] In the meantime, news came from Rome that the Holy See wished to see neither the creation of a separate administration nor the area's integration into the Diocese of Szombathely.[147] No progress was made even when Pehm's activists collected more than 25,000 signatures in favor of the ecclesiastical transfer of the area and submitted the signatures to Prince Primate Serédi. The petition "greatly irritated the [Croatian] clergy. Speaking from their

146. PL Mm. 29. d. Letter of Prince Primate Jusztinián Serédi to József Pehm, November 4, 1941.

147. Ibid., Captain Farkas, head of department at the Ministry of Public Services, to József Pehm, November 6, 1941.

pulpits they called it an anti-clerical measure, for in their view it was Rome's will that the Muraköz area belong to Zagreb."[148] This was, in essence, true. Despite pressure from various Hungarian sources, the Holy See remained politically neutral on the issue until the end of the war and rejected any changes to the diocesan boundaries. Accordingly, the *Muraköz* area, with its ethnic Croat majority, continued to be a part of the Archdiocese of Zagreb.[149]

Although his tasks in the *Muraköz* area left Abbot Pehm with little spare time, he did manage to attend a secret meeting held at the Bishop's Palace in Győr on August 28, 1943. The meeting was attended by members of the Catholic Action (Actio Catholica) group and by several parish priests. They convened to discuss what action the Catholic Church should take under the given circumstances and with a defeat in the war looming. As on so many occasions in the period since 1933, those attending the meeting considered the possibility of founding a new political party that would appeal to the masses, but the majority were still unwilling to drop the traditional party of political Catholicism. Instead, they decided to support an initiative that had been formed under the name of the Catholic Social People's Movement. They also requested the Bishops' Conference to send a circular letter to the clergy "giving general directives on recommended conduct in the current times of crisis and on the position that should be taken regarding the various political approaches."[150] They were addressing an issue of crucial significance: given the complete absence of information, the clergy could merely offer the word of the Gospel as a sure buttress. Often they were at a loss when it came to dealing with everyday life situations. The bishop of Győr, Baron Vilmos Apor (1892–1945), outlined the problem at a meeting of the Bishops' Conference on October 6, 1943, but he did so largely in vain. For Prince Primate Serédi, the domestic political situation in Hungary was so dangerous that the Bishops' Conference could not provide overt political guidance. Moreover, in his view, it was not the mission of the church to do so.

148. Ibid., 28. d. Letter of József Pehm with the invocation "Dear Friends!," May 28, 1942.

149. Ibid., 29. d. Confidential report on the spiritual care of the Levente members in the Međimurje (Muraköz) region, October 15, 1943.

150. PL 7557/1943. Letter of Baron Vilmos Apor, Bishop of Győr, to Prince Primate Jusztinián Serédi, September 18, 1943.

CHAPTER 3

JÓZSEF MINDSZENTY, BISHOP OF VESZPRÉM, APRIL 1944

CHAPTER 3

In the City of the Queens

VESZPRÉM'S NEW BISHOP AND THE FINAL DAYS OF THE WAR

Founded by King Stephen I of Hungary in the early eleventh century, the Diocese of Veszprém covered an area of fourteen thousand square kilometers from the dismemberment of 1777 (which occurred during the reign of Maria Theresa) until 1993, when the most recent changes to the diocesan boundaries in Hungary were made. The territorial changes that took place under the provisions of the Treaty of Trianon (1920) did not affect the diocese. Thus, whereas before World War I it had been a diocese of average size, it became – from 1920 – Hungary's third largest diocese.

The diocese was headed from 1939 until 1944 by Gyula Czapik, who served as diocesan bishop until May 7, 1943, and then, after his appointment as archbishop of Eger, as apostolic administrator until March 1944. (Unusually, the chapter did not appoint a vicar general for the duration of the vacancy.) On March 5, 1944, Pope Pius XII appointed the papal prelate and abbot-priest of Zalaegerszeg, József Mindszenty, as of Veszprém. The appointment took place after a long delay, for there was no consensus as to who should lead the diocese. Indeed, it would seem Mindszenty was appointed as bishop against the will of both the Hungarian government and Prince Primate Jusztinián Serédi.

When Bishop Gyula Czapik was appointed as archbishop of Eger, the search for a successor in the post of bishop of Veszprém began immediately. Initially, Mindszenty was not considered to be a candidate by the government, the apostolic nuncio or the prince primate. Both the government and the regent wanted to see the important Diocese of Veszprém led by a man who was loyal to the regime rather than by someone like József Pehm with his legitimist convictions and perceived disrespectful attitude towards Horthy. The regent's view of Pehm had not changed despite an apparent appreciation for the abbot-priest's activities in the *Muraköz* area. For his part, Prince Primate Jusztinián Serédi had his own favored candidate and even went to the trouble of writing to Rome to explain why he would not recommend Mindszenty:

> Towards his superiors Mindszenty is polite, albeit sometimes excessively solemn, and he speaks as if he wants to win respect for himself and as if he disposes of the same authority. In the company of his equals he behaves as if he were convinced of his own superiority; and with subordinates he is strict and commands respect. Therefore, the clergy do not like him; many respect him but do not like him, and, indeed, a good number have a true aversion to him.[1]

The prince primate then noted Mindszenty's limited erudition, his lack of a university education, his impatience, his forceful nature and coldness. The most serious deficiency, in Serédi's view, was a lack of the flexibility required for the task of governing the Church. The prince primate believed it would be dangerous and, under the circumstances, highly risky to appoint Mindszenty as bishop. Serédi's concern that deficiencies of character would prevent Mindszenty from becoming a wise and discerning bishop, was not groundless. Mindszenty's successful efforts in the field of ecclesiastical organization were known to high dignitaries of the church, but in view of the headwinds from the Hungarian government and the prince primate he stood little chance without effective patronage. Among the clergy it was

1. PL 9369/1944. Prince Primate Jusztinián Serédi's letter in Italian to the nuncio, Angelo Rotta, December 23, 1943.

widely believed that József Pehm had been a candidate for a vacant bishop's seat on two earlier occasions but that his appointment had been successfully prevented by the government and by Prince Primate Serédi.

A new opportunity arose when, on May 7, 1943, two key personnel changes took place: József Grősz, bishop of Szombathely, was appointed as archbishop of Kalocsa, and Gyula Czapik, bishop of Veszprém, became archbishop of Eger. The retired bishop of Szombathely, Count János Mikes, was aware of the unusualness of the situation. Viewing Mindszenty as the guarantor of the church's future, he was determined to make full use of his contacts. Angelo Rotta, apostolic nuncio in Budapest, who played a key role in seeking out potential bishops, had already noticed the pastoral merits of the abbot-priest. At some point in 1943, he had visited the Italian military internees who were being held at a prisoner-of-war camp in Zalaegerszeg. (These men were Italian officers who had been captured by the Germans in the aftermath of the Badoglio Proclamation.) Rotta had also visited the local parish church and had been very satisfied with what he saw there. József Antall, government commissioner for refugee affairs, who had accompanied Rotta on this visit, "was always convinced that Mindszenty had become bishop of Veszprém on these grounds."[2]

In addition to Mikes, others too may well have argued in favor of Mindszenty in discussions with the nuncio. Among such likely advocates was József Cavallier, the unjustly forgotten journalist and the head of the Hungarian Holy Cross Association, a Catholic body established to protect the interests of Jewish converts to Christianity. Cavallier had come into contact with the nuncio Angelo Rotta as the recipient and forwarder of the protective passports issued by the Vatican. Over time the two men formed a friendship, whereupon Cavallier became the nuncio's principal informer. Cavallier worked together with Margit Slachta, the first woman representative in the Hungarian legislature. As the founder of the Society of the Sisters of Social Service and as a legitimist politician, Slachta was well-acquainted with the abbot-priest of Zalaegerszeg. She may well have played a part in the appointment of Mindszenty as bishop of Veszprém.

2. Piarista Rend Magyar Tartományának Központi Levéltára [Central Archive of the Hungarian Province of the Piarist Order] (hereafter: PMKL) IV. 198. Legacy of Vince Tomek: his own manuscripts, 12, Memoirs of Vince Tomek (1968–81), fol. 99.

What is certain is that the Vatican was looking for a candidate who would be capable of maintaining order in a transitional and confused period and of fulfilling the painstaking task of post-war reconstruction. At this time of crisis, there was a need for a determined individual with the ability to lead. It seemed likely that Mindszenty would become such a leader, for he had repeatedly shown an ability to organize and had demonstrated endurance and the unassailable nature of his faith and morals. And if all of this had not sufficed as an argument in favor of Mindszenty, we cannot exclude the possibility that his rock-solid legitimism would anyway have made him a suitable candidate from the Vatican's perspective. In Rome there was already speculation about the possible creation – in East Central Europe – of a Habsburg-led Danube monarchy in the postwar period.

On March 1, 1944, Rotta secretly made the Pope's decision known to the prince primate.[3] When someone enthusiastically made known the decision to Count János Mikes, he simply smiled and then said, as if surprised by the news, "Well I never, my dear son is now a bishop." Secretly, however, he may have murmured: "I have succeeded in having him appointed without [the support of] the prince primate and despite the government."[4] The nuncio Rotta exhorted the new bishop to be *paternus*, or fatherly. "Regrettably, *inter arma* [in times of war] I did not always manage to be so," Mindszenty wrote self-critically decades later.[5] The prelate's oath, which the new bishop was required to make to Regent Horthy, took place only on March 24, 1944.[6] By taking the oath, József Mindszenty acquired the right to administer the episcopal benefice. Despite his reservations about swearing allegiance to a Calvinist regent rather than to the Catholic ruler (as one had to do prior to 1920), Mindszenty did what was required in order to become bishop. This was the sole oath that Mindszenty swore, as prelate, to the Hungarian state and the head

3. PL 9369/1944. Letter of nuncio Angelo Rotta to Prince Primate Jusztinián Serédi, March 1, 1944.

4. László Székely, *Emlékezés Mikes János szombathelyi megyéspüspökről*, ed. Viktor Attila Soós (Vasszilvágy, Magyar Nyugat Könyvkiadó 2009), 146–47; György Feiszt, ed., *Géfin Gyula emlékezete* (Szombathely: Szombathely önkormányzata, 2008), 8.

5. József Mindszenty, *Napi jegyzetek: Budapest, Amerikai Követség 1956–1971* (Vaduz, Mindszenty Alapítvány, 1979), 376. Memo of February 17, 1965.

6. VÉL I.1.44.a. 1483/1944. Text of József Mindszenty's oath of allegiance, March 24, 1944.

of state. Morally, this was the only instrument to which he was bound. And, subsequently, when seeking for points of legal continuity, it was to this that he could – and did – refer.

Mindszenty was consecrated as bishop at Esztergom Cathedral on the Feast of the Annunciation (March 25). The German military occupation of Hungary had begun several days before, on March 19, 1944. The original plan had been to hold the consecration at the main parish church of Zalaegerszeg, but in view of the German invasion the prince primate decided to consecrate the three new bishops at a single ceremony in Esztergom. The mixed reception given to Mindszenty, who arrived at the event with several family members, is made plain in a diary entry by Miklós Esty, personal attendant to Prince Primate Serédi: József Mindszenty, the nominated bishop of Veszprém, "brought with him, surprisingly, his elderly, head-scarfed mother, an older relative, and a younger relative who was lacking even a white shirt, and he said not a word in advance, and now people are running around trying to find them accommodation."[7] More accustomed to the ostentatious trappings of ecclesiastical life, the "protocol chief" evidently looked down on Mindszenty, the provincial priest who may have acted awkwardly in such high circles. For his part, Mindszenty refused to be ashamed of his mother, "an elderly lady in a headscarf," and openly acknowledged his peasant origins.

Entry into Office

Veszprém's new consecrated bishop arrived unobtrusively at his seat on March 28, 1944, a cold and windy Tuesday. Having been welcomed, he presented to the cathedral chapter the papal document of appointment (or more exactly the document issued by the nuncio, Angelo Rotta, in place of the bull). Through this action he formally assumed the government of Veszprém Diocese in accordance with the provisions of the Code of Canon Law. As bishop of Veszprém he also received, in line with tradition, the title of "Queen's Chancellor" and the title of Perpetual Count of Veszprém County.

7. Szent István Társulat Irattára [Archive of the Saint Stephen's Association], Esty Miklós hagyatéka [Legacy of Miklós Esty], 2. d. 6. t. Napló IV. 108r. Entry of March 24, 1944.

In his sermon the new bishop greeted the clergy and the faithful and set out his plan of action as head of the diocese, a key element of which was his desire to remain a serving priest even while bishop. For his coat-of-arms as bishop he chose the figure of Saint Margaret of the House of Árpád, depicted with a lily and holding a book in her hand. Saint Margaret symbolized both the Hungarian saints and Veszprém's past, for she had offered up her life – part of which she spent in Veszprém – in atonement for Hungary. The Latin motto on the coat-of-arms was *Pannonia Sacra*. Curiously, Bishop Mindszenty chose not a scriptural quotation but a slogan that clearly refers to a country, to Hungary. The Latin word *sacra* means here "God-fearing" or "true." Ecclesiastical tradition identified Pannonia with Christian Hungary, and so *Pannonia Sacra* meant "God-fearing Hungary." With this spiritual program Mindszenty was saying nothing less than that he was prepared to live and die for the independent Hungary that had been offered to the Blessed Virgin Mary, "Our Lady of the Hungarians," and that as bishop he wished to lead every Hungarian into this "country," into Pannonia Sacra. It should be mentioned here that the motto was made public only days after German troops began their occupation of Hungary and that Mindszenty kept this motto even when he became archbishop of Esztergom, at the time of the Soviet occupation. In these two words – Pannonia Sacra – the notions of *Homeland* and the Catholic *Church* are interwoven. Just as in earlier stages of his life, the interweaving of these two notions would serve to guide Mindszenty throughout his remaining years.

Mindszenty immediately began performing the tasks that went with the office of bishop: he expressed thanks for the congratulatory messages; he arranged for the telephone and the secret telephone station to be transferred to his name; he had writing paper printed; he audited the confessional and preaching licenses; he made preparations for Easter (arranging for the Bishop's Palace to gift a liter of wine to male members of staff and half a liter to female members of staff).[8] In the spring of 1944, he began performing the sacrament of confirmation. Between May 6 and June 7, 1944, amid ever more frequent air raids, he administered the

8. VÉL I.1.44.a. 1543/1944. József Mindszenty to the steward, József Hankó, April 8, 1944.

sacrament of confirmation in thirty-one parishes. On each occasion he visited the monastic houses in the parish, the head teacher at the local Catholic school, the lay parish chairman, the parents of priests from the area, and exemplary figures in local public life.[9] He also addressed educational issues and the social problems of Catholics in the diocese. In three villages he opened new schools, arranging for teachers to be hired and for the children of Catholic elementary school teachers to receive scholarships. He took charge of the spiritual care of wounded men in the field hospitals and arranged for retired priests to receive assistance. With a view to assisting military families, he founded the Catholic Action Fraternal Service with branches in each parish. He arranged for seminarians in the diocese to attend college and acquaint themselves with the social circumstances of ordinary people and with the opportunities for progress and advancement.

As bishop, he wished to continue the work of organizing parishes which he had undertaken, as bishop's commissioner, in the Zala part of the Szombathely Diocese from 1927 until 1941. In this sphere, his aim was to achieve a drastic reduction in the distances between presbyteries and villages, because, as he said, "Today we have to bring the parish priest close to the people."[10] When making decisions, he took into consideration the census data, the number of Catholics (his aim was for each parish ministry to have around a thousand faithful), the religious composition of a locality, and other demographic data (one child per family). He also gave consideration to such secondary factors as the road system, public administrative anomalies, and local interests. Within a short period, he established fourteen independent ministries within parishes and raised three ministries to the status of parish.[11] Obviously, his proposals as bishop were not enthusiastically received by everyone. One parish priest wrote frankly about the difficulties: local men were having to dig trenches;

9. József Körmendi, "Mindszenty József veszprémi püspöki tevékenysége," in *Mindszenty József emlékezete*, ed. József Török (Budapest: Márton Áron Kiadó, 1995), 11.

10. VÉL I.1.44.a. 5334/1944. József Mindszenty requests contributions from the advowees for setting up the parish of Mezőlak, November 2, 1944.

11. Máté Gárdonyi, "Mindszenty József somogyi plébánia-alapításai," in *Somogy megye múltjából: Levéltári évkönyv*, 33, ed. László Szántó (Kaposvár: Somogy Megyei Levéltár, 2002), 165–80.

refugees were moving into people's homes and barns every night; there was great uncertainty about the future. In the view of this priest, it was not the right time to prioritize the creation of parish ministries. Mindszenty's brief response as bishop rejected the objections.[12] A reluctance to move into the empty houses of deported Jews was also expressed. "...I think with horror about a priest of the Church living in a Jewish house and sitting in Jewish property," a dean wrote in a letter to Mindszenty.[13]

In the Diocese of Veszprém too, the greatest challenge in the field of parish organization was income-related. There were barely any properties suitable for housing the clergy. Moreover, the Hungarian state was willing to pay a salary supplement (the so-called *kongrua*) of just 50–75 percent. The local population was impoverished, and the economic management of the diocese faced grave problems. To promote the economic viability of parishes, Mindszenty wished to sell off parcels of land that would be taken out of the estates owned by the Diocese of Veszprém. Notwithstanding the economic difficulties facing the diocese, selling off the Church's land holdings counted as an audacious and unusual idea. It demonstrates Mindszenty's sensibility and openness towards social issues and towards land reform. In the end, he did not become a "land reformer" because his modern and exemplary initiative failed amid the destruction of war. Since World War I, land reform (subdivision of large estates into smallholdings) had been a matter of concern for other senior churchmen, as well. The issue had been of particular importance to Ottokár Prohászka, who had died in 1927. Interestingly, almost all Hungarian interwar governments had elaborated plans for land reform, but the ideas had failed to materialize or had been barely realized. In its commitment to general land reform the far-right Arrow Cross Party was unique among the various political parties. As we know, however, Mindszenty was hostile to the Arrow Cross.

Occasionally, Mindszenty would visit his priests without giving prior notice. Some priests clearly struggled to meet Mindszenty's high standards. Indeed, he would give detailed critiques of the sermons he heard at the services he unexpectedly attended.

12. VÉL I.1.44.a. 5428/1944. Correspondence between the vice-dean of Kiskomárom, András Gelencsér, and József Mindszenty, Kiskomárom, November 3–21, 1944, and Veszprém, November 6, 1944.

13. Ibid., 4256/1944. Report of the dean, Gyula Noé, August 20, 1944.

> The holy mass did not start on time; it was more like a quarter to nine rather than half past eight. It is not the priest's job to bring the ampullae [little bottles for the communion wine and water] from the presbytery to the church. A sexton should be responsible for such tasks and for the lighting of candles and so forth. The altar candles were not yet lit at the beginning of holy mass. The schoolchildren in the choir and in the pews were not in sufficient numbers. [...] Those standing in the pews were bored and did not even have prayer books.[14]

Bishop Mindszenty was known to have eyes like a hawk; he never missed anything. And he was just as likely to mention a threadbare carpet or the need to replace worn-out Mass-books as he was a neglected sweat-pea plant or creased vestments. His expectation was that Sundays and festival days should be kept holy and free of work. He complained to one parish priest that All Saints' Day was as if invisible, for people were doing the seasonal tasks of the fall like on any other day. He was rather parsimonious in giving praise, but if he found everything in order, then he would also note this down. Throughout his time at the diocese he was adamant that there should be unity and discipline and that no-one should be able to call into question his moral or political standing.

The Sacrament of Baptism and the Holocaust

The mood in the country was one of ominous tragedy; a rebirth seemed a remote and distant possibility. Horthy opted not to resign as regent and the Hungarian army offered no resistance to the invading German troops. The man who had been Hungarian ambassador in Berlin, the avidly pro-German Döme Sztójay (1883–1946), was installed as the new prime minister. His predecessor, Miklós Kállay, and other politicians hostile to the Nazis were forced into hiding. Subsequently, many of them were detained by the Gestapo. Political parties, organizations, and press outlets that were opposed to the war or which had expressed hostility towards Nazi Germany were banned. As a tragic consequence of the occupation, the country's

14. Ibid., 5015/1944. Letter of József Mindszenty to the parish priest of Szentkirály-szabadja, Alajos Krizsek, October 16, 1944.

Jews, whose physical existence had not been endangered until this time, began to be deported to the German death camps. Between mid-May and early July 1944, around 437,000 people – almost the entire Jewish population outside Budapest – were transported out of the country mostly to the extermination camp at Auschwitz-Birkenau. Not until July 7 did Horthy take action to prevent further deportations, following warnings from Pope Pius XII, King Gustav V of Sweden, US President Roosevelt and diplomats of various nations. Emphasis was added to such warnings by developments in the military field (the Normandy landings and the bombing of Budapest on July 5, 1944).

Mindszenty had been bishop for barely two weeks when he issued a warning to Prince Primate Serédi about the dangers posed by far-right extremism, drawing an analogy with the events of the winter of 1918–1919. He politely called upon Serédi to take firm action: "I would request the regent to put a stop to the increasing extremism of the government."[15] This letter not only proves that Mindszenty had a good knowledge of the situation but also that he expected the prince primate, acting in his official capacity and based on customary law dating back to King Stephen I, to safeguard the interests of the nation even if this meant demanding a say in the nature of the government. Prince Primate Serédi assured him merely that "for the sake of the application of justice and the rights of Catholic believers" negotiations had been underway with the competent actors for a month already.[16] An impatient Mindszenty then requested a personal audience with Regent Horthy, but there is no evidence that this then did take place.[17]

Under universal Church law, adults may be administered the sacrament of baptism as soon as permission has been secured from the ordinary (*ordinarius*), who alone is entitled to shorten the time of preparation for baptism. On April 27, Mindszenty issued a circular letter containing the rules of procedure. He requested his priests to show compassion when

15. Ibid., 1614/1944. Letter of Bishop József Mindszenty of April 14, 1944, to Prince Primate Jusztinián Serédi.

16. Ibid., 1954/1944. Letter of Prince Primate Jusztinián Serédi to Bishop József Mindszenty, May 1, 1944.

17. Ibid., 1738/1944. Letter of Bishop József Mindszenty to the head of the Regent's cabinet office, Gyula Ambrózy, April 21, 1944.

approached by Jews seeking baptism. While no-one should be rejected without reason, people should not be baptized without the required preparation. He prescribed a six-month preparatory period during which baptism candidates were to spend two hours each week in preparation classes. This amounted to a doubling of the previous requirement of three months of classes.[18] In May, Mindszenty was still rejecting petitions for immediate baptism that cited exceptional circumstances.[19] Is it possible that he was still unaware of the danger posed to Jews by the deportations and saw no justification for greater flexibility, which would have been permitted under church law? Or, did he consider a more flexible approach to be pointless, given that, under the provisions of the anti-Jewish laws, a recent conversion would not alter the definition of an individual's "race"? In reality it seems that Mindszenty was motivated exclusively by a desire to adhere to the prescriptions of the Catholic faith and to preserve the integrity of the Catholic Church. The spirit of his provisions accorded with the position taken by the Prince Primate's office: the clergy should oppose any attempts to speed up the baptismal process. It was only when Jews were directly threatened by deportation that Mindszenty moderated his stance on baptism. On June 17, 1944 and on several subsequent occasions, he gave permission for exceptions to be made, while insisting on a waiting time and on proficiency in the faith. Then, after the war and following a steep decline in the number of requests for baptism, he re-authorized a shorter time period for preparation for baptism.

The Catholic clergy and the faithful waited in vain for the Bishops' Conference to take a stand against the deportations. Late June saw the drafting of a pastoral letter containing a moderately worded protest against the state-sanctioned persecution of the Jews. In the end, however, Prince Primate Serédi decided for political reasons that the letter, dated June 29, should not be read out in Hungary's churches. While some parts of society demanded a tougher stand from the Church, others condemned its measures as excessive. On June 6, 1944, Bishop Mindszenty spoke about the Church's

18. Ibid., 1844/1944. [April 27, 1944], VÉL I.1.2. 1944/VII. 36. Cf. VÉL I.1.44.a. 6789/1944. Letter of Bishop Nándor Rott to the parish priest, József Serák, December 27, 1938.

19. Ibid., 1674/1944 and 1777/1944. Letter of József Mindszenty to the monk priest of Nagykanizsa, Gellért Gulyás, and the deputy parish priest of Somogyszob, József Sólyom, May 15, 1944.

responsibility at a festive assembly of three church parishes in Nagykanizsa, where he referred both implicitly and explicitly to the issues:

> It is said of the Church, of the clergy and, doubtless, of me that we are pro-Jewish. [Those who say this] forget that the Church and Hungarian clergy were there at the time of Győző Istóczy's first anti-Semitic efforts and later in the anti-Semitic Catholic People's Party. Even in the political struggles of the last century we defended our sacraments and opposed the authorization of mixed marriages, but we shall protect our sacraments. If in Zambezi a black man is baptized, the Church views this through a different lens than it does a heathen. No-one can take it amiss that the Church is not willing to disregard the first sacrament, baptism, as today some people are disregarding it. A church cannot abandon natural law and the Ten Commandments under any circumstances. If someone has been convicted under the law and sentenced for his crime and death is a punishment proportionate with the crime, then let that happen which must happen. But without a proven crime and a legal judgment, the life of no-one can be taken away. This is the position of the Church.[20]

Embedded in Mindszenty's longwinded statement we find at least three messages of grave importance. Historically, the Church has been anti-Semitic (or, in this context, not philo-Semitic), and so there are no grounds to accuse it of being pro-Jewish. Even so, by the grace of the Cross, baptized Jews and their descendants have become fully fledged Christians in the eyes of the Church. For this reason, the Church's duty is to safeguard and protect them – just as it would any other members of the flock. By making this statement, Mindszenty criticized the manner in which the State was dealing on a purely racial basis with the Jewish issue and ignoring the transformative effect of baptism. The final sentences in Mindszenty's statement related – and were addressed – to those Jews who adhered to their religion: "without a proven crime and a legal judgment" the life of no-one, of no Jew, could be taken away. With these words Mindszenty made plain – in this hysterically anti-Semitic era and amid the deportation of Hungary's Jews from the country's rural areas and provincial cities – that

20. *Zalamegyei Ujság* 27, no. 127, June 7, 1944, 2.

the treatment of the Jews had nothing to do with national security or "protecting the Hungarian race" but was quite simply murder and therefore a violation of the Ten Commandments. Mindszenty's words also show that he knew that the aim of the deportations was not to resettle the Jews while depriving them of their rights; rather, the objective was to extinguish life.

The press in the United States had been writing about death camps since the fall of 1942. It is doubtful that the Hungarian prelates would have read such reports. The dramatic realization came when a detailed report by two Auschwitz prisoners reached Hungary. The report revealed the horrendous awfulness of the death camp. A copy of the *Auschwitz Protocol*, a translation into Hungarian, seems to have been received by Prince Primate Jusztinián Serédi no later than on May 20, 1944. It was also received by several other senior Catholics in Hungary, who confidentially forwarded it to others. Serédi must have informed members of the Bishops' Conference of the essence of the report. In this connection he made an unexpected visit to Veszprém on June 9.[21]

No record was made of the conversation in Veszprém between the prince primate and the bishop, but the treatment of the Jews evidently concerned the two men. Serédi had already requested that Jews who counted as Christians be exempted from having to wear the yellow star – or, at least, that they be permitted to replace the star with a white cross. The government had acknowledged his request without making any changes to the law.[22] Serédi had then suggested to his fellow bishops that, by way of protest, Jewish converts place a cross alongside the yellow star. Mindszenty refused to support this proposal.[23] It was not the consequences of the protest that he feared. Rather, he argued that a Christian should wear a cross or nothing; wearing the symbols together would weaken the message of baptism, namely that the power of the sacrament was stronger than any mundane prejudice and overrode a person's ancestry. Mindszenty's suggestion instead was to arrange for the Church's efforts on behalf of "baptized non-Aryans" to be leaked to a source in neutral Switzerland.

21. VÉL I.1.44.a. 2640/1944. Papers relating to the visit of Primate Jusztinián Serédi.

22. MNL OL K64 KÜM Reservált pol. iratok [Reserved political documents], 1944. 43. t. 77. fol. Döme Sztójay's reply to Primate Jusztinián Serédi, June 19, 1944.

23. VÉL I.1.44.a. 2747/1944. Letter of József Mindszenty to Primate Jusztinián Serédi, June 13, 1944.

More than once Mindszenty asked for an exception to be made. For instance, on May 25, 1944, he requested that the Pátkai family from the town of Pápa be exempted from internment in a ghetto.[24] He also wrote a letter to Prime Minister Döme Sztójay on behalf of the famous Szombathely surgeon Ernő Pető, who had thrice operated on Mindszenty's thyroid gland and whose son had been a classmate at the Premonstratensian grammar school.[25] The Jewish inhabitants of the town and district who had not been exempted were transported to the death camps on June 19, 1944. In a letter to Regent Horthy, Mindszenty requested measures to prevent baptized Jewish children from being taken away.[26] His efforts were fruitless. The local "Christian political newspaper" covered the emptying of the ghetto in a short and dispassionate article entitled "Away from the ghetto."[27] The Catholic priest of Románd, György Kis, who had Jewish ancestry, wrote a letter to Bishop Mindszenty informing him of the newspaper article's outrageous content, which was of particular concern, given that the *Veszprémi Hírlap* (Veszprém Newspaper) was the diocese's own newspaper. In his response Mindszenty agreed with Kis but also made excuses, saying that he had warned the newspaper on several prior occasions and was warning it again now, but that his protests in the past had been without effect. In his view, the Church needed to strike a balance between the two extremes of rescuing Jews and dogmatic betrayal. In this way, the Church would be able to defend the interests of Christians in line with its duty. The room for maneuver was limited, albeit – as he added – "*...we could have done more and been more forceful. I suggested just that.*"[28]

The shock felt by Mindszenty as events unfolded is signaled by his condemnation of those who put in claims for possession of vacated Jewish properties. In the spring of 1944, it seems he still had no qualms about changes of ownership from Jews to Christians; indeed, at that time, he even considered the purchase of minor Jewish properties to be a desirable

24. Ibid., 2716/1944. Intervention by József Mindszenty on behalf of Lajos Pátkai and his family of Pápa, May 25, 1944.

25. Ibid., 3172/1944. Letter of József Mindszenty to Prime Minister Döme Sztójay and Minister of Interior Andor Jaross, July 6, 1944.

26. Ibid., 2895/1944. Letter of József Mindszenty, bishop of Veszprém, to Regent Miklós Horthy, June 19, 1944.

27. *Veszprémi Hírlap* 52, no. 50, June 21, 1944, cover page.

28. VÉL I.1.44.a. 3262/1944. József Mindszenty's reply to György Kis, July 5, 1944.

course of action.[29] After the deportations, however, his moral assessment of the situation was quite different. Indeed, in five short months, Mindszenty had gone from emphasizing the lawful – and thus acceptable – nature of the transactions to being confronted with the bloody reality: the homes left vacant after the deportations, the subsequent plundering, and the arbitrary seizure of properties. In Veszprém, the "re-allocation" of vacated Jewish dwellings began in the first half of September 1944. On September 25, 1944, Mindszenty issued a pastoral letter in Latin prohibiting the institutions of the Catholic Church from participating in this process.[30] He did not wish to become – even indirectly – an accomplice of the Nazis.

Can we, on account of these actions, add József Mindszenty's name to the imaginary memorial plaque that commemorates the heroism of Bishop Áron Márton (Transylvania), Bishop Vilmos Apor (Győr), Bishop Endre Hamvas (Csanád), and Angelo Rotta, the papal nuncio? It is, above all, posterity that has cast Mindszenty's efforts to defend the persecuted as insufficient and lacking in credibility. Assessments of his role written at the time or shortly after the tragic events tended to be more positive. For instance, in his memoirs, Samu Stern, who served as president of the Jewish Council, wrote admiringly of the bishop of Veszprém.[31]

Undeniably, József Mindszenty's attitude towards Jews changed over time. In his early years, as parish priest in Zalaegerszeg, he might have rebuked his own chaplain for purchasing something from a Jew, because he believed in the need for "Christian self-defense."[32] Now, as bishop of Veszprém, he felt sympathy for the persecuted Jews and attended to their needs, just as he strove to help other distressed people. Unlike others, he never professed to being a philosemite; nor did he ever claim to have organized large-scale rescue actions in his diocese. He had expected a firm stand to be taken by Rome or by Esztergom, and so he had awaited instructions from his superiors – but these never came. While he obviously considered the measures taken by the leadership of the Catholic Church

29. Ibid., 1971/1944. Confidential letter of József Mindszenty, bishop of Veszprém, to several parish priests, April 28, 1944.

30. Ibid., 4598/1944; VÉL I.1.2. 1944/XI. 61.

31. Samu Stern, Emlékirataim. *Versenyfutás az idővel: A "zsidótanács" működése a német megszállás és a nyilas uralom idején*, ed. Gábor Ács (Budapest: Bábel Kiadó, 2004), 325.

32. PL Processus, V–700/27. 106. fol. Szombathely, incomplete document from January 1945.

to be insufficient, he continued to show obeisance to his superiors, and he expected his clergy to do the same. In terms of his own actions, he went as far as what was compatible with church doctrines and church law. Principally, therefore, he sought to protect Jews who had become Catholics, because it was in this field alone that his efforts had a realistic chance of success. To go beyond this meant, in 1944, risking one's own life. Indeed, only the exceptionally brave or audacious dared defy a heavily armed militaristic foreign power and its domestic accomplices.

Memorandum of the Bishops in Western Hungary

The Bishop's Palace began receiving increasingly alarming reports on the situation of the Jews in the ghettos, on the failed ceasefire, on the Arrow Cross takeover of power, and on the resignation of the government. Ferenc Szálasi, the leader of the far-right Arrow Cross Party, became both prime minister and head of state. Two-thirds of the country was already a war theater, and the Red Army was steadily advancing on Budapest. Meanwhile, the Arrow Cross minister of war was demanding suicidal perseverance from the Hungarian troops. As the weeks passed, however, the fighting spirit subsided and the front could no longer be held. Arrow Cross members wearing red and white armbands (Árpád stripes) swarmed into the city of Veszprém, and the streets were awash with placards urging resilience as well as refugees who had arrived in the city on their way westward.

Mindszenty suffered greatly from his incapacity to act. On November 13, he traveled to Budapest to make known to the government the prelates' common position, which urged the authorities to spare the inhabitants of Western Hungary (Transdanubia) the destruction of warfare. "An individual may sacrifice himself for the nation. Tens of thousands of our nation even in this World War died for their fatherland; but to push a whole nation to suicide just for your ideas is impossible. A sense of responsibility and conscience will not allow this,"[33] stated the memorandum of October 31, 1944, which was signed by Mindszenty and three other leading churchmen: Vilmos Apor (bishop of Győr), Lajos Shvoy (bishop of Székesfehérvár), and the archabbot of Pannonhalma, Krizosztom Kelemen.

33. *Új Ember* [New Man] 1, no. 16, November 25, 1945, 2; cf. József Mindszenty, *Memoirs* (New York: Macmillan, 1974), 253.

Notably missing from the document is the signature of the prince primate. Archbishop Serédi was, first and foremost, a man of negotiation, law, legal intricacies, and science. It was simply not his style to express his opinion in a petition in the manner of a *homo politicus*. Even so, he was similarly concerned for the fate of the nation and aware of his responsibility to society. Perhaps his dislike of Mindszenty explains his unwillingness to support the plan or attribute any significance to it. The signatures of other bishops are also missing from the memorandum. Evidently, some bishops must have disagreed with the initiative, albeit the sticking point in most cases was probably the form of the memorandum rather than its content. Those who did sign the document were clearly putting their lives at risk. Hopeless in terms of its aims but nonetheless a valuable gesture, the memorandum offers insights into the underlying mentality of Mindszenty and his attitude towards public life and politics. Despite the apparent hopelessness of the situation, for Mindszenty the importance of the initiative was its moral message, as he firmly believed that the Church and the bishops must do their utmost to protect the nation and the people.

On the evening of November 13, Mindszenty personally submitted the memorandum to Deputy Prime Minister Jenő Szöllősi. The unusual nature of the memorandum and the even more unusual content "caused Szöllősi great consternation, and he asked whether we were seeking a capitulation. [...] He kept his cool, but one could see his disquiet. He indicated to me that the matter would be discussed as a matter of urgency."[34] Three days later, the deputy prime minister forwarded Szálasi's sarcastic response: the prelates were promoting with their "so very necessary and courageous stand" their own moral authority. In Szálasi's view, rather than merely formulate their expectations, the bishops should have made some specific suggestions.[35] Of course, Mindszenty had no intention of offering military advice.[36] He believed, however, that the main priority of the Hungarian and German

34. Viktor Attila Soós, "Apor Vilmos és Mindszenty József kapcsolata," in *In labore fructus: Jubileumi tanulmányok Győregyházmegye történetéből*, eds. Gábor Nemes and Ádám Vajk (Győr: Egyházmegyei Levéltár, 2011), 382.

35. VÉL VIII.35. Legacy of József Mindszenty, 1. d. Letter of Jenő Szöllősi to József Mindszenty, November 16, 1944.

36. Egyházmegyei Levéltár, Győr – püspökségi levéltár [Diocesan Archive, Győr: Episcopal Archive] (hereafter: GyPL) Legacy of Apor Vilmos, Letter of József Mindszenty to Ferenc Szálasi, November 27, 1944.

forces was to prevent the Red Army from crossing the Danube. Even if they failed in this endeavor, he would not support a solution that required the evacuation of the population, the removal of assets, and the demolition of buildings. Mindszenty was concerned primarily for human lives, for the fate of assets, real estate and animal stocks, and for the preservation of church buildings. Failure in these areas would render the physical and spiritual survival of the Hungarian nation hopeless. This stance was diametrically opposed to the Szálasi government's military strategy, which foresaw the evacuation of the civilian population. Mindszenty's willingness to express his opinions under these circumstances bears testament to his personal courage. This, in itself, was sufficient pretext for the Arrow Cross regime to remove the troublesome bishop from his post.

AS A PRISONER OF THE ARROW CROSS REGIME

The Arrow Cross could barely wait to find grounds for removing the bishop of Veszprém from his post. The occasion was not long in coming. Concerning the reasons for his arrest, many rumors and half-truths were circulated. Some claimed that Mindszenty had refused to allow church buildings to be used as accommodation for wounded soldiers. Others asserted that his arrest had been made under German orders rather than at the behest of the Arrow Cross. The Germans, it was claimed, "were not squeamish about dealing with some Hungarian prelates."[37] For decades after 1948 the communist regime's official version of events was that Mindszenty's wartime "resistance" had amounted to nothing more than a dispute with an Arrow Cross prefect over 1,800 underpants.

The "Arrow Cross Mass"

In his memoirs, Mindszenty also gives a detailed account of the events. He notes that his arrest was due in part to the personal revenge of a lawyer named Ferenc Schiberna, who was the Arrow Cross Party leader in Veszprém: Schiberna's younger brother had been fired from his position at the bishop's estate on account of the misappropriation of funds.

37. *Haladás* [Progress] 4, no. 30, July 22, 1948, 3.

Moreover, according to his memoirs, Mindszenty had dented the prestige of the Arrow Cross leader by prohibiting the celebration of Holy Mass and Te Deum at the Franciscan church in Veszprém on the "successful" conclusion of the deportation of the town's Jews (around a thousand Jewish individuals were deported, of which no more than fifty returned to the town after the war). Schiberna was undeniably the most influential person in Veszprém at the time. It is also true that on June 20, 1944, a day after the emptying of the Jewish ghetto in Veszprém, Schiberna asked the local head of the Franciscan order to hold a service of thanksgiving for the deportation of the Jews. The Franciscans agreed to this request, publicly announcing the holding of the Mass on the following Sunday (June 25).

The request greatly irritated Mindszenty, who firmly opposed the most holy sacrifice being turned into a political sympathy protest in support of a morally reprehensible and shameful act (the deportation of the Jews). He reprimanded the Franciscan prior for having agreed to the theme of the church service and instructed him on the content of the homily, but he could not prohibit the service, for his jurisdiction did not extend to the Franciscan prior but was limited to pastoral issues affecting the congregation of the Franciscans' church. The prerequisite for peaceful monastic life is namely the *exemptio* granted in the Code of Canon Law. The Franciscans conducted their church services on the basis of this exemption. Accordingly, Mindszenty had no choice but to acknowledge the Mass would be held. He made two requests: that the *Te Deum* hymn not be sung at the service and that Arrow Cross members refrain from attending in their uniforms. In the end, however, the church service – which had been publicly advertised on flyers – was attended by Arrow Cross men in black jackets and green shirts, who quickly filled up the Franciscan church, which had a capacity of no more than 120. The Franciscan priest held the Mass, dressed in a green vestment.[38] The matching of colors was coincidental: green is the liturgical color on Sundays after Pentecost and until Advent, the beginning of the new liturgical year.

38. An account of this event was given in a telegram sent by Reich Plenipotentiary Edmund Veesenmayer. The contents of the telegram were first made public in 1963: Randolph L. Braham, ed., *The Destruction of Hungarian Jewry: A documentary account* (New York: Pro Arte for the World Federation of Hungarian Jews, 1963), 625.

Mindszenty stayed away from the service in protest. As on almost every Sunday since his induction, he was traveling in the diocese. On this particular Sunday, he went first to Ajka, visiting the glass factory, the bauxite mine, the aluminum factory, an industrial plant, and even a school. Then, in the evening, he paid a visit on the former bishop of Szombathely, János Mikes, who was convalescing in Balatonfüred.[39] In the meantime, in Veszprém, the Arrow Cross mass was held without incident. Contrary to Mindszenty's express request, the Te Deum hymn was indeed sung at the end of the service. Many people, even among the congregation, were shocked by the theme of the Mass. The Arrow Cross supporters, however, sought an explanation for Mindszenty's absence. They were convinced that the purpose of the bishop's visits to the various military industrial sites was to gather intelligence, which he could then forward to the British using a secret transmitter. On these grounds they sought to have Mindszenty arrested on the charge of "treason."[40] Mindszenty could have informed the faithful of these events from his cathedral pulpit the very next Sunday, but he chose not to do so. Still, he did inform the Marian Provincial, Fr. Thedorik Vargha, who evidently reprimanded the Franciscan prior for conflating politics with the Gospel, for the latter then wrote, in an apologetic letter, the following: "I am ashamed that this happened, but I can assure the Father Superior, that something like this will not happen again."[41] Why did the prior ever agree to hold the Mass? Perhaps his covert aim was to conceal the fact that the Franciscans were providing refuge to hundreds of desperate people.[42]

The story offers evidence of the mutual antipathy between Mindszenty and Schiberna. The arrest of the former was evidently due in part to the hatred of the local Arrow Cross leader. A few months later, on October 29, 1944, Schiberna received a promotion, becoming the prefect of Veszprém County. In a departure from tradition, after his appointment he refused to

39. *Veszprémi Hírlap* 52, no. 52, June 28, 1944, cover page.

40. VÉL I.1.44.a. 3254/1944. Petition of the deputy parish priest of Ajka, János Némon, to József Mindszenty, July 3, 1944, and the latter's reply of July 4, 1944.

41. MNL OL P233 FRL, 16. cs. 1/a. t. 99. fol. 462/1944. Letter of the prior, Lambert Pulyai, to the provincial, Theodorik Vargha, July 17, 1944.

42. According to the data, the Franciscans gave refuge to some 500 people, see: Piusz Rácz, *Ferencesek az ország nyugati részén* (Zalaegerszeg: A Szűz Máriáról nevezett Ferences Rendtartomány kiadása, 2004), 168.

pay his respects to the bishop. Accordingly, his first visit to the Bishop's Palace came on November 27, 1944, "in the company of eleven policemen and a porter who had been dismissed from service some time earlier."[43]

From his Refusal to Take an Oath until his Arrest

The controversy surrounding the oath of allegiance arose after the Arrow Cross takeover. Ferenc Szálasi was granted the executive powers of the head of state on November 3, 1944. It was his expectation that public employees and officials take an oath of allegiance, as had been the practice at the time of the Dual Monarchy and under Regent Horthy. In a draft paper, Mindszenty explained why he could not be considered a public official and why he would not take an oath of allegiance to the Szálasi regime. He also gave reasons for his general opposition to the new "revolutionary" government (Szálasi's "Government of National Unity"). The title of his draft paper was *Juramentum non*, or "No Oath." The subtitle speaks for itself: It is impossible to serve the revolution and the Church concurrently.[44] Mindszenty reasoned that National Socialist ideology and the Arrow Cross movement it had spawned were contrary to the Catholic faith, as they promoted a false notion of God (namely a racist God), were contemptuous of the significance of baptism, supported the right to divorce, subverted Christian moral principles, and disregarded the rights of the Church. In essence the document reiterates the official position of the Church on Nazism as outlined by Pius XI in his encyclical *Mit brennender Sorge* (With Burning Concern). Although it was never finalized, Mindszenty's draft paper nevertheless proves his antipathy towards, and scorn for, the Arrow Cross and Nazi ideology. He viewed the Arrow Cross as the "scum" of the political underworld. Elsewhere he called Szálasi a "non-entity" and a "brigand" with a dangerously skewed vision.[45]

43. PL Processus, V–700/32. 120. fol. Mindszenty's handwritten insertion into an undated letter addressed to Prime Minister Ferenc Szálasi but written in fact to Deputy Prime Minister Jenő Szöllősi.

44. PL Mm. 17. d. Envelope inscribed with "1943–45": Original handwritten draft by József Mindszenty. For the contents, see István Mészáros, "Juramentum non – Nincs eskü! Mindszenty veszprémi püspök írása 1944. november elejéről," in *Mindszenty-mozaik: Írások a bíborosról* (Budapest: Ecclesia, 2010), 53–56.

45. MMAL 50. d. Chapter 12: "Egy különös sorsú nemzet."

In Veszprém, the passive resistance of local inhabitants to the new regime greatly irritated the Arrow Cross, which had expected to receive their support. On October 29, 1944, martial law was proclaimed in the city. Many local people were interned in punishment for spreading rumors (about an impending German defeat in the war) or for refusing to accommodate refugees. The greatest consternation in the city, however, arose when news spread that the bishop was being taken to prison.

The precise nature and order of events were established by Mindszenty himself in a petition submitted to Minister of Interior Gábor Vajna.[46] On November 27, 1944, eleven policemen came to the Bishop's Palace in order to prepare a cantonment for military personnel, but they were refused entry by two of the bishop's staff, who were then arrested on the orders of the prefect. When the bishop found out what had happened, he protested, whereupon he too was arrested at the prefect's behest. The police wanted to take Mindszenty away in a car, but a group of seminarians stood between them and the bishop. In the end, a rather odd procession – eleven policemen, three detainees, and an accompanying group of seminarians – set off for the police station. This spectacle sufficed to cause outrage among the people of Veszprém. Indeed, the bishop did not have to do anything during the 1.5 kilometer trek to stir the crowds. On reaching the police station, Mindszenty said a blessing and then instructed his priests and seminarians to return home. "The government commissioner Schiberna raved and ranted on hearing of the procession and the powerlessness of the armed police force."[47]

During the next two days, several other priests were also arrested and the seminarians who had accompanied the bishop on the procession were detained. Two official searches of the Bishop's Palace were made. In Mindszenty's room a rather insignificant letter was found, dated March 6, 1944. It had been written by a Catholic priest named Béla Varga, who had been vice president of the Independent Smallholders' Party at the time. Later on, the records of the communist secret police (the State Protection Authority) referred to the legitimist content of the letter as having been

46. VÉL VIII.35. Mindszenty József hagyatéka [Legacy of József Mindszenty], 1. d. Letter of József Mindszenty to Minister of Interior Gábor Vajna, December 30, 1944.

47. VÉL I.1.44.a. 541/1945. József Mindszenty's petition to the Political Committee of the Provisional National Assembly, April 30, 1945.

the grounds for the bishop's internment.[48] Aside from the letter, the house search also revealed 1,800 hidden shirts and 1,800 hidden underpants. Mindszenty had purchased these clothing items for the wounded soldiers, the refugees, and the impoverished seminarians.[49] Four years later, communist propaganda was citing this clothing initiative as evidence that the bishop's arrest in the fall of 1944 had been, in reality, on grounds of stockpiling. According to this communist-inspired version of events, Bishop Mindszenty had sought private gain by stockpiling underpants. He was, therefore, nothing other than a selfish, cold and petty figure whose political resistance was rooted in his own inner conflicts. Communist propaganda thus belittled the persecution Mindszenty had suffered at the hands of the Arrow Cross, transmuting it into his rightful punishment for the "concealment of underwear."

Yet, according to the final judgment issued by the prefect on November 30, 1944, the grounds for Mindszenty's detention were his opposition to a regulatory provision during an onsite inspection aimed at securing accommodation for the troops. As the judgment also stated, Bishop Mindszenty had committed a violent act against officialdom, and he had then attempted to incite a public rebellion by holding a protest march together with his associates – all of which had greatly threatened public order and security, as well as military operational interests.[50] The Arrow Cross leadership in Veszprém had received a direct hit; it had become an object of ridicule among the town's inhabitants. The prefect reported the events to his superior, the minister of interior, who had the right to decide on public administrative matters. The minister of interior, however, dithered. Fearing for his office or simply out of caution, he referred the decision upwards to Szálasi. Clearly, he did not want to let the "big prey" get away. On the other hand, he did not wish to shoot himself in the foot, if the matter became politically embarrassing. And so, he thought it better

48. ÁBTL 3.1.8. Sz–222/9. 22–23., 25. and 29. fol. Records of witness statements of Lajos Farkas, county police chief, Capt. Antal Molnár (police investigator), and Capt. Kálmán Zsedényi (state police officer), made on February 5, February 10, and February 23, 1946.

49. VÉL I.1.44.a. 3701–3845/1945. A document entitled "*Tartani!!* 1945" [Keep!! 1945] with no inventory number and placed at the end of the box: inside a letter dated November 5, 1944, about the purchase.

50. Ibid., 10.147/1959. Ruling no. 1622/1944 of Prefect Ferenc Schiberna on the placement of József Mindszenty in police detention, November 30, 1944.

to pass the responsibility on to someone else. Subsequently, all decisions in the matter were taken by Ferenc Szálasi, "leader of the nation."[51]

Mindszenty protested at every imaginable forum. He denied all the charges in his petitions: "...no kind of defiance took place. [...] I know of no violence, nor of rebellion," he emphasized.[52] Two and a half months later, on February 14, 1945, a so-called "general's court" summarized the reasons for the detention of the bishop of Veszprém:

> Bishop József Mindszenty and the people close to him are, based on the findings of years-long surveillance, anti-National Socialist, anti-German, pro-English and legitimist in their sentiments. [...] ...since the takeover of power, the bishop and the clergy have, in general, shown complete disinterest or indeed, as one might say, passive resistance. The '*Veszprémi Hírlap*' [Veszprém Newspaper], which is owned by the bishopric, has undertaken no patriotic or anti-Bolshevist propaganda. On the contrary, the articles have sought, in a covert and tendentious manner, to highlight the difficulties arising from the country's current situation. [...] The defeatist, anti-Hungarist, Anglophile and Russophile propaganda of the clergy and of the episcopal center in Veszprém in particular, is very detrimental to the mood of the leading sections [of society], the army and the populace...[53]

This summary is testimony to József Mindszenty's antipathy towards the Arrow Cross.

Mindszenty's recollections may need some revision in terms of the details. Even so, the evidence strongly suggests that the true reasons for his arrest were: the ominous memorandum of the bishops of Western Hungary, his criticism of the holding of a service of thanksgiving, his personal antipathy towards and detachment from the Arrow Cross. These

51. Budapest Főváros Levéltára [Budapest City Archives] (hereafter: BFL) XXV. 1.a. Budapesti Népbíróság, büntetőperes iratok 293/1946. Szálasi-per [Budapest People's Court, criminal case documents 293/1946. The Szálasi-trial], 248. d. XVI-10/45. 1759. and 1761. fol. Minutes of main hearing, held on February 16, 1946, on the matter of Ferenc Szálasi and his associates.

52. VÉL VIII.35. Legacy of József Mindszenty, 1. box, Arrow Cross imprisonment: The petitions made to the Arrow Cross authorities can be found here almost in their entirety.

53. Ibid.

were the various irritants that so annoyed the Hungarists and which the Arrow Cross leadership in Veszprém County interpreted as opposition to their goals and an attempt to prevent the realization of such goals. Nor should one ignore Szálasi's personal demand that the Bishop's Palace be used as accommodation for the wounded: it was simpler to remove the far from congenial host.

Mindszenty was detained at Veszprém police station and in a local jailhouse from November 27 until December 5, 1944. Thereafter and until December 22, he was held at the prosecutor's prison in Veszprém. His personal freedom was restricted, but he did not suffer physical abuse or religious humiliation. He was still permitted to administer the affairs of the bishop's office and hold a Mass every morning with daily meditation. On December 7 and 8, a memorable event took place in the corridor of the prosecutor's prison: out of the sixteen imprisoned seminarians Bishop Mindszenty ordained ten fifth-year seminarians as priests.[54] On December 10, the second Sunday in Advent, he ordained five further novice priests who had fled from Kolozsvár (today Cluj-Napoca, Romania) to Hungary. From his prison cell, he also founded the Veszprém parish of Saint Margaret of Hungary, signing the deed of foundation of the parish on December 3.

Despite the relatively favorable conditions, it was still a prison. Moreover, rumors came that all the inmates were to be deported to Germany, which naturally led some to consider making an escape. The escape attempt failed and an investigation ensued. Soon the prosecutor's prison was being guarded by armed gendarmes with Arrow Cross armbands.[55] Finally, on December 22, Mindszenty and his priests and seminarians – 27 men in total – were placed on a bus and transported to Sopronkőhida with a gendarmerie escort. It would seem they were regarded both as hostages and as persons requiring protection. The conditions were far worse in Sopronkőhida than they had been in Veszprém:

54. József Körmendy, "Mindszenty József veszprémi püspök plébánia- és iskolaszervező munkája 1944–45-ben," in *Ministerio: Nemzetközi történész konferencia előadásai 1995. május 24–26.*, ed. István Bárdos and Margit Beke (Esztergom: Esztergom-Budapesti Érsekség, Komárom-Esztergom Megye Önkormányzata, and Kultsár István Társadalomtudományi és Kiadói Alapítvány, 1998), 83.

55. "*A veszprémi papság és papnevelő intézet kiállása a Szállasi* (sic) *rendszer ellen*" [The stand of the Veszprém clergy and seminary against the Szállasi (sic) regime], Recollections of Lénárd Kögl, 3. Privately owned.

...mockingly, they put us in a dirty place for two nights. We washed ourselves at a trough in the courtyard. For two days they failed even to provide us with food. [...] We could go to the toilet, which was sixty meters from the storeroom and across the courtyard, but only in a group and accompanied by a guard. One did not know whether to laugh or cry, at the sight of bishops, canons, and college teachers and so forth standing in front of the toilet, as shoppers nowadays do in front of shops,

Mindszenty complained with naturalistic detail in a lengthy letter to the Arrow Cross deputy prime minister.[56] For the Christmas vigil, a musty and dank storeroom in the prison was made available to them. Finally, on December 29, they were transported to the mother convent of the Daughters of the Divine Redeemer in Sopron.

With the Nuns

As Soviet troops approached Budapest, the two houses of the Hungarian Parliament moved to Sopron. Around a third of the parliamentary representatives also relocated to the town, where they were joined by Ferenc Szálasi and the Arrow Cross general staff. In the eastern part of the country, the Provisional National Assembly had already begun to function, basing its authority on popular sovereignty and having broken with the notion of legal continuity. On December 21, 1944, the Provisional National Government was formed, its members having been pre-approved in Moscow. One of its first measures was to declare war on Germany. Having accepted the Soviet Union's terms of peace and signed an armistice, the new government began to reorganize public administration and promptly launched a program of land reform. The armistice treaty stipulated – as was also the case for the other two Nazi allies, Romania and Bulgaria – the operation of an Allied Control Commission (ACC) in Hungary. The ACC was a joint body of the occupying powers. In each of the three countries, the ACC was chaired by the general of the army of the country that had occupied the defeated state. In Hungary this person was Kliment Yefremovich Voroshilov,

56. VÉL VIII.35. Legacy of József Mindszenty, 1. d. Letter of József Mindszenty to Deputy Prime Minister Jenő Szöllősi, January 12, 1945.

marshal of the Soviet Union. Representatives of the Western Allies – the United States, the United Kingdom and France – were required to contact the Hungarian government bodies exclusively through the Soviet High Command. There was no doubt that Hungary's administration would be subordinated to Soviet interests and that the sovereignty of the national government and of the country would be limited, at least until the signing of a peace treaty.

Mindszenty dispatched his New Year's message from the isolation of the nunnery in Sopron; the message was then printed at a printing press in Budapest, which by this time lay under siege. In this circular letter Mindszenty summarized his accomplishments as bishop of Veszprém: the opening of three parish churches, the creation of fifteen chaplaincies, and the establishment of new Catholic schools in seven villages. Mindszenty also described how he had employed 23 refugee priests for temporary service in the diocese. He barely made reference to his own fate, but he praised at length the heroic stand of the clergy. From his room in the nunnery he was able to conduct much of his ecclesiastical organizational work in an undisturbed manner: his room was full of papers, and even today the diocesan archives include several documents that arose here. Not only could he freely correspond with others, but also someone would visit him almost every day. Indeed, as spring approached, he could even do some gardening in the courtyard.[57] In his memoirs Mindszenty mentions tolerable conditions at the nunnery. Indeed, the conditions of his imprisonment under the Arrow Cross regime were far better in general terms than what he would later experience as a prisoner of the communist regime.

Seeking his own release, József Mindszenty wrote countless letters to members of the Szálasi government and to the speaker of the Upper House. As time passed, he grew increasingly upset and his petitions became ever lengthier. He could not understand the accusation being made against him or the reason for his continued detention. He found it difficult to cope with the confinement and the uncertainty. On the evening of February 22, 1945, Mindszenty's "accomplices" were released. The bishop, however, had to stay where he was. This was contrary to all previous pledges, but the

57. Gergely Mózessy, "Noteszlapok Shvoy Lajos fogságából," *Soproni Szemle* 60, no. 1 (2006): 32.

purpose may have been to protect Mindszenty. Mindszenty's three court priests – Szabolcs Szabadhegÿ, Tibor Mészáros, and László Lékai, who became the apostolic administrator of Esztergom in 1974 and then archbishop of Esztergom – as Mindszenty's successor – in 1976, stayed with him voluntarily. Why did the Arrow Cross authorities keep Mindszenty under house arrest? Mindszenty suspected, not without reason, that it was his status as bishop, rather than his person, that made him important to Szálasi. At the time, the Arrow Cross leader was characteristically fantasizing about obtaining for himself – through blackmail – the right of Hungarian rulers to appoint the country's prelates. What had been, in November, no more than an abuse by the local Arrow Cross leader in Veszprém, seemed now to be a cunning opportunity. But history was to follow a different course: the adoption of the new "Hungarist" constitution, which had already been elaborated in substantial detail, and the election of the national leader (i.e., Szálasi) as palatine never took place. Accordingly, Szálasi did not receive the customary right of Hungarian rulers to choose the country's prelates.

On March 9, 1945, the inhabitants of the priory were joined by two new co-prisoners: Lajos Shvoy, bishop of Székesfehérvár, and his brother, Lieutenant-General Kálmán Shvoy. The latter mentioned in his memoirs his first meeting with Mindszenty:

> The sister led us into the shelter, where Mindszenty was sitting with two or three priests. [...] We introduced ourselves... I was struck by the fact that Mindszenty, who had been bishop for only a year, compared with Lajos's [Lajos Shvoy's] eighteen years of service as bishop, did not offer his place in the armchair to Lajos but let him sit on a small chair, in a worse place. I did not like this man at all, with his arrogance, conceit and posturing. He was full of his own importance. Sitting beside him, modest Lajos was so much greater and more appealing.[58]

Doubtless Kálmán Shvoy was somewhat biased towards his own brother. Even so, it is noteworthy that in his view Mindszenty's behavior

58. Mihály Perneki, ed., *Shvoy Kálmán titkos naplója és emlékirata, 1918–1945* (Budapest: Kossuth Kiadó, 1983), 317–18.

was rigid and officious. The fact that Mindszenty held "seniority" in terms of the length of time spent in prison did not excuse his apparent rudeness.

In view of stubborn rumors that the prisoners were shortly to be sent off to Germany, Mindszenty flirted with the idea of making an escape. The man seen in a portrait photograph made for this purpose is in civilian clothes and wearing a beret, a tie, and a moustache. The other prisoners immediately dissuaded Mindszenty from going ahead with the plan. In the end, the matter was effectively settled with the hasty departure of the Arrow Cross on March 28, 1945, and the arrival of Soviet troops in Sopron on April 1. At that time, the town's mayor invited Mindszenty to give a speech at a reception to be held in honor of the liberators. Mindszenty, however, declined the invitation. As he clarified in his memoirs, "I was not liberated but merely left behind by the fleeing police."[59] Mindszenty's reticence towards the Soviets is explained by his knowledge of the Soviet Union, the Red Army, and the situation on the front, which was overwhelmingly negative. He was already envisioning the persecution of the Church and Hungary's complete subjugation. His distrust of the Soviets did not diminish subsequently.

While Mindszenty was trapped in Sopron, the Catholic Church in Hungary suffered a series of blows: on March 28, 1945, the titular archbishop and former bishop of Szombathely, János Mikes, died of a heart attack at the sight of rowdy and drunken Soviet soldiers. The next day Prince Primate Jusztinián Serédi passed away in Esztergom. And on the third day, Bishop Vilmos Apor of Győr was fatally wounded by a drunken Soviet soldier in the cellar of the Bishop's Palace. Consequently, during this most critical period, the Catholic Church was left leaderless. For a temporary period, the archbishop of Kalocsa, József Grősz, took over direction of the Bishops' Conference.

"UNDER GOD'S FREE SKY"

Mindszenty had no wish to avail himself of the assistance offered by the Soviet military. In consequence, he spent three further weeks in a state of enforced inaction at the priory. Finally, on April 20, 1945, after a journey

59. Mindszenty, *Memoirs*, 24.

lasting three and a half days, the bishop arrived at his seat in Veszprém.[60] Throughout the journey – made in a freight wagon, an oil tanker and a cart – he had seen the destruction wreaked by war. On arrival in Veszprém he found that the Bishop's Palace had been ransacked and plundered by Szálasi's men. "Furniture, clothing, artwork, and groceries in the twenty-eight rooms were missing. I was left with not a single towel or tablecloth."[61] The building had been used for accommodation in rapid succession by the German army, by the Soviet military municipal command, and by a hospital. For the time being, Mindszenty opted to stay with one of the canons. Only in mid-summer could he move back into his palace.

On April 30, 1945, Mindszenty traveled to Budapest. He and József Grősz, archbishop of Kalocsa, requested a meeting with leading members of the new Provisional National Government. At the meeting, the two prelates made known their grievances, protested against the treatment of detained priests, urged the authorization of a Catholic daily newspaper, drew attention to the untenable situation of ethnic Hungarians in the occupied areas and of the men held at Russian prisoner-of-war camps, and related the injustices committed against ethnic Germans in Hungary who were loyal to the state. The two prelates then discussed the chaos caused by land reform with the executive head of the National Land Reform Council.[62]

A New Beginning amid the Ruins

Life at the Bishop's Palace in Veszprém was slow to resume normality. Both the bishop and his staff lived modestly and practiced self-denial. "At first, there was just one change of clothes and of bed linen," one of the sisters recollected later on.[63] As soon as the difficulties relating to food and transport had been overcome, Mindszenty directed all his efforts at reconstruction, a new beginning, and the "normalization" of daily life.

60. VÉL I.1.44.a. 414/1945. Letter of József Mindszenty to the Veszprém Municipal Command of the Red Army, April 20, 1945; Ibid., 422/1945. Letter of József Mindszenty to the superior general of the Daughters of the Divine Redeemer in Sopron, April 25, 1945.

61. Ibid., 541/1945. Petition of Bishop József Mindszenty, April 30, 1945.

62. Margit Beke, ed., *A magyar katolikus püspökkari tanácskozások története és jegyzőkönyvei 1945–1948 között* (Cologne and Budapest: Argumentum, 1996), 33–36.

63. SZTTTI 1192/111. Sister Kolumba Ádám's witness statement on the matter of the beatification of József Mindszenty, Buffalo, May 1985.

A priority for Mindszenty was to arrange for the re-opening of the schools that had been closed during the war. He instructed the Transylvanian priests who had come to the diocese as refugees to return to their congregations. He then petitioned for the payment of the so-called "kongrua" (a stipend paid by the state), the age allowance and other entitlements which had not been paid on time. Soon enough, the payments were received. Services of remembrance were held in commemoration of the wartime martyrdom of seven of the diocese's clergy. A particularly large number of priests in the Veszprém diocese had been apprehended by the Arrow Cross or by the Germans: 31 of the 55 priests detained in Western Hungary (Transdanubia) had come from the Veszprém Diocese. Mindszenty viewed his decision to stay as setting a good example to other priests. Indeed, all but two of the parish priests stayed with their flocks throughout the battles.

In the early summer, Mindszenty began visiting the parish churches in the diocese. In the course of the summer, he succeeded in visiting three-quarters of them, often traveling in a horse-drawn carriage. Many church properties had been seized for use as military accommodations, hospitals or administrative centers. This was particularly so in the urban areas and less so in rural areas. Everywhere there were signs of destruction, violence, and robbery. Mindszenty could see for himself the sufferings of ordinary people.

Mindszenty resumed, with a passion, the church construction work, which had been abandoned in the fall of 1944. In view of the impoverishment of the local population and the church's lack of land, the project was even more problematic now than it had been previously. Yet, despite all the difficulties, thirty parish churches, three Catholic boarding schools, and nine new Catholic schools were established within a year and a half.[64]

Since the German invasion of March 1944, the inhabitants of the diocese had known the meaning of a foreign military occupation. Still, the brutality of the Soviet army exceeded people's fears and confirmed Mindszenty's anti-Soviet prejudices, which he had nurtured for decades. Mindszenty wrote a whole series of angry letters to various government ministers. In one, he dramatically summed up the situation as follows:

64. VÉL I.1.2. 1945/IX. September 29, 1945.

Not a single woman is safe. Our priests have buried women of 76 and 82 years of age. In Világos, a husband and wife were buried, who had been killed together by Soviet officers on account of their resistance. In Felsőpáhok a father who tried to protect his daughter was killed, here too by an officer. I do not understand why weapons are used for such purposes. Crimes against property are seen on the roads and along the routes. The stirrups are taken from a horse belonging to a Veszprém priest, the necklace is stolen from another priest, a third is attacked in the vicinity of Kaposvár. Trains are stopped and then plundered. 2000 soldiers descend at night on the village of Balatoncsicsó and hold it to ransom. They take what is left of the clothing; farm animals and animal feed are lost.[65]

At the bishop's place a gruesome report was heard of the tragedy of a local printer: on the night of August 6, two armed Soviet soldiers had come to his house. The soldiers had bound the printer to his bed, and while one of the soldiers raped his wife in the garden, the other did the same thing to his 16-month-old (!) baby daughter. The soldiers had then stolen as much as they could. The printer's wife and daughter had been infected with venereal disease.[66] Such events greatly influenced Mindszenty's attitude towards the occupation force and the country's new authorities. Neither at the time, nor later did Mindszenty recognize the dual role played by the Soviets (and their allies): on the one hand, they liberated the country from Nazi occupation and the terror of the Arrow Cross regime (for a substantial section of the population this truly was a liberation); on the other, as the new occupation force, the Soviets carried out further destruction and plundering, while humiliating Hungarian women and transporting tens of thousands of the men against their will to Soviet territory for "malenkiy rabot." Yet, in a pastoral letter adopted on May 24, 1945 at the first Bishops' Conference in the post-war period – a conference presided over by József Grősz, archbishop of Kalocsa – the tone was one of understanding and recognition of the actions of the Soviet army and the military bodies:

65. PIL 274. f. 7/247. ő. e. 28. fol. Letter of József Mindszenty to Prime Minister Béla Dálnoki Miklós, July 11, 1945.

66. Arkhiv Vneshney Politiki Rossiyskoy Federatsii [Archive of Foreign Policy of the Russian Federation] (hereafter: AVP RF) f. 0453. [ACC-files] op. 2a. papka (paper folder) 20a., delo (file) 67. l. 14. Memorandum, December 4, 1945.

"...the news that has been spread concerning the Russian army's intention to liquidate the Church, has not been substantiated. Our churches are still standing and church services are proceeding without hindrance."[67]

The fact that the Red Army's actions came as a pleasant surprise to the Hungarian prelates is linked with Joseph Stalin's earlier decision to subordinate church policy strategy to the greater purpose of victory in World War II. For decades, the reports reaching East Central Europe on the situation of churches in the Soviet Union had inspired no optimism at all. Still, in the spring of 1944, the world witnessed a remarkable reversal: on April 29, *Pravda* published a photograph of Stalin and Molotov in conversation with a Catholic priest from Springfield, Stanislav Orlemanski. In an interview with Radio Moscow, the American priest stated that he had concluded with much satisfaction that Stalin was a friend of the Catholic Church... An American priest of Polish ancestry, Orlemanski had requested and received a visa to travel to the Soviet Union for the purpose of meeting with Stalin and discussing with him issues surrounding the status of religion. Surprisingly, Orlemanski had been successful in his endeavor; indeed, thanks to him, the Western world had learned of Stalin's new strategy. In the knowledge of the tragedy of 80,000 priests executed in the Soviet Union, it is difficult to view Stalin's intentions as honest rather than as cynical and calculating. He stated no less than that the authorities should strive for dialogue and cooperation with the churches and that "the Soviet government had abandoned its hostile position on religion. [...] There must not and will not be any kind of religious retribution. The Soviet Union will seek retribution against those who persecute religion."[68]

Subsequent developments, however, did not engender loyalty on the part of Mindszenty. Indeed, the circular letter's failure to criticize the actions of the Soviet military personnel was a serious omission in his view – one that he was determined to make up for. Although he acknowledged

67. József Vecsey, comp., *Mindszenty okmánytár: Pásztorlevelek, beszédek, nyilatkozatok*, vol. 1, *Mindszenty tanítása* (Munich: [s. n.], 1957), 34.

68. T. V. Volokitina et al., eds., *Vostochnaja Europa v dokumentah rossiyskih arhivov 1944–1953, Tom 1, 1944–1948* (Moscow and Novosibirsk: Sibirskiy hronograf, 1997), 36–42; T. V. Volokitina, G. P. Murashko, A. F. Noskova, and D. H. Nokhotovich, eds., *Vlasty i cherkov v Vostochnoy Evrope 1944–1953: Dokumenti rossiyskih arhivov. Tom 1. 1944–1948* (Moscow, ROSSPEN, 2009), 29–35.

that during the military conflict Soviet military personnel had generally shown respect to priests, monks and nuns and had respected the right of people to hold church services, he nevertheless drew attention to the multiple instances of brutality and destruction: the plundering of Veszprém Cathedral and Saint Margaret's parish church, the use of vestments to wash military trucks, the death of five parish priests in the diocese, the murder of Vilmos Apor, bishop of Győr, and the rape of four nuns in Sümeg and another nun in Agyagosszergény.

Mindszenty suspected that a "secret hand" – instructions issued by the senior leadership in Moscow – lay behind such events. The evidence currently at our disposal suggests his suspicions were as yet unfounded. For example, a memorandum containing the reasons for the reprimanding of Sándor Zöld, Hungary's minister of interior, by Major General A. M. Belianov – a senior member of the domestic affairs section of the Allied Control Commission, who was essentially the Budapest representative of the NKVD (People's Commissariat for Internal Affairs) – mentions that the political police, a body controlled by the Hungarian Ministry of Interior, had used unacceptable force against civilians.[69] The ideological and political power struggle resulted inevitably in the construction of enemy stereotypes, but the atrocities suffered by church figures and institutions in 1945 did not take place on the orders of the Soviet authorities or even of the communist party. Rather, it is closer to the truth to attribute such acts of violence to the overzealousness of local organs and to the random aggressiveness and uncouthness of war-hardened and half-starved soldiers, especially those who were not serving in regular forces. Department No. 1 of the Ministry for Religious Affairs and Education requested from each diocese the names of priests and nuns who had been detained, interned or arrested. For the period until July 1945, only a small number of cases were reported from the Diocese of Veszprém. In most deaneries there were no reported police violations in the first half of 1945.[70] In the second half of the year, however, the situation deteriorated, and six more priests were arrested between July and September.

69. AVP RF f. 0453. op. 4. papka (paper folder) 43., delo (file) 11. Memorandum. Talks between Maj. Gen. A. M. Belianov and State Secretary Sándor Zöld, May 25, 1945.

70. VÉL I.1.44.a. 966/1945. Reports by deaneries.

As time passed, there was growing evidence of church actions that were hostile to the Soviet Union or at least perceived as such. The Soviet military commanders increasingly took the view that Catholic priests were politicizing and making statements that insulted the communists or which could easily be misinterpreted. A pastoral letter issued by Mindszenty on measures taken against youth dances certainly fell in this category. In the letter Mindszenty drew, for the first time, an analogy between the circumstances that had arisen following the defeat in war with the symbolic sites of ancient defeats suffered by Hungarians: Muhi, Mohács, Majtény, and Világos. On account of Mindszenty's pastoral letter, the parish priest of Marcali got into trouble with the local Russian commander, who had the letter seized on suspicion of it being "fascist propaganda." Mindszenty deemed the confiscation of the letter to be interference in Hungarian domestic affairs. On September 14, 1945, in one of his first official protests, he wrote the following words to the United States Mission in Budapest: "The secular authorities should not enter the churches, for that would be a grievous violation of the freedom of conscience. [...] If the Hungarians refuse to dance, they are certainly not harming the interests of the United Nations," he stated in his defense of the Church's terrenum.[71] As bishop and subsequently as prince primate, Mindszenty refused to allow anyone – and certainly not the secular powers – to interfere in the matters of the Church.

In consequence of the land reform legislation of March 15, 1945, an enormous burden was placed on József Mindszenty's shoulders. On entering the Arrow Cross prison, he had been a landowner prelate. On his release, owing to the land reform, he was a poor bishop facing substantial financial burdens and with a duty to provide for 305 parish churches, 550 priests and 600 schools. The episcopal estate of Veszprém had practically ceased to exist: only 700 acres remained of the original more than 42,000 cadastral acres, and the farm equipment was gone. The wartime battles had depleted livestock to a mere fraction of their pre-war numbers: there remained 17 out of 1,321 cattle and 3 out of 295 horses.[72] The estate's charity

71. National Archives and Records Administration, College Park, Maryland (hereafter: NARA) Record Group (hereafter: RG) 84. Department of State, Hungary, Budapest Mission 1945, Box 65. 840.0–840.7 Catholic Church. Letter of József Mindszenty to H. F. Arthur Schoenfeld, September 14, 1945.

72. PL Processus, V–700/39. 34. fol. Annual report of the auditor Lénárd Kögl, January 1, 1946.

pensioners lost their incomes. To pay wages, salaries and pensions, state aid was required by the cathedral chapter, the diocesan central office, the episcopal aula, the schools' inspectorate, the diocesan court, and the auditing body. Formerly, none of these bodies had received state assistance, as their expenditures had been covered by the episcopal benefice.

Under Section 15 of the Land Reform Decree, 300 cadastral acres could be retained in cases of verified anti-fascist activity. József Mindszenty acted quickly to make use of this opportunity. On June 1, 1945, after some debate, the Political Committee of the Provisional National Assembly gave a positive assessment of his claim.[73] However, the implementation of this decision was slow to proceed, and he received the 300 acres in several pieces.

The pastoral letter issued by the Bishops' Conference on May 24, 1945 included a multifaceted analysis of public life: it criticized the operation of the national committees and of the new government bodies in general and called for the restitution of the country's traditional and professional public administration. In the pastoral letter, the bishops also strongly condemned the activities of the political police, a force controlled by the communist-led Ministry of Interior. They then gave their assessment of the land reform program, noting that, for the first time since the foundation of the state by King Stephen, Hungarian bishops had been excluded from the process of reordering the country. Indeed, even though the land reform program had utilized 765,000 of the Catholic Church's 862,000 acres, the authorities had failed even to consult the Catholic bishops. The pastoral letter frankly admitted that the Church faced a funding crisis: revenue would not cover expenditure on Catholic schools, cathedrals, and parish churches. Nonetheless, the bishops gave their blessing to the land that had been distributed and to the new owners. They acknowledged that the land reform legislation gave attention to the Church while failing to provide for the existential basis of those church-managed institutions that had previously been maintained using income from landholdings. The prelates also mentioned the ill-considered implementation of the provisions of the decree and their exploitation for political purposes to the benefit of the Communist Party.[74] Although the land reform had shaken the very

73. MNL OL XVIII–5. 4. fol. Record of resolutions, June 1, 1945.
74. Vecsey, *Mindszenty okmánytár*, vol. 1, 37.

foundations of the Catholic Church's financial status, it had nevertheless opened up new horizons: the Church could now turn towards the faithful with new vigor.

The Search of Political Catholicism for its Place

Political Catholicism's wartime search for its place in Hungarian society had most closely resembled a cul-de-sac. The younger generations, however, had not been prepared to give up, and finally, on October 13, 1944, the Christian Democratic People's Party was formed with the goal of placing Catholic party politics on new social foundations. The word "Christian" in the name of the party was a reference to its interdenominational nature, but from the spring of 1945 it was known simply as the Democratic People's Party and the emphasis was placed firmly on the people's party character of the new formation in an effort to avoid even the impression of a "clerical" party. Count József Pálffy, the nephew of Bishop Apor, became leader of the party. The landowner Pálffy had acquired some political experience as a member of Parliament from 1939 supporting the program of the governing party. On October 15, 1944, Pálffy informed Prince Primate Jusztinián Serédi about the newly constituted party. Serédi approved its formation and pledged his support for rejuvenation in several fields.[75] However, there was still no official recognition for the Christian Democratic People's Party. While several Jesuits, having crossed the front, had managed to secure, from one or other members of the Provisional National Government, the tentative (verbal) authorization of the party, this subsequently proved to be of little value amid the administrative chaos that followed the conclusion of the war.

Looking back at Mindszenty's earlier stances on the Christian Party, we repeatedly find him among the reformers and those seeking new approaches. It comes as no surprise, therefore, that at the time of the post-war resumption of political life in Hungary, Mindszenty opted to support the founders of the new Christian party rather than those individuals who were presenting themselves as the successors of the Christian People's

75. KFL I.1.a. 990/1945. Letter of the university professor Gyula Szekfű to József Grősz, archbishop of Kalocsa, April 10, 1945.

Party of 1943. Mindszenty's decision was motivated not only by his close relationship at the time with the new party's Jesuit organizers, namely Jenő Kerkai and Töhötöm Nagy, but also by his recognition that their movement, the Catholic Agrarian Youth League (KALOT, Katolikus Agrárifjúsági Legényegyletek Országos Testülete), with its commitment to the country's peasant farmers and its modern social program, could engender mass support. The feeling of goodwill was mutual, as demonstrated by Töhötöm Nagy's role at the time of Mindszenty's appointment as prince primate.

The initial unity, however, soon belonged to the past. The refusal of the prelates, Mindszenty at their head, to countenance personnel changes at church institutions widened the existing cracks in political Catholicism. It is at this point that the first signs of a bipolarization in Catholic public life can be observed. We find, on the one side, those who wished to resume the traditional, pre-1945 approach to politics and public life, including the leaders of the former Christian Party and Catholic Action, and, on the other side, an evolving group of Catholics who supported Christian Democracy and who had been in contact with, or even participated in, the anti-fascist resistance. This was the fracture line along which the Christian Democratic People's Party became divided into two factions by mid-summer, with a conservative group headed by the party chairman, Count József Pálffy, and a progressive wing headed by István Barankovics, the party's general secretary.

Obviously, the legitimist and aristocratic József Pálffy stood closer to Mindszenty than did István Barankovics, an intellectual who supported a republican form of government. That Mindszenty chose nevertheless to support Barankovics may be explained primarily by Pálffy's disorderly personal life and by his aristocratic background, which was disadvantageous at the time. He acknowledged Pálffy's removal from the head of the party, which followed several months of inter-factional rivalry. Mindszenty monitored Catholic party political developments throughout this period. Indeed, making full use of his authority, he sought to influence if not determine the course of events in this field.

At the meeting of the Bishops' Conference in May it was József Mindszenty who summarized the rather unfavorable party political situation: "...perhaps it is not impossible that we too should fight in a party led by a Protestant preacher; yet, even so, the current situation gives grounds for worry." Mindszenty was referring here to the Independent Smallholders' Party and its chairman, the Calvinist minister Zoltán Tildy.[76] The tone of his remarks well illustrates the mentality of Mindszenty and, more generally, of the clergy prior to the Second Vatican Council. Beyond the theological differences that divided Protestant and Catholic Christians, another factor was Mindszenty's desire to reorganize Christian society on a legitimist foundation, an aim flatly rejected by the Smallholders, Hungary's most popular political force at the time. This political difference between Mindszenty and the Smallholders' Party did not arise in 1945 but dated back to an earlier period in the 1930s.

In the aftermath of the war Mindszenty immediately urged the launching of a Catholic newspaper, but according to the practice at the time political newspapers could only be published by recognized political parties. The failure to found a party meant that the country's Catholics, who made up more than 60 percent of the population, did not have their own newspaper. While the monthly magazine *A Szív* (The Heart), several periodicals, and – as of August 9 – the weekly newspaper *Új Ember* (New Man) could be published, a daily newspaper remained lacking. This fact, which was made worse by the authorized newspapers' difficulties in securing an adequate paper supply, was to become one of the Church's most frequently expressed grievances.

76. Beke, *A magyar katolikus püspökkari 1945–1948*, 49.

CHAPTER 4

MINDSZENTY'S INSTALLATION
AS THE ARCHBISHOP OF ESZTERGOM AT THE BASILICA IN ESZTERGOM

CHAPTER 4

The Hungarian Mount Zion

APPOINTMENT AS PRIMATE

The burial of Prince Primate Jusztinián Serédi took place in Esztergom on April 2, 1945. At the modest funeral wake after the ceremony the question of who should succeed him was raised. The bishop of Győr, Baron Vilmos Apor, who had Transylvanian ancestry, was considered the most likely candidate. Those attending the wake did not know that Bishop Apor had sadly passed away, having been shot just days earlier by an angry drunken Soviet soldier as he sought to protect a group of women who had fled to his residence. Two days after Archbishop Serédi's funeral the papal nuncio, Angelo Rotta, was expelled from the country. Today we know for certain that this measure had been ordered by the Allied (Soviet) Supreme Command rather than by the Provisional National Government. This expulsion was the first disappointment for those who had envisioned a rapprochement with the Soviet authorities. Meanwhile, for those Catholic leaders – among them Mindszenty – who deemed cooperation impossible, the expulsion of the nuncio served as further proof of the Soviet authorities' underlying hostility towards the Church. The legal justification for the expulsion was the nuncio's decision to remain at his post even after the Arrow Cross coup. This decision – it was argued – had amounted to *de facto* recognition of the collaborationist Szálasi government. Such an argument disregarded the fact that the nunciature had been kept open for the purpose of rescuing the persecuted.

Candidates and Nominees

József Cavallier accompanied the nuncio to the railway station: "...as he was accompanying Angelo Rotta, he mentioned to him once again that there was no better candidate for the archbishop's seat in Esztergom than József Mindszenty, bishop of Veszprém... For he had shown bravery against the Nazis, and because he was uncompromising..."[1] Angelo Rotta needed no persuasion; he had been a supporter of Mindszenty at the time of the abbot-priest's nomination as bishop of Veszprém, and nothing had happened since then to alter his good opinion of Mindszenty.

In terms of relations between church and state, the choice of prince primate had never been incidental. The government now wished to utilize an opportunity provided for in the *intesa semplice* (simple arrangement) of 1927. This meant that although the Apostolic See had asserted its right to select prelates as of 1918, the Hungarian government could make its comments prior to the filling of an ecclesiastical office falling under Rome's jurisdiction and could, furthermore, make a suggestion concerning the persons it deemed suitable for a post within two months of it having become vacant. In this specific instance, the two-month period after the death of Prince Primate Jusztinián Serédi was to expire on May 29.[2]

At its meeting on May 25, 1945 (i.e., before the expiry of the two-month period), the government addressed the issue of the new prince primate. Minister of Culture Géza Teleki put forward five names, the last being that of József Mindszenty.[3] In the end, the Council of Ministers considered three men to be suitable candidates for the office of prince primate. The first of these was the provost *László Bánáss* (1888–1949), vicar of Debrecen;

1. Béla Saád, *Tíz arckép* (Budapest: Ecclesia, 1983), 96.

2. MNL OL XIX–A–1–j–XXIII–1631/1945. Az INK iratai [Documents of the Provisional National Government] (1944) 1945–49. 27.971/pol.–1945. Verbal note to the Allied Control Commission, May 19, 1945.

3. MNL OL XIX–A–83–a/30. sz. 2. fol. Minutes of the meeting of the Council of Ministers on May 25, 1945.

the second was *Áron Márton* (1896–1980), diocesan bishop of Gyulafehérvár; and the third was Benedictine Archabbot *Krizosztom Kelemen* (1884–1950).[4] Hence, none of the candidates was József Mindszenty, and this fact doubtless remained no secret to him.

The government turned to the Allied Control Commission, requesting that it contact the Holy See concerning the choice of prince primate. In late July, however, Georgiy Maksimovich Pushkin, the Soviet political representative, ruled out any such measure "in view of the fact that they have no means of proceeding in the absence of diplomatic relations."[5] It is doubtful, therefore, that the Vatican received any kind of list from the Provisional National Government. It is more likely that, owing to the breach in diplomatic relations, the temporary nature of the Hungarian state authorities, and the country's occupation and lack of sovereignty, the Catholic authorities in Rome decided to proceed in accordance with the 1917 Code of Canon Law as it had been interpreted before the *intesa semplice*. That is to say, the Holy See had the right, in all cases, to appoint bishops. At any rate, we know that Rome did not choose one of the government's candidates.

In Rome, other Catholic figures spoke up in support of József Mindszenty. In the summer of 1945 the Jesuit Töhötöm Nagy traveled to the eternal city to seek funding for the Catholic Agrarian Youth League. At the time, the Jesuit leaders of the League maintained favorable relations with the bishop of Veszprém. Indeed, Mindszenty expressly supported the work of the League. One of his first letters to the US representation in Budapest had been devoted to presenting the work of the League.[6]

Töhötöm Nagy was the first visitor to Rome from the territories occupied by the Red Army. Consequently, his visit was met with great interest. In his report he detailed the physical and moral damage to the country (plundering, brutality, the killing of Bishop Apor, the deportation of half a million men to the Soviet Union) and the ideological and political balance

4. MNL OL XIX–A–1–j–XXIII–1631/1945. Az INK iratai (1944) 1945–49. Letter of Count Géza Teleki, minister of education and religious affairs, to the minister of foreign affairs, May 31, 1945.

5. Ibid., Pro domo, July 30, 1945.

6. NARA RG 84, Department of State Hungary, Budapest Mission 1945, Box 66, 843–850.7 Catholic Agrarian Youth League (KALOT). Letter of Bishop József Mindszenty to the "American Mission," August 24, 1945.

of power ("the Russians are seemingly not interfering in matters," but "the Hungarian communists are doing everything" and "the Communist Party is the blind tool of the Soviets, implementing their direct instructions").[7] Perhaps with the ulterior motive of the Jesuits controlling Mindszenty, Nagy gave the following characterization of him to the Secretariat of State and, in a private audience on August 14, to Pope Pius XII:

> Arguments for him:
> 1. A consequential and determined man who does not shrink from difficulties.
> For years he lobbied in many counties to have them demand changes in the Civil Marriage Act. He firmly condemned the unjust provisions of the civil authorities. When a government minister rebuked him (at the time he was still a priest) for these things and emphasized his own power, his response was: your power is greater, but mine is more enduring.
> As dean he founded and consecrated eighteen parish churches within a period of twenty years, and he also opened more than twelve Catholic schools. As bishop of Veszprém, he founded sixteen new parish churches in the first year alone. In the second year, detailed plans for continuing the work were prepared, but the Russians arrived and everything came to a halt.
> 2. An excellent and talented organizer.
> As the parish priest of Zalaegerszeg, in an exemplary manner he organized people of every social class in the town into different Catholic organizations.
> 3. Social awareness.
> For many years he strove to help poor Roma people. Just weeks after his appointment as bishop, he raised the wages of day laborers on the church estates. The laborers had previously been living in true poverty.
> 4. A priest with an exemplary life.
> Coming from a poor family, on his appointment as bishop he distributed all his personal property among his relatives, warning them that they should not expect any financial assistance from him in the future.

7. JTMRL II.1. Copies from the material in the Rome archive of the order, Epistolae Singulorum 1913–49/1942–45. "Notes sur la situation actuelle de la Hongrie et des mouvements catholiques en Hongrie, Jusqu'au 14 juin 1945," Rome, le 14 juillet 1945.

Even his most vehement enemies could never accuse him of moral failures. Many times I myself have seen him praying alone and at length in the church. He is a docile person with an open soul.

5. An educated man.

He has written several books: alongside several historical studies of minor significance, a three-volume monumental work full of godliness on the duties of Christian mothers.

6. Even the communists hold him in high esteem, because the Nazis carried him off using force.

Arguments against him:

1. Excessively rigid (strict).

He literally forced the priests and catechists in the town to live in a community housed in the extended presbytery building. The strict discipline that he kept there was such that the presbytery came to be known as the "Pehminarium" (because, at the time, his surname was still Pehm).

2. Sometimes he tells the truth in a rather brusque fashion,

and this happens so frequently that it is pointless to list the examples. For this reason, many are afraid of him, and although he is respected, he is not loved.

3. His willpower is excessive.

Whatever he comes to know as the truth he mercilessly imposes on everyone else. He arranged for a county deputy prefect to be dismissed after the man in question had sought to hinder him in his struggle against civil marriage. Thus he destroyed the man's political career.

4. Active role in Hungary's re-annexation of the Vendish (Slovene) territories.[8]

The territories have now been returned to Yugoslavia.

8. Töhötöm Nagy made no distinction between the Muraköz area (Međimurje), with its Croatian majority, and the Muravidék area (Prekmurje), which had a Vend (Slovene) population. Mindszenty's efforts had been directed primarily at the re-annexation of the Muraköz area (Međimurje), as described in another chapter of this book. (In 1941, the Holy See had temporarily entrusted the ecclesiastical administration of the Vend region to the north of the River Mura to József Grősz, bishop of Szombathely, as the apostolic governor of Muravidék.)

5. He is known for his royalism.
A permanent fixture in his room was a portrait of Otto von Habsburg, heir-to-the-throne; each year, on the anniversary of the death of Charles IV, the last King of Hungary, he held a solemn funeral mass.
6. Recently, the communists have become indignant against him, because the communists sought to use his prestige to benefit their own interests and he managed to thwart their plans.
Conclusion: all the virtues and defects of the most excellent statesmen are to be found in József Mindszenty.[9]

The Jesuit – who was barely known in Rome other than by one or two fellow Jesuits – characterized Mindszenty in a fitting manner (although posterity has usually ignored him, for Töhötöm Nagy subsequently pursued an adventurous life, developing a rather ambiguous attitude towards the Church).[10] Nagy highlighted a number of Mindszenty's characteristics, including an aspect that is undeservedly neglected in the biographies: not only did Mindszenty have an unmatched capacity for work manifested in his contribution to public life as bishop, but he also lived a fervent and prayerful priestly life.

On August 6, 1945, Miklós Tóth, who was studying theology in Esztergom, set out for Rome with a semi-official list of candidates. He arrived in the city on the night of 17 August. For the lower clergy and a majority of influential churchmen whose opinion had been sought, the first preference for the post of prince primate was József Mindszenty. There was universal agreement that filling the post was the priority, while the choice of candidate was of secondary importance. As Miklós Tóth wrote, "The question remains: Does the Vatican want a strong personality with a

9. Töhötöm Nagy, *Jezsuiták és szabadkőművesek* (Buenos Aires: Danubio, 1965), 198–200.

10. When the pope received Töhötöm Nagy in a further private audience on April 29, 1946, he said "half in earnest and half in jest [...]: You recommended him! Whereupon I explained that even today I consider him the most suitable [man for the job], because firstly he conducts himself differently now and, secondly, we should not forget that with his forceful statements he shook a nation out of its stupor and became the hope of the people. The Holy Father repeated three or four times that it was his hope that the prince primate would now conduct himself in a smarter manner." OSZK Kt. 216. f. 236. ő. e. Letter of Töhötöm Nagy to Jenő Kerkai, May 3, 1946. – For more about his career, see Éva Petrás, "'Álarcok mögött': Nagy Töhötöm élete," *Századok* [Centuries] 149, no. 1 (2015): 203–12.

firm hand – in which case Bishop Mindszenty has been sent by Providence – or does it consider a more conciliatory policy to be more suitable, in which case Archbishop Grősz would be the right choice."[11] Grősz, however, had informed Nuncio Rotta at Archbishop Serédi's funeral that he would not be putting himself forward as candidate for succession.

The Decision

At the Vatican the decision was taken without much hesitation. On August 16, 1945, just two days after receiving Töhötöm Nagy in a private audience, Pope Pius XII, who had yet to be informed about the candidates on the Esztergom list, selected József Mindszenty, bishop of Veszprém, for the post of archbishop of Esztergom.[12]

Why did the pope appoint Mindszenty to this important and politically sensitive office? Why did he not choose a more flexible and conciliatory figure to deal with Hungary's post-war government leadership? There were more than a few monsignori in the papal apparatus who questioned the suitability of the "peasant bishop," viewing his lack of political sagacity as his weakest point. Others, however, felt that Hungary had already been irrevocably lost, and so Mindszenty – as both a tried and tested antifascist and an anticommunist – was the best person to wage the "final battle."[13]

The pope needed to select an unchallengeable prelate who was firm in his beliefs and principles and exemplary in his lifestyle. Owing to his legitimist views, Mindszenty had not identified with the fallen Horthy regime, and his hostility towards the Arrow Cross movement was known throughout the country. His anti-Nazi stance was also public knowledge, but his rejection of Nazism had never been accompanied by hostility towards Germans as a nation. This fact may have been an important consideration for Pope Pius XII, a Germanophile who still regarded Ger-

11. "*Riguardo alla persona del Primate il parere del clero inferiore e manifesto e chiaro: Giuseppe Mindszenty vescovo di Veszprém.*" OSZK Kt. 216. f. 490. ő. e. Miklós Tóth's summary in Italian, August 24, 1945.

12. *Magyar Kurír* [Hungarian Courier] 35, September 17, 1945, second edition.

13. Hansjakob Stehle, *Die Ostpolitik des Vatikans 1917–1975* (Munich and Zurich. R. Piper und Co. Verlag, 1975), 285; Stehle, *Geheimdiplomatie im Vatikan: Die Päpste und die Kommunisten*. (Zurich: Benziger, 1993), 241.

many as the main defensive bastion against communism in postwar Europe. Meanwhile Hungary's conservative and bourgeois political forces needed the consistent support of Hungarian Catholicism in order to repulse the communists, who were steadily advancing in society. All in all, in view of the Bolshevik threat to Hungary, a strong and tough personality such as József Mindszenty – the youngest of Hungary's bishops and a complete unknown in the world church – seemed to be the guarantee for the proper government of the Hungarian Catholic Church.

On September 8, József Grősz, archbishop of Kalocsa, personally informed Mindszenty of the pope's intent. It must have been a poignant moment in Mindszenty's life when he read the notice in Latin that Grősz had received from the Vatican: "Above all, inform His Excellency Mindszenty of his appointment as archbishop of Esztergom and request his consent. Keep the matter as a secret of the Sanctum Officium until His Excellency Mindszenty states that he will accept the office to which the Holy Father has called him."[14] Mindszenty hesitated and made no immediate decision, requesting three days' grace. He wrote in his memoirs,

> Suffice it to say that after two days of reflection I agreed. The decisive factor for me was the confidence of Pope Pius XII. He knew my character, knew that I was more concerned with the care of souls than politics,[15] and it was he who had also proposed me for the diocese of Veszprém, although the government at the time had raised objections. The nuncio had fully informed the Holy Father about my administration of the diocese and also about my imprisonment. In addition, time was pressing. Archbishop Grősz pointed out to me that it would be highly disadvantageous to Hungarian Catholicism if the seat of the primate, which had already been orphaned for half a year, continued vacant. When I gave my consent, I was trusting wholeheartedly in our people, brave defenders of their faith who had so often and so movingly proved their attachment to Christianity. But

14. VÉL I.1.44.a. 2168/1945. Archbishop Grősz of Kalocsa included the information he had received in his letter to József Mindszenty, September 6, 1945.

15. In the original Hungarian version of *Memoirs* it is not stated that Pius XII knew that Mindszenty was more concerned with the care of souls than politics. (In view of his life course, Mindszenty may have sought the inclusion of the statement in the English version by way of self-justification.)

I confess that I was also hoping somewhat to obtain support from the Allied Control Commission...[16]

The deceased prince primate, Archbishop Jusztinián Serédi, had lacked an ambition for leadership and an interest in secular matters. Mindszenty, however, had both. Even so, the absence of formal qualifications bothered him even more than it had done before. He had studied theology at a provincial college and not at a famous university, and he feared that his authority as archbishop would suffer as a result. His knowledge of foreign languages was limited; German was the only one he spoke adequately. While his knowledge of Latin was good, this was of no benefit to him when meeting with secular visitors. Moreover his approach to interpersonal relations and his manner of negotiation had long caused him problems. Another source of uncertainty was the still untested nature of his leadership capabilities, for he had been a bishop only for a short time. On the other hand, his book publications meant that he was known to the country's clergy and many lay persons. Having suffered at the hands of the Arrow Cross, he seemed likely to receive the trust of the government. Mindszenty had considerable self-awareness. In notes written at the time, he highlighted, among his objections to taking on such a senior post, the following admission: "I am not a diplomat or a tactician, but possess merely the strength of my principles."[17] Mindszenty then noted his arguments for accepting the post, ranking them as follows:

1) At some time or other I will be put in some kind of prison. 2) I will not reject work or martyrdom. 3) Reports [of the appointment] are already being spread – by whom? 4) Relations with the Apostolic See are very difficult, and so it will be at least a year before they find another person. 5) The two cardinals have no ambitions. This is certain in the case of K[alocsa]; what about Eger?

16. Mindszenty, *Memoirs*, 33. – Note: The cardinal's memoirs mention a 24-hour period of grace, but a note made by Mindszenty clarifies the time period: "For a period of three hours, he [Archbishop Grősz] kept on urging me [to make a decision] but I did not give my consent. I asked for three days." PL Processus, V–700/16. 9. fol. Note in Latin of József Mindszenty, September 9, 1945.

17. PL Processus, V–700/16. 9. fol. József Mindszenty's note, September 9, 1945. (The following quotation is also taken from the same place – the author.)

As he pondered the possibilities, a clear motive for Mindszenty was the opportunity to testify for the faith. Indeed, for the sake of his principles, he was willing to make a personal sacrifice and even to countenance martyrdom. On September 11, Mindszenty called on Töhötöm Nagy; he knew, by this time, that Nagy had brought Pius XII's letter to Hungary from Rome. The Jesuit told him truthfully everything that had been said at his private audience with the pope. At the end of their conversation, Mindszenty touchingly pronounced the word "*affirmative*" that signaled his acceptance.[18]

Mindszenty was evidently aware both of his foibles and of his virtues. He finally drew the conclusion that from the window of his parsonage in Zalaegerszeg he had been able to see, not only the county hall, but also the house of the nation. Public administration, decrees and regulations were known to him. He had dealt with hundreds of petitions and applications, acting when needed and sometimes resorting to tough talk. At the time, county officials had viewed him – rather than the deputy prefect – as the primary inspector. The wide range of experiences he had gained at that time endowed him with the self-confidence he needed to govern the Hungarian Catholic Church and, in his role as prince primate, to seek influence over Hungarian society and government as a whole. By the time Mindszenty decided to accept the appointment, he had firmly concluded that he was the right person to show direction to Catholics throughout the country. As a man of 53 years, he was ready to rise to the task.

Mindszenty let Archbishop Grősz know of his affirmative decision without any further delay on September 14, 1945. The pope's intent to appoint Mindszenty could now be made public, and Grősz took immediate action to this effect. (In the end, the official announcement was preempted by a report appearing in several Budapest newspapers that had gotten wind of the appointment.)[19] Unusually in a formal sense (but unsurprisingly in view of the difficulties of keeping in touch), both the papal bull of appointment and the notification to the chapter were issued on a later

18. Nagy, *Jezsuiták és szabadkőművesek*, 206–07.

19. *Magyar Kurír* 35, September 17, 1945, second edition; PL 2925/1945. 69. fol. József Grősz's document no. 1945/1945 in Latin on the appointment of József Mindszenty, September 14, 1945. For an account of the events, see Török, *Grősz József naplója*, 259; for an analysis, see István Mészáros, *Prímások, pártok, politikusok 1944–1945: Adalékok a magyar katolikus egyház XX. századi történetéhez* (Budapest: Szent István Társulat, 2005), 188–99.

date: October 2, 1945 (the day of the inauguration to the chapter), which the Papal Chancellery dispatched on October 19, almost a fortnight after the installation ceremony.[20] Given that József Mindszenty's appointment has been variously dated, it is worth reiterating that the date of the papal bull (October 2, 1945) is to be regarded under church law as the official date of József Mindszenty's appointment as archbishop of Esztergom.

The first letter of the new prince primate was addressed to Pius XII. The letter was sent from Esztergom on September 20, 1945:

> I received with the deepest respect the truly magnificent grace of Your Holiness, with which you deemed me, your useless servant, of being worthy of being placed in the seat of the Archbishopric of Esztergom. I could give my consent only three days later, because the tasks that go with the office are extraordinarily difficult in these times in Hungary. The divine hand has become weightier over us. For thirty years I taught the faithful to be obedient to the Apostles' Creed, and now I must show obedience. While I am unfit for this office and weak for the burden, I shall not decline to offer my efforts and my enthusiasm for the flock, for the Church, and for the country, against the wolves that are running amok."[21]

The newly appointed prince primate soon experienced the nature of the circumstances in which he was to govern the Hungarian Church. On September 24, between the villages of Csipkerek and Kám in the vicinity of the Vas County highway, three drunken Russian soldiers fired shots at his car. He was not hit, but he felt the bullets whizz past his body. On September 26, he informed the prime minister of the incident and sent a note to the British, American and French delegates of the ACC. The prime minister subsequently informed the chairman of the ACC, Marshal Voroshilov.[22]

20. PL 1647/1946. Pius XII's appointment bull for József Mindszenty. Rome, Seat of St. Peter, October 2, 1945, with Papal seal; PL Székesfőkáptalani Levéltár 109/1945. Bull addressed to the Chapter about József Mindszenty's appointment, October 2, 1945.

21. JTMRL II.1. Copies of the papers in the Order's archive in Rome, Epistolae Singulorum 1913–49/1942–45. József Mindszenty's letter in Latin to Pius XII, September 20, 1945.

22. PIL 274. f. 7/247. ő. e. 32. fol. József Mindszenty's letter to Prime Minister Béla Dálnoki Miklós, September 26, 1945.

On September 14, 1945, a peel of church bells, rung throughout the country for half an hour, heralded József Mindszenty's appointment as archbishop of Esztergom. The joy of the faithful was reported on positively in the press and was given a favorable reception in political public life. As József Antall, a state secretary from the Smallholders' Party, wrote in the Catholic weekly *Új Ember* (New Man), Mindszenty's appointment meant that a "man of steel" had been placed at the head of the Catholic Church in Hungary.[23]

The government acknowledged the appointment and expressed hope for a speedy normalization of relations with the Holy See. The regime could not really raise any political objections, for it itself had recognized Mindszenty's past in the resistance by awarding him the 300-acre exemption with respect to the Veszprém benefice. Prime Minister Béla Dálnoki Miklós saluted, on behalf of the government, the new archbishop, who responded with thanks in a telegram dispatched from the town of Pápa at 8.45 a.m. on September 22, 1945: "I thank you heartily for your warm congratulations; the country's first dignitary stands at the disposal of the nation. Prince Primate."[24] With an incredulous shrug the prime minister showed the telegram to several of his staff members, whereupon one of them commented: "He's probably abnormal." The prime minister gave an affirmative nod, remarking something like "Crazy people can cause a lot of trouble."[25]

Mindszenty left no doubt that, similarly to his predecessors, he wished to make his voice heard in Hungarian public life. No-one objected to this in principle. However, his self-description as the country's first dignitary had clearly ruffled feathers, for it could only mean that he, as the new prince primate, intended to ignore the National Ruling Council, which had been vested temporarily with the powers of the head of state. On top of representing divine power, Mindszenty seemed also to be demanding a certain amount of earthly authority. Tradition dictated that he would play some kind of role in the exercising of public authority. An open question, how-

23. József Antall, "'Az új hercegprímás arcképe.' Az acélember" ['The portrait of the new prince primate'. A man of steel], *Új Ember* 1, no. 8, September 30, 1945, cover page.

24. PIL 274. f. 7/247. ő. e. 16. fol. Telegram.

25. Ákos Major, *Népbíráskodás – forradalmi törvényesség: Egy népbíró visszaemlékezései* (Budapest: Minerva Kiadó, 1988), 264.

ever, was the exact nature of his public role and its significance as Hungarian statehood underwent its postwar reestablishment and consolidation. For the time being, no-one wished to address this issue.

Further documents shine light on Mindszenty's interpretation of his role: in two lengthy letters to Archduke Otto von Habsburg, son of the deceased king of Hungary, he wrote in the humble style of a loyal subject that was at complete variance with the terseness of his telegram. In the letters, he addressed the archduke as "Your Majesty," calling him "my king-in-waiting." These titles were customarily used in Hungary to address the lawful king and the heir-to-the-throne.[26] In the end, however, the archduke received neither of the two letters, for the Jesuit vicar-general refused to approve a journey to Paris by Töhötöm Nagy, who was to have served as "postman."[27] Yet, the assignment given to the courier Jesuit by the prince primate extended to negotiating on his behalf with the archduke and heir-to-the-throne, "assuring him that the new prince primate will do everything to bring about a Habsburg restoration, but requesting His Majesty to facilitate the matter by making efforts towards obtaining the entire territory of Greater Hungary."[28] All of this would have amounted to a gross intervention in politics, and as such it could not be countenanced by the vicar-general, de Boynes. This was especially true, given that the most influential men at the Roman Curia, as well as Pius XII himself, considered Mindszenty's vision of a Habsburg restoration to be untimely to say the least. Töhötöm Nagy made this clear to the prince primate in a report on his private audience with the pope, which took place on October 23, 1945: "A Habsburg restoration would be very salutary for a Catholic block in central Europe, but who will do this now? We are very far from this today," Pius XII had stated, according to Nagy's report.[29]

26. OSZK Kt. 216. f. 486. ő. e. József Mindszenty's letters to Crown Prince Otto von Habsburg, September 18, 1945, and September 22, 1945; The latter is published in Nagy, *Jezsuiták és szabadkőművesek*, 209.

27. ÁBTL 3.2.3. Mt–975/2. 120. fol. Data on Mindszenty's political role. Cf. Nagy, *Jezsuiták és szabadkőművesek*, 208 and 214.

28. Ibid.

29. OSZK Kt. 216. f. 19. ő. e. 301–302. fol. and 48. ő. e. 3. fol. Töhötöm Nagy's report for József Mindszenty, October 23, 1945; Cited – in a different style but with the same content – in Nagy, *Jezsuiták és szabadkőművesek*, 213.

On October 2, 1945, József Mindszenty was installed as archbishop by the vicar capitular. The inaugural ceremony took place at Esztergom Cathedral at 11 a.m. on October 7. The cathedral was packed with people, all of whom wanted to see this rare event, as thitherto, there had been only two primate inaugurations in the twentieth century: in 1916 and in 1928. Government ministers, diplomats, and local notables attended the ceremony at the cathedral where they were joined by the mayor of Esztergom and by delegations from the local Calvinist and Lutheran congregations.

In a sermon laced with historical analogies, Mindszenty spoke in stirring tones of his despair at the unfolding situation: "Today we are staring at the blind depths of a swirling abyss; wounded Hungary is suffocating in our history's greatest vortex, a legal but also moral, political and economic vortex."[30] The tone was one of emotional duality: indignation and bitterness were accompanied by hope and optimism. He sketched a picture of a defeated and impoverished nation, concluding, however, on a note of confidence: even if churches have been destroyed, God can never be defeated, and it is He who can give his people the mercy of repentance. Faith and hope must be stronger even if "we are sitting by the rivers of Babylon." The metaphor refers to the Babylonian captivity recorded in Psalm 137, with the Israelites having refused to sing the songs of joy that their captors – not satisfied with merely oppressing the captives – had demanded from them. It was not difficult for educated Mass attendees to draw an analogy between the Biblical examples and the country's situation. They could also hear the new prince primate's rather eccentric idea of history and witness his aristocratic and traditionalist attitude, which provided a frame for his approach to the present and to recent centuries in Hungarian history.

Mindszenty also spoke of his belief that Hungary had just one option: to purify itself in a moral sense. Indeed, in his view, the country required a moral renaissance grounded on religion. Amid the desperation and lethargy of the aftermath of war, Mindszenty saw a particular role for the Catholic Church in the reconstruction of society. His sermon included a brief mention of financial matters.

30. PL 2925/1945., VÉL I.1.44.a. 3206/1945. Prince Primate József Mindszenty's inaugural sermon; VÉL A 44 4095/1945. Eighth Circular of the Archdiocese of Esztergom, October 17, 1945. (The following quotations are taken from the same place – the author.)

> I do not come with the fantastic wealth of Széchényi and Kopácsy.[31] Yet, how good that would be for the Hungarian nation which is now more impoverished and more quashed [elsewhere: more bled to death] than it was in the Ottoman era! I say this without weeping about the lands and without recognizing as legitimate something that happened without a legal basis.

This digression was important because it related not only to the land reform of 1945 but also to all other subsequent instances of the confiscation of property. For Mindszenty the grievance was the bypassing of the constitutional route and the fact that the provisional (i.e., temporary) government was adopting measures that were far from transitional. Even in the absence of a legal basis, he did not cast doubt on the historical necessity of land reform (the subdivision of large estates into smallholdings). Further, he made no attempt to demand the return of land from the beneficiaries of land reform.

At the inauguration ceremony, he reiterated the public legal status of the country's prince primate, but he did so without expressing the meaning of this in substance:

> We are lacking more than one constitutional factor. But if, as the severity of the misfortune diminishes, the wisdom of the nation builds a bridge, as it has always done and as, indeed, it needs to do now if it wishes to survive above the vortex, your cardinal, the country's primate, will be there in the reestablishment and continuance of our public life as Pontifex, the bridge builder, the country's first knight banneret, based on more than 900 years of law.

Mindszenty called himself the country's "first knight banneret," a title that had been used by the press to describe him for some weeks. At the time a legal vacuum surrounded the office of head of state in Hungary. The powers of the former lawful head of state, Miklós Horthy, had ceased to prevail as of October 15, 1944, while the regime headed by Ferenc Szálasi

31. György Széchényi (1605–1695) and József Kopácsy (1775–1847) were archbishops of Esztergom and prince primates of Hungary.

had been swept away at the end of the war and postwar multi-party parliamentary democracy was taking shape within a narrowly defined framework of statehood that lacked sovereignty. The trauma of the war had engendered radical and fundamental changes, including the tearing into pieces of the fabric of the state and the collapse of the old political hierarchy. In the aftermath of war, the representatives of the former regime had no credibility; the traditional economic and social elites were in disarray; and the system of laws and customs had collapsed. The entire Horthy regime had been discredited, because it had culminated in the German occupation of the country, the Holocaust, and the running amok of Ferenc Szálasi and his Arrow Cross accomplices. The Provisional National Government gained Soviet recognition on September 22 and American recognition on September 29, but the British decided to wait until after the national assembly elections. (British recognition thus came only on November 17.) Even after the elections, the powers of the head of state continued to reside with the three-man National Ruling Council, which had been formed on April 17, 1945 at the time of the public legal interregnum. The National Ruling Council continued to exercise these powers until February 1, 1946. During this period, Hungary remained a kingdom in a constitutional sense, but the direction of legal and political developments strongly suggested that a monarch would never return to the throne. A social, political and economic *tabula rasa* came into being, whereby the "strong threads and fine grain" of legal continuity were lost.

When Mindszenty talked about his dignitary status in public law, he was referring to a centuries-old custom of coupling prerogatives with the office. In Hungarian history, among the various ecclesiastic dignitaries, the primate had the strongest and most important public legal role: for a thousand years or so, the primate had been both an ecclesiastic and public legal dignitary.

The title of primate is an ecclesiastical rank that was in use as early as the thirteenth century, at which time it meant in terms of canon law "the first prelate [or primate] of the Hungarian Church." From 1394, the title and nature of "born papal legate" was added (*legatus natus*). Because of being primate, therefore, Mindszenty bore the tasks of spiritual pastor for the entire country, and it was in this sense that he called himself the "country's prelate." The intertwining of certain secular tasks and ranks with the post of archbishop of Esztergom contributed to the development of the ecclesiastical rights of the primate. For instance, since the reign of King Stephen I (Saint Stephen), the archbishop of Esztergom had been the permanent crowning prelate. Thanks to Christian August of Saxe-Zeitz (Hungarian: Keresztély Ágost), who served as archbishop of Esztergom between 1707 and 1723, the holder of the archbishopric of Esztergom became, from 1714, a prince of the Holy Roman Empire. The latter status is the origin of the title of prince primate, which was used until the use of secular titles by priests was prohibited by the Hungarian legislature in 1947 and by Pope Pius XII in 1951. Act XIX. of 1937 mentioned, in the event of a vacancy in the office of regent (head of state), the archbishop of Esztergom as one of the members of the competent national council.

Accordingly, alongside the nobility (both secular and ecclesiastical), the archbishop of Esztergom was, on account of his being an ecclesiastical dignity, a constituent part of public authority from the medieval era until the mid-twentieth century. Did this mean, therefore, that whoever was archbishop was the first public legal dignitary or the first knight banneret?

The "first knight banneret" was a particular status of the archbishop of Esztergom in the Hungarian feudal state. From the fourteenth century, the knights banneret were national dignitaries that joined the royal army with their own banderia (or company of troops) and under their own banner. Later on, the country's most senior secular officials were referred to as knights banneret. Some have claimed that the supreme secular knight banneret was the palatine, while the supreme ecclesiastical knight banneret was the prince primate. Moreover, since the ecclesiastical knights banneret took precedence over the secular ones, the prince primate was considered – until as late as the mid-nineteenth century – the first public legal dignitary in the country after the ruler.[32] True, within the elite the ecclesiastical dignitaries clearly constituted the first estate, as the salvation of the king depended on them. Hence, throughout Europe, the ecclesiastical estate had been given precedence over the secular estate on spiritual grounds ever since the Carolingian Mirrors of Princes with its portrayal of the exemplary good king. Even so, primacy in political affairs had belonged to the secular

32. István Mészáros, "Az 'első zászlósúr' cím," in *"Állok Istenért, Egyházért, Hazáért:" Írások Mindszenty bíborosról* (Budapest: METEM, 2000), 73.

elite. Neither in the medieval period nor in modern era had the members of the ecclesiastical estate – among them the prince primate – been included among the country's knights banneret. Accordingly, József Mindszenty's "self-identification" in 1945 as the country's first knight banneret was not only unusual but also historically erroneous.

It was, furthermore, disputable that the prince primate held first place among the public dignitaries. The acts of the year 1485 stated that the palatine was the second person in the country after the ruler. All subjects were obliged to show obedience to the palatine in the same way as to the king. In the absence of a palatine, however, it is true that the archbishop of Esztergom was appointed, on several occasions, as royal locotenential (*locumtenens regius*). Yet, the royal locotenential did not have to be the archbishop of Esztergom; he could also be chosen from among the bishops of Transylvania, Eger, Győr, and Nyitra or the archbishop of Kalocsa. And this was true even when the see of Esztergom was not vacant. In other words, a prince primate did not automatically become the royal locotenential. While a vacancy in the post of palatine often resulted in the archbishop of Esztergom becoming royal locotenential, it cannot be concluded that the primate was, in general, the first public legal dignitary.

Rivalry between the palatine and the primate marked Hungarian history over a period of several centuries. This was, in essence, a political power struggle between the secular estates and the ecclesiastical elite. By the sixteenth and seventeenth centuries, the establishment of a modern state administration saw an irrevocable shift of power towards the palatine and the secular elite. The year 1848 saw the discontinuation of the tenth, or tithe. This latter step also removed any basis for the requirement that the Church raise a battalion in times of war. Subsequently, Act XLII of 1870 transformed the perpetual countship into a mere dignitary. The ruler's recognition of the right of the archbishop to receive revenue for control of the mint began to falter as early as in the sixteenth century; it was finally withdrawn at the end of the nineteenth century.

After the failure of the revolutions of 1918–1919, the foundations of the new state were laid in Act I of 1920. The members of the national assembly determined to elect, for the period until a final settlement, "a regent by secret vote and from among Hungarian citizens, who would perform the tasks of the head of state." The process of choosing a successor to the regent was governed by Act XIX of 1937, which established the institution of a national council. When the post of regent became vacant, the national council was to serve as the temporary head-of-state body, whereby the prince primate was mentioned as the fourth of the body's seven members. None of the members of the body had any rights as individuals to take action. In other words, the Act did not consider the prince primate to be the exclusive deputy head of state. Moreover, the Act stipulated that the speakers of the two houses of the national assembly – rather than the prince primate – were to have the right to convene the national council and to chair its meetings.

At the end of 1944, two administrations operated concurrently on the territory of the Kingdom of Hungary. One of them was the Government of National Unity, which was established on October 16, 1944, after the coup that had removed Horthy from power. Its leader – Ferenc Szálasi – styled himself as both prime minister and head of state. The other administration was that of the Provisional National Assembly, which convened in Debrecen on December 21, 1944, claiming to be the sole representative of Hungarian state sovereignty. In the end, military and political developments (power relations) rather than legal theoretical arguments or self-definitions determined which of the two administrations would become the legitimate authority and government. The government of national unity fled the country, while the Soviet occupation forces accepted the Provisional National Government as their negotiating partner in Hungary. On April 17, 1945, the National Ruling Council was formed for the express purpose of exercising "the various rights due to the head of state" until "the Hungarian people decide upon the means of exercising the powers of the head of state." In this way the rights of the head of state were divided into at least three parts, resulting almost immediately in a political debate about the associated constitutional issues. Once again, the public legal role of the office of prince primate was not even considered in this debate.

In the light of the above, what conclusion can be drawn concerning the public legal functions of the prince primate? It would seem that by the mid-twentieth century the original public authority tasks of the primate, which had been an important facet of the feudal state, were no longer pertinent. Indeed, the primate's various positions or ranks had become merely symbolic. When József Mindszenty became archbishop of Esztergom on October 7, 1945, the sole remaining public legal task of the primate – a formal task, but one that still existed in theory given that the country remained a kingdom – was the crowning of the king. But even this theoretical task existed only until February 1, 1946, when the republic was proclaimed. After the coronation of Franz Joseph I in 1867, there had been just one instance of a royal coronation in the twentieth century: in 1916, János Csernoch, archbishop of Esztergom and Prince Primate, accompanied by the Calvinist Count István Tisza, who was deputy palatine and prime minister, had placed the Holy Crown on the head of Charles IV, king of Hungary. In the kingdom without a king in the period between the two world wars, even this task had been consigned to the dustbin of history. Consequently, the prince primate was one of the public dignitaries only in a representational sense, and he was so because of his right to crown the king and because of a Christian worldview in which spirituality and faith take precedence over financial factors, ergo ecclesiastical figures take precedence over the secular ones.

In terms of its form of government, in 1945 Hungary was still *de jure* a kingdom. This formed the basis of the prince primate's claim to competences and powers in the public sphere, even while the Provisional National Assembly completely ignored the issue. Amid the provisory legal confusion – which prevailed at least at the level of legal theory – the position of prince primate remained a firm and legitimate source of power and authority, a source that embodied historical legal continuity and was supra-party. So, one might say that József Mindszenty, by making his statement about his being a knight banneret and the country's first public legal dignitary, was perhaps seeking to dust off the unwritten constitution or even thinking that he needed, for the time being at least, to fill the public legal vacuum. Ultimately, however, he gave the impression not only of seeking to reinvigorate the moral authority of the primate's function but also of wanting to revive its past public legal content. And it is true that Mindszenty kept on referring to this historical role and duty until his death. His efforts in this field would lead to manifold conflicts, because, for instance, his defense of the crown inevitably led him to oppose the proclamation of the republic, which he viewed as the harbinger of communism. Moreover, as a consequence of his monarchist stance, he became alienated from the first postwar government, which was far from being communist. Yet, in 1945 – amid the confusion of the liberation-cum-occupation and the revolutionary societal changes – the domestic and international balance of political power ruled out any "resurrection" of the kingdom and with it the possibility of an ecclesiastical dignitary – in this case, the prince primate – being once again endowed with a public role.

The Elections of 1945

While the festive inauguration of the archbishop took place in Esztergom, in Budapest an election was underway for the municipal council of Greater Budapest. A strong leftist majority was anticipated, particularly in view of the fact that the candidates of the Social Democratic Party had formed a joint list with the communists. In the end, however, the Independent Smallholders' Party won the election with 50.54 percent of the popular vote.

A week later, on October 17, 1945, the Bishops' Conference met for the first time under József Mindszenty's chairmanship in the Primate's Palace in Buda Castle, which lay for the most part in ruins. At the meeting the bishops addressed many church matters as well as several political issues. In their general view, there was no justification for reiterating the drawbacks of land reform to the competent authorities, as prior efforts in this field had been fruitless. For his part, however, Mindszenty announced that, in protest at the unlawful aspects of the implementation of the land ownership decree, he intended to reject the salary offered by the government and paid for from the state budget as a "livelihood possibility." The remuneration offered would have been twice the prime minister's salary.[33]

The Bishops' Conference also examined the Hungarian–Soviet economic and trade agreement, which, in the absence of the prime minister's express authorization, had been countersigned by Ernő Gerő, minister of trade, and Antal Bán, minister of industry, on August 27, 1945. According to Mindszenty, who submitted the matter to the Bishops' Conference, the agreement foresaw the removal from the country of all its natural resources and it also planned new "communist sites." The treaty did

33. Beke, *A magyar katolikus püspökkari 1945–1948*, 55. (Point 7 of the minutes of the meeting of the Bishops' Conference convened on October 17, 1945.)

indeed empower the Soviet Union to exploit Hungary's major industrial sectors, its natural resources, its agriculture, and its air and water transport for its own purposes. Government ministers from the Smallholders' Party also opposed the treaty, but in the absence of Western economic assistance they could not prevent the signing of the agreement. The Bishops' Conference – on account of it not being informed about squabbles within the government – authorized the prince primate to issue protests against the agreement, which were to be addressed to the prime minister and to the "foreigners," that is, the Allied Control Commission. Mindszenty clearly saw the dangers of the agreement: if the Soviets gained a footing in the economic sphere, Hungary would be "just one step away" from political dependence, so he protested about the agreement to the prime minister and recommended its rejection.[34] Two days later, on October 19, Prime Minister Béla Dálnoki Miklós responded to Mindszenty in an exhaustive letter. The contents of the letter emanated an air of incomprehension: What business was all this of the prince primate? Indeed, one senses veiled criticism:

> As prince primate you have rightly pointed to the immeasurable responsibility that rests today upon the shoulders of statesmen. But when determining responsibility, one must search primarily for the causes that plunged the nation into this current depravity, and here the responsibility lies not only with those who took an active part but also with those who, on account of their passive stance or their cautious reserve, made no attempt to prevent the nation from sliding further on the slope of destruction.[35]

Mindszenty underlined the final sentence. Evidently, the prime minister was implying that the Catholic prelates were in part responsible for the absence of broad social resistance to fascism.

34. PL Processus, V–700/10. 308–309. fol. József Mindszenty's letter to Prime Minister Béla Dálnoki Miklós, October 17, 1945. For a more detailed account, see Péter Sipos and István Vida, "Az 1945. augusztus 27-én megkötött szovjet–magyar gazdasági egyezmény és a nyugati diplomácia," *Külpolitika* [Foreign politics] 12, no. 4 (1985): 102–18; László Borhi, *A vasfüggöny mögött: Magyarország nagyhatalmi erőtérben 1945–1968* (Budapest: Ister, 2000), 31–36.

35. PL Processus, V–700/10. 311–312. fol. Letter of Prime Minister Béla Dálnoki Miklós to Prince Primate József Mindszenty, October 19, 1945.

The Bishops' Conference also discussed how Marshal Voroshilov, chairman of the ACC, having noted the failure of the communists in the local elections, was seeking to persuade the political parties to establish joint lists and to divide the parliamentary seats according to some kind of formula rather than on the basis of the actual election results – a system that would have negated any meaningful role for the opposition parties at the election. Following a motion by the archabbot of Pannonhalma, the bishops adopted a principled objection to such plans, which Mindszenty then included in his letter criticizing the Soviet–Hungarian trade agreement. On this matter too, Prime Minister Béla Dálnoki Miklós's response was evasive: the joint electoral lists were an internal matter for the parties, and no final decision had been taken on the issue. Nothing more came of the matter, because both the Smallholders and the Social Democrats decided against forming joint lists with other parties. The prime minister then went on to remind the prince primate, who once again began referring to his status as a public dignitary, that, owing to its defeat in war, Hungary's room for maneuver was extremely limited. He also pointed out that the Soviet chairman of the ACC wielded the real political power, while the Americans, British and French were mere assistants, which meant that one could hardly accuse the government of "endangering the independence" of the country.

The Bishops' Conference approved the contents of Mindszenty's letter, which became known as the election pastoral letter. Published on October 18, the letter was written in the name of the Bishops' Conference, but it was signed by Mindszenty alone.[36] The draft of the letter met with the consternation of several bishops, who noted that the Bishops' Conference, even while making recommendations on public issues, had always refrained from issuing pastoral letters in the run-up to a national election.[37] For the first time this was now happening, which suggested a change of style, one that was clearly tied with József Mindszenty, the new chairman of the Bishops' Conference. Further, the tone of the pastoral letter

36. PL 3482/1945. Pastoral letter of the Bishops' Conference, October 18, 1945, first and second edition. The bishops' letter was also published in the Western press. See, for instance, *La France Catholique* 20, no. 870, December 28, 1945.

37. Margit Beke, ed., *A magyar katolikus püspökkari tanácskozások története és jegyzőkönyvei 1919–1944 között*, vol. 2. (Munich and Budapest: Aurora, 1992), 485.

differed from that of the pre-1945 circulars of the bishops, which had been unctuous in a "priestly fashion." While such earlier letters may have been largely ineffective, they had never brought trouble on the Church. The new letter also differed in tone from the first post-1945 pastoral letter of the Bishops' Conference, dated May 24. That letter had denied, with a sense of relief, the Red Army's hostility towards the Church and had asked for God's blessing on the new landowners. The dissenting bishops rightly sensed that in the post-1945 era the boundaries of freedom of speech would be set by the Soviet-led ACC. The same bishops then accurately predicted the consequence of this state of affairs: the Church would be subjected to hefty attacks from the left-wing political parties. They were proved right, as the pastoral letter precipitated the first political scandal of 1945.

Even though the final version of the letter – the one taken to the printers – had undergone several refinements, it still caused a stir. Indeed, the head of the printing unit in Esztergom reported it to the local branch office of the ACC. On October 25, the police seized the letter at the command of a lieutenant-colonel. The galley proofs were taken by special courier to Marshal Voroshilov. The marshal did not ban the publication of the pastoral letter. Rather, he requested István Balogh, a state secretary at the Prime Minister's Office who in "civilian" life was a parish priest in Szeged, to arrange for the removal from the letter of several sentences that were considered embarrassing in foreign policy terms.[38]

The passage to which Voroshilov objected quoted Ernest Bevin, Great Britain's new chief diplomat. The sincere albeit inexperienced British foreign minister had openly stated his view that totalitarian governments had been formed in Hungary, Romania, Bulgaria, and Yugoslavia. At a meeting of the Council of Foreign Ministers of the "Big Five" (the United States, Great Britain, the Soviet Union, China, and France) on September 12, 1945 (the so-called London Conference), Bevin had warned that if the elections held in the four countries were unfair and the new governments were insufficiently representative, they should not count on diplomatic recognition. The original version of Mindszenty's pastoral letter had quoted Bevin's words as follows: "Regretfully, we must agree with the British

38. István Balogh, "Vádolom magam" [I accuse myself], *Magyar Nemzet* 4, no. 222, September 26, 1948, cover page.

foreign minister who said that Hungary seems to have simply exchanged one totalitarian regime for another."[39]

The Hungarian prime minister also requested a "correction" from Mindszenty, who accepted a deal with the following proviso: he would be willing to omit the crucial sentences if the prime minister could arrange with Marshal Voroshilov for the removal of the obstacles to diplomatic relations between Hungary and the Holy See and inform him (Mindszenty) [of efforts to this effect] by telegram by 12 noon the following day (October 28).[40] The comforting reply to the ultimatum came just in time: "Talks on the matter in question began on Friday. A Church initiative on behalf of the faithful and addressed to the government would seem necessary. I shall send information about this in a letter."[41] Thereafter the circular letter was reprinted with the omission of the four ominous sentences. It was then distributed around the country by courier, before being read out in churches on All Saints' Day (November 1).

Although Mindszenty had accepted the deletion of the British foreign secretary's words, the pastoral letter's remaining passages were barely less masked. In the letter, Mindszenty characterized the past as "frivolous, mistaken and culpable," going on to express his doubts about the future. Whereas the errors and frailty of the new system had once been regarded as mere teething problems, with the passage of time such optimism had dissipated, as there had been a surge in the number of abuses of power and a perceptible deterioration in public security. The regime was inclining towards violence: the political police were threatening priests with deportation to Siberia and placing many defenseless citizens in internment camps. In the pastoral letter, Mindszenty made no mention of the postwar reconstruction efforts, but he wrote in detail about the ill-considered

39. József Mindszenty, *Emlékirataim* (4th ed., Budapest: Szent István Társulat, 1989), 100. The original Hungarian version of the memoirs is cited here, as the quoted passage is not included in *Memoirs* (New York: Macmillan, 1974), the English translation; PL 3482/1945. Pastoral letter of the Bishops' Conference, October 18, 1945, first edition.

40. PIL 274. f. 7/247. ő. e. 39. fol. Letter of József Mindszenty to Prime Minister Béla Dálnoki Miklós, October 27, 1945. Cf. Béla Ispánki, *Az évszázad pere* (Abaliget: Lámpás Kiadó, 1995), 25–27.

41. PL 3482/1945. Telegram of Prime Minister Béla Dálnoki Miklós to Prince Primate József Mindszenty, October 28, 1945, 8.25 a.m. For an analysis of the letter, see István Mészáros, "Választás 1945 őszén", in Mészáros, *Mindszenty-mozaik*, 109–11.

aspects of the land reform decree and the biased methods and intent of its implementation. "Concerning land reform, party politics have prevailed, and our soldiers have been left out of the process of land redistribution," stated Mindszenty in a frank assessment of the irrefutable truth. He then added that he did not criticize the reform itself, "but the vindictive spirit it manifested." Here, his criticism clearly targeted the Hungarian communists and the ACC, which, he believed, were implementing land reform on a class basis. Over time the prince primate's critique was distorted into a false accusation and rendered as the first proof of his "reactionary stance." Mindszenty, it was said, opposed land reform and was seeking the restoration of the system of large estates.

The political essence of the pastoral letter was its call for Catholics to vote against the communists. True, it did not explicitly take a position for or against any of the political parties; nor did it mention by name any of the parties or politicians. It did, however, urge the faithful to judge candidates by moral standards and not to fear "the threats of the sons of evil." Catholics should vote for candidates who "will stand up for moral purity, the law, justice, and order, and who will be capable of fighting against the abuses of the current sorrowful conditions." Regardless of the sophistication of these words, they evidently served to orient Catholics towards the Smallholders, the largest non-communist party. The pastoral letter, not unwittingly, promoted unity among the bourgeois forces, identifying Mindszenty and the Catholic Church as a major conservative actor in Hungarian politics.

For the time being, an overt battle between church and state, which some had feared, did not occur. Even so, the pastoral letter caused an enormous stir, for it amounted to the first critique of the regime made with the explicit authority of the Church. People listened to the letter with jubilant spirits. There was a general awareness of an insuperable contradiction between the leftist political vision and Mindszenty's own vision for the future. In one stroke, the Hungarian primate, who had been largely unknown to the general population, became the most popular man in the country.

At a meeting of the Council of Ministers on November 2, it was concluded that Mindszenty had, by writing the pastoral letter, "launched an attack on the various democratic actors and on the government."[42] According to a joint statement by the parties – which was published by the press a day before the elections – the pastoral letter amounted to unprecedented interference in the election battle in support of reactionary politics, seeking by deceitful means to influence Catholic believers. The joint statement urged the prince primate to refrain from interfering in public matters.[43] By this time, the events were – even if in slightly distorted form – beginning to catch the attention of the United States. By making a great fuss, the leftist politicians achieved just the opposite of what they had intended: even non-churchgoers who had heard nothing of the pastoral letter soon came to know all the essential aspects of the story, for even on the radio, news reports focused – for a day and a half – on the statements of the political parties and on the pastoral letter that had elicited them. In response to the fierce reception, the "competent ecclesiastical place" (i.e., Mindszenty's office in Esztergom) issued a statement: The Bishops' Conference had proceeded in accordance with tradition and with its duties when it addressed publicly certain lugubrious issues of public life.[44]

At the elections of November 4, 1945, six parties competed for parliamentary seats, none of which represented political Catholicism. Under the provisions of Act VIII of 1945, political parties that were not included in the Hungarian National Independence Front were required to request permission (a license) in order to put forward candidates in elections. In the summer, the Christian Democratic Party had split in two. The wing of the party led by József Pálffy, which enjoyed Mindszenty's support the most, managed to obtain a license, but it was only valid for Budapest and not for the entire country. Meanwhile, owing to its detachment from the clergy and its good relations with the political left wing, the Democratic People's Party led by István Barankovics received all the necessary licenses. Yet, in the end, the DPP did not field candidates in the election. Even though the party's internal disputes had been resolved, there

42. MNL OL XIX–A–83–a/65. sz. Minutes of the meeting of the Council of Ministers on November 2, 1945. See László Szűcs, ed., *Dálnoki Miklós Béla kormányának (Ideiglenes Nemzeti Kormány) minisztertanácsi jegyzőkönyvei, 1944. december 23.–1945. november 15.* (Budapest: Magyar Országos Levéltár, 1997), 530–31.

43. *Szabad Nép* 3, no. 181, November 3, 1945, cover page.

44. *Magyar Kurír* 35, November 5, 1945, first edition.

was simply not enough time to prepare for the election. István Barankovics and his supporters – on this issue they and the prince primate took the same position – supported the Smallholders in the national elections, as a result of which two of the Smallholders' candidates announced after the elections that they were now representatives of the DPP rather than the Smallholders. In this way, with its two representatives the DPP constituted a mini-faction in the new Parliament. Noiselessly, the party began preparing for the next election contest.

Another grouping that did not field candidates in the election was the Christian Women's League, but the League's leader, Margit Slachta, one of the Sisters of Social Service, entered into an electoral alliance with the Civic Democratic Party, as József Pálffy and his group had also done. This party alliance, however, was frowned upon by Mindszenty. The latter had committed himself to the Smallholders' Party, having met with the party's senior leaders and secured a pledge from them that – in return for the Catholic Church's support in the elections – they would refrain from adopting a critical stance on the Christian worldview and would support, where possible, the wishes of the Catholic Church.[45] Slachta subsequently became a member of Parliament, having been elected on the Civic Democratic Party list. József Pálffy, however, did not obtain a seat. Overall, the Civic Democratic Party performed rather poorly in the elections; voters in Budapest showed little enthusiasm for the "Catholic list mixed with people who were evidently Jews."[46]

Based on land reform and the presence of the Soviet army, the communists had been confident of success at the elections. The results, however, confounded their expectations. The left-wing rout in the local elections was repeated. The Smallholders gained an absolute majority of 57 percent, while each of the two leftist (or workers') parties received 17 percent. In Mindszenty's native Zala County, the Smallholders received twelve of the fourteen seats, with the Communist Party winning merely a

45. ÁBTL 3.1.9. V–700/2. 352. fol. "Pótlólagos feljegyzések olyan eseményekről, melyek jelentősnek látszanak és eddig nem szerepeltek" [Additional notes on events that appear to be significant and have not been reported on so far], notes of András Zakar, secretary to the primate.

46. PL 2551/1945. Report of the protonotarian canon, Zsigmond Mihalovics (national head of Catholic Action), to József Mindszenty, November 8, 1945.

single seat, represented by party leader Mátyás Rákosi. Even so, under pressure from the ACC and by way of compensation for the abandoned joint electoral list, the Smallholders' Party refrained from forming a government on its own or with natural allies. Rather, the Smallholders consented to the formation of a Grand Coalition. Several vital ministries were then given to the communists, including the Ministry of Interior, which directed the police and state security bodies. A rare opportunity to limit communist influence had been missed. Prime Minister Zoltán Tildy, Ferenc Nagy (Speaker of the National Assembly), and Béla Varga (a parish priest and leading Smallholder politician) became the three members of the National Ruling Council, which undertook the tasks of head of state.

The communists' share of the vote – 17 percent – was an excellent result in view of the formerly clandestine nature of the party and the fact that many senior communists had been living in the Soviet Union. The problem, however, lay in their expectation of an election win. In the aftermath of the election, rather than face up to their defeat and seek explanations for their unpopularity, they naturally began looking for scapegoats. In his position as minister of state, Mátyás Rákosi became one of the deputies of the new head of government, Zoltán Tildy. Rákosi identified three factors that had led to failure in the elections: food shortages, inflation, and the role of the Church. This was the first time, that he had identified the prince primate as one of the political adversaries of the Communist Party. Which, incidentally, he truly was...

The Kingdom at Stake

At the turn of 1945–1946, a question that had been raised after World War I returned to the agenda: What form of government should the country have? Should Hungary, which had not had a king for twenty-four years, remain a kingdom or should it become a republic? It was around this issue that chasm arose in November 1945 between the political parties and the prince primate.

On November 16, having presented his government to Parliament, Prime Minister Zoltán Tildy – a Calvinist minister in "civilian" life – visited Cardinal Mindszenty in accordance with the old tradition at his residence in Buda Castle. During their discussions much was said about Hungary's form of government. At the time the country was still a monarchy. The prince primate stated that in principle he was opposed to raising this issue at national level. If, however, it was impossible – owing to pressure from the communists and their allies – to postpone a discussion of the issue, then he would suggest the holding of a referendum. France served as an example, for on October 21, 1945 the French people had voted on France's constitutional future, as a result of which the Fourth Republic had been established. (At the time, referendums were becoming increasingly popular means of determining controversial questions: for example, in 1946 the Italians voted to abolish their monarchy, while the Greeks and the Belgians voted to retain their monarchies.) Tildy, who was rumored to be a legitimist, told Mindszenty that he shared his views. He then informed him of the government's wish "to establish diplomatic relations with the Vatican as soon as possible."[47]

Mindszenty's support for the monarchy comes as no surprise. As prince primate, his political attitude was consistent with his earlier view: the country must remain a monarchy. If Hungary's politicians failed to support this view, then the Church and its leader (i.e., Mindszenty himself) would have to save the kingdom, to which the Church had been attached for 900 years. This stance did not breach any laws; nor, however, did it reflect the political realities or the domestic balance of power. On the other hand, even the slightest sign of monarchism was bound to elicit a strong political counter-reaction. The effect, therefore, was to accelerate the process whereby Hungary became a republic.

Oft-used expressions in Mindszenty's vocabulary were "historical constitution" and "ancient constitutionality." The legitimists considered the sum of legislative practice since the beginning of the reign of King Stephen I (the first Hungarian king) to be the *unwritten* – hence historical – constitution of the Hungarian state. This constitution included the *Corpus Iuris*, the "body of law" (all the laws recorded in this body were in effect, while any other unrecorded law had no effect) and the *Doctrine of the Holy Crown*, which even today influence Hungarian constitutional thinking.

In Hungary, statehood and the idea of public authority were realized – during the period in which Mindszenty lived – in the legal personification

47. Beke, *A magyar katolikus püspökkari 1945–1948*, 66. Minutes of the meeting of the Bishops' Conference on December 20, 1945, (agenda item 2).

of the *Holy Crown*, which was viewed as the intermediary of divine authority (and therefore holy) and was juxtaposed with royal authority of a personal nature. Hungarian constitutional thinking had long considered the state as a society organized in the public interest and embodied in the Holy Crown. In Hungary, the powers of those who exercised public authority were derived from the Holy Crown rather than from the ruler. Indeed, public officials swore loyalty to the Holy Crown rather than to the king. It is no coincidence, therefore, that royal privileges were due only to crowned monarchs. The Hungarian state was a monarchy in which the king was sovereign but where enshrined rights were – especially when it came to exercising these rights – shared between the king and the (political) nation, that is, the "members of the Holy Crown."[48]

The second most cited legal premise of legitimism – after the Doctrine of the Holy Crown – was the *principle of legal continuity*, which simply meant that the country's valid laws were those that had been an integral part of the development of law in Hungary over a thousand years. Collaboration between king and diet, as the manifestation of the national will, represented the main thrust of legal continuity. In other words, the continuity lay in the legislation that had arisen out of the resolutions of the diet (the national assembly) and the royal assent given to them. Anything that came about in another fashion or was contrary to the laws established in this manner was alien to the nation. In instances where this happened, a return had to be made to the point where legal continuity had been broken.[49]

From the "cult" of the ancient constitution arose the notion of loyalty to the king. For adherents to the principle of legal continuity, Charles IV had remained king even after he became unable to exercise his power. After his death in 1922, the legitimists had had no option but to accept the status quo and to continue their political struggle against the abolition of the monarchy using the legal means that had been granted them by the new regime. For his part, Mindszenty continued to devote all his authority and

48. Ferenc Eckhart, *A Szentkorona-eszme története* (Budapest: MTA, 1941); József Kardos, *A Szent Korona és szentkorona-eszme története* (Budapest: IKVA, 1992); Béla Szathmáry, "Keresztény értékek az alkotmányozásban," in *Történelmi tradíciók és az új Alkotmány*, ed. András Téglás (Budapest: Országgyűlés Alkotmányügyi, igazságügyi és ügyrendi bizottsága, 2011), 18–24.

49. ÁBTL 3.1.9. V–700/9a. 68. fol. (Jusztin Baranyay), *A jogfolytonosság visszaállítása* [Restoring Legal Continuity].

the resources of Hungarian Catholicism to a struggle aimed at conserving the foundations of traditional Hungarian society (kingdom, dynasty, church, national culture) and upholding "constitutionalism." His advisors in this area came exclusively from staunchly conservative circles. Indeed, based on the company Mindszenty kept, it seemed that the Hungarian Catholic Church had become fatally tied to the country's aristocracy, to the interests of big capital, and to reform-hostile conservatism. Mindszenty's error was, therefore, his failure to recognize that Hungarian Catholicism's ultra-conservative stance would inevitably attract extremist elements, thereby compromising and discrediting the Church. The links with extremism would then be exploited by left-wing propagandists to the full. For instance, Hungary's exiled former leader, Miklós Horthy, whom Mindszenty (in his earlier life as the Abbot-Priest Pehm) had considered illegitimate, was quick to seek contact with Mindszenty, telling the prince primate that he still considered himself to be regent. Mindszenty, however, took notice of Horthy only on a personal level; when it came to Hungary's future, the prelate was not counting on him at all.[50] Mindszenty came to be seen as the embodiment of the conservative line. His tough personality meant that his stance would have been the same even in the absence of his advisors, whom, incidentally, he viewed as mere consultants. Meanwhile, at his palace in Esztergom, Mindszenty was receiving ever fewer people with different views on the challenges and opportunities facing the country. For their part, the communists, the country's real rulers, were beginning to consolidate their power in line with their long-term ambitions.

Mindszenty's royalism was that of a man who clung to the authoritarian and hierarchical structures of the past and who ignored the possibility of new paths. For him, the monarchy symbolized stability, as did the Church. Moreover, the structures of the monarchy were interwoven with those of Catholicism. The hard reality, however, was that the Soviet Union had extended its influence to half of Europe. Further, many people sincerely believed that a republican form of government would be more capable of promoting and upholding constitutional rights than a monarchy, a form of government viewed as a relic from the past synonymous with tyranny.

50. PL Processus, V–700/1. 67. fol. Memorandum on József Mindszenty's interrogation on January 2, 1949.

Obviously, we now know that monarchy – where the powers of the ruler have constitutional limits – is not contrary to democracy and that royalists are not always hostile to democracy. Indeed, a lesson of twentieth-century history is that a republican form of government and democratic freedoms do not always go hand in hand. Indeed, a republic can be authoritarian or even dictatorial.

Legitimism was not the default position of a Catholic primate in Hungary. Mindszenty, however, had expressed a loyalty to the Habsburg family ever since his youth. Even after 1945, he was and remained one of the main advocates for legitimism. It was his conviction that the restoration of the monarchy was of vital interest to Hungary. The country's greatness, security, and independence depended on it, in his view. It is worth reminding ourselves of the criteria of legitimism: a legitimist was a monarchist who wished to see Charles IV on the Hungarian throne and then, after Charles's death, his son, Otto – as foreseen under the strict rules of succession set out in the Pragmatic Sanction of 1723. A true legitimist could not help to the throne someone who, under these strict rules, was not the legal successor. This applied even when the person in question was a member of the Habsburg family. For an "ordinary" monarchist the conditions would have been simpler. Mindszenty supported the order that had been established by law, and so he regarded Otto as king. Still, in late 1945 and early 1946, it was the monarchy as a 1000-year-old institution rather than the person of the king that was at stake.

In Hungary republican traditions had been almost negligible until 1944, whereby the republican idea had not really permeated national consciousness. According to a public opinion survey conducted in December 1945, however, 76 percent of Budapest inhabitants would have voted for a republic, compared with just 20 percent who would have voted for a monarchy. These percentages reflected the Hungarian public's desire to move on from the past and seek renewal in the present – a desire (or endeavor) symbolized by a change in the form of government. In this way, the republic became synonymous with change, democracy, and the self-determination of peoples. To support the republic meant to protest against any kind of restoration of the Horthy regime. Opponents of republicanism were perceived as dangerous "reactionaries" rather than as mere royalists or supporters of the interwar regime.

Hungary's form of government was not debated in the run-up to the parliamentary elections of the fall of 1945. It was only after the elections – judged free and democratic by the Allied powers, the international press, and domestic public opinion – that the political parties began to address the issue.[51] More accurately, the form of government was mentioned in just one party's program: the Social Democrats declared the introduction of a people's republic to be a necessity.[52] The programs of the other parties mentioned democracy, the equality of citizens, freedom, and independence. In other words, they focused on ideas grounded in the modern principles of a republic. All this resonated with the Yalta Declaration on "Liberated Europe" (February 11, 1945), which, rather than give the Soviet Union "a free hand" in Central and Eastern Europe, actually sought to strengthen the rights of peoples, with the aim of enabling them to decide on their form and system of government and on national policy. (The declaration's lack of sanctions for violations of these fine principles is another matter, as is also the fact that some weeks before the elections, Soviet politicians were referring to the choice of a republican form of government as a fait accompli.)

At a rather slow pace, the government determined to change the form of government. The stubborn reoccurrence of reports concerning the proclamation of a republic led the prince primate to write the following, in a letter addressed to Prime Minister Zoltán Tildy and dated December 31, 1945:

> I have heard that the National Assembly intends shortly to place constitutional reforms on the agenda, including the introduction of a republic accompanied by a plan to get rid of the thousand-year-old Kingdom of Hungary. If this report is true and even if I have received no official information about this, I raise an objection to these plans based on the public legal office practiced by Hungarian primates for more than 900 years."[53]

51. László Hubai, "Viták és álláspontok a II. Magyar Köztársaságról," *Múltunk* [Our Past] 50, no. 2 (2005): 218. For a detailed analysis of the issue, see Gizella Föglein, *Államforma és államfői jogkör Magyarországon* 1944–1949 (Budapest: Osiris Kiadó, 2001).

52. Sándor Balogh and Lajos Izsák, eds., *Magyarországi pártprogramok* 1944–1988 (Budapest: ELTE Eötvös Kiadó, 2004), 42.

53. PIL 274. f. 7/248. ő. e. 5., 8. fol. Letter no. 53/1946 of József Mindszenty to Zoltán Tildy, December 31, 1945. Photocopy. – Note: the letter was first published in the so-called "Fekete Könyv" [Black Book], published by the Hungarian government. See *Mindszenty József a népbíróság előtt* (Budapest: Állami Lapkiadó, 1949, 70–72). Later on, the essence of the letter

The Hungarian primate urged the authorities to deal with the country's socio-economic problems rather than raise constitutional issues in such an untimely manner. If the authorities were determined to put the form of government on the agenda, then it would "be appropriate to ask the people." In other words, Mindszenty urged the holding of a referendum. He reminded Tildy that on this issue the two men had expressed agreement during the prime minister's brief visit to Esztergom on November 16. Gyula Ortutay, who subsequently became minister of culture, viewed this particular letter from Mindszenty to Tildy as the starting point for a confrontation between the government and the Church.[54] In the mosaic formed by historians, the right form of government for Hungary became a bit of a landmark issue. Issued shortly before the election, the pastoral letter had resulted in a crisis of trust. The situation might have been resolved and trust reestablished, but for the primate's stance on Hungary's form of government, which elicited a grave crisis of legitimacy.

Mindszenty arranged for a copy of his letter to Tildy to be forwarded to the parish priest Béla Varga, a member of the National Ruling Council. In 1921, Varga had been among those fighting for the king against Miklós Horthy at Budaörs. Now, however, he was a key supporter of republicanism within the Smallholders' Party. Mindszenty sought to set Varga straight, telling him that he had "no choice but to stand on the side of the monarchy... The list of candidates is unfavorable to Catholicism. A Catholic cannot take part in this, still less a priest."[55] Varga replied on January 2, 1946. He wrote that, in view of the country's foreign policy interests and despite his legitimist convictions, he considered the proclamation of a republic to be an inevitable development. The next day Mindszenty responded in an even more condemnatory tone: "A tough stand should have been taken on the issue of the form of government. I have not seen this from anyone. The most dedicated have failed to take the initiative, and I have yet to see them

was published in the first volume of Vecsey, *Mindszenty okmánytár*, vol. 1, 107–8), where the editor questioned the letter's authenticity. Since then, the document's authenticity has been proven.

54. PL Mm. 17. d. 1948 – Foreign press outlets: *Le Monde*, July 18 and 19, 1948. – Note: In the cited interview, Ortutay denied that any priests were being held in internment camps in Hungary. According to the Catholic Church, however, 63 priests had been arrested.

55. ÁBTL 3.1.9. V–700/9a. 7. fol. Letter of József Mindszenty to Béla Varga, December 31, 1945.

support the secular initiatives. In public life, one must stand up for one's principles, rather than make excuses."[56] Clearly, the Hungarian primate had been disappointed by Varga. He had evidently expected the priest to strengthen the Catholic and legitimist line within the Smallholders' Party, which Varga had failed to do. For his part, Béla Varga was of the opinion that the primate had lost touch with reality and was living in a delusionary world that denied the actual political balance of power.[57] A few months later Varga characterized Mindszenty as a man who was tormented by fearful nightmares, whose eyes "were burning with crazed fanaticism," and whose words betrayed "a sense of utmost hatred for the democratic republic."[58]

After two months of hesitation, the Smallholder fraction in the Hungarian Parliament gave their approval to a republican form of government. In doing so, their primary motive was to secure a more favorable outcome at the peace talks by implementing what would widely be perceived as modern constitutional reform.[59] On January 31, 1946, the Hungarian Parliament adopted Act I of 1946, which abolished the monarchy and proclaimed Hungary to be a republic. In effect, the foundation for a new constitution had been laid. During the parliamentary debate, Margit Slachta was the only representative to defend the monarchy. In a high-pitched voice, she tried, somewhat unctuously, to win over lawmakers to her view, but the intrepid nun was rudely interrupted by angry shouts. On February 1, 1946, the chairman of the Smallholders' Party, Zoltán Tildy, who had been prime minister until this time, was elected president of the republic. The parish priest Béla Varga was elected speaker of the Parliament.

The choice of a Protestant reverend as president of the republic in a country with a Catholic majority was not particularly shocking after the long regency of the likewise Protestant Miklós Horthy. The prime ministership passed from Zoltán Tildy to Ferenc Nagy, who was also a Protestant. Ferenc Nagy's appointment meant the rejection of Mindszenty's preferred candidate, the Catholic and onetime legitimist Dezső Sulyok. The new

56. PL Mm. 4. d. Letter of József Mindszenty to Béla Varga, January 3, 1946.

57. ÁBTL 3.1.9. V–82.897/1. 22–23. fol. Pencil-written prison confession of Vendel Endrédy, abbot of Zirc, November 1, 1950. Cited in Eszter Cúthné Gyóni, ed., *Egy fogoly apát feljegyzései: Endrédy Vendel zirci apát feljegyzései az ÁVH börtönében* (Budapest: METEM–ÁBTL, 2013), 46.

58. ÁBTL 3.1.8. Sz–222. 221. fol. Report, April 1, 1946.

59. István Vida, *A Független Kisgazdapárt politikája 1944–1947* (Budapest: Akadémiai Kiadó, 1976), 140–44.

prime minister, Ferenc Nagy, represented – both personally and politically – Hungary's peasant farmers. He hoped to preserve Hungary's national integrity until the country regained full sovereignty and could freely take control of its own destiny.

While national and church flags were raised throughout the country in honor of the republic, the prince primate was pondering a protest against the promulgation of the parliamentary act. In the end, however, he decided against such a measure. On February 1, 1946, when the act was promulgated, Mindszenty limited himself to a concise summary of some indisputable facts: "...I conclude that the debate [on the form of government] has been conducted under foreign occupation, without consulting the Hungarian people, and with restrictions on the freedom of speech of representatives within the political parties; in consequence, the nation has been thinking about and judging events with these in view."[60] His main criticism was that the national assembly had decided upon the form of government under external pressure from the occupiers and prior to the signing of the peace treaty by the national assembly (i.e., the restoration of the country's national sovereignty). Another fundamental weakness, in his view, was the failure to hold a referendum on such a major issue. In fact, there had been no precedent for holding referendums under the historical constitution. Indeed, the national assembly (Parliament) had been the main repository of government power and the single mode of expression of the popular will. Accordingly, there had been no option but to render the right to elect a president a competence of the national assembly.[61]

This marked the conclusion of the debate surrounding Hungary's form of government. The significance of the debate was, however, more far-reaching. Indeed, the introduction of a republican form of government brought with it the termination of the prince primate's public roles, which had been rooted in the "historical constitution." Moreover, the establishment of a unicameral national assembly and the subsequent proclamation

60. MNL OL XIX–A–1–j–XXIII–1602/1946. Letter of Cardinal József Mindszenty to the chairman of the National Assembly and the Prime Minister, February 1, 1946. Published in Ádám Somorjai and Tibor Zinner, *Majd' halálra ítélve: Dokumentumok Mindszenty József élettörténetéhez* (Budapest: Magyar Közlöny Lap- és Könyvkiadó, 2008), 264–65.

61. MNL OL XVIII–1–b. Meeting of the National Assembly's Committee on Public Law and Constitutional Law, January 28, 1946, 62. fol.

of the republic destroyed any remaining prerogatives enjoyed by the Catholic prelates and by the prince primate in particular. The Upper House (of Parliament) was not reconstituted; rather, it was simply omitted from the list of political institutions of the new republic. Thus, under the new system, Catholic bishops were no longer ex officio members of the legislature; the Bishops' Conference could no longer debate and express an opinion on parliamentary legislation prior to its adoption; the right of the prince primate to crown the king was abolished; and the title of perpetual count used by bishops was also scrapped. The president of the republic received the rights, powers, and duties of the office of head of state. That is to say, it was his task to represent the Hungarian state both domestically and abroad. Further, subject to certain limitations, he could exercise executive power by way of the government. Meanwhile, the prince primate – the country's "first knight banneret" – became, after the adoption of the act on the republic and the signing of the Paris Peace Treaty (February 10, 1947), merely the first priest and eternal father of a truncated Hungary.

Another decree provided for the abolition of the use of the royal symbols, but its implementation was not immediate. On the stamps and official stationary of the authorities and in state institutions, the Hungarian abbreviation for kingdom – "kir." – and the royal coat of arms remained visible for a long time. Still, any attempt to dispute the public legal changes or to practice aspects of the primate's former political role would have amounted to a denial of the results of the national elections and of the change in the form of government. This was true even though this republic had not yet become a conscious community of free and equal citizens, as certain forces had begun striving, soon after the proclamation of the republic, for its abolition and its replacement with a "people's republic." In 1949, these forces achieved their aim in the distorted form of a Stalinist dictatorship.

With the Eyes of a Diplomat

Mindszenty's overt royalism and his thinly-veiled hostility to the republic backfired. When, on February 10, 1946, he gave Mass in Budapest, the faithful flooded the streets after the service and cheered the prince primate. However, what began as an innocent demonstration soon became a political protest; those present called not only for a Catholic political party and a Catholic press, but also for the re-annexation of Transylvania, a Hungary free of Jews, and the dismissal of communist and social democratic politicians. A small number of the protestors even hailed Szálasi and Imrédy.[62] Mindszenty took the view that a group of troublemakers had infiltrated the crowd of faithful Catholics. The political left, however, argued that the prince primate's speech had roused the crowd. This latter view was repeated by the left-wing press in their reports on the incident. In this way, Mindszenty was placed alongside the discredited leaders of the Arrow Cross and other war criminals, simply because his name and their names had been cheered together. There followed a heated parliamentary debate on the events. The Smallholders spoke of a mob hired for a day's wages, while the left-wing parties condemned the extremism of the prince primate's supporters. The traditionally anti-clerical Social Democrats and the fervently atheistic communists protested against the "acts of the fascist cardinal" by holding demonstrations against the primate and by going on strike. This, at any rate, was the story reported in the Soviet newspaper *Novoye Vremya*.[63] In Szeged, protestors even bore placards with the words "Down with Mindszenty," and one rather extreme group cried out for "a noose for Mindszenty." This marked the beginning of a process whereby Mindszenty's name was increasingly conflated with both the Horthy regime and the Arrow Cross terror.

Inevitably, the attention of the political police was drawn to the Hungarian primate. In the spring of 1946, at the behest of Mátyás Rákosi, a special political police body for church affairs was formed as Section III of the State Protection Department (ÁVO). Its primary task was gathering intelligence about, and reporting on, meetings of the Bishops' Conference and on the intentions of the Church. A secondary task related to security. At first, the political police must have had scant information, for it needed time to infiltrate the primate's immediate circle. The ACC's Soviet repre-

62. ÁBTL 3.1.8. Sz–222. 140. fol. Report of Gábor Péter, Head of Department, Budapest Police Department, Hungarian State Police, February 11, 1946; *Új Ember* 2, nos. 7 and 8, February, 17, 1946, 1–2 and February 23, 1946, 3; *Népszava* [People's Voice] 74, no. 35, February 12, 1946, 3.

63. MNL OL XIX–J–1–j KÜM TÜK-documents 1945–64. Soviet Union, 8. d. 28. Report in *Novoye Vremya*, March 1, 1946.

sentative for the county even complained about the difficulties: "Twice a week a meeting is held at the cardinal's residence, which can only be attended with a special permit and by passing through a secret entrance. The political police find it difficult to get a foot in."[64] In the course of 1946, the shortage of informers was overcome: among the new recruits were one of Mindszenty's legitimist brother-in-arms, as well as a lay priest chamberlain, a university professor, an archdiocesan school inspector, and several members of staff at the primate's palace. Relatives of Mindszenty were among those placed under surveillance.

Even the authorities in Moscow began to show an interest in Mindszenty. Deputy Foreign Minister Dekanozov asked Gyula Szekfű, the new ambassador to Moscow, "what is Mindszenty doing?"[65] For his part, the prince primate chose not to respond to the criticism. Thereafter, however, he rejected all government gestures and attempts at rapprochement. Mindszenty not only spurned the communism that had arrived part and parcel with the Soviet occupation; he also had reservations about the democratic experiment of the change of regime. In Mindszenty's eyes everything that had happened under the Soviet occupation and with the active collaboration of Hungarian communists was uniformly negative. His stance could only be one of repudiation. This precluded, however, an understanding of the urgency of social changes and of the need for general reforms. For the bourgeois (conservative) political forces, Mindszenty was, at one and the same time, the respected head of the church, a cardinal and archbishop of the Catholic Church, and a figure who was unsteady on his feet in the postwar system and who lacked experience in politicizing and was sometimes downright vexatious. Meanwhile the Catholic faithful waited patiently for an improvement in their fate and prayed zealously that the country's liberators might soon return to the peace and comfort of their own homeland. They began to refer to Mindszenty as the bravest Hungarian, as he was almost unique in daring to criticize the Soviet occupation. The emerging halo fanned the glowing embers, and the primate's

64. AVP RF f. 0453. op. 2a. papka (paper folder) 11. delo (file) 8. l. 58–59. Minutes of the meeting of ACC representatives in Hungary with authority as of May 15, 1946.

65. MNL OL XIX–J–42–a KÜM, TÜK-documents of the Hungarian Embassy in Moscow. Report of the envoy Gyula Szekfű, Moscow, April 14, 1946. (It is noteworthy that Mindszenty also received a copy of the report – presumably from Szekfű himself. See PL Processus V–700/16. 327. fol.)

name was put on the banners and standards of people who had never agreed with him before.

Mindszenty remained a royalist even after the enactment of the law on a republican form of government. In the depths of his soul, he still considered the regime illegal,[66] but he never said this openly – at least not in Hungary. Rather, he implicitly acknowledged the new form of government. While he never declared his recognition of the republic, he did not publicly reject it. When abroad, he was far more open about his real opinions. In Rome he requested Sir D'Arcy Osborne, the British envoy to the Holy See, to inform his superiors of the following:

> ...the present Hungarian government does not represent the Hungarian nation, many of its members being by nationality, training or sympathy more Russian than Hungarian and consequently ready to sacrifice Hungarian interests to Russia's vindictiveness towards Hungary. He urged that in order to avert a treaty of revenge we should allow patriotic Hungarians now in exile to express their views or even set up a rival Hungarian Government abroad. I told him the latter was clearly out of the question and that I thought the same applied to the former.[67]

According to the British diplomat, "it is quite clear that the cardinal feels it his duty to play a political role in defence of his country's interests against the present Hungarian Government." As he had done once before, he suggested that the Vatican warn Mindszenty to stay out of politics. Even so, he saw little chance of being able to stop him.

> He is a grimly unsmiling fanatic, who would I have no doubt readily accept martyrdom in pursuit of what he conceived to be his duty to his Church or his country. Unless, as I hope may be the case, he has been categorically ordered by the pope to confine his crusading to ecclesiastical matters,

66. He put this into writing in his will of the fall of 1948, a fact he subsequently mentioned in his memoirs: Mindszenty, *Emlékirataim*, 264.

67. PIL 508. f. 1/45. ő. e. 56. t. TNA FO 371/59004, R 3565/256/21. Report no. 34 of Sir D'Arcy Osborne, British minister to the Holy See, to the Foreign Office, March 6, 1946. (The two following quotations are taken from the report – the author.)

> I fear it can only be a question of time before he provokes an open conflict with the present Hungarian Government and its Russian supporters.

The British foreign ministry drew a grave consequence:

> The attitude of the cardinal towards the present Hungarian Government as expressed to Sir D'Arcy Osborne is a dangerous and foolish one and we should be careful to avoid associating ourselves with it. The Hungarian Government was elected by popular vote and attacks on it by a man in the cardinal's position do not seem to be in the best interest of his country. You and members of your mission should avoid contact with the cardinal as much as possible,

stated the instruction sent to Budapest.[68] Mindszenty's political intransigence had already backfired. As a responsible prelate, he could not condemn as illegal a government that was regarded internationally as legitimate. Nor could he encourage the formation of a government-in-exile. Why did he then think it was his right and duty to do so? The explanation is once again his argument, drawn from the historical constitution but disputed by legal historians, that, in the absence of the head of state (the king), the country should be run by the prince primate. This is the only argument that he could use to justify his political activity. An insistence on historical and legal traditions was clearly alien to the Soviet communist milieu. It clashed, furthermore, with the worldview of postwar Hungary's budding and then withering democratic system.

Until 1956, Mindszenty refrained from tying the interruption of legal continuity to a specific date, lest he should become embroiled in the constitutional debates and disputes. Although the issue may seem a petty one, there was disagreement among both the Hungarian émigré community and domestic political forces about which events and pieces of legislation could be used to derive their own legitimacy. Even the royalists gave different dates. The essay entitled *Restoring Legal Continuity*, which was attached to the Mindszenty trial papers and which may have been authored by the Cistercian law professor Jusztin Baranyay (the second defendant in

68. Ibid., Draft telegram to the British Legation in Budapest.

the trial) in 1946, dated the interruption in legal continuity to November 1918, because Charles IV's abdication statement could not be considered valid in the absence of the formal accessories of enforcement and the confirmation of the Hungarian legislature.[69] Baranyay cast doubt on the legislative rights of the 1945 legislature in view of the exclusion of certain parties from the electoral system and the resultant restriction on the will of the people. By extension, the law professor also questioned the validity of the laws, provisions and other measures adopted by that assembly.

None of the available sources indicate whether Mindszenty shared the law professor's opinion. Of course, his support for legitimism was a known fact. In his letter to US President Truman, Mindszenty wrote that in his view the parliamentary elections of November 4, 1945, had been the legitimate result of the people's will, but that subsequent events, including the change in the form of government, had made a mockery of democracy.[70] Without a doubt, Mindszenty trusted initially in the game rules of parliamentary democracy. Over time, however, he gathered negative experiences concerning "the people's democracy of Hungary." He now dated the breach in the continuity of law, or the boundary between constitutionality and lawlessness, to March 19, 1944 (rather than to 1918, which had been his position as a legitimist): "The thread of Hungarian constitutionality was broken in March 1944 at the time of Hitler's occupation. This is where we have to return on the basis of the continuity of law. Only 1944 can be 'normal year'. [...] Stalin and Voroshilov cannot be sources of Hungarian constitutional law."[71] After 1956, Mindszenty's clearly stated view was that all developments in the country after March 19, 1944 had been illegitimate. By that time, the primate no longer pondered

69. ÁBTL 3.1.9. V–700/9. 70. fol. (Jusztin Baranyay), *A jogfolytonosság visszaállítása* [Restoring Legal Continuity].

70. ÁBTL 3.1.9. V–700. 151., 155., 162. fol. Letter of József Mindszenty to President Truman, June 12, 1947. Typed text in Hungarian and in English translation, no signature, and Mindszenty's original handwritten draft.

71. NARA RG 84, Records of the Foreign Service Posts of the Department of State, Hungary, Records Relating to Cardinal Mindszenty 1956–72. Box 1, Mindszenty–Classified 1958. Letter of József Mindszenty to Deputy Under Secretary Robert D. Murphy, January 10, 1958. Published in Ádám Somorjai, *Mindszenty bíboros követségi levelei az Egyesült Államok elnökeihez 1956–1971 – Letters to the Presidents. Cardinal Mindszenty to the Political Leaders of the United States* (Budapest: METEM, 2011), 464–66.

over the issue and no longer took into account Hungary's wartime defeat and the factors of political reality. In view of the unilateralism of the Soviets and of Hungary's domestic communists, he came to reject *everything* that had taken place in late 1944 and early 1945. This meant, in effect, that he also called into question the Paris Peace Treaty of 1947. A long path, however, led to his recognition and expression of this state of affairs. In the midst of events, his perceptions were rather different, particularly on account of the consensus that surrounded the government and the legislature elected at the legitimate elections of November 1945.

The new political system adopted laws for its own protection. It became a punishable crime even to call into question the republican form of government: on March 23, 1946, the National Assembly adopted Act VII of 1946 on the "effective protection of the democratic political system and the republic." In the ensuing years, this act of legislation became the main point of reference for the growing number of show trials. Death sentences were issued on several occasions to those who plotted against the republic (i.e., did not recognize the republican form of government) and to those who conspired against the government (i.e., wished to see it overthrown). The Smallholder-dominated Parliament approved these tough regulations, as they seemed to be suitable means for clamping down on the left wing, which it viewed as a threat to the republic and its institutions. The same hope – the opportunity to eradicate political opponents – was, however, shared by the communists. Under the law, the overt expression of private opinions on the form of government could lead to a death sentence. Even Mindszenty had to abide by the laws of the republic – unless he wished to forfeit his life. The issue of the form of government was discussed for the last time at a meeting of the Bishops' Conference on April 2, 1946. As the minutes recorded, "On the issue of the form of government the idea of making a declaration was raised. The Archbishop of Eger notes that no-one now expects such a statement. He motions for the Bishops' Conference to remain silent on the matter."[72] This is what happened. The Bishops' Conference took no position on whether to reject or accept the republic, and a sort of balance was reached.

72. Beke, *A magyar katolikus püspökkari 1945–1948*, 95.

Neither the Hungarian government nor the ACC sought to hinder the new primate, who was accompanied by his secretary, from flying to Italy on an aircraft belonging to the British Military Mission (Hungary). He arrived in Rome on December 2. The official reason for the trip was the need to fill the vacancy of two episcopal sees. Evidently, Mindszenty also wished to introduce himself to the heads of the Holy See's offices and be given an audience by the pope.

The Issue of Diplomatic Relations

Mindszenty's stay in Rome was an eventful one. In the offices and state secretariats of the Holy See he conversed in Latin in what were, almost exclusively, one-to-one meetings. He met first with Giovanni Battista Montini, the substitute for general affairs (internal ecclesiastical matters), who was often referred to as deputy state secretary. Then he paid a visit on Domenico Tardini, the secretary for the Congregation for Extraordinary Ecclesiastical Affairs (foreign affairs), thereafter meeting with all the superiors general stationed in Rome. In addition, he met with representatives of the Hungarian colony in Rome.

Pope Pius XII received the Hungarian primate on December 8, the Feast of the Immaculate Conception. Mindszenty thus became the first prelate from the Soviet-occupied part of central Europe to inform the Vatican in person about the situation in the region. The two men were already known to each other, for the pope – at the time as papal legate – had visited Budapest seven years earlier, at the time of the 34th International Eucharistic Congress. Mindszenty expressed gratitude for the canonization of Blessed Margaret of Hungary in 1943 (a Hungarian delegation had not been present at the canonization ceremony, owing to the wartime conditions). He informed the pope of the recovery in religious life in Hungary and of the events that had occurred on August 20, the Feast of Saint Stephen (King Stephen I of Hungary, founder of the Christian Hungarian state). For that occasion, the Americans – thanks in part to an intervention by the pope – had returned the Holy Right Hand, a Christian relic, which the Arrow Cross had taken with them at the time of their flight from Hungary.[73] With the return of Saint Stephen's right hand, a large crowd, still sensing great relief at the conclusion of the war, had been able to take part in the traditional festive procession, which had been held every year since 1819. Mindszenty described to the pope, whom he judged to be well-informed, the domestic political conditions in Hungary, illuminating for him the actions of the power-hungry communists and the indifference of the Smallholder-dominated government. The Hungarian primate then "brought up Premier Tildy's request for the restoration of diplomatic relations. The pope was at once ready to send Nuncio Angelo Rotta back to Budapest. But I revealed my distrust and suspicions, and described to him the antireligious attitude of the communists."[74] Mindszenty refrained from detailing his suspicions, but it would seem that in his view the Hungarian government was seeking to appear in a favorable light at the Vatican, and that both the Soviets and the Hungarian government wished to exploit the accreditation of the nuncio for their own legitimization, thereby disguising their anticlerical actions.

Mindszenty returned to Hungary from Rome on December 13, 1945. The Hungarian primate expressed optimism wherever he spoke. He informed the government and the public that the Vatican welcomed the initiative to restore diplomatic relations. In conversations with members of the Bishops' Conference, he said something similar. Indeed, both publicly and in private, he mentioned nothing that would have implied reservations on his part.

A few weeks later, however, the British envoy to the Holy See informed the foreign secretary in London of very different developments, or, more accurately, of the absence of any developments: "The Vatican is more than ever mystified as to the position. It has had no further report from the Primate of Hungary, but on the other hand a Jesuit priest [Töhötöm, Nagy] has reached Rome from Budapest and has repeated that the Hungarian prime minister has suggested that the nuncio return."[75] The primate's silence arose

73. MNL OL XVIII–4. 1. d. 2. cs. Letter of Béla Witz, vicar-general in Budapest, to Béla Zsedényi, speaker of the National Assembly, requesting the return of the Holy Right Hand, June 26, 1945.

74. Mindszenty, *Memoirs*, 49.

75. TNA FO Religious affairs: proposal to accredit Vatican representative to Hungary: position of Prince Primate, Cardinal Mindszenty, Archbishop of Esztergom: Soviet reactions.

from his hesitation to act, which reflected, in turn, the domestic political developments that occurred between October and December 1945 – the elections and the change in the form of government. Mindszenty's initial enthusiasm had clearly been dented by these developments. Still, according to a centuries-old custom, whoever was the acting primate was also *legatus natus*, or the native papal envoy. One of the primate's official tasks was, therefore, to mediate between the Holy See and the Hungarian government. Indeed, until the arrival of a nuncio, Mindszenty would remain the sole official interpreter in Hungary of the pope's will. Of course, the same was also true in reverse: in Rome, he was the sole representative of the Hungarian Catholic Church. The presence of a nuncio would have meant an alternative channel of communication, both for the government and for the Holy See. Such an alternative channel would have limited Mindszenty's scope for political action. Evidently, the issue was not the existence or absence of diplomatic relations. Rather, it was the timeframe for the restoration of relations. Should they be restored as soon as possible, regardless of the domestic political situation? Or should the process be a more gradual one, with no final decision being taken at least until the signing of a peace treaty. The situation was undeniably awry from whichever angle it was viewed.

In response to the leaks about Mindszenty's trip to Rome, the Jesuit József Jánosi (whose name had come up several months earlier in connection with the primatial succession) traveled to Rome at the prime minister's behest and with the task of counterbalancing the Hungarian primate's accounts of the domestic situation. Prior to his departure, Jánosi held talks with Marshal Voroshilov, the chairman of the ACC, with Mátyás Rákosi, general secretary of the Communist Party, and with Árpád Szakasits, leader of the Social Democrats. He also received a letter of recommendation from Arthur Schoenfeld, the head of the US political mission to Hungary. The letter was addressed to Harold H. Tittmann, who was the diplomatic assistant to Myron Charles Taylor, the United States president's personal envoy to the pope.[76] Jánosi became the first churchman to undertake a government-ordained assignment, doing so in effect against the will of the

Code 21 File 436, FO 371/59014, 1946, Doc. no. 16/1/46. Letter of Sir D'Arcy Osborne, British minister to the Holy See, to Foreign Secretary Ernest Bevin, January 3, 1946.

76. MNL OL XX–10–k LÜ PO 18.300/1989. US archive papers. Memorandum no. 1143 of Ambassador H. F. Arthur Schoenfeld to the secretary of state, December 21, 1945.

Hungarian primate, Mindszenty. A direct consequence of this in the short term was an irrevocable rupture in the Jesuit Jánosi's relationship with Mindszenty. Even so, it was now plain to everyone that there was a desire on both sides to restore diplomatic relations. The Vatican wished to see Rotta return to Budapest. Indeed, if his previous status (nuncio, thus doyen) was now unacceptable to Budapest, the Vatican authorities would have consented to the lesser rank of internuncio.[77]

Since 1815, when the international rules on the hierarchical ranking of diplomats were established in Vienna, the pope's envoy (who was called the *decanus* or *doyen*, that is, the first or eldest) was – regardless of the timing of his commission – the doyen of the Diplomatic Corps at all times in Catholic countries and in most instances in other countries. After 1945, the first foreign diplomat to be appointed as envoy or ambassador to Hungary was none other than the Soviet envoy G. M. Pushkin, who was aged thirty-six years at the time. The customary diplomatic choreography suddenly became a matter of prestige between an atheistic world empire and the Catholic Church, which necessarily decided the issue. On July 9, 1946, with reference to reliable sources, the head of the British political mission in Budapest informed the Foreign Office in London that the Soviet leadership had categorically prohibited the Hungarian government from permitting the arrival in Hungary of a papal nuncio.

> This Soviet decision seems all the more regrettable because of the personality of the present prince primate, since it might have been hoped that if a representative of the Vatican were accredited, he might have had some success in restraining the activities and language of Cardinal Mindszenty,

commented Knox Helm the decision.[78] By the end of 1946, the efforts of the Hungarian Jesuits to reach an accommodation with the Soviets had clearly failed.

77. TNA FO Religious affairs: proposal to accredit Vatican representative to Hungary: position of Prince Primate, Cardinal Mindszenty, Archbishop of Esztergom: Soviet reactions. Code 21 File 436, FO 371/59014, 1946, Doc. no. 16/1/46. Letter of Sir D'Arcy Osborne, British minister to the Holy See, to Foreign Secretary Ernest Bevin, January 3, 1946.

78. TNA FO Religious affairs: proposal to accredit Vatican representative to Hungary: position of Prince Primate, Cardinal Mindszenty, Archbishop of Esztergom: Soviet reactions.

On the last day of 1945, József Mindszenty gave a New Year's Eve address, which was broadcast on the radio. It was his first radio broadcast. As is customary at this time of the year, in his address he urged the country's people to examine their consciences. Although his words were interpreted by some as a critique of the Soviet army, the Hungarian primate did not criticize the occupation force. He did, however, indirectly condemn Hungary's postwar governments by inquiring what they had done in the course of 1945 for human rights, freedom of the press, and the realization of the Ten Commandments. In this field, even people on the political left acknowledged the deficiencies and failures. Still, they regarded such problems as the teething problems of democracy rather than as constituting an underlying weakness of the system, which was the view of Mindszenty, however. Even Alvary D. F. Gascoigne, the head of the British political mission to Hungary, judged it necessary to inform his superior of "the great deal of truth" contained within the Hungarian primate's speech.

> But coming soon after his Pastoral Letter, which formed the subject of my despatch No. 446 of the November 5, and coming moreover from a man who in the eyes of the Leftists is considered to be a legitimist (vide his reference to the Crown) and as a defender of "reaction", it was not a well-timed pronouncement. It is to be hoped that Cardinal Mindszenty, with his great potential power for good, will not broadcast such public utterances in the future; for they will only tend to bring him, and the Catholic Church, into bad odour not only with the Leftists but also with the present coalition government.[79]

Becoming a Cardinal

In late 1945, for the first time since the war, Pope Pius XII appointed thirty-two new cardinals. With his excellent sense for diplomacy, Pius XII did not wait until the signing of the peace treaties. Rather, in advance of the treaties, he selected outstanding churchmen from all parts of the world,

---

Code 21 File 436, FO 371/59014, 1946, Doc. no. 10528/436/21. Report of Alexander Knox Helm, British Political Representative in Hungary, July 9, 1946.

79. PIL 508. f. 1/52. ő. e. 72. t. 15. fol. TNA FO 371/59002 R. 858. Report of Alvary D. F. Gascoigne, head of the British Political Mission in Hungary, January 7, 1946.

whose task would be to realize Vatican policy. In accordance with the historical custom, one of the new cardinals was the archbishop of Esztergom, whose activities as chief pastor of Hungary had visibly impressed the pope. The list of prospective cardinals was made public on December 23, 1945, and it was immediately broadcast on the radio. Owing to the Christmas holidays, the world press and the *Magyar Kurír* (Hungarian Courier – the semi-official newspaper of the Hungarian Bishops' Conference) published the details only several days later, on December 28. From the time of the announcement, Mindszenty started to call himself cardinal, a rank which was, according to the official position of the Roman Curia, equal to that of a royal prince by blood.

A US military plane took off for Rome with József Mindszenty on board at 7.50 a.m. on February 18, 1946. According to the rather theatrical account given in Mindszenty's memoirs, the aircraft had stood ready for take-off in a field on the outskirts of Esztergom, so that the primate could be flown to Rome as quickly as possible.[80] In reality, however, the plane departed from the airport at Mátyásföld (a suburb of Budapest), which had been Hungary's first airport and one of the busiest in Central Europe. From 1945 until as late as 1990, it functioned as a Soviet military base. Mindszenty was accompanied on the journey by his secretary, András Zakar, and by the papal chamberlain, Miklós Esty. British, American, and even Soviet officers were also on board the plane.

Among the churchmen invited to the ceremony in Rome, Mindszenty was the last to arrive. Originally, he was scheduled to travel on January 11, but he failed to receive a passport from the Soviet authorities. He was allowed to travel only after his absence in Rome had become a source of embarrassment and following wild accusations concerning his house arrest in Hungary or, indeed, his being sentenced to death. In his memoirs, Mindszenty wrote that he was the only absentee. In fact, however, owing to illness, neither Jules-Géraud Saliège, archbishop of Toulouse, nor Jan de Jong, archbishop of Utrecht, were able to attend. Still, whereas the press made only brief mention of their absence, Mindszenty's obstruction by the authorities in Hungary, as well as the political background to this development, received wide coverage in the media. Indeed, the name of the Hungarian

80. Mindszenty, *Emlékirataim*,112.

prince primate appeared on the cover pages of major newspapers around the world.[81] The tensions stemming from the pettiness of Soviet bureaucracy were confounded by a death in the family: József Mindszenty's father passed away on February 3, 1946. The prince primate himself conducted the funeral Mass and burial at Csehimindszent.[82]

The consistory lasted a whole week.[83] On February 18, the pope held a secret conference with the participation of the old cardinals, during which he created thirty-two new cardinals. The simultaneous appointment of such a large number of cardinals was unprecedented, as was also the large proportion of non-Italians: twenty-eight of them were natives of other countries. The College of Cardinals had had a similar composition on two prior occasions: in 1517 and in 1816. Nine years before, Pius XI had created cardinals on December 13, 1937. Pius XII, however, who had been pope since 1939, had not created any cardinals until this point in time. The new cardinals were not allowed to attend the secret consistory, and so, even though he was delayed, Mindszenty missed nothing of particular significance. The pope gave him an audience on the morning of February 20. Then, in the afternoon, at the Aula delle Benedizioni, Mindszenty received, in a semi-public consistory, the *mozetta* (the short elbow-length sartorial vestment in scarlet color) and the cardinal's *biretta* (also in scarlet).

On the morning of February 21, 1946, the public consistory, the most spectacular part of the series of ceremonies, took place in a packed Saint Peter's Basilica. During the ceremony, Pius XII sat on a scarlet adorned throne. The new cardinals, who were dressed in scarlet gowns and grouped according to their seniority, were then led one by one to the throne.[84] Aged 54, Mindszenty was one of the last in line, along with the other younger priests. Mindszenty, whose late arrival had been widely reported, was greeted

81. MNL OL XIX–J–1–k USA admin., 1945–64. IV-28. The Consistory in Rome and the appointment of Prince Primate Mindszenty as Cardinal in the US press, April 5, 1946; "Cardinals' fetes to be restricted," *New York Times*, January 22, 1946.

82. "Meghalt a Hercegprímás édesapja" [The father of the prince primate has died], *Új Ember* 2, no. 7, February 17, 1946, 2.

83. Mindszenty's appointment as cardinal is analyzed in László Imre Németh, *Mindszenty megvalósult álma: A Santo Stefano Rotondo és a Szent István Ház* (Budapest: Szent István Társulat, 2009), 37–50.

84. The atmosphere at the ceremony can be experienced by watching the following: http://www.youtube.com/watch?v=O-NkIccZHxs Consistory A.D. 1946. Pope Pius XII.

by the attendees with a round of applause. In accordance with the rules, he kneeled in front of the pope and kissed his foot. The pope then embraced Mindszenty and placed the cardinal's hat on his head. Pius then said the following words: "Of the thirty-two you will be the first to suffer the martyrdom whose symbol this red color is!"[85] In this way, the pope demonstrated his conviction that under communism, martyrdom awaited the church. As early as 1945, Pius XII was integrating into his statements the following two ideas: the atheism of communism was fatal for religious faith, and so Catholics must oppose it with all their strength. And why did the pope express this famous sentence to Mindszenty rather than to someone else? There were two new cardinals from East Central Europe, and so the pope might have addressed his words to the Pole, Adam Stefan Sapieha as well. The Polish prelate, however, was already seventy-nine years old. Evidently, he would not bear the brunt of the "great clash." The pope was correct in his judgment of the spirit of the young new Hungarian primate, for in Mindszenty a combatant prelate stood at the head of the Hungarian Catholic Church. Mindszenty would doubtless have willingly renounced the newly acquired title of cardinal if such a step might have served his goals. On two occasions subsequently, he did indeed determine to do this.

The next day the new cardinals received their rings, and a titular church was assigned to each cardinal. In József Mindszenty's case, the assigned church was Santo Stefano Rotondo, whose title he could now bear and in which he was due the same liturgical rights as at his own cathedral. Built in the fifth century in honor of Saint Stephen, the first Christian martyr, the church had been managed in the fifteenth and sixteenth centuries by the Pauline Fathers (Order of Saint Paul the First Hermit), an order founded in Hungary. Thereafter it had become the seat of the Hungarian Seminary in Rome. In 1580, under this legal title, it became the property of the Collegium Germanicum et Hungaricum. It came to be regarded as the

85. Mindszenty, *Memoirs*, 50. The incident was also recalled by Sister Pascalina Lehnert, who served as Pope Pius XII's housekeeper: "'Aber, wie konnten Eure Heiligkeit wissen, was Sie dem Kardinal sagten? Und ist es nicht furchtbar für ihn, aus dem Munde des Heiligen Vaters eine solche Voraussage zu vernehmen?', erwiderte Pius XII, dass er selber erschrocken sei, als er sich sagen hörte: 'Unter diesen 32 wirst Du der Erste sein, der das Martyrium erleidet, dessen Symbol diese rote Farbe ist.'" Sr. M. Pascalina Lehnert, *Ich durfte Ihm dienen: Erinnerungen an Papst Pius XII* (Würzburg: Verlag Naumann, 1983), 149–50.

unofficial church of the Hungarians in Rome and was looked after by the Jesuits. The walls of the church are – like those of many other churches – decorated with frescoes portraying the sufferings of the martyrs.

In the ensuing days, Mindszenty had to attend tiring protocol events and meet various other obligations. On March 4, he was given a further audience with the pope,[86] and on March 12 he was present at the Mass held on the seventh anniversary of Pius' coronation. For the first time in history, the Mass was celebrated in the Armenian rite (the pope was seated and the liturgy was conducted by Armenian prelates, priests and deacons).[87]

Knowledge of the details of Mindszenty's meetings with the pope is limited, but the two men must have discussed Hungarian–Vatican diplomatic ties. In December 1945 there had been little reason for the Hungarian primate to dissuade the pope from hastily establishing relations. However, since then, following the proclamation of the republic and the press attacks against his person, Mindszenty's position had hardened. In the end, the pope chose not to allow Rotta to resume his duties as nuncio in Budapest.[88] Although Pius XII was persuaded by Mindszenty on this issue, nevertheless it seems he did not entirely approve of the Hungarian primate's stance on relations with the state authorities. According to Töhötöm Nagy, who paid a third visit to Rome in mid-March 1946, the pope twice used the following expression in connection with the primate: "*troppo imprudente*," that is, excessively imprudent.[89] Still, the pope had no wish to influence Mindszenty when it came to Hungary's domestic affairs. Indeed, he later refrained from instructing the Hungarian primate to tone down his public statements.

The second journey to Rome was important – in addition to Mindszenty's being made a cardinal – from the perspective of the subsequent show trial. Some of the prosecution's accusations related to contacts Mindszenty made at this point in Rome with West European and North American cardinals – contacts that were, incidentally, natural and understandable under the

86. PL Processus, V–700/32. 240. fol. Notification of the chamberlain, F. C. di Vignola, Vatican City, March 3, 1946.

87. *Magyar Kurír* 36, March 19, 1946, 3rd edition.

88. Lapo Lombardi, *La Santa Sede e i cattolici dell'Europa Orientale agli albori della guerra fredda* (Roma–Budapest: Editrice Pontificia Università Gregoriana–METEM, 1997), 103.

89. ÁBTL 3.2.3. Mt–975/2. 121. fol. Data on Mindszenty's political role; Nagy, *Jezsuiták és szabadkőművesek*, 229.

circumstances. The prosecution argued that, during his time in Rome, Mindszenty may well have passed on information concerning Hungary to these churchmen and that, in the manner of a spy, he subsequently supplied these contacts with regular information. And what information could he have passed on? Nothing more, than what anyone in Hungary could experience firsthand. When the American prelates became aware of the squalid conditions in Hungary, they, in Mindszenty's words, "put their money on the table."[90] However, Mindszenty's receipt of cash donations – including 30,000 dollars from Montini and 5,000 Italian lire from the archbishop of Toledo[91] – led to accusations of foreign currency speculation, as he managed to avoid exchanging the sums at the official rate.

Mindszenty met with many members of the Hungarian émigré community in Rome, among them Miklós Kállay, the former prime minister. This meeting, too, was later used against him in the show trial. The prosecution claimed that a "counter-government" (a government-in-exile) had been formed in Italy under the leadership of Miklós Horthy, with Miklós Kállay as prime minister and József Mindszenty as minister of culture.[92] There may have been some basis for the rumor, as both the British political mission to the Holy See and the counterpart mission in Hungary reported something similar to London.[93] For his part, Kállay declined to play an active role, fearing for the fate of family members still in Hungary. Mindszenty struggled to accept Kállay's reticence, given that "he had been, after all, the last constitutional prime minister" prior to his flight to the Turkish embassy on March 20, 1944, which took place shortly before the arrival of SS men charged with his arrest.[94]

90. Beke, *A magyar katolikus püspökkari 1945–1948*, 88. Point 1 of the minutes of the Bishops' Conference meeting on April 2, 1946.

91. ÁBTL 3.1.9. V–700/39. 307–308. fol. Letter of Enrique Pla y Deniel, archbishop of Toledo, to József Mindszenty, February 1, 1946.

92. ÁBTL 3.1.8. Sz–222/6. 101. fol. Report on Prince Primate József Mindszenty; Nagy, *Jezsuiták és szabadkőművesek*, 228; Zoltán Nyisztor, *Vallomás magamról és kortársaimról* (Rome: Magyar Ny. St. Gallen, 1969), 244.

93. PIL 508. f. 1/45. ő. e., Item no. 56, TNA FO 371/59004, R 3565/256/21. Report no. 34 of Sir D'Arcy Osborne, British minister to the Holy See, to the British foreign secretary, March 6, 1946; PIL 508. f. 1/46. ő. e., Item no. 53, TNA FO 371/59005. Report of the British Political Mission in Hungary, August 10 (or 18), 1946.

94. PL Processus, V–700/1. 65. fol. Report on the interrogation of József Mindszenty on January 2, 1949.

It was in connection with the same visit to Rome that the rumor arose of a "conspiracy" between Mindszenty and Otto von Habsburg. What actually happened was that Cardinal Josef-Ernest van Roey, archbishop of Mechelen-Brussels (Belgium), passed on to Mindszenty Prince Otto's congratulations and his letter requesting a meeting.[95] At this time, however, no meeting took place. Mindszenty wished to avoid provoking the month-old Republic of Hungary, and Otto did not even travel to Rome. It was more than a year later, in the summer of 1947, that the two men met in Chicago.

Mindszenty reported on his visit to Rome and on the widening rift between the wartime allies at a meeting of the Bishops' Conference on April 2, 1946.

> In the fall the situation was still such that Central Europe was of no interest to the Anglo-Saxons. They were simply pleased the war had ended. Bolshevism left them cold. Now, however, a sense of Christian solidarity is perceptible among them... Along with Churchill, they too mentioned the Iron Curtain and the peril faced by Christendom. The Trieste, Iranian and Manchurian issues were at boiling point, which is why the American cardinals suddenly returned home ahead of the arranged time, on their own airplanes and government-owned battleships. The general view now is that Bolshevism is a danger to Europe and will be a danger to the world later on. In British and American public opinion, war is, according to some, the only solution at hand.[96]

The American prelates did not mislead Mindszenty when they spoke of the collapse of cooperation among the Allied powers, for there were increasing signs of this being the case. It suffices to mention Winston Churchill's famous speech on the Iron Curtain that had descended across Europe, dividing the continent in two. According to a Gallup public opinion survey, 69 percent of the US population believed that the United States would become embroiled in a war within 25 years, while just 19 percent thought that peace would prevail (a year earlier, the ratio had been 38:45).[97]

95. Ibid., 203. fol. Handwritten confession of József Mindszenty, January 1–11, 1949.

96. Beke, *A magyar katolikus püspökkari 1945–1948*, 88.

97. MNL OL XIX–A–a–e–IV/2–35/pol.–1946. 60. fol. Report of Aladár Szegedy-Maszák, envoy extraordinary and minister plenipotentiary in Washington, April 2, 1946.

At the Vatican too, a war scenario was regarded as a possibility, but not exclusively so. Pius XII recognized that for Stalin it was vital to maintain the antifascist coalition for some time at least after the end of the war. He believed this explained why Stalin had left scope for the various nations to follow different paths, rather than force them to adopt the Soviet model straightaway – even in relation to religion and the official policy on the churches. Consequently, communism would have to be reckoned with in the long term. In Hungary too, the public discourse did not rule out the possibility of renewed war. Indeed, war was foreseen by the Soviet officers stationed in Hungary, who, after some heavy drinking, would confidentially share their "news" with the Hungarians who fraternized with them.

Mindszenty did not resolve the dilemma of war or peace by coming out in favor of war. Still, he evidently believed in the coming demise of communism, which had been rumored by the American prelates. He was counting on a reversal in East Central Europe, a change in the balance of power as anticipated by the "man on the street" throughout the region. The new balance would reflect the West's economic strength and technological superiority rather than Soviet military power. Would the cardinal have pursued a different political course in the absence of this pessimistic vision of impending war? He probably would not have done so, for his conduct and tactics were being driven by his innate personality, to which was merely added a genuine belief in the closeness of the anticipated reversal. He wanted to be a hero, a hero of opposition to Bolshevism, rather than a master of compromise. He lacked the capacity for self-reflection that he would have needed in order to discern the condition of Hungarian society and the challenges facing the Hungarian nation at this critical juncture in history (the year 1945 and the subsequent period) and after such fundamental changes in the law, affecting both constitutional law and the primate's public legal role.

The removal of the Soviet Union from the status quo of victor would indeed have required a new war. With our current knowledge we are aware that Mindszenty was chasing illusions, as were also – it should be noted – the majority of Hungary's "Christian middle class." Neither of the two superpowers had an interest in renewed war, and so the idea of an impending "liberation" of countries in East Central Europe, brought about through the intervention of external powers, was nothing more than a dream. The Western powers had conceded the region to the Soviets while the war was still being fought. Only after the collapse of the Soviet Union would they finally intervene. They were more interested in the security of the Mediterranean, the defense of Greece and Turkey, and the future status of Germany and Austria. Meanwhile, East Central Europe was to be found somewhere towards the end of the list of priorities.

János Drahos, the archbishop's vicar, who served four princes primate during his life, perceived the change as follows:

> When law and order still prevailed in Hungary, Providence placed an excellent legal expert in the archbishop's seat of Esztergom. [...] Now the era of calm reasoning and argumentation has come to an end. The time has come for a fight. On the street strapping young lads are running about in combat boots and with submachine guns around their necks. Thus, Providence has sent us a "submachine gun" primate. Prince Primate József Mindszenty is in his element in a fight.[98]

FOR THE RULE OF LAW

In 1945–1946, the Catholic Church made "reconciliation" its watchword: love and forgiveness needed to replace war and hatred. Mindszenty put this into practice when, as the prelate of the nation, he considered it his duty to find out what was going on in public life and speak out against unlawfulness, abuses of power, injustices, and brutality. On the very same day he would write longer or shorter letters to a number of politicians, cabinet members, and diplomats, even doing so in the case of individual grievances and always calling for people to be treated fairly. One might even say that he became the "advocate" of the Hungarian people and nation.

A growing number of people turned to him for help in locating family members, for instance. In the absence of a Catholic newspaper – the permit for which the authorities continued to deny on various pretexts – Mindszenty used his pastoral letters to inform ordinary Catholics and the clergy about vital issues facing the Hungarian nation. Every Sunday a Mass was broadcast

98. MMAL 010. dosszié, Csaba Szabó's collection.

on the radio, and every two weeks there was a half-hour religious radio broadcast. Neither of these broadcasts, however, was a forum for the provision of information. In 1945, the only Catholic newspapers were *Magyar Kurír* (a simply designed "lithographic") and the two weeklies *Új Ember* (New Man) and *A Szív*. From November 1946, the magazine *Vigilia* resumed publication, but the circulation was far less than before the war. A shortage of paper was not only an excuse for the lack of publications; it was also a genuine and longstanding problem. Indeed, no more than a tenth of the requirements for paper could be met, and so it had to be rationed out for the various purposes, from printing banknotes to school textbooks. Paper was often distributed according to undisguised political sympathies.

The "New Persecuted"

The Hungarian State Police was faced with an increasing number of tasks, when, from early 1945 onwards, the internment of Nazi sympathizers, other far-right supporters, and warmongers began. At least according to the law, the maximum term of internment was twenty-four months. The number of internees was swollen by instances of simple error or calculated (sometimes political) revenge. Moreover, conditions in the internment camps and the treatment of internees left much to be desired. While he was still bishop of Veszprém, Mindszenty was already requesting the minister of the interior to release the innocent, to prevent the abuses of the political police (a new department created within the Hungarian State Police), to arrange for the spiritual care of the internees, and to improve meals in the camps.[99] As archbishop of Esztergom, he paid even closer attention to the fate of the "new persecuted."

In mid-October 1945, there were more than 10,000 internees in Budapest alone. Mindszenty received a detailed report concerning the Buda-Dél Internment Camp, which described the atrocious conditions and the brutality of the forced interrogations.[100] Ten days later, in reaction to what

99. VÉL I.1.44.a. 2383/1944., ÁBTL 3.1.8. Sz–222/9. 12., ÁBTL 3.1.9. V–700/56. 177–178. fol. Letter of Bishop József Mindszenty to the prime minister and the interior minister, August 25, 1945.

100. PL Processus, V–700/17. 195–198. fol. Letter of the residents of the Buda-Dél Internment Camp to József Mindszenty, November 8, 1945.

he had read, he visited the camp, where he found 4,000 starving internees in unheated and windowless rooms. His visit to the camp must have been anticipated, for the camp commander was waiting at the gate to shake Mindszenty's hand and the national anthem was played on his arrival. The commander had "dressed in uniform for the occasion, which was unusual for him, for it had not happened since he began serving at the camp."[101] Mindszenty gave a speech to the assembled, in which he made it clear that he saw in every prisoner a person who was suffering rather than a sinner, regardless of whether the person had been interned on account of his Arrow Cross past or for black marketeering or out of error. Without a doubt, his own time in prison meant that he was entitled to say this. He caused a further stir when, on December 9, 1945, citing the approach of Christmas, he requested the government to declare an amnesty for the internees and for prisoners convicted of minor political crimes. The press rushed to tell the public that the Hungarian primate was knocking on open doors, as a general amnesty was anticipated shortly. Still, nothing of merit happened for some time. Indeed, the first general amnesty did not take place until the spring of 1948.

When, at Christmas 1945, Mindszenty attempted to visit the internment camp in Csepel (a suburb of Budapest), where 2,400 people were being kept in cramped conditions, the camp's commander, citing an order from his superiors, refused the Hungarian primate entry to the building. The authorities were visibly annoyed by the activism of Mindszenty, who departed from the scene, saying "I yield to coercion."[102] In the new year, he returned to the camp, this time bearing a permit. His visit was reported on in the Hungarian-language newspaper of the Red Army, *Új Szó* (New Word), in a rather pointed fashion: "...His Eminence, Prince Primate Mindszenty (Pehm) made a protest visit to the Csepel Internment Camp on Monday. He went first to the SS men. Laying open his arms, he moved towards them asking 'How are we, my boys?' He did not respond to their complaints, telling them merely that he was the first priest of Hungary and that 'for me the internees are just as dear as the freemen.' Then he visited the gen-

101. PIL 274. f. 7/246. ő. e. 11. fol. Report of the political group of the Kingdom of Hungary's Police Force at the Buda-Dél Internment Camp, November 20, 1945.

102. Ibid., 13. fol. Visit of the prince primate to Csepel, December 24, 1945.

darmes."[103] The Soviet newspaper, citing Cicero, sent a warning message to Mindszenty, one that was designed to make him think: "*Quousque tandem abutere patientia nostra?*" – How much longer will you abuse our patience?

At the Archbishop's Palace, the petitions of the internees became ever more numerous: The Hungarian primate received many heart-wrenching letters from the various camps, which left him unable to remain silent. The complaints, grievances, requests, and cries for help were answered – to the extent that was possible – by the "Prince Primate Inquiry Office." One of the received letters had been written at the Soviet-run internment camp in Kiskőrös. The Hungarian citizens kept at the camp tended to be men whom the Red Army, citing security factors, had "taken into protective custody" in the course of the battles in Hungary. This security measure could be justified in the final days and hours of the war as one that had saved military officers, politicians and better-known civilians who were regarded by the Germans as "traitors" and "collaborators." With the end of the war, however, it had lost any real function. The circumstances of the protective custody were deemed "accommodating" or "exceptional" even by those being protected. Indeed, compared with the average internment camp, conditions were favorable. The unacceptable aspect was the situation itself: those under "protection" were being denied their personal freedom for no real reason; they must have felt like hostages or prisoners. On Christmas Day, Mindszenty wrote a letter to the prime minister in which he requested the release of the prisoners held at the internment camps in Kiskőrös, which were being run by the Russian military administration. He even named one of the prisoners whose release he sought: Colonel General Lajos Dálnoki Veress.[104] Why did Mindszenty make special mention of this military leader and ignore other internees such as Count Károly Apponyi (a member of the Upper House), Géza Lakatos (former prime minister), and Count Nándor Zichy (a former member of Parliament)? The reason seems to have been that in the fall of 1944, Regent Miklós Horthy had appointed Lajos Dálnoki Veress as *homo regius*, or "the king's man," to act

103. *Új Szó* 2, no. 24 (213), January 29, 1946, 2; ÁBTL 3.1.8. Sz–222. 75. Report, January 4, 1946. Cf. Mindszenty, *Emlékirataim*, 117. (Mindszenty seems to have confused in his mind the unsuccessful attempt at Christmas and the second attempt, which did result in a permit.)

104. PL Processus, V–700/10. 24–25. fol. Letter 5 of the prince primate, Cardinal József Mindszenty, archbishop of Esztergom, to Prime Minister Zoltán Tildy, December 25, 1945.

as his substitute in case of his own incapacitation. However, on October 16, 1944, the Arrow Cross had arrested Dálnoki Veress, imprisoning him at Sopronkőhida, where Mindszenty was also being held temporarily. In this way, the two men could become acquainted. In March 1945, Dálnoki Veress had escaped, but two months later he had been detained by soldiers of the Red Army and sent to the internment camp in Kiskőrös. Thanks in part to Mindszenty's intervention and in part to the commencement of the closure of prisoner-of-war camps throughout Europe, Dálnoki Veress was released on January 28, 1946. Mindszenty received immediate notification of his release.[105] A further report from the camps so upset Mindszenty that, after the Christmas holidays, he wrote another letter, dated December 29, 1945, to the prime minister and to the interior and justice ministers. On this occasion, he told of the fate of the internees at the Csillagerőd Camp in Komárom: 1,586 people were crammed on wooden bunks in a casemate, "like, for instance, at Buchenwald in Germany. There is no washroom, no dining area, and all the more lice, bedbugs, and roaches for it. The only heating is the animal warmth of the people themselves, who await their fate in a state of spiritual collapse, their faith in truth and humanity having been dented, and without an accusation."[106]

Seeing that the anticipated general amnesty had not taken place, Mindszenty compiled a new summary on November 12, 1946. He wrote about the depressing moral conditions, the manner of treatment which showed no regard for the needs of children, the elderly, and the sick, the inadequate food provisions, the inhumane housing, and the boredom that wore down the internees mentally. "Human rights, how mockingly they illustrate you! Democracy, how do they make you so loved?" This was Mindszenty's rhetorical question.[107] The authorities must have regarded as excessive the primate's petitions relating to the internees, but he refused to give up.

105. Ibid., V–700/27. 319. fol. Letter of István Balogh, state secretary at the Prime Minister's Office, to József Mindszenty, January 30, 1946. It should be noted that Lajos Dálnoki Veress had less than a year of freedom ahead of him, for he was detained once again on December 24, 1946 and accused of participating in the so-called Hungarian Community "conspiracy." On January 16, 1947, he was sentenced to death by the Budapest People's Court. On appeal, his sentence was reduced to 15 years' imprisonment.

106. Ibid., V–700/17. 67. fol. József Mindszenty's letter draft, December 29, 1945.

107. Ibid., 24. fol. Summary entitled *"Az internáltak: A Buda-Dél internáltjai"* [The internees: The internees of Buda-South] and dated November 12, 1946.

On August 8, 1945, in London, the three great powers – the Soviet Union, Great Britain, and the United States – signed an Agreement for the Prosecution and Punishment of the Major War Criminals of the European Axis (the London Charter). Under the agreement, a crime against peace refers to the "planning, preparation, initiation, or waging of wars of aggression, or a war in violation of international treaties, agreements or assurances"; a war crime is an act that constitutes "a serious violation of the laws or customs of war"; a crime against humanity is an act of "murder, extermination, enslavement, deportation, and other inhumane acts committed against any civilian population." In other words, the people as a whole are the aggrieved party in cases of war crimes and crimes against humanity. The "collective" nature of the aggrieved party is justified by the fact that war is, by nature, a historical disaster. A principle emerged whereby no-one has the right to treat a people or a nation in an irresponsible manner or drive it to war or into some other disaster. States that acceded to the agreement were required to extradite war criminals whose crimes had been committed on the territory of a country. The organized return to Budapest of former Hungarian political and military leaders who had been captured in the West began on October 3, 1945. (The head of the Hungarian political police, Gábor Péter, held talks – on the return of these men – with Allen Dulles, a senior staff member of US intelligence in Europe. A photograph taken of the two men at that time was used in 1953 as evidence of Gábor Péter's treason: he was portrayed as the newly recruited "spy" shaking hands with the US spy boss...)

In most European countries, including Hungary, a special institution of law – the People's Court – was established to bring to justice those who had committed war crimes or crimes against humanity (formerly "crimes against the people") during World War II. The tribunal, which had no precedents in Hungarian law, served not only for the prosecution of war criminals but also as a means for the Communist Party to rid itself of its political adversaries. It is worth dwelling on the structure of the People's Courts, because, in 1949, József Mindszenty would be convicted by one. Each People's Court initially consisted of five members, but soon the number was increased to six. The five members were delegated by the political parties, while the sixth member was chosen by the National

Council of Trade Unions. The people's judges tended to be laymen (non-jurists), as only the lead judge was required to have a law degree. Hence, the composition of the panel of judges arose in a complex manner and formed part of the broader political struggle. Whenever the number of votes on both sides was equal, the lead judge would cast a deciding vote, whereby he would obviously favor whichever party that had won his sympathy/support. The National Council of People's Courts served as the court of (or forum for) appeal. Compared to earlier times, the system of prosecution also underwent a change: at the People's Courts, the prosecution was represented by a public prosecutor, whereas at the court of, or forum for, appeal it was represented by the chief public prosecutor. The historical experts differ on the number of prosecutions of war crimes and the number of prosecutions of crimes against humanity. According to a parliamentary statement made on January 26, 1949, the People's Courts had dealt with 43,850 cases between 1945 and 1948. Acquittals had been made in 38.8 percent of almost 39,000 concluded cases.[108] The proceedings and verdicts of People's Courts were public, and there was no mechanism for holding a closed session. A drawback of this circumstance was that proceedings often descended into farce, as the courtroom "audience" could interrupt at any time.

There were no large-scale trials until the extradition to Hungary of the political and military leaders who had fled to the West. Thus, the first trials dealing with war crimes and crimes against humanity were launched around the time of the parliamentary elections (November 4, 1945). The identity of the accused and the nature of the indictments were determined by political – sometimes party political – factors. This applied in particular to major war criminals. In the first major trial, the Budapest People's Court sentenced the former prime minister, László Bárdossy, to death on November 3, 1945. Twenty days later, another former prime minister, Béla Imrédy, received the same sentence.

108. *Országgyűlés Naplója* [Diary of the National Assembly], 1947, Volume 5, Column 760. Sitting no. 104 of the National Assembly, on January 26, 1949. – According to a British historical analysis, the number of fascists and collaborators sentenced in Hungary as a percentage of the total population did not exceed the percentages found in postwar Belgium or the Netherlands. See Tony Judt, *Postwar: A History of Europe Since 1945* (New York: Penguin Press, 2005).

In view of the harshness of sentences, Pope Pius XII requested politicians throughout Europe to halt capital punishment for political actions.[109] In doing so, the Pope gave inspiration to Mindszenty, who, with reference to his duties stemming from his ecclesiastical and public legal status and to his own imprisonment, submitted – on the day of the verdict in Béla Imrédy's case (November 23, 1945) – a lengthy petition to Prime Minister Zoltán Tildy in which he protested against "popular judgment," which, as he argued, had no precedence in Hungarian criminal law or practice.[110] In another letter written at the same time, he argued against the execution of war criminals (on the same day he attempted to meet with Marshal Voroshilov, with the vain aim, it would seem, of gaining a reprieve for Imrédy). Drawing on classical Roman law, Mindszenty argued that the principle of *nullum crimen sine lege* ("no crime without law") meant that a person could only be punished on the basis of the law in force at the time the act was committed. The People's Courts, however, were applying the law retroactively, thereby calling into question this age-old legal principle. Moreover, the tribunals seemed in particular to be punishing those acts that had not been unlawful at the time they were committed. "...No-one could have abided by a law that did not exist when the act was committed, and so, for this very reason, it is the greatest injustice today to bring anyone to justice for such an action," Mindszenty wrote.[111]

In making this conclusion, Mindszenty effectively struck the Achilles heel of the People's Court trials, as the issue was fast becoming a test for judges throughout Europe – all of them educated in Roman law – as they began giving verdicts and sentences.[112] In press articles and in books on international law, there were great debates about the legality of prosecuting and punishing war criminals. Those who denied the legality of the process would often use the same arguments as Mindszenty: the legal provisions had been established only after the war, and criminal law should not be

109. *Magyar Kurír* 35, November 20, 1945. First edition.

110. PIL 274. f. 7/247. ő. e. 51–56. fol. Letter of József Mindszenty József to Prime Minister Zoltán Tildy, November 23, 1945.

111. Ibid., 52. fol.

112. Johannes Fuchs and Flavia Lattanzi, "International Military Tribunals," in *The Max Planck Encyclopedia of Public International Law*, ed. Rüdiger Wolfrum (Oxford: Oxford University Press, 2012), 1016–37.

applied retroactively. Other legal experts and, above all, politicians and public opinion were of the view that the war criminals had violated provisions of international law that had already been in force.[113] Moreover, the fact that legislation had lagged behind events (the Hungarian Criminal Code dated from 1878) and had failed to regulate how to bring someone to justice, could not absolve them of their responsibility and culpability. Further, Hungary's commitment – as expressed in the armistice – to punish war criminals overrode the classical principle of law.

In the modern history of humanity, the crimes of World War II were unprecedented in terms of the scale of brutality. And so, while a particular crime may not have been in breach of the law in force, it was more than likely to have violated natural law. Norms of a higher order – moral laws of natural or divine origin – whereby man has an inherent right to life, freedom, and property, do exist, and the task of the state should be to protect such rights. During the war, however, human life had become so devalued that the issuing of so many death sentences in the immediate postwar period had encountered little opposition. Moreover, the process of bringing criminals to justice met with society's sense of justice, which was dented only when clearly innocent people were convicted or when party political factors manifestly prevailed over all others.

It must be emphasized that Mindszenty was not speaking out in favor of the politicians who had been accused of crimes against the people. Rather, his demand was that the rule of law should be upheld. His sense of rightness led him to protest against popular justice and the injection of political factors – by way of party delegates in the People's Courts – into the professional world of law. Mindszenty did not make any moral arguments in defense of the pre-1945 political leaders. Neither then nor subsequently – for instance, in the memorandum drawn up in connection with the peace talks[114] – did he dispute their culpability. On the other hand, he did strongly criticize the means of bringing them to justice, because, when it came to punishing former government members, the relevant legal passages were – in the absence of new regulations – Sections 32–35 of Act

113. Thus, for instance, the Hague Conventions of July 29, 1899 and October 18, 1907 for the Pacific Settlement of International Disputes; the Versailles Peace Treaty of June 28, 1919; the Geneva Convention (1929) on the Treatment of Prisoners of War.

114. *Új Ember* 2, no. 25, June 23, 1946, 3; Vecsey, *Mindszenty okmánytár*, vol. 1, 221.

III of 1848 and the statutes of the two houses of the Hungarian Parliament. According to these provisions, government ministers could only be brought to justice by the Parliament (and not by the People's Courts). Among the 189 people executed after having been accused of war crimes, we find three former prime ministers – László Bárdossy, Béla Imrédy, and Döme Sztójay – and the former "Leader of the Nation," Ferenc Szálasi. At their respective trials, the four men did not complain about the retroactive application of the law or cite the principle of *nullum crimen sine lege* (whereas the defendants in the Nuremberg trials did do so). Rather, in their case, another principle was applied: *rebus sic stantibus* (in these circumstances), which is to say that everything should be interpreted according to its own circumstances and that, where conditions have changed, the law is normally extended to the new situations.[115]

In his letter written on the final day of the year, Mindszenty requested humane treatment for the people who had been held captive for several months and were awaiting trial. Though he did not mention the word amnesty or identify anyone by name, it would seem that the trials of Bárdossy and Imrédy had led him to request the suspension of sentences, citing the need for public relief and reconciliation.[116] In the end, however, none of the condemned former prime ministers were shown mercy. The only concession related to the means of their execution: they were shot rather than hanged. Ferenc Szálasi, onetime Arrow Cross "Leader of the Nation," was denied even this concession; he was taken to the gallows and executed like a common criminal.[117]

Mindszenty also wrote on behalf of Lieutenant-General Szilárd Bakay, and this time the letter was sent to both the British and the US envoys.[118]

115. Tibor Zinner, "Háborús bűnösök perei: Internálások, kitelepítések és igazoló eljárások 1945–1948," *Történelmi Szemle* [Historical Review] 28, no. 1 (1985): 119–40; Pál Pritz, *A Bárdossy-per* (Budapest: Kossuth, 2001), 76–77; Péter Sipos, *Imrédy Béla* (Budapest: Elektra Kiadóház, 2001), 129–30.

116. PL Processus, V–700/20. 406–407. fol. Letter no. 16/1946 of József Mindszenty to Minister of Justice István Ries, December 31, 1945. Published in Somorjai and Zinner, *Majd' halálra ítélve*, 253–55.

117. László Bárdossy was executed on January 10, 1946, Béla Imrédy on February 28, 1946, Döme Sztójay on August 22, 1946, and the "national leader," Ferenc Szálasi, on March 12, 1946.

118. PL Processus, V–700/15. 16. fol. Note of Alvary D. F. Gascoigne, the British political representative in Hungary, acknowledging the letter of József Mindszenty of April 14, 1946,

Favorably inclined towards the Allies and hostile towards the Germans and Nazis, Bakay had been the principal orchestrator of Hungary's attempt to exit the war. For this reason, on October 8, 1944, just days before the planned realization of the action, the Germans had kidnapped him. At the end of the war, he had been liberated at Mauthausen and had then returned to Hungary. Subsequently, he had undergone a screening at the People's Court, a procedure which had allowed him to clear his name. On April 11, 1946, the Soviet military authorities detained Bakay. Just three days later, Mindszenty's letter of protest was lying on the desks of the British and US envoys. Yet Mindszenty's efforts were to be in vain. Even though he managed to draw international attention to Bakay's plight and then keep the US envoy informed of developments,[119] and even though others too intervened (including the Hungarian Ministry of Foreign Affairs), Lieutenant-General Szilárd Bakay was executed by the Soviet military authorities on March 17, 1947.[120]

Mindszenty sensed that the arrests and detentions were now affecting military officers and civilians who had been hostile to Germany and had participated in the resistance movement. Indeed, some of the new detainees had even cooperated with Moscow. It seemed as if a strange ambiguity had arisen in morality: some could be executed on account of their political beliefs, while others could not. Mindszenty, however, never made such distinctions and never applied a double standard. When judging past actions, he preached Christian love rather than hatred. His guiding principle was forgiveness rather than vengeance. Meanwhile, he had no real confidence in the justice delivered by the People's Courts, which might have constituted a middle road between the two extremes. By taking such a stance, he made himself vulnerable to accusations of being a reactionary or a friend of war criminals.

---

concerning the arrest of General Szilárd Bakay, April 19, 1946; Ibid., V–700/17. 141. fol. Note of H. F. Arthur Schoenfeld, the US envoy, acknowledging letters of József Mindszenty of April 13 and April 14, 1946, April 19, 1946.

119. NARA RG 84, Records of the Foreign Service Posts of the Department of State, US Legation, Budapest, Hungary, General Records (hereafter: GR) 1946–63, Box 4, 1947 – 840.4. Letter of József Mindszenty to H. F. Arthur Schoenfeld, the US envoy, January 6, 1947.

120. Szilárd Bakay was officially rehabilitated on the basis of Russian laws on September 22, 1992.

PRISONERS-OF-WAR, DEPORTEES, AND THE DEFENSE OF HUMAN RIGHTS

In his role in public life, József Mindszenty was at his noblest when defending the persecuted and the rights of prisoners-of-war. He also protested against the collective punishment of the German ethnic community in Hungary and of the Hungarians in postwar Czechoslovakia.

Prisoners-of-War and Refugees

Mindszenty watched closely as Catholic Hungarians were dispersed around the world in the course of the postwar migrations. In the West, almost 280,000 Hungarian soldiers had been captured and placed in POW camps,[121] while more than twice that number – 600,000 Hungarians, almost a third of whom were civilians – were being held captive by the Soviets.[122] The situation of the prisoners – whether held in British, American, French or Soviet camps – was miserable. In his quest to secure their return to Hungary, Mindszenty tried all means, from pastoral letters, to sermons, to prayerful pilgrimages for the release of the prisoners. While he was still bishop of Veszprém, he requested effective measures from the prime minister.[123] Later on, as the Hungarian primate, he urged the members of the ACC to arrange for the return of the Hungarian prisoners-of-war to Hungary before the onset of winter. Representatives of the victorious Allies discussed the Hungarian primate's intervention at their meeting on November 28, 1945. Since, in their view, the prisoners-of-war were returning home on schedule, they determined that special measures were not required. Moreover, those present at the meeting – Marshall Voroshilov (ACC chairman), Major General William S. Key (head of the US military mission), and Major General Oliver P. Edgcumbe (head of the British military mission) – noted that clerics should not be interfering in political matters...[124]

121. Gyula Borbándi, *A magyar emigráció életrajza 1945–1985* (Budapest: Európa, 1989), vol. 1, 22; Tamás Stark, *Magyarország második világháborús emberveszteségе* (Budapest: MTA Történettudományi Intézete, 1989), 47–62.

122. Tamás Stark, *Magyar foglyok a Szovjetunióban* (Budapest: Lucidus Kiadó, 2006], 105–10.

123. VÉL I.1.44.a. 4068/1945. Letter no. 4883/1945 of Prime Minister Béla Dálnoki Miklós to József Mindszenty, July 15, 1945.

124. István Feitl, ed., *A magyarországi Szövetséges Ellenőrző Bizottság jegyzőkönyvei 1945–1947* (Budapest: Napvilág Kiadó, 2003), 112–13.

In fact, in the summer and fall of 1945, sick and infirm prisoners were the only ones released from the Soviet camps. The return of the other Hungarian prisoners from Soviet camps began a year later, after the closure of the United States' POW camps in Europe. Several camps in Hungary were closed at this time, but in late 1946 there were still over 400,000 Hungarian prisoners in the Soviet Union. On behalf of these unfortunates, Mindszenty sent more than a dozen letters to the British and American diplomats in Hungary, seeking the assistance of their governments.[125] His efforts were largely in vain, and it became clear that neither the United States nor Great Britain had any desire to exploit the prisoner-of-war issue so as not to open a new front against the Soviet Union.

Mindszenty, however, did not give up. After the signing of the Paris Peace Treaty (February 10, 1947), which, people hoped, would promptly resolve the prisoner-of-war issue, he sent off several more letters seeking assistance for the Hungarian prisoners, including a letter dated February 27 to the archbishop of New York (Francis Joseph Spellman) and the archbishop of Westminster (Bernard Griffin), a letter dated March 31 to the US secretary of state, and a letter dated May 12 to the Board of the American Red Cross.[126] On February 14, 1947, he requested Pope Pius XII to intervene. Albeit delayed, the response to this request was a positive one: the Pope asked the competent American and British bodies to address the release of the Hungarian prisoners-of-war, and he separately reminded the personal representative of the US president to the Holy See, Myron C. Taylor, about this matter.[127] Taylor had already been approached by Mindszenty in person, when the latter was in Rome for his elevation to the rank of cardinal.[128] At that time, Mindszenty's concern had been the

125. Several letters are cited in Stark, *Magyar foglyok a Szovjetunióban*, 238–41.

126. NARA RG 84, Records of the Foreign Service Posts of the Department of State, US Legation, Hungary, GR 1946–63, Box 4, 1947 – 840.4. Report of H. F. Arthur Schoenfeld, US envoy in Budapest (May 6, 1947), with Mindszenty's letter attached, according to which 16,000 of approximately 500,000 prisoners-of-war had returned to Hungary. Historians have since given a more accurate figure: by 1947, around 120,000 prisoners-of-war had returned to Hungary; see Tamás Stark, "Magyarország háborús emberveszteség," *Rubicon* 11, no. 9 (2000): 44–48.

127. ÁBTL 3.1.9. V–700/17A. 496–497. fol. Letter of Giovanni Battista Montini, substitute secretary of state, to József Mindszenty, July 22, 1947.

128. PL Processus, V–700/17A. 444. and 443. fol. Letter of Franklin C. Gowen, a member of staff working for Myron C. Taylor, to József Mindszenty, March 2, 1946.

Hungarian prisoners-of-war in the US zone of Germany. On April 14, 1947, Mindszenty requested, by way of Taylor among others, that the US government intervene on behalf of (seek the release of) the Hungarian prisoners-of-war that were still being held by the Soviet Union.[129]

US diplomacy welcomed only half-heartedly the actions of the Hungarian primate. While supporting his efforts to improve the spiritual care of the prisoners and in other areas that were strictly church-related, American officials dodged all other requests. When Mindszenty sent a list of the names of the Hungarian prisoners-of-war to Schoenfeld, the US envoy in Budapest, the latter simply sent the list back with a note saying that repatriation was not part of his purview.[130] The government became increasingly active in the lead up to the 1947 parliamentary elections, and many prisoners-of-war were released at this time. The communists were quick to seize the advantage, with the party's propagandists claiming that Mátyás Rákosi had secured the release of each and every prisoner-of-war. The truth is that the release of the Hungarian prisoners-of-war from Soviet captivity was a drawn-out affair lasting until as late as 1956. Moreover, out of around 600,000 Hungarian prisoners-of-war, approximately 200,000 disappeared or died (many of them in transit camps in Romania, where they were kept prior to transportation to the Soviet Union).[131]

The Deportation of the Ethnic Germans from Hungary

Although their forebears had settled in the Kingdom of Hungary centuries earlier, the ethnic Germans became – as elsewhere in Central and Eastern Europe – *personae non gratae,* as the Hungarian public sought to identify those responsible for the wartime destruction and a number of politicians began to exploit the hostile public mood. When, in the fall of 1944, the

129. NARA RG 84, Records of the Foreign Service Posts of the Department of State, US Legation, Budapest, Hungary, GR 1946–63, Box 4, 1947 – 840.4. Report of H. F. Arthur Schoenfeld, the US envoy in Budapest, May 6, 1947.

130. PL Processus, V–700/17A. 492. H. F. Letter of Arthur Schoenfeld, the US envoy, to József Mindszenty, May 26, 1947. The letter contains a reference to Mindszenty's letter of May 7, 1947, to which a 46-page list of the names of POWs had been attached.

131. For a comprehensive analysis of the issue, see Éva Mária Varga, *Magyarok szovjet hadifogságban (1941–1956) az oroszországi levéltári források tükrében* (Budapest: Russica Pannonica, 2009).

front reached Hungary's borders, the Soviet army began – as payment in kind for reparations – to transport tens of thousands of ethnic Germans from Hungary to camps in the Soviet Union, doing so in advance of a Soviet military command to this effect.[132] Under the terms of the provisional armistice agreement (January 20, 1945), Hungary undertook to "intern the German citizens." This applied, first and foremost, to those ethnic Germans who had lost their Hungarian citizenship on account of their membership of the SS or of the Volksbund. In practice, however, the postwar authorities interned all of Hungary's ethnic Germans, many of whom still had Hungarian citizenship. The targeted group constituted about five percent of the country's total population.

The initial reports of the impending deportation of the ethnic German population were published in the spring of 1945 in connection with the land reform program. The land reform decree made no distinction between fascist leaders, war criminals, and ordinary members of the Volksbund. Their land was confiscated in a uniform manner and used to alleviate the problems facing landless peasants and for the purpose of resettling ethnic Hungarian refugees from outside Hungary and the Székelys of Bukovina. Thus, from the very outset, an economic and social aim – land reform – was tied to the need to punish that part of the ethnic German population that had sympathized with Hitler's Germany. In the course of 1945, the legal basis for internment and resettlement (deportation) was gradually established and then extended by lawmakers. Several forward-looking politicians warned of the consequences of these measures: the resettlement (deportation) of the ethnic Germans would provide Hungary's neighbors with legal and moral grounds to take similar measures against their ethnic Hungarian populations. A number of government ministers disagreed with the collective punishment of the German ethnic group and with the dismissal of an approach based on individual assessment. Perceptions of the national interest clashed with humanitarian principles and with human rights.

132. Hungarian historians have estimated that 40–60,000 ethnic Germans were forcibly taken from Hungary to the Soviet Union for "malenkiy rabot," but according to recent Russian research a more realistic estimated figure is 30,000. See B. Konasov and A. V. Tereshchuk, "Berija és a *malenkij robot*: Dokumentumok Ausztria, Bulgária, Magyarország, Németország, Románia, Csehszlovákia és Jugoszlávia polgári lakossága 1944–1945-ös internálásának történetéről," *Történelmi Szemle* 46, nos. 3–4 (2004): 345–402.

In the end, such expressions of concern had no impact on policy: the Hungarian government – following the example of the governments of Czechoslovakia, Yugoslavia, and Romania – requested the consent of the Allied powers to deport 200–250,000 (ethnic) Germans.[133] The Hungarian government's "diligence" in effect gave impetus to the ideas of Czechoslovakia's president, Edvard Beneš, for in the absence of the Hungarian request, the talks in Potsdam (August 2, 1945) might have ignored the Germans of Hungary. As it was, however, the Allied powers stated in a resolution that the German-speaking minorities were to be relocated to Germany not only from Poland and Czechoslovakia but also from Hungary. Subsequently, the deputy head of the ACC in Hungary, Lieutenant-General Vladimir Petrovich Sviridov, instructed the Hungarian prime minister that his government was to carry out the expulsion (deportation) of 400–450,000 ethnic Germans.[134]

At its first post-war meeting (May 24, 1945), the Catholic Bishops' Conference discussed the fate of the German-speaking minority in Hungary, requesting fairness and justice for ethnic Germans who had remained loyal to the Hungarian state.[135] As preparations for the expulsions began, József Mindszenty, who had just been appointed as archbishop of Esztergom, wrote a second letter to Prime Minister Béla Dálnoki Miklós, having received no response to his first letter. In this second letter, Mindszenty strongly criticized the authorities for failing to distinguish between ethnic Germans who had been enthusiastic members of the Volksbund and those who had remained loyal citizens of the Hungarian state.[136] A week later, on October 17, 1945, the Bishops' Conference repeated – in a pastoral letter that declared a commitment to conscience and compassion – the principal message of Mindszenty's letter to the prime minister, juxtaposing the responsibility

133. MNL OL XIX–J–1–a–II–28–41/res/Be–1945. Ministry of Foreign Affairs: papers of the department preparing for the peace treaty, Verbal note to the government of the Soviet Union, May 26, 1945.

134. MNL OL XIX–A–83–a/44. sz. Minutes of the extraordinary meeting of the Council of Ministers on August 13, 1945.

135. SzfvPL no. 7338 185/1945. and VÉL I.1.44.a. 1187/1944.

136. PIL 274. f. 7/247. ő. e. 35v. Letter no. 4001/1945 of Prince Primate József Mindszenty to Prime Minister Béla Dálnoki Miklós, October 10, 1945. Published in Csaba Békés and Ágnes Tóth, "'Ha csak a bűnösöket büntetnék, hallgatnánk…' Mindszenty József levelei a hazai németség ügyében," *Forrás* 23 (1991): 58.

of the individual with that of the collective. The pastoral letter referred to the Hungarian people's millennium-old tradition of inclusiveness and its ability to live peacefully with foreign peoples:

> If the transgressors alone were to be punished, we would remain silent, but people who have committed no proven crimes are called friends of the bad; indeed, they are accused of doing something that is their due under natural law, for instance, speaking in the mother tongue. [...] we feel the elevating consciousness that in a country inhabited by [several] ethnic groups, there can only be space for love, mutual understanding and respect.[137]

On November 28, 1945, Mindszenty sent yet another letter to the ACC expressing concern for the fate of Hungarians of German ethnicity who had been transported to the east. He received a reply from the Hungarian Ministry of Foreign Affairs, informing him that the Hungarian ambassador in Moscow had already been instructed to seek the return of the captives from the Soviet Union.[138] Even so, Mindszenty's endeavors achieved little of substance. Indeed, on December 22, 1945, the Hungarian Parliament adopted, in a roll-call vote and with a large majority, a decree on the transfer to Germany of Hungary's German minority. The decree, which was clearly based on the principle of collective punishment, cited the Allies' decision on this issue, made in Potsdam on November 20, 1945. The legislation stipulated the resettlement in Germany of all Hungarian citizens who had self-identified as ethnic Germans and/or German native speakers at the most recent population census (1941) or who had Germanized their surnames or who had been members of the Volksbund or any German armed unit (e.g., the SS). Leaving behind everything that had been accumulated since the arrival of their forebears two centuries earlier, the Germans of Hungary were forced to begin new lives in their old/new homeland.

137. MNL OL XIX–J–1–a–II–28–4529–7/1946, 627v. Ministry of Foreign Affairs: Papers of the department preparing for the peace treaty, Prince Primate József Mindszenty's pastoral letter on behalf of the Bishops' Conference, October 17, 1945.

138. PL Processus, V–700/19. 29–30. fol. József Mindszenty's manuscript draft, dated November 28, 1945, according to which 12–15,000 men and women had been taken off to the east.

Hungarian public opinion, the press and politicians gave various assessments of the decree. There were some who spoke of an historical act and proudly flaunted their support for the measure. Others, eager to assuage their guilty conscience, referred to the large number of unsatisfied claimants for land and to the obligations laid down in the international treaty. On December 26, 1945, Mindszenty wrote once again to Prime Minister Zoltán Tildy. His condemnation of the mass expulsions and of the multiple abuses of power – of which he gave specific examples – was even more adamant on this occasion than in his earlier letters.[139] After the promulgation of the decree, on the last day of the year the Hungarian primate wrote a further letter to Prime Minister Tildy, requesting the suspension of the expulsions at least until the end of the winter. This time he did receive a reply, albeit one of rejection. Tildy explained that there was nothing he could do, as the deadline for the completion of the resettlement action was July 1946. While claiming that a suspension was impossible, Tildy did promise to ensure the humane administration of the process.[140] In the end, Mindszenty had no option but to authorize priests serving in German-speaking parishes to accompany the faithful to Germany, insofar as they wished to do so. It should be noted that he did not compel the priests to accompany their congregations (nor could he have done so).[141] The evidence shows that Mindszenty recognized the danger of the resettlement decree serving as a precedent for similar actions against the Hungarian minorities in the neighboring countries. Moreover, perhaps he alone among the protesters saw through the greed to which so many prosperous ethnic German families had fallen victim. It is a fact that some had been put on the list of expellees simply because of the extent of the property that could be confiscated.

The first trains left Budaörs on January 19, 1946. Within a six-month period, 150,000 persons of German ethnicity were expelled from Hungary

139. MNL OL XIX–J–1–a–II–28–4529–7/1946. Ministry of Foreign Affairs: papers of the department preparing for the peace treaty. Letter of József Mindszenty to Prime Minister Zoltán Tildy, December 26, 1945.

140. Ágnes Tóth, *Telepítések Magyarországon 1945–1948 között* (Kecskemét: Bács-Kiskun Megyei Önkormányzat Levéltára, 1993), 110–11.

141. SzEL AC 132/1946. Pastoral letter signed by József Mindszenty and dated January 8, 1946.

and resettled in Germany. Throughout this period, Mindszenty regularly besieged the competent authorities, petitioning them on behalf of vulnerable people and the unfairly punished. The expulsion of people from Hungary was accompanied by resettlement programs within the country. Indeed, the population exchange agreement between Czechoslovakia and Hungary (February 27, 1946) had added a new element to the process of resettlement: room was now needed for the Hungarians of southern Slovakia.

Efforts on Behalf of the Hungarians of Slovakia

The collective punishment of ethnic minorities quickly became a contagion in Central Europe. The spread of the "disease" was facilitated by Stalinist policy, which respected the goal of the young nation-states to free themselves of their national minorities. With a view to creating a "pure" nation-state, the government apparatus in Czechoslovakia determined upon the complete removal of the Hungarian minority. In Czechoslovakia, a whole series of disenfranchising measures were taken in the spring and summer of 1945. There were mass job dismissals and many ethnic Hungarians were interned. Forced public work was introduced in the fall of 1945, a program that had affected 10,000 ethnic Hungarians by late December.

While still bishop of Veszprém, Mindszenty had called on the Slovakian Bishops' Conference to take actions against the persecution of the Hungarians in Czechoslovakia, but he had not received a response.[142] On the day of his installation as archbishop (October 7, 1945), he had then written to the heads of the US and British missions, telling them about the persecution and harassment of Hungarians whose native regions were once again controlled by Czechoslovakia (having originally been ceded to that country under the Treaty of Trianon). To resolve the problem, he had proposed a border adjustment:

> It is now evident that this (the problem of the hostility towards Hungarians – the author) can be satisfactorily settled only by adjusting the border to Hungary in accordance with the desire of the Hungarians living there in

142. Mindszenty, *Emlékirataim*, 145; Katalin Vadkerty, *A kitelepítéstől a reszlovakizációig 1945–1948* (Bratislava: Kalligram, 2007), 70.

> a solid group for centuries. The Czechoslovak Government will the result of the plebiscit [sic. orig] make smaller, therefor [sic. orig], certainly, persecute and expell now the Hungarians from this territory. I feel sure, that Your Excellency's Government already up to the present made much in the cause of truth and particularly in the interests of the Hungarian People, but I beg Your Excellency again, that You take steps, that the measures which injure people's rights and are unlawful be urgently remedied and that suitable reparations be made.[143]

We do not know the diplomats' response to Mindszenty's letter, but presumably they wrote no more than a few polite lines in acknowledgement. A rather bumpy road had led to the population exchange agreement between Czechoslovakia and Hungary, signed in Prague on February 27, 1946. The British and Americans had called on the two parties to the dispute to settle the issue among themselves. In the end, the two countries agreed that the number of ethnic Hungarians to be expelled from Czechoslovakia could be no more than the number of Slovaks living in Hungary who signed up to be voluntarily resettled in Czechoslovakia. In the light of the Hungarian census of 1941, this would have meant the resettlement of 104,819 ethnic Slovaks living in Hungary. In addition, Czechoslovakia undertook to suspend the confiscation of property and to resume payment of the deducted sums and pensions. The Hungarian government agreed to accept unilaterally a thousand persons deemed minor war criminals.

During the implementation of the agreement, the Czechoslovak side found countless loopholes, and the confiscation of property continued apace. Moreover, it rapidly became apparent that the authorities were seeking to establish – in place of the expelled Hungarians – a series of Slovak-inhabited villages along the Danube, whereby the objective was to drive a wedge between the Hungarian-inhabited southern region of Slovakia and Hungary. Concurrently, there was a rapid increase in the number of ethnic Hungarians that were to be expelled from Slovakia and resettled in Hungary. This increase particularly affected those ethnic

143. PL Mm. 2. d. Letter of József Mindszenty to the British and US envoys, October 7, 1945. For the copy of the letter received by the US envoy, see NARA RG 84, Records of the Foreign Service Posts of the Department of State, Hungary, Budapest Mission 1945, Box 65, 840.0–840.7 Catholic Church.

Hungarians who had been classified as war criminals. War criminal proceedings were initiated against entire villages, and sufficient pretext for such proceedings was that someone in the village had publicly celebrated the arrival of Hungarian troops in 1938. Despite substantial efforts on the part of the Czechoslovak government to persuade Hungary's ethnic Slovaks to resettle in Czechoslovakia, the number of ethnic Slovaks registering for voluntary resettlement was far fewer than the number of Hungarians targeted for expulsion by the Czechoslovak authorities. There was general consternation when, in the summer of 1946, it was rumored that Czechoslovakia was planning the unilateral expulsion of 200,000 ethnic Hungarians and the forceful "re-Slovakization" of the remaining 300,000. The Allied powers, however, denied the Czechoslovak government authorization for implementation of the plan. Yet the Czechoslovak authorities were still intent on radically altering the ethnic map of southern Slovakia and breaking up the contiguous ethnic Hungarian areas. Accordingly, in late September and early October 1946, the authorities began the deportation of tens of thousands of ethnic Hungarians from southern Slovakia to villages in the Czech lands that had been left empty following the expulsion of the local population of ethnic Germans.

In an appeal based on historical arguments, Mindszenty called on the Hungarian government to annul the population exchange agreement; he requested the same from the British foreign secretary.[144] In his letter he cited in particular the 1,028-year history of the Hungarian community in southern Slovakia with its population of almost 700,000. He also condemned, in the strongest terms, the Beneš government's policies (the ban on the use of the Hungarian language, the confiscation of land owned by Hungarians, the imprisonment or internment of many members of the community, and the deportation of ethnic Hungarians and Hungarian-speaking Jews to Bohemia and Moravia for the purpose of forced labor). The letter described in detail the propaganda of the Czech authorities – which did not shy away from blackmail – and their attempts to cajole ethnic Hungarians into declaring themselves Slovaks on the basis of a single ancestor with a Slovak surname. Those who refused were to be hounded

144. PL Processus, V–700/19. 70–83. fol. Letter of József Mindszenty to Minister of Foreign Affairs János Gyöngyösi, April 25, 1946; Ibid., 433–434. fol. Letter of József Mindszenty to British Foreign Secretary Ernest Bevin, April 29, 1946.

out of southern Slovakia. The choice was a stark one: nation or livelihood; human rights or intimidation. Mindszenty envisaged the complete destruction of the Hungarian community in Slovakia. In his view, the only way to save the community was to persuade the great powers to reject the validity of the population exchange agreement and to return the territory to Hungarian sovereignty. As we know, there was no chance of this happening.

In numerous subsequent letters, the Hungarian primate addressed measures taken by the Czechoslovak authorities that violated the earlier agreement. He sent the letters to diplomats, minister of foreign affairs, and leading churchmen. He arranged for a pastoral letter, dated October 28, 1946, to be sent on behalf of the "*bishops of the Kingdom of Hungary*" (Episcopi Regni Hungariae) to bishops around the world.[145] (Eight months after the proclamation of the Hungarian Republic, it was rather odd and certainly telling that Mindszenty made this reference to the Kingdom of Hungary – even if he did so in Latin...) The letter requested the understanding of ecclesiarchs and their assistance in protecting the rights of Hungarians in Slovakia. The tone of the letter was harsh and acrimonious; it branded the Slovaks undisguised turncoats for having put themselves on a moral pedestal in spite of their spearhead role in the recent, Hitler-inspired persecution of the Jews. Mindszenty wished to see the situation himself, so he requested permission from the Czechoslovak authorities for a visit to the Hungarians who had been deported to the Czech areas of the country and for a meeting with Archbishop Beran of Prague. The government in Prague, however, opted to deny him an entry visa.[146]

During these months, Mindszenty authored two lengthy memoranda on the various stages of the deportation of Hungarians from Slovakia. He substantiated his findings by providing a wealth of data. He then sent both documents to the state secretariat at the Vatican. His initiative clearly

145. Ibid., 7–8. fol. (The pastoral letter was successfully delivered abroad, and an original copy – signed by József Mindszenty – is kept at the Archives Historiques de l'Archevêché de Paris in Box "9 K 2, 5 Hongrie.")

146. Ibid., 262–263. fol. Letter in Latin of Josef Beran, archbishop of Prague, to József Mindszenty, January 18, 1947; Mindszenty, *Emlékirataim*, 147; István Janek, "Mindszenty József tevékenysége a felvidéki magyarok megmentéséért 1945–1947 között," *Századok* 142, no. 1 (2008): 179–80.

served a purpose, for it transpired that these were the first reports the state secretariat had received of the events.[147] On December 22, 1946, Mindszenty requested Pius XII's support for an initiative that sought to persuade the great powers to set up a special international commission in view of the "escalation in Slovakia of the extraordinarily violent persecution and deportation of the Hungarians."[148] Then, on January 9, 1947, he dispatched a further poignant letter to the pope:

> The Hungarians are being taken by force from their thousand-year-old homeland to the so-called Sudeten region, being transported in rail wagons at temperatures of 16–22 degrees below zero (2– -8°F), for 5–6 days, and with infants that are barely clothed and nourished, with women who are pregnant and close to giving birth, and with the elderly and the sick. During this time their property and their real estate at home is being taken away from them. The well-disposed railway workers and soldiers are aghast at these egregious injustices.[149]

On January 31, 1947 (according to Mindszenty's memoirs, on February 5), he repeated his protest. This time he sent a telegram to King George VI of England, US President Harry S. Truman, and Montini, the substitute for general affairs to the secretary of state (Holy See), requesting them to assist the Hungarians in the same way as they had previously helped the Jews.[150] In February, he wrote once again to the British foreign secretary, Ernest Bevin, about the legal deprivations and the forcible mass transfers of people.[151] These letters were the same in terms of their content, all of them protesting against the deportations and condemning the domestic political course in Czechoslovakia. Their graphic accounts of human tragedies served almost to shock the reader. Mindszenty treated the dismemberment of Hungary and the situation of the resultant Hungarian minorities in the

147. Ibid., 218. fol. Letter of Secretary Domenico Tardini to József Mindszenty, December 15, 1946. (Diplomatic relations between Czechoslovakia and the Holy See were restored on May 13, 1946, whereafter Archbishop Saverio Ritter arrived in Prague as apostolic internuncio.)

148. Ibid., 220–221. fol. Letter of József Mindszenty to Pope Pius XII, December 22, 1946.

149. Ibid., 239–242. fol. Letter of József Mindszenty to Pope Pius XII, January 9, 1947.

150. PIL 274. f. 7/248. ő. e. 184. fol. Summary, May 12, 1948. Subject: József Mindszenty.

151. PL Processus, V–700/19. 128–129. fol. Letter of József Mindszenty to British Foreign Secretary Ernest Bevin, February 15, 1947.

neighboring countries as related subjects. Even when a response was received to one of his letters, it was either no more than a polite acknowledgement of receipt or – even worse – a rejection of what he had requested.

On February 10, 1947, the day on which the Paris Peace Treaty was signed, József Mindszenty turned to the participants in the peace conference. Despite his despair at the hopelessness of the situation, he once again argued for a revision of the borders based on the ethnic principle, for without a border correction and the resolution of the nationality issue, the Paris conference would simply repeat and uphold "the errors of the peace treaties that followed World War I and lay the basis for further wars."[152] Even a Slovak Catholic prelate – and the Slovak clergy were known for their nationalism – requested a more humane approach in a letter addressed to Czechoslovakia's political leadership.[153] The man in question, Bishop Pavel Jantausch of Nagyszombat (Trnava), may have written the letter under gentle pressure from the Vatican. Whatever the case, he was the only major public figure in Czechoslovakia to openly voice opposition to the forcible resettlement of the Hungarians. True, his request was merely that the deportations be put on hold until the winter frosts had passed... The Hungarian government also made substantial diplomatic efforts, but ultimately those were proved right who had predicted a repeat of the procedure used against the ethnic Germans in Hungary. Indeed, in the eyes of the world, Hungary had lost – through its own actions – the moral right to protest against the expulsion and deportation of Hungarians in Czechoslovakia. Evidently, however, the issue was less about morality than about power.

The exchange of population began, accompanied by general dissatisfaction and leaving wounds that even today remain unhealed. Hungarian families from Slovakia were transferred to properties in Hungary formerly owned by ethnic Slovaks who had been voluntarily resettled in Slovakia and

152. Cited in Vadkerty, *A kitelepítéstől a reszlovakizációig 1945–1948*, 70.

153. Praha Ministerstvo Zahraničných Vecí (Prague), Ministry of Foreign Affairs – Praha Teritorialni odbory – obyčejné 1945–59. Maďarsko, krabica 3. 33283/1947. Letter of Pavel Jantausch on behalf of the Slovak Catholic Bishops' Conference to Minister of Foreign Affairs Ján Masaryk, Trnava, February 1, 1947; The bishop also sent the letter to President Beneš. For the text of the letter, addressed to the presidium of the Slovak National Council, see Vadkerty, *A kitelepítéstől a reszlovakizációig 1945–1948*, 518–20. For more on the issue, see Štefan Šutaj, *Maďarská menšina na Slovensku v rokoch 1945–1948 (Východiská a prax politiky k maďarskej menšine na Slovensku)* (Bratislava: Veda, 1993), 105–06.

by ethnic Germans who had been expelled earlier. The outward expulsion and inward resettlement programs caused chaos and havoc. Reluctance and mistrust poisoned the public mood, and in some places the atmosphere resembled that of a civil war. In a further letter to the US envoy, dated April 5, 1947, Mindszenty outlined this situation. He referred repeatedly to the grievances, the inhumane treatment, the abuses, and the injustices.

Since the number of available properties in Hungary was inadequate, the Hungarian authorities determined to resolve the problem of accommodating the Hungarians arriving from Slovakia by expelling additional groups of ethnic Germans. On hearing word of this intent, Hungary's leading churchmen issued renewed protests. The Catholic prelates submitted two memoranda to the prime minister: one had been drawn up by the Hungarian primate himself, while the other was signed – unusually – by two bishops on behalf of the Bishops' Conference.[154] The prelates reaffirmed their support for those Germans who had remained loyal to Hungary during the war. They also condemned the principle of collective punishment and raised the issue of historical responsibility. Mindszenty was among the first to demand an end to "all types of deportation" and that, at the very least, "all those who had not committed grave sins" be permitted to remain in Hungary.

In an exceptional act, the government put the Hungarian primate's letter on its agenda. Interior Minister László Rajk, who was chosen to lead the debate, noted frankly the economic advantages of the resettlement programs, including the opportunities for seizing property from the diligent German ethnic community. After an explosive debate, the Council of Ministers decided to continue the policy of resettlement in line with the original schedule. At the same time, Rákosi stressed that "a polite response should be given to Mindszenty."[155] Just as there was no chance

154. For József Mindszenty's letter, see the Manuscript Archive of the Hungarian Academy of Sciences: Mihályfi Ernő hagyatéka [The legacy of Ernő Mihályfi], Ms 6266/149. Letter of József Mindszenty to Prime Minister Lajos Dinnyés, July 28, 1947. For the letter signed by Hamvas and Péterv on behalf of the Bishops' Conference, see ibid., Ms 6266/148. (In the publication entitled *Mindszenty okmánytár* the letter is erroneously attributed to Mindszenty. See Vecsey, *Mindszenty okmánytár*, vol. 2, *Mindszenty harca*, 110–13.)

155. László Szűcs, ed., *Dinnyés Lajos első kormányának minisztertanácsi jegyzőkönyvei 1947. június 2. – szeptember 19.* (Budapest: Magyar Országos Levéltár, 2000), 827–28 and 834. Agenda item 20 of the minutes of the Council of Ministers meeting of August 21, 1947.

of making the proposed changes to the international treaties, neither was there a political will in Hungary to mitigate domestic policy on resettlement. The resettlement (expulsion) of the ethnic Germans continued, albeit the destination was now the Soviet zone (i.e., East Germany), for the Western powers were refusing to accept further "human deliveries." This new reluctance seems to have had both economic and political roots, but Mátyás Rákosi was convinced that Mindszenty's protests lay behind it, as it had been his request to the American government.

Mindszenty never really gave up; he repeatedly sent a flood of letters to every imaginable forum. He wrote, for instance, to Pius XII on multiple occasions. The anticipated vigorous response failed to materialize, however. It was at this point that Mindszenty pondered taking a highly unusual step: if the pope failed to assist the Hungarians of Slovakia, he would resign as cardinal. He must have been beset by various emotions, including bitterness, frustration, helplessness, anger, worry, and compassion. But he also felt pride and a need to show defiance. It is worth reminding ourselves how he had threatened to resign even as a parish priest when his ideas had clashed with those of his bishop. On this occasion, however, the gravity of such a step was incomparably greater, even if his purpose was simply to put pressure on the Vatican and on world public opinion with a view to eliciting more effective assistance. On August 27, 1947, he wrote and dispatched his resignation to Pius XII, but rather than make specific mention of the office of cardinal, he wrote instead of resigning "from his post," while twice referring to the "crimson light that was burning at his conscience."[156] The pejorative reply from the Vatican, signed by the secretary for the Congregation for Extraordinary Ecclesiastical Affairs, Domenico Tardini, must have caused him great disappointment: the civilian authorities had not responded with sufficient good will to the Holy See's proposal that love and justice should govern relations between the peoples. And while the pope was doing his utmost on behalf of the Hungarians of Slovakia, he could not intervene directly. Rather than offer specific promises of assistance, the pope sent an Apostolic Blessing. The letter addressed the matter of Mindszenty's resignation inasmuch as to give him

156. PL Processus, V–700/19. 297–299. fol. Letter of József Mindszenty to Pope Pius XII, August 27, 1947.

a polite admonition: the pope trusted that "rather than be overwhelmed by the problems, you wish to continue guarding in a wakeful fashion the faithful who have been entrusted to you, showing everyone an example of strength, patience and the Gospel of love."[157] Mindszenty understood the warning and chose to continue bearing his cross.

The true effects of the population exchange program were vividly illustrated in a pastoral letter to the faithful, which was issued by Mindszenty on behalf of the Bishops' Conference on September 9, 1947:

> Just as what happened to the Jews during Hitler's time, so now hundreds of thousands if not millions of people are being driven from their centuries-old villages, homes and properties and forced into migration and oppression, having been condemned on the basis of their ancestry and their mother tongue. It is called resettlement. It is claimed to be a major modern means of promoting and ensuring peace, and it is forcibly put into effect and implemented. In reality, however, the very dangerous seed of further unrest is being disseminated.
>
> In Czechoslovakia 700,000 Hungarians are deported or hounded out from the land that has been inhabited by their ancestors in compact communities for almost a thousand years, a region above the Danube that was ceded to the new state only after the previous world war, that is, barely a quarter-century ago. This resettlement – even if it is being carried out in part on the basis of an embarrassing bilateral agreement – is, in fact, [a program of] expulsion, and the circumstances of its realization are, in many instances, very cruel. This is one of the desperately painful Hungarian wounds."[158]

With its dramatic exaggeration of the facts, the pastoral letter equated – not for the first time among such writings on this subject – the resettlement program with the Holocaust. While postwar resettlement was undeniably brutal and inhumane, unlike the Holocaust the aim was never to extinguish human life.

Mindszenty's protests, regardless of their target or the addressee, proved ineffective. His fervency for writing letters diminished somewhat

157. Ibid., 346–348. fol. Letter of Domenico Tardini to József Mindszenty, Vatican City, November 5, 1947.

158. SzEL AC 1954/1947.

after the entry into force of the Paris Peace Treaty (September 15, 1947), but it did not cease altogether. When the "working time" of the Hungarian forced laborers in Sudetenland was extended by a further six months, Mindszenty mentioned the issue in a letter to the new US envoy to Hungary, Selden Chapin. The primate explained to Chapin – as he had done to his predecessor – that the measure reflected the Beneš policy on national minorities, which sought to break up the Hungarian community in southern Slovakia by reintroducing the Hitlerite principle of collective punishment. Moreover the expulsion of the Germans from Sudetenland had created a situation in which people were required to cultivate their lands.[159] On September 25, 1948, having been informed that thirty Catholic priests were about to be resettled, Mindszenty wrote another letter to Prime Minister Lajos Dinnyés. "Through this and other measures – and instead of the minority rights that have been promised in the press for months – the government is consenting to the liquidation of the Hungarian community in Slovakia, to the loss of its leaders, to the complete eradication [of the community], and to a renewed process of re-Slovakization," stated the indefatigable Hungarian primate, whom the left wing already regarded as their enemy.[160] He went on to accuse the leadership of the Hungarian Working People's Party of committing an act of treason: by agreeing to the resettlement of the minorities, the government had betrayed the Hungarian minority in Czechoslovakia. László Rajk, who in the meantime had become Hungarian minister of foreign affairs, proposed that the Council of Ministers declare that Mindszenty "is not entitled to play the role of the country's first knight banneret and is not a competent forum on this issue."[161] On this occasion too, Mindszenty chose to go beyond the Hungarian government: in the summer of 1948, he contacted the (communist) minister of justice in Czechoslovakia, Alexej Čepička,

159. NARA RG 84, Records of the Foreign Service Posts of the Department of State, Hungary, Budapest Legation, GR 1948, Box 167, 840.4. Letter of József Mindszenty to Selden Chapin, US envoy, August 10, 1948.

160. MNL OL M–KS 276. f. 67/214. ő. e. 56–57. fol. Letter of József Mindszenty to Prime Minister Lajos Dinnyés, September 25, 1948.

161. MNL OL XIX–A–83–a/259/a. sz. Minutes of the closed meeting of the Council of Ministers on October 22, 1948.

criticizing the Czechoslovak government's abject failure to make good on its promises regarding freedom of worship.[162]

It would be naive to believe that Mindszenty's protests resulted in the cessation or mitigation of the deportations in Czechoslovakia, the confiscation of properties, and the mass sentencing of citizens by People's Courts. Indeed, the expulsion of ethnic Germans from Hungary to Germany continued until mid-June 1948, while the expulsion of Hungarians from Slovakia to Hungary went on until the end of 1948. Still, when Mindszenty made his cry for help to the Western powers, his appeal clearly had weight: as head of the Hungarian Church, he was able to criticize – as a representative of the universal church – the collective punishment of the Hungarians in Slovakia (and that of the Germans in Hungary) and condemn the Beneš policy of treating the expulsion of people from their native regions as "a national revolutionary goal." Evidently, if the Western democracies had conducted themselves differently at the Paris peace negotiations, the government in Prague might well have eradicated the Hungarian minority community. In the minds of many, Mindszenty's proposal for changes to the Trianon border conjured up Hungary's revisionist endeavors. Indeed, the proposal incensed public opinion in those states which would have been affected by any border changes (above all Czechoslovakia, with its young statehood). Yet the context in which the proposal was made (the violation of the rights of Hungarians) was, ultimately, the only one that afforded the possibility of eliciting sympathy in the West for a defeated country that had fought alongside Nazi Germany until the end.

People and Rights

Mindszenty made his voice heard on many other issues in the field of human rights. It was he who drew the prime minister's attention to the atrocities of Tito's partisans in the Vojvodina region and to the murders and mass deportations affecting the Hungarian minority there. And he did

162. NARA RG 84, Records of the Foreign Service Posts of the Department of State, Hungary, Budapest Legation, Box 167, 1948/814.2–840.4. Letter of József Mindszenty to Alexej Čepička, Czechoslovak minister of justice, July 6, 1948, copy from the US Embassy in Prague.

so at a time when many already knew of these events, but no-one was protesting against them.[163] He reacted with concern to signs that the Soviet army was preparing for a long-term stay in Hungary. Meanwhile, based on complaints made to him, he wrote reports about the situation of the Hungarians in the Carpathian region, on the grievances they had suffered, and on the efforts of the Soviet authorities to stifle church life.[164]

On several occasions, the cardinal spoke out against the discrimination of certain public employees – their placement on the so-called *B list* as part of the "cold terror" – as a means of achieving staff reductions. While there was indisputably a need to rid the public service apparatus of Arrow Cross, Nazi and fascist sympathizers (this being the original goal of the "B list"), the screening procedures targeted not only the real enemies and adversaries of the postwar system, but also the *potential* ones. An avalanche of abuses ensued, and since a person could be declared innocent or guilty as the party saw fit, many innocent public officials lost their jobs while real criminals evaded justice. In connection with the placement of people on the "B list," Mindszenty drew Prime Minister Ferenc Nagy's attention to the real problem of the resurfacing of antisemitism.[165] While Hungary's Jews were never able to regain their pre-war positions in the economy and society, many of them did manage to find employment in the police force, at the People's Courts, and in the bodies that oversaw reparation payments and the crop quota system (the obligatory supply of agricultural produce by peasant farmers). Naturally, the rumor soon spread that the Jews were seeking revenge, a rumor that Mindszenty did not refute. Meanwhile, foreign aid packages specifically targeting Jews gave rise to envy and resentment among the general population. Moreover, many of the country's leftist and liberal politicians had Jewish ancestry. While they themselves had no interest in this ancestry and had long broken away from their religion, in the eyes of the people they were, in spite of their assimilation,

163. PIL 274. f. 7/247. ő. e. 84. fol. Letter of József Mindszenty to Prime Minister Ferenc Nagy, July 17, 1946.

164. PL Processus, V–700/10. Thematic collection, original documents. Note in the margin of the letter on page 163: "It has been sent to the British and US embassies in Prague and in Budapest."

165. Ibid., V–700/16. 474–476. and 482. fol. Letter of József Mindszenty to Prime Minister Ferenc Nagy, August 22, 1946.

"Jewish communists." The Hungarian primate also attributed the reemergence of virulent antisemitism to these factors.

In the summer of 1948, Mindszenty once again mentioned the problem of antisemitism.

> Jewry, if it had conducted itself wisely after 1945, could have rendered the country philosemitic, simply because of the compassion that was felt by the Hungarian people towards the Jews who had been persecuted by Hitlerism in 1944. This is not what happened. Hungarian public life is threaded through and through by Jews and their excessive power. Either the leading politicians are Jews or their wives are. The governing parties, in particular the influential Communist Party, are largely controlled by Jews (Rákosi, Gerő, etc.). All those points in public life that represent power or are suitable for inciting hatred have been covetously occupied by Jewry, especially its youth, in disregard for the future,

the Hungarian primate wrote in a letter to the US envoy to Hungary, Selden Chapin. The text of the letter then read as follows:

> The Church will naturally oppose any individual actions, but it would be desirable that the government of the United States, by way of its sizeable Jewish community, which gave such assistance to Hungarian Jewry at the time of the persecutions and has done so since then, should make the latter [Hungarian Jewry] understand that it should pull back, lest the strings are stretched to the point of breaking.[166]

As Mindszenty saw it, the survival of the nation was threatened by alien elements that sought its destruction, by the Jews who were imposing communism on society and whose arrogance was simply nourishing Hungarian nationalism. Accordingly, with a view to halting the spread of antisemitism, the Hungarian primate recommended that self-restraint be exercised by the country's 100,000 Jews, who mostly resided in Budapest. Whereas he had been the one to protest against the collective punishment

166. NARA RG 84, Records of the Foreign Service Posts of the Department of State, Hungary, Budapest Legation, GR 1948, Box 167, 840.4. Letter of József Mindszenty in Hungarian to Selden Chapin, US envoy to Hungary, July 31, 1948.

of Hungary's ethnic Germans and Slovakia's ethnic Hungarians, he now seemed to be condemning the entire Jewish community on account of the transgressions of a few politicians who had long ago cut off their ties with Judaism. Moreover, he viewed the Jewish population as uniformly pro-communist, whereas in reality most Jews were – similarly to non-Jews – repulsed by communism and fearful of it. He failed to discern that ordinary Jews were supporting the left wing and sometimes even becoming party members either because they perceived the left-wing movement (and not US or British democracy) as the true and credible representative of the struggle against fascism or because – less idealistically – they believed that it would be the leading political force in the future and that opposing it would be disastrous for their livelihoods. Whatever the case, evidently their primary motivation was not a desire to take part in constructing a communist society. Mindszenty's admonitions were unfair, because they ignored such issues as moral responsibility, collective repentance, and complicity and disregarded the failings of Christians. Yet, one can only speak of true repentance when one has already acknowledged one's own sins.

When a reporter for the Viennese newspaper *Welt am Abend* asked the cardinal to state his opinion on the destruction of eight million European Jews – including 600,000 Hungarian-speaking Jews – Mindszenty's immediate response was to correct the exaggerated figures: as far as he knew, in total five million Jews had died in Europe, of whom "only" 400–500,000 had been Hungarian Jews, and several hundred presumed victims had turned up alive...[167] The loss of Jewish lives so interested him that he made serious efforts to calculate the losses, which he resumed in November 1948 while awaiting his arrest. Even today various figures are cited regarding Jewish losses in the Holocaust, and this has nothing to do with philo- or antisemitism or even Holocaust denial. Rather the discrepancies reflect the difficulty of documenting facts and/or the uncertain nature of knowledge in this field. Even so, Mindszenty's reaction is hard to understand. Indeed, it would seem likely that Mindszenty belonged to the school

167. "Besuch bei Ungarns Fürstprimas in Esztergom." *Welt am Abend*, no. 194, June 18, 1947, 4; Gosudarstvennyi Arkhiv Rossiyskoy Federatsii [State Archive of the Russian Federation] (hereafter: GARF) f. 6991. op. 1. delo (file) 78. l. 111. Information on the international Catholic congress in Canada. (Slightly different data but essentially the same content are cited in *Mindszenty József a népbíróság előtt*, 16.)

of thought that was incapable of acknowledging how the silent protests of the Christian Churches had led, ultimately, to a silent complicity. Even in his memoirs, Mindszenty failed to mention pre-war Hungary's anti-Jewish laws, the forced labor servicemen, the murders committed by "royal Hungarian" officers. Like others too, his natural reflex was to shirk responsibility in this area. Indeed, not only did he refuse to admit even token responsibility, but he also identified Jewry with those who were occupying positions of power in the postwar era, particularly in the political police force, which was perceived as the embodiment of terror and persecution.

At the same time, Mindszenty threw the full weight of his authority as primate – without prejudice and judgment – into preventing human rights violations. Almost whenever he spoke, he would emphasize the Church's duty to speak out against violations of God's unwritten (i.e., natural) and written (i.e., revealed) moral laws and to protect anyone whose human rights have been breached, regardless of family background, nationality, religion or social status. Despite all his efforts, he achieved tangible results only in individual cases, with the exception of a decree of the Ministry of Interior that authorized the holding of church services for internees. The resettlement programs, however, were not halted; the internments continued; and the abuses of power became, if anything, more and more frequent. Yet in Hungary and around the world, people knew of the primate's brave stand on behalf of his flock, his fellow Hungarians, and the interests of Catholicism. His integrity and credibility demanded respect and admiration. As the Jesuit Töhötöm Nagy wrote, "the many cowardly people are pleased that someone is being courageous in their place, and this is sufficient to prevent their spiritual collapse. Today the prince primate is keeping the spirit for an entire nation. And people are indeed aware of, and uplifted by, the fact that we have a heroic cardinal."[168] The primate became a representative of the integrity and conscientiousness of the nation. His friends watched him with inner exultation, his enemies with an audible gnashing of teeth. "The man has a wonderful charisma," – these were the words the legitimist Jusztin Baranyay used to describe Mindszenty to Prince Otto von Habsburg. "And this explains why he has become the

168. OSZK Kt. 216. f. 50. ő. e. Töhötöm Nagy's report on the situation of Hungarian Catholicism, Rome, November 12, 1946. In Italian: JTMRL II.1. Copies of the Order's archive material in Rome, Epistolae Variorum 1946–50/1946.

anchor of hope for every Hungarian. As things stand now, we have to believe that as soon as the clock of political free expression strikes, the strongest party will be the one under his auspices. In the eyes of Protestants, a Hungarian prelate has not had such respect and such integrity in four hundred years."[169] At this point, his authority stemmed not only from his position as prelate but also from his personality. Still, he was immediately accused of going beyond his remit and of politicizing whenever he spoke out in response to the political events of the era.

169. ÁBTL 3.1.9. V–700/49. 167. fol. Report, January 17, 1949. Letter of Jusztin Baranyay to Otto von Habsburg, n. d. [1947]

CHAPTER 5

CARDINAL MINDSZENTY,
ARCHBISHOP OF ESZTERGOM (1945–1974)

CHAPTER 5

Frontlines

IN THE CROSSFIRE

In the spring of 1946, the Hungarian Communist Party, having suffered a defeat in the elections, began a systematic offensive to overturn the political balance of power. With the establishment of the Left Bloc on March 5, 1946, it bound to itself both the Social Democratic Party and the National Peasant Party. In this way, the communists were able gradually to consolidate their power and reduce the influence of the Independent Smallholders' Party. The alliance of leftist parties was directed against the political right (principally, the Independent Smallholders' Party) rather than against the churches, but the ramifications of the political power struggle were felt by the Catholic Church as an institution and by Cardinal Mindszenty personally. It was during this period, for instance, that the leftist press shocked its readers with horror stories about reactionary, bomb-making, homosexual, and pedophile priests, whereby the aim was to incite anticlericalism and the scapegoating of priests. An unstoppable avalanche had been triggered. As part of a general campaign against so-called reactionary forces, the authorities ordered searches of Catholic schools and monasteries, resulting in the unveiling of armed "conspiracies" and the unmasking of "assailants" who intended to strike at Soviet soldiers. The gravest instance related to a Franciscan named Szaléz Kis: his alleged incitement to murder Soviet soldiers served as a means both to undermine the Independent Smallholders' Party and to exert control over the Catholic Church. The left wing focused on the responsibility borne by the clergy and on the need for the "provocations" to be met by "consequences."

Protecting Religious Freedom and the Catholic Church
The Politics of Grievance

Some Communist Party members – those with limited experience of a tactical approach to politics – became convinced very early on (in 1946) that the domestic political situation was favorable to a general attack on the Catholic Church. During this period, Mátyás Rákosi was the one who held back his comrades, as the following shows:

> One cannot chase two hares... Clerical reaction has altered its tactics. Mindszenty's provocative speeches and pastoral letters have now ceased, because the Church is afraid that if it tightens the string too much, it will snap. [...] The systematic struggle against the Church cannot be launched in a haphazard fashion. Everyone knows what kind of force we are up against. A fight is unavoidable, but the timing of its commencement is an important political issue, and it should be initiated when the relative balance of power [between the communists and the Church] is favorable. If it [the Church] conducts itself in an unruly manner, we shall hit it on the nose.[1]

Cardinal Mindszenty, however, did become "unruly," particularly when he saw challenges to Catholic morality and natural law. Assessing the domestic political situation – the establishment of the Left Bloc, the weakening of the governing coalition, and the exposure of "conspiratorial" clergymen – he concluded that a culture war had begun in Hungary, a struggle that was accompanied by moral degeneration. Morality in life was always close to Mindszenty's heart. Indeed, he regarded children born out of wedlock as the fruits of moral decay, branding Act XXIX of 1946 on the

1. PIL 274. f. 2/34. ő. e. 55–56. fol. Shorthand minutes of the meeting of the HCP CL meeting on May 17, 1946. Mátyás Rákosi's reply to questions.

legal equality of such children as a measure that would "bring polygamy into the family, as well as the trashing of loving relationships."[2] He complained about excessively libertine attitudes, "in late 1945 and early 1946, at the time of the greatest paper shortage, practically the entire Hungarian press delved into the love-making and tasteless stories of Mussolini, Hitler and their associates," while the supply of paper was barely sufficient or insufficient for the Catholic newspapers.

To achieve his goal of establishing a broader framework for the practice of religious belief, Mindszenty needed to maintain contact with the government. Such contact was also a prerequisite for the continued existence of the Catholic dailies and for Catholic political action and freedom of association. Mindszenty had, incidentally, been socialized in a world accustomed to the centuries-old alliance of "throne and altar." In this world, a man who became a bishop was due glory and power on account of his status alone. This traditional relationship soon fell apart after the momentous events of 1945. If we remove the conservative veil from Mindszenty's declarations and statements (his claims to the status of knight banneret, public dignitary, etc.) and discount the raw emotions of a man who has been offended, we see his vision of an autonomous, yet hierarchically structured Church which would be independent of the state while operating in partnership with it. According to this vision, the clergy were to play the leading role in the Church.[3] True, this image of the Church adheres to the mores of the pre-Vatican II era. Even so, within this triumphalist ecclesiastical model, there was also sensitivity on social issues.

On June 19, 1946, Cardinal Mindszenty, in a protest letter addressed to Prime Minister Ferenc Nagy, summarized the complaints and grievances of the Catholic Church: the absence of contact with Rome; the refusal to grant a license to a Catholic political party and to a Catholic political daily; the hurdles placed in front of Catholic associations; unethical attacks by the press against the pope and against prelates and clerics in general; the failure to pay compensation to the Church after the land reform program; the weakening of ecclesiastical autonomy; the unjust imprisonment

2. PL Mm. 45. d. [Mindszenty József:] Typed document entitled "Against the Moral Teachings of the Church." (The following quotation is also from there – the author.)

3. András Fejérdy, "Mindszenty József szellemi portréja," *Kommentár* [Commentary] 1, no. 4 (2006): 43.

of priests and monks; and the growing number of assaults. He criticized the system of spies in churches, the failure to ensure Catholics were employed in proportion to their share of the population, and the (politically-motivated) obstructionism of the state authorities, which often prevented charitable work and placed restrictions on Sunday processions. Evidently, the political left was not the only group responsible for such measures, as none of the parties in the governing coalition wished to see the establishment of a party that would operate on ideological grounds or that of a Catholic daily. On other matters, each statement of the Hungarian primate was based essentially on facts, but his acerbic style led even those who sympathized with his arguments to question his politics of grievance. For instance, Béla Varga, a Catholic priest who had been elevated to the position of Speaker of the National Assembly, spoke, in a private conversation, of the "prince primate jumping about."[4] In his reply to Cardinal Mindszenty's letter, dated July 9, Prime Minister Ferenc Nagy referred to his own political powerlessness: it would be up to the Allied Control Commission to assess the listed grievances.[5]

The unresolved problems merely accentuated feelings of grievance. In the October 6, 1946 issue of *Új Ember* (New Man), a sermon by Mindszenty was published. In the sermon, the Hungarian primate drew a contrast between the followers of Saint Gerard (Hungarian: Gellért), the first bishop of Csanád, and the murderous Magyar heathens. Then, having transposed the story onto the present, he juxtaposed his own camp of supporters with that of "the murderers and arsonists." He argued that "those men" should not even be approached, for to do so "would demean us." Mindszenty's simple and ruthless exposition of the truth made him extraordinarily popular among ordinary people. Owing to his strong character, Hungarian Catholicism came to have the strongest profile in the whole of Central Europe – apart from Poland. At the same time, Mindszenty failed to anticipate, or was simply indifferent to, the potential negative impact of his outspoken and scoffing manner on the Church. Moreover many priests, having heard his sermons, began preaching in a similar style and with exaggerated rhetoric. Thus, in late October 1946, the authorities arrested

4. PL Processus, V–700/32. 87. fol. Statement by János Kóródy-Katona, June 21, 1946.
5. Beke, *A magyar katolikus püspökkari 1945–1948*, 105 and 113.

a canon who had stated in a sermon that he saw no difference between Hitler and Stalin. By the end of August 1946, 111 priests had been placed in custody or under police supervision. Other than protest at their detention, Mindszenty could do little for these men.[6]

The rapid deterioration in relations with the occupying forces and with the domestic political left wing had long-term consequences. In 1945, the Soviet military administration encountered a dynamic and well-organized Church in Hungary. At the time, it was in the Soviet Union's interest to be acknowledged as a European negotiating partner. For this reason, it opted to pursue a policy of tolerance towards European traditions, first among which was religion. For tactical reasons, therefore, no churches were closed in Hungary, no ban was imposed on religious education, and Catholic schools were allowed to remain open. Funding was even made available for the restoration of church buildings. None of this impressed Mindszenty. Indeed, the receipt, as an act of mercy, of something that was, in his view, an acquired right, merely accentuated his feelings of grievance. For a Church accustomed to working in partnership with the government, the radical social and economic transformations meant a clear restriction of its influence. Cardinal Mindszenty thus reacted with measures designed to protect the faith and the Church. The other side, however, regarded these measures as the politics of grievance.

The Holy See viewed Mindszenty as a useful obstacle to the spread of communism in East Central Europe. Even so, its support for the Hungarian prelate was far less robust than was implied by Mindszenty or perceived by the Soviet authorities and the leftist parties in Hungary. The various currents of opinion have yet to be described in full, but many documents show that in 1945–1946 several senior Vatican figures favored a policy of compromise and disagreed with the Hungarian primate on Europe's future course. Töhötöm Nagy even wrote that by the second

6. MNL OL XIX–A–1–e–VI/3–1901/46. Margit Slachta's report for Prime Minister Ferenc Nagy about detained priests, August 29, 1946. – According to Russian researchers, only 200 Catholic ecclesiastical persons were arrested in the people's democracies between 1946 and 1953: 45 in Poland; 48 in Czechoslovakia, 24 in Hungary, 16 in Yugoslavia, 10 in Romania, 9 in China, 7 in Albania, 6 in Bulgaria, 1 in North Korea (GARF f. 6991. op. 3. delo (file) 134. l. 1–14. A. Report of A. Polianskiy, the chairman of the Council for Religious Affairs working alongside the Council of Ministers of the Soviet Union, June 15, 1956).

half of 1945, Vatican officials had accepted the need for a *modus vivendi* with the Soviet Union. Indeed, the pope himself had authorized him to contact Boris Pavlovich Osokin, the deputy political advisor to the ACC, who was reputed to be the "head" of the NKVD in Central Europe.[7] Evidently, despite criticism of Mindszenty's approach, no-one at the Vatican doubted that he was the man to decide in concrete situations. The Vatican took a similar stance in its dealings with Beran in Czechoslovakia, with Áron Márton in Transylvania, and with Wyszyński in Poland, each of whom responded differently to similar issues. The government in Moscow, however, could not comprehend such local "sovereignty": the aforementioned Osokin stated on several occasions that in his view Mindszenty was the Vatican's vanguard soldier, a man who was following instructions issued in Rome. Osokin also believed that Mindszenty would portray the return of the nunciatura to Hungary as his own triumph, and so this advantage had to be denied him.[8]

Many Hungarian Catholics viewed Cardinal Mindszenty's approach as just one of several possible options. Some took the view that a sensible *modus vivendi* should be sought in place of confrontation. They argued for a proper assessment of the opportunities for coexistence, thereby acknowledging the likelihood of a long-term Soviet presence in Central Europe. Mindszenty, however, remained determinedly opposed to a policy of placating the Soviets. In his view, rather than reflect foresight or tactical strategy, such a policy amounted to being in league with a hated adversary. When, on the tenth anniversary of the foundation of the Catholic Agrarian Youth League, a spokesman for the Soviet Antifascist Youth Committee also spoke, Mindszenty's patience broke. He demanded an explanation for what he perceived to have been a grave error. In a long letter, the two Jesuit leaders of the Association explained that for the sake of preserving values,

7. OSZK Kt. 216. f. 19. ő. e. 300–303. fol., Diary of Töhötöm Nagy S. J., Rome, October 23, 1945; Ibid., 48. ő. e. 10. fol. "Report on the achievements of my second stay in Rome (October 11 – November 9, 1945)" November 21, 1945, with the signature "Alessandro" [= Töhötöm Nagy] for Prince Primate József Mindszenty.

8. OSZK Kt. 216. f. 20. ő. e. 21. fol. Memorandum on the talks between the Jesuit Töhötöm Nagy and B. P. Osokin (Embassy counsel), September 6, 1946. (Osokin was detained – probably while still in Budapest – transported to the Soviet Union and murdered by Soviet secret servicemen. See Zamertsev, Ivan Terentevich: *Cherez gody i rasstoyaniya*. http://militera.lib.ru/memo/russian/zamertsev_it/index.html.)

they were willing to cooperate in social and cultural fields with other associations and bodies but would not make concessions on ideological issues.[9] In their view, this was the only option, if the greater evil – the closure of the vibrant Catholic associations – was to be avoided. Mindszenty rejected such arguments and called the contents of the letter "scandalous." Thereafter he ostracized both Jenő Kerkai, who had once been his pupil and confidential advisor, and Töhötöm Nagy, the Jesuit who had nominated Mindszenty for the post of prince primate. Yet, for the good of the Catholic Church, the two approaches should have been employed concurrently, as there was a strong argument for both.

The Closure of the Catholic Associations

In the end, it was Interior Minister László Rajk – rather than Mindszenty – who ordered the closure of the uniquely successful Catholic Agrarian Youth League. He did so after an incident on June 17, 1946, when someone fired shots from a Budapest rooftop at Soviet soldiers in the street below. Two Soviet officers were killed and several others were wounded in the attack, which negatively impacted on Hungary's image abroad. According to the official version of events, which was altered several times, when investigators arrived at the scene, all they could find was the charcoaled corpse of the suicide "attacker" in an attic. Mysteriously, the suspect sniper's Catholic Agrarian Youth League membership card had mysteriously survived the inferno. Soviet retaliation for the death of the Soviet officers came swiftly. On June 28, 1946, Lieutenant-General Sviridov, executive chairman of the ACC, demanded the dissolution of all "pro-fascist" youth organizations.[10] The government chose to concede: within a period of a few weeks and beginning on July 4, 1946, it dissolved 1,500 religious associations and organizations, seizing their premises, assets and records. The

9. Nagy, *Jezsuiták és szabadkőművesek*, 234–50.

10. Kisgazda Örökség és Levéltár Alapítvány [Foundation of Smallholders and Archives] 285. f. 6/160. ő. e. 7–10. fol. – According to contemporary Soviet reports, there were 26 attacks against Soviet soldiers in Hungary at this time, while 22 similar attacks were recorded in the Soviet occupation zone in Austria. Rossiiskii Gosudarstvennyi Arkhiv Sotsial'no-politicheskoi Istorii [Russian State Archive of Socio-Political History] (hereafter: RGASPI) f. 17. op. 128. delo (file) 116. l. 145.

dissolution struck a blow at the Church's influence in Hungarian society and public life, while also giving an impetus to leftist associations.

On July 10, 1946, Mindszenty wrote anew to the Allied Control Commission. He wrote in a wise and considered manner that contrasted with the style of his earlier letters.[11] His apparent concern was the general attack demanded by Lieutenant-General Sviridov on the institutions of the Catholic Church rather than, specifically, the dissolution of the Catholic Agrarian Youth League. Still, this time the cardinal's fury paid off: on June 16, 1946, the British government sent a note – at the time this was a rare event – to the Soviet commander of the ACC expressing disagreement with the actions of the Soviet side. Four days later the US government dispatched a note to the Soviet government in which it argued that the reparation policy pursued in Hungary was detrimental to the country's reconstruction and the associated economic opportunities.[12] This was the first significant disagreement in Hungary between the Western powers and the Soviet Union. For Mindszenty, the British and US notes reaffirmed his belief in the necessity of resistance. On July 22, 1946, as the "head of the accused Catholic Church in Hungary," he sent a letter of protest, unprecedented in its vehemence, to Minister of Foreign Affairs János Gyöngyösi. Demanding the annulment of all previous measures, he made the following ultimatum: if his demands were rejected, he would bring the entire matter to the world's attention. Moreover, he would have no qualms about excommunicating those who had drafted and were implementing the decree.[13] Such a response would have been uniquely harsh.

On July 26, the prime minister soberly replied to the cardinal's letter. With unusual frankness, he stated that in his view the attack on the Soviet

11. Mindszenty sent the letter to the US Legation on July 25, 1946, to which he attached a copy of the letter (dated July 22) that he had received from the Hungarian minister of foreign affairs: NARA RG 84, Records of the Foreign Service Posts of the Department of State, Hungary, Budapest Legation, GR 1946, Box 103, 840.4.

12. RGASPI f. 17. op. 128. delo (file) 125. l. 26–32. Report of Lieutenant-Colonel V. Mudrikov on political events in Hungary, August 8, 1946. Published in Lajos Izsák and Miklós Kun, eds., *Moszkvának jelentjük: Titkos dokumentumok 1944–1948* (Budapest: Századvég, 1994), 114.

13. PIL 274. f. 7/247. ő. e. 73–76. fol. József Mindszenty's letter to Minister of Foreign Affairs János Gyöngyösi, July 22, 1946. For a copy of the letter, see: NARA RG 84, Records of the Foreign Service Posts of the Department of State, Hungary, Budapest Legation, GR 1946, Box 103, 840.4.

soldiers had served merely as a pretext for action against the Catholic Church, which was, in reality, the result of a process and a consequence of the Hungarian primate's anti-Soviet stance and his blatant opposition to official Hungarian foreign policy. The Soviets' distrust of Mindszenty dated back to the pastoral letter he had issued at the time of the election. As the prime minister explained, "Since that time, they have viewed with suspicion everything done by the clergy or by the Catholic associations."[14] There was, therefore, a causal relationship between the antagonistic gestures of the Catholic Church and the measures taken against it. The prime minister concluded his letter by emphasizing that the dissolved associations would, in all likelihood, be permitted to reconstitute themselves under new leaderships. Moreover, there were no plans to close down other Catholic associations, which would only be subject to closure where there were specific objections.

Mindszenty's response to the prime minister's letter came within a few days. He summarized once again the grievances suffered by the Church, insisting that the failing relationship between church and state was due to the other side's actions rather than to his electoral letter or to any other of his endeavors. In his view, the Catholic Church had been forced to defend itself. The internment, harassment, and torture of clergy could not be blamed on him, because these were the intimidating and retaliatory measures of the political police. Finally, he firmly rejected the accusation that the church had somehow instigated or organized the murder of the Soviet soldiers on Teréz Boulevard in Budapest. Despite his various complaints and objections, Cardinal Mindszenty still would not exclude the possibility of reconciliation and concluded his letter amicably as follows: "While having no choice but to establish these facts, I think with understanding about the government's difficult situation and about the efforts it is making."[15] Mindszenty's denial of the detrimental and provocative effect of his pastoral letter on the elections can hardly have been a sincere one, for several members of the Bishops' Conference had warned him in advance of the dangers his letter would unleash. On account of his

14. Ibid., 65–68. fol. Letter of Ferenc Nagy to József Mindszenty, July 26, 1946.

15. PL Processus, V-700/10A. 572–576. fol. Letter of József Mindszenty to Prime Minister Ferenc Nagy, July 31, 1946.

provocative anti-Russian stance, the Soviets had opted to discount the Hungarian primate and regard him as their adversary.

Mindszenty's ultimatum and the metaphorical tightening of the string were given coverage in the reports of diplomats. The head of the British Mission deeply regretted that in such grave times the Hungarian primate's tactical and strategic sense was so lacking. In the British diplomat's view, Mindszenty's combative approach and his "constant goading" might well accelerate Russian efforts to separate church and state.[16] The diplomat was claiming nothing less than that Mindszenty's personality and conduct were serving as a pretext for restrictions on the Church in excess of what might otherwise have happened as part of the communist takeover. US Envoy Schoenfeld reached a similar conclusion. In his view, the cardinal was incapable of understanding the political realities in Hungary.[17] Ultimately, however, Mindszenty's efforts were not entirely fruitless: Lieutenant-General Sviridov, in his capacity as deputy chairman of the ACC, granted authorization – under certain conditions – for the operation of some associations. Accordingly, the Catholic Agrarian Youth League could resume its activities under the new name of Catholic Peasant Youth League. Even so, the new organization was a mere shadow of its predecessor. Overall, the effect of the hostile official measures was to paralyze civil society.

In a dramatic development, in September 1946, many of the Catholic priests and students who had been detained in the spring or early summer on charges of armed conspiracy against the Soviet army or of the murder of Soviet soldiers, were sentenced to death or to forced labor (7–10 years of hard labor). The accused had pleaded not guilty, and the investigators had failed to produce conclusive evidence of their guilt. Soon, however, the real reason for the punishment of the priests and students became

16. "It is highly regrettable that the Leader of the Roman Catholic Church in Hungary at this time should have so little sense of tactics and of statesmanship. By his actions he is doing grievous harm to his flock and to the Hungarian people. Events of the last few days suggest that the Russians are going slow, at any rate for the time being, but nothing seems more likely to make them turn the heat on again than the constant goading which they are receiving from the prince primate." TNA FO Religious affairs: proposal to accredit Vatican representative to Hungary: position of prince primate, Cardinal Mindszenty, archbishop of Esztergom: Soviet reactions. Code 21 File 436, FO 371/59014, 1946, 11506/436/21. Report of A. K. Helm, head of the British Political Mission in Budapest, July 30, 1946.

17. MNL OL XX–10–k LÜ PO 18.300/1989. US archival sources. H. F. Arthur Schoenfeld's proposal no. 1829, August 13, 1946.

clear: their refusal to give their support to communism. In a noteworthy decision, the People's Prosecutor's Office in Budapest released the Hungarian citizens to the Soviet authorities. This action violated a clause in the armistice agreement that had made it incumbent upon the Hungarian authorities to hear the cases of such defendants. József Mindszenty's intervention in the matter bore no fruit,[18] as he was not on good terms with any influential Soviet politicians or military officers. Indeed, he found himself in a vacuum, and there was nothing that he could build upon other than his own self-indignation. Prior to this period, a consecrated priest had never been put to death in Hungary. Father Szaléz Kis was the first cleric to be executed at Sopronkőhida. For some decades, however, no-one knew for certain that the priest had been executed.

Assistance from Abroad and Internal Struggles

For the resolution of Hungary's domestic problems and a successful outcome to the peace negotiations, Mindszenty counted first and foremost on assistance and support from the Americans. The US diplomatic representation in Hungary, however, was only moderately supportive of the cardinal's activities. On December 27, 1946, Envoy Schoenfeld – in response to several letters he had received from Mindszenty – rejected Mindszenty's request for US intervention:

> In this connection you are of course aware of my Government's long-standing policy of non-interference in the internal affairs of other nations. This policy has proven over a long period of time and through many trying situations the best guarantee of spontaneous, vigorous and genuine democratic development. It will be clear to Your Eminence that it necessarily precludes action by this Legation which could properly be construed as interference in Hungarian domestic affairs or which lies outside the normal functions of diplomatic missions.[19]

18. NARA RG 84, Records of the Foreign Service Posts of the Department of State, US Legation, Hungary, Budapest, GR 1946–63, Box 4, 1947 – 840.4. Franklin C. Gowen's report no. A-1, Vatican City, January 8, 1947.

19. MNL OL XX–10–k LÜ PO 18.300/1989. US archival sources. Annex to the US Legation dispatch no. 2408 of January 8, 1947.

Mindszenty found Schoenfeld's reply inadequate. He had expected far more support from the world's democracies and did not believe that Hungary could be a strategic irrelevance for the postwar foreign policy of the United States. For the cardinal, the envoy's reply was acceptable under only one set of circumstances: if it was merely a mask and a gesture to the outside world; and he could otherwise be trusted. In a further letter, Mindszenty demanded to know whether the promises made by the British and Americans would be kept:

> Thinking back to 1942–44 when we were promised democracy rather than Siberia and Russian and Marxist prisons in Hungary, I request your Excellency, Envoy and Minister, to take action to give effect to the human rights that have been guaranteed by the Allied powers and to bring an end to torture and to the constant persecution of people."[20]

Among Mindszenty's proposals for effective action to be taken by the Western democracies was a large increase in the number of soldiers in the British and US military contingents.[21] The cardinal's stance, which ignored both Yalta and Potsdam, was an illusion, as was also his expectation that the United States and its Western allies would unreservedly accept his opinion – or that of anyone who, even if persecuted by the Arrow Cross, had been tied in any way to the prewar regime. His disappointment was all the greater when, in Paris on February 10, 1947, the Allied Powers signed the peace treaty with the Republic of Hungary.

In response to this decision by the great powers, the only sensible course of action would have been one of resignation. Mindszenty, however, chose to hold a devotional session for the nation at Saint Stephen's Basilica. With heightened pathos he spoke of the country's dismemberment, arguing that the Paris Peace Treaty was even more serious than had been the Treaty of Trianon (1920) after World War I. The only hope for reconciliation was Jesus Christ himself, as the unfailing source of truth. In his

20. NARA RG 84, Records of the Foreign Service Posts of the Department of State, US Legation, Hungary, GR 1946–63, Box 4, 1947 – 840.4. József Mindszenty's letter of January 6, 1947 to H. F. Arthur Schoenfeld.

21. PL Processus, V–700/1. 129. fol. Interrogation report of the suspect, January 11, 1949, including text of József Mindszenty's letter of May 4, 1946 to the US and British envoys.

search for the causes of the calamity, he soon stumbled upon his favorite analogy: the dichotomy of sin and punishment. The Hungarian people had neglected the divine laws, so they were now atoning for their transgressions and walking the way of Calvary.[22]

Towards a better understanding of Mindszenty's disappointment, it is worth outlining his efforts to secure a more advantageous peace for Hungary. On July 22, 1946 – a week before the commencement of the peace conference in Paris – he wrote to the British, American, and Soviet ministers of foreign affairs, appealing for them "to seek the truth."[23] In the letter, he not only pointed to the injustices of the national boundaries but also requested the protection of human rights throughout the territory of the former Kingdom of Hungary. The three addressees received the primate's letter, but none of them reacted in substance. Soviet Minister of Foreign Affairs Molotov simply wrote a little note to himself on it: "Оставить без ответа" (Leave unanswered).[24] The archives also contain a draft letter that Mindszenty intended to send to the US president and to George VI of England with a view to preventing "a repetition of the mistakes of the Treaty of Trianon."[25] Yet, as at the time of the Trianon decision, so also now the principle of the stability of the nation-states outweighed the historical factor (the 1000-year history of Greater Hungary). The great powers decided in favor of Hungary on just one issue: they prohibited the government of Czechoslovakia from unilaterally expelling the Hungarians residing in a contiguous area in southern Slovakia. The reaction in Hungary to the peace treaty was one of dismay. Even so, the Hungarian government opted to sign the treaty in the hope of a swift end to the Soviet occupation, which would allow Hungary to become a European state with full rights. Several months later, it became evident that, contrary to initial expectations, the Soviet troops were to remain in Hungary in order to secure the supply route to the military divisions stationed in Austria. For Hungary, this dispelled all remaining hopes linked to the peace treaty, and the Soviet occupation was from this moment increasingly seen as a permanent feature

22. *Magyar Kurír* 37, second edition of February 11, 1947.

23. Beke, *A magyar katolikus püspökkari 1945–1948*, 130.

24. AVP RF f. 06. op. 8. papka (paper folder) 27. delo (file) 420. l. 26. Cited in Galina P. Muraskova, "Kak i gde reshalas' sud'ba vengerskogo men'shinstva v Slovakii," Manuscript.

25. PL Processus, V–700/19. 223–224. fol. Typed draft with Mindszenty's corrections.

of the postwar era. And there was no question as to which political forces would gain advantage from the Soviet military presence.

The country was just beginning to recover from the shock of the Paris Peace Treaty when a new chapter in the policy of domestic criminalization opened: the members of a harmless secret society – the Hungarian Community – were accused and found guilty of "conspiring against the republic." In the course of this prototype show trial, many activist supporters of the governing Independent Smallholders' Party were branded as accomplices. In this way, the crushing of the largest political party continued. On February 25, 1947, the Soviets forcibly took away and deported to Siberia the general secretary of the Independent Smallholders' Party, Béla Kovács. (His release did not come until the spring of 1956.) If Hungarian society had not been sobered by the terms of the peace treaty, this event certainly had such an effect. If even a member of Parliament with parliamentary immunity was unsafe, then what should others expect? The threat was far from being based on a delusion. In connection with the "conspiracy," the authorities detained around 260 people.

Despite such disappointments, Mindszenty's faith in US diplomacy was undented, in part because of the Truman doctrine, which promised political assistance for countries struggling against communism. On June 12, 1947, József Mindszenty – "on account of the rights of the prince primate stretching back 950 years" – candidly requested the US president to make known his country's plan for Hungary, which had suffered so much both in war and peace and had experienced so many crises. His description of the situation was naturalistic, detailed, and accurate, even if somewhat overdramatic:

> In the prison of Hungary there are no civil rights. Freedom of speech, of the press, and of association are lacking, as is also equality before the law. Benefitting from foreign weapons, a small section of society rules with terror and fury. Everything is characterized by the following slogan: he who is against the communists is an opponent of democracy. There is no freedom of religion.[26]

26. ÁBTL 3.1.9. V–700. 151., 155. and 162. fol. Letter of József Mindszenty to US President Truman, June 12, 1947.

He outlined the government crisis in Hungary and requested that American soldiers monitor the upcoming elections. In his show trial, these words were interpreted as a request for military intervention rather than as a means to ensure the integrity of the elections. Moreover, in the end, the letter, which Mindszenty always referred to as no more than a "draft," was not sent. Thus it cannot be found even in the otherwise rich and precisely archived Truman Library. Not only have researchers failed to find the letter in the US archives, but also, on March 5, 1990, the US State Department officially informed Hungary's Ministry of Foreign Affairs that it has no copy of the letter.[27]

BATTLE AXE AND PEACE PIPE – THE EVENTS OF 1947

While Mindszenty – based on his appearances and actions – may seem to have been unskilled or inept in diplomacy, it should be acknowledged that, in spite of his stubbornness, he was perceptive enough to understand that a kind of political duality characterized the government in Hungary in the post-1945 era. On the one hand, political parties could freely organize themselves, elections were held, a broad diversity of opinions could be heard in Parliament, and ordinary people could converse about politics in smoke-filled cafes. While still in its early stages, a Western-type civil democracy was steadily being constructed, whose playing rules determined, on the surface at least, the functioning of the system. At the same time, however, Hungarians were asking: Who truly holds power? Was it the Independent Smallholders' Party, with its absolute parliamentary majority (the result of general and secret elections), or the Hungarian Communist Party, which enjoyed the support of the occupation forces and was gradually expropriating executive power? Mindszenty had no faith in the slick slogans, because they stemmed from the communist "atheists and Soviet lackeys," whom he completely distrusted. Equipped with his knowledge of Hungarian historical traditions and drawing strength from his faith in God, he struggled against abuses of power and moral decline. At the same time, he was distrustful of the bourgeois parties. He doubted the ability of politicians in those parties – aside from a few notable exceptions – to defend the national

27. MNL OL XX–10–k LÜ PO 18.300/1989. Letter of John R. Crook, foreign affairs counsel, to the consul, Pál Éliás, March 5, 1990.

interest, given their willingness to enter a coalition with the communists. The events of 1947 merely strengthened his views in this field.

A Proposal for Voluntary Religious Education

Until 1948, Hungarian law did not question the legality of church schools (schools founded and/or maintained by one of the denominations). Such schools had been around for centuries. The Catholic Church had founded schools as early as the sixteenth century, while other denominations had begun to do so later on. In the postwar period, the main task for the Hungarian government in the field of education was the introduction of compulsory primary education (grades 1 to 8), a measure perceived as part of the effort to modernize the country. Universal primary education also served the government's aim of ensuring equal opportunity as well as other political goals. Alongside the transformation of the institutional structure, there were also changes in the content of education.

The new system could not be implemented overnight. In 1946, there were in Hungary as few as 816 state elementary schools (barely more than ten percent of the total number of primary schools). The government viewed the educational quality of church schools as poor and their teaching methods as outdated. It contrasted their performance with the high educational standards and modern teaching methods of the state schools.[28] In October 1945, József Mindszenty protested to the prime minister about the introduction of eight-grade elementary schools, citing the absence of the necessary conditions. In his view, the measure violated the autonomy of the churches and their right to maintain and operate schools. He suspected that the reforms were merely a precursor to the introduction of a uniform system of state schools. His suspicions proved correct: the government's program for universal compulsory primary education struck first at the role of the churches as maintainers of schools.

At the Third Congress of the Hungarian Communist Party, General Secretary Mátyás Rákosi told his comrades that, as the next step in the fight against reactionary forces, the problem of compulsory religious

28. For education policy, see Éva Kovács, "*A magyar közoktatásügy története 1945 és 1956 között (A magyar közoktatás-politika ideológiai változásai)*," (PhD thesis, Faculty of Humanities, ELTE, Budapest, 2003).

education was to be "resolved."[29] In spring 1947, the issue of voluntary religious instruction increasingly gave rise to tensions between church and state. Purportedly, the Independent Smallholders' Party – rather than the communists – wished to make religious instruction voluntary. On March 6, 1947, the coalition parties came to an agreement on three issues: the merger of small village schools with multi-grade teaching; the nationalization of school textbook publishing and the publication of standard and uniform textbooks; and the introduction of voluntary religious education (in place of compulsory classes) in connection with the freedom of conscience and religion guaranteed in Act I of 1946.[30] In combination, the three measures – had they been imposed – would have amounted to the nationalization of church schools. Cardinal Mindszenty stressed, therefore, that he would never authorize the use of state textbooks in church schools and would oppose the educational reforms.[31]

Minister of Culture Dezső Keresztury, a member of the National Peasant Party, was ill-prepared to implement the coalition's proposal on state textbooks and the introduction of universal primary education. Consequently, on March 14, 1947, he resigned (this was not his first resignation, but this time it seemed to be a final decision). His replacement as minister was the ethnographer Gyula Ortutay, a member of the Independent Smallholders' Party who was renowned for his radical and centralizing tendencies. He summed up his educational policy in ten points, whereby the main trend was clearly directed at eradicating the role of the churches in the public education sector. For this reason, and although voluntary religious education was evidently a modern approach and, indeed, a requirement for freedom of conscience, none of the churches was prepared to make any concessions in this area. For his part, Mindszenty urged faithful Catholics to avoid being misled by anyone and to maintain their firm support for compulsory religious education.[32] Soon the offices

29. PIL 274. f. 1/12. ő. e. Mátyás Rákosi's speeches at the Third Congress of the Hungarian Communist Party. September 29, 1946.

30. Ibid., 7/161. ő. e. Memorandum on the inter-party conference, March 6, 1947.

31. Archives du Ministères des Affaires étrangères (Paris) Archives diplomatiques (hereafter: AMAE AD) Série: Europe, 1944–1949, sous-série: Hongrie, dossier 16, Politique intérieure, Sept. 1946–Août 1947. Report no. 27/EU of Henry Gauquié, French legate in Budapest, [date of arrival] February 4, 1947.

32. PL 3020/1947. Pastoral letter of Primate József Mindszenty, March 13, 1947.

of national politicians were being swamped by thousands of protest letters and telegrams. On March 20–21, 1947, university and high school students protested in Szeged against the introduction of voluntary religious education. For the first time in postwar Hungary, the police used water cannons to disperse the crowd.[33] On March 29, Mindszenty protested on behalf of the Bishops' Conference.[34] He sent a copy of his protest letter, which criticized the entire system, to the US envoy.[35] Elementary and high school teachers of religious education had their pupils write "letters of loyalty" to Cardinal Mindszenty. Various meetings and mission days and weeks were held, with the Hungarian primate in attendance at some of them. On April 12, all fourteen members of the Bishops' Conference requested, in a letter sent to Prime Minister Ferenc Nagy, that the issue of voluntary religious instruction be taken off the agenda. They suggested that the issue be reexamined as part of the "*modus vivendi*" talks with the Vatican.[36] In response to the government's church policy measures, the Bishops' Conference underlined that the proposed measures affected general ecclesiastical law. For this reason, under the terms of canon law, they were a matter for the Apostolic Holy See.

The joint and vehement protests from the churches came as a surprise to the country's politicians. According to a report dispatched to Moscow,

> the Hungarian Catholic Church is one of Europe's best organized churches. Hungarian Catholics are the most fanatic and they are very united. A majority of women in rural areas are very much under their influence. The Catholic Church is a strong force, which has clashed with the communists. For the time being, the Communist Party has not found a way to fight against them.[37]

33. *Magyar Kurír* 37, third edition of March 21, 1947; *Új Ember* 3, no. 13, March 30, 1947, 4.

34. PL Processus, V–700/13. 20. fol. Letter of József Mindszenty to Prime Minister Ferenc Nagy, March 29, 1947.

35. NARA RG 84, Records of the Foreign Service Posts of the Department of State, Hungary, US Legation, GR 1946–63, Box 4, 1947 – 840.4. Letter of József Mindszenty to H. F. Arthur Schoenfeld, March 24, 1947.

36. MNL OL XIX–A–1–e–VI/3–894. Ferenc Nagy sent a copy of the Bishops' Conference's letter no. 313/1947 to Minister of State Mátyás Rákosi.

37. Memorandum of G. J. Korotkevich of the Foreign Affairs Department of the CPSU CC on a conversation with V. P. Sviridov, deputy head of the ACC. Budapest, early April 1947, in Volokitina et al., *Vostochnaja Evropa*, vol. 1, 605.

Furthermore, public opinion had been only partially persuaded that the Smallholders, rather than the Communist Party, were seeking the introduction of voluntary religious education. The Communist Party rapidly distanced itself from the unpopular initiative and refused to take responsibility for it. Rather, it pretended now to be a friend of the Catholic Church. This trend was particularly strong in Nógrád County, where, at the Easter resurrection procession, the district secretary of the Communist Party carried the crucifix, while local miners guarded the holy grave in the church. All of this had a significant effect: the priests "sat down, after the procession, with the miners for a glass of wine, expressing their hope that the miners would turn with greater courage to the county committee with a view to arranging for the repair of the church."[38] In several places, the local branch organizations of the Communist Party offered their support to church renovation projects.

The government's drive to make religious education voluntary had a detrimental effect on local initiatives aimed at reconciliation. Evidently, action at a higher level was needed in order to resolve the relationship between church and state in the long term. The solution appeared to be a direct agreement – or concordat – between the Hungarian state and the Holy See. With the agreement of the Hungarian prime minister and the party leaders, László Tóth, chancellor of the University of Szeged, traveled to Rome as a semi-official representative of the Hungarian government – the first in the postwar era. Originally, his task was to negotiate on the introduction of voluntary religious instruction. Mindszenty, however, "undermined" Tóth's original assignment in a letter sent to the pope.[39] Accordingly, by the time the university chancellor arrived in Rome, his mission had been altered: his task now was to acquire a statement from the Holy See recognizing the results of the Hungarian government's postwar reconstruction efforts. This statement too he failed to obtain,[40] for such a document would have amounted to the condemnation of Cardinal Mindszenty's stance, which the Holy See wished to avoid. In a report issued

38. PIL 1/16. ő. e. 69. fol. Second National Conference of HCP functionaries, April 12–13, 1947.

39. ÁBTL 3.1.9. V–700/13. 22. fol. Letter of József Mindszenty to Pius XII, May 30, 1947.

40. MNL OL XIX–J–1–j–IV–14. 258/pol. res./1947. Vatican classified papers. Memorandum of István Kertész, minister plenipotentiary, on the assignment in Rome of László Tóth, the university chancellor.

at a meeting on August 14, 1947, the Bishops' Conference summarized the matter as follows: "The result is barely anything or nothing at all."[41]

The semi-official assignment ended in failure: diplomatic relations and the matter of a concordat both ran aground on the issue of voluntary religious education. As time passed, the government realized that no progress had been achieved at the Holy See. Rather than achieve the dispatch to Hungary of a nuncio, the government had, in effect, strengthened Mindszenty's position, who now received a free hand from Rome. The government's plan, which anticipated the gradual and democratic secularization of Hungary's schools, had clearly failed, owing to the churches' influence on the masses, their efficiency, and their unity. Consequently, in early June 1947, the introduction of voluntary religious instruction was taken off the government's agenda (for the time being at least).

Mindszenty's First Visit to North America

On May 30, 1947, while on a trip to Switzerland, Hungarian Prime Minister Ferenc Nagy resigned from his post, having been implicated by his communist rivals in the conspiracy known as the Hungarian Community, which was mentioned in the foregoing. Minister of Defense Lajos Dinnyés became the new prime minister. Over time, Dinnyés, a man with considerable political experience but without a strong personal charisma, gradually became a fellow traveler of the communists. The summer of 1947 saw fundamental changes within the various coalition parties, including the largest coalition party, the Independent Smallholders. In each party, right-wing members were excluded and those who were prepared to cooperate with the communists became the leaders. Success in the matter of voluntary religious instruction, a governmental crisis, and, in particular, the prospect of elections in the near future, resulted in a more conciliatory stance on the part of the left wing. Indeed, Mindszenty characterized the months between April 15 and August 31, 1947, as the period of the "olive branch of peace" or the "cooking of the broth" (i.e., the softening up of the opposition).[42] It was during this time that he received, without hindrance, a passport and visa for his travels abroad.

41. Beke, *A magyar katolikus püspökkari 1945–1948*, 232.
42. Ibid., 251.

In January 1947, the Canadian archbishop, Alexander Vachon, invited Cardinal Mindszenty to attend the Marian Congress that was to be held from June 18–22 in Ottawa, in celebration of the centenary of Ottawa Cathedral. At the time, Marian congresses were being held around the world, following Pope Pius XII's appeal to Catholics (an appeal made in 1946) for their support for the dogma of the Virgin Mary's assumption into heaven. Mindszenty accepted Vachon's invitation. On June 13, 1947, he traveled by way of Vienna and London to Canada, whence he paid a visit to the United States. He was accompanied on the journey by his secretary, András Zakar, who also served as his interpreter. Various people close to Mindszenty criticized his decision to leave his flock in the immediate run-up to the elections in Hungary. "It seems such an excursion is more important to him than the fate of Hungarian Catholics" they said indignantly.[43] However, in addition to exploring new places, Mindszenty sought, through his attendance at the events, to strengthen the image of the Hungarian Catholic Church and to establish good relations with influential US figures in the world church.

The Marian Congress was immediately followed by an international conference of the *Jeunesse Ouvrière Chrétienne* (Young Christian Workers). Mindszenty chaired the opening of that conference at the University of Montreal on June 24. Delegates came from forty-eight countries on five continents. They gave a ten-minute ovation to Cardinal Mindszenty as he entered the hall. The welcome given by delegates and local Catholics exceeded all expectations. June 24 is also the day of Canada's patron saint, St. John the Baptist, and during the procession, held on the feast day, a Hungarian flag was held high at the front of the crowd in honor of Mindszenty. Those present also celebrated Hungary and the Virgin Mary.[44]

After the Marian Congress, Cardinal Mindszenty traveled to New York, stopping off in Chicago on June 28, where, at a local monastery, he met – for the first time since 1924 – with Otto von Habsburg.[45] For Mindszenty it was this meeting that gave true purpose to what was a very tiring journey.

43. ÁBTL 3.1.8. Sz–222/4. 28. fol. Report, June 24, 1947.

44. "Il Cardinale Mindszenty al Congresso jocista canadese." *L'Osservatore Romano* 87, no. 155, July 6, 1947, 2.

45. PL Processus, V–700/50. 172–177. fol. "The US trip of the Prince Primate," "Discussions with Otto," "Conversation with Cardinal Spellman."

András Zakar was absent from the meeting, but he later learned from the cardinal that the discussion had touched upon a Habsburg-led Catholic federation in Central Europe – an idea that had previously been supported by the United States until the abandonment of the plan in late 1943 or early 1944. In statements made subsequently during his trial, Mindszenty recalled the meeting with Otto von Habsburg:

> Otto pointed out to me that the legitimists should refrain from establishing a separate party; rather, they should work cautiously and unobtrusively, in order to minimize risk. If possible, they should seek representation in existing suitable parties, take up jobs, and seek to sustain the legitimist ideal by way of social contacts. Concerning his plans, he stated that although he regarded the issue of Austria as distinct from that of Hungary, nevertheless he was thinking in terms of a personal union, with harmony in economic life. Thus, Austria would further develop its industry, while Hungary would perfect its agricultural sector, whereby it would supply, in addition to its own industry, Austrian industry too. This dual formation would, Otto stated, be a defensive bastion against materialism, in particular because it would be based on the gospels. [...] We agreed to keep the meeting secret and, for this very reason, a statement to the outside world was not possible.[46]

Mindszenty acknowledged, therefore, that Otto, acting out of caution, had rejected the establishment of a separate legitimist movement. (Other sources confirm that this was Otto's stance.) Instead, he called for cohesion, advising that the legitimists seek a presence in the political parties, in public life, and in the major positions. Mindszenty told the legitimist politician Baron István Kray, who was, by this time, an agent of the Hungarian political police, about his confidential meeting with Otto von Habsburg. According to Kray, Mindszenty told him that the crown prince had stated that "as long as the Russian occupation continues, you should not risk your freedom," whereupon Mindszenty had stated "that the Hungarian legitimists were organizing themselves with sufficient caution,

46. PL Processus, V–700/1. 75–76. fol. Interrogation record of the suspect József Mindszenty, January 5, 1949. With verifier's signature.

and that they would continue to do so until they achieved their goal."[47] In a 1993 interview, Otto von Habsburg denied that the two men had envisioned the restoration of the kingdom. "Because that would have been rather grotesque. We did exchange views on how to help Hungary, how to organize assistance towards mitigating poverty in Hungary, and how to assist the Church in Hungary."[48] (Of course, something which, from the vantage point of 1993, seemed nonsensical might have been, in 1947, dreamt about by an ambitious young man with only a superficial knowledge of Hungarian domestic politics.) After Mindszenty's arrest, the meeting of the two men became a matter of controversy: citing the crown prince's spokesman, as well as Archbishop Spellman, the foreign press and public opinion cast doubt on whether the meeting had truly taken place. For his part, Otto von Habsburg later stated that he had first heard about it in Chicago from the newspapers...[49] The Hungarian political police, however, had its own information sources. And they suspected a conspiracy based merely on the fact that the meeting was kept secret. Thus, the meeting would be an important "piece of evidence" that Cardinal Mindszenty had sought to overthrow the republic and place Otto von Habsburg on the Hungarian throne, as part of a legitimist conspiracy backed by the United States. Moreover, Mindszenty, it would be claimed, had brought with him "instructions" from Otto concerning future tasks.

In New York the Hungarian primate was the guest of Cardinal Spellman. The two men had been created cardinals at the same time, and they had developed a warm friendship as a result. On July 6, 1947, both men, accompanied by James Duhig, archbishop of Brisbane (Australia), celebrated a Mass at St. Patrick's Cathedral (Manhattan). In his pocket diary, Spellman made mention of the Hungarian cardinal's visit: "Cardinal Mindszenty left. I had the impression I was saying goodbye to a martyr. He asked me smilingly if I would name a school after him if he were

47. PIL 274. f. 7/248. ő. e. 153. and 187. fol. "Summary, Budapest, May 12, 1948. Subject: József Mindszenthy." [Comprised by Gábor Péter] – The same words can be read in the interrogation record of István Kray: ÁBTL 3.1.9. V–700/6. 81. fol. and PIL 274. f. 7/248. ő. e.

48. *Magyar Nemzet* 56, no. 72. March 27, 1993, 7.

49. *L'Osservatore Romano* 88, no. 303, December 30, 1948. First reports of the denial of the meeting came from the Reuters news agency. The US press reported the same in 1962: *New York Herald Tribune*, March 24, 1962.

imprisoned."[50] Mindszenty's frame of mind when posing this question is revealed in a letter he wrote to Pius XII prior to his departure from New York:

> Having attended the Marian Congress in Ottawa, I came to the United States, with a view to providing and receiving information concerning our unfortunate country, the Virgin Mary's country. According to reports, war is drawing close. My experiences in Hungary tell me that the changes and the crisis there are getting worse and worse. In Hungary, everyone now sees that the Bishops' Conference was right to state that it was wrong to concede to the Marxists and to the Russians. I now seek to return to Hungary to suffer together with my people. With God's help, I am prepared to go to prison or to be put to death. I humbly ask the Holy Father to love and help our people, and to prevent the deportation by the Russians. To this end, I request the mediation of the Americans and the British to direct the conflicts in this way and to ensure that Hungary can be evacuated. I entrust to the Holy Father's protection the soldiers and civilians who fled to the West or who were deported to Russia.[51]

From the vantage point of the free United States, it seemed that Mindszenty was returning home to die behind the Iron Curtain.

Mindszenty arrived back in Hungary on July 11, 1947. He reported on his travels to the Bishops' Conference on July 25. In retrospect he identified the aims of his journey as follows: to collect and provide information; to express gratitude for the support already received; and to visit Hungarians émigrés. To his fellow bishops, Mindszenty made no mention of his meetings with members of the Habsburg royal family and with other politicians; only a very small number of confidants were told about these. Why did the Hungarian primate keep these developments secret? Evidently, he was aware of the risks of the course he had set for himself. The Bishops' Conference disapproved of meetings with the Habsburgs, fearing accusations of its support for the restoration of the monarchy. But the

50. Archives of the Archdiocese of New York (hereafter: AANY) Spellman diaries, entry of July 7, 1947.

51. AANY Collection 007 Box S/D-10. Folder 5. Letter of József Mindszenty to Pius XII. New York, July 7, 1947.

Hungarian bishops were not alone, for the Holy See also looked critically on these developments, as the impression had been given that Rome had an interest in embracing the constitutional demands of the Habsburg family. He refrained from collecting donations, while accepting unrequited sums. Mindszenty spoke in glowing terms about religious life in Canadian and American congregations and about the Catholic schools in the two countries. He drew attention to the absence of a Catholic daily newspaper in the United States. In his view, Hungarian Catholicism was greatly respected in North America: "They do not speak of our sins as accomplices; rather, they merely conclude that we do not want to be an accomplice now."[52] He reported that in the United States many communists were being arrested. "The thread appears to be breaking. Bellum in proximo," he wrote, confidently predicting an impending war.

After Mindszenty's departure, Cardinal Spellman had the crucial task of helping to determine the fate of the Holy Crown of Hungary. In 1945 this national relic had fallen into the hands of the US army stationed in Germany. As early as on February 10, 1946, Mindszenty had proposed to the pope that the Holy Crown be kept at the Vatican.[53] This idea reflected the change in the form of Hungary's government. Without stating its own position on the matter, the Secretariat of State (Holy See) made known Mindszenty's request in a memorandum sent to the emissary to the pope for the president of the United States: "As long as the Holy Crown of Saint Stephen cannot be returned in safety to Budapest, it should be kept by the Holy See."[54] Meanwhile, Cardinal Spellman asked US Secretary of War Robert P. Patterson to ensure that the United States Military Command handle the Holy Crown, the ancient symbol of Hungarian statehood, with the greatest care. He passed on Mindszenty's proposal that the Holy Crown be given to Pius XII for safekeeping or – and this would seem to have been Spellman's own idea – that it be kept in the United States. His arguments were not derogatory with respect to the domestic political regime in Hungary; nor did he suggest that the relic had to be kept safe from the

52. Beke, *A magyar katolikus püspökkari 1945–1948*, 218.

53. PL Processus, V–700/9a. 8. and 9. fol. Draft letter to Pius XII, February 10, 1946.

54. NARA RG 59, GR of the Department of State, Decimal Files 1945–49, Box 6887. State Secretariat of the Apostolic Holy See, verbal note no. 123423/SA, April 25, 1946.

communists.[55] In the end, Patterson ignored the letter, as he was about to resign from his post. It was left to his successor, Kenneth C. Royall, to make an evasive response: "Since the restitution of sacred relics other than to the government of origin is not properly within the discretion of the Military Government authorities..."[56] Nevertheless, Royall sent a copy of the letter to the State Department, which he believed was competent on the matter. Within the US government apparatus three possible scenarios were raised concerning the fate of the Holy Crown: *a)* it would be given to the Holy See for safekeeping in line with Mindszenty's proposal; *b)* it would be brought from Europe to the United States and deposited there; *c)* it would be left in Germany until its safe return to Hungary became possible.[57]

In the meantime Mindszenty had begun to lobby the new US envoy to Budapest. His arguments now contained a new element: the transfer of the Holy Crown to Rome was crucial "because the valuable relic might end up in unfortunate circumstances in the course of military action."[58] Mindszenty was implying that the Holy Crown needed to be protected from the dangers of a possible war. Convinced of the gravity of this danger, the Hungarian cardinal requested other prelates, including the archbishops of Vienna, Munich, and Salzburg (Theodor Innitzer, Michael Faulhaber, and Andreas Rohracher), to intervene. At Mindszenty's behest, Archbishop Rohracher then wrote a letter, dated November 18, 1947, to Cardinal

55. AANY Collection 007 Box S/D-10. Folder 5. Cardinal Spellman's letter to Robert Patterson, US secretary of war, July 26, 1947. Having received word of Mindszenty's arrest, on January 9, 1947, Spellman published his correspondence with the Hungarian primate. When the letter was retyped at that time, the date was changed by mistake to July 28, 1947, and it is this erroneous date that appears in Robert I. Gannon, *The Cardinal Spellman Story* (Garden City, NY: Doubleday & Company, 1962), 344. Cf. AANY Collection 007 Box S/A-21, Folder 10; NARA RG 84, Records of the Foreign Service Posts of the Department of State, Hungary, Subject Files Relating to Cardinal Mindszenty 1956–72, Box 2, SOC 12–Mindszenty 1964.

56. AANY Collection 007 S/D-10. Folder 5. US Secretary of War Kenneth C. Royall's letter to Cardinal Spellman, August 11, 1947. The text of the letter appears in Gannon, *The Cardinal Spellman Story*, 344.

57. MNL OL XX–10–k LÜ PO 18.300/1989. US archival sources. Proposal no. 1342 of the American political advisor Robert D. Murphy to the US State Department, May 31, 1946.

58. PL Processus, V–700/9a. 21–22. fol. József Mindszenty's letter to Envoy Chapin, August 31, 1947. – On September 12, Chapin confirmed receipt of the letter: "Permit me to assure you, my dear Cardinal, that your suggestion will be given due consideration at such time as the disposition of this relic is brought to the attention of this Legation." PL Processus, V–700/9a. 30–31. fol.

Spellman of New York, who was considered by all to be the most influential churchman. The request made in the letter accorded with Spellman's own view that "the Crown of Hungary may not be turned over to the present regime. It should be sent to the Holy Father in Rome."[59] Spellman discussed the contents of the letter with James H. Griffiths, Chancellor of the Military Ordinariate, who, in turn, consulted on the issue with some Hungarian émigrés including Ferenc Nagy, former prime minister, and Tibor Eckhardt, former Smallholder politician. Griffiths concluded that while the Americans could treat the crown as if it were a work of art that had been stolen by the Nazis, it would be inadvisable to ship it to America, as this might strengthen anti-American Soviet propaganda. Indeed, the Soviets might then claim – not without foundation – that the United States had no legal basis to keep an historical relic that belonged to the Hungarian people. For similar reasons, Griffiths was opposed also to the idea of transferring the Holy Crown to the Vatican. Thus, Griffiths, despite his respect for the intent of Mindszenty and Rohracher, was of the view that it would be wrong and impractical to remove the Holy Crown from Germany. When asked to outline the right solution and how the Holy Crown could be prevented from falling into the hands of the communists, Griffiths acknowledged he had no idea.[60] In the end, it became the official position of the United States that the Crown had been accepted from the Hungarian authorities for safe-keeping. This meant, in turn, that the return of the Crown to Hungary could not be part of the ceasefire conditions.

An Ideological Struggle Requires an Ideological Party

During the national elections of November 1945, it became evident that neither the Communist Party nor the Independent Smallholders' Party had an interest in the emergence of political Catholicism in the political arena.

59. Given the circumstances of the court case, historians have doubted the authenticity of the letter. It does, however, exist; an original copy is preserved in Cardinal Spellman's legacy: AANY Collection 007 S/D-10. Folder 5. We still do not know, however, how an original copy of the letter came into the possession of the Hungarian political police and how it then came to be published in the political brochure entitled *A Mindszenty bűnügy okmányai* (Budapest: Athenaeum, 1949), 39–42.

60. AANY Collection 007 Box S/D-10. Folder 5. Letter of James H. Griffiths, auxiliary bishop of the Archdiocese of New York to Cardinal Spellman, December 9, 1947.

For this reason, Catholic society in Hungary was left with no representation in Parliament. Mindszenty was keen to see the establishment of a Catholic political party, but efforts towards this end were slow. He had never sympathized with the views of István Barankovics, who had become the new leader of the Democratic People's Party after the party split in two in the summer of 1945. Indeed, the policy of *modus vivendi* was alien to Mindszenty. Meanwhile, Count József Pálffy, the leader of the conservative wing of the Democratic People's Party, allied himself with Dezső Sulyok, who, having been thrown out of the Independent Smallholders' Party, founded a new party called the Party of Hungarian Freedom (Magyar Szabadság Pártja). Pálffy, who became the deputy chairman of the new party, assisted Sulyok in obtaining Mindszenty's support. The coming together of Mindszenty and Sulyok required that both men show willingness for compromise. While Sulyok assured Mindszenty that he, as a Catholic, would adhere to the rules of the Church, he also told him that he was unwilling to lead a party that was Catholic in name or in terms of its party emblems. Further, Mindszenty acknowledged that the time was not yet ripe for legitimism. As a result of the compromise agreement, Mindszenty renounced for a time the establishment of an overtly Catholic political party. Still, he asked Sulyok to refrain from recommending non-Catholics (for membership of the party), for otherwise he would be left with no choice but to express his clear opinion that "*in Hungary there was a dominance of Calvinist clerics.*"[61] Accordingly, even while he acknowledged and accepted the non-sectarian approach of Sulyok and his party, he could not enthuse about the idea.

When the Party of Hungarian Freedom applied for a license from the ACC, rumors of Mindszenty's support for the party were an obvious disadvantage. Indeed, the Soviet chairman of the ACC called in Sulyok and allegedly threatened that "the Soviets would not tolerate the Party of Hungarian Freedom if it were to cooperate with the Catholic Church."[62] Sulyok, however, proved rather adept at maneuvering in this political milieu, and so on October 11, 1946, his party received a license from the

61. ÁBTL 3.1.8. Sz–222/2. 146. fol. Report on the talks between Sulyok and Mindszenty, June 30, 1946.

62. MNL OL XX–10–k LÜ PO 18.300/1989. US archival sources. Legate H. F. Arthur Schoenfeld's proposal no. 1730 to the US secretary of state, September 13, 1946.

ACC, signed by Lieutenant-General Sviridov. Still, the merger of the two political groupings – that is, the part of the Democratic People's Party that was loyal to Pálffy and the Party of Hungarian Freedom – was less than a satisfactory outcome from Mindszenty's perspective. At the founding general meeting on November 24, József Pálffy placed great emphasis on "Christian democracy" and the "Christian worldview," but no mention was made of Cardinal Mindszenty or the Catholic Church.[63]

In the absence of a Catholic party, Mindszenty now aimed to ensure the representation of Catholics in local councils and in Parliament – by means of Catholic candidates in Sulyok's party. He believed that such representatives might soon become the builders of a new party based on the Gospel. In a rather mysterious fashion, the foundation of a "Gospel Party" was indeed announced on June 20, 1946. In the *Magyar Kurír*, an announcement was made, with reference to the "competent ecclesiastical body" (i.e., the Esztergom Diocesan Office), that "a decision has been taken to establish a new party on the basis of the worldview of the Gospel" and that this party "will not be identical to any of the licensed parties in today's political life."[64] This sentence not only declared the foundation of a new party but served also to distance it from the Democratic People's Party. The text of the announcement made no mention of the character of the new party, but as the Gospel belongs both to Catholics and to all other Christians the implication seemed to be that the party would be Christian rather than exclusively Catholic. The announcement did not include the names of the founders, but the choice of the passive voice ("the decision has been taken") rapidly gave rise to rumors that the Bishops' Conference was behind the initiative – rumors that appeared to be confirmed by the inclusion of the words "competent ecclesiastical body."[65] On the other hand, the Catholic Church had, for some generations, avoided giving even the impression of participating in the establishment of a political party, fearing that a

63. SzCsPL I.1.a. 320/1947. *A Magyar Szabadság Párt zászlóbontó nagygyűlése 1946. november 24-én* [The founding general meeting of the Party of Hungarian Freedom on November 24, 1946.] (Budapest: 1946), 17–18.

64. *Magyar Kurír* 36, June 20, 1946, second edition.

65. SzCsPL I.1.a. 1595/1946. Joint letter of Sándor Bálint, Sándor Eckhardt, and István Barankovics to Bishop Endre Hamvas, July 16, 1946. Published in Jenő Gergely, "A Demokrata Néppárt 'igazoló jelentése' a Mindszenty József bíboros hercegprímással keletkezett konfliktusról," *Századok* 127, no. 5–6 (1993): 764–76.

Church-supported grouping could easily be perceived as a clerical, rather than Christian or Catholic, political party.

The initiative to create a new party was indeed the work of Mindszenty. In the period 1946–1948 the foundation of a new party was his dream, even though he sometimes deviated from this goal and sought contact with various right-wing parties. As he stated,

> We need an ideological party, because an ideological struggle is underway, and democracy in its Western sense does not exclude ideological parties; rather, it requires them. Whether the party should include in its name the word Catholic or Christian is something that must be weighed up by those launching it.[66]

The Cistercian jurist Jusztin Baranyay (co-defendant in the Mindszenty trial) recalled how the issue of the nature of the party led to a disagreement between him and Mindszenty: whereas Baranyay's idea was for a party founded on a broad national consensus (which might even have Jewish members), Mindszenty believed the future lay in an intrinsically Catholic party.[67] The Hungarian primate appointed Vendel Endrédy, the Cistercian abbot of Zirc, to launch negotiations on the foundation of the party. The talks, however, failed to reach a conclusion, as the targeted persons were "unwilling to undertake the tasks designated for them. While they agreed essentially with the program, they nevertheless regarded the launch of the party as untimely," noted Vendel Endrédy in his prison diary. Endrédy told Mindszenty he was unable to complete his task in view of the lack of a consensus.[68] There were, indeed, a broad range of opinions concerning the timeliness of a political party, its name and program, the composition of its leadership, and its relations with other parties. The constitutional form of government and the issue of the monarchy were also raised, but Mindszenty did not comment upon these matters and refrained from giving his support to any of the legitimist groupings. Moreover, he took no part in

66. PL Processus, V–700/11. 131. fol. József Mindszenty's handwritten note on a letter he received from Vid Mihelics. N. d. [June 1946]

67. ÁBTL 3.1.9. V–700/2. 29. fol. Interrogation record of the suspect Jusztin Baranyay, December 26, 1948.

68. Ibid., V–82.897/1. 25. fol. The prison notes (written with a pencil) of Abbot Vendel Endrédy, November 1, 1950. Cited in Cúthné Gyóni, *Egy fogoly apát*, 47.

the efforts of certain legitimists to find a way forward after 1945, even though the monarchists regarded him in part as their spiritual and intellectual leader. In essence, Mindszenty followed Otto von Habsburg's advice, focusing his attention on developing a presence of legitimists in public offices, other parties, and movements rather than on founding a legitimist party.

The presence or absence of a party became a particularly important issue when, after the resignation of Prime Minister Ferenc Nagy (on June 1, 1947), the Social Democrats called for the dissolution of Parliament and the holding of new elections. While it was not their goal to ensure the communists held power in the period after the peace treaty, their proposal had just that result. The political authorities were aware of the significance of religious voters in the election, but they also knew that, with the exception of the Independent Smallholders' Party, the existing parties were unlikely to gain their support. Accordingly, they employed the principle of "divide and rule": many parties were allowed to take part in the elections in the hope of voter fragmentation. The Party of Hungarian Freedom (Dezső Sulyok's party), however, was excluded from the election, even though it could count on significant support from the Church. The reason for this was that the electoral law had been formulated in such a way as to exclude individuals who had been politically active under the previous regime. During the 1930s, Dezső Sulyok had been a member of Parliament for the government party, and so he could not take part in the elections. On July 21, 1947, Sulyok's party dissolved itself, and so the party's Catholic wing led by Pálffy also crumbled. Dezső Sulyok and József Pálffy opted to go into exile.

Under these circumstances, a coming together of national forces and the establishment of a united opposition party – or, at least, an electoral alliance – might have radically altered the political situation. Yet, such a development was not to be. What was lacking was an authoritative but charismatic personality who would have stood above all the parties and been accepted by their leaders. "József Mindszenty could not fulfill this task," concluded Zoltán Pfeiffer, founder of the Hungarian Independence Party, who otherwise admired the Hungarian primate.[69] Yet, in a survey

69. József Varga, "Magyar Függetlenségi Párt (1947. júl. 26. – 1947. nov. 20.)," in *Jelenkori magyar történelmi dokumentumok*, 4. (Washington D.C.: American Hungarian Cultural Center, 1988), 49.

conducted in July 1947 on the popularity of public figures, one in four people in Budapest named Mindszenty as their favorite.[70] The respect of the public did not, however, translate into a unification or alliance of parties. Undeniably, the differences of opinion among the politicians were great, but the reason why Mindszenty failed to remain above the parties was that, unlike his predecessors as primate, he did not abstain from efforts to establish a Catholic party or from involvement in party political decisions. Indeed, he sought more than a ceremonial role; he wanted to participate in the decision-making as a kind of "gray eminence." To his confidants, he stated the following: "The newspapers are seeking in vain to make out of me a party leader and out of the Bishops' Conference a party leadership; I am, first and foremost, a primate, and it is my duty to defend the interests of my Church under all circumstances." It would seem, therefore, that he had no wish to become a party politician, not even in a symbolic sense.[71]

There was failure, however, both in terms of forging a united party and in terms of establishing a Catholic/Christian party. Ultimately, an opaque and tortuous political situation arose, and the national elections were held against the backdrop of fragmentation and a lack of preparedness in Catholic society. In this situation, Cardinal Mindszenty would have been prepared to give his support to the Democratic People's Party and designate it a Christian party, in return for the party signing up to a six-point declaration. Under the terms of the declaration, the party would have come under the direct control of its hierarchy and the party chairman, József Mindszenty, while István Barankovics would have resigned from his role within the party (general secretary), doing so, however, only after the elections, as was Mindszenty's wish.[72] (The idea had been to exploit his

70. President of the Republic Zoltán Tildy was in first place, while in second and third place were the deputy prime ministers Mátyás Rákosi and Árpád Szakasits. (A year and a half later, József Mindszenty had fallen to fifth place; Minister of Transport Ernő Gerő had overtaken him.) The only woman in the top list of public figures was the legitimist Margit Slachta, who was named by just 0.3 percent of respondents. MNL OL XIX–I–1–v–12. t.–11–1947. Gyula Ortutay's papers. Confidential report no. 29/1947 of the Hungarian Public Research Institute on public opinion research concerning the popularity of men in public life, July 31, 1947. The results were also forwarded to Moscow: RGASPI f. 17. op. 128. delo (file) 913. l. 156.

71. ÁBTL 3.1.8 Sz–222/4. 66. fol. Report, July 24, 1947.

72. PMKL IV. 213. Legacy of István Albert, Papers, Item no. 4, file named "Néppárt [People's Party]." Two versions of the statement are published in György Szakolczai and Róbert Szabó, *Két kísérlet a proletárdiktatúra elhárítására* (Budapest: Gondolat, 2011), 286–88.

popularity to win votes.) The impossible conditions meant that the talks were soon abandoned. Accordingly, at a meeting of the Bishops' Conference, Cardinal Mindszenty, who was presiding, stated that he would no longer support Barankovics's People's Party and that, under the prevailing circumstances, the launch of an ideological party was impossible.[73] While it would be inaccurate to claim that a united bourgeois front failed to materialize on account of Mindszenty, it is nevertheless true that the Hungarian primate refused to recognize in István Barankovics a leading figure in Hungary's postwar democratic experiment and to tolerate his specific brand of Christian Democracy. Mindszenty evidently allowed himself to be driven by his antipathy towards Barankovics rather than by a calm presence of mind. It might even be said that the cardinal tragically sacrificed the unity of the opposition on the altar of intrigue. Despite Mindszenty's rancor, the Democratic People's Party still enjoyed the support of several diocesan bishops. Moreover, in the end, several conservative and legitimist politicians were elected to Parliament as candidates on the Democratic People's Party's list.

In the course of the election campaign, on August 13, 1947, the new US envoy to Hungary, Selden Chapin, paid a visit to Esztergom. Archbishop Spellman of New York had described Chapin as a fervent Protestant. He differed, therefore, from his predecessor Schoenfeld, who had shown little interest in religion.[74] Legitimist circles in Hungary placed great hopes in the new legate, a former sailor who admitted to having become a diplomat by accident. The expectation placed on Chapin was no less than that he would "change Hungarian domestic politics."[75] Chapin, however, had very few means to pursue a more forceful and active foreign policy than that of his predecessor. Moreover, his enthusiasm for the cause did not mean the abandonment of US diplomatic detachment.

After the new US envoy's introductory visit, Cardinal Mindszenty immediately dispatched a letter to Brigadier General George Hatton Weems, who had been the chief of the United States Representation on the Allied Control Commission for Hungary since the summer of 1946. He asked the brigadier general to delay the elections, as the electoral law

73. Beke, *A magyar katolikus püspökkari 1945–1948*, 219.
74. PL Processus, V–700/1. 22. and 273. fol. Memorandum, December 28, 1948.
75. ÁBTL 3.1.9. V–700/6. 76. fol. Minutes of suspect István Kray, n. d.

had denied hundreds of thousands of people the right to vote.[76] In a formal legal sense, there was no reason to hold elections just two years after the 1945 vote. However, in view of the impending departure of the ACC (which the terms of the peace treaty foresaw happening in September 1947) and the resulting reduction in Soviet power, the left-wing parties were keen to establish their dominance in the legislature and strike a lasting blow to the bourgeois parties.

The elections thus went ahead on August 31, 1947. Mindszenty, in protest, refrained from voting, and in an interview with foreign journalists called the elections a circus. On their return journey from Esztergom to Budapest, a group of journalists made jokes about the Hungarian primate. According to a report, one of them said, in mock incomprehension, the following: "...the prince primate wants the Americans to march into Hungary and liberate the poor and oppressed people from Russian-supported communist subjugation? 'And I was told this man was a politician!'."[77]

The election result brought no surprises: the governing coalition parties won the election, and, owing partly to election fraud, the Hungarian Communist Party secured a relative majority of the votes. The Independent Smallholders' Party, which had been victorious two years previously, received two million fewer votes. The opposition received almost 40 percent of the vote, and the Democratic People's Party, with 16 percent, became the second-largest party after the communists. Doubtless the result would have been even better if Cardinal Mindszenty had given the party his support. Rather than praise the party's success in the elections, however, Mindszenty reiterated his view that "the unity of Hungarian Catholicism is in ruins, and you have destroyed it."[78] This accusation was addressed primarily at the four prelates in whose dioceses the Democratic People's Party had been particularly successful in the election. Mindszenty then mockingly stated that Barankovics had used communist agitators "and so Barankovics is a traitor because he is liked in Soviet circles."[79]

76. Péter Sipos and István Vida, "Mindszenty József és az amerikai követség," *História* [History] 5, no. 5–6 (1983): 42.

77. PIL 274. f. 7/248. ő. e. 82. fol. Memorandum, September 4, 1947.

78. ÁBTL 3.1.8. Sz–222/4. 130. fol. Report. Budapest, September 6, 1948.

79. Ibid., 131. fol.

The Soviets' partiality for Brankovics may explain why Mindszenty was so determined to undermine the politician's position. On September 6, 1947, the cardinal informed, in confidence, Knox Helm, the British political representative in Hungary that "Barankovics's party is pro-Moscow, and that although it seeks to represent the Catholic worldview, it is not under the control of the Church."[80] By way of conclusion, he noted that he was writing all this with a view to preventing a misunderstanding in the event of a decision on the part of the international forces to declare the national elections invalid. The people around Mindszenty mockingly referred to Barankovics's party as "His Majesty Rákosi's loyal opposition." The Hungarian primate would probably have been of the same view even if he had known that around this time the highest body of the Hungarian Communist Party instructed Interior Minister László Rajk to arrange for the Hungarian State Police State Protection Department (ÁVO) "to produce some compromising data on Barankovics."[81]

The antipathy between Mindszenty and Barankovics was multifaceted. The Hungarian primate's "human resources policy" had always prioritized reliability, while aptitude – the importance of which many of his fellows underlined – was deemed of secondary importance. The two men made very different assessments of the political situation, both of which were illusory. Accordingly, whereas the primate put his faith in Western intervention in Hungary, the politician believed in finding a *modus vivendi*. They also had different views on the nature of the Christian state: Mindszenty was thinking in terms of the historical constitution, whereas Barankovics placed the focus on the Christian Democratic ideal of the state, and in a Gospel-inspired Socialism. The primate was driven by a kind of "holy mission," whereas the politician –Barankovics – had to be willing to make compromises.[82] As time passed, such differences of principle, attitude and constitution created an unbridgeable chasm between the two men. Obviously, for the left wing, the tension between Mindszenty and Barankovics was grist to the mill: it resulted in the Democratic People's Party

80. PIL 508. f. 1/117. ő. e. 7. fol. TNA FO 371/67185. Letter of József Mindszenty to Political Representative Knox Helm, September 6, 1947.

81. PIL 274. f. 3/120. ő. e. 2. fol. and RGASPI f. 17. op. 128. delo (file) 309. l. 95. Minutes of the meeting of the HCP PC (Politburo) on November 20, 1947.

82. Zsolt Semjén, *Két pogány közt* (Budapest: Barankovics Alapítvány, 2013), 80.

distancing itself from the primate and thus from the "official" Catholic Church. In this way, the party lost the moral and political support of the Church. What then happened is public knowledge: the nascent totalitarian dictatorship spared neither the conservative brand of political Catholicism nor its Christian Democratic counterpart. The suppression of both, which took place almost concurrently, was greatly facilitated by the squabbling between Mindszenty and Barankovics.

Soon there were reports of an event that turned out to be a historical milestone: following talks at the Polish resort of Szklarska Poręba (September 22–27, 1947), Cominform (the Communist Information Bureau) was formed. With the entry into force of the Paris Peace Treaty (on September 15, 1947), the ACC ceased to exist, but the Soviet Union accelerated the Sovietization of the region by way of the Cominform. Some authors have linked the launch of the anti-clerical strategy in East Central Europe to the meeting in Szklarska Poręba. In fact, however, the issue of religion and the churches was addressed only marginally on that occasion.[83] The Hungarian delegates sensed that participants in the conference regarded the churches as serious adversaries yet not as the most dangerous opponents. Diplomatic relations with the Holy See – which had thitherto been deemed beneficial – were being wound down by the Poles and were considered to be a burden by the Yugoslavs. Still, in Italy the communists were about to enter a coalition with the Christian Democrats.[84]

The Hungarian primate expected nothing good to come from the dawning of the new era. At a general meeting of the St. Stephen Association held on December 11, 1947, he weighed up developments in Hungary in the preceding three decades. He concluded that the foundations of the state and of society had been damaged, as had also morality, law and order, the family, marriage, duty, justice, love and peace.

> Today, the churches – in a fundamental shift after nine and a half centuries [of stability] – have no say in the adoption of laws, and their opinion is

83. *Szabad Nép* 5, no. 226, October 5, 1947, cover page; *A Kommunista és Munkáspártok Tájékoztató Irodájának határozatai* [Resolutions of the Information Bureau of the Communist and Labor Parties] (Budapest: Szikra, 1950), 8.

84. PIL 274. f. 10/14. ő. e. 4., 12., 22., 34. and 50. fol. Notes of József Révai and Mihály Farkas on the founding meeting of the Information Bureau.

> not even sought in connection with legislative bills that affect faith and morality; my occasional utterances have mostly been left unanswered; [the churches] have no free pastoral letters, and they have today no daily newspapers or weeklies.[85]

At the same time, Mindszenty made it crystal clear that he would not renounce "the right of the country's primate to voice an opinion promptly on legislative bills affecting, in any fashion, the Church or the country." Mindszenty's speech caused a stir because he had once again reiterated his role and rights in the public legal sphere, which was a sensitive issue for the republican government. Mindszenty's thinking was permeated by a conviction – one that overstated the importance of Hungary – that a battle of life and death between Christianity and paganism would be determined here. Yet, for him, victory was not the primary aim; rather, the priority was to bear witness, and this was what he encouraged his priests and the faithful to do.

As had been expected since the establishment of Cominform, the Hungarian Communist Party now broke with its tactic of long-term transition and began seeking immediate "revolutionary" change. Between late 1947 and March 1948, there was a systematic attack on those forces that were opposed to fusion with the two workers' parties (the Hungarian Communist Party and the Social Democratic Party). State control was expanded to include a far broader area of economic life: the three-year plan was launched; and the banking system was nationalized. In the end, the left wing occupied every significant position, trampling underfoot the principle of a numerical majority. It stressed repeatedly that it had the financial resources, the talent, the authority, and the support of the Soviets. The choice of political parties became ever duller and more uniform. With the gradual liquidation of the opposition in Parliament, the Catholic Church and its chief shepherd, József Mindszenty, came to play a leading role in opposing the communist forces.

85. *Magyar Kurír* 37, December 11, 1947, fourth edition.

The Catholic Church endeavored to hinder the communist advance through its own means, by centralizing the power of Catholicism and offering prayers. A suitable occasion for the Church to act – particularly in the extra-ecclesiastical sphere – was the Year of the Blessed Virgin Mary (the Marian year), which had been announced in the workplan of Actio Catholica (Catholic Action) for 1947–1948. It began a month after the Hungarian primate returned from Canada, and lasted from August 15, 1947 until December 8, 1948.[86] The revitalization of the centuries-old Marian cult, as well as the tradition of local pilgrimages, offered great opportunities for Mindszenty in the pastoral field. The phrase Regnum Marianum (the country of Mary), was used by many Catholics and stemmed from the tradition that King Stephen I of Hungary, who had been left heirless, had offered the Holy Crown and the country to the Virgin Mary prior to his death. Over the centuries Regnum Marianum had come to evoke the historical Kingdom of Hungary. Now, however, the phrase symbolized the nation's drawing strength from the Virgin Mary for its recovery and that the only means to achieve a communist-free Hungary was through the spiritual realization of the country of Mary. "A fight using the power of prayer!": this was the spiritual declaration of war for a series of events that proved very popular with the masses. The Marian year comprised, in the main, well-organized devotional events. And even though the interweaving of Christianity and national identity was less significant in Hungary than it was, for instance, in Poland, the various events aimed to create a new, albeit tradition-based, image both for the Church and for the nation. In terms of their depth, influence and magnitude, the series of events were uniquely significant in the era. They served principally to energize Catholic public life.

Among the various events held during the Marian year, St. Stephen's Day (August 20) was particularly memorable. While the public debate was dominated by the rivalry of the political parties in the run-up to the election, the day saw a procession of an estimated half a million people, with the crowd being led by Mindszenty, who was dressed in a *cappa magna*.

86. *Magyar Kurír* 37, August 17, 1947, third extraordinary edition. For a detailed account of events, see István Mészáros, *Boldogasszony Éve 1947/1948: Mindszenty bíboros evangelizációs programja* (Budapest: Ecclesia, 1994).

Bishops, monks, nuns, and the faithful took part in the procession. Since 1819, a Christian relic, namely the right hand of Saint Stephen (Hungary's first Christian king), had been carried through the castle district of Buda on this day. Since 1945, owing to the ruined state of Buda and the Royal Palace, the right hand had been carried through the other half of the city, Pest. (The new route, which had been inaugurated in 1938, the Year of Saint Stephen, led from the Basilica to Heroes' Square by way of Andrássy Street.) The new procession route was lined by the townhouses of the nobility and the upper class. The monarchic venue had been replaced by a modern bourgeois nationalist milieu. The seating plan for the event was surprisingly familiar: behind the main podium there were seats for the prime minister, Lajos Dinnyés, and for other government ministers, the country's military and police chiefs, and the heads of the diplomatic representations to Hungary, most of whom were accompanied by their wives. Also in attendance were the staff members of the Allied Control Commission, as well as the Soviet commander and the Yugoslav counsel. Delegates from the political parties were, however, absent. In his sermon, József Mindszenty contrasted the sanctity of the ancient relic (Saint Stephen's right hand) with the conduct of contemporary "statesmen" (i.e., weak politicians), who were, in his view, responsible for the moral impoverishment of the country. He then underlined that the defense of the Christian faith was the priority of the era. (His words were still in the ears of the faithful when they turned out to vote in the national elections some ten days later.) At the end of the event, a new ceremony took place: the blessing of industrial and agricultural tools. As a reporter noted, workers and peasants placed their tools on a table in front of the main altar, ready to be blessed. The procession itself included agricultural machinery and vehicles, which were decorated with the national flag and floral tributes. In this way, hundreds of thousands of people expressed their support for the Christian worldview and moral stance, which, acting in combination, were generally considered to constitute the foundation of the Hungarian state. The procession amounted to a true *Ecclesia militans*.

On September 7, 1947, Mindszenty consecrated the rebuilt cathedral in Szombathely , the reconstruction of which – following wartime destruction – had been funded by donations from the faithful. The celebrations continued the next day with a Marian day. Throughout the country, large numbers of pilgrims set out for the various Marian shrines. On September 14, the day of the Exaltation of the Holy Cross,[87] Cardinal Mindszenty led 100,000 men by foot on a pilgrimage to Máriaremete, which lies fourteen kilometers from Budapest. (The women pilgrims made the same journey a week later, on September 21.)[88] Having confessed and partaken of the Sacrament, the pilgrims walked to their destination, singing Marian songs and praying the Holy Rosary with enthusiasm and confidence.

Based on the model of the international Catholic congresses and as a substitute for them, a National Catholic Marian congress was held on October 4–7, 1947. A police observer, who evidently sought to meet the expectations of his superiors, reported that 60–65 percent of those in attendance were women and "only a negligibly small fraction of them, 5–10 percent, were consciously fascists."[89] Not even this police observer, however, characterized the event as political. On October 7, Mindszenty spoke to a crowd of around 90,000 who had gathered on the square in front of the Basilica in Budapest. A delegation presented the resolutions adopted at the congress – including the launch of a Catholic daily newspaper – to Lajos Dinnyés, who had remained prime minister after the elections. A visibly fatigued Dinnyés, who had already received a number of delegations on that day, gave the Catholic delegation a rather frosty reception. He repeatedly interrupted them as they were speaking. On being told that the congress resolutions had been approved by 100,000 people, he cynically responded as follows: "A hundred thousand! Oh please, if a hand grenade had been thrown among them, they would all have run away, leaving only the prince primate and perhaps one or two others."[90] When, in a bid to secure a license for the proposed Catholic daily newspaper, the head of the delegation argued in favor of freedom of conscience and the ratification of the peace treaty, Dinnyés mockingly dampened hopes. On

87. On this day, Catholics commemorate the discovery of the cross used in the crucifixion of Jesus.

88. SzCsPL I.1.a. 1430/1946. Actio Catholica's working program for 1947/48. Zsigmond Mihalovics, national head of the AC to the bishops, May 27, 1947.

89. PIL 274. f. 2/246. ő. e. 34. fol. Report on the Marian days.

90. SzCsPL I.1.a. 2058/1947. "Minutes. Taken on October 10, 1947. Subject: Actio Catholica delegation's meeting with the prime minister." – The minutes were leaked to the US Legation. See NARA RG 84, Records of the Foreign Service Posts of the Department of State, Hungary, US Legation, GR 1946–63, Box 4, 1947 – 840.4.

hearing the prime minister's response, Mindszenty angrily demanded that Dinnyés stick to his word, noting that he had earlier promised Archbishop Czapik of Eger and the Cistercian jurist Jusztin Baranyay that a license for a Catholic daily would be issued after the elections: "There is paper for pornography as well as for besmirching the Church. Meanwhile the Jews have some press publications, and the Calvinists can make their voice heard..." – only the Catholics were to remain silent.[91]

The Marian year continued to make an impact even in its second part. As well as honoring Mary, it targeted atheism, materialism, and communism (the latter being viewed as a derivative of materialism). The political police were given control over the various events, but it was not their task – in the initial stages at least – to cause "provocations." On average, 165 secret policemen were in attendance at the church services and at the festivities. They reported, in great detail, on what they saw and heard, including actions by the police to restrict events. In the late afternoon of May 13, 1948, the police broke up – apparently by mistake – a devotion to Fatima that was being held at the Cave Church on Gellért Hill. It proved to be a fateful error. The immediate vicinity of the Cave Church had become overcrowded, and so some of the crowd had walked down to Gellért Square. On the same afternoon, the communist leader Mátyás Rákosi was meeting with the members of a Polish delegation at the Hotel Gellért. The security men, whose task was to clear a path for Rákosi's entourage, told the crowd to cheer the leader as his car passed. The assembled crowd, however, were anticipating Mindszenty rather than Rákosi. As the car went by, they shouted "Long live Mindszenty!", not knowing that the deputy prime minister was inside the vehicle. The police quickly silenced the crowd.[92]

On September 8, 1948, the Hungarian primate visited the town of Zalaegerszeg, the scene of his earlier ministry. Owing to police intimidation, the attendance numbers were far smaller than the anticipated one hundred thousand. Even so, the crowd was still a large one – the psychosis of fear had already affected people. The left-wing press reported

91. PIL 274. f. 7/247. ő. e. 101–2r–v. Letter of József Mindszenty to Lajos Dinnyés, October 18, 1947.

92. Of course, the contemporary report of the State Security Department did not mention any violence. It reported that "the crowd broke up in an orderly fashion at 8 p.m.." ÁBTL 3.1.8. Sz–222/9a. 196. fol. Report, May 13, 1948.

that the "Voice of America" had been heard at the event which "honored Mary and dishonored Hungarian democracy."[93]

The crafty yet clumsy approach of the political police was laid bare by a series of measures aimed at preventing the Marian Day events in Celldömölk on September 12. Many people were expected to attend the events, because 1948 marked the bicentenary of the placement of a statue of the Virgin Mary in the town's Pilgrimage Church. The authorities attempted to halt preparations for the celebrations by withdrawing the official permit, citing a meningitis epidemic. To counter the epidemic, 380 armed policemen were sent to the site of the events and a ban was imposed on the consumption of alcohol. Steps were taken to prevent the crowds finding accommodation; visitors needed a registration card in order to move around the town. In spite of these measures, thousands of people arrived in the town on Sunday morning. During Holy Mass, vehicles belonging to the fire department kept going around the church, spraying slurry onto bystanders. Before he even began his sermon, Mindszenty issued a solemn protest, criticizing the presence of "a police force near the church on the day of a Marian pilgrimage. I have to regard it as interference in the most intimate matters of the Church."[94] In his sermon, which was non-political, Mindszenty spoke of the veneration of Mary. He addressed contemporary developments only to the extent of condemning the replacement of a vow by state officials that had pointed to their religious convictions by a new vow that was neutral in terms of their worldview. (The original wording of the vow had ended as follows: "So help me God." Now it was being replaced by the words "I pledge by my honor and my conscience." Mindszenty perceived this change as an indication of the strengthening of the left wing rather than as the normal separation of church and state.) According to a State Protection Authority report,

> After his sermon in the church, Mindszenty left the town. His departure marked the full defeat of the Reaction. The rumor was put about by policemen and agitators that, on account of the epidemic, everyone at the municipal hospital was being stripped naked and disinfected. A false

93. *Keszthelyi Újság* [Keszthely News] 4, no. 37, September 12, 1948, cover page.

94. SZEK, ős. XXVIII/alsó I. József Mindszenty's sermon at Celldömölk on September 12, 1948.

> rumor was that people arriving in Celldömölk were to be taken off to Siberia... After Mindszenty had left the church, the crowd spilled out of it. A jeep and two large police cars drove into the crowd. This was a mistake. One of the jeeps almost knocked down Mindszenty.[95]

The events profoundly shook the Hungarian primate. An otherwise resilient man, he grew tearful and "trembled with rage" on being told of the excesses of the authorities.[96]

Mindszenty created much work for the inquisitive staff of the political police. As his secretary observed, his tight schedule left him mentally and physically exhausted. His voice was hoarse, and he suffered recurring bouts of Graves' Disease. He dwelt little on these problems and attended many events during the year of the Assumption of Mary, speaking in front of tens of thousands of people, leading pilgrimages, and presiding over meetings. He made good use of the experience he had gained as parish priest, dean, bishop's commissioner, editor, and social organizer. The men who were watching him could not possibly write their reports in a manner that would evoke the atmosphere and at the same time meet the expectations of their superiors. For instance, one of them "heard" when, during a Mass, Mindszenty was interrupted by applause and the following cry from the congregation: "Long live Mindszenty, the apostolic king of Hungary!" According to another report, at an event during a Marian congress, Mindszenty gave a speech in front of 25–30,000 people that was clearly intended to incite them: "...the fascist part of the crowd applauded his hateful words and cheered him on, while at the same time decrying democracy. (Down with Ortutay! Now let's see whether Matyi [Mátyás Rákosi] dares to speak; down with the Jews, long live the English! etc.)"[97] Undeniably, people did sometimes shout out slogans that had nothing to do with the Virgin Mary, but the mood of an event was never determined by such comments.

By May 1948, 3,891,000 people had taken part in events and pilgrimages held in Hungary as part of the Marian year. By the end of the series

95. ÁBTL 3.1.9. V–700/29. 317–319. fol. Memoranda on the Marian days at Celldömölk; Mindszenty, *Memoirs*, 77.

96. ÁBTL 3.1.8. Sz–222/13. 98. fol. Report, September 13, 1948.

97. PIL 274. f. 7/246. ő. e. 34. fol. Report on the Marian days.

of events, the figure had risen to around 4,600,000.[98] In the light of these numbers, no one can doubt that the Catholic Church – despite the restrictions imposed upon it – continued to exert great influence on the people. Even in his cardinal's robe, Mindszenty remained a simple priest. He was famous for his spartan quarters, his strength of will, and his huge capacity for work. Throughout the winter he slept in an unheated room, and during the day he worked in a modest study. He took simple meals, and expected his priests to show moderation in all things. When a confirmation ceremony was being planned, Mindszenty's secretary stressed that "in line with the express wish of His Eminence, the lunch should be modest." "When ordinary members of the public are going without, the primate cannot eat with a big spoon (i.e., indulge in a feast)," he explained.[99] He refused to accept the state salary offered to him in lieu of church estate revenue, and he distributed among the poor the donations made to him. Consequently, his primatial palace became a place of frugality, and the palace gardens were used to cultivate vegetables. He found harmony of soul in renunciation; he fasted on two or three days in each week, which greatly exceeded the prescribed number of strict fasting days. Self-denial, a valuable part of the fasting process, was directed towards supplication to divine mercy. He had just one weakness: a light cigar, which he cut in half. He would smoke one half after lunch and the other half after dinner.[100]

Mindszenty made many – perhaps too many – public appearances. There was, however, a price to pay for the popularity he achieved: Hungary's politicians came to view him as an adversary rather than as an opponent. The masses, meanwhile, regarded him as a veritable oracle, for there was no issue that he declined to address from the perspective of faith. He became the embodiment of a critique of everything that people feared or despised. His rhetoric was characterized by a self-confident style that could seem harsh and patronizing. A deeply-ingrained hostility towards communism drove his actions. In Mindszenty's view, the nature of pastoral work left him with

98. PL Mm. 9. d. Report of the Archbishop's High Commissioner; *Magyar Kurír* 38, December 12, 1948, first edition.

99. PL Mm. 11. d. Information on the confirmation ceremonies in the fall of 1946, June 23, 1946.

100. Ispánki, *Az évszázad pere*, 51; Statement made by the Salesian monk János Szőke, June 7, 2010.

no option but to take a position on political issues. For him, political activity was a necessary evil. In the shadow of Soviet armor, however, Mindszenty had no real chance of successfully opposing the regime.

THE DISPUTE OVER SCHOOLS

At its meetings on December 30, 1947 and January 7, 1948, the Political Committee (Politburo) of the Hungarian Communist Party debated a new policy towards the churches. Rákosi summarized the essence of the new policy as follows: Clerical reaction must be done away with by the end of the year [1948].[101] Concerning the means to achieve this goal, he mentioned "agreement," "settlement," and "termination." Rákosi was not so reckless as to attack the spiritual mission of the Catholic Church. Rather, in a lengthy speech, he referred to Mindszenty exclusively in a political context.

It must be acknowledged that Mindszenty had several vulnerabilities. The Hungarian primate exploited every opportunity to express his antipathy towards the communists, to criticize the government's decisions, and to expose police tyranny. Provocation of the authorities was not alien to him. Indeed, he kept in contact with "enemies of the regime," doing so, in some cases, even after they had gone into exile. Such behavior merely nurtured suspicions of his involvement in anti-state activities. Further, he fostered relations with Western diplomats, who, however, reacted somewhat ambiguously.

> We respect his courage, his determination, and the dignity with which he conducts himself. At the same time, it must be acknowledged that at least some clergy and the country's most informed Catholics disapprove of his intransigence, his narrow-mindedness, his authoritarian and brash manner, his capacity for provoking incidents, and, finally and most importantly, his reactionary spirit understood in the strongest of terms. He is characterized by arrogance, a refusal to accept things as they are, a 'no, no, never' attitude, which is not without magnitude but is full of risks. The feudal Hungarian of the Horthy era is embodied in this prelate, who, however, has no aristocratic roots. [...] It seems that he shares the view

101. PIL 274. f. 1/22. ő. e. 39. fol. Minutes of the HCP's Third National Conference of Functionaries, January 10–11, 1948; Mátyás Rákosi, *Válogatott beszédek és cikkek* (Budapest: Szikra, 1951), 267.

> of those who think that there has been no lawful government in Hungary since the fall of Horthy and that the current regime is based on the bayonets of the occupiers,[102]

the French ambassador to Hungary wrote about the cardinal in a perceptive report.

Rákosi's speech, promising to bring about the defeat of clerical reaction, was more than a party-political strategy. As the Communist Party's leader was also the Hungarian deputy prime minister, the policy could be viewed as part of the government's program. People began to wonder how the policy should be interpreted: Did it amount to the digging up of the hatchet and the advent of a war on the churches? Or was it merely political bluff, whose purpose was to persuade the Holy See to recognize the Hungarian government? Here, it is worth noting that the government's repeated attempts to revitalize relations had so far proved fruitless. The biggest diplomatic fiasco had involved the Hungarian envoy in Rome, László Velics, who had been personally acquainted with the pope for two decades. In October 1947, Velics had submitted his credentials to the Vatican authorities, indicating to them that all moderate political forces in Hungary supported the prompt restoration of diplomatic relations – which, in turn, had become a possibility upon the termination of the ACC's mandate. Velics had then confidently awaited the Vatican's response. When the reply came, however, his surprise could not have been greater: "The Holy See considers that the time is not yet ripe for negotiations with the Hungarian government and for the restoration of diplomatic relations, as in its view the Hungarian government – albeit through no fault of its own – does not have complete freedom of action."[103] Velics was not even given an audience with the pope, on the grounds that the latter could not receive an envoy who was accredited to the Republic of Italy.[104]

102. AMAE AD Série: Europe, 1944–1949, sous-série: Hongrie, dossier 18, Questions religieuses, 1944–49. fol. 19–22. Report no. 40/EU of Henry Gauquié, French legate in Budapest, January 24, 1948.

103. MNL OL XIX-J-1-j, Vatikán-IV-14-487/pol. res./1947. Report of the Hungarian envoy in Rome, László Velics, November 7, 1947.

104. AMAE AD Série: Europe, 1944–1949, sous-série: Hongrie, dossier 18, Questions religieuses, 1944–49. fol. 19–22. Report no. 40/EU of Henry Gauquié, French legate in Budapest, January 24, 1948.

The Holy See's rejection of Velics and the growing international tension led the authorities in Hungary to view the Catholic Church as an enemy of the state and the embodiment of "clerical reaction." Here it is worth noting how, in May 1946, Rákosi had told his comrades that it was not possible to chase two "hares," but that the day would come when the Catholic Church would be the hare. And on that day the Communist Party would be holding a gun. At the turn of 1948, the "hunt" began, slowly but surely. For the time being, however, Rákosi strove to maintain the impression of a democratic Hungary. He therefore launched all-embracing reforms of education, calling the various parties to the negotiating table.

Meetings of "Private Individuals"

For a time both the government and the other actors had an interest in negotiations, for they all wished to avoid a mutually damaging conflict. Having liquidated or co-opted the other political parties, the Communist Party now found itself up against the only organized force in Hungarian society that was capable of opposing the regime – the Catholic Church. Moreover, the Church continued to have substantial control of an essential element of the country's future development, namely the education of its young people. Religious education at school remained compulsory. Significantly, the religious denominations still ran 60 percent of elementary schools, 80 percent of male primary teacher training colleges, and 75 percent of female primary teacher training colleges. Such church schools and colleges outperformed the state-run institutions in terms of both pupil numbers and the quality of education. The minister of education and religious affairs even acknowledged this fact in an unguarded but truthful remark.

On January 8, 1948, at a meeting of Hungary's Catholic prelates, Gyula Czapik, Archbishop of Eger, stated unexpectedly that the time had come for negotiations with the government. The surprise of those in attendance was heightened when Cardinal Mindszenty raised no objection to the proposal. He wrote in an unpublished manuscript for his memoirs the following: "I did not oppose the talks. And they did take place. It would have been difficult to avoid them, because completely isolating oneself simply irritates the other party – even more so when the other party is like the one we faced. And by entering negotiations we did not breach our principles."[105] On several occasions, Mindszenty discussed tactics with Gyula Czapik, Archbishop of Eger, who had been asked to head the delegation. The two men agreed that the Church would negotiate subject to the fulfillment of four conditions: 1. Restoration of diplomatic relations between the Holy See and Hungary; 2. Authorization for the Catholic associations that had been banned in 1946; 3. The granting of a license for a Catholic daily newspaper; 4. The cessation of anti-religious attacks by the Marxist parties.

Meanwhile the Politburo of the Hungarian Communist Party was finalizing its own prerequisites for the start of negotiations: "The first demand from our side in the talks should be that the Church take an official and positive stance on the issue of democracy and the three-year plan."[106] Rákosi personally headed the government delegation, and the apparent aim of the talks was to reach an agreement. Similar talks were also undertaken with the Protestant Churches. The conciliatory style was a means of distracting attention from the real nature of the proposed measures. Similarly to the salami tactics used against the political parties, the underlying purpose was to sow divisions among the various denominations and cause splits even within the various churches. In the case of the Catholic Church, the government even hoped to provoke a split with Rome. Signs of a division between Catholics and Protestants were already apparent. Some of the tension stemmed from the fact that the president of Hungary was a Calvinist minister who was widely regarded as a supporter (and guarantor) of a policy of accommodating the governing coalition and communism. The Soviets were also interested in strengthening groupings within the Catholic Church that were opposed to Mindszenty: a memorandum issued by the Soviet Union's foreign ministry mentions this possibility and discusses how the Vatican might view such a development.[107] Two years later, the Politburo of the Hungarian Working People's Party concluded self-critically that "our attempts to break up the Bishops' Conference have brought little success."[108]

105. MMAL 070. sz. A red file containing Mindszenty's manuscripts.

106. PIL 274. f. 3/130. ő. e. Minutes of the meeting of the HCP PC (Politburo), February 5, 1948.

107. Volokitina et al., *Vlasty i cerkov*, vol. 1, 363.

108. MNL OL M–KS 276. f. 53/15. ő. e. 46. fol. Minutes of the meeting of the Hungarian Working People's Party PC (Politburo) on November 25, 1948. See also RGASPI f. 17. op. 128. delo (file). 521. l. 215.

The period was a rather anachronistic one. On the one hand, the two sides shared a mutual hatred; on the other, they were inquisitive about each other. Each side carefully observed the other, and sometimes even polite conversation was made. A Soviet memorandum even decries the lack of consistency on the part of the Hungarian communists. According to the memorandum, the Hungarians were casting aspersions on Mindszenty, while also renovating church buildings and arranging for priests to consecrate newly opened Communist Party offices. Indeed, in one party office in Hungary "a crucifix hung on the wall between portraits of Stalin and Rákosi."[109] Diplomats stationed in Budapest were surprised when Marshal Voroshilov suddenly expressed a desire to visit the Basilica in Budapest and then, during the visit, told the episcopal vicar that "religion is greatly esteemed in the Soviet Union."[110] Meanwhile, in a significant shift, Mindszenty authorized Catholic schools to take part in the government-sponsored festivities that were being held to mark the centenary of the revolutionary events of 1848. Even so, he stipulated that the Church should not be subjected to senseless criticism.

The first unofficial negotiations between the Hungarian government and the Catholic Church took place in a private residence on February 7, 1948. The Bishops' Conference was represented by Gyula Czapik, Archbishop of Eger. On the government side, Deputy Prime Minister Mátyás Rákosi was accompanied by several communist politicians. Although Rákosi swore to be discreet and the parties agreed not to draw up a memorandum, nevertheless the political police made a secret tape-recording of the proceedings. The recording even includes the sound of spoons being stirred in coffee cups and the rustling of letter paper, on account of which sometimes the conversation is difficult to hear.[111] Czapik had no such technology at his disposal; he later made notes based on what he could recall:

109. Information bulletin of the Foreign Policy Department of the CPSU CC for the Hungarian Working People's Party on the lessons to be drawn from the errors of the Yugoslav Communist Party. Moscow, before June 12, 1948. See István Vida, ed., *Iratok a magyar–szovjet kapcsolatok történetéhez 1944. október – 1948. június* (Budapest: Gondolat Kiadó, 2005), 334–35.

110. AMAE AD Série: Europe 1944–1949, sous-série: Hongrie, dossier 18, Questions religieuses, 1944–49. fol. 34. Report no. 100/EU of Henry Gauquié, French legate in Budapest, March 21, 1948.

111. PIL 274. f. 7/261. ő. e. Typed text of recording made of negotiations between representatives of the HCP and of the Catholic Church.

> I had to be very cautious, lest I said something that might subsequently be used against me, and lest I said more than what had to be said and used up my arguments (new ones being needed subsequently) and offered them a deeper insight into how we were conducting ourselves.[112]

The tone of the discussion was a polite one; it was far from the oversimplified style of the press. Rákosi requested that the Catholic Church issue an official statement in support of both the republic and the land reform program. For him it did not suffice that the Church had refrained from actively opposing the authorities and the three-year plan, thereby acquiescing to the changes. Archbishop Czapik stated that the Church could not come before the faithful with positive statements about the regime until the government abandoned its hostile stance towards the Church. For the Church, the form of government was not an essential issue; acknowledging that Hungary was now a republic would not give rise to any particular difficulties, in his view.

On February 14, 1948, the Government Minister Ortutay visited Mindszenty in Esztergom for the express purpose of discussing the grievances of the Church. At the meeting, no mention was made of the nationalization of schools. The two men did, however, discuss the timing of the launch of official negotiations. Mindszenty evaded the issue by claiming that under canonical law the Apostolic Holy See was exclusively entitled to sign an agreement.[113] Overall, the meeting between the government minister and the primate took place in good spirits. At the end of the meeting, Mindszenty accompanied Ortutay to the stairwell. His politeness contrasted starkly with his words in a speech given the next day at Saint Stephen's Academy, when he spoke – in connection with the government – of a "yoke of lies."[114] At the behest of Mindszenty, a subsequent meeting of the Bishops' Conference, held on March 18, 1948, drafted an ecclesiastical warning (*monitum*) that could be used as the clergy saw fit: "A self-aware person cannot become a member of [one of] the Marxist parties; a person

112. PMKL IV. 213. Legacy of István Albert, item no. 4, Pro memoria on the informative discussion of February 7, 1948.

113. Beke, *A magyar katolikus püspökkari 1945–1948*, 335.

114. SzCsPL 581/1948. Speech of József Mindszenty at St. Stephen's Academy, February 15, 1948.

that does join, must be condemned and may not partake of the Sacrament of Penance and may not obtain absolution."[115] The warning was modeled on an encyclical that had been issued by Archbishop Alfredo Schuster of Milan in February, whereby communists were not to be administered the sacraments. The dissemination of the *monitum* was to be carried out in secret. However, on the very same day a copy of its text already lay on the desks of several senior ministerial officials. On hearing of the leak, Mindszenty acknowledged that some kind of retaliation was likely in view of the rising tension between church and state.[116] On March 20, 1948, with the aim of ameliorating the situation, Mindszenty paid a visit on Gyula Ortutay, minister for education and religious affairs. The meeting, however, did not progress beyond formalities. It was the last time the two men met. Indeed, Mindszenty subsequently refused to take part in any event attended by Ortutay. The measures taken against the Church continued. The nationalization of the Stephaneum Catholic Printing Company resulted essentially in the cessation of Catholic book publishing in Hungary.

It was against this backdrop that informal talks between representatives of the government and of the Bishops' Conference were resumed on April 16, 1948. Whereas the meeting in February had been almost jovial, on this occasion the mood was subdued. Rákosi accused Mindszenty of persuading the Bishops' Conference to facilitate the excommunication of communists and socialists. He questioned Mindszenty's legitimacy, stating that he believed the cardinal would rather have his arm cut off than recognize the republic. He frankly acknowledged that the authorities could not be indifferent to the actions of the Hungarian primate, because "Mindszenty is not just anyone! He is not your run-of-the-mill priest – albeit one often has the feeling that he's still in that role – forgive me if I am being disrespectful, but he has not moved beyond this level. [...] There is a difference between a no-name chaplain daydreaming about plans for the restoration of the monarchy in the spirit of legitimism and the same being done by the head of the Hungarian Catholic Church."[117] He then asked: "Cannot the bishops somehow stop this man from ruining everything?" Czapik responded

115. PIL 274. f. 7/248. ő. e. 128. fol. Report on the conference of March 18, 1948. Cf. Beke, *A magyar katolikus püspökkari 1945–1948*, 312.

116. PIL 274. f. 7/248. ő. e. 131. fol. Report, Budapest, April 11, 1948.

117. PIL 274. f. 7/261. ő. e. 100. fol. Typed text of recording made of negotiations on April 16, 1948.

laconically as follows: "You might just as well ask me to change the trajectory of the moon."[118] In the end, Rákosi offered an agreement that was essentially the same as the one made with the Protestants, holding out the prospect of as many as sixteen Catholic high schools.

Archbishop Czapik promptly reported to Mindszenty on the talks. It was his impression that the government had no real interest in reaching an agreement but was seeking to place the blame for the failure of the talks on the Church. Mindszenty was aware of his responsibility and found himself in a quandary. On April 27, he sent a confidant to Chapin, the US envoy, to ask whether he should adhere to the Christian moral foundation or accommodate the situation at hand. Chapin gave no tangible advice. His reticence was related either to his being a diplomat or to a visit Czapik had paid on him a couple of weeks earlier, when the archbishop had expressly requested that Mindszenty be denied unconditional support, as such support would be – in Czapik's view – detrimental to the interests of the Church.[119] In response, Mindszenty's representative revealed that the cardinal wondered whether the Church "had to come to terms with a short- or long-term accommodation with the communists, since apparently war was inevitable." Chapin then told his superiors the following:

> I told him that I did not personally share the opinion that war was inevitable, I said that I felt I could go so far as to say that US certainly would never attack first and to best my knowledge and belief Soviet Government itself did not wish war but that of course there was always a possibility that some irresponsible persons might bring about a prestige situation which would have serious results.[120]

The US secretary of state agreed with Chapin: "It is not (rpt not) advisable for US to intervene in current issues between church and state."[121]

118. Ibid., 121–122. fol.

119. ÁBTL 3.1.9. V–302/1. 33–34. fol. Minutes of interrogation of Jenő Kerkai, February 17, 1954.

120. MNL OL XX–10–k LÜ PO 18.300/1989. US archival sources. Report no. 688 of Legate S. Chapin, April 26, 1948.

121. MNL OL XX–10–k LÜ PO 18.300/1989. US archival sources. Telegram no. 522 sent by US Secretary of State George C. Marshall to Legate S. Chapin. Washington, May 21, 1948 Washington.

Mindszenty was thus required to come to his own decision. Although – having been told by the Vatican that the Holy Father would like to see a *modus vivendi*[122] – he did not categorically rule out further talks, he nevertheless had no wish to add to the regime's credibility by signing an agreement with it. He was clearly counting on the regime being short-lived. For him, therefore, the downside of cooperation with the regime was its potential negative impact on relations between the Church and the state after the fall of the regime.

Nationalization

The minister for education and religious affairs made an official announcement concerning the government's unilateral decision to nationalize schools on May 15, 1948. Subsequent, rather desperate attempts to put a stop to the state takeover of schools ended in failure. Mindszenty responded to the authorities' demands by making some of his own, stipulating, for instance, that the grievances of the Church must be addressed before the commencement of official negotiations. His main demand was the renunciation of the government's plan to take control of schools.

On May 30, 1948, amid torrential rain, 250,000 Catholics attended a ceremony commemorating the tenth anniversary of the Eucharistic World Congress of 1938, which had been held in Budapest. The commemorative ceremony amounted to one of the largest Catholic demonstrations in postwar Hungary. The crowd listened to a radio speech by the pope. The speech, which the Interior Ministry had intended to ban, was delivered through loud speakers. In his speech, the pope encouraged Mindszenty and his bishops to show endurance, which, he said, would further enhance the authority and prestige of the Hungarian primate.[123] The occasion had another special feature: Mindszenty, citing a bout of sciatica, had not taken part in the Corpus Christi procession held three days earlier. His illness may have been "diplomatic in origin," as the procession had been attended, on behalf of the government, by Gyula Ortutay, minister for education and religious affairs.[124] In view of the government's intent to take control

122. ÁBTL 3.1.8. Sz–222/6. 119. fol. Report. Budapest, March 5, 1948.

123. *Magyar Kurír* 38, May 30, 1948, fourth extraordinary edition.

124. *Magyar Kurír* 38, May 27, 1948, second edition.

of schools, Mindszenty had not wished to brush shoulders with any government minister. In reality, the Hungarian primate's stubbornness had benefited the government, for it could condemn the Church for its "reactionary opposition" to its plans while happily proceeding with their implementation. While the Church had shown resolute determination, the government too was unwavering.

A whole series of heated meetings were held, and there were overt and veiled propaganda campaigns on both sides. Letters by the sackful were sent, with demands both for and against the nationalization of schools – but they always arrived at the other side's address. In the highly charged atmosphere, a mere spark could set off a blaze... The spark came on June 3 in the village of Pócspetri (Szabolcs County), where a policeman, who had been stationed outside the village hall, died after a gun accident. The authorities claimed that the man had been murdered. Indeed, the communist political leadership treated the incident as a provocation on the part of reactionary forces. The regime gave the impression that the Catholic Church, in its determination to keep its schools, would even be capable of criminal action. In this way, what had been an accident became a murder, with the witnesses as the murderers and the local priest as the instigator. Pócspetri also became a symbol for the "intellectual darkness" prevailing in the eastern part of the country, which, in turn, served as justification for the nationalization of schools within a general educational reform framework. The government argued that such reform was necessary in order to modernize Hungary.

People's passions were unleashed, and in many places there were disturbances that sometimes escalated into violence. The press demanded the incarceration of the head of the "black [clerical] reaction." Concurrently, however, both sides in the dispute – the Communist Party and the Catholic bishops – received signals that there was no purpose in heightening tensions. The masses had grown tired of the propaganda thrown at them from both sides. The annual harvest was approaching, and people's livelihoods had more importance than anything else. Therefore it was expected that the nationalization campaign would soon draw to a close. As the last act in this war of nerves, Mindszenty took steps to mobilize support among American Catholics: on June 8, 1948, he sent word to Cardinal Spellman about the regime's efforts to nationalize the schools and the various waves of subsequent protest. The Hungarian primate then expressed a request: "Please bring to the attention of every Catholic institution, school and parish that they should, as quickly as possible, send telegrams and letters to our government or to our Parliament, therein taking a stand against the worsening persecution of the Church in Hungary."[125] Mindszenty subsequently drew the following analogy: when a man is judged guilty and sentenced to death, there is often a flood of telegrams demanding the man's deliverance; now, with the nationalization and the spiritual and physical suppression of the youth, the life to come has been sentenced to death. What might the Church lose by refusing to negotiate? In the cardinal's view, barely anything, for the [Catholic] schools, as well as state funding for such schools, had already been lost. True, there were still some things of a material nature that could be lost (congrua, the salaries of teachers of theology, pensions, etc.), but in his view, one could not abandon or compromise one's principles for the sake of material gain. For Cardinal Mindszenty, the only way forward was to seek to win some time.

Meanwhile, the Fourth Congress of the Hungarian Communist Party and the Thirty-Seventh Congress of the Social Democratic Party were held on June 12, 1948. The two parties convened separately in the morning and then held a joint congress in the afternoon, at which the merger of the two parties was announced. After the merger, the new united party was called the Hungarian Working People's Party (which soon became known as the "vanguard of the proletarian dictatorship"). This marked the end of a major battle for power: right-wingers among the Social Democrats were removed from leading positions. The slogans chosen for a procession held in celebration of the party merger did not spare the Hungarian primate: "Mindszenty is doomed; now give us our nationalized schools!"[126]

Concerning the case in Pócspetri, a martial-law trial was held on June 11, 1948. The next day the "murderer" of the police officer was sentenced to death and then executed by hanging. A death sentence was also received by János Asztalos, the local priest. However, in a presidential act of clemency, this sentence was later commuted to life imprisonment in a high-security prison. (Both the local notary, who was executed, and the

125. AANY Collection 007, Box S/D-10, Folder 8. Letter of József Mindszenty to Archbishop F. J. Spellman. Esztergom, June 8, 1948.

126. PL Mm. 30. d. Typed text preserved among a collection of articles from *Szabad Nép*.

priest were exonerated by a Hungarian court in 1990.) The day of the execution (June 12) saw the publication of a pastoral letter by the Bishops' Conference. The bishops imposed the most severe ecclesiastical discipline on individuals who voted for or collaborated in the implementation of legislation on the nationalization of schools. This action on the part of bishops caused a crisis of conscience in many people, because state officials, bureaucrats or judges knew they would lose their jobs if they refused to implement the provisions of the law. The ramifications of the bishops' instruction were also a matter of concern for the lower clergy.

On June 15, the bishops met once more, prior to the parliamentary debate on the school nationalization bill. Mindszenty was of the view that his earlier measures had been justified, for Bishop Hamvas of Csanád, having returned from his so-called *ad limina* visit to Rome (which a bishop was supposed to make at least every five years), brought the following message from the Papal Secretariat of State: "They approve of our conduct in the matter of the schools."[127] On the same day (June 15), writing in the newspaper *Szabad Nép* (Free People), Mátyás Rákosi vehemently criticized Mindszenty and his church policy. The outcome of the battle was already decided, even though (or perhaps precisely because) three thousand state schools stood against as many as five thousand church schools. Of that latter number, 3,148 were Catholic schools (1,706 elementary schools, 1,205 so-called people's schools, 52 grammar schools, 87 middle schools, 32 teacher training schools and lyceums, 3 kindergarten teacher training schools, 27 workers' schools, 36 other schools in such sectors as nursing, farming, industrial, commercial, shorthand and typing schools). There were 463,405 pupils at these schools (run by the Catholic Church).[128] On June 16, the Parliament – in a session interrupted by shouting and heckling – voted to adopt Act 33 of 1948 on the nationalization of church schools. There were 230 votes in favor of the adoption of the act and 63 votes against. The names of representatives were recorded against their votes, a practice that was not repeated for some decades afterwards... Representatives of the

127. Beke, *A magyar katolikus püspökkari 1945–1948*, 359.

128. Statistics for Catholic schools (February 1, 1947). Mindszenty sent the statistics to Archbishop Spellman, Esztergom, June 8, 1948 (AANY Collection 007, Box S/D-10, Folder 8.) Note: different data appear in various historical works, but the order of magnitude is the same.

Democratic People's Party and the Christian Women's League voted against the legislation.

More than 2,500 teachers from the religious orders were forced to abandon their careers, as a bishops' directive prohibited them from teaching in nationalized schools. Teachers of religious education were the only exceptions, as religious education lessons remained compulsory until September 1949. The decision of the bishops was a precipitous one as it left many monks and nuns in a precarious state in terms of their livelihoods. With a view to protecting the interests of these monks and nuns, the heads of several religious orders – Pál Sárközy (Benedictine abbot primate), Vendel Endrédy (Cistercian abbot), Sándor Sík (Piarist provincial superior), and István Borbély (Jesuit provincial superior) – embarked on negotiations with the Ministry of Education and Religious Affairs, doing so, however, without Mindszenty's permission. When Cardinal Mindszenty heard what had happened, he publicly disavowed the monks, given that they had received no instructions from the Bishops' Conference to negotiate.[129] This action ruled out the possibility of further talks.

Vince Tomek, Father General of the Piarist Order, concluded that he should attempt to persuade Mindszenty to change his mind. Tomek thus returned home to Hungary from Rome on July 25, 1948, in order to speak out on behalf of schools run by the religious orders and their teachers. He did so, even though the Papal Secretariat of State had cast doubt on whether anything could or should be done: "Regarding the matter of schools, we should do what the primate tells us to do. If he says that we should negotiate with the government, then we should negotiate. If, however, his position is a negative one, then we should obey him: one's view of the situation is better at home than in Rome."[130] Evidently, the Vatican believed that Mindszenty held the key to resolving the situation. On August 11, 1948, Tomek traveled to Esztergom, having already met with Archbishop Czapik, who was of the view that "the greatest problem is that they thought we were strong, and now it is obvious that we are weak. And the cause of all

129. PMKL Tartományfőnöki levelezés, vegyes ügyek [Correspondence of the Provincial, miscellaneous issues], N. 1267/4. Pro memoria on the talks held with the heads of the teaching orders.

130. PMKL IV. 198. Legacy of Vince Tomek, own manuscripts, item no. 12. Recollections of Vince Tomek (1968–81). 64. fol.

this is the primate. The primate is a sick man full of hatred."[131] The meeting between Mindszenty and Tomek brought no change to the situation. Tomek failed to persuade the Hungarian primate that communism was unlikely to collapse in the near future and that a world war was similarly unlikely. Having achieved nothing, he returned to Rome.

Even after Tomek's failed attempt, Archbishop Czapik and others who were in favor of negotiations refused to abandon their struggle. Czapik forwarded to Mindszenty a proposal for a settlement that had been drafted by the Democratic People's Party. Under the terms of the proposal, certain Catholic schools would have been exempted from the provisions of the nationalization law for a period of one year. Thereafter the provisions of the law would have been implemented unless, in the meantime, an agreement had been reached between the Church and the government. For Mindszenty, however, the proposal was no more than communist trickery. Meanwhile, the minister of education and religious affairs let it be known that for him the proposal would have been an acceptable one.[132]

Concerning the nationalization of schools, Mindszenty informed the pope and several other leading churchmen, including Cardinal Spellman of New York:

> There is no doubt that if our country were democratic, our schools would have remained Catholic, in accordance with the spirit and intent of the majority of the people. But all of this is happening against a backdrop of threats, violence and – for some weeks now – military deployments, detention of leaders, lies and deceit, efforts to prevent Catholics from speaking, prohibitions on jubilee celebrations, the disruption of religious processions, imprisonment of hundreds of thousands of people and their being persuaded into 'switching sides in prison,' and the coercion of people into making false statements. And what is now to follow is the confiscation of agricultural produce from our farming folk. We ask for your prayers that now – with three and half years having already passed – the Lord will

131. Ibid., 65. fol.

132. PMKL IV. 213. Legacy of István Albert, item no. 4, Barankovics's proposal for schools; PL 6087/1948. József Mindszenty's report to Pius XII. Esztergom, September 6, 1948.

shorten the time of 'his visit'[133] and will protect the fortunate nations of this world from the ideas and rule of atheism.[134]

The school year began in the nationalized schools on September 6 without any serious disturbances. Mindszenty was confident that the government would be incapable of finding replacements for those teachers who had been removed because they were clergymen or members of religious orders. In the end, the authorities succeeded in employing 1,500 new teachers by offering "accelerated" teacher training courses to unemployed intellectuals. The policy was facilitated by the high rate of unemployment among intellectuals in postwar Hungary. The explanation for the smaller number of new teachers (1,500) relative to the larger number of teachers who had lost their jobs in the Catholic schools (2,500) was that most of the teachers in the Catholic elementary schools had a secular background and could continue teaching in the state-run schools. Even so, serious difficulties arose (including a fall in educational standards) as a result of the absence of teachers from the religious orders.

On the eve of the new school year, Cardinal Mindszenty's pastoral letter was read out in every Catholic church throughout Hungary. Mindszenty reminded congregations that in the nationalized schools there would be – for the first time in a thousand years – a complete absence of Catholic educators working alongside the children. He also explained why the government's offer to priests and members of the religious orders concerning their jobs had been unacceptable. He stated that, in his view, education in the nationalized schools would not be neutral, for if the government had no intention of indoctrinating the children, why had it insisted on taking control of the schools? He advised parents to prevent their children from joining "anti-Christian and anti-Hungarian" clubs and societies at school. Parents should, on the contrary, enroll their children in

133. The reference may be to Luke 19:43–44 (cf. Deuteronomy 28:52; 29:2–3; Jeremiah 6:6; Zechariah 14:2): "For the days shall come upon thee, that thine enemies shall cast a trench about thee, and compass thee round, and keep thee in on every side, and shall lay thee even with the ground, and thy children within thee; and they shall not leave in thee one stone upon another; because thou knewest not the time of thy visitation."

134. AANY Collection 007 Box S/D-10. Folder 6. József Mindszenty's letter in Latin to Archbishop Spellman. Esztergom, July 21, 1948. (Date of arrival: August 18.)

Catholic youth organizations. At the end of the pastoral letter, Mindszenty strongly urged parents – in lieu of the monks and nuns that had formerly educated the children – to teach their children about Christian ideals and morality. The forceful but sober tone of the circular letter differed greatly from the Hungarian primate's earlier statements on the issue.

In consequence of nationalization, from June 1948 until September 1950 there were no Catholic schools in operation in Hungary. When, in 1950, the Catholic Church signed an agreement with the Hungarian state, only eight schools were returned to it, whereas under the proposed deal of 1948, it would have been given control over as many as 16 high schools. In a way, therefore, the Catholic Church was punished for its intransigence. Even if unwittingly, the policy of adhering to its principles resulted in a reduction in the regime's original offer on the number of schools that could be retained by the Church. This, in turn, led to problems later on in terms of finding young Catholic intellectuals who could follow in the footsteps of the older generation. Of course, no-one can be sure whether the communist regime would have fulfilled its promises... Clearly, for the time being, Mindszenty had lost a battle but not the war. Meanwhile, a series of negotiations commenced by the government with the Protestant Churches and the Jewish denomination led – after a number of personnel changes and, in the case of the Lutherans, the prosecution of Bishop Lajos Ordass – to the signing of agreements over a period of several weeks between October and December. Paradoxically, in order to survive, these churches subsequently had no choice but to acknowledge and accept the death sentence imposed on churches and religions by the Marxist approach to history.

"WE WILL DESTROY MINDSZENTY-ISM!"

The Sovietization of Hungarian society and the eradication, by economic and then political means, of opportunities for self-organization progressed rapidly during 1948. The merger of the two workers' parties (more precisely the disappearance of the Social Democratic Party), the nationalization of industrial plants, and the nationalization of schools were all milestones in the ideological and political struggle. The multiparty political system had become no more than a formality. The evolving relationship between the Catholic Church and the Hungarian state became a key domestic political factor in Hungary. The authorities' ongoing disputes with the churches, however, were a source of potential problems with unforeseeable consequences for the Hungarian rural masses and in the field of Hungary's international relations. The nationalization of church schools transformed the gap between the Catholic Church and the state into a seemingly unbridgeable chasm.

Towards a "Tougher Political Line"

On one side of the political arena stood the Hungarian Working People's Party (formed through the merger of the Communist Party and the Social Democratic Party), together with the State Protection Authority. On the other side stood the Catholic Church and its prince primate, József Mindszenty. It soon became evident that Mindszenty would personally be targeted. Archbishop Czapik pointed out at a meeting of the Bishops' Conference on June 24, 1948, that according to information he had received "they want to find something that could be used to compromise Your Eminence." They were examining Mindszenty's contacts with people abroad and investigating his currency transactions.

The wrath of Deputy Prime Minister Rákosi had by this time turned on the Catholic Church and on Mindszenty, who was the same age as him (the two men having been born in the same month). For Rákosi, Cardinal Mindszenty was the embodiment of the principles he despised and of the constitutional order – the former regime – that had locked him up in prison. Indeed, Rákosi hated and looked down on Mindszenty. In his memoirs, he wrote openly and frankly of the antipathy he felt for the cardinal: "Prior to World War I, people in the movement were well acquainted with a type of cleric that was called a 'joker chaplain' – an uneducated and slow-witted heckler priest who was based in a village or small town and who hated socialism and despised workers."[135] The antipathy was mutual; the two men were at opposite ends of the ideological spectrum.

Rákosi often pondered how he might remove Mindszenty from public life. When, in February 1948, he visited Moscow in order to sign the Soviet–Hungarian treaty, he told his Soviet comrades that "for the time being we

135. Mátyás Rákosi, *Visszaemlékezések 1940–1956* (Budapest: Napvilág Kiadó, 1997), 516.

shall not openly oppose the Church, but if they [the Church] declare war on us, we will find some good psychiatrists willing to declare Mindszenty insane."[136] István Barankovics noted in his diary how Rákosi would have preferred a "less painful" (Rákosi's words) method of silencing the cardinal. In private conversation, Rákosi would often accuse Mindszenty "of wanting to be a martyr at any price, but I will not do him the pleasure of making a martyr out of him."[137] Mihály Károlyi, who had earlier served as Hungary's first president, was Hungary's envoy in Paris at the time. Károlyi, who not only was indifferent to Catholic interests but also supported the regime's policy of coming down hard on the clerical opposition, advised the government to show caution, lest it made an error that would be seized upon by the Americans. In his view, the US government was not only threatening Hungary but also seriously planning for war: "Putting such a major figure in jail would be exploited by them to get public opinion behind a 'holy' war. It's better for us to lose a battle today than a war tomorrow. Before you decide on a final reckoning, it must be discussed with the Kremlin. Only you can do this," wrote Károlyi to Mátyás Rákosi.[138] Stressing the need for caution, Károlyi referred to a meeting he had with the Soviet ambassador to France, A. J. Bogomolov, during which he had attempted to fathom the official Soviet position. When Károlyi had made the provocative suggestion that the Hungarian government imprison Mindszenty, the ambassador had rejected such a move by "shaking his head, although he had not said a word." A similar opinion appeared in a Soviet report on the situation in Hungary: while the report approved of the nationalization of church schools, it showed no enthusiasm for combining the measure with a fight against "clerical reaction," for exacerbating divisions between Catholics and Protestants, or for arranging for the dismissal of Mindszenty.[139]

136. Volokitina et al., *Vostochnaja Evropa*, vol. 1, 761–762, Memorandum of L. S. Baranov to Mátyás Rákosi, the general secretary of the HCP, and to M. A. Suslov, secretary of the CPSU, on the discussions in Moscow. February 19, 1948.

137. Árpád Pünkösti, *Rákosi a csúcson: 1948–1953* (Budapest: Európa, 1996), 76–77.

138. PIL 274. f. 10/10. ő. e. 28–29. fol. Letter of Mihály Károlyi to Mátyás Rákosi. Paris, May 31, 1948. Published in Tibor Hajdu, ed., *Károlyi Mihály levelezése V. 1945–1949* (Budapest: Napvilág Kiadó, 2003), 534. (The next quotation is also from this source.)

139. Vida, *Iratok a magyar–szovjet kapcsolatok történetéhez*, 334–335. Information bulletin of the Foreign Policy Department of the CPSU CC on the lessons to be drawn from the errors of the Yugoslav Communist Party. Moscow, before June 12, 1948.

Mátyás Rákosi replied to Mihály Károlyi on June 10, responding also to concerns about the fate of Mindszenty:

> In this area, if I may express myself in this way, we are on the defensive; we are merely returning the blows, literally. Whether Mindszenty will or will not be detained, is of course a political question. It is something that requires much consideration, because it is difficult to find someone like him, who has blindly made a series of such grave political errors and has a compromised past going back thirty years. Seen from this perspective, he is not such a bad opponent.[140]

Rákosi did not rule out the possibility of getting rid of Mindszenty, but for him it was crucial to wait for the right moment. In the meantime, he was evidently overstepping his competences as the deputy prime minister of a supposedly democratic state.

Preparations for the prosecution of the Hungarian primate took more than six months. In May, in addition to the customary state security surveillance, Rákosi ordered the targeted gathering of data about Mindszenty. He requested Gábor Péter, the head of the State Security Department, who went on to head the successor institution – the State Security Office of the Interior Ministry – to compile a dossier of "problematic" churchmen, namely Mindszenty, as well as several Lutheran church leaders. A tailor by trade, Péter had been a member of the clandestine communist movement under the Horthy regime. A man of limited imagination, he always adhered to Mátyás Rákosi's instructions, doing so in a rather pedantic and unscrupulous fashion. And so it was with the data Rákosi had requested. Péter had, at his disposal, abundant material: The State Security Department received, week by week, reports from every village, town and city in the country on the content of Sunday's sermons in the local churches.

Meanwhile, Mindszenty was increasingly a lone voice in the desert when it came to protesting against the regime. Most of the leaders of the political opposition as well as crucial figures in ecclesiastical life had opted to go

140. PIL 274. f. 10/10. ő. e. 30–31. fol. Letter of Mátyás Rákosi to Mihály Károlyi. June 10, 1948. Published in Hajdu, *Károlyi Mihály levelezése*, 535.

into exile rather than risk imprisonment. Interestingly, as the strength of the Parliamentary opposition waned, so the Catholic Church – with Mindszenty at the fore – took an ever greater role in uniting the anti-communist forces. Among Catholics going into exile were Zsigmond Mihalovics, the national director of Actio Catholica, and Sándor Csertő, the organization's secretary in Budapest. It seems likely that the authorities encouraged Mihalovics's departure from the country. In this way they were able to remove Mindszenty's most trusted confidant, who had worked hard to ensure a close relationship between the cardinal and the Catholic faithful. A further hope on the part of the authorities was that Mihalovics would seek to contact Mindszenty from abroad, thereby compromising him further. Their expectation proved correct: the rather reckless letters that Mihalovics sent Mindszenty from abroad did indeed cause substantial damage to the cardinal. The former director of Actio Catholica was subsequently prosecuted *in absentia*, receiving a ten-year prison sentence as punishment for anti-democratic activities and treasonous relations with foreign parties. Mihalovics was the first well-known priest that the regime sent before a People's Court. His trial was still underway when the press began reporting that the true guilty party was Mindszenty. These actions represented the first steps towards creating a public atmosphere in which Mindszenty could be put on trial.

Criticism of the Hungarian primate and slander against him continued throughout the summer. Efforts were made in the press to portray the cardinal as a retrograde and reactionary individual or, indeed, as a laughable figure. More and more churchmen were being arrested on the charge of "activities against the democratic constitutional order" (Act VII of 1946). On July 25, 1948, Mindszenty informed the pope in a letter of the detention and court sentencing of 225 priests and members of the religious orders; 24 of them had been arrested expressly for defending church schools.[141] Subsequently, he wrote to several leading figures in the world church about the harassment and persecution suffered by Catholics in Hungary. As a result, on August 25, 1948, the annual conference of German bishops issued a solemn protest against the suppression of religious

141. ÁBTL 3.1.9. V–700/17. 8–9. fol.

freedom in Hungary.[142] Mindszenty's letters to Catholics abroad clearly focused the attention of the world church on Hungary. An atmosphere of impending civil war in Hungary was exacerbated by the unexpected cancellation – after a political spat between church and state – of the Saint Stephen's Day (August 20) procession of the Holy Right Hand. The dispute arose when the Budapest police department unilaterally shortened the route of the procession. In response to this decision, Mindszenty declined to organize the procession, assigning the task of protecting the Holy Right Hand to several parish churches.[143] The Hungarian primate then held a celebratory mass at the Basilica at 10 a.m. on August 20. On that day the state security organs did not remain inactive: they sent a member of staff to all the churches in Budapest, each of whom was required to submit frequent reports. There were no disturbances or provocative acts, and the priests refrained, in their sermons, from criticizing party policy. Whereas a year earlier the feast day had been a spectacular and joyous occasion for Catholics in Hungary, it now constituted a silent display of resolute opposition to the regime.

On August 20, Deputy Prime Minister Mátyás Rákosi traveled to Kecskemét, where he celebrated the day as the "festival of the new bread." In a speech, he once again accused Mindszenty and his staff of "reactionary tendencies." This, he claimed, explained why the government needed to address concurrently the reorganization of agriculture on socialist lines (i.e., the introduction of agricultural cooperatives) and the eradication of the clerical reaction.[144] This was an important and cunning declaration on the part of the authorities. Evidently, the communist leadership believed that efforts to break up the peasantry – which was regarded as the social foundation of the Church – would inevitably weaken religious life and ecclesiastical influence. Indeed, the Hungarian Working People's Party stepped up its campaigns against both Mindszenty and the "kulaks" (rich

142. PL Processus, V–700/17. 326–327. fol. Joint letter from the cardinals Faulhaber, Frings, and von Preysing to Prince Primate József Mindszenty. Fulda, August 26, 1948.

143. MNL OL M–KS 276. f. 67/214. ő. e. 16–18. fol. Report. Budapest, August 17, 1948. – Note: Until 1950 the Holy Right Hand was kept in the cloister of the Sisters of Loreto (i.e., the Institute of the Blessed Virgin Mary). Then, after the Hungarian state withdrew the license for the religious order, it was kept in the safe of St. Stephen's Basilica. Until as late as 1988, public processions in honor of the Holy Right Hand were prohibited.

144. Mátyás Rákosi, *Építjük a nép országát* (Budapest: Szikra, 1949), 310–11.

peasant farmers). In the meantime, desperate efforts were being made behind the scenes to accomplish the discreet removal of Mindszenty and a compromise agreement between church and state.

Efforts towards a Diplomatic Solution

On September 21, 1948, Archbishop Czapik of Eger traveled to Rome on an *ad limina* visit.[145] As has already been discussed, Czapik and Mindszenty disagreed on the proper nature of the Church's relations with the state. Archbishop Czapik was not given an assignment by the government, but he did consult with Rákosi prior to his departure for Rome. According to the Communist Party leader's memoirs, Czapik was informally requested to ascertain whether the Vatican would be willing to come to an unofficial agreement with the Hungarian Communist Party leadership concerning Mindszenty's future.[146] Rákosi revealed to Czapik the position of the party's supreme organ as of September 2. He let it be known that a precondition for an agreement with the Catholic Church was the following: "Mindszenty, as well as several other persons whose activities are hindering an agreement, should be dismissed from their positions at the head of the Church. As part of this, the Hungarian democracy would be willing to sign an agreement, similar in essence to the one it has signed with the Reformed (Calvinist) Church."[147] The prelate Czapik, however, was far too independent-minded and disciplined to play the role of "postman" at Rákosi's behest. Even though Czapik held Mindszenty in low esteem and viewed his actions and policies as a burden, he would never have betrayed Mindszenty. "We have to support and count on him; we must lead the fight from the second row, endeavoring to reduce the gravity of the blows that are being struck against us because of him," Czapik wrote in a note addressed to himself.[148] At the same time, it was his opinion that the Soviet occupation (and with

145. For more on this issue, see Balázs Rétfalvi, "Czapik Gyula 1948-as római útja és az apostoli vizitáció ügye," *Egyháztörténeti Szemle* [Ecclesiastical History Review] 12, no. 2 (2011): 3–38. On the Internet: http://www.uni-miskolc.hu/~egyhtort/cikkek/retfalvibalazs.htm.

146. Rákosi, *Visszaemlékezések*, 513–15.

147. RGASPI f. 17. op. 128. delo (file) 519. l. 45. and MNL OL M–KS 276. f. 53/8. ő. e. 1. fol. Minutes of the meeting of the Hungarian Working People's Party CL PC on September 2, 1948.

148. PMKL IV. 213. Legacy of István Albert, item no. 4. The necessity of an agreement, VII.

it communism) would continue in the long term, and so a means of coexistence had to be found.

Archbishop Czapik was received by Pius XII on September 29, 1948, and by Domenico Tardini, secretary for the Congregation for Extraordinary Ecclesiastical Affairs, on October 2. Reportedly, the pope initially criticized the archbishop for his refusal to support Mindszenty but then rapidly became more open to a different view of recent developments in Hungary, subsequently consenting to the dispatch of a visitation committee to the country.[149] Tardini, on the other hand, argued that it would be a waste of time to negotiate with a government that did not keep its promises anyway.[150] Czapik naturally disputed this, arguing that coexistence was an inherently acceptable and decent option. The archbishop then held conversations with several other senior Vatican figures. The most fruitful of these was a discussion with Montini, an official who supported the republican form of government. The men Czapik met complained that they knew next to nothing about the negotiations in Hungary between church and state. In response, Archbishop Czapik drafted a report on the discussions held with Rákosi in 1948, which had ended in a stalemate. By the time he was due to travel home, Czapik had become more optimistic. Indeed, he was far more hopeful on his departure from Rome than he had been on his arrival in the city.

Czapik had not traveled to Rome in order to persuade the Vatican to remove or dismiss Mindszenty. Rather, he sought an elegant and reassuring answer to the question of how, in a given situation, progress could be made in relations with the state while upholding the authority of the Hungarian primate. A solution to his quandary was found: the pope would dispatch to Hungary an *apostolic visitator* in the person of Angelo Rotta, who had previously served as nuncio in Budapest. This visitator (Rotta) would listen to the opinions of both church and government figures and then offer stern advice to the Hungarian primate, which the latter would then be required

149. MNL OL M–KS 276. f. 67/214. ő. e. 56–59. and 61–81. fol. Reports on Archbishop Czapik's visit to Rome. Budapest, October 8, 1948; PMKL IV. 213. Legacy of István Albert, item no. 4. Czapik's handwritten notes in the file "Római megbeszélések" [Meetings in Rome].

150. PMKL IV. 213. Legacy of István Albert, item no. 4. In the file "Római megbeszélések": "Tardini véleményére tett megjegyzéseim" [Meetings in Rome: my comments on Tardini's opinion].

to act upon. In essence, therefore, the proposal would have put restrictions on Mindszenty's authority.[151] It was only on October 20 that the Vatican informed the Hungarian primate of the proposal, by which time it had become a definitive plan of action. The proceedings seem to accord with Moscow's impression of Vatican policy, according to which the Holy See was advising the heads of Catholic churches in East Central Europe to refrain both from exacerbating relations with the respective governments and from making concessions to them. In other words, they should strive for a situation in which the faithful saw the repression suffered by the Church and believed that the clergy were not to blame for such repression.

It seemed at first as if the Hungarian government would welcome the apostolic visitator, but then there were lengthy delays in the issuing of a visa. The formal excuse for the denial of a visa was the publication in *L'Osservatore Romano*, the Holy See's semi-official daily newspaper, of three short commentaries critical of the domestic political situation in Hungary. (The three commentaries were published on October 10, 23, and 28, 1948.) Citing such "belligerence," the Hungarian authorities refused to issue an entry visa to the apostolic visitator. Unwittingly, therefore, the Hungarian government found itself on the same side as Mindszenty, who viewed the possible dispatch of a visitator as a restriction of his rights and as the direct result of Archbishop Czapik's efforts to undermine unity.[152] Ultimately, the decision to delay and then refuse the issuing of a visa can be traced to Soviet Ambassador Pushkin and to the authorities in Moscow.[153]

The Vatican's announcement of its intent to dispatch a visitator to Hungary signaled that relations between Hungary and the Holy See had developed to a point where the Soviet ambassador needed to be kept informed about developments. Indeed, the issue had taken on a broader, international significance, and so Hungary's politicians were reluctant to take the initiative without prior Soviet approval. It was Defense Minister

151. MNL OL M–KS 276. f. 65/352. ő. e. 10. fol. Legate László Velics's encrypted telegram. Rome, October 11, 1948, 7.35 p.m.

152. MNL OL M–KS 276. f. 67/215. ő. e. Report. Budapest, November 24, 1948. Subject: Catholic Church; György Gyarmati: A Mindszenty-ügy „diplomáciai" rendezésének kudarca [The failed attempt to find a "diplomatic" solution to the Mindszenty-case], *Történelmi Szemle* 42, no. 1–2 (2000): 69–90.

153. Diplomatic ties between the two countries were raised to the ambassadorial level on May 8, 1948.

Mihály Farkas who, on October 14, 1948, told Pushkin that the Holy See had requested a visa for Angelo Rotta. At the same time, Farkas provided Pushkin with a summary of prior events. For the experienced Soviet intelligence agent and diplomat, Mindszenty's stance and the Vatican's policy were inseparable; the one could not be juxtaposed against the other, in Pushkin's view. He determined that "the Vatican might agree to Mindszenty's dismissal if it came to the view that such a move would be beneficial, but we should be in no doubt that the Vatican will not dismiss Mindszenty from his office as cardinal [*sic*] until it receives substantial concessions from the Hungarian government or guaranteed rights for the Hungarian Catholic Church, or until it signs an agreement with the Hungarian government that it deems beneficial."[154] He let it be known to the Hungarian leader that he peremptorily opposed "the signing of an agreement with the Vatican and even negotiations with it." The stance of the ambassador, who was acting in accordance with the will of the authorities in Moscow, prevented the Hungarian government – regardless of its own position – from allowing the Vatican diplomat to enter Hungary. (Thereafter it was merely a case of finding a pretext for rejecting the visa application: the unfriendly commentaries in *L'Osservatore Romano* came as a godsend in this respect.) In the end, Pushkin also told Farkas – and this is the truly surprising development – that in his view "there is no need to urge Mindszenty's removal from the cardinal's seat, since his dumb policies are helping the communists rather than the Catholic Church. A new cardinal would probably be smarter and thus also more dangerous than Mindszenty." His words clearly show that Soviet diplomacy had no wish to see Mindszenty's detention or his "peaceful" removal.

Pushkin's reaction served as a lesson to Hungary's politicians. Just as real progress was about to be made in the Hungarian state's relations with the Catholic Church (including the initiation of the much-discussed involvement of the Holy See), the Hungarian government had to retrace

154. AVP RF f. 077. op. 28. papka (paper folder) 125. delo (file) 6. l. 100. Ambassador Pushkin's report on the discussions with Mihály Farkas on October 14, 1948. (The next two quotations come from that report – the author.) – Please note: The Soviet ambassador evidently did not grasp the difference between the office of archbishop (and prince primate) and the rank of cardinal. Clearly, he was speaking of the office of archbishop rather than Mindszenty's status as cardinal.

its steps rapidly. The only chance now was that Rákosi, who was due to return to work in two weeks' time after a stay at a sanatorium, might succeed in changing the Soviet ambassador's mind. In the end, however, the ambassador did not change his mind, and Rákosi was left to utter a series of rather embarrassing excuses. He assured Pushkin that he had never regarded negotiations with the Vatican as a serious possibility. He had engaged with the Catholic prelates for tactical reasons alone, seeking to persuade them to renounce some of their rights. Pushkin viewed with mistrust Rákosi's efforts to make excuses: "Rákosi is now endeavoring to portray his negotiations with the Catholics in a different light," he reported to the Ministry of Foreign Affairs in Moscow.[155] Indeed, Pushkin viewed the party leader's conduct as nothing other than a pathetic attempt to conceal his own actions. Even some months later, Pushkin still stuck to his position on the matter. Concerning the content of the Soviet ambassador's words, it is inconceivable that, without the knowledge of his superiors, he would have criticized the Hungarian communist leaders for negotiating with the Holy See or cautioned them against removing Mindszenty.

In contrast, *L'Osservatore Romano* treated as credible information a report from Vienna that the Hungarian authorities had arrested Mindszenty in response to a Cominform directive.[156] Based on the documents accessible to researchers today, we have no direct evidence that Cominform played a decisive, "malevolent" role in Mindszenty's detention.[157] The secondary evidence for such a role is also rather thin, consisting of prejudicial press reports. Evidently, the function of Cominform was different: its aim was to establish and maintain unity in the international communist movement rather than to assist in the "creation" of criminal proceedings. Of course, it is quite possible that, on such occasions, the comrades informed each

155. AVP RF f. 077. op. 28. papka (paper folder) 125. delo (file) 6. l. 102. Ambassador Pushkin's report on the discussions with Mátyás Rákosi on October 23, 1948.

156. "L'arresto del Cardinale Mindszenty ripetutamente ordinato dal Cominform," *L'Osseratore Romano* 89, no. 6, January 9, 1949.

157. Minutes of meetings and other papers of the Cominform have been published: G. M. Adibekov, A. Di B'yadzho, L. Ya. Gibianskiy, F. Gori, and S. Pons., eds., *Soveshchaniya Kominforma 1947, 1948, 1949. Dokumenty i materialy* (Moscow: ROSSPEN, 1998); Francesca Gori and Silvio Pons, eds., *Dagli archivi di Mosca: L'Urss, il Cominform e il PCI (1943–1951)* (Rome: Carrocci, 1998).

other about their domestic political problems. Still, this does not amount to the making of an institutional decision on intervention.

At a more general level, an instruction had clearly been received by the satellite countries from the Kremlin: "Anything that is to the right of us should be chopped down, including the Catholic Church with its broad social appeal and support." The policies pursued by the people's democracies in relation to the churches – policies that communist politicians justified by citing the churches' collaboration with fascism and their subsequent collaboration with US imperialism – contain so many similarities that they must have been coordinated to some degree. Even so, it is doubtful that specific instructions (of the *ukase* type) were given by the authorities in Moscow or that those same authorities ordered or proposed Cardinal Mindszenty's prosecution and determined the tactics used in the proceedings. Based on the documents currently known to researchers, it may be concluded that although the Soviet government doubtless had control, it did not initiate the proceedings against the Hungarian primate, which ended in his criminal conviction. However, by preventing the visitator from coming to Hungary, Pushkin accomplished the opposite of what he intended: he effectively accelerated Mindszenty's arrest. Regarding the events leading to this outcome, the personal responsibility of Hungarian politicians, in particular that of Mátyás Rákosi, is far greater than historians had realized or assumed until now.

Rákosi, an experienced politician, knew that he could not simply ignore the Soviet ambassador's words of caution. The Hungarian communist leader acknowledged that he must abandon the plan for a visitator, even though the plan appeared to be an effective means of neutralizing Mindszenty. But how could Rákosi step back without a loss of prestige? The only solution was to launch a further offensive against the Church and against Mindszenty, and to ensure that this new offensive would surpass all previous ones and would ultimately remove Mindszenty from Hungarian public life. The offensive had two possible outcomes: either Mindszenty would resign (under pressure from the Bishops' Conference or having been pushed aside by the Holy See) or criminal proceedings would be launched against him. Since Rákosi had already succeeded in getting a prime minister (Ferenc Nagy) and, indeed, the president of the republic (Zoltán Tildy) to resign, he was confident of his ability to bring about the Hungarian primate's (forced) resignation. To further this idea, on November 2, 1948, the Agitation and Propaganda Committee of the Hungarian Working People's Party was formed in József Révai's office at the government ministry. The committee identified as its primary task the resumption of the fight against Mindszenty and against "clerical reaction."[158] The next day (November 3), Mátyás Rákosi, the party's general secretary, announced, at a meeting of the Budapest executive committee, a veritable declaration of war: "Democracy, after having been on the defensive, will now switch to a comprehensive offensive against the Catholic Church. [...] The warnings submitted to the Church have been ended. Priests who politicize from the pulpit will be taken straight to an internment camp or to a prison."[159] Protest, dismissal, and imprisonment – these became the key words in the methodology of the chosen strategy. It was a frank speech – made behind closed doors. In the meantime, a more detailed personal file on Mindszenty had been compiled, together with various summary reports on his public appearances, on the people who visited him, on his correspondence, and on his past. On the opening page to one of the reports, Gábor Péter wrote, in his characteristically neat handwriting, "Comrade Rákosi, I have underlined those sentences which will provide a basis (when the time is ripe) for criminal proceedings against Mindszenty."[160] The essence of these confidential decisions was leaked out to Mindszenty, who thus came to know that the regime was about to launch a punitive campaign against the clergy.[161]

Rákosi now openly advanced towards his goal. On November 27, he announced the collectivization of Hungarian agriculture. Concurrently, in an effort to reassure religious peasant farmers, he stated that his aim was not to attack the church but to remove the "clerical reaction" and, in particular, Mindszenty and his followers. Developments in the other countries of the region also indicated growing hostility towards the Church on the part of communist political leaders. For instance, in 1945, *Josyf Slipyj*, major archbishop of Lviv, was accused of having collaborated with the

158. MNL OL M–KS 276. f. 86/1. ő. e. Resolutions of the meeting on November 2, 1948 of the Agitation and Propaganda Committee of the Hungarian Working People's Party.

159. ÁBTL 3.1.9. V–700/11. 324/8–9. fol. Secret memorandum found in material about the search of Mindszenty's residence.

160. PIL 274. f. 7/248. ő. e. 172. fol.

161. ÁBTL 3.1.9. V–700/6. 56–57. fol. Interrogation record of the suspect József Földényi. Budapest, November 30, 1948.

German occupiers and having spied for the Vatican. He was sentenced to eight years of hard labor. Slipyj's real "crime" had been to reject the forced merger of the Ukrainian Greek Catholic (Uniate) Church with the Russian Orthodox Church.[162] On October 11, 1946, *Alojzije Viktor Stepinac*, archbishop of Zagreb, was sentenced to sixteen years of forced labor, having been charged with treason and war crimes.[163] Until Mindszenty's trial, prelates in Central and Eastern Europe had been accused of complicity or collaboration with Nazi Germany. In Mindszenty's case, however, the accusation could not be collaboration with the Germans, for his anti-fascist past was public knowledge.

In the fall of 1948, there was a noticeable increase in the number of anti-church demonstrations, press articles, speeches, and "revelations." In prefabricated telegrams and notices, the country's state institutions demanded that the government put a stop to the cardinal's anti-democratic activities. In Hungary's schools, students were required to fill out vigilance questionnaires entitled *With Open Eyes*. All the questions were directed against Mindszenty. The Hungarian primate was also repeatedly targeted by a joke magazine with a circulation of a hundred thousand: alongside the figure of a potbellied capitalist, Mindszenty was mockingly portrayed as a similarly overweight man who hid weapons beneath his cassock and represented symbolically the "clerical reaction." Unscrupulous prejudice and overt threats were expressed against Mindszenty with increasing frequency.

Not only was there a surge in primitive hate speech against the Church, but also the Hungarian people were increasingly subjected to the process of Sovietization. The authorities let it be known that the Soviet model was to be copied. This Soviet way of life, with its agricultural collectives (*kolkhoz*) and state-owned farms (*sovkhoz*), was popularized in literature and film, at mass public meetings, and by the media. Leftist progressive politics

162. Ivan Choma, *Josyf Slipyj* (Milan: La Casa di Matriona, 2001), 48–53.

163. Historians still disagree about the role played by the archbishop. According to the most recent Croatian research, although Stepinac indulged the "independent" (Ustaša) Croatian state and endowed it with a certain amount of credibility, his actions were driven throughout by his love for the Croatian nation and his desire for a free Croatia. Tvrtko Jakovina, *Američki komunistički saveznik: Hrvati, Titova Jugoslavija i SAD 1945–1955* (Zagreb: Profil International, 2003), 152; Zdenko Radelić, *Hrvatska u Jugoslaviji 1945–1991: Od zajedništva do razlaza* (Zagreb: Hrvatski institut za povijest, Školska knjiga, 2006), 109.

morphed into cult-like fanaticism, accompanied by demagogic propaganda. The brash campaigning and propaganda left the populace feeling jaded. As a counter-reaction, hundreds of thousands of Catholics spontaneously expressed their love of, and respect for, Cardinal Mindszenty, and they were joined in this by many non-Catholics and non-believers.

People's benign feelings for the cardinal could not, however, alter the course of events: the noose around Mindszenty's neck was tightened and the pressure raised, both metaphorically and literally. The primatial palace in Esztergom had been under the surveillance of the political police for some time. Dressed as costermongers, secret policemen watched the comings and goings from a hideout disguised as a fruit and vegetable stall (its real function was, of course, common knowledge among townsfolk). The secret policeman on duty on November 15 doubtless reported to his superiors the visit on that day of the US envoy, Chapin, who had come to Esztergom at Cardinal Mindszenty's request. We know what Mindszenty and Chapin discussed from the contents of a telegram the legate sent to Washington after the meeting.[164] As Chapin reported, the Hungarian primate voiced his concerns over Hungary's future. He sketched two likely political developments: the liquidation of an independent (self-supporting) peasantry and the internment of the clergy.

Mindszenty correctly identified the communists' political intent: having successfully broken up the urban middle class – the social class that was most capable of withstanding Sovietization in an economic and ideological sense – the party leadership now wished to eradicate the middle peasantry. Mindszenty's other fear also came to be substantiated, albeit not quite as he had anticipated and at a different point in time. Mindszenty asked Chapin to take steps to ensure – in the event of the internment of the clergy – a forceful diplomatic reaction from the West. Chapin, however, was reluctant to give any assurances and placed the emphasis on the effectiveness of publicity and the implementation of the terms of the peace treaty. Chapin's impression was that the cardinal believed the meeting would be their last and was anticipating his own arrest. The American diplomat therefore offered the cardinal his assistance in the event that

164. MNL OL XX–10–k LÜ PO 18.300/1989. US archival sources. Legate Selden Chapin's report no. A-695. Budapest, November 17, 1948.

Mindszenty should decide to leave the country.[165] This, however, was not to be his path. The Hungarian primate was a saintly, benevolent, courageous and tough man, who, despite his somewhat outdated attitudes, would have been a valuable and spirited leader against decent adversaries. The adversaries he encountered, however, were far from being decent. His armory was lacking in everything that would have been vital for the impending battle: sober-mindedness, diplomatic skills, a smart cunningness, and a capacity for pretense.

THE FINAL ACT

In the fall of 1948 József Mindszenty rarely left the primatial palace in Esztergom. He was preparing himself for the inevitable. He drafted a letter to the nation, in which he responded to the accusations that had been made against him. He also rejected, in the same letter, claims that the Church had been responsible for the cancellation of the planned negotiations with the Hungarian government. The domestic press naturally refrained from publishing the cardinal's letter. In contrast, members of the Hungarian émigré community in the United States judged Mindszenty's piece to be so important – as "the only voice of it's [sic. orig.] kind that is reaching us not only from Hungary, but from behind the whole iron curtain." – that they forwarded the letter to President Truman.[166] On December 3, Mindszenty wrote the same rather "odd" Christmas greeting to forty cardinals: he bid them farewell by citing the words of Advent masses and hymns. In the greeting, he asked the cardinals to pray for him and for the Catholic faithful who were being pursued by Satan.[167] On December 18, he wrote a detailed report to Pius XII. The report was a further record of the Hungarian government's actions against the Church (the nationalization of schools, measures

165. ÁBTL 3.1.9. V–700/2. 281. fol. Memorandum on the interrogation of József Mindszenty on December 28, 1948. With verification signature.

166. Harry S. Truman Library, Independence, Missouri (hereafter: Truman Library), Official File (OF) 226 Hungary Misc. to Of 227 Farm Matters Misc. (1950–53), Box 970. Mindszenty Folder. Letter of László Boros, publisher of the *Amerikai Magyar Népszava*, to President Truman. New York, December 6, 1948. – For the text of the Mindszenty's piece, see Vecsey, *Mindszenty okmánytár*, vol. 3. *Mindszenty áldozata*, 263–65.

167. AANY Collection 007, Box S/C-10, Folder 6. Letter no. 8414/1948 in Latin of József Mindszenty to Archbishop Spellman. Esztergom, December 3, 1948.

to prevent the legal operation of Catholic associations, the undermining of the livelihoods of the faithful, police terror, fear and the disruption of internal church unity). In his letter to the pope, Mindszenty also frankly described his confusion on hearing the reports concerning Archbishop's Czapik's *ad limina* visit to Rome in September and on seeing that Czapik was "working hard on a possible compromise" but being unsure whether the archbishop had received authorization to do so from the Holy See. "My office was searched by police [November 22]. My house is surrounded by ten secret p[olicemen]. I do not consider myself to be free. On the other hand, I do not feel I have the authorization to take a decisive step."[168] He urgently requested information and guidance, which should be relayed "in such a manner that only I will be able to understand it." Mindszenty's words are also rather mysterious: What did he mean by "a decisive step"? In the knowledge of all the various circumstances, we may assume he was not talking about whether to leave the country. Rather, the greatest dilemma was whether to fight or remain passive, whether to negotiate or refuse to talk. This may seem surprising, but it is the inference to be drawn from subsequent developments. On December 22, 1948, he sent copies of the authorizations he had received from Rome to József Grősz, archbishop of Kalocsa. Mindszenty instructed the archbishop to exercise the authorizations in the event of his own inability to do so.[169] By taking this measure, Mindszenty made sure that the Church would continue to have leadership in the event of his being prevented from fulfilling his duties.

The Noose Tightens – The Detention of András Zakar

The first trial of resistance had to be overcome by the Hungarian primate's secretary, András Zakar. A qualified mechanical engineer, Zakar had been ordained priest in 1940, aged 28. He had come into the service of Mindszenty in 1944. He was known as a model theologian with a soft voice. He adhered to the rules even when they were considered rather insignificant. His

168. PL Processus, V–700/14. No page numbers. Letter of József Mindszenty to Pius XII. December 18, 1948.

169. KFL I.1.c. Folder 7. Letter no. 8760/1948 of József Mindszenty to Archbishop Grősz of Kalocsa. Esztergom, December 22, 1948.

asceticism appealed to Cardinal Mindszenty, who required Zakar's English skills. The young priest rapidly won the cardinal's trust.[170]

"Zakar – Mindszenty's secretary – must be arrested if he really did telephone the embassies," stated the minutes of a meeting of the supreme body of the Hungarian Working People's Party, held on November 18, 1948.[171] The information received by the party headquarters turned out to be correct. Indeed, not only had Zakar phoned various embassies, but also, on the night of November 18, he had received, in Esztergom, a US diplomat of Hungarian ancestry named Stephen Andrew Koczak, who was serving as second secretary at the US embassy. All of this was more than suspicious for the party bureaucrats. They suspected that Mindszenty was planning to flee Hungary. In reality, Koczak's intent in visiting Esztergom had indeed been to arrange for Mindszenty's "rescue": twenty-two years later he told how he had been informed by Iván Boldizsár, the Hungarian state secretary for foreign affairs, that Zakar was to be arrested the next day. It was this knowledge that had motivated him to travel to Esztergom at such a late hour in the day. According to Koczak, on his arrival in Esztergom, Zakar had refused to wake the cardinal, and so the US diplomat's plan for rescuing the cardinal and his secretary had to be aborted.[172] A degree of fatalism perhaps explains Zakar's decision. Only a few hours later, on the morning of November 19 (i.e., merely four days after the US envoy, Chapin's visit to Esztergom), András Zakar was intercepted and detained by the Hungarian secret police as he returned to the primatial palace after Holy Mass.

In an act of courage, András Zakar initially refused to make a statement, citing his obligation, as the Hungarian primate's employee, to confidentiality. Several days later (on November 22), however, he made his first detailed statement on Mindszenty's political intentions and actions, doing so with the zeal of an eminent bureaucrat. Zakar subsequently made a series of compromising statements on various issues.[173] In response to Zakar's

170. BTL 3.1.8. Sz–222/3. 69. fol. Miklós Boér on Catholic affairs and the political situation. October 15, 1946.

171. MNL OL M–KS 276. f. 54/17. ő. e.; RGASPI f. 17. op. 128. delo (file) 522. l. 186. Minutes of the meeting of the Secretariat of the Hungarian Working People's Party on November 18, 1948.

172. Archivio Generale dei Scolopi (hereafter: AGS), Legacy of Vince Tomek, Diaries, 7., vol. 86. Vince Tomek's memorandum of October 10, 1971. (Kálmán Peregrin's collection.)

173. ÁBTL 3.1.9. V–700/2. 120–130. fol. Record of András Zakar's interrogation, November 19 and 22, 1948.

initial statement, Gábor Péter, head of the political police, asked Rákosi for further instructions: "I want Comrade Rákosi to discuss with me the direction of future inquiries and how far I should go? Nov. 22, 1948."[174]

What could have lain behind Zakar's sudden willingness to assist the inquiry? The most likely explanation is that the state security agency blackmailed Béla Witz – having accused him of being a pedophile – into releasing Zakar from his confidentiality oath. A second possibility is that Zakar was forced into making the statements after his sister, who was working for the Ministry of Agriculture, became a party to a "conspiracy" trial which had ended just a few weeks earlier with the criminal conviction of numerous employees of the Ministry. At the time of that trial, Mindszenty had been mentioned as a possible accomplice to the supposed leader of the conspiracy, whereby their alleged common goal had been to sabotage the work of the government in the field of agriculture.[175] A third possible scenario is that the political police had some compromising information on Zakar, which was used to force him into making a statement. The former military judge Ákos Major mentioned in his memoirs, for example, that when Mindszenty and Zakar's arrest was announced in the media, their room-maid admitted, amid tears, that the Hungarian primate's secretary had been her lover.[176] The affair would appear to have been an innocent liaison dating to the period before Zakar's ordination. If it had been anything otherwise, the secret services would doubtless have exploited the story for their own designs, broadcasting the details more widely. (Whatever the case, the story was clearly one that could be used for the purpose of blackmail.) On the other hand, Zakar – who was an ascetic by character and had taken the strictest oath of celibacy – was unlikely to have had an affair with a woman.

Supposedly, Zakar was not beaten or tortured. On the contrary, he allegedly attended Mass each morning, and – during a house search on December 23 – was even allowed to take his home altar with him.[177] This

174. MNL OL 275. f. 67/215. ő. e. 20/a. fol. Handwritten memorandum.

175. ÁBTL 3.1.8. Sz–222/12. 293–296. fol. Report. Budapest, July 26, 1948; PL Mm. 27. d. *The Tablet*, July 31, 1948. For an analysis of the trial, see Éva Cseszka, *Gazdasági típusú perek, különös tekintettel az FM-perre (1945–1953)* (Budapest: Gondolat, 2012).

176. Major, *Népbíráskodás*, 393.

177. MNL OL M–KS 276. f. 67/215. ő. e. 88. fol. Report. Budapest, December 25, 1948.

version of events, however, does not seem credible and is contradicted by the statements of others. For instance, citing reliable sources, the US envoy reported to his superiors that Zakar had been both grievously mistreated and narcotized. The envoy made no similar claims with regard to Cardinal Mindszenty.[178] Several factors explain why Zakar proved willing to talk: the threat of physical violence, emotional pressure, and his own disciplined and dutiful personality. It would seem that the police fully exploited Zakar's good manners and upbringing. When asked a question, he would answer. And he could not lie, because the imperative "Tell the truth!" worked like a reflex in him. Indeed, he would have been ashamed to lie even to his interrogators. In his memoirs, Mindszenty gives no explanation for Zakar's behavior. We know, however, that he forgave his secretary, based on the evidence provided in his will: Mindszenty left to his secretary, who had suffered so much on his account, the precious pectoral cross that he had been gifted by Bishop János Mikes several years earlier.[179]

Whatever the case may be, one thing is certain that Zakar, rather than hinder or prolong the work of the police investigators, ended up assisting them. Gradually, the other actors in the planned court case were detained: Béla Ispánki and Miklós Nagy (on November 24 and 26, 1948), and Jusztin Baranyay and Pál Esterházy (on December 24 and 26, 1948). As of December 29, all these men were being held in pre-trial detention.[180] Another accused individual, the journalist László Tóth, was placed in pre-trial detention on January 25, 1949.

Only a narrow circle – four senior leaders – within the Hungarian Working People's Party appear to have known that the political police intended to create a "case" and take it to trial by exploiting statements made by Zakar and the others. The party's Political Committee adopted a new set of anti-clerical propaganda measures at a meeting on November 27.

178. Truman Library, RG 46. Record of US Senate. Senate Committee on Foreign Relations. Selected Documents, January 25–April 5, 1949. Box 5. Resolutions re Joseph Card. Mindszenty. March 12, 1949. 17–18.

179. Gergely Kovács, "Isten szolgája, Mindszenty József tárgyi hagyatéka," in *"Szenteltessék meg a Te neved…"*, ed. Viktor Attila Soós (Lakitelek: Antológia Kiadó, 2012), 96. – Note: The Mindszenty Foundation (Hungary) still has the cross; it can be viewed in the Treasury of St. Stephen's Basilica, Budapest.

180. ÁBTL 3.1.9. V–700/7. 9–10. , 576. fol. Budapest People's Court judgment no. IX.254/1949/10.

In the minutes, the following words are legible, even though they were crossed out: "In the course of the [anti-clerical] campaign, physical assault should be treated gingerly." In the ensuing weeks, events proceeded according to the plans concocted in the witch's kitchen of politics. "Arrest or removal by other means" read the proposal.

Only an agreement between Hungary and the Holy See would have prevented Mindszenty's detention. The chances of such an agreement, however, were negligible. The arrest of the cardinal was the obvious intended outcome of police strategy. Even so, diplomatic efforts to resolve the situation continued to be made for a period of two weeks. For instance, István Barankovics, general secretary of the Democratic People's Party, proposed a "gentlemen's agreement" between the Hungarian government and the Vatican, comprising the following points: 1. A ceasefire on the radio and by the media. 2. The Hungarian government permits Angelo Rotta, Apostolic Visitator, to visit Hungary, together with his staff. 3. The Hungarian government makes known to the Holy See the prosecution's case against Mindszenty prior to his actual indictment, thereby enabling appropriate action to be taken by the Vatican. 4. The Hungarian government makes no unilateral changes to the status quo of the Hungarian Catholic Church.[181] On making his proposal, Barankovics could not have known that the Soviet ambassador to Hungary had already vetoed the granting of a visa to Angelo Rotta. Révai and his associates, however, must have known about the Soviet position, and so their support for a "gentlemen's agreement" was evidently mere positioning. Or was there really some faint hope of avoiding a prosecution?

An effort to resolve the situation was also made by people within Mindszenty's camp who were opposed to his policies. Indeed, on December 8, Mindszenty received a visit from the composer Zoltán Kodály, the historian and diplomat Gyula Szekfű, and the journalist József Cavallier. All three men sought to persuade him to change his mind. Cavallier frankly asked whether Mindszenty should not become a cardinal of the Roman Curia. Noticeably irritated, the Hungarian primate responded as follows: "We have come together to negotiate about grave things, rather than to

181. MNL OL M–KS 276. f. 65/352. ő. e. 41. fol. Pro memoria concerning the hearing on December 2, 1948, signed by József Révai.

make jokes."[182] The group of three men was not the first to have requested a meeting with Mindszenty with a view to persuading him of the errors of his ways. A group of nine men – all of whom had been excommunicated on account of the school nationalization policy – had done the same on November 20, 1948.[183] Similarly, János Drahos, archbishop's vicar, had informed Archbishop Czapik of Eger that several senior priests in the diocese had asked him to persuade the Hungarian primate to resign.[184] None of these initiatives had been successful, however. Mindszenty, who knew that he still had the support of the Bishops' Conference, was reluctant even to countenance the possibility of his voluntary retirement or the idea that he should become a cardinal of the Roman Curia.

On the day of the visit of Cavallier, Kodály, and Szekfű to Esztergom, the "three-man committee on church policy" of the Hungarian Working People's Party convened. The "troika" were Mátyás Rákosi, József Révai, and Mihály Farkas. A topic of discussion at the meeting was the prosecution's case against Mindszenty, which comprised five distinct aspects:

1. The conspiracy with Crown Prince Otto;
2. Spying on behalf of the United States;
3. Information on Mindszenty's alleged fascist past;
4. Foreign exchange violations;
5. Perfidy and treachery in the matter of the Holy Crown.[185]

The three senior communists were still hoping for a breakthrough in the talks and a change in Mindszenty's position by early January (his resignation or transfer to Rome). The Jesuit teacher Imre Mócsy (a confidant of Archbishop Czapik) and László Velics, Hungarian envoy in Rome, were tasked with persuading the competent Vatican officials to take firm action on Mindszenty. On December 10, Imre Mócsy traveled to Rome with the government's approval but without informing Cardinal Mindszenty. His

182. Pécsi Püspöki Levéltár [Episcopal Archives of Pécs] (hereafter: PPL) Rogács Ferenc püspök hagyatéka, 44. iratköteg [The legacy of Bishop Ferenc Rogács, bundle of documents 44]. Notes on the meeting of the Bishops' Conference, Esztergom, December 11, 1948.

183. *Szabad Nép* 4, no. 292, December 18, 1948; *Népszava* 76, no. 292, December 18, 1948, cover page; *Szabad Esti Szó* [Word of the Evening] 50, no. 292, December 19, 1948.

184. MNL OL M–KS 276. f. 67/215. ő. e. 17. fol. Report. Budapest, November 22, 1948.

185. MNL OL M–KS 276. f. 54/20. ő. e. 9. fol. Minutes of the meeting of the three-man ministerial commission for church affairs of the Hungarian Working People's Party. December 8, 1948. Ibid., RGASPI f. 17. op. 128. delo (file) 522. l. 327.

task was to submit the text of the "gentlemen's agreement" (of December 2) to the appropriate Vatican officials and to tell them that, in the Hungarian government's view, the best solution for Mindszenty – the only way of saving him – was for the Holy See to arrange for his immediate transferal to Rome.

If Rákosi and his group had succeeded in removing Mindszenty from the Hungarian domestic political scene in this way, then they might well have added a further element to their accusations against the Catholic Church. They might have said that the pope, acting as an accomplice to US imperialism, had rushed to rescue the Hungarian vassal before he could be subjected to the weight of the law in a people's democracy. This scenario, however, was soon rejected, and Mócsy's journey to Rome was derived of its original purpose. According to Mihály Károlyi, the plan to have Mindszenty transferred to Rome was aborted because Rákosi and his group were profoundly concerned that "the cardinal, after his arrival abroad, might have crowned Otto with the 'Holy Crown,' which was being held in the US zone [of Germany]."[186] This supposition reveals the communists' complete misunderstanding of the coronation rules: a coronation of a Hungarian king performed outside Hungary would automatically be invalid. If there was never any real likelihood of Mindszenty's being transferred to Rome, what real chance did he have of avoiding arrest? It would seem that the officials at the Vatican were playing high stakes: Mindszenty would remain in Hungary because the arrest of a cardinal by the regime would be an act so shameful that it would cause great damage to Hungary's fledgling "people's democracy." Moreover, by extension, it would also deal a blow (perhaps fatal) to Soviet bolshevism.

On the Home-Stretch

There is no doubt that the detailed statement provided by András Zakar, the Hungarian primate's secretary, tipped the scales onto the side of action against Cardinal Mindszenty – his criminal prosecution. The first summary statement (fifty pages in length) was completed on December 13, 1948, based on the interrogation records drawn up since November 22. The

186. PIL 704/1. f. 232. ő. e. Hit, illúziók nélkül, III. Manuscript, 295 and 537 fol., and vol. 4, 3037. fol.

summary presented sufficient evidence for Mindszenty's indictment. Rákosi now possessed the conclusive evidence that he had previously lacked. Zakar's statement covered every major aspect of the case that would subsequently be made against Mindszenty. Subsequent memoranda in the case contained only minor additions and amendments.

The next day (December 14), at a session of the Hungarian Parliament, several representatives reiterated the accusations made against the Church and against Mindszenty. Prime Minister István Dobi, a member of the Independent Smallholders' Party and a one-time member of KALOT (the Catholic Agrarian Youth League), condemned Cardinal Mindszenty in the harshest terms: "The forces of reaction in Hungary are primarily assembling under the black flag of Cardinal Mindszenty. Mindszenty is the main patron and organizer of the reactionaries, the fascists, and the war criminals."[187] Dobi slavishly met Rákosi's expectations, leaving no doubt as to the government's real intent. The brutal mood of the Hungarian Parliament was revealed when one of the communist deputies (Kálmán Jászai) shouted out the following: "Mindszenty is the new Führer!"[188] On December 21, concerning the accusations heard in parliament, the newspaper *Magyar Kurír* published a full denial by "the competent ecclesiastical body" (i.e., József Mindszenty).[189] This was to be Mindszenty's last statement in the semi-official church press.

Minister of Foreign Affairs László Rajk promptly informed the Vatican authorities about the government's change of view on Mindszenty. Rajk rescinded the government's earlier offer made by way of Imre Mócsy. He then instructed envoy Velics to inform the "competent authority" at the Vatican of the following: "the Hungarian Ministry of Interior has come into the possession of data which make it impossible for us to continue our policy of making apologies and waiting things out."[190] The "competent authority" was the nuncio, Angelo Rotta. Velics informed him by telephone

187. *Országgyűlés Naplója* [Diary of the National Assembly], 1947, volume 5, column 8. The 91st session of the Parliament, December 14, 1948.

188. Ibid., column 114. The 92nd session of the Parliament, December 15, 1948.

189. *Magyar Kurír* 38, December 21, 1948, third edition.

190. MNL OL XIX–J–1–j–IV–14–15/1948. Vatican. Secret papers, Minister of Foreign Affairs László Rajk's letter to László Velics, the legate in Rome. Budapest, December 14, 1948.

on December 18, but as Rotta was away, the official written information could not be delivered until after Mindszenty's arrest (December 27).

All aspects of the subsequent indictment were included in the letter. If Rákosi and his associates had believed that the pope's startled response would be to send, by return of post, a plan for a concordat or to publicly acknowledge the Hungarian political regime, they were to be greatly disappointed. Velics's oral communication and the subsequent submission of the letter were separated by nine days of drama, as the competent members of staff were busy with their Advent spiritual exercises. Even the Jesuit Mócsy, who submitted a memorandum on the "gentlemen's agreement" (which had already been revoked) to the State Secretariat of the Holy See on December 22, was only given an audience with Tardini on December 28. In this way, Vatican officials received the Hungarian government's threatening message only after some delay, by which time it was already too late for the Vatican to take appropriate action.

In effect, Mindszenty's destiny was decided with Rajk's letter of December 14. Of course, for the decision to become final, it had still to be approved by Moscow. For just as it is unimaginable that Ambassador Pushkin, when expressing his opposition to Mindszenty's removal from Hungarian public life to Mihály Farkas and Mátyás Rákosi, had been expressing his own private opinion, so it is just as unlikely that Rákosi would have implemented his plan on such an important matter against the will of the Soviets. We know that the Hungarian party leadership was distrusted in Moscow and that Stalin had long had grave reservations about Rákosi. Although Rákosi decided on Mindszenty's arrest and detention after several months of hesitation and without having received instructions from the Soviet government, nevertheless it would seem a nod of approval from Stalin was still required before he could proceed with his plan of action.

Rákosi was not only driven by a desire to prove himself and demonstrate his own merits. His chosen course of action also reflected the lessons – the "methodology" – he had learned as a Hungarian exile in the Soviet Union in the 1930s. He had personal experience of such methods. Now, however, he was caught between his own megalomania and the risk of a fiasco. The stakes were enormous. Mindszenty was far from being a run-of-the-mill political adversary. Rather, he was the head of the Hungarian Catholic Church and a member of the College of Cardinals, a body with barely more than fifty members. His name was known in Moscow, London and Washington. Further, he would be the first prelate in a Soviet satellite country to be put on trial for clashing with the postwar political regime. All other such defendants had been tried as war criminals or for their collaboration with the Axis powers. For this reason, Rákosi presumably wanted Stalin's personal approval for Mindszenty's arrest, thereby going above Pushkin.

Accordingly, Rákosi wrote a humble petition to Stalin. An audience was then granted by Stalin. It was an exceptional event, for between 1946 and 1949 Stalin received Rákosi on just five occasions. We know that Rákosi spent a couple of hours inside the Kremlin on December 16, 1948 (from 10.05 pm until 01.15 am). When the doors of Stalin's study finally opened, he beckoned several persons to enter simultaneously. Thus, Rákosi was joined by three Romanian politicians: Gheorghe Gheorghiu-Dej (general secretary of the Romanian Communist Party), Ana Pauker (minister of foreign affairs), and Vasile Luka (minister of finance).[191] In view of Stalin's busy schedule, this was the only way he could meet with Rákosi, who had desperately sought a consultation with the Soviet leader. What issue was so important to Rákosi? There was nothing that more concerned him than the Mindszenty issue, and so it is almost certain that he asked Stalin for his opinion on the cardinal's impending arrest. We shall never know how much information Rákosi passed on to Stalin about the case. In all likelihood, he told him very little. But there was no need for him to say any more, for Stalin quickly responded to his question of whether he could have the cardinal arrested as the "principal adversary of the people's democracy" in Hungary or whether such a move would be contrary to Moscow's interests. The Soviet leader may have employed the strategy he often used in such situations: Rákosi was given a seemingly free hand. He could put the cardinal on trial if he was certain that this was the right thing to do. Stalin doubtless cared little whether a Hungarian priest would live or die: for the Eastern Orthodox the Catholic "heresy" was a greater evil than paganism. And Stalin, it appears, had imbibed such beliefs while attending a school for Orthodox priests in his youth. Moreover, in the Soviet

191. A. A. Chernobaev, ed., *Na prieme u Stalina: Tetradi (zhurnaly) zapisei lits, priniatykh I. V. Stalinym (1924–1953 gg.)* (Moscow: Noviy Hronograf, 2008), 514.

Union, court proceedings were rarely employed against priests and bishops. Instead, they were simply executed or deported. True, in the course of World War II, Stalin had adopted a position of greater benevolence towards the churches, for he knew that victory in the war was at stake (c.f. Stalin's conversations with the American priest, Father Orlemanski). By 1948, however, little of the former benevolence remained. Further, Stalin had failed in his aim of establishing an anti-papal ecumenical "Vatican in Moscow," and in his view the work of the Russian Orthodox Church was inadequate against the backdrop of a nascent Cold War. Consequently, instead of seeking to win over the churches, Stalin now focused on advancing home-grown leftist and radical ideas. If, during Stalin and Rákosi's conversation, the Romanians were also in the negotiating chamber (and the records make no mention of their departure), it would seem even more likely that Rákosi was given a free hand, for Stalin rarely issued instructions in front of others. Was Rákosi unhappy about having to discuss his concerns over clerical reaction in Hungary in front of the Romanian politicians rather than in a one-to-one meeting? Apparently, he was not. Moreover Gheorghiu-Dej and his fellow communists likely approved of Rákosi's approach, for they too were seeking to deal with members of the Catholic clergy who were opposed to communism.

While Rákosi was in Moscow, Hungary's domestic press welcomed enthusiastically the signing of agreements between the government and the Protestant Churches and between the government and the Jewish denomination.[192] Press reports contrasted this development with the defiance shown by Mindszenty and the Catholic Church. On December 10, a narrow circle of Hungarian bishops met to discuss possible tactics. Mindszenty maintained his opposition to talks, while Czapik argued for a negotiated settlement. In the end, the bishops sought to bridge their differences; they expressed a willingness to negotiate while upholding the authority of the Hungarian primate. They also agreed to issue a joint statement, formulating a draft which would be finalized at the plenary meeting of the Bishops' Conference on December 16. At that meeting, the bishops

192. The Hungarian government signed agreements with the Calvinist (Reformed) Church and the Unitarian Church on October 7, 1948, with the Jewish Denomination on December 7, 1948, and with the Lutheran Church on December 14. The four agreements covered around thirty percent of Hungary's population.

did indeed debate, finalize and then officially issue the statement, which, it should be noted, contained a clear reference to the Church's unwillingness, as perceived by the government, to negotiate a settlement on church and state relations.[193] The value of the statement was reduced when Mindszenty changed his mind and withdrew his support for the statement formulated on December 10. He requested the bishops to adopt a list of grievances (several pages in length) rather than issue a statement declaring their willingness to negotiate. This was the moment when differences of opinion among the bishops resulted in a noticeable split. Archbishop Czapik asked for it to be recorded in the minutes that he could not accept the list of grievances proposed by Mindszenty. In Czapik's view, in this crisis situation, Mindszenty was unable to show moderation, whereas a display of moderation is a virtue in any leader. Ultimately, the majority of bishops voted in favor of the original version of the statement, which, however, was abbreviated and no longer contained their support for the land reform and for the republic. The primate refused to give his approval and support to the statement even in its much-abbreviated and altered form. From his perspective, the Bishops' Conference, through its silence, was giving the green light to the humiliation of the Hungarian primate. Finally, he requested the bishops to refrain from signing any coercive agreements in the event of his imprisonment.[194] The events demonstrate that Mindszenty's arguments were always justified, in the sense of being based on real grievances. Still, the positions he took were not always necessary. The never-ending protests and the lack of self-reflection reduced the gravity of his arguments – especially where the weight of any grievances was willfully exaggerated.[195]

193. *Magyar Kurír* 38, December 17, 1948. – The importance of the statement is underlined by the fact that Chapin forwarded the text to the US State Department. See: NARA RG 84, Records of the Foreign Service Posts of the Department of State, Hungary, Budapest Legation, GR 1948, Box 167, 840.4. Telegram from the envoy S. Chapin, December 20, 1948.

194. MNL OL M–KS 276. f. 65/352. ő. e. 55–56. fol. Top secret memorandum on the meeting of the Bishops' Conference on December 16, 1948.

195. This is the impression gained from some of the diplomatic reports. For instance, the British political representative in Hungary, Knox Helm, commented in the following fashion on Mindszenty's characterization of events as "mass deportations": "The other parts of the cardinal's letter contain the usual exaggerations. The idea of mass deportations is based on the case of a single person." PIL 508. f. 1/114. ő. e. 40. t. TNA FO 371/67175 R 7813/11/21. Knox Helm's letter to Foreign Secretary Bevin, May 28, 1947.

On his return from Moscow, Rákosi no longer doubted the necessity of Mindszenty's arrest and imprisonment. The only remaining question for the communist leader was when to have the cardinal arrested. On December 23, 1948, at Rákosi's behest, Police Colonel Gyula Décsi oversaw the police search of the primatial palace in Esztergom, a search that lasted from the early afternoon until late evening.[196] The house search began in Zakar's office (the police had taken Zakar to the scene) and it went on to encompass the entire building. Zakar, who was acting strangely and was – unusually for him – in jocular mood, showed the place in the cellar of the palace where, on October 27 at Mindszenty's behest, he and the archivist János Fábián had buried a "secret archive," a metal case one meter in length and 20 centimeters in width. A photograph "revealing" the metal case was soon being published around the world: a tall, lean priest (András Zakar), accompanied by a stockier and shorter man (János Fábián), points at a metal cylinder that had once been used to store maps. In his memoirs, Mindszenty – who was still trying to protect his irresponsible secretary – wrote that on suspecting that his arrest was near, he had instructed his secretary to destroy all dangerous papers and documents. Mindszenty was therefore convinced that the metal cylinder had been planted by the secret police. On their "discovery" of the cylinder, the police had then placed in it copies of fake and burnt documents, which they had seized from a typist.[197] In fact, however, the metal container, full of documents, had actually existed. Rather than incinerate sensitive documents, Zakar, acting out of caution, had simply removed the names of correspondents from their letters to the cardinal.

Ignác Csepregi, who was serving as priest of the primatial aula in Esztergom and who – alone among Mindszenty's staff and not coincidentally – escaped arrest both at the time and subsequently, told the following story about the "metal cylinder," doing so as canon and parish priest in Budapest and as head of the Archbishop's Office in Esztergom. The secret police had

196. The first vehicle arrived from Budapest a few minutes after midday on December 23, 1948; András Zakar, Cardinal Mindszenty's secretary, was a passenger. Shortly before 1 p.m. Lieutenant Colonel Décsi arrived with a team of policemen. (ÁBTL 3.1.8. Sz–222/17. 78. fol. Report, December 23, 1948.) In 1952, Décsi was appointed as minister of justice, partly in recognition of his efforts in the Mindszenty affair. However, in December 1953, he received a court sentence for Zionist activities. He was released in 1957, subsequently working for the publishing house Akadémiai Kiadó until his retirement.

197. Mindszenty, *Memoirs*, 87.

no knowledge of the archives, and so they would have found it difficult to identify the documents of interest to them. They therefore played a trick: they sent an agent to Zakar shortly before his arrest, and this agent confided that a house search would soon take place, for which reason, it would be advisable to conceal politically sensitive papers.[198] The archival sources affirm this anecdotal story: Baron István Kray, the agent codenamed Magasházi, had indeed visited Esztergom, advising that all letters, reports, petitions and confidential information be destroyed or, at least, removed from Cardinal Mindszenty's office and his residential quarters.[199] Thereupon Zakar had expertly selected what he considered to be the most sensitive documents, placed them in an old metal map container, and put the metal container in a hole dug in the cellar. Zakar even showed the investigators where the metal container had been hidden.

Cardinal Mindszenty had never imagined that his seemingly tried and tested secretary would so quickly reveal these secrets and allow the compromising documents to fall into the hands of the State Protection Authority (ÁVH). The metal container was not opened in the cellar; rather, it was removed by the police, who made a record of its contents only some days later.[200] This meant there was time for other documents to be smuggled into the container, including some that had indeed been destroyed, for since 1946 the political police had been making copies of suspicious letters received by Cardinal Mindszenty in the post.[201] The metal container was kept by the police as an object of criminal interest until 1952 when it was released for educational purposes to a School for Police Investigators.[202]

Mindszenty was arrested seventy-two hours after the police search of his quarters. On December 24, Margit Slachta contacted the British envoy, whom she barely knew, to ask whether the Western powers could

198. Statement by Pál Rosdy, retired head of the Primatial Library, September 27, 2010; MNL OL XX–10–k LÜ PO 18.300/1989. Record of the hearing of the witness Ignác Csepregi, January 12, 1990.

199. ÁBTL 3.1.8. Sz–222/15. 197. fol. Report, October 20, 1948.

200. ÁBTL 3.1.9. V–700/49. 73–75. fol. Minutes, December 28, 1948, with József Mindszenty's signature of verification.

201. See ÁBTL 3.1.8. Sz–222 for the files, in chronological order, containing Mindszenty's personal papers, including many letters and telegrams (copies thereof), which were clandestinely obtained by the secret services, from the fall of 1946 onwards.

202. Ibid., V–700/7. Vol. 2, judgment no. B.II.461/1950, October 23, 1952.

do anything to prevent the arrest of Cardinal Mindszenty.[203] The response to Slachta's question was negative: the experienced diplomat Knox Helm knew that he should avoid making rash promises. His main concern was whether the investigators might have found something in the course of their search that would compromise the legation. Other than Slachta, no-one took any action to help the cardinal. Indeed, the head of the Primatial Office noted Mindszenty's disappointment at the failure of other Hungarian bishops to contact him.[204] In contrast, Mindszenty himself sought to assist others until moments before his arrest. For instance, on December 24, 1948, he requested Archbishop Spellman's assistance for twenty people who were seeking entry visas to the United States.[205] In view of the incriminating nature of the papers found (or planted) in the metal container and in the light of various witness statements pertaining to the appointment of Cardinal Mindszenty as temporary head of state, the authorities had no reason to defer his arrest.

203. TNA FO Legation, Vatican: General Correspondence, FO 380/148: Hungary, 1949, doc. no. 67/94/48. Letter of A. Knox Helm, British legate in Budapest, to G. A. Wallinger, Southern Department, Foreign and Commonwealth Office, December 29, 1948.

204. ÁBTL 3.1.8. Sz–222/17. 80. fol. Report, December 24, 1948.

205. PL Processus, V–700/27. 517–518. fol. Letter of József Mindszenty to "His Eminence" [based on the contents of the letter, the addressee was Cardinal Spellman, archbishop of New York], December 24, 1948.

CHAPTER 6

JÓZSEF MINDSZENTY,

HUNGARY'S PASTOR-IN-CHIEF AT THE PEOPLE'S COURT

CHAPTER 6

"I Will Smite the Shepherd, and the Sheep of the Flock Shall Be Scattered Abroad" (Matthew 26:31)

THE ARREST

The tension was so great that it could have been cut with a knife, especially in the seat of the archdiocese, Esztergom, as well as in the Hungarian capital, Budapest. On hearing rumors of a demonstration in support of Mindszenty, the authorities sent a group of armed secret servicemen (State Protection Authority) to watch over the primatial palace. Based on evidence gathered in the course of house searches and interrogation sessions, the political police regarded it as proven that "under József Mindszenty's leadership, important church figures had conspired to bring about the demise of the Republic of Hungary."[1] Now, no other option remained; the cardinal had just hours left as a free man.

"The End of Personal Freedom"

At 6 p.m. on December 26, 1948, Cardinal Mindszenty, who was in his 57th year, was taken into police custody, having been accused of treachery,

1. Ibid., V–700/50. 246. fol. Report, December 26, 1948.

espionage, foreign currency manipulation, and conspiring to overthrow the republic. All of these charges were stereotypical accusations made by totalitarian regimes. The timing of the arrest was cynical to say the least. The authorities were demonstrating their indifference to the Christian festivals: at Christmas, Christians commemorate the birth of Jesus Christ. The next day, December 26, is the Feast of St. Stephen, the first Christian martyr, who was stoned to death. The head of the State Protection Authority unit that was sent to Esztergom, Lieutenant Colonel Gyula Décsi, a law graduate, had received personal instructions from Deputy Prime Minister Mátyás Rákosi (general secretary of the Hungarian Working People's Party) about how he should proceed in the case. Rákosi had impressed on Décsi the importance of "adhering in full to the law" and of refraining, under all circumstances, from the use of force.[2] For some days, Rákosi withheld information from the Council of Ministers about the plan of action. The government, which had met on December 23, did not meet again until December 31. Mátyás Rákosi opened that meeting by congratulating Prime Minister István Dobi – whom he called the son of the people – on his 50th birthday. Only then did the minister of interior provide information on the recent arrest of Cardinal Mindszenty.[3]

In detention, Mindszenty at first insisted on his innocence, forwarding, by way of a confidant, a declaration to the bishops:

> Personal freedom has ceased. What has now happened, R.[ákosi] had sworn in May, by way of a personal envoy, to do, if... Certain circles were even plotting an assassination. What they are announcing now, and, even more importantly, what they will be announcing soon, should not be given any credibility. Nullius conspirationis particeps fui et sum. [I have not been and am not any part of a conspiracy.] Any kind of resignation or abdication, and so forth, can be ruled out. If such things are reported, it will either be to mislead people or it will be invalid on account of coercion exceeding human strength.[4]

2. MNL OL XX–10–k LÜ PO 18.300/1989. Witness interrogation record for Gyula Décsi, January 30, 1990.

3. MNL OL XIX–A–83–a/270. sz. 2. fol. Minutes of meeting of the Council of Ministers, December 31, 1948.

4. PL Processus, V–700/1. 271. fol. József Mindszenty's handwritten notes, n. d. – The letter reached the US embassy, whence it was received by British diplomats, who immediately forwarded it to London.

The contents of this letter became particularly relevant when, later on, the Bishops' Conference received repeated requests from Mindszenty – via official channels – to accede to his temporary retirement, which the authorities seemed to be setting as a condition for treating his case separately from the others or even, subsequently, as a condition for his release.

Between November 19, 1948 and mid-January 1949, twenty individuals, among them Mindszenty, were arrested in the case. In January, the State Protection Authority carried out a further "casting of the actors" for the show trial. Ultimately, therefore, there were only seven defendants in the Mindszenty case. From the perspective of the authorities, the seven individuals comprised three groups: "legitimist conspirators" (Jusztin Baranyay and András Zakar), "traitorous spies" (Béla Ispánki and László Tóth), and the "foreign currency speculators," who were the alleged financiers of the conspiracy (Pál Esterházy and Miklós Nagy). The Hungarian primate was the link between these three groups and acted as their leader. Five of the seven defendants were ordained Catholic priests (at the trial hearings, however, only Cardinal Mindszenty and his secretary were permitted to wear clerical collars). The two non-priests were the landowning aristocrat Pál Esterházy and the journalist László Tóth. The "residual" thirteen individuals were initially called as witnesses. Subsequently, however, as was not uncommon under such circumstances, many of them became defendants themselves in related trials.

On December 27, the Hungarian envoy in Rome, László Velics, informed the Holy See of Cardinal Mindszenty's arrest. Both orally and in writing, he then made it plain that, regardless of the events, the Hungarian government was willing to negotiate.[5] The Vatican's response came in the late hours of New Year's Eve: in the Holy See's view the Hungarian government's willingness to come to an agreement was incompatible with the authorities' harsh treatment of the head of the Hungarian Catholic Church, as such action violated the Holy See itself.[6] News of the Vatican's stance of rejection rapidly became public knowledge – thanks to a report in the January 4, 1949 edition of *L'Osservatore Romano*. Despite the Hungarian government's swift efforts to alter the Vatican's position, the Holy See

5. MNL OL M–KS 276. f. 65/356. ő. e. 66. fol. Cipher telegram, Rome, December 30, 1948.
6. MNL OL XIX–J–1–j–IV–14. 1946–49. TÜK-documents of the Vatican, 1. d. Chronology.

proved unwilling to treat Mindszenty's arrest separately from the Church's general operations in Hungary. The Hungarian authorities thus failed in their endeavor to portray Mindszenty's arrest as a mere criminal matter. Evidently, the Vatican was fully aware that the true goal of the communist regime was to break the will and spirit of the Hungarian Catholic Church.

At the Vatican, there were, incidentally, at least two interpretations of the situation. Domenico Tardini, the secretary of the Congregation for Extraordinary Ecclesiastical Affairs, was fundamentally opposed to making any accords with countries in the Soviet bloc. Indeed, he regarded communism as a blight on humanity. Meanwhile, however, Giovanni Battista Montini, the substitute for ordinary affairs, refused to rule out negotiations and a search for compromise. When, in 1954, Montini was unexpectedly appointed as archbishop of Milan – which meant his departure from the Curia – he was, in effect, being punished for his efforts to seek closer relations with the communist countries. The ideas and mentalities of these two officials continued to influence Mindszenty's fate in subsequent periods too. In early 1949, relations between the communist-led Hungarian regime and the Catholic Church reached deadlock, and negotiations between the two parties were put on hold. Tardini's tough stance greatly influenced the Vatican's position until his death in 1961. Thereafter, Pope John XXIII began to set his own course, gradually developing what became known as the Vatican's Eastern policy. His successor, rather than tear up the foundations laid by John XXIII, opted to build upon them. This came as no surprise, for the man who became Pope Paul VI in 1963 was none other than Giovanni Battista Montini, who had been removed from the Vatican nine years earlier.

The world was shocked to hear of the arrest of the Hungarian primate, Cardinal Mindszenty. The news agencies were overwhelmed by a flood of both true and false news reports. Several newspapers reported that Mindszenty had been deported to Siberia. Robert A. Lovett, the US under-secretary of state, voiced his support for the Hungarian cardinal on December 28, while President Truman did the same at his end-of-year news conference. Cardinal Spellman of New York issued a statement to the *Reuters* news agency, condemning the Hungarian communist regime's persecution of the Church. A protest demonstration was held outside the Hungarian Legation in Paris. Meanwhile, the international communist press organs were alone in their support for Mindszenty's arrest. For its part, the Holy See imposed the gravest discipline on Catholics: on December 28, 1948, it excommunicated all those individuals who had "raised a sacrilegious hand against His Eminence and Cardinal of the Church of Rome, Archbishop József Mindszenty of Esztergom."[7] Within days, the offices of Pius XII were awash in a sea of telegrams. Protests were received from archbishops, bishops, priests and ordinary Catholics all around the world. Dezső Sulyok, the former leader of the Party of Hungarian Freedom who had emigrated to the United States, wrote to President Truman calling for the cessation of diplomatic relations between Washington and Budapest.[8] The Hungarian Legation in Washington received a great number of protest letters. One of the first protest demonstrations was held outside the Hungarian consulate building in New York on January 5, 1949.[9] Hungarian and non-Hungarian Americans avidly watched the developments, and the first protests were soon followed by larger public demonstrations.

Almost without exception, the foreign diplomats serving in Budapest reminded their respective ministries of foreign affairs that the arrest of Cardinal Mindszenty was more than a domestic matter for Hungary, because it could not have occurred without the prior approval of the Soviet government in Moscow. There was, indeed, a radical shift in the Soviet Union's religious policy at this time, and the rise of anti-clericalism throughout Central and Eastern Europe was merely one sign of this. The new strategy aimed, in the short term, to accomplish a rupture in religious and other relations with Western Europe and to silence overt opposition. The longer-term objective was the complete eradication of religion and its institutions.

In Hungary, the peaceful mood of Christmas was replaced by feelings of shock and horror. In the press, articles of expressly hateful intent were published for the first time. The writers of such articles did not spare their words: the cardinal was repeatedly called "cowardly," "vile," "a worm,"

7. R. Kothen, ed., *Documents Pontificaux de Sa Sainteté Pie XII 1948* (Paris and Louvain: Éditions Labergerie – Éditions Warny, 1950), 464–65.

8. "La dolorosa indignazione mondiale per l'arresto del Cardinale Mindszenty," *L'Osservatore Romano* 88, no. 304, December 31, 1948, 1 and 4.

9. MNL OL XIX–J–1–d KÜM – Washingtoni Nagykövetség [Hungarian Embassy in Washington] 1949–52. 5. d. Report of Béla Balassa, head of office, New York, January 5, 1949.

"insane," "miserable," and "criminal." Perhaps the "zenith" was reached when Mindszenty was called the "preacher of death."[10] Meanwhile, Catholic news outlets opted for eloquent silence. Reports reaching the Hungarian Working People's Party were mixed: the bitterness and outrage of the people were noted, but there was also a good deal of apple-polishing and the spreading of malicious rumors. Here and there, someone was brave enough to call Mindszenty a martyr. The endless demagogy and fear had a dual effect. While no-one cried out "crucify him," some Catholic priests and laypersons began – amid the chill of fear and the deluge of lies – to behave "smartly." Even the Bishops' Conference opted to refrain from speaking out publicly against the arrest of the Hungarian primate. This lack of action surprised the Catholic faithful, who would have expected a call for public prayer and/or a pastoral letter protesting Mindszenty's arrest. The flock and the shepherds were understandably frightened.

The First Days on Remand

Public opinion was still coming to terms with news of Cardinal Mindszenty's arrest when, in Budapest, in the cellar of No. 60 Andrássy Road (which later on became an emblematic site of political terror),[11] Lieutenant Colonel Gyula Décsi undertook the interrogation of the cardinal, in accordance with Mátyás Rákosi's specific instructions.[12] Mindszenty's cell was a rather stuffy and dark room (20 square meters) on the first floor of the building. The cell was a heated one. No cellmate informant was put into Mindszenty's cell; rather, his cell was watched over night and day by a team of guards.

It was not the first time that Mindszenty had been denied his freedom. Even so, the first night spent in his cell shook him up. We can reconstruct the events based on seventy hefty files, which were drawn up during the

10. "A halál prédikátora" [The preacher of death], *Szabad Nép* 6, no. 240, October 17, 1948, 5.

11. The building had served in 1940 as a base for the Arrow Cross Party. In February 1945, it was taken over by the new political police force, which turned the cellars into a prison. Since 2002, the building has functioned as a museum known as the House of Terror.

12. In his memoirs, Rákosi wrote that he was in constant receipt of the interrogation records for Mindszenty, which were forwarded to him by Gábor Péter, head of the State Protection Authority. Rákosi, *Visszaemlékezések*, 712.

police inquiry. Mindszenty himself was interrogated from immediately after his arrest. This first interrogation session lasted from 11 p.m. until dawn. It is the interrogation record of the following day however which tells us more or less what happened:

> I was greatly humiliated, which I had not experienced before, and well, the manner in which they spoke in the course of the interrogations, and what was going on in the other room, well, somehow it was for me a great act of self-control, that I should be at their disposal in whatever respect... The shameful and dirty language that was used in my presence; it is deeply depressing that even in the case of intelligent members of the Hungarian police, such vulgar behavior is possible. [...] So much chivalry is shown to a prelate, a cardinal, of which there are only 51 throughout the world, and then, at the offices of the Hungarian police, they demonstrate such behavior.[13]

Mindszenty's outrage suggests that he was subjected to profanity and lewd behavior but was not actually beaten. The profanity and lewdness would have been difficult for anyone to stomach. For a God-fearing prelate whose message was one of love for one's neighbor, the situation must have been particularly upsetting. Compared with the uncouthness of the prison guards, it seems Gyula Décsi was the embodiment of civility and politeness. Throughout the interrogation he addressed Mindszenty as "Prince Primate" and referred to the questioning session as a "conversation," thereby giving the impression that nothing significant was at stake. Mindszenty answered the questions with great caution and brevity; he did not wish to incriminate anyone and responded, "I don't remember" on several occasions. More than once he referred to confidentiality and his duty of non-disclosure, claiming that he needed a permit from the Holy See to make a statement. Whatever Mindszenty was thinking in his austere prison cell, he must have been greatly surprised to discover how much the authorities knew about him.

The amicable "conversation" with Décsi was followed by a merciless night of intimidation at the hands of the secret police. Décsi's task was to produce

13. ÁBTL 3.1.9. V–700/5. 21–22. fol. Transcript of shorthand notes on Mindszenty's interrogation, December 27, 1948, evening. – The maximum number of cardinals at this point in time was seventy. However, Pius XII had left fifteen cardinal seats empty, and some of the cardinals had died.

a signed interrogation record. What could not be obtained with fine words, had to be squeezed out of the cardinal in the course of regular beatings. As the Hungarian primate told his defense attorney a few weeks later,

> ...I did not want to sign the interrogation record, because they had not recorded my statement, and so it was a made-up story [...] they took me into the next room, and there a police major hit me with a rubber truncheon, removed some of my clothing, and when I could no longer bear the thrashing, well, I climbed under [the table].[14]

This is how the first interrogation record was made, with each of the three pages bearing Mindszenty's signature.[15] Two of these three signatures show his faint and spidery handwriting, while the third is distorted beyond recognition, which seems to indicate that he was suffering from strong pain or was about to pass out. Indeed, his signed name is almost falling off the edge of the paper. In front of all three signatures, there are two letters: *c. f.* It would seem that when signing the record drawn up on December 27, Mindszenty was following the example set by Christian prisoners at the time of the Ottoman wars who would write the letters "c. f." (*coactus feci*) by their names to indicate that they had been coerced into making their statements.

When reading the interrogation records, Mátyás Rákosi noticed the unusual signature. He inquired about the meaning of "c. f.", whereupon Gábor Péter told him that it was "some kind of religious nonsense" for he had been told by Mindszenty that it was an abbreviation for cardinalis foraneus, that is, a provincial cardinal, rather than a curial one. Rákosi, however, was smarter than this: "No, this is not religious nonsense, but means rather that 'not a word is true'."[16] He was right. Indeed, on January 3, 1949, Mindszenty himself admitted in writing to having performed the trick: "In the records, the signature with c. f. (coactus feci) means an act of coercion; in other words, I wanted to signal that I had made my statement

14. Ibid., 136–138. fol. Cardinal József Mindszenty's second conversation with his defense attorney, Dr. Kálmán Kiczkó, January 28, 1949.

15. PL Processus, V–700/1. 19–20. fol. Interrogation record for suspect, December 27, 1948.

16. MNL OL M–KS 288. f. 9/1962/51b. 27. fol. Gábor Péter, *Mi az igazság?* [What is the truth?] Manuscript, July 10, 1956.

under coercion."[17] Thereafter the beatings began once again. The same day he was prohibited from smoking tobacco, and the opportunities to say Mass were temporarily rescinded.[18] Although the circumstances of his detention explained why he could not say Mass daily, nevertheless the prelate, who had been raised on the basis of the Code of Canon Law of 1917, still felt a burden on his conscience.

Mindszenty initially stood firm. Indeed, on December 29, 1948, he appealed against the prosecutor's decree ordering his pretrial detention. The subsequent interrogation records (those of January 5, 9, 11, 1949) clearly reflect, however, the style and methods of the State Protection Authority: a series of self-accusatory and factitious sentences are to be found in the manipulated and montage-like texts, and each page bears the cardinal's signature of endorsement. In the course of the interrogations, the main emphasis was laid on the cardinal's contacts in the United States and on the legitimist "conspiracy" to bring about the fall of the Hungarian republic. Spice was added to the case in the form of the alleged "foreign currency dealing" and the matter of the Holy Crown. These latter accusations, however, were also designed to show that the authorities were not attacking the Church as a whole, but merely a single "sinful priest." In making its case, the prosecution cited Mindszenty's past in Zalaegerszeg and his support for certain political parties. They even dug up information from the press trials. Essentially, they were searching for a petty and greedy man who was always nagging others and who customarily abused his power and influence.

The Letter of Pope Pius XII

Prime Minister István Dobi invited members of the Bishops' Conference to talks scheduled for January 4, 1949. Prior to this conference, the bishops met behind closed doors to determine their course of action.[19] Many of the

17. PL Processus, V–700/1. 9. fol. József Mindszenty's handwritten notes, January 3, 1949.

18. Mindszenty could say Mass on December 30 and 31, 1948 and on January 1, 1949, but then, for a period of twelve days (until January 13), he was prohibited from doing so. Ibid., V–700/33. 250. fol. Memo of József Mindszenty, March 31, 1949.

19. MNL OL XIX–A–2–ab, 3. d. Papers of Prime Minister István Dobi, 070/1949. – For the material relating to the meeting of the Bishops' Conference on January 4, 1949, see Margit Balogh, ed., *A Magyar Katolikus Püspöki Kar tanácskozásai 1949–1965 között: Dokumentumok* (Budapest: METEM, 2008), 39–48.

bishops had already been threatened, and called upon by the minister of interior to step down. In the end, a statement was formulated that neither judged the state authorities nor protested their actions. In essence, the bishops' position was that, in spite of events, they should adhere to their declaration of December 16, 1948, in which they had shown a readiness for negotiation and compromise. They also reiterated that any talks would have to be made in collaboration with the Apostolic Holy See.

Fourteen bishops attended the meeting on January 4. They were expecting to be treated as partners and to receive information from Mátyás Rákosi in person about developments in the Mindszenty case, for they had no more knowledge of the case than the average newspaper reader. They left the meeting in disappointment and having been humiliated. For his part, Rákosi was dissatisfied with the statement issued by the bishops, because it failed to declare an anti-Royalist stance. As the report of an informer surveilling the bishops concluded: "...all of the bishops are in despair. All of them reckon on being detained sooner or later. They expressed this among themselves as follows: 'First, two [of us] will be detained, and then another two.'"[20] The official report of the Hungarian News Agency – MTA – mentioned none of this. Instead, it noted that negotiations had been conducted "in a spirit of understanding" and would be resumed in the future. The leftist press in Hungary and abroad welcomed the talks, which had left Western propaganda "in ruins", because while the Vatican authorities in Rome had opted for a policy of excommunication, representatives of the Catholic Church in Budapest had refused to abandon dialogue and had even signed a new agreement.[21]

The next day Rákosi informed the Secretariat of the Central Leadership of the Hungarian Working People's Party (HWPP CL) about what had happened. He received authorization to continue negotiations with the aim of obtaining a "a statement that can be used politically to the full" and which stated in black and white that Hungary was a country of religious freedom. If such a statement were to be issued, the bishops would receive

20. ÁBTL 3.1.5. O–13.405/1. 170. fol. Report, January 5, 1949.

21. MNL OL XIX–J–1–j–IV–14–1637–1948. TÜK-documents of the Vatican 1. d. Open telegram of Envoy László Velics, December 28, 1948, 2.20 p.m.

permission to view the material gathered on Mindszenty and even to travel to Rome.[22]

A new round of negotiations was scheduled for January 8, but owing to the unfolding of events, they became superfluous. On January 7, Imre Mócsy, the Jesuit who had taken the Hungarian government's offer to Rome in December, returned from his stay at the Vatican. While there, Mócsy had managed to hold talks with Robert Leiber, an influential Vatican insider who was the confessor priest of, and advisor to, Pope Pius XII. On December 22, he had passed to Secretary Domenico Tardini a German translation of the Hungarian government's church policy memorandum,[23] but the pope himself had been unable to examine the Hungarian matters prior to Christmas. On hearing of Cardinal Mindszenty's arrest, the Jesuit Mócsy, a man of great decency, blurted out: "Here am I and those stupid men throw such a bomb in my way!"[24] By the time he was given – on December 28 – fifteen minutes to talk with Tardini in person, his mission had lost its relevance and urgency, for Mindszenty had already spent two days in police custody. Tardini informed Mócsy that he was going to take a tough stance: "There is nothing left to do but to protest against the violation that has befallen Mindszenty and, through him, the entire Bishops' Conference, the College of Cardinals, and the pope himself."[25]

Mócsy set out for Hungary on the evening of January 3, carrying the following written message from Pius XII:

> Abide loyally in protection of your faith and of morality and in the struggle that the good Lord has placed upon you, so that, in the people of your country, famous for its ancient faith, there should be no weakening of the Christian principles according to which the country's people have lived for centuries. The heroic stand taken by Cardinal Mindszenty has offered a true example. He has not acted in any other way than what stems from

22. MNL OL M–KS 276. f. 53/24. ő. e. Minutes of the meeting of the Secretariat of the HWPP CL on January 5, 1949, Agenda item no. 1. For a copy, see RGASPI f. 17. op. 128. delo (file) 665. l. 10.

23. JTMRL II.1. Copies of the Rome archive material, Epistolae Variorum 1946–50/1947–49. Papers from December 1948.

24. MMAL 020/c. folder, Typed manuscript of József Mindszenty's memoirs, item no. 7.

25. ÁBTL 3.1.9. V–19.441 73. fol. Suspect interrogation record for Imre Mócsy. January 17, 1949.

> his apostolic office and is his duty; that with all his strength he should protect and defend the faith, the teaching, the free operation of the Church, and the preservation of schools that ensure the education in the Christian faith of future generations.[26]

The Vatican authorities acted without hesitation in defense of Mindszenty. From Rome's perspective, József Mindszenty was a cardinal who, even after his arrest, remained the head of the Hungarian Catholic Church and continued to be a symbol and embodiment of Catholic principles. The Vatican understood that Mindszenty perceived sharing in the fate of his flock as his duty.

The pope's letter contained no explicit instructions, but it did warn of the duty to show resistance. In view of this warning, the bishops decided to cancel their attendance at talks with the government on January 8. On January 17, Mócsy informed the bishops of the details of his visit to Rome. He told them that Vatican officials were fully behind Mindszenty and that the whole world was going into action on his behalf, including "even the Czech bishops, leaving us as the only exceptions."[27] Although it was now evident that efforts aimed at securing an agreement had failed, the Hungarian Bishops' Conference chose not to protest at Cardinal Mindszenty's arrest. Further, the bishops kept Hungarian Catholics in the dark when it came to the contents of the pope's letter. Meanwhile the Hungarian authorities took steps to silence the "courier to Rome," Imre Mócsy, whom the State Protection Authority arrested as he was leaving the meeting. As his "reward" for his work as "spokesman," the Jesuit priest was placed in an internment camp for several years.[28] The bishops became increasingly desperate: officially, they were not allowed to negotiate, but, at the same

26. The letter was originally written in Latin using lithographed handwriting. It was signed personally by the pope, thus comprising four pages: ÁBTL 3.1.9. V–700/54. 6–7. fol. Report, January 12, 1949. The text of the letter is published in Somorjai and Zinner, *Majd' halálra ítélve*, 577–78.

27. ÁBTL 3.1.5. O–13.405/1. 183. fol. Report, January 18, 1949.

28. Imre Mócsy, *Hagytam magam szerettetni* (Budapest: Szent Jeromos Katolikus Bibliatársulat, 2007); Gábor Bánkuti, "Mócsy Imre jezsuita szerzetes római küldetése, és ami utána következett," in *Megértő történelem. Tanulmányok a hatvanéves Gyarmati György tiszteletére*, edited by Magdolna Baráth, Gábor Bánkuti, and János Rainer M. (Budapest: L'Harmattan Kiadó, 2011), 173–81.

time, they dared not walk out on the government. Accordingly, they decided to remain in contact with the government and negotiate on minor issues, lest they gave the impression of a unilateral rupture.

The parliamentary session on that day – January 17, 1949 – dealt at length with the Mindszenty affair and the danger of "Mindszenty-ism" gaining a foothold in the country. Several representatives spoke of the prelate as if he were a common criminal. The leaders of the Reformed (Calvinist) Church in Hungary then issued a statement condemning Mindszenty, which also received the support of the chairman of the Alliance of Free Churches in Hungary and the leaders of several independent churches.[29] The Lutheran Church in Hungary subsequently issued a statement in support of the government and critical of Mindszenty.[30] After a delay of several weeks, representatives of the Jewish denomination in Hungary added their voice to the critics. Both the Protestant churches and the Jewish denomination were required to make these pro-government statements for the sake of their respective agreements with the Hungarian state.

THE SCRIPT FOR THE TRIAL AND ITS "UNDOING"

The prince primate of Hungary became the ideal hero of the Hungarian people's struggle for independence and of their loyalty to the Christian faith. Mindszenty was also an exemplary figure in the struggle against political oppression and dictatorship; the whole world viewed him with awe and wonder. He was among the few individuals in Hungary who – without resorting to coercion – could exercise power over the masses. As time passed, he even won the affection of the Arrow Cross émigrés, who had so disliked him (and had even imprisoned him) during their rule.

Opposing the Government is a Crime

Until the Mindszenty affair, Rákosi had shown little interest in the work of the political police. Now, however, he followed developments on a daily

29. MNL OL M–KS 276. f. 65/356. ő. e. 57–58. fol. Typed statement.

30. PIL 508. f. 1/125. ő. e. 122. t. 4. fol. (=TNA FO 371/78580, R. 676/1785/21.) Knox Helm's telegram to the British Foreign Office, January 20, 1949.

basis, in effect steering proceedings from the background. He rightly surmised that his political career could be at risk if he failed to bring the matter to a satisfactory conclusion. Years later, Rákosi complained to the Hungarian representative at the Cominform that

> "the Soviet bodies and the Soviet comrades did little to help and sometime failed to give their attention to the numerous spy groups that had been arrested by the Hungarian authorities" and since there were no properly qualified cadres "on a daily basis I spent much of my working time leading the investigation, and this lasted almost the entire year (the trials of Mindszenty, Rajk, Vogeler, and others)".[31]

It is tragicomical that Rákosi, the powerful communist party leader, pitied himself while simultaneously taking pride in his achievements.

Despite his hands-on approach, Rákosi was dissatisfied with the results of the somewhat rushed investigation. On reading the interrogation record of January 9, 1949, he sharply criticized the work of the political police. In his view, the interrogation record "was absolutely ignorant of policy; it was the work of men who had not the slightest idea of state security."[32] Yet, the interrogation record in question was, in fact, full of "admissions of guilt" on the part of Mindszenty. In his impatience, Rákosi then dictated his expectations: "The objective: 'a federative Central European kingdom' with Hungary, Austria, and, if possible, Bavaria. Headed by Otto von Habsburg, by whose side Mindszenthy [sic] would have been 'first violinist' after having placed the Hungarian crown on his [Otto von Habsburg's] head. This would only have been possible by overthrowing the Hungarian Republic with American assistance." Accordingly, Mindszenty, who was "in all respects at the disposal of the Americans," made use of the support

31. S. G. Zavolzhskiy's report on the negotiations with Mátyás Rákosi on March 6–7, 1950. Moscow, March 9, 1950, in Volokitina et al., *Vostochnaya Evropa v dokumentah rossijskih arhivov 1944–1953, Tom II, 1949–1953* (Moscow and Novosibirsk: Sibirskiy hronograf, 1998), 318 (Document no. 105).

32. MNL OL M–KS 276. f. 65/356. ő. e. 39. fol. Typed, unsigned document. (The following quotations are from this document – the author.) – Note: Rákosi was similarly unsatisfied with the results of the interrogations in the Rajk case: "He banged his fist on the table, saying that the secret service people were incompetent, and the matter was not progressing." MNL OL M–KS 288. f. 9/1962–51/a. ő. e. 10. fol.

of the former political elite and undertook large-scale espionage. Had he achieved this goal, he would evidently have annulled the land reform program, nationalization, and all the achievements of democracy. Playing his "*unwanted*" role of unofficial prosecutor, Rákosi also instructed that the interrogation record should show

> Mindszenthy as he really is: a reactionary, dull-witted, narrow-minded, and cynical political adventurer. The interrogation record should make it clear to all segments of the Hungarian working people – the workers, the new farmers, the middle peasants, the democratic petit bourgeoisie – as well as to people abroad, who Mindszenthy is. For this reason, one must expose not only his reactionary and fascist past but also his dim-wittedness and bigotry. Do not forget that the case will have repercussions that reach far beyond the borders of Hungary and will mark the defeat of the entire international reactionary forces. Continue your work bearing these aspects in mind.[33]

In accordance with Rákosi's instructions, the interrogation records were amended and rewritten several times. The "draft version" of Cardinal Mindszenty's summary record is full of corrections, additions, and stylistic changes. In places, the handwriting is certainly not Mindszenty's.[34] Unsurprisingly, the corrections serve to highlight Mindszenty's responsibility ("I acknowledge," "I admit") and the continuity of his incorrigibility (he had done or thought something "already" in his youth). Reading through the text, one can see how sentence construction becomes increasingly artificial. The key element was Mindszenty's legitimist stance, which was public knowledge. Legitimism was not, in itself, a crime, and he could not be accused of conspiring against the state on the basis of having a political belief that differed from the official line. However, the fact that Mindszenty had met with Otto von Habsburg in the United States in the summer of 1947 could be framed as part of a conspiracy.

The authorities in Budapest then instructed Hungary's diplomatic representations abroad to hold press conferences at which the Mindszenty affair was to be portrayed as an "ordinary reactionary conspiracy" rather

33. Ibid., 41. fol.
34. PL Processus, V–700/1. 147–167. fol. Draft of József Mindszenty's summary record.

than as an ecclesiastical matter.[35] It was at these press conferences that the results of the State Protection Authority's investigation were presented, in the form of an 86-page brochure (officially titled *The Mindszenty Criminal Papers*), which came to be known (on account of its canary yellow color) as the "*Yellow Book*." The *Yellow Book* is an object lesson in how to mislead the unsuspecting reader by means of distortions, misrepresentations, and false references, so that in the end he or she believes that the criminal of the century has been caught by his tail. Moreover, the overt criticism of an accredited diplomat of a foreign state – namely, the US envoy – was unprecedented in a government brochure published in peacetime. The picture drawn was of a man who had commissioned Mindszenty to work as a spy, supplying secret information on Hungary and on the Soviet troops stationed in the country. Having read the *Yellow Book*, no-one could be in any doubt that the two men were accursed evildoers who had conspired against the democratic Hungarian state with a view to restoring the Habsburg monarchy. Through his actions, the US diplomat had become "useless" in the sense that no Hungarian now dared speak to him, either publicly or privately. Even though his official position had become untenable, the US government refused to recall the diplomat, as it feared this would be interpreted as an acknowledgment of guilt.

Was there any truth to the allegations made against the US diplomat? What is true is that, in August 1947, the newly appointed envoy had presented himself – as was the custom at the time – to Cardinal Mindszenty, Hungary's prince primate. Subsequently, at the beginning of 1948, he had sent the cardinal a New Year's greeting. In sum, the two men had met on five separate occasions, conversing together for, in total, five or six hours with the help of an interpreter – which meant a "net" conversation time of three hours at most. The fact that the cardinal had invited the envoy and his family on an excursion to Esztergom, including lunch, indicated that the relationship had gone beyond mere protocol. On a separate occasion, the cardinal had requested the envoy's assistance in arranging for four people to obtain refuge abroad. Their most recent meeting had taken place on November 15, 1948. On that occasion, Mindszenty had spoken openly of his concerns for the country's future and for his own prospects. In

35. MNL OL XIX–J–30–a, 19. d. TÜK-documents of the Hungarian embassy in Paris.

response, the US envoy had offered to assist Mindszenty in leaving the country, if that became his wish. But all of this did not mean that the US diplomat had encouraged Mindszenty to engage in espionage. It was even less likely that the two men might have conspired to bring about a change of regime or the restoration of the kingdom.

Treachery, Conspiracy, and Foreign Currency Dealing

Although, based on the information at its disposal, the State Protection Authority must have known that the legitimists were an insignificant political force, it nevertheless portrayed them as a real threat and as monarchist conspirers. For his part, Mindszenty had never denied his legitimist convictions, and nor did he do so to his interrogators. Rather, he acknowledged that in the spring of 1947 he had been greatly concerned about what would happen to the country in the event of a political vacuum. In view of the terms of the Paris Peace Treaty, it had seemed certain at the time that the Soviet army would withdraw from the country by no later than the fall. For the police investigators, however, Mindszenty's admission in this regard indicated the point in time at which the "conspiracy" had become a serious undertaking, culminating in Mindszenty's meeting with Otto von Habsburg in the summer of 1947.

In early 1947, the Cistercian monk and university professor Jusztin Baranyay – a prominent supporter of the legitimist movement – had indeed drafted a paper in preparation for the situation that would arise in the aftermath of the signing of the peace treaty. Among other things, Baranyay's paper had discussed the constitutional role of the prince primate in the event of such a "transitory" political situation.[36] The monk and legal expert, who, as late as September 1948, had been hired by the Ministry of Interior to serve as its expert on canon law in certain negotiations, was now – just a few months later – made the secondary co-defendant in the Mindszenty trial. Baranyay's indictment stemmed from the conclusion he had made in his paper that the prince primate, in view of his public legal function, would be in a position to restore legal continuity. Further, the monk had included in his paper a list of possible

36. ÁBTL 3.1.9. V–700/2. 17–18. fol. Jusztin Baranyay's memorandum, December 25, 1948.

members of a grand coalition government, capable of governing the country for a temporary period. The name of the proposed prime minister had not featured in the list, but Baranyay had made no secret of his view that – similarly to the postwar role in Greece of Damaskinos Papandreou, archbishop of Athens and All Greece – the prince primate, as temporary head of state, would be in a position to appoint the head of government.[37] We can only surmise as to Mindszenty's opinion of all this. Since 1918, the royal throne had been vacant and the country had been headed by a Calvinist regent rather than by a Catholic Habsburg ruler. On April 17, 1945, the three-man National Ruling Council had been formed with the task of exercising the powers of the head of state, but its composition (a military officer, a Lutheran professor, and a communist politician) had evidently not been to Mindszenty's taste. After the proclamation of the republic on February 1, 1946, the former prime minister and Calvinist preacher Zoltán Tildy became the first president of the republic. He was followed by Árpád Szakasits, the Social Democratic Party leader. The mere sight of these names had resulted in consternation in the legitimist Mindszenty.

A legitimist conspiracy would have been completely worthless without a crown and a king. Therefore, the investigators began examining Mindszenty's ideas for the depositing of the ancient royal crown of Hungary at the Vatican. Not only had the cardinal wished to safeguard the crown from the vicissitudes of a renewed war, but also his other aim had been to keep the Holy Crown – viewed by many Hungarians as the source of all authority and rights – out of the hands of the pro-Soviet governments. In the indictment, the facts were cleverly mixed up and distorted, whereby the impression was given that Mindszenty's daydreaming concerning a change of regime were part of a plot – as if Mindszenty's only reason for seeking to have the crown moved to Rome was that he could then have placed it on Otto von Habsburg's head. We know for certain that Mindszenty would not even have considered a coronation in *Rome,* for such a coronation would have been entirely ineffectual, given that, under the terms of Hungary's historical constitution, a coronation performed outside the country was necessarily invalid. For his part, Otto von Habsburg had neither the power

37. Ibid., 32. fol. Interrogation record for Jusztin Baranyay, December 28, 1948; PL Processus, V–700/1. 15. fol. Memorandum on József Mindszenty's interrogation, December 27, 1948; Ispánki, *Az évszázad pere,* 147.

nor the means to reoccupy his throne. After his visit to the United States and the failure of his plans to have the crown removed to Rome, Mindszenty accepted that the West was unwilling to lift even a finger for Otto and his kingdom in Hungary. Mindszenty's signed statement, in which he "acknowledged" that it had been his intention to crown Otto von Habsburg, is misleading and clearly the result of coercion. Throughout the court hearing, József Mindszenty consistently emphasized that his sole consideration had been to protect the crown and that his idea for placing it at the Vatican had been aimed at sparing the crown the vicissitudes of a new war and any possible claims from the successor states.

The accusation that Mindszenty had been making efforts to overthrow the regime would have sufficed to remove him from public life. Rather than strengthen the case, the other accusations – espionage, foreign currency dealing, and so forth – had the effect of discrediting the entire proceedings. For the ordinary public, however, "wheeling and dealing in foreign currencies" was far easier to understand as an accusation than a complicated tale of conspiracy. It is a fact that, on account of his foreign contacts, Mindszenty had had some foreign currency at his disposal, certain amounts of which he had distributed to the bishops for the purchase of goods needed by the churches and for charitable purposes. A further amount had – without Mindszenty's specific instruction – been sold by his accountant at an excellent rate to Prince Pál Esterházy and others.[38] (In 1948, the official exchange rate was one dollar to 11.74 forints, but on the black market a dollar was worth almost double this amount. Prince Esterházy had paid even more – around 30–35 forints.) The prosecution sought to portray this business deal as a political act. In its view, a series of confessions that it had gathered together served as "proof" that Pál Esterházy had sponsored the alleged legitimist conspiracy.

Foreign currency exchange at the official rate was highly disadvantageous, owing to the hyperinflation that had accompanied the country's economic collapse. The rate of exchange after the introduction of the forint in place of the "paper pengő" was unrealistically low. At the same time, foreign currency – its exchange into forints and even its sale on the black

38. MMAL 34. d. Folder with heading "Ispánky [!] Béla által átnézett fejezetek" [Chapters reviewed by Béla Ispánky (!)], without pagination. Pages that were omitted or corrected during the editing of Mindszenty's memoirs.

market – had become vital for the operation of ecclesiastical institutions. Lénárd Kögl, the one-time auditor of the Veszprém Diocese, stated in 1990 (i.e., at a time when he was no longer subject to coercion or pressure) that Mindszenty

> did not recognize the right of the state to freely determine the value of a foreign currency, which, under certain circumstances, could be lower than the real market value, whereby the state would benefit financially to the detriment of the Church. [...] ...with regard to donations, based on the sovereignty of the Church, he did not accept laws and regulations applying to foreign currency.[39]

It would seem that Mindszenty did indeed violate the legal rules applying to foreign currency, for rather than exchange the full sum of the foreign currency (all of which had been received from abroad) at the Hungarian National Bank, he used it as he saw fit. Under the laws in force, dealing in foreign currency was a financial crime that was punishable with a death sentence. On these grounds, all Hungarian bishops and a substantial share of the clergy could have been brought to trial. (In the case of the Lutheran bishop Lajos Ordass, this is exactly what the authorities did: on September 8, 1948, Ordass, having been accused of "a crime that violates the country's management of foreign currency," was sentenced by the Budapest Usury Court to two years' imprisonment and a five-year ban on the exercise of his office. Ordass's trial was, in many respects, a dress-rehearsal for the Mindszenty trial. Here too, the proceedings made a mockery of the service of justice. The Ordass trial was, however, less dramatic and gave rise to a lesser reaction, in view of Hungary's far smaller Lutheran population.)

Lénárd Kögl recalled that the sale of currency on the "free market" was "public knowledge in that period" and that the government leadership had not protested against it. That the churches had received favorable treatment was confirmed by Miklós Nyárádi, the finance minister who had resigned on December 3, 1948 and had thereafter remained abroad. In a statement, he pointed out that the churches had been exempt from the foreign currency

39. MNL OL XX–10–k LÜ PO 18.300/1989. II. Witness interrogation record for Lénárd Kögl, February 13, 1990.

regulations in the case of certain noble causes.[40] Even one of Rákosi's own statements reveals that there had been a differentiated approach. He predicted the end of a policy of tolerance that had treated with indulgence "spies, traitors, and currency smugglers who have been running around in priestly robes or dressed as cardinals...."[41] His statement in effect reveals that there had been a policy of tolerance relating to the use of foreign currency, whereby the churches had been permitted to freely use foreign currency sent or brought from abroad for charitable purposes or, indeed, to exchange it at a higher rate. This is what had happened to Mindszenty. He had left in the United States some of the money and checks he had received in the course of his 1947 visit to the USA and Canada for the purpose of a Hungarian Catholic Foundation. A further amount – 4,200 US dollars – he had exchanged at the Hungarian National Bank, while the rest he had placed in the ecclesiastical treasury. This latter amount had then been used to distribute sums to the poor. All of this he kept to himself until some ten years later when he informed a member of staff at the US embassy in Budapest.[42] It would seem, however, that at the time this way of proceeding accorded with the interests of the national economy and of the churches. Years later, Rákosi himself admitted that the game rules had been unilaterally suspended when he stated in a tape-recording that the accusation concerning foreign currency dealing had "not been true," while also claiming that the discovery of the "secret archive" in the metal container had been his particular achievement.[43] Evidently, the authorities were able to fully exploit the implicit nature of the permission that had been granted.

40. *Katolikus Magyarok Vasárnapja [Sunday of the Hungarian Catholics]* (Cleveland), February 18, 1949, 5.

41. "Rákosi Mátyás elvtárs nagy beszéde az MDP Központi Vezetőségének ülésén [The grand speech of Comrade Mátyás Rákosi at the Central Committee meeting of the Hungarian Workers' Party]," *Szabad Nép* 6, no. 275. November 28, 1948, 4.

42. NARA RG 84, Records of the Foreign Service Posts of the Department of State, Hungary, Records Relating to Cardinal Mindszenty 1956–72, Box 1, Mindszenty–Classified 1959, 570.3. Minutes of conversation with the cardinal, n. p. [February 27, 1959.]

43. Magdolna Baráth and István Feitl, eds., *Lehallgatott kihallgatások: Rákosi és Gerő pártvizsgálatának titkos hangszalagjai, 1962* (Budapest: Napvilág Kiadó–ÁBTL, 2013), 155.

Original or Forgery?

One of the documents in the *Yellow Book* – the publication containing the documents relating to the Hungarian primate's "crimes" – was Mindszenty's statement, or confession, of January 11, 1949, which amounted to a handwritten account of his ancestry, his career, and his political views. This statement is probably the most important in the series of admissions he made during the 39 days of his interrogation while in detention. A striking feature of the statement is that the grammar of Mindszenty – a painstakingly exact man who had edited a magazine for a period of twenty-five years – becomes noticeably poor in the second half. In his memoirs, Mindszenty not only denies that he had written the statement, which is full of errors (e.g., he "miswrote" the date of his appointment as prince primate), but also names the married couple who carried out the forgery: László Sulner and his wife, Hanna Fischhof. Sulner and Fischhof were handwriting experts.[44] Fischhof's father, Gyula Fischhof, had been a pioneer in handwriting analysis and graphology. In 1899, at the time of the Dreyfus trial in France, he had even been appointed as a handwriting expert. Then, after World War I, he had worked for the Hungarian government as its forensic document and graphology expert. After his death, his daughter had continued his work. A reference was made to Hanna Fischhof, the "international handwriting expert," in an article published in the January 7, 1949 edition of *Szabad Szó* (Free Speech), a newspaper with ties to the National Peasant Party. The article contained the following character description of Cardinal Mindszenty:

> Mindszenty is an ambitious and finicky person. For him externalities are important and he likes flashy stuff. He wants to make a mark and enjoys being given attention. The form of his handwriting suggests a stubborn man, who is also indiscrete. He is passionate and a man with an obsession; he is clever, but he is no diplomat, for he is opinionated and obstinate.[45]

44. Mindszenty, *Memoirs*, 115.

45. "Nemzetközi tekintélyű írásszakértő véleménye: Mindszenty írása és jelleme Winkelmann SS-tábornokéval azonos" [Opinion of an internationally renowned handwriting expert: the handwriting and personality of Mindszenty is identical to that of SS General Winkelmann], *Szabad Szó* 51, no. 5. January 7, 1949, 5.

Up until this point, the opinion of the graphologist could be said to have been roughly correct in terms of Mindszenty's character. The next segment of the newspaper article, however, is mere manipulation. It compared Mindszenty's handwriting to that of Otto Winkelmann, higher SS and police leader in Hungary during World War II, and to that of Sári Fedák, the infamous Arrow Cross primadonna.[46] The conclusion to be drawn by the reader was evident: Mindszenty bore a resemblance to Winkelmann and Fedák, both in terms of his personal nature and in terms of his political sympathies.

The events leading up to the graphology analysis and the circumstances of the forgeries first became known to US intelligence when the young couple made a statement after their escape to Austria.[47] According to Fischhof and Sulner's statement, the Hungarian police had come to their apartment on January 4, 1949. Having given them twenty photocopies of Mindszenty's handwriting, the police had then ordered a character analysis. A specific request on the part of the police had been that Sulner and Fischhof prove that Mindszenty's handwriting resembled that of a war criminal. They were instructed to pick out, from among the verified handwriting samples of German war criminals, the one that most closely resembled Mindszenty's handwriting.

In return for producing the graphology analysis, Hanna Fischhof requested and received an exit visa for her mother to travel to the United States, where she could meet with her son. On February 5, 1949, the mother left Hungary. Meanwhile Fischhof and Sulner systematically gathered together and photocopied all the documents relating to the Mindszenty case that were at their disposal and then, on February 6, in the middle of the Mindszenty case, they left the country illegally by way of an unguarded border. (Such an act was extremely rare on the part of individuals whom the political police regarded as reliable and had even employed.) For

46. The actress Sári Fedák (1879–1955) had agitated on behalf of the Republic of the Councils in 1919. In 1944, as a staff member of the German Nazi radio broadcaster Donausender, she had called for the continuation of the war. Accordingly, in 1945, the People's Court had sentenced her to prison for eight months. Her true punishment, however, was being banished from the stage.

47. NARA RG 59, GR of the Department of State, Bureau of European Affairs, Office of Eastern European Affairs, Records Relating to Hungary 1941–77, Box 9, Sulner Case. Statements of László Sulner and Hanna Fischhof made under oath, Salzburg, March 18, 1949.

months, the couple lived in a refugee camp at Sankt Gilgen in Austria. During this time, US military intelligence sought to verify their story. The young couple realized that they were making a poor impression on the intelligence staff. They handed over their evidence on 970 microfilm reels and in other forms. Allegedly, however, some of the material subsequently went missing. These events gave rise to a lengthy dispute between the graphologist couple, US intelligence, and staff at the State Department.

US military intelligence thoroughly examined the ominous microfilms, concluding that they contained little clear evidence. The reports drafted at the time indicate that a positive assessment was made of Sulner and his wife's statements. Still, the general perception among US intelligence personnel was that, in the hope of being granted a new life overseas, the couple had exaggerated both their role and the significance of the documents. Indeed, the information provided by them was treated with growing suspicion. Their credibility was dented by the way in which they seemed to be withholding information or framing their story.[48] On July 8, 1949, Sulner and Fischhof were finally permitted to leave the camp in Austria. Their lives did not, however, take a fortunate turn. Aged barely thirty years, László Sulner unexpectedly died in the summer of 1950, as he was making his way to a hearing at the United Nations. Contemporary reports saw the "helping hand" of the Soviet secret service behind his death.

The first newspaper to report on Sulner and Fischhof's account of the forgery of papers in the Mindszenty trial was *Wiener Kurir* in its editions of February 14 and 15, 1949. The newspaper was published in the US occupation zone of Austria. After a year's silence the *New York Herald Tribune* and the *Chicago Sun-Times* published the story as a series of articles. It was this somewhat dramatized version of the story that became known to the world – and decades later to Mindszenty himself. Allegedly, a thousand US dollars were paid for the story.[49] According to these articles, the political police had – under threat of death – persuaded Sulner and Fischhof to use their knowledge and skills to provide evidence that would incriminate Cardinal Mindszenty. In the articles, László Sulner admitted to having

48. Ibid., Summary report of Colonel Lewis E. Perry, January 31, 1951.

49. Ibid., and *New York Herald Tribune*, European edition, July 3, 1950, and the following issues; *Chicago Sun-Times*, July 9, 10, 11, 13–14, 1950.

forged just three "pieces of evidence." He claimed to have undertaken the forgeries using the device for copying handwriting invented by his father-in-law.

What is the truth about the statements and letters that Mindszenty was alleged to have written but which he, in his memoirs, claimed not to have written? As noted above, in his memoirs Mindszenty makes it clear that in his view the "work" of Sulner and Fischhof was critical when it came to the statement that began with the words "*Magyar nemes vagyok*" (I am a Hungarian noble). For his part, however, László Sulner claimed that the statement was not a forgery but had indeed been written by Cardinal Mindszenty, because if he or his wife had produced it, they would not have made so many simple errors. He also stated that while several paraphs proved that it had been written by Mindszenty, as a graphologist he could also prove that the statement had been written under duress. The hand that wrote the statement had been that of Mindszenty, but the spirit was alien to him.

When the case was reopened in 1989, Hungary's chief public prosecutor commissioned linguists and handwriting experts to examine several documents. It was their unanimous opinion that there could be no doubt that the records, statements and signatures had stemmed from a single person, József Mindszenty.[50] They also ruled out the possibility that the statements had been dictated or copied. Concerning the authenticity of the statement beginning with the words "*I am a Hungarian noble*", they concluded that at the time of its drafting, Mindszenty had been mentally exhausted and physically weak, as demonstrated by the increasingly uncoordinated handwriting and the poor train of thought. In the view of these experts, the statement had clearly been made under "extremely subjective conditions of writing." The experts did not rule out the possibility that the statement had been drafted on the basis of a "thematic sketch" or in line with specific expectations. Even so, linguistic analysis proved that, even in this case, the writer-author had indeed been József Mindszenty.

Even without knowledge of graphology, one can, on reading the statement beginning with the words "I am a Hungarian noble" sense the

50. MNL OL XX–10–k LÜ PO 18.300/1989. Expert opinion of a group of linguists, April 18, 1990.

duress and dreadful internal struggle experienced by its writer. Doubtless Mindszenty did feel that he was violating his own moral norms as he wrote down one lie after the other. Perhaps the first part of the text was indeed dictated; the rising and falling of the letters would seem to mirror Mindszenty's deep feelings of anxiety and resistance. Then, Mindszenty appears to have found a solution. Indeed, it would seem that the grammatical and spelling errors are indicative of Mindszenty's conscious intent rather than of a poor forgery, for the cardinal, who had been a writer and editor for decades, would not have made such elementary mistakes. The errors may have been made with a view to distorting the text or in order that Mindszenty could later deny authorship. The most likely scenario, however, is that the errors constituted a message to posterity. Mindszenty could no longer use his first method of showing defiance (the abbreviation "c. f."). And there was no other way of warning unsuspecting readers that they should not believe what they see, for the content had been made up. This explanation is contradicted by the fact that Mindszenty makes no mention in his memoirs of this clever strategy. It may well be, however, that he wished to forget the details of the time spent in captivity and erase them from his memory. Having made his self-accusatory statement, Mindszenty was promptly "rewarded." As of January 13, he was once again allowed to take Mass in his cell.[51] The opportunity to take Mass – its use as a reward or punishment – became a part of the spiritual pressure placed upon Mindszenty, whereby the goal was to break his spirit. The prisoner soon came to perceive – even if only subconsciously – that the only way to obtain his everyday needs was to offer something in return (his signature to a document, an admission of guilt, etc.).

A few days later a further interrogation record was produced. The marks of a dictated piece are evident even to the uninitiated reader, for the sentence structure is so wordy and complicated that the text is obviously the work of several people and could not have been written by a cultivated prelate who undertook intellectual tasks on a daily basis. Even so, we find, at the bottom of every page, Cardinal Mindszenty's original signature. The manner in which it is written, however, betrays his agitated state of mind.

51. PL Processus, V–700/33. 250. fol. József Mindszenty's memorandum, March 31, 1949.

Compared with the beatings, a far more refined method of interrogation was to have Mindszenty write down his statement repeatedly. On each occasion he had to answer the same questions. In this way the interrogators could bend and distort his words until the original style had been replaced by a text that was more artificial and mechanical and which ultimately met the interrogators' expectations. In this way, an innocent meeting could be morphed into a secret gathering of plotters, while Mindszenty's efforts to safeguard the crown could be framed as part of a conspiracy to restore the monarchy. Moreover, making the cardinal rewrite his statements was an effective means of exhausting him until he lost his self-control. None of this proves that the forgery of documents was alien to the Hungarian political police. Indeed, we know from Fischhof and Sulner's account that forgery was a police practice at the time. Nevertheless, their statement also shows that even if "decisive" forgeries were made in the Mindszenty case, they must then have been put to one side. Clearly, the authorities simply could not risk making them public. Perhaps there will never be full certainty on this matter.

"...Those who Held me Captive... Beat me"

By mid-January 1949, a sufficient number and "quality" of admissions had been squeezed out of Mindszenty and his co-defendants. The various men involved subsequently had different recollections about whether physical abuse had been employed during the interrogations. In the secret interviews conducted at the time and in their statements to the chief public prosecutor in 1990, the one-time interrogators were unsurprisingly unanimous in their denial of the use of force. According to Lieutenant Colonel Gyula Décsi, the department dealing with the churchmen had a very good reputation and was a "very respectable and normal department that did not use force. [...] The department 'institutionalized' the use of beatings from the Rajk case onwards [from mid-1949]." Décsi did, however, admit that without his knowledge one or another of the guards might have abused Mindszenty, but this would have amounted, in his view, to at most a kick or a punch.[52]

52. MNL OL XX–10–k LÜ PO 18.300/1989. Witness interrogation record for Gyula Décsi, January 30, 1990.

In his memoirs, Mindszenty gives a very different account, telling of multiple beatings. His statements on the matter are backed up by the presence in the investigation documents – contrary to the intent of the interrogators – of several isolated references to torture. In conversation with an investigator who had won the trust of the Hungarian primate, Mindszenty referred to one of his interrogators as a "henchman" who hit and beat him, pushed him up against the wall, and made him stand on his tiptoes with his face to the wall. At other times, according to Mindszenty, the man had "merely" been rude to him. He also told his defense attorney about the physical abuse:

> ...they beat me with a rubber truncheon. Then they wanted to squeeze priestly secrets out of me and obtain data on my priests; [...] they gave me a good beating, and then the one who was there kicked me three times on the spine in the back and I fell against the wall [...] and they hit me just below and in the heart, and I do not know ... I am in the grave here... they called my mother a whore ... As a matter of self-esteem, I can't cope with this. Physically too, I am finished.[53]

The lawyer advised Mindszenty to remain silent about these matters: in the absence of evidence, the court would not give credence to the complaint, as almost all defendants made such claims.

Although Mindszenty had knowledge of police methods, nevertheless he had not been expecting such abuse. Years later, Rákosi recalled how the cardinal

> had repeatedly said, I, Joseph, Hungary's prince primate, and so forth. This is how he spoke to us. You lost children of mine, and so forth. In response, I said, give him two healthy punches, and then he will come to his senses and will understand how things are run here and that here he is not the prince primate. And they did give him two punches, and from then on, he was not the prince primate.[54]

53. ÁBTL 3.1.9. V–700/5. 136–138. fol. Cardinal József Mindszenty's second conversation with his defense attorney, Dr. Kálmán Kiczkó, January 28, 1949.

54. Baráth and Feitl, *Lehallgatott kihallgatások*, 156.

Rákosi thus admitted – and in this respect, his statement is decisive – that the cardinal had been beaten "to teach him a lesson."

In Mindszenty's case, however, there does not seem to have been sustained brutality, otherwise he would have let such conduct be known at the public hearing. Subsequently, Mindszenty himself barely spoke of his humiliation. It was only on November 4, 1956, at a press conference given after he had sought refuge at the US embassy, that he answered questions concerning his treatment before and during the show trial. The published version of his experiences added a bit more color to the events: "For days on end, he was beaten with a rubber hose," wrote Leslie Balogh Bain, the Hungarian-born editor of the magazine *Look*. "'They chose my chest because they knew I had a weak lung from childhood,' he explained. They undressed him and stood him nude for hours in a cold, damp cell, berating and ridiculing him. They brought "devilish devices" into play, to humiliate and hurt. The cardinal said he was dragged to a room where he was compelled to watch the most obscene orgies."[55] In order to cause a sensation and get the story on the cover page, Balogh Bain appears to have exaggerated events. Decades later, Béla Ispánki thus suggested to Mindszenty that he should leave the journalist's name out of his memoirs, for he was undeserving of being included in it, as he had made a mockery of the press by publishing this untrue story.[56] Cardinal Mindszenty accepted Ispánki's advice and removed Balogh Bain's name, effectively denying the journalist's assertions. The next time Mindszenty opened up was in 1960 during an interview with a French journalist in the aftermath of hearing the shocking news of his mother's death:

> A rubber truncheon [matraque] was often used and the most diverse physical punishments were suffered; the cardinal's face grimaces as he remembers the unbearable sufferings that were inflicted upon him by a State Protection Authority major, a specialist in torture, who liked to deal with him between 10 p.m. and 5 a.m. The interrogations went on night and day. They did not let him sleep or rest (the cell-mates [which meant the four prison guards who were interrogating or guarding Mindszenty] were

55. *Look* 20, no. 26, December 25, 1956, special Christmas issue.
56. MMAL 34. d. Folder with heading "Ispánky [!] Béla által átnézett fejezetek."

vile and worthless men; it was their determined intent to humiliate the cardinal and break his spirit). Since the cardinal feared he would be given drugs, he rejected all food for a period of thirteen days, which added to his weakness. Moreover, he was unable to treat his medical condition (Graves' Disease – an overactive thyroid) from which he had been suffering for a long time, as he was not permitted to see his chosen surgeon. This explains why the judges could see only a human wreck in front of them.[57]

In addition to the naturalistic description, it is worth noticing the reference to Graves' Disease, for the condition will be of significance later on.

"Oh my Goodness, What if they Get their Hands on This"

Rákosi sought documents that would be even more incriminating. As none could be found, the interrogators persuaded Mindszenty to compose additional self-incriminating documents. In this way several further letters arose, including a few to the US envoy, Selden Chapin, as well as a petition addressed to Minister of Justice István Ries and Prime Minister István Dobi.

The issue of escape or abscondment was present throughout the proceedings against Mindszenty. An attempted escape would have proven his guilt to the whole world, as guilty parties are the ones who make escapes (or lonely and desperate people in the knowledge of their innocence...). Whilst in prison, Mindszenty too began to put together an escape plan, having been encouraged to do so by the 31-year-old political investigator, József Jámbor. Employing his excellent acting skills, the police captain managed to persuade the Hungarian primate that he, Jámbor, was a lamb among wolves. Having tricked Mindszenty into trusting him, the police captain then sought to awaken in him the hope of liberty. The cardinal liked to hear Jámbor tell stories about the preparations that were needed in order to make an escape, such as clearing the meadow that was to serve

57. AMAE AD Série: Europe, 1956–1960, sous-série: Hongrie, dossier 103, Questions religieuses, juillet 1958–décembre 1960, 221. fol. Memorandum of Edouard Hutte, advisor at the French embassy: interview with Cardinal József Mindszenty on February 5, 1960. For a copy of the interview, see: NARA RG 84, Records of the Foreign Service Posts of the Department of State, Hungary, Subject Files Relating to Cardinal Mindszenty 1956–72, Box 1, Mindszenty–Classified 1960. 570.3 Religion (Mindszenty).

as a runway in order to prevent the wheels of the plane from hitting a molehill. He even talked about when and in what clothing they should try to sneak out of the building. The dream of freedom resulted in false hopes being embedded in Mindszenty's heart. Pensive about the escape, he dealt "with the moon, the wind, and with everything."[58] He calmed his conscience by telling himself that he would not be escaping but would be saving himself for the good of the nation.

Key roles in the implementation of the plan of escape were received by Chapin, the US envoy, and by Margit Slachta of the Sisters of Social Service. Since the US mission in Budapest lay under strict guard, Jámbor was to forward Mindszenty's messages to Slachta rather than directly to the US envoy. Mindszenty wrote three letters to Chapin, two of which were dated January 7 while the other was dated January 23. Mindszenty discussed the contents and style of each letter in great detail with Jámbor, who suggested that he should write down the things he had admitted to and, by way of reassurance, "those things he had not said."[59] The cardinal swallowed the bait. Until then, his interrogators had tormented Mindszenty with accusations of an attempted escape. Now he was the one reminding the US diplomat of the latter's November 1948 offer of an escape. One of the letters dispatched on January 7, 1949 read as follows:

> Your Excellency!
> Remembering the good relationship that was sustained between us, I request that you address my matter for the sake of an important public interest and for the sake of the interest of the direction represented by you [sic], and do what you offered to do in Esztergom in mid-November. I have reached this new position because not only the Church and the Nation but also your own country will suffer greatly if I remain here until the trial hearing. All my statements in the interrogation records are false. But I have not said everything about your country and about you. This should be a reassurance. Nor have I said everything about the Hungarian situation. Not for personal reasons, but for the sake of an important

58. ÁBTL 3.1.9. V–700/5. 69. and 81. fol. Conversation between Mindszenty and Jámbor on January 7, 1949.
59. Ibid., 86. fol.

general interest, I request in confidence the above, the fulfillment of which cannot fail in view of the old warmth [between us].
January 7.

†József [60]

The other letter, also dated January 7, makes no secret of the plan for an escape and deals with the reward to be granted to Jámbor (a job, US citizenship for the police captain and his family, as well as 2,000 Hungarian forints in cash).[61] Mindszenty must have been aware of the significance of the message, for when composing the second letter, he sighed and wrote: "My goodness, what if they get their hands on this."[62] Original copies of both letters were left in the investigation file of the State Protection Authority. In other words, neither letter was delivered – or, more exactly, successfully delivered – to its addressee.

What actually happened was that, on January 10, 1949, Captain Jámbor rang the bell at the gate to the convent of the Sisters of Social Service. He asked the nun who came to the door whether he could see Margit Slachta. By way of explanation, he then handed over Cardinal Mindszenty's handwritten terse instruction: "Sister M.[argit]! Forward urgently to Ch[apin]. †J."[63] The nun at the gate told Jámbor that Slachta was staying elsewhere, but she took the note and went inside. She then came back and asked the captain what the "Ch." meant (the abbreviated form of Chapin, the name of the US envoy). As Captain Jámbor wrote subsequently in his report: "I saw that they treated every visitor with great caution; indeed, I understood that not all of the nuns knew where Slachta was staying."[64] Jámbor left the note containing the short message with the nuns, but he did not give them the letter that was addressed to Chapin. This marked the

60. PL Processus, V–700/33. 10. fol. One of József Mindszenty's handwritten letters of January 7, 1949, to the US envoy Chapin.

61. Ibid., 247. fol. Another of József Mindszenty's handwritten letters of January 7, 1949, to the US envoy Chapin.

62. Ibid., 78. fol. Conversation between Mindszenty and Jámbor on January 7, 1949.

63. ÁBTL 3.1.9. V–700/49. 127. fol. Copy of Mindszenty's handwritten memorandum. The original copy was not returned to Jámbor.

64. Ibid., 126. fol. Report, January 10, 1949. – Four decades later, the same József Jámbor, in a statement at the Mindszenty retrial, named a female acquaintance as the letter carrier in place of himself. His statement in 1949 would appear to be the more creditworthy.

conclusion of the first act in the escape drama. The attempt to have Margit Slachta, the head of the Sisters of Social Service, sitting on the defendants' bench next to Mindszenty had failed.

It was some two weeks later – between 5 and 7 a.m. on January 21 – that Jámbor met with Mindszenty once again. Jámbor's lengthy absence had greatly worried the cardinal. What had become of the helpful captain, he had asked the investigator, who had told him that Jámbor had been sent on a border patrol. At the meeting with Jámbor on January 21, Mindszenty complained about the treatment he had received in the intervening two weeks: "Since we last met, I have been through a tremendous amount of rudeness. Many times they beat me and tormented me, and they made me sign records of interrogation which they drew up elsewhere, subsequently placing them under my nose for me to sign."[65] Rather than encourage Mindszenty to write further letters, Jámbor now attempted to determine how the Hungarian primate intended to conduct himself at court. The sense of justice had not been extinguished in Mindszenty. On the contrary, it was now even stronger than before. And he made this plain to Jámbor: "I think the right thing to do is to state that I do not identify myself with the records of interrogation, but only with that for which there is documentary evidence. I have also considered saying – but only to the judge – that I was beaten here."[66] The cardinal was thus preparing to make a statement emphasizing his innocence and revealing the procedures employed by the authorities!

The political police now had to put their thinking caps on and elaborate a plan of deceit that would prevent the "enemy of the people" from revealing to the public the true nature of the accusations and the conduct of his interrogators. All those who came into contact with the cardinal during these days sought to persuade him that it would be better to refrain from following through with his plan, but József Jámbor was the best at manipulating the cardinal. He not only managed to talk him out of his plans, but also made him come to terms with the idea of admitting his guilt. Appealing to his pride and to his self-esteem, Jámbor argued that the cardinal should not show himself to be a coward. Something significant

65. ÁBTL 3.1.8. Sz–222/17. 143–144. fol. Agent's report, January 21, 1949.
66. Ibid., 145. fol.

still needed to happen, however, to dissuade Mindszenty from pursuing his chosen course and to have him write a further letter to Chapin.

On January 21, 1949, several hours after Mindszenty's early morning conversation with Jámbor, the people's prosecutor Gyula Alapy made known the indictment to the cardinal. It became clear to the Hungarian primate that the trial would be based both on his admissions of guilt (which he could rescind) and on additional documentary evidence. While he admitted to the authenticity of the documents presented to him, he continued to deny his guilt: "I have understood the suspicions raised against me, but I do not feel myself to be guilty at all."[67] The cardinal's firm stance points to a clear and determined mind. As there were barely two weeks left before the start of the trial, the authorities had to act quickly and persuade Mindszenty to lodge a guilty plea.

What cards were the political police still holding? In the final third of his time in detention, Mindszenty was subjected to a series of threats interspersed with outright flattery. In private conversations Mindszenty spoke of how the interrogators' rude manner had changed to a show of concern for his wellbeing. For instance, they even inquired whether he was satisfied with the meals he was receiving and with the accommodation. Understandably, Mindszenty began to draw conclusions. Indeed, he wrongly concluded that something important had happened in the outside world – an event that might even bring about his release. This, he concluded, would explain why his captors were now giving him better treatment. The indictment, however, alarmed him – despite the firmness with which he had denied his guilt. He was aware that, based on the gravity of the indictment, he might even be facing a death sentence. Emotionally, he swung back and forth between two extremes. In this state of flux, he failed to realize that the chance of there not being a court hearing or a sentence was simply a trap to make him reconsider his views on church-state relations. His confusion as to the best course of action grew: Should he abscond, negotiate, concede, grovel or go to the gallows? As he tried to establish his chosen course, he was influenced by a sense of being called

67. PL Processus, V–700/1. 169. fol. Record of József Mindszenty's interrogation by the people's prosecutor, January 21, 1949.

to martyrdom as the head of the church, by the sacrificial service to the Hungarian nation, and by a very human fear of death.

It was in this complex psychological situation that Mindszenty's captors once again put forward a plan for the cardinal's escape. Acting out of panic, voluntarily, or as the victim of a devious trick, Mindszenty wrote another letter to the US envoy, which Captain József Jámbor agreed to smuggle out. This time there was to be no intermediary; rather, Jámbor would deliver the letter directly to the US mission, for Slachta had gone underground. In a few short and desperate lines, the cardinal asked for the diplomat's help:

> Dear Minister,
> Action must really take place by Thursday. The trial is ready. This trial is directed against America and they want to prove that I obtained money from America for secrets.
> I beg for a motor car and an aeroplane.
> There is no other solution.
> With warmest regards
>
> Mindszenty
>
> January 23
> P.S. I beg Mr. Koczak to make arrangements to meet the bearer of this letter to talk over everything.
>
> Mindszenty
>
> P.S. Please offer in response of this letter 4000 dollars to the pilot, which sum I will repay.
>
> Mindszenty[68]

This third letter did not conceal the essence of Mindszenty's request and even sketched some of the technical details. The original version of this letter remained in the investigation file; it too was never delivered to Chapin.

Stephen Andrew Koczak, who was mentioned in the letter, was political under-secretary at the US mission in Budapest. He was in fact employed by the Federal Bureau of Investigation in the field of political intelligence. In

68. Ibid., V–700/33. 128. fol. József Mindszenty's letter to the US envoy Chapin, January 23, [1949]. Original, handwritten.

a 1992 interview, he recalled the events. While his memories must have faded with the passage of time, he still remembered the major developments:

> A man with a letter from Mindszenty contacted me. He told me that he was working as a coal loader in the prison where the cardinal was being held and that the prisoner Mindszenty had recently taken him into his confidence. He said that he would even be able to arrange for the cardinal's escape in a coal truck; he just needed to bribe the guards. A plan of action had been elaborated, which had now to be implemented. He requested the assistance of the embassy [in fact, at the time, it was still a legation], as stated in the primate's letter. I immediately contacted the ambassador and made known to him my visitor's offer, telling him that, in my view, they were evidently trying to provoke us. We could, however, draw benefit for ourselves by keeping the letter and making it public. The ambassador did not, however, accept this reasoning. He was of the view that we could not take such a risk: the letter should not be accepted; rather, it should be given back to the individual that had brought it to us. I attempted to fulfill the instruction. I told the deliverer of the letter that the embassy was not in the business of assisting escapes and that they should take back the letter. The man in question, whom, of course, I never saw again, protested despairingly. The building was surrounded by secret policemen and, he said, if he were to be caught with the revealing evidence – Mindszenty's letter – it would mean the end for both the cardinal and for himself. Right then, I said, and I burnt the letter in front of the letter carrier.[69]

The credibility of the story is enhanced by the fact that, twenty years earlier in Rome, Koczak had given the same details to Vince Tomek, the former superior-general of the Piarist Order.[70] The story as a whole shows the importance attributed by the political police to the letter reaching its addressee. Perhaps they were hoping that staff at the US Legation would, in some way, incriminate themselves.

69. László N. Sándor, "Ő szöktette volna meg Mindszenty bíborost" [The man who would have helped Cardinal Mindszenty escape from prison], *Magyar Hírlap*, no. 236, October 7, 1992, 8.

70. AGS, Legacy of Vince Tomek, Diaries, 7., vol. 86. Vince Tomek's memorandum of October 10, 1971. (Peregrin Kálmán's collection.)

Again the question arises: If the original copy of the letter remained in the archive, what did Police Captain Jámbor seek to deliver to the envoy Chapin? We can only suppose that it was a forgery, which the Americans might have considered to be an original, as they were unfamiliar with Mindszenty's handwriting. Meanwhile, the original copy was needed as "evidence" for the court hearing. In his memoirs, Mindszenty explains the emergence of the letter at the court by retelling the story he was told by Lieutenant Colonel Décsi one day as he left the courtroom: "As for the failure of the plan of escape, Koczak, an official at the embassy [the US Legation], was responsible for that."[71] According to Décsi, Koczak, who had since been expelled from the country, had foolishly left Mindszenty's letter to Chapin in the drawer of a desk in his vacated apartment. The new resident of the apartment had then found the letter and had then taken it, in shock, to the political police. Naturally, all of this was a lie. We know, for instance, that Koczak was only expelled from the country on February 11, 1949. By that time, the sentence in Mindszenty's court case had already been announced.

To summarize what we know of the letters addressed to the US envoy Chapin: All three letters – two letters dated January 7 and one letter dated January 23 – were written by Mindszenty while he was in possession of his mental abilities but lacking common sense. Their authenticity is beyond doubt; the handwriting is certainly Mindszenty's – which is what László Sulner, the handwriting expert involved in the forgery, also claimed.[72] Original copies of the letters are to be found among the evidence relating to the case. The strength of this evidence was such that Mindszenty could not simply deny that he had written the letters. Indeed, he did not do so during the trial. It was only later that he claimed to have been acting under coercion. All of this also means that we can be sure that the provocateurs of the State Protection Authority did not give these original letters to legation staff. For her part, Slachta did contact the US Legation and then show the brief note of one line to Chapin. The envoy himself informed Washington of his meeting with Slachta: "And the facsimile of the piece of paper and the words written upon it, which the man claiming to be the

71. Mindszenty, *Memoirs*, 135.

72. MMAL 10. dosszié, 16. ő. e. "The Story of the Mindszenty Forgeries," *Chicago Sun-Times*, July 13–14, 1950.

cell guard brought. Evidently, they wanted to catch three people with one strike: His Eminence, Mr. Chapin, and Sister Margit."[73]

Evidently, the whole procedure had two aims – to discredit and to provide evidence. In this limited sense, therefore, the truth content of the details of the story – whether or not the letter was accepted by the legation, whether the delivered copy was an original or a forgery, whether or not the letter was burnt on the steps of the legation – is unimportant, as the writing of the letter was, in itself, proof of an intent to escape. In a figurative sense, Rákosi and his associates were seeking, by means of Mindszenty's letter requesting US assistance for his escape, to place the United States of America on the defendants' bench. Here, it should be noted that since September 15, 1947 – on which date the provisions of the Paris Peace Treaty had entered into force – the United States had no longer been a member of the Allied Control Commission, because that institution had ceased to exist. In other words, at the time of the elaboration of the escape plan, the United States no longer exercised partial control over Hungary. Its collaboration in the escape plan would, therefore, have counted as unauthorized interference in the domestic affairs of Hungary. In addition to its provocative elements, there is another reading of the story: Mindszenty firmly intended to escape from the prison and evade punishment. Ergo, the cardinal was seeking to avoid being called to account. For his part, Mindszenty explained his conduct as an attempt to defend the higher interests of the Church: "If I get to the court hearing, the politicians will do what they want with the entire Bishops' Conference and with the Catholic Church. This has to be understood by Chapin," the agent provocateur, Captain Jámbor, recounted the words of the cardinal.[74]

Entrapped by the Petitions

An important milestone on the psychological journey that ran from defiance to concession and agreement was the indictment. The evident aim

73. NARA RG 59, GR of the Department of State, CDF 1945–49, Box 6888, 864.404/2–849. Appendix to Selden Chapin's report no. 81, dated February 8, 1949, the note from Mindszenty containing the sentence ("Sister M[argit], Forward urgently to Ch[apin]. †J.").

74. ÁBTL 3.1.9. V–700/49. 121. fol. Report on the interrogation of József Mindszenty, January 6, 1949.

of the prosecutors was to represent the position of the authorities. Even so, they still sent their work to Mátyás Rákosi for his approval.[75] The people's prosecutor of Budapest accused József Mindszenty and his six co-defendants of grave crimes that were punishable by death. Cardinal Mindszenty himself was accused of leading recurrent and organized attempts to overthrow the democratic state order and the republic, of treachery, of "failing to report the exchange of foreign currency," and of foreign currency manipulation.

The indictment was already complete, but the strategy of the defense – which would be so vital in the case – was still under development. The authorities drew up background reports not only about members of the court but also about the defense lawyers. These reports were then sent to the Communist Party headquarters. The request of Cardinal Mindszenty that the highly regarded lawyer József Gróh, a member of Parliament for the Christian Women's League, be his defense attorney was rejected. In the end, the political choice fell on Kálmán Kiczkó, a nominal Catholic and a man who had been openly collaborating with the communists for years. Kiczkó, who practiced law in Budapest, lived amid modest circumstances. The authorities succeeded in persuading Mindszenty to authorize Kiczkó to undertake the task of defense attorney. Formally speaking, therefore, the cardinal's right to choose his own attorney was not breached. In practice, however, this was not the case.

Mindszenty met with his defense attorney Kálmán Kiczkó on January 27 and 28. At the time, the stance he would take at court was still unknown. Would he show defiance and reveal the truth about his interrogators or would he admit to his "guilt"? One thing was certain: he was now less sure of himself than he had been earlier on. The information he had received from his defense attorney had largely brought about this change in attitude. Cardinal Mindszenty gave more credence to the lawyer's words than he had done to those of the political police. Accordingly, what he heard from his attorney came as a shock and left him traumatized. The first bombshell was the realization that he would not be able to count on outside help; he would have to bear the sufferings of the trial until the very end. The second

75. MNL OL XX–10–k LÜ PO 18.300/1989. Witness interrogation record for Gyula Décsi, January 30, 1990.

trauma was related to the reactions of his fellow bishops and the Catholic faithful: his defense attorney purposely told him of voices of criticism rather than expressions of sympathy. (For instance, the attorney told of the great number of people who had signed petitions condemning him and that most of the bishops were already negotiating with representatives of the state.) Concerning the expected sentence, Kickó then informed the cardinal that under the provisions of Act VII of 1946 he could even be sentenced to death. Jámbor had already told Mindszenty that a death sentence was possible, but the cardinal had doubted the sincerity of the police captain. Now, however, he had to face the fact that a death sentence was not necessarily an empty threat. It was at this point, as Mindszenty listened to his defense attorney, that his Don Quixote fight came to an end. Having experienced both obsolescence and disappointment, he now felt an instinctual need to survive. He wanted to defend himself as best he could and try his hardest to come out of the trial alive. For only if he was alive could he do anything for his church. It may well have been this realization that led Mindszenty to change his stance. This train of thought seems to be confirmed by the impressions of the defense attorney Kiczkó:

> In terms of [his general] condition, he is well, but he has deathly fears and would like to see an acceptable outcome. [...] His Eminence will state that everything which he wrote is true and that it was he who wrote those things. [...] the sentence is ready (the will of the Russians is realized in it) – his impression is that it will not be a death sentence. [...] When the presiding judge convened a meeting of leftist defense attorneys, he said that they [the court authorities] wanted to see quick and uninterrupted proceedings with punishments that serve to reassure public opinion.[76]

Exploiting the cardinal's trepidation and his emotional collapse, the authorities set a further trap for him. This time it was Gyula Décsi, the man leading the investigation, who persuaded the cardinal to write a letter to Minister of Justice István Ries. In the letter he admitted to the errors of ecclesiastical policy and offered to retire "for a time" from public life. He

76. SzTTTI 1241/83. Letter signed by "K" and addressed to Margit Slachta, February 1, 1949.

also asked for his case to be severed from the others. Mindszenty radically altered his opinion of the agreement between the state and the Catholic Church. Although he still doubted that his intransigence had had a negative impact on the Church, he began to consider the possibility of a change of tactics that would result in some kind of reconciliation. He thought much about this during the months between the first court trial and the appeal hearing. Decades later, Décsi was still of the opinion that Mindszenty happily made use of the opportunity: "In my view, Mindszenty wrote this letter because he was quite sure that he would not have to take a stand and make a statement on matters about which he wished to remain silent. Of course, we knew that, in such terms, this letter could not be successful."[77]

As if to prove his firmness of mind, Mindszenty sent a similar petition to Prime Minister István Dobi. The contents of the two petitions were in complete contradiction to the earlier statement emphasizing his innocence, which he had written prior to his arrest. Although Mindszenty denied in his memoirs that he wrote the petitions in question, there can be no doubt that he was their author. Evidently, however, at the time of writing, he was in a desperate and agitated state. With the petitions in hand, the public prosecutor's sole task was to wait for the trial, as Mindszenty had, in effect, admitted to his guilt in advance of the court hearing.

Cardinal Mindszenty grew concerned and anxious about whether his petition would be accepted. On January 30, he requested by way of Miklós Dudás, the Greek Catholic (Uniate) bishop of Hajdúdorog, who had come to hear his confession, the intervention of the Bishops' Conference.[78] By this time Mindszenty had altered his position from one of defiance to one of admission of guilt. He told Dudás in confidence that while he had not sinned against natural or divine law, he had erred in terms of the laws of the state: "My conscience is clear in the sense that I have not undertaken a sinful act in itself, but under the title of 'quasi scandalo' I became involved in this matter and I have sinned against some things which, well... others usually sin against."[79] The tactics discussed with Dudás accorded with the contents of Mindszenty's petition: his case should be severed from those

77. MNL OL XX–10–k LÜ PO 18.300/1989. Witness interrogation record for Gyula Décsi, January 30, 1990.

78. ÁBTL 3.1.9. V–700/49. 178. fol. Report, January 30, 1949.

79. Ibid., V–700/5. 143. fol. Bishop Dudás's visit with Mindszenty, January 30, 1949.

of the others; he would retire from public life for a while; and this would remove the obstacle to an agreement. Moreover, Mindszenty even volunteered to make a gesture that would have been unimaginable earlier on: a greeting sent to the president of the republic and his recognition of the republic.

The members of the Bishops' Conference debated Cardinal Mindszenty's request on February 1. They needed to decide whether – in spite of the contents of the pope's recent message – to negotiate with the government and whether to request the severance of Mindszenty's case from the trial of his co-defendants. And before they could decide on these matters they also had to make a judgment about the veracity of the cardinal's message, the contents of which – the archbishop's willingness to retire and the timely need for reconciliation between church and state – fully contradicted Mindszenty's earlier statements. Moreover, shortly before his arrest, Mindszenty had made it plain that all such statements (those made in detention) should be ignored and regarded as invalid. Still, it was not from the press or some other third source that the bishops had learned of Mindszenty's changed position. Rather, the Hungarian primate had personally communicated his new stance to the priest-bishop who was his confessor. The bishops did not know what to do. Although they were well-meaning and honest men, they were not prepared for such a situation. Most of them had started out as ordinary parish priests. None had knowledge of world history grounded in a broad European foundation. Once again, their internal divisions came to the fore. In the end, only four bishops turned up at a 5 p.m. meeting held the next day with Prime Minister István Dobi and Deputy Prime Minister Mátyás Rákosi. The four men were: the archbishop of Eger, the bishops of Csanád and Hajdúdorog, and the archbishop's vicar of Esztergom, János Drahos. Archbishop Czapik announced that there was no support among the bishops for presenting to the government a petition concerning the severance of Cardinal Mindszenty's case from the others. Despite this decision, the bishops' actions may be viewed as a final attempt to win mercy for the cardinal before the start of the trial. The initiative failed, however. Subsequently, each of the four members of the delegation recalled a slightly different version of events. All of them confirmed, however, that the country's political leaders had been expecting something very different – a clearly worded statement or suchlike:

> The proposal was met by surprise; they fell silent, and Rákosi shook his head and murmured something to Dobi. He then said: while this is a position, we were expecting something else. It seems the Ecclesia is still militant. Dobi: I acknowledge what has been said.[80]

In the Hungarian press, it was reported, somewhat inaccurately, that "the Bishops' Conference has no position on the Mindszenty case" and "will leave the matter to the wise discretion of the government."[81] Whatever our view of these events, ultimately the Bishops' Conference capitulated and removed itself from the proceedings of the trial. It left judgment in the case to the court. Did the bishops abandon their archbishop? Seemingly, they did so. At the same time, they did not betray him and they also succeeded in preserving the unity of the Church.

The criminal proceedings got back on track: the separation of Mindszenty's case had already been ruled out when the cardinal was still hoping that this might save his reputation and his life. On February 2, two days before the start of the court hearing, Mindszenty requested from Gábor Péter, head of the State Protection Authority, the fulfillment of "the petition for a separate trial."[82] Mátyás Rákosi, however, was playing cat and mouse with the prisoner primate. His goal now was to fully humiliate and then destroy his opponent. The communist leader had no reason to forgo the "pleasure" of watching Mindszenty declare himself guilty in front of the country and the world. Thus, the petition for a separate trial was next heard at the court hearing itself, at which time Mindszenty acknowledged he had written it and said that he stuck by its content.

80. PPL Rogács Ferenc püspök hagyatéka, 44. iratköteg [The legacy of Bishop Ferenc Rogács, bundle of documents 44]. Note, February 1, 1949.

81. "Dobi miniszterelnök fogadta a püspöki kar képviselőit" [Prime Minister Dobi received the representatives of the Bishops' Conference], *Szabad Nép* 7, no. 27, February 2, 1949, 3. The visit was noted by the Soviet Ministry of Foreign Affairs: AVP RF f. 77. op. 28. papka (paper folder) 27. delo (file) 10. l. 28. Bulletin, No. 26, February 2, 1949.

82. PL Processus, V–700/33. 22–23. fol. József Mindszenty's letter to Gábor Péter, February 2, 1949.

The hearing began at 9 a.m. on February 3, 1949 at the Budapest People's Court, in front of a special panel of judges headed by Vilmos Olti. The indictment had been prepared by the people's prosecutor, Gyula Alapy. The leadership of the Hungarian Working People's Party had already determined when the court hearing should start and when it should end: "On the 8th of this month, a sentence should be brought in the Mindszenty affair. After the sentence, we shall ask for Chapin to be recalled. Concurrently, by way of the Ministry for Religious Affairs and Public Education it must be determined who is the head of the Catholic Church in Hungary."[83] The fact that a political party determined the schedule for a court hearing is proof in itself of the partiality of the justice system. The question as to who headed the Catholic Church is also revealing: they did not know that until the pope decided otherwise (which would not be the case until February 5, 1974) József Mindszenty would remain – under ecclesiastical law – archbishop of Esztergom and chairman of the Hungarian Catholic Bishops' Conference, and this would be so, regardless of any convictions imposed by a secular court. As of December 26, 1948 – and with the notable exception of a period lasting several days in 1956 – József Mindszenty was unable to exercise his authority and his rights as Hungarian primate for the simple reason that the government authorities prevented him from doing so.

On the Defendants' Bench

The People's Court performed its role in line with the political expectations. Both the judge and the public prosecutor had reasons to be grateful to the regime, and both men featured on the top secret list (as did also the head of the appeals court and the attorney general) containing the names of judges and prosecutors employed as agents/informers by the political police.[84]

When constituting the People's Court, efforts were made to ensure the complete exclusion of Jews and Protestants; the court was to be made up of Catholics alone. Amid the very detailed preparations, it dawned on no-

83. MNL OL M–KS 276. f. 53/20. ő. e. and RGASPI f. 17. op. 128. delo (file) 664. l. 43. Minutes of a meeting of the HWPP PC held on February 3, 1949.

84. ÁBTL 2.1. IX/62. 44. fol. Material relating to the informers and agents involved in the show trials.

one (or, if it did, the matter was ignored) that composition of the People's Court, which had otherwise been thoroughly controlled, was in fact unlawful. According to Act 34 of 1947 on the Panels of the People's Courts, the members of the People's Courts had to be delegated by the local organizations of the Independent Smallholders Party, Agricultural Laborers and Civil Party, the Hungarian Communist Party, the National Peasant Party, and the Social Democratic Party. However, in June 1948, the two workers' parties – the Hungarian Communist Party and the Social Democratic Party – had merged, whereby the organizing provisions in the act of law had lost their validity, for a single party had remained, the Hungarian Working People's Party (established by way of the fusion of the two predecessor parties). Meanwhile, the Hungarian Parliament had not authorized the Hungarian Working People's Party to continue delegating two judges to the councils of the People's Courts in accordance with "its original right." The court's unlawful composition raises the question of whether its judgments were to be considered valid.

The hearing was held at the Markó Street jail in downtown Budapest. That area of the city was then hermetically sealed off from the outside world. Although no other hearings were being held in the building at the time, a small-sized army was brought in to deal with any disturbances: during the night the force consisted of "only" seventy personnel, while during the day 250 personnel from the State Protection Authority (investigators and police officers) were deployed. Policemen armed with submachine-guns stood guard outside the courtroom. Wherever he went, Mindszenty was accompanied by the same six investigators. Hungarian Radio reported on the events using sound medleys. The first report was broadcast at 9 p.m. on February 3. There was a general prohibition on photography and the making of film or tape recordings. A sole photographer, who had been commissioned by the State Protection Authority, was permitted to take pictures at the hearing. Meanwhile, however, technicians ensured that Rákosi could listen in his own room to the proceedings as they unfolded.

The authorities made efforts to persuade both domestic and foreign public opinion that Mindszenty was guilty. Their efforts began with the publication of the "fact-bearing" *Yellow Book*, which was translated into English, and the ubiquitous embassy press conferences. There followed generous promises to allow foreign reporters to attend the trial. By the time the court hearing began, however, these promises had shrunk like the "skin of the wild ass" in Balzac's novel and none of the Western diplomatic missions received the pledged trial attendance credentials. In sum, twenty-three thoroughly screened foreign journalists were allowed to be present, all of whom were pre-examined for personal background, party political sympathies and worldview.[85] The authorities' rejection of the request of other journalists to be present boomeranged: it was more widely reported than the fact that twenty-three reporters had been permitted to report from the scene of the trial.

Neither Great Britain nor the United States were permitted to send observers to the hearing, but some of their reporters were allowed in. During the hearing, at the behest of Iván Boldizsár (a state secretary at the Ministry of Foreign Affairs in charge of communication), the pro-communist US citizen Peter Furst had journalists covering the trial sign written statements that they had not been censored by the Hungarian authorities, that the court had not mistranslated the proceedings to the foreigners present in the courtroom, and that they rejected Western accusations that only communists and communist sympathizers could attend the trial. This proved insufficient to whitewash the proceedings. On the contrary, US diplomacy sardonically asked: What was this magical device that enabled Furst to determine the accuracy of the translations despite his ignorance of Hungarian?[86]

Two days before the judgment was due, in a leading article the communist daily *Szabad Nép* heaped verbal abuse on the cardinal: he was a "pitiable worm," a "cowardly scoundrel," an "unmasked Tartuffe," who, at the court, "puts aside his principles and aims and does not care for anything except his wretched life." Hungarian Radio, on the evening of the sentencing, told the world that the Cardinal was a "bloodthirsty beast."[87] In communist propaganda, Mindszenty came to embody all potential adversaries. He was portrayed as the implacable enemy of Hungarian democracy, an

85. NARA RG 59, GR of the Department of State, CDF 1945–49, Box 6888, 864.404/2–349. Telegram no. 195 sent by Chapin to the US State Department, February 3, 1949.

86. Ibid., 864.404/2–549. Chapin's telegram no. 196 to the US State Department, February 5, 1949.

87. Ibid., 864.404/2–1749. Gabriel Pressman's report – the appendix to the US Mission in Vienna's report no. 97, February 17, 1949.

accomplice of the imperialists, who, in view of the weight of the evidence, would be left with no option but to confess all. Those listening in on the radio, however, heard neither a fanatical Savonarola nor even a political criminal. The authorities' efforts proved counterproductive: public opinion even came to doubt things that really had happened.

The judge, Vilmos Olti, began the hearing with a surprise move: he had the prosecution lawyer read out the cardinal's letter addressed to the minister of justice, in which Mindszenty had not only called for the suspension of the trial and the separation of his case from the others, but had also made known his willingness to retire from public life and – even more importantly – had withdrawn the statement made before his arrest concerning the invalidity of any subsequent confession or admission of guilt (which would only be, as he had claimed, attributable to physical weakness). This was a rather odd element in the proceedings against the cardinal. It might even be described as an "own goal" on the part of the communist "justice system." Rather than seek to have the cardinal deny that he had ever written such a letter, they forced him to withdraw it. In doing so, they rendered the existence of the letter a definitive fact.

Whatever people thought of the cardinal, no-one disputed that he always stuck to his principles and that he had been unwilling to leave the scene of the fight, even after his secretary's arrest. For this reason, the Hungarian public was greatly surprised by his offer in the letter to withdraw from public life (which some erroneously interpreted as his resignation as archbishop and prince primate). The objective of the propaganda, which had already judged the cardinal guilty even before a final court judgment was made, was to discredit the image of Mindszenty as a patriotic man of courage and to portray him instead as someone who was unwilling to face the consequences of his actions and convictions.

The request for the separation of his case – which the court flatly rejected, thereby setting the tone for the whole trial – was interpreted by parts of the press as cowardice, since it made the cardinal seem rather willing to abandon his co-defendants to their fate. Cardinal Mindszenty had walked into each of Rákosi's traps, and on the very first day of the hearing he had managed to present himself in unfavorable colors. He willingly admitted to having written the letter, and this was to be the first in a whole series of admissions and expressions of regret, to which he added a pledge to adhere to Hungary's laws in the future.

The accusations against the defendants were more or less the same as those made throughout Central and Eastern Europe at the time against anyone whom the authorities wished to remove from public life. The manipulations of the propaganda publications reveal the scandalous nature of the case. The questions posed during the hearing left little room for a proper response; rather, the answers were in the questions. Indeed, the word said most often by the judge was "Ugyebár?" (Is it so?), which could only be answered affirmatively. If the judge felt a defendant's response was going in the wrong direction, he would simply interrupt him. In spite of all this, the judge still managed to mess up, mixing up the various pieces of evidence, which were rather unconvincing anyway. Mindszenty acknowledged – as he had already done during a session with the people's prosecutor on January 21 – that he had authored the documents attached as evidence to the case. However, in the case of one of these documents (several sentences of which are cited in the *Yellow Book*), the claim that Mindszenty was the author was clearly a crass manipulation. The compromising document in question contains such statements as:

> "Much of [Hungary's] provincial Jewry has been destroyed, but almost all the Jews of Budapest remain. The danger in this is that the capital city's Jewish spirit has also survived..." "This is a permanent ulcer and infectious force, whose painless removal is our priority task ..." "It is our good fortune, however, that the great Galician and Bukovina Jewish reservoir, the million-strong ghetto Jewish mass, has been reduced – in consequence of the German destruction and war – to around 500,000 souls." "By fixing the date of legal continuity to March 19, 1944, anyone appointed after that date can be removed from public office, and so, therefore, all the Jews and half-breeds can be and should be removed."[88]

If we were to attribute all of this to Mindszenty – and the Budapest People's Court did attribute these sentences to him – then we would have

88. PL Processus, V–700/16. 396–399. fol. "Gondolatok a zsidókérdés rendezéséről" [Thoughts on resolving the Jewish question], cited in *A Mindszenty bűnügy okmányai*, 79.

to draw the grave conclusion that the cardinal approved of genocide. This, however, would be pure slander. Mindszenty had never been an anti-Semite who incited pogroms. Nor was he, as the prosecutor called him, "a cheerleader for racial persecution." His critical stance towards Jewry had never been driven by racial aspects. Rather, his critique had been made on Biblical/dogmatic grounds or on the basis of economic and social factors. But what, then, is this document and what could have happened during the proceedings? The answer is very simple: the ominous document is a summary of views that was sent to Mindszenty rather than a piece authored by Mindszenty himself. Owing to its content, however, it was put in the same file as some notes that had indeed been written by the Hungarian primate on the Jewish question. So, when the prosecutor made known to Mindszenty the indictment and showed him the pile of documents, he acknowledged them in good faith as his own. How can Mindszenty's authorship be ruled out for certain? The main reason is the alien nature of both the content of the sentences and the expressions and words used to form them. At the end of the typed document, there is a handwritten section which was clearly not written by Mindszenty, who, however, had underlined in red, as was his custom, those sentences he regarded as important. The use of the document as "evidence" illustrates the underhand methods of the State Protection Authority and the prosecutor, inasmuch as they were seeking, by means of the document, to prove Mindszenty's antisemitism and even his depravity.

The bulk of the evidence comprised, however, letters written by Mindszenty and acknowledged by him as his own. The cardinal said the following about these papers:

> I would divide these documents into three groups. In the first group, there is a sub-group of letters that were drafted and addressed to someone but which were never sent and so came to be among the evidence. [...] The majority were indeed sent. The primary aim of these [...] was not to uncover errors; and it was not their primary aim to cause harm or to defame; somehow the aim was to help, but something that was good or correct took place in a way that was not correct. At any rate, it would have been better if these letters had not been dispatched. Now I regret having sent them. And then there was a third group, which actually also falls into the

> second category, and... these, you know, were sent for the sake of the Hungarian prisoners-of-war, and then they were sent to foreign powers and concerned the controls exercised by the Red Cross with regard to the Hungarian prisoners-of-war, and then they were sent on behalf of the Hungarians who were being deported and persecuted in Czechoslovakia. [...] I could not get out of writing these; I had to write them and my regret does not extend to these matters, because here I was fulfilling a pastoral and a humanitarian duty.[89]

Even during his court hearing, Cardinal Mindszenty, archbishop of Esztergom, continued to speak up for the protection of human rights and for the truth. For these same noble goals, he had already and without hesitation risked his own life and livelihood. Despite the trials he now faced, he had no intention of abandoning this struggle.

The performance of Mindszenty's defense attorney, Kálmán Kiczkó, was atrocious. Rather than defend the defendant, he protested about having to defend him. He called no corroborating witnesses and his speech in defense of the cardinal was more about himself than about Mindszenty. In the speech, he spoke at length of the extent of his loyalty to the Hungarian government, while largely ignoring Mindszenty's alleged disloyalty. At the same time, he rejected foreign claims about the dishonesty and unfairness of the trial. Finally, in the remaining part of his speech, he spoke of Mindszenty as a man of good faith who had nevertheless failed to appreciate the gravity of his actions. Here, it should be noted that the defense attorneys of the other defendants were more active, both during the initial trial and during the preparations for the trial at the court of appeal. The third actor in the case, the prosecutor Gyula Alapy, tried to "score points" with his arrogant and high-handed behavior.

According to the witnesses, József Mindszenty, albeit looking tired and rather drawn, conducted himself in an apparently normal and reasonable manner. When prompted to speak, he spoke calmly without conviction. Sometimes the judge instructed him to speak louder. He responded to the questions willingly but with some hesitation. As he spoke, he pledged

89. Magyar Rádió Hangarchívuma, "dr. [!] Mindszenty József és társai pere" [The trial of Dr. (sic) József Mindszenty and his associates]. Reel no. 6.

several times and without hesitation to amend his behavior. Overall, he was clear-worded and logical. Although he exhibited the listlessness of a man who knows his fate is sealed, he was nevertheless ready and willing to debate. Throughout the court trial, he defended his faith with determination and resilience. On the other hand, he did not become a lionhearted fighter for a Catholic Church that had been deprived of its estates, its schools, and its privileges. "Essentially" – he often used this word to express himself – he admitted to his guilt. Yet, attentive listeners may have noticed that when accused of serious crimes, he would repeat the principles of the Church and speak of his regret for his actions rather than of his guilt. Alternatively, he would express regret for having come into conflict with the laws of the state, while also pleading for peaceful relations between church and state. On occasion he disputed or argued against what had been said. Nevertheless, a surprised public could now hear from Mindszenty's mouth the fictitious "events" documented in the interrogation records.

Paralysis of Will or a Paralyzing of his Will?

Later on in life, Mindszenty was greatly troubled by his own conduct during the trial. A US diplomat who spoke to him about the matter wrote of his "haunting guilt complex based on the thought that he weakened before..."[90] Several theories have been put forward to explain this out-of-character behavior. Two of the most popular are, in fact, simple explanations that one might even call primitive interpretations. The first explanation – which was disseminated above all by people working for the Hungarian government – propagated the false idea that Mindszenty had never been a hero of freedom but was rather a paltry, weak and petty man who had betrayed both his country and – following his imprisonment – the Church. This explanation, however, was so contrary to the cardinal's personality, his nature and his past, that perhaps even its disseminators could not bring themselves to believe it.

90. NARA RG 59, GR of the Department of State, CDF 1960–63, Box 2681, Doc. No. 864.413/11–1760. 3–3161. H. G. Torbert Jr.'s letter to Harold C. Vedeler, head of the Eastern Europe Division at the US State Department, March 31, 1961. For the text of the letter, see Somorjai, *Mindszenty bíboros követségi levelei / Letters to the Presidents*, 554.

The second theory or explanation stubbornly lives on in certain circles even today: Mindszenty made his confessions under the influence of some "truth" or "confession" drug. Some see the hand of István Bálint, the State Protection Authority's medical officer, in this matter. Bálint became the object of people's suspicions because he was a qualified neurologist and psychiatrist. Meanwhile, however, in émigré publications and, by way of transmission, in domestic far-right forums, the prime suspect has usually been Emil Weil, the communist physician who "restructured" the Hungarian medical profession in line with communist expectations after 1945. Weil, who went on to become Hungarian envoy to the US in the period 1950–1953, is suspected of having injected Mindszenty with narcotic drugs or substances that weaken a man's will. On January 28, 1952, in the United States Senate, Alexander Wiley, Republican senator from Wisconsin, accused Weil and two other doctors of using injections to compel Mindszenty to make an admission of guilt.[91] According to Senator Wiley, the poison was the same as the one that had been used in Moscow in 1937 to break the spirit of Mikhail Tukhachevsky, marshal of the Soviet Union, as well as his associates. The senator's accusation revealed how little understanding people in the freer half of the world had of Soviet political methods. In the trial of Tukhachevsky and his associates, the proceedings – if one may even call them that – had taken place behind closed doors. There had been no defense attorney and the death sentence had been implemented immediately after its announcement. All of this had not required the use of narcotics in order to squeeze out a confession, as no-one had been interested in whether or not the defendants admitted to their alleged crimes.

Two chemical substances were typically mentioned by the press in the aftermath of Mindszenty's trial: the drugs *Actedron* and *Scopomorphine* (or *Scopolamin*). One of them tended to loosen a person's tongue, while the other made him or her listless. Citing a "reliable letter" that it had received from Budapest, the Italian Catholic daily *Il Quotidiano* raised the possibility of the use of such a drug. The newspaper speculated that Mindszenty had

91. "Weil követ kiutasítását követelik a szenátusban" [The Senate is demanding the expulsion of Envoy Emil Weil], *Amerikai Magyar Népszava*, February 2, 1952, cover page. See Hoover Institution Archives, Tibor Eckhardt, Box 17, Subject File, Mindszenty, Cardinal Jozsef.

been given the drug during his pre-trial detention and interrogation. The international press soon took up the story. The right-wing French newspaper *L'Époque* claimed to know that the narcotic substance had been administered to Mindszenty in a glass of water after eighty-two hours of interrogation, during which time the prisoner had been fed nothing other than salted fish. Having lost his sense of taste, Mindszenty had been oblivious to the presence of the chemical in the water.[92] Based on their contacts inside the police, László Sulner and his wife, the graphology experts who had fled abroad, claimed that the cardinal had been drugged. However, as noted in the foregoing, US law enforcement agents had strong doubts about the veracity of their claims.[93] In a secret consistory held on February 14, 1949, Pius XII formulated – in a rather understated fashion – the suspicion of the use of a "secret inducer." With its strong belief in the rule of law and the justice system, the West could only explain the inexplicable – the failure of the defendant to protest against the absurd accusations – by pointing to the use of consciousness-altering drugs.

In Hungary too, it was widely believed that Mindszenty had made his admission of guilt under the influence of narcotic injections or otherwise administered drugs. The historical literature, however, is cautious and uncertain, because none of the authoritative sources prove anything for certain. The Mindszenty files, created by the State Protection Authority, contain nothing that might suggest that the cardinal had been in a consciousness-altered state. Evidently, an absence of sources does not mean that such or similar methods were never employed by the political police. Conversely, we do not have to regard the documents of the State Protection Authority as "conclusive evidence."

Did there really exist a drug that would cause a man to incriminate himself day after day and then repeat, like a parrot, the things he had been taught to say? A drug that was a hundred percent effective and whose dosage regime – despite resistance from the "patient" – could be strictly adhered to for the sake of a successful "performance" at a public trial. Some of the

92. François Le Grix, Les aveux spontanés, *L'Époque* 12, no. 2241, February 1, 1949, 1. The same version of the story was recounted in several Hungarian émigré newspapers.

93. NARA RG 59, GR of the Department of State, Bureau of European Affairs, Office of Eastern European Affairs, Records Relating to Hungary 1941–77, Box 9, Sulner Case. László Sulner and Hanna Fischhof's sworn written statement, Salzburg, March 18, 1949.

drugs used in psychiatry do indeed affect an individual's personality and his or her behavioral patterns. However, there does not and did not exist a psychoactive substance that can cause an individual to lose his or her will but still create out of the person a puppet able to play its role. As the experts underline, there is no substance that will completely destroy a person's will. "Brainwashing" can be achieved through extortion, through sleep deprivation, or by beating the subject or "breaking" him or her psychologically. And this process can be enhanced by administering drugs – but only indirectly.

Supporters of the theory that Mindszenty was drugged cite the calmness he exhibited even during the prosecutor's indictment speech. Indeed, eyewitnesses reported that Mindszenty seemed strangely oblivious to what was going on around him in the courtroom. Tape recordings of the hearing confirm Mindszenty's muteness, but this may have reflected the weariness of a man of high office rather than a drug-induced state. Neither during his pretrial detention nor at the court hearings did Mindszenty behave like a helpless puppet. Nor, however, was he a lion growling at everyone. He did not appear disorientated even when he spoke. On the contrary, he paid attention to the questions and gave coherent and thoughtful responses, often seeking to construct an argument. The cardinal not only made admissions but also sometimes disputed what had been claimed – which would have been impossible after a lengthy course of amphetamines.

It was not only among Mindszenty's political adversaries that there was doubt about the cardinal having been drugged. British diplomats in Budapest, as well as the US Legation, expressed similar skepticism.[94] The recalled US envoy, Selden Chapin, arrived on the Queen Mary ocean liner in New York on February 25, 1949. At a press conference on his arrival, Chapin stated that there was no proof of the Hungarian primate having been drugged.[95] Three weeks later, he restated his doubts at a hearing of the Foreign Affairs Committee of the US Senate, albeit he provided no concrete

94. TNA FO Legation, Vatican: General Correspondence, FO 380/148: Hungary, 1949. British Foreign Secretary Ernest Bevin's telegram no. 6/168/49 to the British plenipotentiary minister to the Vatican, Victor Perowne. February 14, 1949, and MNL OL XX–10–k LÜ PO 18.300/1989. US archive material. Report no. 316 of the US Legation in Budapest, February 25, 1949.

95. *Katolikus Magyarok Vasárnapja – Catholic Hungarians' Sunday* 55, no. 9, March 4, 1949, 1.

information.[96] An interesting report drafted in 1951 by the British mission in Budapest, which contains information from an informer who had worked as the assistant to the prison doctor and had been freed in an amnesty, also denied that Mindszenty had been drugged:

> The highly skilled process of inducing mental exhaustion in the prisoners made the use of drugs entirely unnecessary. He alleged that people who had gone through this treatment and then had been tried had little or even no recollection afterwards of having been through a trial.[97]

Readers rightly expect a historian to take a position, but a lack of tangible evidence makes it very difficult, in this case, to draw a well-founded conclusion. It might be easier and simpler to state that Mindszenty was drugged throughout his time in detention and during the trial. Still, based on the circumstances, the time schedule, and the observations made at the time, the only proper conclusion is that the use of consciousness-altering substances cannot be verified. What factors indicate that the use of such substances can be ruled out? First – and in a seemingly paradox fashion – Mindszenty's admissions of guilt in pretrial detention. As mentioned earlier on, Mindszenty himself warned that he was acting under coercion, marking his statements with the Latin abbreviation (c.f.) until his captors discovered the ruse. The warning thus given is a further indication that his consciousness had not been altered. He was also behaving "normally" – albeit naively, to say the least – when he considered escaping. Mindszenty did not give way to the prosecutor; he refused to lodge a guilty plea. Until he met with his defense attorney, he complained on several occasions, requested a copy of the Code of Civil Procedure, and prepared for his defense. He did not seem to have accepted his circumstances. The threat of a death sentence, however, spurred him to look anew for a way out. Yet, he could not see through the intrigues, and his thyroid disease plagued him. His sense of purpose would seem to rule

96. Truman Library, RG 46. Record of US Senate. Senate Committee on Foreign Relations. Selected Documents, January 25–April 5, 1949. Box 5. Resolutions re Joseph Card. Mindszenty. March 12, 1949. 18. fol.

97. TNA FO Political Departments, General Correspondence from 1906–66. SOUTHERN: Hungary, FO 371/95231: Code RH file 1651/1. December 14, 1951.

out an altered consciousness. Still, why is it we see the cardinal at the trial – in photographs taken by the international press – with bulging eyes? The explanation may well be an overactive thyroid rather than his being in a narcotic state. The thyroid problem may have been particularly severe because – as Mindszenty indicates in his memoirs – he was afraid to take medicines. Whenever he could, he would sabotage efforts to medicate him, and so his condition – Graves' Disease – from which he had suffered since childhood, went untreated. But the physical symptoms of anxiety arising from the special situation in which he had found himself also included bulging eyes, shaking hands, and excessive sweating. The forensic experts commissioned by the prosecutor general in 1989 warned that non-medics might suspect, when confronted with the symptoms of Graves' Disease, the use of the stimulant Actedron.[98]

If all of this fails to convince, it is worth looking at what Mindszenty himself said about the possibility that he had been drugged. On November 4, 1956, a journalist expressed the suspicion (widely believed around the world) that he had been "under influence" during the court hearing: "No, not drugs," the cardinal replied, "only the influence of 29 [sic – in fact, it was 39] sleepless nights and a congested lung. I shall explain more about the trial in my book."[99] Thus, the cardinal himself rejected the theory of a drug serum! Further, he did not only make such a statement to this one journalist. He told Major Antal (Pallavicini) Pálinkás the same thing when, after eight years of imprisonment, they met – now as free men – on the evening of October 30, 1956: "The officers that had come into the office then asked about the method of his earlier interrogations. Mindszenti [!] said that they had not mistreated him and that he had not been given injections; nor had he had any complaint about his board and lodging."[100] By the time his book, Memoirs, was actually published (in 1974), however, even Mindszenty no longer had any doubt that psychoactive drugs to break his willpower and narcotic drugs had been mixed into his food; his only uncertainty concerned their use during the final days of the trial. It seems

98. MNL OL XX–10–k LÜ PO 18.300/1989. Medical expert opinion, March 2, 1990.

99. *Look* 20, no. 26, special Christmas edition (December 25, 1956).

100. HM HIM Hadtörténelmi Levéltár, Budapesti Katonai Bíróság [Military History Archives of the Ministry of Defence, Military Court of Budapest], B.II. 071/1957. Court records in the case of Major Antal Pálinkás and his associates, September 2, 1957. Sheet 10.

that by the time he wrote his memoirs, Mindszenty had himself been influenced by the views of others who could not conceive of an acceptable explanation for the cardinal's conduct in court, other than his having been drugged. As time passed, Mindszenty himself came to believe that the drugging story was true, saving thereby his conscience and driving the memories of his pretrial interrogation to the depths of his consciousness and seeking to forget them.

Still, the question remains unanswered: How can the events be explained if not by chemical substances? Physical and mental torture, humiliation, psychological suggestion on the part of the interrogators and emotional and psychological collapse on the part of the defendant. An important element in the pretrial interrogation and in the court trial was the undermining of Mindszenty's human dignity, his identity and consciousness. His interrogators were professional experts at destroying an individual's will; they were more skilled in influencing an individual than any hypnotherapist and could achieve better results than any hypnotic substance. They could practice their methods on a daily basis and they knew something which the drugs did not: how to tailor to a specific individual such methods as sleep deprivation, twenty-four-hour interrogations, threats, the accentuation of the fear of death, incessant indoctrination (regarding the accusations), inadequate provision of food and the resultant loss of weight and debilitation, psychological torment, raising and then dashing a person's hopes. In combination, these methods inevitably bring about a psychological collapse. A more drastic effect cannot be achieved using drugs.

During the thirty-nine days of pretrial detention and interrogation, Mindszenty's spirit was successfully broken. It was evident anyway that Rákosi and his associates would not countenance a trial in which the cardinal might proclaim his version of the truth in his role as "leader of the opposition." Rather, in the envisioned trial, the cardinal was to show regret and reveal himself to be a somewhat pathetic figure rather than a hero. To accomplish this, Mindszenty's *will had to be broken*. The trial shows that the authorities succeeded in this goal. The continuous flow of questions gradually made him sink into apathy, and he even began "to believe" the accusations, as he wrote in a shockingly frank manner in his memoirs:

> My powers of resistance gradually faded. Apathy and indifference grew. More and more the boundaries between true and false, reality and unreality, seemed blurred to me. I became insecure in my judgment. Day and night my alleged 'sins' had been hammered into me, and now I myself began to think that somehow I might very well be guilty. Again and again the same theme was repeated in innumerable variations; they always steered the dialogue in the same direction. I was left with only one certainty, that there was no longer any way out of this situation. My shaken nervous system weakened the resistance of my mind, clouded my memory, undermined my self-confidence, unhinged my will – in short undid all the capacities that are most human in man.[101]

Mindszenty perfectly describes the process, or *suggestive situation*, whereby pressure was exerted upon him incessantly.

The cardinal's shattered ego did not revive during the court hearings. "*Quo vadis, Domine?*" Peter, who is fleeing crucifixion in Rome, asks of the risen Jesus. The message of this New Testament story is the command to stay put. The good pastor stays with his flock, even at risk to his own life. Mindszenty could have retired from public life or even have left the country. But he did not do so. He knew that in order to have a hope of drawing the world's attention to the church-state conflict in Hungary and to the unscrupulous nature and methods of the totalitarian regime, he would have to accept his own personal humiliation and "working over."

The Judgment

By way of an indictment, the prosecutor gave a political propaganda speech full of theater and demagogy. In effect, the speech revealed the show-trial nature of the proceedings: the decisive factor would not be forensic clues and unambiguous criminal evidence but "evidence" arrived at by way of an "extraordinarily complex logical thinking process." This suggested that there would be much room for false argumentation and explanation. Prosecutor Alapy requested an "exemplary" judgment, which meant, in effect, the gravest punishment (i.e., a death sentence).

101. Mindszenty, *Memoirs*, 110–11.

Cardinal Mindszenty made use of his right to the last word. In his memoirs, he wrote that this speech was not really his own, in view of the admissions of guilt, the humiliation, and the feelings of regret. On hearing the sound recording of the speech and having read up on the sources, we are left with no choice but to dispute Mindszenty's later assertion, for it is in this particular statement that we can recognize something of his old self. Mindszenty's oratorical skills became more evident and determined than they had been at the time of his admissions and confessions of guilt. His words were easy to understand and clear, and he chose every word in a thorough and thoughtful manner and then pronounced it clearly. This was the first occasion, it seemed, when he wanted his words to be put on record – not for the benefit of the judges, but for that of the public, or posterity! The dignified words with their ambiguous meaning could not have been dictated to the cardinal. Nor could they have been said by a man under the influence of drugs: "I was not and am not an enemy of the Hungarian people. I did not and do not have a problem with the Hungarian working class, with the Hungarian peasant society, to which I belong, together with my family."[102] In these two sentences, the cardinal skillfully concealed his real message. Now if ever would have been the best occasion to say a few words about how he had been mistreated during his pretrial detention, which could then have discredited the whole proceedings. But he did not do so; nor did he withdraw his admissions of guilt. Instead, he chose merely to clarify some of the conclusions that had been drawn in the indictment: he denied that he had conspired to overthrow the republic. Did he still have an irrational trust in the inviolability of the office of primate and in the Hungarian justice system? Or was he getting bogged down in the tactics of seeking a way out? Or had he recognized that there was a need to mitigate the pressure exerted by the authorities on the faithful? That there was a need to rescue those ecclesiastical institutions that could still be saved? If this was the case, he must also have known that he could only achieve this goal by consciously refraining from playing the role of hero at the trial. His words acquiescing to and acknowledging guilt carried with them a sense of the whole horror of the time spent in detention awaiting trial.

102. *Mindszenty József a népbíróság előtt*, 155.

From its own standpoint, communist propaganda had scored an important victory. Even the US legation submitted a report detailing how the Hungarian authorities had succeeded in destroying the image of the cardinal as a symbol of the domestic opposition by showing him to be a cowardly and spineless figure. This had been achieved through a well-orchestrated press campaign and a thoroughly prepared trial that had seen the cardinal admit to his guilt and express regret for his conduct.[103] Still, with the destruction of the myth, something else had been born. Among ordinary people, a sense of offended justice prevailed – not because the cardinal had been sentenced for something that may indeed have been a criminal offense under the law, but rather because he had been forced to express regret for these crimes. In other words, the sense of offended justice stemmed, not from the falsification of the proceedings, but from the falsification of the man.

The People's Court promptly announced the judgment at 9 a.m. on February 8, 1949 – in exactly the manner that had been determined by the Political Committee of the Hungarian Working People's Party on the first day of the trial. According to eyewitnesses, the grisliest moment was when the presiding judge, who would otherwise barely look up when reading out judgments, got up from his chair, leaned over the podium, and read out to "Defendant No. 7," the hard of hearing László Tóth, his judgment. Tóth leaned forward and held his hands to his ears, so that he might hear better. The presiding judge kept shouting out the sentence until the 59-year-old Catholic newspaper editor finally understood that he was to be sent to prison for ten years.

When his own sentence was read out, Cardinal Mindszenty stood with his head slightly bowed and his hands clasped. His face twitched slightly, but this was the only visible sign of the emotional storm raging inside him. József Mindszenty was found guilty on seven counts of the indictment: 1. leading a conspiracy to overthrow the republic; 2. committing treason continually; 3. failing to report foreign currency; 4. failing to report a claim relating to substantial amounts of foreign currency; 5. foreign currency trafficking; 6. continually exporting foreign currency; 7. possession,

103. MNL OL XX–10–k LÜ PO 18.300/1989. US archive material. Submission no. 129 of the US Legation in Budapest, February 23, 1949.

without a license, of valuable objects that are subject to a notification requirement. As punishment for these crimes, the People's Court sentenced József Mindszenty to life imprisonment in a high-security prison; it deprived him of his political rights and ordered the confiscation of his entire assets. (His release on probation might have been possible after fifteen years. Accordingly, Mindszenty might in theory – if "nothing untoward happened" – have been released in 1964.) The co-defendants received sentences ranging from three years to life imprisonment. In view of the age and poor health of the defendants, the court imposed prison sentences rather than hard labor. (Forced labor had been introduced in April 1945 as a punishment that lay between a death sentence and imprisonment. The justification given for its introduction was that those who had destroyed Hungary should contribute to its reconstruction.)

The two assessors representing the Hungarian Working People's Party submitted a minority opinion requesting the death sentence for both József Mindszenty and the three other defendants, as well as far more stringent sentences for the remaining defendants. The prosecutor, Gyula Alapy, appealed against the judgment: he too requested the appeal court to issue a death sentence.[104] Alapy seems to have been working in a great hurry, for his appeal was dated February 5, which was earlier than the judgment itself! If not a typing mistake, there is only one logical explanation for this: the judgment had been ready in advance of the conclusion of the proceedings. In his cynicism, Rákosi had indeed considered the possibility of a death sentence, but he knew that such a judgment would raise Mindszenty's status to that of a martyr and would also serve as a never-ending source for anticommunist propaganda. Given the moral and political state of the country, it was "more useful" to arrange "merely" for Mindszenty's life imprisonment. After the court of first instance issued its judgment (which could be appealed), Mindszenty faced six more months of uncertainty: Would his life sentence be mitigated or sustained? Or might he even be sentenced to death by the National Council of the People's Courts? He had, years earlier, prepared his soul for possible martyrdom. Even so, he had never before felt death so tangibly close to him.

104. ÁBTL 3.1.9. V–700/7. 2. 457. fol. Final motion, February 5, 1949.

For as long as Stalin had even the slightest chance of rebuilding the destitute Soviet Union using Western, principally US, financial assistance, he continued to make concessions in the field of religious policy. With the advent of the Cold War, however, the Bolshevik regime no longer had any reason to show any other face than its true essence: complete domination of the social, economic and ideological plane. Accordingly, the period saw the rapid homogenization of policies in the so-called Socialist countries and the launch of a vicious campaign – in line with Cominform's Bucharest Resolution of June 1948 – against the "Trotskyite nationalist cliques" in Yugoslavia. The trial of Mindszenty in Hungary took place at this historical juncture. An era was about to end, but it had not yet died off; and a new era was about to emerge, but it had not yet been born.

There is no evidence of direct Soviet involvement in the planning of the Mindszenty trial. Rather, Stalin seems to have given Rákosi a free hand when he received him on December 16, 1948. We cannot be so sure, however, when it comes to the execution of the trial. On January 15, 1949 (i.e., after Mindszenty's arrest and not in preparation for it), the Soviet Union's minister of internal affairs, Sergei Kruglov, sent a letter to Minister of Foreign Affairs Vyacheslav Molotov, telling him that the interior ministry was in possession of compromising material, namely Major General István Ujszászy's statement on "the plans of influential circles in America and the Vatican that were aimed at the restoration of the Habsburg dynasty and the establishment of a Danubian confederation with a monarch." Kruglov proposed that the material be forwarded to the Hungarian leadership, which is what then happened.[105] Until 1942, Ujszászy had worked for Hungarian intelligence and counter-intelligence. Between 1942 and 1944, he had headed the State Protection Center of the Ministry of Interior (of the Kingdom of Hungary) and had been a key player in Hungarian attempts to exit the war. He had been taken prisoner by the Germans in 1944 and then by Soviet forces in 1945. The document that is of interest to historians of the Mindszenty trial is a statement addressed to the "Soviet government"

105. GARF f. 9401 op. 2. delo (file) 240. l. 40. Interior Minister S. N. Kruglov's cover letter to Minister of Foreign Affairs V. M. Molotov, January 15, 1949; See Volokitina et al., *Vostochnaya Europa*, vol. 2, 14–15 (Document no. 3; the archival reference differs from that given in the volume); *Vlasty i cherkov*, vol. 2, 29 (Document no. 7).

and translated from German into Russian. It contains multiple errors and is undated. According to the statement in question, in the spring of 1943 important discussions had been held at the Vatican on the future of East Central Europe, with József Mindszenty representing the Hungarian legitimists. While the meeting probably did happen, the parish priest from Zalaegerszeg is unlikely to have taken part in it. The Ujszászy statement seems to have played no role in preparations for the Mindszenty trial. It could have been a factor in the appeal, but there was no reason to present it as evidence by then. The statement said nothing new about Mindszenty's legitimism; his support for a Habsburg restoration did not need to be "revealed" or "proven," as it was public knowledge.

On March 12, 1949, Erik Molnár, Hungary's ambassador in Moscow informed Andrey Vyshinsky, the Soviet deputy foreign minister, about the results of the Mindszenty trial. Doubtless Molnár had a great wish to accommodate the Soviet comrades, but perhaps he himself disbelieved the lie he then told: "Among other things, he said that Mindszenty was, furthermore, a homosexual but that the decision had been taken to refrain from mentioning this issue at the court, lest the political significance of the trial be so diminished."[106] The State Protection Authority, as part of its effort to meet political expectations, had collected data about the sexual indiscretions of churchmen, with a view to discrediting their moral authority and that of the Church. The regime, however, made use of this method only two years later, at the time of the trial of the archbishop of Kalocsa.

The countries that called themselves "people's democracies" were united in their support for the actions taken by the Hungarian authorities, whereas the civilized world was shocked and scandalized by them. The evidence provided by the Hungarian prosecutors was, according to standards recognized by the western world, deficient or false, but it sufficed as a pretext for a trial. For this very reason, diplomats from the world's major powers were unsure how their governments should react: Should they protest officially through diplomatic channels or should they take the unofficial route, making known their distaste in the public arena? The

106. AVP RF f. 077 op. 22. papka (paper folder) 24. delo (file) 4. l. 44. Published in Volokitina et al., *Vostochnaya Europa*, vol. 2, 35 (Document no. 12).

arguments in favor of an official protest included the pressure of public opinion, the associated political advantage, and the view that the protests would not increase communist hostility towards the cardinal or lead to his execution, for regardless of whether he was deported, imprisoned or executed, Mindszenty had already ceased to be the focus of the domestic anticommunist opposition. The arguments against an official protest included the realization that by means of the accusations brought against Mindszenty – foreign currency manipulation, espionage, treason – the communists had cleverly evaded the matter of religious freedom and human rights. In the end, the choice fell on an official protest.

Neither the Americans nor even the French decided straightaway to make a formal protest. It was only after the proclamation of the judgment that their positions firmed up. In New York, five thousand people demonstrated in support of Mindszenty. On February 8, Secretary of State Dean Acheson accused the Hungarian government of steadily depriving the Hungarian people of their basic human rights and freedoms. He announced that the US government wished to bring the Mindszenty affair and other unfavorable developments in Hungary before the United Nations. The next day President Truman called Hungary a police state, adding that the Hungarian people are not responsible for the actions of the country's government.[107] The US Senate Foreign Affairs Committee put a discussion of the events in Hungary on its agenda. On March 12, committee members listened to Selden Chapin, the envoy who had been recalled from Hungary. Chapin gave a comprehensive account of developments in Hungary since 1945, including the land reform program, the elections, and the attacks on the church. He described Mindszenty to the politicians as follows:

> I think he was quite prepared for martyrdom himself. At least he always gave that impression. [...] I think he is very shrewd and I think he is an intelligent man. I do not know that he would perhaps be, so far as intelligence is concerned – and I say this with due humility – one of the greatest leaders in the history of the Catholic Church, so far as intelligence is concerned. It is, of course, a mystery to all of us who were there in Budapest, just as much of a mystery, really, to us, as it is to people here in the United States as to

107. ÁBTL 4.1. A–3240. 20. fol. Hungarian US relations in the period 1945–65.

> what happened to this man to turn him from the lion that we all thought he was into this sort of meek lamb as he appeared in the trial.[108]

Around 20,000 people attended a mass demonstration in Paris in support of Mindszenty. On February 9, in the Italian parliament, Mario Scelba, the interior minister, condemned the events in Hungary – to the consternation of the Italian leftists. On February 11, a group of around 150 people protested in front of the Hungarian embassy in Rome. The protests went on for months. One of the biggest public demonstrations against the persecution of the Catholic Church in Eastern Europe took place in Dublin, Ireland on May 1, 1949. Around 150,000 people – amounting to a third of Dublin's population – attended the demonstration. As well as local citizens, bishops and the speaker of parliament expressed sympathy for the victims of the events in Eastern Europe, including Archbishop Stepinac and Archbishop Mindszenty. They reassured the pope of their loyalty to the Catholic Church as it found itself in the grip of communism and atheism.[109]

On February 12, 1949, Pope Pius XII addressed the world's bishops, declaring a firm stand against "certain forces" that prevailed "in certain countries." He stated that he welcomed "certain allies" against these forces. Pius was alluding to the nascent North Atlantic Alliance that would be capable of taking up the fight against Soviet expansionism and against communism. Two days later, on February 14, at a secret extraordinary consistory of the College of Cardinals – attended by just seventeen cardinals – Pius spoke in general terms of the efforts of the communist regimes to eradicate religion and the Church. On February 16, at an audience with diplomats accredited to the Holy See, and again, on February 20, in a speech to the people of Rome, who had gathered on St. Peter's Square, the pope condemned the conviction and sentencing of Cardinal Mindszenty. The pope used strong and tough words, which may have seemed disproportionately harsh in comparison with the slippery and evasive wording of his condemnations of war crimes only a few years earlier.

108. Truman Library, RG 46. Record of US Senate. Senate Committee on Foreign Relations. Selected Documents, January 25–April 5, 1949. Box 5. Resolutions re Joseph Card. Mindszenty. March 12, 1949. 13–14.

109. ASDMAE AP 1946–50, Ungheria, Busta (envelope) 11, Fasc. 2. Report of the Italian Embassy to the Holy See, June 3, 1949.

In the eyes of the Stalinists of the Soviet bloc, such rhetoric merely added oil to the fire, whereby the flames of the anticlerical struggle rose ever higher. In fact, however, the proceedings of the consistory, the tone of the pope's speeches, and the general nature of the arguments made, would seem to indicate a degree of confusion in Vatican circles as to the best tactics. Ever since the beginning of the Mindszenty trial there had been two distinct schools of thought: the hard line had wished, from the outset, to utilize the affair for the initiation of a large-scale anticommunist "crusade" in collaboration with US diplomacy. Supporters of this hard line regarded political evocations as unnecessary; they advised imperturbability, which essentially meant rejecting change. For this stance to hold, they needed to be able to point to victims of persecution, such as Mindszenty. Proponents of a softer line desired a more cautious policy. In view of the political gaffes of Mindszenty and his feudal and clerical excesses, they considered the Mindszenty affair to be an unsuitable or suboptimal stage for the anticommunist struggle.

Pope Pius XII favored a strategy of imperturbability and intransigence. On July 1, 1949 – partly in order to influence the Italian parliamentary elections – the Holy Office (once known as the Inquisition, then as the Supreme Sacred Congregation of the Holy Office, and currently as the Congregation for the Doctrine of the Faith), proclaimed, with the approval of Pius and for the first time in the 20th century, the excommunication of those who professed, defended or promoted materialistic communist doctrine, or who joined or showed favor to communist parties, or who published, distributed, or read publications that supported communist doctrine or activity, or wrote for such publications. Yet, just three years after the excommunication decree, Pius XII set out on a more conciliatory course. In the *Sacro Vergente anno* (July 7, 1952), an Apostolic Letter to all peoples of Russia (*Ad universos Russiae populous*), Pius drew a distinction between (erroneous and false) teachings and the people who were disseminating them (people who were worthy of mercy and love). In this way, Pius XII wished to express that his rejection of communism was not directed against the peoples of the Soviet Union.[110] At the same time,

110. Philippe Chenaux, *L'Église catholique et communisme en Europe (1917–1989): De Lénine à Jean-Paul II* (Paris: Les Éditions du Cerf, 2009), 220.

however, a condition for any sort of relationship was the cessation of religious persecution and the restoration of religious freedom.

What Was at Stake in the Trial and What Lessons Were Learned?

The essence of Mindszenty's prosecution lay in the methods and procedures employed in the trial rather than in his being sentenced to life imprisonment or long-term imprisonment. In a technical sense, everything spoke against him. Yet, the trial came to be seen as a mockery of the truth. Moreover, the proceedings, which followed the Soviet model, gave rise to revulsion and fear among the Hungarian public.

Much was at stake in the trial – first and foremost the relationship between the Catholic Church and the Hungarian state. After the verdict was proclaimed on February 8, 1949, no one knew how long the Church, having been deprived of its pastor, would remain on the defensive. Another open question was to what extent the communists would succeed in removing Catholics from public life and isolating the Catholic Church. The trial of Mindszenty gave a boost to the Hungarian regime's anticlerical policy, which the communists justified by arguing that the Catholic Church had variously colluded both with the fascists and with imperialism.

A further objective of the Mindszenty trial from the communist perspective was to prove that no ecclesiastical body or public figure would be capable of defending the Catholic faithful, the clergy or indeed itself/himself from the communist authorities. In this regard, the trial served as a model and as a disciplinary device for clergy in Hungary and in the other countries of Eastern Europe. In Czechoslovakia, as an immediate consequence of the Mindszenty trial but also as part of the repression of the Hungarian minority, a series of arrests were made, beginning in the spring of 1949. One lesson of the Mindszenty trial – a lesson that seems to have been learned by various communist regimes – was that it was better to avoid a public trial. In Romania, the authorities subsequently opted for the "disappearance" method. In addition to six Greek Catholic (Uniate) bishops, who had refused to join the Romanian Orthodox Church, the Romanian authorities also detained two Roman Catholic bishops: Áron Márton, bishop of Transylvania, was kidnapped on June 21, 1949, as he was making his way to talks with the government. Only after two years of secrecy did it become known that he had been sentenced to lifelong hard labor. Anton Durcovici, bishop of Iaşi, who was beatified in 2014, died in 1951 at the infamous Sighet prison in Sighetu Marmației (Máramarossziget). In Hungary, the justice system was "more advanced" inasmuch as Archbishop Grősz of Kalocsa – even though he had signed the agreement between church and state – was tried at a court in 1951. His trial was not broadcast on the radio, however. With the Mindszenty trial and the Rajk trial (September 1949) behind it, the country was fertile ground for witch-hunts. The atmosphere of mistrust facilitated Soviet efforts to extend control over the communist parties and governments of the entire region.

There is a further lesson in the remarkably frequent observation that criminal proceedings were directed against a single "guilty" prelate rather than against the entire church. Here, we see tangible evidence of the tactics employed by the communist regimes after 1948 in the field of religious policy: the objective was to sow divisions within the Catholic Church, initially by launching a series of intimidating arrests and then by establishing the "peace priest"[111] movement as a mouthpiece for the Kremlin's "peace" propaganda. Just days after the end of the Mindszenty trial, Cominform's top gremium convened, on February 11–12, 1949, in Karlovy Vary (Karlsbad), Czechoslovakia. The meeting, from which the Hungarians were absent, evaluated the Mindszenty trial as the end of the first chapter of the fight against the Church in Hungary. At the same time, concerns were expressed about the resilience of religious belief in the face of retaliatory measures. With a view to eradicating Vatican influence, participants at the conference proposed the establishment of an "eastern [i.e., Orthodox or national] church" that would be independent of Rome and which would have its seat initially in Warsaw and then in Prague, where Hussite traditions could be built upon.[112] Hungarian politicians likewise

111. The so-called "peace priest" movement was established by governments of the countries in the communist bloc. Its aim was to sow divisions within the Church, intimidate the priests who were perceived as "enemies of the regime", and create a sense of uncertainty among the faithful. In Hungary, the "peace priest" movement was launched in the summer of 1950, and had been in operation for several decades, formally until 1989. The activities of the "peace priests" varied: there were those who did little harm, but others slavishly served the ecclesiastical policies of the party state.

112. *Der Spiegel* 3, no. 7, June 23, 1949, 14–16; For the role of Cominform based on Czech archival sources, see Karel Kaplan, *Stát a církev v Československu 1948–1953* (Brno: Doplněk, 1993), 23.

sought to separate the Catholic Church from Rome and establish a national church, but their efforts were unsuccessful.

The prosecution and trial of Mindszenty also acted as a *coup de grace* against multi-party democracy in Hungary. In his consternation at the Mindszenty trial, István Barankovics, the leader of the major opposition party, chose exile. Having lost its leader, the Democratic People's Party dissolved itself, and so there remained no significant democratic opposition parties in Hungary, aside from the Christian Women's League led by Margit Slachta, who, however, fled to Austria on the night of June 22, 1949. The parliamentary elections of May 1949 finally sealed the fate of the multi-party system.

At the same time, however, the trial was the first nail in the coffin for communism: those who had sympathized with Bolshevism and had called for dialogue, could no longer take this path out of their own volition. Contrary to the intent of the communists, the Mindszenty affair eroded the authority of the Hungarian Working People's Party, which was then further undermined by the Rajk trial. The charges against Mindszenty appeared to confirm the view of world politics that had been repeatedly proffered by the leftist press: The Vatican had formed a united front with "Yankee imperialism" against communism. In reality, however, the Holy See had retained full political independence and freedom of action, even though its policies were fundamentally defined by defensive strategies aimed at halting the advance of communism. This defensive policy had arisen in response both to growing Soviet influence in Europe and to developments in China where, by the end of 1948, the communist troops of Mao Zedong (Mao Tse-tung) had occupied Manchuria and northern China and were in the process of destroying Chinese Catholicism and the achievements of missionary work stretching back decades.

Finally, but importantly, as a consequence of the trial, the perception of the United States and the West as the world's moral leader was severely dented, because ordinary people living to the east of the Iron Curtain could experience firsthand how, in spite of the human rights declarations and the protests, the holders of power could violate religious freedom with impunity, ignore public opinion, and trample on civil rights. Mindszenty trusted in the United States as the savior of democracy, but – contrary to the claims made in the indictment and at the trial – his political opposition to the regime was at the behest of neither Washington nor the Vatican. Hungarian Radio not only broadcast the voices of the accusers and the accused; the country's people could also hear the lengthy, thundering applause of the crowd in the grand court chamber as it celebrated the verdicts and the sentencing. The totalitarian regime had won. Thereafter and until the death of Stalin in the spring of 1953, the country lay frozen in the grip of fear.

CHAPTER 7

FREE AGAIN AFTER NEARLY EIGHT YEARS OF IMPRISONMENT:
CARDINAL MINDSZENTY IN THE COURTYARD OF THE PRIMATIAL PALACE IN BUDA,
OCTOBER 31, 1956

CHAPTER 7

The Third Term of Imprisonment and a Brief Interlude of Freedom

A CONVICTED CRIMINAL

The decisions of the court of first instance were appealed[1] both by the defendants (through their attorneys) and by the prosecutors. There were, however, two exceptions – the defendants Pál Esterházy and András Zakar, whose sentences were not appealed and thus became final. The cases of the other defendants advanced to the National Council of the People's Courts (the court of appeal), but it would be months before that body reached a decision.

At the Reception Prison

Those convicted were transported to the Budapest Prison, which was also known as the "reception prison." Mindszenty was not housed with the "ordinary" prisoners. Instead, he was placed in what the secret servicemen called a "residence," a prison hospital room, whose conversion into living

1. Strictly speaking, both the defense attorneys and the prosecutors lodged 'complaints of nullity' rather than substantive appeals.

quarters had been overseen by Gábor Péter, the head of the State Protection Authority. Eight years later, Péter himself would await sentencing in the relative comfort of this special room.[2] The accommodation was, in truth, a cold if relatively spacious chamber, with an adjoining bathroom. It was furnished but infested with bedbugs.

Mindszenty's master prison record contained not only basic personal information (his name, characteristic features, sentence, etc.) but also an exceptional piece of data: "Taking meals separately as of February 11, 1947." This suggests that the food served to Mindszenty – public enemy no. 1 in Hungary – was more nourishing than that received by the other prisoners. We know from the recollections of Béla Ispánki, a fellow prisoner, that the Hungarian primate was also exempted from having to clean his cell. Furthermore, even at the reception prison, he was able, as he himself recorded in his memoirs, to celebrate Mass every day, which he regarded as a true mercy.[3] Despite such differential treatment, there is no denying that Cardinal Mindszenty lost both his liberty and the chance to undertake meaningful work. As he waited for the final verdict (possibly even the death penalty), he spent his days trying to manage his anxiety.

There is no record of Mindszenty having committed a disciplinary offense in prison, whereas infractions – mostly minor ones, albeit punishments were severe – were recorded in the case of most of his fellow prisoners. For instance, Ispánki "wrote non-permissible things in a serial letter" and, on another occasion, "failed to remove the nails and twines from his prison cell, despite having been ordered to do so." Prince Pál Esterházy "organized a protest about the meals being inadequate," and then "while out of his cell failed to pay attention to the guard, subsequently refusing to obey him." Jusztin Baranyay "accepted from a fellow prisoner a 'black' letter [i.e., a letter than had been smuggled into the prison]." As punishment for such offenses, the offenders were placed in a dark cell or their right to correspond with the outside world or to receive visits was withdrawn.[4]

2. Vladimir Farkas, *Nincs mentség: Az ÁVH alezredese voltam* (Budapest: Interart, 1990), 129.

3. "Since my arrival I have performed holy Mass on a daily basis, using ordinary bread and wine." Mindszenty, *Emlékirataim*, 330.

4. Budapesti Fegyház és Börtön Irattára [Archives of Budapest Prison], Fegyencgyűjtőkönyv "16/49. 2997–3295" [prisoner master record nos.] P 913/49, 3114 (Esterházy), P 05/49, 3116 (Ispánki), P 915/49, 3115 (Baranyay).

Mindszenty's 75-year-old mother visited her son in prison on three occasions during 1949. By the time of her death in 1960, she had made around thirty such visits. Her first visit to the reception prison came around two weeks after the hearing at the court of first instance. A lady of great inner strength, she found her son – on this first visit – to be in good spirits and a healthy condition. During renewed visits on August 25 and September 25, however, she perceived him to be thinner and in a more neglected state. Her perception was correct: the prisoner-prelate's spirit was gradually being worn down, and this in turn was weakening him in a physical sense.

In the immediate aftermath of the lower court hearing, Mindszenty had appeared to be full of energy. His first wish had been to discuss with his attorney the submission of an appeal (a complaint of nullity) to the National Council of People's Courts. To this end, he had then ordered a book on foreign currency law, "a bilingual (Hungarian–German) book as reading material, and a more powerful lamp, as according to him, his cell was very dark in the evening. Finally, he requested 8–10 ordinary cigars."[5] On February 12, he made the following offer to Minister of Justice István Ries: the cancellation of his own legal complaint subject to the prosecutor agreeing to withdraw his.[6]

On the same day, he wrote a letter to the archbishops of Kalocsa and Eger, which, in an act of indiscretion, the press then printed in full. "Earlier on, we chose to fight rather than seek reconciliation, but now at least I would like to further the cause of peace. I now acknowledge that we were viewing the problems from just one side and we were not seeking to understand the problems of Hungarian democracy. [...] To the extent of my possibilities, I would like now to promote reconciliation between church and state," he wrote – neither for the first time, nor for the last – regarding the necessity of negotiations with the state.[7] Archbishop Grősz of Kalocsa received the letter by post, but it was delivered to Gyula Czapik, archbishop of Eger, by two detectives, who demanded to know his response. What

5. ÁBTL 3.1.9. V–700/49. 203. fol. Report on controls imposed on József Mindszenty, February 10, 1949.

6. PL Processus, V–700/33. 146. fol. József Mindszenty's letter to Minister of Justice István Ries, February 12, 1949.

7. KFL I.1.c. Dossier 6. József Mindszenty's handwritten letter to József Grősz, February 12, 1949.

could Czapik say? He wisely stated merely that the Hungarian primate should send his request to the Holy See. Czapik's tactic was to win time, so that he could consult with the bishops. On February 18, 1949, the two archbishops informed the bishops of the contents of Mindszenty's letter. In the view of Archbishop Grősz, the Hungarian primate's words reflected the fact that he had been kept in the dark about developments since December 26 and did not know that the Holy See had already ruled out negotiations with the Hungarian authorities. The bishops found themselves in a fix: the Hungarian government had offered talks, Mindszenty wished to strike a deal, but the Vatican's firm position was one of rejection.

On February 25, 1949, Béla Witz, the archbishop's vicar in Budapest, visited Mindszenty in prison. Naturally, their conversation was secretly recorded, and so we know that after the confession Mindszenty suggested that the three-man delegation that had visited him in December 1948 – József Cavallier, Zoltán Kodály, and Gyula Szekfű – request the Hungarian government in a petition to apply "the spirit of reconciliation" and to speak out also on behalf of his fellow prisoners, lest their petition "appear to be a one-sided attempt to rescue the primate."[8] In his solitude, Mindszenty was clutching at all straws. He even gave instructions concerning the schedule of negotiations: "My situation [must] be the first matter for discussion." He continued by stating that "talks can be held, but [an agreement] cannot be perfected without the Holy See. What we are talking about is that [...] the Bishops' Conference gives its support to my case and can say that I am not a nobody but one of its own. Now and for the first time, I am the one who needs help; if I am released, I will find it easier to negotiate than I do now as a prisoner."[9] He even considered it possible that he would be permitted – in return for certain guarantees – to travel to Rome with a view to advocating for talks.

Confined to his prison cell, Mindszenty had no inkling of the outside world's concern for his wellbeing. Nor could he know that a man whom he regarded as a traitor and an adversary had spoken out on his behalf. This man was the one-time president of the republic, Mihály Károlyi, who was serving as Hungarian envoy to France. Károlyi, who had raised objections

8. ÁBTL 3.1.9. V–700/5. 159. fol. Visit of Béla Witz, archbishop's vicar in Budapest, to József Mindszenty at the reception prison, February 25, 1949. Copy of shorthand notes.

9. Ibid., 161–162. fol.

even at the time of Mindszenty's arrest, condemned the trial's methods and the sentence passed. Although for a short time he continued to give public support to the decisions of his communist friends, he was agonizing inside:

> What was the reason for my not resigning? The fact that my actions would have been misunderstood and then interpreted as meaning that I had changed sides and now supported the United States, the Vatican, and Spellmann [!]. The side that was seeking to bring back the old regime. I was also aware that if I defended [the actions of] the government I would be placing myself alongside those who were consciously seeking to direct the case in such a manner that the defendant should have no chance of making a defense. This was the biggest dilemma of my political career.[10]

Several Hungarian diplomats – among them even some who rejected Mindszenty's position – resigned from their posts, signaling their unwillingness to be associated, even indirectly and in the manner of Pontius Pilate, with the trial of Cardinal Mindszenty. Others – like Károlyi – remained in their posts but had grave doubts about their chosen course. Many among those working for the state apparatus found themselves torn between personal integrity and obedience to the party, between honor and livelihood.

In response to the outcome of the trial, on February 9, 1949, the United States expelled János Flórián, the secretary at the Hungarian Legation, from the country. In a tit-for-tat measure, the Hungarian authorities then expelled Stephen Andrew Koczak and another American diplomat, having accused both men of actions tantamount to human smuggling.[11] (It was indeed a fact that several opposition politicians – among them István Barankovics, leader of the Democratic People's Party – had escaped from the country in Koczak's automobile.) On February 12, the Hungarian government requested in a diplomatic note that Selden Chapin, the US envoy, be recalled to

10. PIL 704. f. 232. ő. e. Hit, illúziók nélkül, III. 588. fol. Report of 1953 entitled "Mindszenty."

11. AVP RF f. 77. op. 28. papka (paper folder) 27. delo (file) 10. l. 101–102. Bulletin, No. 34. February 11, 1949.

Washington "in view of his links to the conspiracy relating to Mindszenty."[12] The State Department preemptively recalled Chapin "for consultations." In the absence of such a maneuver, the US government would have been obliged to respond to the note by expelling the Hungarian envoy in Washington D.C. Given there was no formal discharge, Chapin remained in his post as US envoy to Hungary until June 8, 1949. Even so, after his recall, he never again returned to Hungary. This solution meant the United States could avoid severing diplomatic relations with Hungary, which, however, was the desire of some American politicians.

"The Country's Most Miserable Prisoner"

As he was preparing for the hearing at the court of appeal, Mindszenty put forward several proposals that might have formed the basis for an agreement between the Hungarian state and the Catholic Church. None of his proposals evoked a response, however. Indeed, his arguments fell on deaf ears even when he explained – in a message addressed to the Vatican State Secretariat – how he had changed his mind and now supported an agreement.

> Captivity and the opportunity to brood had matured my thoughts. But even if only slowly, these thoughts would also have arisen outside prison. The power of the state authorities, the avoidance of the greater evil, the fatigue of the masses when it came to the struggle, and the desire for peace might also have guided me – even outside prison – to seek, in the fifth year, an accord.[13]

Mindszenty suggested that the Apostolic Holy See instruct the archbishop of Kalocsa that

> with caution the Bishops' Conference should enter into talks with the government while adhering to the teachings, laws and rights of the Church

12. MNL OL XIX–J–1–j–26/a tétel, USA TÜK-documents, 1945–64. 6. d. Calendar of events for Hungarian–US relations, 74. fol.; Endre Sík, *Egy diplomata feljegyzései* (Budapest: Kossuth Könyvkiadó, 1966), 288–92.

13. PL Processus, V–700/33. 3–4., 5–6. fol. Typed letter, with no signature or date. Manuscript draft: 7–8. fol. (The following citation also stems from here.)

> and while reserving the right of the Vatican to decide. The matter of the Prince Primate's release should be made the number one item on the agenda of such discussions. The government is not averse to such a solution. I also request the Apostolic Holy See to attempt my extradition by way of diplomatic channels, either without an exchange or with an exchange, together with another state.

He suggested an exchange of prisoners in another letter he wrote to the pope. Likely, the letter was never sent to the addressee. It seems it was read by members of the political police only, but there was not even the slightest reaction from them.

Mindszenty knew nothing of events in the outside world. Mátyás Rákosi, however, was very informed about what the imprisoned Hungarian primate would or would not do. Just as a child watches the floundering of a butterfly in a killing jar, so Rákosi monitored the Hungarian primate's efforts and his agony. In a report issued by the Central Leadership of the Hungarian Working People's Party that was read out at the meeting on March 5–6, 1949, he referred with satisfaction to Mindszenty's volte-face, calling him a harbinger of World War III. Two months later, on May 12, Rákosi made the surprising proposal to S. G. Zavolzhsky, the Cominform's desk officer for Hungary, that Mindszenty be exchanged for pro-Republican Spanish prisoners, claiming that the idea for such an exchange stemmed from the Hungarian Catholic Bishops' Conference. The Cominform bureaucrat refused to take responsibility for such a decision and replied as follows: "You have already requested my advice on several occasions and you know with whom you should consult on this issue."[14] The mysterious person with whom it was worth conciliating can only have been Stalin. Rákosi shared the idea for a prisoner exchange with his fellow comrades, arguing that Mindszenty could even be exchanged for some Greek communists. No-one commented upon his proposal. In the end, even Rákosi was unwilling to implement it and thus made no requests to Stalin. Still, Rákosi seems to have been less than happy with the Cominform bureaucrat's prevarication, for when he reported to Ambassador Pushkin on the Mindszenty trial, he

14. RGASPI f. 575. op. 1. delo (file) 44. l. 91. Report of S. G. Zavolzhsky to L. S. Baranov, head of the International Information Department of the CPSU CC, May 17, 1949.

noted that "it was easy for Comrade Zavolzhsky to watch the struggle from the sidelines."[15] This complaint shows once again that the Soviets were rather disinterested in the fate of the Hungarian primate. Indeed, it was Rákosi who had a personal stake in the staging of the trial.

Meanwhile, Mindszenty, who had grown increasingly desperate and was struggling with his own inertia, wrote another letter to the archbishop of Kalocsa, reminding him of his earlier promise to ensure that in the event of his arrest, his fate would be the priority in any discussions: "At least you, my friends, should beg, if for no other reason than having regard for Catholic faithful. I can only expect mercy from others, if mine are compassionate."[16] However, the minister of justice described Archbishop Grősz's request to visit as "insincere" and rejected it. The air around Mindszenty grew thinner. Whereas before he had enjoyed privileges, now he was a man who had been pushed to one side. It was during the six-month wait for the appeal ruling rather than while he was on remand that he became truly shaken. His nerves could not bear the public's seeming indifference or his own fear of death. He had no company other than his former interrogator, Gyula Décsi, who paid rare visits, as well as Lieutenant General Gábor Péter, the head of the State Protection Authority, whose visits were even less frequent. "You were here two weeks ago," Mindszenty told one of them, exclaiming on another occasion: "It was such a long time ago that you visited me!"[17] In profound bitterness, he signed his letters as "the convict," "the inmate," and "convicted archbishop." Between the two sentences (issued by the court of first instance and the court of appeal), he wrote forty-three letters to Gábor Péter, eighteen letters to István Ries (minister of justice), ten letters to Gyula Décsi, nine letters to Prime Minister István Dobi, and a further nineteen letters to eight other people. In total, therefore, he wrote ninety-nine letters – these, at least, have survived in the interrogation files. Apart from him, no other person had an interest in writing these letters; they were not forged, and nor did he write them after having been beaten or drugged. The authorities simply let him turn in on himself in the solitude of his cell.

15. Ibid., l. 95.

16. PL Processus, V–700/33. 50–51. fol. József Mindszenty's letter to József Grősz, archbishop of Kalocsa, March 9, 1949.

17. Ibid., 56, 44, and 45. fol. József Mindszenty letters to *a)* Col. Gyula Décsi, March 10, 1949; and *b)* Gábor Péter, March 6, 1949.

Not only was Mindszenty mentally unwell; he was also physically weak. Barely able to walk and suffering from rheumatism and physical cold, he requested and received attention from a doctor. Even so, his zest for life brought him a new set of endeavors and personal trials: On April 7, he believed that he had found, in the prison cleaner, the right man to smuggle out a letter. Once again, the State Protection Authority had succeeded in tricking him, for in fact the cleaner was an undercover investigator... In the secret letter, which he wrote in capital letters to hinder identification, he urged his fellow bishops to intervene in an effective fashion. He requested the "highlighting of the head" and the cancellation of the case against him, emphasizing his innocence in respect of the political accusations. He also mentioned that it was very cold in his cell...[18] His loss of any sense of reality points to a spiritual crisis, the seriousness of which we cannot gauge but may have been bottomless.

Months went by without any word of the date of the appeal hearing. Perhaps this was owing to the international outrage which reached unanticipated heights in the aftermath of the trial. Another possible reason for the inaction on the part of the authorities was their wish to avoid provoking the populace prior to the national elections on May 15. Mindszenty himself asked for a delay, suggesting that there be an adjournment for a period of one year, during which time he and three fellow prisoners would be freed on bail. This would give him time to accomplish – together with members of the Bishops' Conference – a reconciliation between church and state.[19] By mid-June, he had made this proposal to several influential personalities. All of this indicates that Mindszenty was attempting to gauge what conciliatory decisions could or should be taken in view of his behavior prior to his arrest and the emergency that had arisen due to his conviction by a court of law. At stake was not simply the need to bring principles and actions into harmony, but also his credibility as prelate, thinker and person faced with the despair of life imprisonment or death. What would better serve the faithful, who wished fundamentally for no more than to hear the Good News of salvation and receive the sacraments? Would it be to see their chief pastor defer to the atheist state

18. Ibid., 272–273. fol. Letter in upper case to Béla Witz, archbishop's vicar, and Kálmán Papp, Bishop of Győr.

19. Ibid., 159. fol. József Mindszenty's letter to Prime Minister István Dobi, March 10, 1949.

authorities? Or would it be to exercise self-denial and offer his right arm to his enemies for the sake of the flock? Neither the Bible nor the practice of the popes offered him a clear answer. Having been influenced by constant self-examination, Mindszenty was prepared to abandon several basic elements of his established strategy. Indeed, he was even prepared – for a temporary period – to leave his post as archbishop and as primate. Evidently, in making this offer, his aim was not to assist in the construction of a totalitarian communist system but rather to place relations between the communist regime and the Catholic Church on new and firmer foundations that would guarantee the survival of the Church. If Rákosi and his clique had paid any attention to Mindszenty's intimations, they might have recognized an opportunity for reconciling the integrity of the Hungarian Catholic Church with the anticlericalism of the political regime.

The criminal case against József Mindszenty and his associates was heard by the National Council of People's Courts on July 6, 1949, with a final judgment being issued on July 9. Gábor Péter personally informed Mindszenty about developments in the hearing. In reaction to the unsuccessful initiatives, the absence of a proper defense, six months of entreating the authorities, and the holding of the trial in spite of his request for a delay, Mindszenty withdrew his previous statements, claiming that he had made them involuntarily and under coercion.[20] As in the case of the court of first instance, the composition of the panel of the appeal court was irregular in the sense that even though they had merged more than a year earlier, the two workers' parties were represented by two persons at the court. Hence, the decision on the appeals was taken, not by the judges, but by the Central Leadership Secretariat of the Hungarian Working People's Party, which proclaimed on June 28, 1949 that "Next week the National Council of the People's Court will discuss the Mindszenty affair and uphold the judgment [of the court of first instance]."[21] Unconcerned by the need to keep up appearances, this organ of the regime was grossly interfering in what should have been independent court proceedings. Under the rules in force, the defendants were not permitted

20. Ibid., 244. fol. József Mindszenty's letter to the National Council of People's Courts, July 7, 1949.

21. MNL OL M–KS 276. f. 54/51. ő. e. 125. fol. Minutes of the meeting of the Hungarian Working People's Party CL Secretariat on June 28, 1949.

to be present during the appeals procedure; nor were the judgments delivered to them in person. Thus, on July 22, Mindszenty made the following request to Gábor Péter: "Please inform me about the judgment."[22] At the reception prison, a response did not arrive until August 16.

The trial was now over. The only change in Mindszenty's sentence related to his agency in the crime (which was reduced). Still, the gravity of Mindszenty's sentence remained unchanged, even while the sentences of the other co-accused were somewhat reduced. It is telling that the verdict was made in two versions, with stylistic differences. As far as the Hungarian primate was concerned, mitigating circumstances included his essential admittance to the crime, his remorse, and his unpractical and gullible nature, all of which had been exploited – the judges noted – by the US envoy, Selden Chapin. On the other hand, his being a high-ranking Church dignitary and a learned scholar were viewed as aggravating circumstances.[23]

The court argued, nonsensically, that the sentences had been mitigated because "the Mindszenty case has lost its original significance." Such reasoning was very telling, for while criminal charges can expire under statutes of limitations, a crime never loses its significance – unless, of course, the judges decide that no crime has been committed. The decline in significance was, of course, correct in a political sense. By this time, domestic politics in Hungary had been distracted by a new "conspiracy": on May 30, 1949, Minister of Foreign Affairs László Rajk had been arrested. A member of the inner circle of the Communist Party leadership, Rajk had – like Mindszenty – been imprisoned by the Arrow Cross at Sopronkőhida in 1944. The regime was beginning to consume its own children.

The proclamation of a final judgment dispelled any remaining hopes of a normalization of church governance. Such hopes had been illusory anyway. Until his own arrest on May 18, 1951, Archbishop Grősz of Kalocsa performed the tasks of chairman of the Bishops' Conference. Still, significant confusion surrounded the leadership of the Archdiocese of Esztergom. Matters were initially overseen by the episcopal vicar, János Drahos, who, however, died on June 15, 1950. Since the *de jure* Archbishop

22. PL Processus, V–700/33. 119. fol. József Mindszenty's handwritten letter to Gábor Péter, July 22, 1949.

23. ÁBTL 3.1.9. V–700/56/A–B. 383. fol. Nb. IX.254/1949/22. Memorandum, Special Council of Budapest People's Court, August 16, 1949.

of Esztergom, József Mindszenty, was in no position to appoint a new archbishop's vicar, the cathedral chaplain exercised his rights and arranged for the election, *sede plena,* of a vicar-general. In a secret vote, which was held despite opposition from the regime but with Mindszenty's approval, the Auxiliary Bishop Zoltán Meszlényi was elected. (Meszlényi was beatified in 2009.) The regime reacted by switching to the language of coercion. Indeed, on June 29, 1950, the political police abducted both the newly elected vicar-general and the other potential candidate. Having been terrified by the arrests, the cathedral chaplain submitted to the will of the authorities and on July 5, 1950 he arranged for the appointment of the regime's candidate, Miklós Beresztóczy, as vicar-general. The fixing of the election result resulted in a situation that was incompatible with canon law. On July 18, 1950, the Holy See restored legality by appointing Bishop Hamvas of Csanád as apostolic governor. Hamvas's appointment was to last until October 30, 1956, when Mindszenty was finally able to make a return. Despite all this, until Archbishop Grősz's release and his resumption of his tasks as the head of the Archdiocese of Kalocsa and as chairman of the Bishops' Conference (a position he held until June 13, 1956), there were two representatives from the Archdiocese of Esztergom in attendance at meetings of the Bishops' Conference: Endre Hamvas and Miklós Beresztóczy. The former's presence at such meetings was in line with the provisions of canon law, while the latter's attendance had no justification in canon law, but it was accepted by the Hungarian state.

The Mindszenty Affair at the United Nations

On April 2, 1949, the United States and Great Britain submitted diplomatic notes to the Hungarian and Bulgarian governments stating that both Hungary and Bulgaria – where, between February 25 and March 8, fifteen Protestant pastors had received prison sentences (5–15 years) for allegedly conspiring against the state – had violated their obligations under the peace treaties in the field of human rights and fundamental freedoms. The two Western powers called upon the Hungarian government to cease and remedy the violations. The official Hungarian response, which came on April 8, branded the diplomatic notes a flagrant attack on the sovereignty of the People's Republic of Hungary. Concerning the American note, the

Hungarian authorities were of the view that it was nothing other than "a series of vacuous statements that were unspecific and ignorant of the facts and arguments, whereby its evident objective was to serve as incitement propaganda."[24]

Concurrently with the exchange of diplomatic notes and in line with an earlier announcement by US Secretary of State Dean Acheson, the violation of the peace treaties by Hungary and Bulgaria was brought before the United Nations at the initiative of Bolivia and Cuba. The involvement of the United Nations broadened the scope of the issue, which was no longer limited to a bilateral exchange of diplomatic notes. Now, the entire Soviet camp was affected, and the Soviet Union had to prepare itself for the ramifications. The Soviet delegation to the special session elaborated a detailed report, amounting to a Cold War dossier and containing the relevant clauses from the Charter of the United Nations. The members of the delegation were tasked with rejecting the inclusion of the Mindszenty judgment on the agenda of the General Assembly, whereby they were to argue that it was exclusively a domestic matter for Hungary. If, despite their protests, the issue was put on the agenda, they were to point out that

> an inquiry into the issue in question contradicts both the principle of the sovereignty of states and the Charter of the United Nations. [...] It must be shown that placing the Mindszenty issue on the agenda of the General Assembly is a part of the hostile campaign which the leading circles of the United States, Great Britain, and several other countries are pursuing against the people's democracies with the aim of inciting hatred against the peoples of these states. Similarly, Mindszenty's true face must be exposed, as the agent of aggressive circles in the United States, which are seeking, with his collaboration, to organize the overthrow of Hungary's democratic order, destroy the people's republic, and restore the Habsburg monarchy. If an attempt is made to accuse the Soviet Union – in connection with the Mindszenty affair – of interfering in Hungarian domestic affairs, such attempts must be rejected, by stating that such accusations are

24. MNL OL XIX–J–1–d/1. 3. ő. e. I. Document entitled "Mindszenty Affair – Human Rights"; MNL OL XIX–J–1–j–1945–64/26/a. Memorandum on hostile actions taken by the US against Hungary, March 9, 1950.

slanderous and serve to cover up the real interference of the United States and Great Britain in the internal affairs of Hungary and other countries.[25]

At a plenary session on April 30, 1949, the U.N. General Assembly debated – in the absence of a Hungarian representative, as Hungary was admitted to the U.N. as a full member only in December 1955 – the implementation of human rights and fundamental freedoms in both Hungary and Bulgaria.[26] The General Assembly decided that the governments of the two countries be required to respond to the accusation that the court cases against their churchmen amounted to a breach of the peace treaty. On May 31, the US and British Legations announced that the matter was to be handed over to a committee comprising the envoys to Hungary of the United States, Great Britain and the Soviet Union. In response, the Soviet Union announced that it was declining to take part in the committee, given that in its view Hungary was conscientiously implementing the provisions of the peace treaty.

The issue of Eastern European human rights violations was debated by an ad hoc political committee of the U.N. General Assembly on October 4, 1949 and at the fourth session of the General Assembly on October 21–22, 1949 (by which time, Romania had been added to the list of countries involved).[27] Once again, there was no Hungarian presence at the forum. The Hungarian envoy to the United States received indirect information, according to which the representatives of the "fraternal countries" "had revealed the machinations of the imperialists" and the Soviet delegation had defended Hungary's interests in the most effective manner.[28] Finally, a joint proposal submitted by representatives from Bolivia, Canada, and the United States, received the approval of forty-seven countries, with five

25. Volokitina et al., *Vostochnaya Evropa*, vol. 2, 36–37 (Document no. 13); Volokitina et al., *Vlasty i cherkov*, vol. 2, 52–53 (Document no. 15, n. p.).

26. United Nations, *Official Records of the third session of the General Assembly. Part II. Plenary Meetings of the General Assembly. Summary Records of Meetings, 5 April – 18 May 1949*. Lake Success, New York, n. d., 241–58.

27. United Nations, *Official Records of the fourth session of the General Assembly. Plenary Meeting of the General Assembly. Summary Records of Meetings, 20 September – 10 December 1949*. Lake Success, New York, n. d., 130–50.

28. MNL OL XIX–J–29/a–450/1949. Report of Legate Imre Horváth, Washington, October 21, 1949.

countries voting against. In line with this proposal, on October 22, 1949, the United Nations requested the opinion of the International Court in The Hague on four questions: 1. Do the show trials in Hungary, Bulgaria, and Romania violate the human rights provisions of the peace treaties; 2. Are the governments of these three countries required to nominate representatives to the committee charged with reviewing the treaties; 3. If the countries in question are unwilling to do the above, can the U.N. Secretary-General appoint a "super judge" as if representatives had been appointed; 4. Will a committee with representatives from merely one side, have the competence to resolve once and for all the disputed issues? The Soviet delegation protested; in its view, all four points were in breach of the Charter of the U.N. and amounted to interference in the internal affairs of the affected states.[29]

On November 7, 1949, the International Court in The Hague called on all three countries to make known their positions on the matter. In its response, dated January 13, 1950, the Hungarian Ministry of Foreign Affairs, having consulted with the foreign ministry in Moscow,[30] reiterated its previous arguments. It further made known that neither the United Nations – to which Hungary had still not been granted membership on account of the ongoing inquiry into human rights violations – nor the International Court in The Hague had authorization to examine the "supposed" debate concerning the peace treaty or to interfere in the domestic affairs of Hungary. In Hungary's view, the entire procedure at the international court was illegal, and so it would refuse to take part and would not even comment in substance on the matter. The International Court in The Hague announced its decision in the form of an "advisory opinion" on March 30, 1950. For the court, the matter had been concluded, and thus it did not address subsequent developments. It concluded that there was a dispute about the interpretation and implementation of the terms of the peace treaty and that Hungary was obligated to submit to the ruling of the three-man arbitration committee, as established in Article 40 of the peace treaty. On October 5, 1950, the U.N. General Assembly expressed, in a resolution,

29. RGASPI f. 82. op. 2. delo (file) 1079. l. 174–178. Report of Minister of Foreign Affairs A. J. Vyshinsky to J. V. Stalin, December 28, 1949.

30. Ibid., delo (file) 1152. l. 26. Report of Deputy Minister of Foreign Affairs A. A. Gromyko to J. V. Stalin, October 22, 1949.

its condemnation of Hungary, Bulgaria, and Romania for the human rights violations. Hungary's reaction was consistent with its earlier view: neither the international court nor the United Nations had jurisdiction, the procedure was unlawful, and the resolution passed under "imperialist pressure" was unacceptable. The General Assembly's resolution marked the end of the matter, as the attention of the international community was soon drawn to events in China and Korea. The Mindszenty affair – which had arisen essentially at the propaganda level of the Cold War – did not precipitate a profound crisis between East and West.

Prisons and Cells

József Mindszenty was held captive – under house arrest, in prison or at a prison hospital – from December 26, 1948 until October 30, 1956. He was deprived of his liberty for nearly eight years. After the proclamation of the final sentence, it was some weeks before his health condition began to stabilize. Then, on September 27, 1949, he was taken in a car with curtained windows from the reception prison to the State Security Prison (penitentiary) on Conti Street. Mindszenty thus remained in Budapest, whereas his convicted co-defendants were transferred, in the spring of 1950, to the town of Vác and held captive there at the National Prison.

After his release, Mindszenty rarely spoke of his prison years. He first did so in November 1956, mentioning them again on February 5, 1960, the day on which he was informed of his mother's death.

> He spent five of the eight years that followed the court hearing in an underground cell with no air or light and above an open sewer. It was here that he caught TB and Malaria [sic]. Secrecy was kept in full (he was kept in ignorance), and so even now he does not know the location of this hell, this inferno, worthy of Dante.[31]

The penitentiary on Conti Street was, indeed, incomparably worse than the reception prison. Even prior to World War II, it had been regarded as

31. AMAE AD Série: Europe, 1956–1960, sous-série: Hongrie, dossier 103, Questions religieuses, juillet 1958–décembre 1960, 217–220. Memorandum of French Embassy Counselor Edouard Hutte: Interview with Cardinal József Mindszenty on February 5, 1960.

one of the most unhealthy and notorious prisons in the country, where, from 1938 onwards, people convicted of military or anti-state crimes – or, during the war, of espionage or treason – had been held and incarcerated. At the time of Mindszenty's detention, the prison was "operated" by the State Protection Authority. Mindszenty was only removed from this prison and taken to the establishment in Vác when he was due to meet with his mother or required medical treatment.

In his memoirs, Mindszenty wrote at length of the events of October 15, 1949, the day on which László Rajk, the proven warrior of the workers' movement, and his associates were executed in the prison courtyard. These men had been leading officials of the ruling communist party rather than the regime's party political adversaries or supporters of the "clerical reaction." The executions took place at dawn, whereafter the regime's henchmen and the assembled party leaders drank coffee and hard spirits. For their entertainment, a vulnerable Mindszenty was brought out onto the courtyard and mocked at length by the assembled crowd.[32] Some of those who at this point celebrated Rajk's death and who scorned Mindszenty were soon to suffer their own deathly fate. The first of these was Ernő Szűcs, who was arrested in 1950 and beaten to death – together with his brother, Miklós – during interrogation. Minister of Justice István Ries did not survive until his own court hearing; he died in prison in September 1950. János Kádár was arrested in 1951, by which time he was no longer minister of interior; he was rehabilitated in 1954. Gábor Péter, the head of the State Protection Authority, was arrested in 1953 and sentenced to life imprisonment. Gyula Décsi, a colonel at the State Protection Authority and subsequently minister of justice, was charged with being an American spy and sentenced to nine years in prison. Mihály Farkas, who, despite his lack of military training, was serving as minister of defense, was brought to trial in the matter of an infringement of the law committed by the State Protection Authority. He was the only top communist leader who was brought to trial after 1956 and he received a 16-year prison sentence on April 19, 1957. With the passage of time, all these prisoners were subsequently granted clemency and released.

32. ÁBTL 3.1.9. V–150.019/5. 118. fol. Handwritten admission of Gyula Décsi, April 24, 1956. Cited in László Varga, ed., *Kádár János bírái előtt: Egyszer fent, egyszer lent 1949–1956* (Budapest: Osiris Kiadó–Budapest Főváros Levéltára, 2001), 63.

As the Hungarian primate later wrote, the most tortuous aspects of prison life were its unending nature and its soul-destroying uniformity, which sooner or later drove a man crazy. "Prisoner-dreams" both tortured and healed. Coarseness and indecency were pervasive. Daily, he was expected to sweep floors and then sometimes scrub them, either lying on his belly or kneeling. He could shave once a week. Correspondence with the outside world was forbidden. His mother's visits represented the only break in the loneliness and boredom, but the visits were limited to a few occasions in each year. After the visit of September 25, 1949, it was not until June 17, 1950, that she was permitted to see her son again. For that visit, Mindszenty was taken to the prison in Vác, lest his mother find out where he was really being held. She was relieved to hear how the cardinal was celebrating Mass every day and was devoting his time to contemplation and prayer. He prayed six rosaries a day, read from the Holy Scriptures, and took a regular, daily stroll. His hair, however, had become a little thin...[33] Archbishop Spellman of New York learned that Mindszenty was in an adequate mental and physical condition. Indeed, the Hungarian primate even sent him a greeting in flowery language.[34]

Imprisonment saved Mindszenty from having to reach an accord with the communist regime. This became the task of the Bishops' Conference, as with the dispersion of the religious orders in Hungary and the founding of the peace priests' movement it felt obliged to enter into negotiations with the government, and so on August 30, 1950 it signed the agreement. A year later, Archbishop Grősz of Kalocsa, who had signed the agreement, was "rewarded" with a fifteen-year prison sentence. The day of his arrest marked the foundation of the State Office for Church Affairs, a body charged with implementing communist policy towards the churches. Hungary's most senior archbishop, Gyula Czapik (archbishop of Eger), was chosen to preside over the Bishops' Conference. Under his leadership, the Bishops' Conference swore an oath of loyalty to the Constitution of the People's Republic of Hungary.

Stalin died on March 5, 1953. Within weeks of his death, there was a significant weakening of repression in countries belonging to the Soviet

33. MMAL 10. dosszié, 15. ő. e. 10. fol. "The imprisonment of Cardinal Mindszenty" (a report by József Vecsey); ÁBTL 3.1.5. O–13.405/1. 246. fol. Report, June 20, 1950.

34. AANY Collection 007, Box S/D-10, Folder 8. Typed memo.

"camp." Faithful communists were released from prison and rehabilitated. Even some imprisoned priests regained their freedom. The communist leader Rákosi was left with no option but to transfer some of his power to Imre Nagy, who became prime minister. While adhering to the policy of repressing religious practice, the new prime minister recognized that détente could have positive impacts. At this point, the Hungarian envoy in London made the startling proposal that Mindszenty and Grősz be exchanged for the Rosenberg couple.[35] (A similar idea was raised a few years later: in 1960, two Soviet pensioners suggested namely that Mindszenty be swapped for Manolis Glezos, a Greek politician who had been sentenced – on charges of espionage – to nine years in prison.)[36]

Even within the prison walls, there were several minor signs of the political "thaw" occurring outside. For instance, Mindszenty received both a pencil and an exercise book, whereafter the days passed by somewhat more quickly. Still, his health continued to be a concern, as he suffered from the recurring effects of Grave's Disease. He also developed a serious case of shingles, which was accompanied by painful cramps, fever and mental depression. A further affliction was weakness of the heart. On January 28, 1954, he wrote one more letter to the authorities. In the letter, he referred to his illness, his desire for confession, his mother's old age, and the pledge he had received from Gábor Péter on the day of the appeal hearing: "'I shall come after some years and I shall bring a release.' He even gave a reason for this statement. He said he would do the above 'because you did not get nasty during the hearing or in captivity.'"[37] Mindszenty could not have known that by this time Gábor Péter was no longer a free man... Hungarian Interior Minister Ernő Gerő wrote a little note on the letter and forwarded it to Prime Minister Imre Nagy and to the non-cabinet member Mátyás Rákosi:

35. His proposal was forwarded to Andor Berei, who was not only the party's primary figure at the Ministry of Foreign Affairs, but also an informer for the State Protection Authority. Berei scribbled onto the letter "Does not require attention," whereby the matter was placed ad acta: MNL OL XIX–j–1–d/1.

36. Zoltán Ólmosi, ed., *Mindszenty és a hatalom* (Budapest: Lex Kft., 1991), 60.

37. MNL OL M–KS 276. f. 65/356. ő. e. 63. fol. Photocopy of Mindszenty's handwritten letter.

> This is a rather disturbed letter. He does not suggest directly that we should release him, but this is the rough sense of what he writes. In my view, we should allow for [religious] confession. [...] The thought occurred to me that the right course of action might be to allow Mindszenty (in accordance with the Polish example) to move to a monastery. [...] Perhaps this could also be used as an opportunity to make some progress among Catholics and the clergy. It is clearly worth thinking about this issue. [...] What is the opinion of the comrades?

Rákosi wrote down his opinion the very next day:

> As far as I know, Poland's Archbishop Wyszyński[38] is doing time [in prison]; the Vatican, at least, claims as much. Whatever we might do with Mindszenty and whatever he might promise, he will, within a few months, carry on from where he left off. Despite all this, we must examine the question, albeit at first sight the harm seems to be greater than the benefit.[39]

Rather than offer clemency to Mindszenty, Prime Minister Imre Nagy proposed the suspension of his prison sentence and his banishment to a monastery. Nagy was evidently aware of the embarrassment his government would suffer if the Hungarian primate were to die in prison. At the same time, he was evidently reluctant to restore Mindszenty's freedom.

In the end, Mindszenty was moved from the penitentiary to the hospital of the reception prison on May 13, 1954. Although Mindszenty received adequate provisions and better treatment at the prison hospital, his health showed no improvement. A further concession was made by András Hegedüs, who became prime minister in April 1955. On July 16, 1955, radio listeners in Hungary were informed that József Mindszenty's life prison sentence had been suspended in view of his poor health and advanced age and at the behest of the Bishops' Conference and at the primate's own request. The next day Mindszenty was secretly transported to Püspökszent-

38. Stefan Wyszyński (1901–81), archbishop of Warsaw and Gniezno, head of the Polish Bishops' Conference, had been detained in 1953. On October 26, 1956, he was permitted to return to Warsaw and resume his duties as archbishop.

39. MNL OL M–KS 276. f. 65/356. ő. e. 64. fol. Note with Rákosi's handwriting, 1954. II. 7. Underlining in the original.

lászló in Baranya County, where he was housed at an episcopal summer residence dating from 1797.[40] He remained in custody even though he was no longer a prisoner. His living conditions at Püspökszentlászló were somewhat more favorable, but he was still isolated from the outside world and subject to strict controls. What was the motive for the decision of the authorities? When asked this question by a Soviet diplomat, the head of the Office for Church Affairs cited the cardinal's appalling physical condition: in the confines of prison, his weight had fallen by a half to forty-eight kilograms (105 pounds).[41] In fact, the objective of the regime was to improve its image abroad and preempt a negative reaction. The authorities were aware that Mindszenty's death in prison would be followed by the publication of hostile articles in the international press concerning the barbarity of the Hungarian communist regime. The timing of the Hegedüs government's decision was not coincidental: the suspension of Mindszenty's sentence was announced just thirty-six hours before the commencement in Geneva of a summit of the heads of government of the United States, Great Britain, France, and the Soviet Union. The Geneva Summit was the most important high-level meeting of the four powers since Potsdam. The concession made by the Hungarian authorities came at no cost, and yet it put to rest the judgment made six years earlier, which had been exposed so graphically by Cardinal Mindszenty's vacant seat at the 36th Eucharistic International Congress (held in Rio de Janeiro in the summer of 1955).[42]

The conference of the four great powers in Geneva failed to end the Cold War, but it did amount to a major milestone in East-West relations. After the summit, there was a general belief that unresolved international

40. Interior Minister László Piros initially suggested that Mindszenty be sent to the village of Hejce in Borsod-Abaúj-Zemplén County, where Bishop Pétery of Vác was being held. Perhaps this suggestion was rejected because holding three leading churchmen (Mindszenty, Pétery, and Archbishop Grősz) in custody at the same place was considered too risky. MNL OL M–KS 276. f. 53/240. ő. e. 59–60. fol. Minutes of the meeting of the Political Committee of the Hungarian Working People's Party on July 7, 1955.

41. GARF f. 6991. op. 3. delo (file) 133. l. 16. B. Report of Gorbachev, second secretary at the Soviet Embassy, on a meeting with József Varga, head of the State Office for Church Affairs, Budapest, December 20, 1955. By the time of this meeting, Cardinal Mindszenty's life was no longer in danger; after having received medical attention, he had put on weight and now weighed 60 kilograms.

42. NARA RG 59, GR of the Department of State, CDF 1955–59, Box 4805, 864.413/7–2755. Report of Norris B. Chipman, first secretary at the US Embassy in London, July 27, 1955.

issues could be settled through negotiation rather than combat. The gradual thaw in international relations was accompanied by an improvement in Mindszenty's position: he was removed from prison and placed under house arrest. He could take off his prisoner clothes and put on a cassock. He could also take a stroll in the garden and his mother could visit him more often. Indeed, she was even permitted to stay with him for a longer period. Mindszenty then requested that he be joined by another priest. The new arrival was János Tóth, former priest of the Regnum Marianum Church (Budapest), which had been destroyed prior to the erection of the Stalin Statue at the same site. It was from Tóth that Mindszenty learned about the country's situation and the fate of the church. Information was also received from Archbishop Grősz of Kalocsa, who was interned at Püspökszentlászló on October 14, 1955. For the time being, Mindszenty was not permitted to receive foreign visitors. Several visitors to Hungary attempted to see Mindszenty: for example, US Senator Estes Kefauver (Democratic Party). Rákosi countered Kefauver's request by telling him: "Mindszenty is in good health, and his political views have changed in recent years."[43]

On November 2, 1955, the prisoners were taken from the damp building at Püspökszentlászló to the Almásy mansion (built in 1902) in the village of Felsőpetény, which lies to the north of Budapest. Discipline was much stricter at Felsőpetény than it had been at Püspökszentlászló. The two prelates were guarded by armed men working for the State Protection Authority and German shepherd dogs.[44] The secrecy of the operation and the presence of guard dogs persuaded local people that a nuclear research station had been established inside the gloomy building. Listeners to Radio Free Europe, however, could know the identity of the new residents in the mansion. Archbishop Grősz's situation soon took a turn for the better: after the death of Archbishop Czapik of Eger, he was granted clemency on

43. MNL OL XIX–J–1–j–USA–26/a tétel (item)/1948–58. Sz. n.–1955. Memorandum on the visit of Senator Estes Kefauver, September 19, 1955.

44. The comparison stemmed from Cardinal Mindszenty. NARA RG 84, Records of the Foreign Service Posts of the Department of State, Hungary, Subject Files Relating to Cardinal Mindszenty 1956–72, Box 1, Mindszenty–Classified 1956–June 1957. E. T. Wailes's telegram to the US State Department, November 25, 1956; MMAL 020/a. dosszié, I. Notes and drafts 12. tétel (item). "Válasz a támadásokra" [Response to the attacks].

May 12, 1956. Thereafter he was permitted to resume his work as Archbishop of Kalocsa and chairman of the Bishops' Conference.

Surprisingly, the State Office for Church Affairs did not initially rule out Mindszenty's return to the post of chairman of the Bishops' Conference. For this to happen, however, the Hungarian primate would have had to acknowledge the achievements of socialism and to request his own release under an amnesty. Mindszenty, however, rejected even the least compromise with the authorities.[45] Yet, if Mindszenty had let go of his pride and had resumed his work as chairman of the Bishops' Conference several months in advance of the revolution (similarly to the recently released Polish primate), he might have been able to steer the Church wisely and influence events in such a way that his flight to the US Legation would have been rendered unnecessary. However, by this time, the Hungarian primate had rediscovered his old self, who refused to make deals and who never flinched or sought mercy. There was no-one in government – neither then nor later – who understood that Mindszenty would not flinch, owing not only to his stubborn character but also to his position. He was not only a Hungarian archbishop but also a cardinal of the Holy Mother Church (Sancta Mater Ecclesiae) in Rome. Without moral recompense (e.g., at the very least, an official pardon), he would not permit himself to be persuaded to cooperate with the authorities. Thus, Mindszenty's "preparation for [...] making a positive statement [...] came to nothing," as the political police concluded in late 1955.[46] Accordingly, the Hungarian primate remained under house arrest. In lieu of amnesty, fate offered him a different chance: On October 23, 1956, the Hungarian revolution and war for independence broke out.

A RETURN TO PUBLIC LIFE

In the summer of 1956, having been encouraged by the Twentieth Congress of the Communist Party of the Soviet Union (CPSU) and the events in Poland, the so-called internal opposition within the Hungarian communist party

45. Mindszenty referred to this in his memoir, but the press and diplomatic reports also mentioned it: AMAE AD Série: Europe, 1956–1960, sous-série: Hongrie, dossier 101, Questions religieuses, janvier 1956–juin 1957, fol. 54–55. Report (No. 121/EU) of Etienne Dennery, French ambassador to Switzerland, May 29, 1956.

46. ÁBTL 3.2.5. O–13405/2. 140. fol. Report, December 9, 1955.

criticized the party leadership and demanded the introduction of "socialist democracy." On July 18, Mátyás Rákosi was deposed as party leader. He immediately moved to the Soviet Union and never again returned to Hungary. The Vatican was made aware of the tensions in Hungary. To mark the 500th anniversary of the victory over the Turks at Nándorfehérvár (Belgrade), on June 29, 1956, Pope Pius XII sent an apostolic letter to the three captive cardinals in East Central Europe: József Mindszenty (Hungarian), Alojzije Viktor Stepinac (Croatian), and Stefan Wyszyński (Polish), as well as to the clergy and laity in eight Central and Eastern European countries. He assured the three cardinals of his special attention, as they were suffering "for the freedom of the Church." He expressed confidence that it was only a matter of time before "the present flood ceases."[47]

Revolutionary Ferment

In early October 1956, a series of decisive events occurred in rapid succession. On October 6, the final respects were paid to László Rajk and his associates, who had been executed seven years earlier. On October 13 and 20, funeral services were held for further victims of the regime. On October 5, the Supreme Court acquitted the Lutheran bishop Lajos Ordass, who had been unlawfully convicted in 1948. This latter event was a true sensation, because the release and rehabilitation of a convicted bishop was unprecedented in a proletarian dictatorship. The Catholic bishops were emboldened by this news: at their meeting of October 17, they called for a general process of rehabilitation and an end to lawlessness. On the afternoon of October 23, the demands of the crowd went well beyond the objectives of the so-called party opposition. Then, at 9.30 p.m., the crowd toppled the statue of Stalin, while a short time later state security personnel stationed inside Hungarian Radio's building shot at protesters outside. In response, the crowd began to lay siege to the building. The armed uprising had begun.

It is a striking fact that the fate of the prisoner Mindszenty was not an emphatic issue in the first ecstatic moments of the revolution. Indeed, his name was not even mentioned in the initial statements and pastoral letters of the bishops. Nor did the crowd cry out his name. Had they forgotten him?

47. "Dum maerenti animo," an apostolic letter of Pius XII. AAS 48 no. 11 (1956): 549–54.

Clearly not. Rather, there was an awareness that the people had not taken to the streets with the idea of saving (or re-establishing) Mindszenty's world. Nor did their protest slogans call for the implementation of his ideology. This was especially true of the generation that became the main actor on October 23. The university student protestors had been mere adolescents at the time of Mindszenty's conviction. Their awareness of social matters stemmed from the post-1949 era, by which time the pro-monarchy primate was no longer the main enemy of the communist regime. Indeed, the authorities may well have believed that he had been banished once and for all. For such youths and for those protestors who accepted the thinking of the internal party opposition, Mindszenty was a relic from the past.

Still, there were, among the clergy, several indications that Mindszenty had not been forgotten. On October 23, a group calling itself Catholic Priests Loyal to Rome sent a list of seven points to the State Office for Church Affairs. The fourth item was a demand for the return to Esztergom of Cardinal József Mindszenty, because "without him the Hungarian Catholic clergy cannot sympathize with the leaders of the Hungarian state."[48] On October 25, Radio Free Europe launched a campaign for Mindszenty's release and subsequent political engagement. The radio station mentioned his name in some context no more than fifteen times between October 19 and October 24 but then on 487 occasions between October 25 and November 4. Still, they subsequently "dropped" him as quickly as they had picked him up. Thus, between November 5 and 12, Mindszenty's name was heard in RFE broadcasts on only twenty-five occasions.[49] On October 29, six days after the revolution broke out, students at the Central Seminary produced a pamphlet demanding not only unfettered religious freedom but also the release of the Hungarian primate, Archbishop József Mindszenty.[50] As was true for the entire nation, the student generation became the prime mover within the church. Young people were drawn into action by the winds of liberty and the forgotten hope of a better future. Further encouragement came in the form of *Luctuosissimi eventus*, an encyclical

48. MNL OL XIX–A–21–a–249/1956.

49. György Vámos, "Itt a Szabad Európa Rádiója, a szabad Magyarország hangja," *Századok* 140, no. 5 (2006): 1163–1233.

50. BFL XXV. 4. f. Fővárosi Bíróság TÜK-documents, 1957. 4016/I. 26–80. Judgment in the criminal case of Albert Egon Turcsányi and his associates, January 10, 1958.

issued by Pius XII on October 28, which urged public prayers for peace and freedom for the people of Hungary.

After the publication of the papal encyclical, Bishop Virág of Pécs published a pastoral letter (his first uncensored pastoral letter for five years) summarizing the principal grievances of the Catholic Church. The letter formulated the wish that "Cardinal Mindszenty, Archbishop of Esztergom, who was innocently imprisoned, should be set free, rehabilitated in full, and be permitted finally to occupy his archbishop's seat after eight years of suffering."[51] It is telling that among the various Catholic bishops it was Bishop Virág of Pécs – 87 years old and infirm – who dared to express such wishes on behalf of the church and seek redress in the matter of the Hungarian primate, József Mindszenty. Such wishes far exceeded any of the requests and petitions that had been made by the Bishops' Conference since 1949. Bishop Virág was aware that silence on the part of church leaders would lead to silence on the part of the faithful and the Church would be left without a voice. Yet, until groups in society began to demand the right to establish political parties, the authorities could ignore such issues as freedom of conscience and religion, religious instruction in schools, and church issues in general.

Release or Liberation?

As the revolution proceeded, many political prisoners were set free. The Hungarian primate, however, remained a captive behind the barbed wire fences of the manor park at Felsőpetény. He had access to newspapers, but he could not listen to the radio or send letters. The revolutionary wave reached the village on October 28. On that day, 200–250 local people marched to the Almásy mansion where Mindszenty was being held. They asked for his release, but after an hour-long dispute they departed without the cardinal. Thereupon, the commander of the State Protection Authority guard at the mansion, Maj. Hugó Németh, concluded that in the event of a firefight he would be unable to guarantee Mindszenty's physical safety. With a view to protecting the Hungarian primate from the "mob," he

51. Gábor Salacz, *A magyar katolikus egyház tizenhét esztendeje (1948–1964)* (München: Görres Gesellschaft, 1988), 142–44; Konrád Szántó, *Az 1956-os forradalom és a katolikus egyház* (Miskolc: Szt. Maximilian Kiadó, 1993), 33–35.

decided that Mindszenty should be moved to a safe place. Németh, of course, would accompany him to this safe place.[52] The cardinal, however, expressed an unwillingness to leave Felsőpetény. He feared that the authorities would exploit him and make him do something against his will. A couple of months later, the US envoy summarized what had happened based on Mindszenty's statements:

> Saying he had taken no one's bread away and spilled no one's blood and therefore stood in no fear of the so-called rabble. Two hefty ÁVH guards then exercised force on the cardinal, tearing his cassock but failing to carry him from the room (the cardinal remarks he was surprised at his own strength).[53]

In the afternoon of the next day (October 29), the head of the State Office for Church Affairs, János Horváth, arrived in Felsőpetény, having been sent there by Prime Minister Imre Nagy. Horváth came in a Soviet armored vehicle and was accompanied by a small party of men. He told the cardinal that the authorities wished to transfer him to a safer location. His offer to Mindszenty was that he be released by mutual agreement and without political rehabilitation. He might then go to his mother's home or even to the Academy of Theology, but in view of the political situation there was no basis for any concessions. Mindszenty proudly answered as follows:

> As long as you are sitting on the back of the horse and I am under its hooves, I shall not conduct negotiations. I am willing to leave this place only to go either to Esztergom or to Buda to the Cardinal's Palace, preferably to the latter since that is where my people need me the most.[54]

52. BFL XXV. 4. f. Fővárosi Bíróság TÜK-documents, 1958. 8017/VIII. 7255. The Council of People's Courts of the Budapest Municipal Court, minutes of the proceedings ending on May 5, 1958; interrogation of the primary defendant, Pál Kósa.

53. NARA RG 84, Records of the Foreign Service Posts of the Department of State, Hungary, Subject Files Relating to Cardinal Mindszenty 1956–72, Box 1, Mindszenty–Classified 1956–June 1957, 570.3 E. T. Telegram no. 315 sent by Wailes to the US Mission in Vienna, January 28, 1957. (The envoy mistakenly dated the described events to October 29, 1956, the day after they had actually taken place.)

54. NARA RG 84, Records of the Foreign Service Posts of the Department of State, Hungary, Subject Files Relating to Cardinal Mindszenty, 1956–72, Box 1, Mindszenty–

Unless he could leave as a free man, Mindszenty would rather stay in the prison. Accepting mercy from the authorities would have strengthened the government's reputation, and he had no wish to come to an agreement with a communist politician.

In the absence of a more favorable instruction, Horváth could not persuade the cardinal to leave. The commander of the State Protection Authority suggested that Mindszenty simply be released, but Horváth was too fearful to take this decision. Instead, in the late afternoon of the following day, Horváth returned empty handed to Budapest. He made the journey in a prisoner transport vehicle, because the Soviet tank had broken down. Having been left to its own devices, the State Protection Authority unit decided – in an unexpected development – to do what Horváth had not done: it elected a revolutionary committee, which then terminated the cardinal's imprisonment at 7 p.m. on October 30. The committee told Mindszenty that he "can go where he wishes."[55] Through their actions, the guards were, in effect, acknowledging and implementing the statement made two days earlier by Imre Nagy, concerning the abolition of the State Protection Authority. Only after these events did the four-man detachment of the training regiment for panzer NCOs arrive from Rétság and take Mindszenty to the safety of its barracks.

Mindszenty's memoirs contain the erroneous claim that he was freed by Maj. Antal Pálinkás (former name: Pallavicini), who was executed in 1957 as punishment for his revolutionary activities.[56] In making this assertion, Mindszenty created a further dramatic turn: one of his predecessors as Hungarian primate, George Martinuzzi (Frater Georgius), had been murdered by General Sforza-Pallavicini and his men on December 17, 1551.

Classified, 1956–June 1957, 570.3, Religion–Mindszenty. Telegram no. 315 sent by Wailes to the US State Department, January 28, 1957.

55. HM HIM Hadtörténelmi Levéltár, Budapesti Katonai Bíróság [Military History Archives of the Ministry of Defence, Military Court of Budapest], B.II. 071/1957. Record of proceedings in the criminal case of Maj. Antal Pálinkás and his associates, September 3, 1957, Sheet 36.

56. Antal Pálinkás (Pallavicini) was the scion of various aristocratic families: by way of his father, he was a descendant of the Italian Pallavicini marchesses. Meanwhile, his maternal grandfather, Count Gyula Andrássy, had been the son of the first prime minister of the Austro–Hungarian Monarchy. The name change – from Pallavicini to Pálinkás – reflected a switch of allegiance to the Proletarian cause under the influence of communist ideology.

Now, four hundred years later, a descendant of Sforza-Pallavicini was restoring freedom to a successor of Martinuzzi. For Mindszenty at least, "the hand of God" had been made visible, especially in view of the subsequent tragic events: A member of the Pallavicini family had murdered a primate, while another had suffered death, having saved the life of another primate.[57] An explanation for this deception of memory comes from the November 1, 1956 edition of the newspaper *Magyar Szabadság* (Hungarian Freedom). Citing Antal Pálinkás, a report entitled "The true story of [József Mindszenty's] liberation" alleged that in the late evening of October 30, soldiers from the barracks in Rétság had, "in the course of a short firefight," driven away the secret servicemen working for the State Protection Authority.[58] There were even claims that men from the district of Újpest had shown photos to their fellows of Mindszenty and some dead bodies (his former captors). In fact, however, no-one had been harmed, and the photograph of the lynched secret servicemen had not even been taken in Felsőpetény. Moreover, there had been no need to liberate Mindszenty, for he had already been released when they came for him on October 30.[59]

Mindszenty was initially cautious when the officers arrived around dinner time; he feared they wanted to execute him. Once things had been clarified, however, he willingly agreed to go with them. The cardinal first bid farewell to some local people and then the party set off for Rétság around 10 p.m. At the barracks in Rétság, he was greeted by Maj. Antal Pálinkás, who used his original aristocratic name – Pallavicini – on being introduced to the cardinal.[60] Mindszenty also met with the commander of the barracks. He was still very suspicious of the intentions of these

57. Tibor Mészáros, *A száműzött bíboros szolgálatában: Mindszenty József titkárának napi jegyzetei (1972–1975)* (Abaliget: Lámpás Kiadó, 2000), 96. Memo from October 23, 1973.

58. Tamás Kocsis, "Mindszenty József hercegprímás kiszabadításának hiteles története" [The authentic story of the liberation of Prince Primate Mindszenty], *Magyar Szabadság* [Hungarian Freedom] 1, no. 2. November 1, 1956, cover page.

59. For more details, see Árpád Tyekvicska, "A bíboros útja: Mindszenty József kiszabadításának története," in Árpád Tyekvicska, *Írások a forradalomról* (Balassagyarmat: Nógrád Megyei Levéltár, 2006), 105–54.

60. HM HIM Hadtörténelmi Levéltár, Budapesti Katonai Bíróság [Military History Archives of the Ministry of Defence, Military Court of Budapest], B.II. 071/1957. Record of proceedings in the criminal case of Maj. Antal Pálinkás and his associates, September 2, 1957, Sheet 10.

military men: "After the introductions, he said 'Soldiers, you are not going to shoot me, are you?' I replied, 'look, comrade' – the phrase slipped off my tongue – 'nothing is going to happen to you, you will sleep here, and tomorrow morning you will be taken away'."[61] Mindszenty then met with some people who had come to Rétság to see him, and then he retired in the early hours for a few hours of sleep before the departure to Budapest in the early morning. At his own request, Mindszenty was taken, not to his seat in Esztergom, but to his palace in Buda Castle. His choice of destination signaled a desire to address the public and to perform the political tasks that were derived from his office, as well as his ecclesiastical duties.

Orientation

At 6 p.m. on October 31, the military unit headed by Antal Pálinkás set off from Rétság with Cardinal Mindszenty. The convoy comprised three tanks, a tank destroyer, two military trucks, and two Pobeda automobiles. The news of Mindszenty's release travelled more quickly than the convoy. The journey to Budapest became a veritable victory procession for Cardinal Mindszenty. "We saw, along the route, flowers laid at the roadside, and the people said that Mindszenty had passed by" said one of the soldiers who had been delayed.[62] The crowds wished to catch a glimpse of Mindszenty and celebrate his release, but even in Vác, the ancient episcopal seat, the convoy stopped for no more than a few minutes.[63]

The cardinal arrived at Buda Castle at 8.55 a.m. He was met in front of the primatial palace by a crowd of twenty to thirty people, whom Mindszenty blessed after they sang the Pontifical Anthem.[64] Recollections of this event vary, and other accounts refer to a crowd of 1,000–1,500 people packed

61. HM HIM Hadtörténelmi Levéltár Budapesti Katonai Bíróság [Military History Archives of the Ministry of Defence, Military Court of Budapest] B.II. 071/1957. Continuation of the record of proceedings in the criminal case of Maj. Antal Pálinkás and his associates, September 3, 1957, Sheet 24.

62. ÁBTL 3.1.9. V–142.947/1. 205. fol. Interrogation record for Antal Vanyek, June 6, 1957.

63. M. Ferenc Horváth, *Vác '56 – Vác 1956-ban és a megtorlás időszakában* (Vác: Váci Levéltár, 2006), 67.

64. ÁBTL 3.1.9. V–142.947 102. fol. Memorandum on Mindszenty's being brought to Budapest. Captain György Országh, January 1, 1956 [sic, 1957].

tightly into the narrow street.[65] Evidently, as news of Mindszenty's arrival in Budapest spread, more and more people flocked to the primatial palace to acclaim him. Maj. Pálinkás reported the successful accomplishment of his task to Minister of State Zoltán Tildy, who then informed Cardinal Mindszenty that the government would shortly be in contact with him. Pálinkás subsequently returned to his barracks in Rétság, leaving behind a force of fifteen men to guard Mindszenty.

At 8.45 a.m., ten minutes before Mindszenty's arrival in Budapest, the radio station "Szabad Kossuth Rádió" (Free Kossuth Radio) broadcast an important public announcement:

> The Hungarian National Government has concluded that the legal case brought against Cardinal József Mindszenty in 1948 lacked any legal basis and that the accusations made by the then regime were groundless. Based on all this, the Hungarian National Government declares that the disqualifications imposed on Prince Primate Mindszenty are invalid, as a consequence of which the Prince Primate may exercise – without restriction – his civil and his ecclesiastical rights. Signed: Prime Minister Imre Nagy.[66]

After the suppression of the revolution, Imre Nagy claimed, while being held on remand, that he personally had disagreed with the above statement, which had been decided upon by the cabinet as a whole. Moreover, Nagy asserted that prior to approval of the statement, the cabinet had demanded that Mindszenty "offer an advance guarantee concerning his future political conduct before his rehabilitation."[67] For Nagy, the announcement had been merely a political gesture. There had been no time for Mindszenty's formal

65. HM HIM Hadtörténelmi Levéltár, Budapesti Katonai Bíróság [Military History Archives of the Ministry of Defence, Military Court of Budapest], B.II. 071/1957. Continuation of the record of proceedings in the criminal case of Maj. Antal Pálinkás and his associates, September 5, 1957, Sheet 80.

66. Jelenkortörténeti Adattár [Contemporary History Database]: http://www.tit.oszk.hu/szer/hangjatszas2.phtml, Sound recording of Free Kossuth Radio, October 31, 1956, 8.45 a.m. For the statement, see MNL OL XX–5–h–8. 1956–58. 104. fol. Imre Nagy and his associates. Investigation documents.

67. MNL OL XX–5–h–8. 1956–58. 166. fol. Imre Nagy and his associates. Investigation documents. Interrogation record for Imre Nagy, September 2, 1957.

rehabilitation, which would have required a judicial decision or a presidential pardon.

After the sensational news of Mindszenty's return and rehabilitation, events began to accelerate. The press besieged the Hungarian primate, who proceeded to give a series of interviews to domestic and foreign media outlets. In a telegram, Pius XII welcomed Mindszenty's return to public life. On the day of Mindszenty's release, more than 2,100 telegrams were received from all corners of the world, with former US envoy Selden Chapin's greetings being among the first ones.[68] The only foreign head of state to express his good wishes was Éamon de Valera, the onetime Irish independence fighter.[69] Mindszenty received a single message from behind the Iron Curtain; it was sent by a parish priest in East Berlin. For the time being, nothing was received from Hungarians living in the neighboring countries.[70] Radio broadcasts in Hungary and abroad gave broadly accurate accounts of the events of the day, albeit with minor variations and some exaggerations. Radio Free Europe even claimed that the reason for the revolution had been the people's desire to liberate Mindszenty. On the first full day of his liberty, Mindszenty took the time to thank Catholic bishops from around the world for their donations and to request their continued assistance and support.[71]

The liberation of the Hungarian primate rapidly became a major international news story. US secretary of State John Foster Dulles, speaking in the National Security Council, referred to Mindszenty as a leader capable of governing Hungary and as an integrating force.[72] Dulles' words were

68. NARA RG 59, GR of the Department of State, CDF 1955–59, Box 4805, 864.413/10–3156 HBS. Chapin's telegram no. 678 to the US secretary of state, Teheran, October 31, 1956.

69. MNL OL XIX–A–21–e–4–3/1973. Information brochures received from the Ministry of Foreign Affairs: Report of Ambassador Lóránd Jókai, The Hague, July 25, 1973.

70. MMAL 020/b dosszié, Manuscript entitled "Az 1956-os szabadságharc" [The 1956 Struggle for Freedom].

71. "To the World's Catholic Bishops!" MMAL 024. dosszié. Published in Viktor Attila Soós, "Mindszenty József a forradalom idején," in Pál Rosdy, ed., *A katolikus egyház 1956-ban* (Budapest: Új Ember, 2006), 132.

72. "In such a heavily Catholic nation as Hungary, Cardinal Mindszenty might prove to be such a leader and unifying force." Dwight D. Eisenhower Presidential Library, Abilene, Kansas (hereafter: Eisenhower Library) Papers as President of the United States, 1953–61, Ann Whitman File, Box 19. NSC Records. Memorandum on meeting no. 302 of the National Security Council. Washington, November 1, 1956, 9.00–10.55 a.m.

restated in a more general fashion by his press spokesman, who asserted that the US government considered the "firm-handed" Mindszenty to be the most qualified man for the post of head of the Hungarian government. In response to a question from a journalist, Mindszenty did not reject categorically the possibility of his joining the government or even heading a government, but clearly his mind was on other things.[73] He too appears to have been swept along by the apparent victory of the revolution. Soon, however, the initial euphoria gave way to an awareness of the external danger. Indeed, the government's actions were increasingly determined by efforts to fend off a Soviet intervention.

On November 1, 1956, the government decided that negotiations should be initiated with Cardinal Mindszenty with a view to "restoring peace and order and to securing a statement from the cardinal in support of the government."[74] There is no doubt that the government wished to win over Mindszenty as part of its endeavor to stabilize the country. Indeed, in the early afternoon of November 1, Minister of State Zoltán Tildy visited Mindszenty, requesting that he refrain from making statements that might disturb the public peace and that he encourage people to resume work and to cease taking the law into their own hands. Tildy made no mention of Mindszenty expressing his support for Imre Nagy's government, but this may have been because Tildy grew so agitated that he almost fainted and Mindszenty had to run for a glass of water.

The Hungarian primate agreed to give a radio broadcast, subject to the proviso that he first be given time to "gain orientation." "As recompense," Mindszenty requested from Tildy the archives of the State Office for Church Affairs, whereby Tildy promised to supply them. (Tildy later denied having made such a promise, and such denials were typical of him concerning anything linked with Mindszenty.)[75] At 8.24 p.m. a short statement by Mindszenty was broadcast on the radio. The Hungarian primate had given

73. NARA RG 59, GR of the Department of State, CDF 1955–59, Box 4805, 864.413/11–356. Letter of Piarist Father, Francis L. Rozsaly to President Dwight D. Eisenhower, November 1, 1956. (Rozsály was asked by the press service of the National Catholic Welfare Conference to interview Mindszenty.)

74. MNL OL XIX–A–83–a. 161. d. Minutes of the third meeting of the government cabinet held on November 1, 1956, Point 2.

75. Ibid., XX–5–h–19. 1956–58. 126. fol. Interrogation record for Zoltán Tildy, July 31, 1957.

the statement earlier on in the day at an international press conference held in the courtyard of the primatial palace. He referred to the events as a war of independence that was unique in world history. Mindszenty avoided the word "revolution" and was taciturn for the time being: "I am still in the process of orienting myself; within two days I shall issue a personal plea to the nation about the way forward." As the events threatened to turn into a civil war, everyone impatiently awaited guidance, reassurance and the truth. Two hours earlier, an announcement had been made of the Hungarian government's unilateral decision to withdraw from the Warsaw Treaty Organization (Warsaw Pact) and to declare Hungary's neutrality. Then, at 7.50 p.m., Imre Nagy had reiterated these heroic steps in a live broadcast. Thus, there was an interval of only a few minutes between Nagy's groundbreaking words and the broadcasting of Mindszenty's recorded statement.

IN THE THICK OF THE REVOLUTION

Mindszenty was ready once again for action, but he ended up spending barely more than a hundred hours – from the evening of October 30 until the morning of November 4 – as a free man. He made no appearances in the street or at public meetings. Indeed, the Hungarian primate remained at the primatial palace on Úri Street, leaving only once to make his radio speech on November 3. Many people visited him during these days. Despite his work tempo and his willingness to go without sleep, Mindszenty did not have enough time to become a major figure of the revolution at national level. It should be noted, however, that some political groupings indicated that they were counting upon the Hungarian primate's guidance.

"Help, Help, Help!"

Among the first to visit Mindszenty was a delegation of seminarians, who demanded the abolition of the State Office for Church Affairs, the seizure of its archives, and the holding to account of the so-called peace priests who had served the interests of the regime. This last demand was one shared by Mindszenty from the moment of his release. Indeed, he even stated that he wished to restore order in the archdiocese, holding the Code of Canon Law in the one hand and the Holy Scriptures in the other.[76] Those clergy who had "excelled" as peace priests or had collaborated in any other manner with the authorities rightly perceived Mindszenty's words as a threat. Mindszenty acted to secure the seizure of the documents held by the State Office for Church Affairs at its premises on Pasaréti Road. Fearing the ransacking of the building by unknown parties, he called on the "personal documents in the archive" to be transferred to his primatial palace, where the material could be used to promote research about the past and to foster ecclesiastical justice.[77] The task of securing the transfer of these documents was given to Albert Egon Turchányi, a retired priest who also served voluntarily as Mindszenty's personal secretary from October 31 until November 8. Owing to his dubious political past, Turchányi was not universally liked by Budapest's Catholic priests. He had won Mindszenty's trust, however, by organizing – in 1948 – a mass meeting attended by a hundred thousand people. Barely an hour after Mindszenty's arrival in Budapest following his liberation, Turchányi had welcomed the cardinal in a letter vouching his loyalty and offering his services.[78]

In the first days of November, Mindszenty spent his time in talks and composing his radio speech. On November 3, he held a meeting with a narrow circle of bishops who were sympathetic to his ideas: Archbishop Grősz of Kalocsa, Bishop Shvoy of Székesfehérvár, and Bishop Pétery of Vác, who arrived uninvited. All three men – even Bishop Pétery, who was an unconditional supporter of Mindszenty – advised the Hungarian primate to exercise great caution. Having examined his draft radio speech, which was to be broadcast that evening, the three men succeeded in persuading him to refrain from publicly declaring the 1950 accord between church and state invalid.[79] Together, they agreed upon the recalling of the peace priests who had served the regime (the "people's democracy"). This

76. Ibid., XX–10–k LÜ PO 18.300/1989. II. Record of the witness statement of the retired episcopal counselor, Zoltán Endrédy, December 14, 1989.

77. ÁBTL 3.1.9. V–150.393/4. 221. fol. Egon Turcsányi's "self-confession," March 28, 1957.

78. MMAL 026. dosszié. MFN 8202, L-3150. Albert Egon Turchányi's letter to József Mindszenty, October 31, 1956.

79. Handwritten memo of Archbishop Grősz of Kalocsa for the meeting of the Bishops' Conference on January 23, 1957. Cited in Peregrin Kálmán, *Dokumentumok Grősz József kalocsai érsek hagyatékából 1956–1957* (Budapest: Szent István Társulat–Hamvas Béla Kultúrakutató Intézet, 2011), 394.

decision followed Mindszenty's call addressed to the diocesan ordinaries for the dismissal of all peace priests from senior posts and the recall to their dioceses of those subjugated to them. This provision desolated five years of work undertaken by the State Office for Church Affairs. After the suppression of the revolution, it would take months to recreate a network of collaborating priests.

Bishop Hamvas of Csanád traveled to Budapest from Szeged, but he did so in vain. Hamvas, whom the Holy See had appointed – *sede plena* – as Apostolic Administrator in place of the imprisoned primate and with the right to administer the Archdiocese of Esztergom, was given an audience lasting no more than three minutes.[80] Mindszenty clearly had an unfavorable view of Hamvas's loyalty to the communist state. Even so, one would have expected Hamvas to have been given more time to report on problems and issues that had arisen in the archdiocese. Also on November 3, such major Protestant figures as Bishop László Ravasz of the Reformed (Calvinist) Church and Bishop Lajos Ordass of the Lutheran Church came to see Mindszenty to pass on the greetings of their respective churches.[81]

Cardinal Mindszenty was besieged by the press throughout this time. He gave several telephone interviews and press conferences. On November 3, he requested the economic and political assistance of the Western nations, in particular the Great Powers, to which he had merely alluded just two days earlier: "Considering the circumstances, he was very considerate in his answers," noted one of the journalists who interviewed him. "but behind the lines we can listen to his call: help, help, help."[82] Another one of Mindszenty's visitors was the Dutch Premonstratensian monk, Werenfried van Straaten, also known as "Speckpater" (Father Bacon), who had received his nickname in recognition of the food donations. Van Straaten informed Mindszenty, who was growing increasingly tired, of the aid transports that were being sent by the Catholic Church in the West with a view to helping the Hungarian Church

80. ÁBTL 3.1.5. O–14.759/7. 328. fol. Report, June 10, 1958.

81. OSZK Kt. 514. f. 127. ő. e. Greeting from Cardinal Mindszenty, read out by the Calvinist pastor Imre Bertalan in New Brunswick on September 30, 1973.

82. NARA RG 59, GR of the Department of State, CDF 1955–59, Box 4805, 864.413/11–356. Letter of Piarist Father, Francis L. Rozsaly to President Dwight D. Eisenhower, November 1, 1956.

and the Hungarian people. "During those days, extraordinary demands were made upon me; I barely stood up and I barely slept," Mindszenty recalled later.[83] A delegation came with a message from Otto von Habsburg: "He requests action in the matter of the Holy Crown," and a decision on whether the Holy Crown should be brought back to Hungary. The reply dispatched to Otto was the same as that given to the Hungarians who had sought Mindszenty's guidance in so many matters: "We are still so far from that point; the situation is remarkably uncertain..."[84] Mindszenty received in person several journalists from the major newspapers. The jaded cardinal sought to persuade them that Hungary was not the Russian people's enemy. Although he then condemned in the strongest terms the communist regime, he showed caution when it came to domestic political issues.[85] Members of the former political elite also appeared in Mindszenty's waiting room. A canon, who had been imprisoned under communist rule, noted how the number of people wishing to see the cardinal increased by the hour, with many of the visitors dressed in traditional black Hungarian parade costume "smelling of mothballs."[86] The political actors of the pre-1949 era were evidently hoping that Mindszenty and the revolution could renew their cause and their careers.

The advice coming from the Vatican was that Mindszenty should not become involved in politics and should keep his distance from those who sought a return to the past. He should not take a position on the legal status of associations, on land reform, or on (the restoration of) private ownership. This was the message that was to be delivered by an Austrian delegation of priests, who set out for Budapest on November 3, 1956. The delegation had received the pro forma task of greeting the Hungarian primate and expressing the gratitude of Austrian bishops for Mindszenty's firm stand and his willingness to be a martyr. In fact, however, the delegation's real aim – if the diplomatic sources are to be believed – was to

83. MMAL 020/a dosszié, I. Notes and drafts, 3.

84. MMAL 020/b dosszié, Manuscript entitled "Az 1956-os szabadságharc [The 1956 Struggle for Freedom]," 51.

85. Thomas Schreiber, *Életmorzsák* (Budapest: I.A.T., 2009), 190–91, and the author's interview with Tamás Schreiber (†2015) in Paris on February 28, 2011.

86. Sándor Petróczi, *Emlékek Pétery József püspökről*, compiled by József Török (Budapest: Szent István Társulat, 1997), 112.

"moderate the cardinal's aggressiveness."[87] Yet there had been no signs of such aggressiveness, given that Mindszenty had not expressed opposition to the Nagy government and had limited his "intransigence" to his dealings with the peace priests.

The Radio Address of November 3, 1956

József Mindszenty's radio address, broadcast live at 8 p.m. on November 3, 1956, had been eagerly awaited by the Hungarian public. The general expectation was that the cardinal would exhibit firmness, intelligence and wisdom. For a nation that had grown accustomed to communist party propaganda, Mindszenty's words were doubtless unusual or even somewhat irritating. It should be noted, however, that the Hungarian primate's message was clearly one of consolidation, balance and patience, rather than incitement or dissatisfaction. Some appraised Mindszenty's speech as brilliant and as befitting a true statesman. Others – particularly those influenced by Radio Free Europe's appraisal – viewed the speech to have been that of Hungary's future prime minister. Still others, however, were disappointed that a political program had been presented rather than guidance from the Gospels. Those who sought sustenance for their anticommunist standpoint drew encouragement from Mindszenty's words. But those who thought they were going to be told what was "right" and what was "wrong" were no cleverer after the speech. Such a demand was clearly unrealistic, particularly of a man who had been living in isolation for eight years. After the suppression of the revolution, the authorities successfully twisted Mindszenty's words given in the speech. They could do this, because few people had access to the full transcript and because the speech had indeed contained several ambiguous passages. The November 4 issue of the newspaper *Népszabadság* published only excerpts from the speech. The subsequent Soviet attack rendered it impossible for the speech to be printed in full. A full version of the speech was published only in the November 4 issue of the provincial newspaper *Szeged Népe* (People of Szeged) and again in Mindszenty's memoirs.

87. AMAE AD Série: Europe, 1956–1960, sous-série: Hongrie, dossier 101, Questions religieuses, janvier 1956–juin 1957, ff. 132–135. Report no. 829/EU of the French Ambasssador to Austria, December 3, 1956.

Mindszenty's radio broadcast is one of the most memorable speeches in Hungarian history. The cardinal was the first public figure to refer to the events as a *struggle for freedom* rather than as merely a revolution. Moreover, in lieu of the term Soviet Union, he used the outdated phrase "Russian Empire," which carried a more negative connotation. The expression "freedom struggle" was bound to be much closer to his heart than the word "revolution," which implied upheaval and chaos. For him, the significance of the Hungarian October lay in the much anticipated and well overdue fall of the communist regime, the ending of the Soviet occupation, and the attempt to establish national independence. His speech was essentially a manifesto grounded in his steadfast ideas and views. It was because he had shown steadfastness throughout his years of imprisonment that Cardinal Mindszenty had become a symbol of resistance to the regime.

He reminded his audience that the most important task was the swift resumption of work, production and reconstruction. He consistently placed himself above party politics, calling instead for national unity. At the same time, he urged the "heirs of the fallen regime" that those responsible for the crimes of the past be held to account by an unprejudiced court, that religious freedom be restored, and that the "institutions and associations" be returned to the Catholic Church. It was apparent from his words that he was not seeking a reformed socialism with a commitment to national values – which, at the time, was the preferred option of many. Even while Mindszenty emphasized the unchanging and steadfast nature of his views, he did not voice support – in public – for legitimism (a Habsburg restoration). According to his secretary, his silence in this area reflected his awareness of the Austrian State Treaty of 1955, which had expressly ruled out a Habsburg restoration.[88]

At the focus of his message was the need to restore the external and internal peace of the country. His vision was that of a neutral Hungary which would be the embodiment of a classless society (he was clearly not thinking of a classless society in the Marxist sense). He stated that "we are for private ownership rightly and justly limited by social interests and we

88. ÁBTL 3.1.9. V–150.393/4. 213. fol. Interrogation record for Egon Turcsányi, February 27, 1957.

want to be a country and nation of strictly cultural-national spirit."[89] Here, the speech was somewhat contradictory. Evidently, Mindszenty had been the recipient of a great number of different impulses in the days preceding the speech, and the transcript suggests the making of repeated stylistic changes. Anybody who heard the speech could be clear of one thing: for the cardinal, private property – the foundation of civil society – was very important. Less clear, however, was what he meant by "culture-nationalism." It was István Bibó, minister of state in Imre Nagy's government, who expounded upon its meaning, in an interview made decades later:

> I was most perplexed by something that I think no-one noticed apart from me, namely when he said that "The future belonged to culture-nationalism rather than political nationalism". No-one understood it then, because under those circumstances it was neither here nor there. But Mindszenty had received his intellectual habits in the 1910s, and culture-nationalism was characteristically an Austrian program. In the Monarchy, they had tried to extend the raison d'etre of the Austrian state by replacing political nationalism with culture-nationalism, whereby the various peoples (nations) would foster their languages but would do so within the framework of the Austrian state. It was, on Mindszenty's part, a clear revocation of the Monarchy, which made, under the circumstances, no sense whatsoever.[90]

Thus, Mindszenty's speech – at least for those who were receptive to such things, like Bibó – could have been interpreted as nostalgia for the Monarchy and thus for the kingdom. Extrapolating a little, we may say that culture-nationalism means a national consciousness where affiliation to the nation is not defined by national borders or citizenship but by linguistic, historical and cultural traditions. By this token, the national borders of 1920 may have sliced up Hungary, but Hungarians living on both sides of the border continued to be members of the same nation just as they had been before. This idea of spiritual interconnection and unity was a very novel approach to the issue of the relationship between the Hungarian

89. Mindszenty, *Memoirs*, 333.

90. István Bibó, "1956. október 23–november 6.: Huszár Tibor interjúja," *Valóság* 32, no. 2 (1989): 59.

minorities living outside the country's borders and the mother country. It also offered a politically realistic view, one which could dispel all illusions and provide a means to break free from the earlier approach that had considered the Treaty of Trianon and the Paris Peace Treaty of 1947 to be a national tragedy.

Cardinal Mindszenty avoided theoretical analysis, seeking instead to offer practical advice, which he could do as someone who was above party politics. Given the state of affairs in the country, he expected the various political parties to entrust the future political system of the country to the result of a free election held under international supervision. The way he referred to his office gave a fine hint of his understanding of the idea of primacy: a primate was not only the country's top prelate but also – if there was no other person who could perform this function – the country's first dignitary, who could play a decisive role in the event of a political vacuum.

When recalling the speech, many spoke of Mindszenty's demand for the return of the Catholic Church's lands. Yet the speech contained no such demand! How were his words misheard by so many? The first distorted account of the speech was published in the May 2, 1957 issue of the newspaper *Népszabadság*. Yet it was not only in communist Hungary that "official" interpretations of the radio speech made mention of such a demand. For instance, the leftist-liberal *Süddeutsche Zeitung* commented that Cardinal Mindszenty had demanded the return of the ecclesiastical estates, and this report was then reiterated by several Western newspapers, including two major Catholic weeklies: *Die Furche* and *The Tablet*. The mistake arose from a misunderstanding of Mindszenty's demand for the return of the Catholic Church's institutions: its schools, colleges, old people's homes, hospitals, printers, and cultural/scientific associations. Evidently, when speaking of such institutions, Mindszenty was not thinking of the ecclesiastical estates. In an article published on March 29, 1962 and marking Cardinal Mindszenty's seventieth birthday, the *Süddeutsche Zeitung* frankly acknowledged its mistake.

The subsequent attacks against Mindszenty were given munition by his mentioning of the financial needs of the great ecclesiastical institutions. In the pre-1945 period, the Church's estates and religious foundations had provided the necessary financial means for the church-run institutions, and these sums had been supplemented by regular and ad hoc grants from the government budget as well as by smaller donations from the Catholic faithful. Cardinal Mindszenty did not address the issue of which of these forms of contribution to the financial needs of the Church the Hungarian people might now – in 1956 – consider as natural or desirable. Nor did he explain – merely citing a circular letter issued by the Bishops' Conference – what exactly was meant by "the direction proven by historical progress" and "healthy development." This could have been interpreted as a threat or as part of a process of internal consultation. In truth, people could interpret these words as they saw fit. Indeed, one could very easily read into these words an attack against any form of expropriation and/or a demand for the return of the large estates. This interpretation, however, amounts to a falsification of Cardinal Mindszenty's real message. Looking back at the period 1945–1948, we can see that Mindszenty never once demanded the return of church lands, whereas he did condemn the abolition of the Catholic associations, the nationalization (secularization) of schools and other institutions, the muzzling of Catholic press outlets and publishing houses, and the withdrawal of the religious orders' operating licenses.

For a restart, Mindszenty would gladly have returned to the immediate aftermath of World War II, when the Catholic Church still had power and the prince primate still exercised influence on Hungarian public life. "The issue of the restoration of the pre-war political regime was never even raised during the struggle for freedom," Mindszenty declared in a statement made to the Associated Press, United Press and Reuters news agencies.[91]

Although the propaganda of the Kádár regime of the post-1956 era asserted that Mindszenty's speech had provoked the Soviets into action, in truth there was nothing in the speech that might have served as a reason for the Soviet armed intervention. Indeed, by the time Mindszenty made his speech, the cogwheels of the Soviet military machine had already been set in motion. Evidently, the Soviet invasion was not ordered in response to a radio speech made by a cleric. Nor did Mindszenty's speech serve to promote or solidify domestic political divisions. The political parties were generally established in the three days between October 30 and November 1.

91. AMAE AD Série: Europe, 1956–1960, sous-série: Hongrie, dossier 101, Questions religieuses, janvier 1956–juin 1957. fol. 139. Report no. 868/EU of Roland de Margerie, French ambassador to the Holy See, December 3, 1956.

Thus, by the time of Mindszenty's radio broadcast, they had already formulated their respective programs or, failing that, had drawn up their principles. At the same time, it cannot be denied that Mindszenty had become a symbol for resistance to communism, and so his very presence on the public stage served to encourage the manifestation of certain restorational ambitions.

The radio speech contained several additional mysterious statements. Many appraised his words "the heirs should not expect certainty" as an attack on the government and as an attempt to undermine national unity. The ominous words could have been understood as a covert threat against the government of Imre Nagy (especially against its communist members). By failing to mention any names, Mindszenty essentially branded with the same brush the Stalinists (Mátyás Rákosi and Ernő Gerő) and the reformers (Imre Nagy and János Kádár). In this way, one of the messages of his speech seemed to be that Reform Communism was incompatible with a political system based on bourgeois democracy. It may well have been the case that Mindszenty simply had insufficient knowledge of the various political actors and their respective positions. It might also imply, however, that his experiences during the three days since his release did not really match his previous impression of the men known in Hungary as the Muscovite communists.

The radio speech received a mixed reception abroad. The US Legation in Budapest referred to the broadcast as the most important speech made to the Hungarian nation.[92] In contrast, the Austrian Catholic hierarchy assessed it as "pure emotional reaction."[93] There were several critical voices at the Vatican, too. According to one Monsignor, "someone who has been isolated from the outside world for eight years should have recognized that he lacked every prerequisite for a clear view of the political situation."[94]

92. NARA RG 84, Records of the Foreign Service Posts of the Department of State, Hungary, Subject Files Relating to Cardinal Mindszenty 1956–72, Box 1, Mindszenty–Classified 1956–June 1957, 570.3. Outgoing telegram from the US Legation in Budapest, January 22, 1957.

93. AMAE AD Série: Europe, 1956–1960, sous-série: Hongrie, dossier 101, Questions religieuses, janvier 1956–juin 1957, ff. 132–135. Report no. 829/EU of the French ambassador to Austria, December 3, 1956.

94. Österreichisches Staatsarchiv, Archiv der Republik, Bundesministerium für Auswärtige Angelegenheiten (hereafter: ÖStA, AdR, BMfAA), Sektion II-pol. Zl. 63–Pol/56. Report of Joseph Kripp, Austrian Ambassador to the Holy See, to Minister of Foreign Affairs Leopold Figl. November 21, 1956.

Criticism of Mindszenty's speech focused on the part in which he had requested the political support of the West. The envoys to the Holy See of both Austria and France jointly stated that Mindszenty's "impassioned" performance had reduced his credibility at the Vatican, in stark contrast to the moderate and cautious approach employed by Cardinal Wyszyński of Poland, who had suffered in a similar manner under the communists but whose forgiving attitude towards the peace priests was more useful for the Catholic Church.[95]

After the radio broadcast, Mindszenty exchanged a few words with the radio station's personnel and then called on Tildy and his wife at their apartment in the Parliament building. Thereafter he returned to the primatial palace. At 4 a.m. he was awoken by his guards from the Rétság barracks: Tildy's secretariat had phoned to say that Soviet troops had begun a general offensive against Budapest and that, for his own safety, Mindszenty should make his way to the Parliament. Mindszenty initially hesitated; he could not understand why he would be safer at the Parliament than in the primatial palace, but Tildy's insistence persuaded him to go.

At the Parliament, the various military commanders came together, expecting to be given instructions, but the general confusion merely grew. In view of the general mayhem, it is small wonder that people's recollections of the details varied so widely: whether he was accompanied by a military escort or merely by his secretary, and whether he went on foot or in a car, it is a fact that József Mindszenty – acting on his own volition – managed to reach the nearest foreign diplomatic mission: the US Legation, which lay barely more than five hundred meters from the Parliament. This act and Mindszenty's subsequent decade-and-a-half-long stay at the legation are unique in world history: there are no other instances of a cardinal of the Catholic Church having sought and received asylum in a foreign mission of the United States.

95. Ibid., and AMAE AD Série: Europe, 1956–1960, sous-série: Hongrie, dossier 101, Questions religieuses, janvier 1956–juin 1957, fol. 146. Telegram no. 904 of François Seydoux de Clausonne, French ambassador to Austria, December 8, 1956.

CHAPTER 8

IN THE REFUGE OF THE US DIPLOMATIC MISSION
IN BUDAPEST, NOVEMBER 1956

CHAPTER 8

The Guest
A Decade and a Half Spent at the US Embassy

"THE CARDINAL IS AT THE DOOR..."

The revolution led to Cardinal Mindszenty's release from captivity on October 30, 1956, and it was the suppression of the revolution that brought him – around 8 a.m. on November 4 – to the doors of the US Legation in Budapest. At this historic juncture, Mindszenty faced two key decisions: should he seek asylum and, if this was his chosen course, at which country's embassy should he do so?

Martyrdom or Asylum?

Mindszenty was not counting on a lengthy period of asylum, but did he realize that from the moment he requested asylum he would no longer be a victim or a martyr? According to a Vatican monsignore, the Catholic authorities in Rome immediately drew this conclusion on hearing of Mindszenty's action, for it was the Church's expectation that a cleric should remain with his flock and share in their fate.[1] In a strictly legal sense, however, the matter was not so simple: whereas under international law Mindszenty was not resident in Hungary for as long as he stayed in the US mission, canon law did not recognize extraterritoriality, and so from the Catholic Church's perspective Mindszenty was still present in the territory of the Archdiocese of Esztergom. Therefore, under the provisions of the Council of Trent, he was considered resident in the archdiocese. And while it was true that he was isolated from his flock, he had not abandoned them.

The voices of criticism were not isolated and they reached the very top of the Catholic hierarchy, as some information provided by the Italian envoy in Budapest shows: According to the Italian diplomat, Pope John XXIII – while dedicating his photograph to Cardinal Mindszenty and expressing sorrow for his fate – pointed out that "the primate of Hungary, having been required to make a choice in the early hours of November 4, 1956, should have chosen the prisons of the regime rather than American asylum."[2] Reports even reached Moscow that there were some at the Vatican who viewed Mindszenty's request for asylum as an act of cowardice: "A head of the Church cannot place himself in such an embarrassing situation; in the history of the Church over the past two centuries, such conduct is unprecedented."[3]

As Soviet troops poured into Budapest, the Hungarian revolutionaries who continued to resist them also accused the prelate of having prematurely sought refuge at the legation. In view of his active political role during the days of the revolution, they regarded his actions as somewhat ignoble. As the revolutionaries saw it, Mindszenty should have stuck with them, whereby – even at risk to his own life – he could have morally opposed the Soviet invasion and rejected a surrender to the Kádár government. Such a course of action would have been a uniquely effective means of stirring the conscience of the free world and awakening it to the drama being played

1. ÖStA, AdR, BMfAA, Sektion II-pol. Zl. 63–Pol/56. Report of Joseph Kripp, Austrian ambassador to the Holy See, November 21, 1956.

2. AMAE AD Série: Europe, 1956–1960, sous-série: Hongrie, dossier 103, Questions religieuses, juillet 1958–décembre 1960, fol. 86. Report no. 631/EU of Jean Paul-Boncour, the French legate in Budapest, on information supplied by the Italian legate concerning the Vatican's position. Budapest, December 9, 1958.

3. Rossiiskii Gosudarstvennyi Arkhiv Noveishei Istorii [Russian State Archive of Contemporary History] (hereafter: RGANI) f. 5. op. 28. delo (file) 476. l. 80–81. Report of the CPSU CC on the Vatican's policy towards Hungary, Poland, and Yugoslavia. March 26, 1957.

out in Hungary.[4] In 1957, researchers from Columbia University undertook a survey among the Hungarian refugees in the United States. The results of the survey revealed that most of the refugees saw in Mindszenty the conservative turn in the revolution. Moreover, no more than 15 percent of them mentioned him as a possible future leader of the country. Forty-six percent of survey respondents had a favorable view of Mindszenty, while 33 percent were indifferent, and 21 percent hostile to his person.[5]

Unlike his critics, many people refused even to countenance calling Mindszenty to account for having evaded a renewed threat to his life. Leaving aside the "fight or flight" dilemma, we do well to note the critical remarks of the Austrian ambassador:

> The cardinal, whose most striking characteristics – according to all who know him – are not exactly wisdom and political sensitivity, did the greatest service to the regime by fleeing to the most hated enemy; through this act, he turned himself into an object of the Cold War between the Americans and the Hungarians, and the US Legation here [in Budapest] into a pawn of the regime.[6]

It is true that, by seeking asylum at the US Legation, Mindszenty provided the Kádár regime with a valuable propaganda theme. On the other hand, Mindszenty was also an "asset" for the Americans. By welcoming the Hungarian primate to its legation, the United States could rebut accusations that the country had betrayed its role as the protector of democracy through its failure to support the Hungarian revolution.

It was once claimed that when Mindszenty heard of the Vatican's critique of his actions, he immediately offered his resignation to the pope and pledged to leave Hungary. There is no evidence for this claim in the documents accessible to researchers. According to a report that appeared

4. AMAE AD Série: Europe, 1956–1960, sous-série: Hongrie, dossier 101, Questions religieuses, janvier 1956–juin 1957, ff. 105–106. Letter of Étienne Manac'h, head of the Eastern European Department of the French Ministry of Foreign Affairs, to Roland de Margerie, French ambassador to the Holy See, November 23, 1956.

5. Vámos, *Itt a Szabad Európa Rádiója*, 1176.

6. ÖStA, AdR, BMfAA, Sektion II-pol. Zl. 21.–Pol/58. Kardinal Mindszenty, zu Telegrammerlass Zl. 58029 3-fach. Report of Walther Peinsipp, Austrian legate to Hungary, October 27, 1958.

first on this subject in the Brussels newspaper *La Libre Belgique* and which made this claim, Mindszenty had just one ambition: to write a book about his sufferings and the methods employed by the communists. The report then stated that Pius XII had rejected Mindszenty's resignation, expressly requesting that he stay in his post.[7] Irrespective of the veracity of the report, there is no doubt that Mindszenty was already thinking about writing his memoirs. In December 1956, in a letter to Cardinal Spellman, he wrote the following: "I do not know what I should do with myself here. I was thinking of publishing a memoir of the eight years."[8] Meanwhile, a rumor spread among the clergy in Hungary that the government would allow Mindszenty to leave the country. Endre Marton, a press reporter for the Associated Press – who had also been given refuge at the US Legation for a period of some weeks prior to his emigration from Hungary – was asked by a lieutenant colonel in the State Protection Authority to take Mindszenty with him. According to the family legend, the lieutenant colonel reasoned as follows:

> Mindszenty at the American Legation is a nuisance for us and for the Americans. If he gets out, he will be on the front pages of your newspapers for how long? For three days perhaps. Then he will disappear behind the thick walls of a monastery somewhere in Rome and the world will soon forget him.[9]

Marton told the legate (Edward T. Wailes) about the offer, who, however, viewed it as far too risky. He thus refrained from telling Mindszenty about it.

In choosing refuge rather than the uncertain fate that was bound to be his after the Soviet invasion, Mindszenty was doubtless influenced by his

7. AMAE AD Série: Europe, 1956–1960, sous-série: Hongrie, dossier 101, Questions religieuses, janvier 1956–juin 1957. fol. 161. Report no. 901/EU of Roland de Margerie, December 21, 1956.

8. MMAL, 024. dosszié, MFN 8167, L-3115. Letter of József Mindszenty to his "Eminence" [based on its contents, the letter was addressed to Cardinal Spellman of New York]. December 3, 1956. Please note: 1. Mindszenty changed the month in the date from December to November, because he had to date his letters written at the US legation to a time before his arrival there. 2. The US State Department did not forward the letter to its addressee.

9. Kati Marton, *Enemies of the People: My Family's Journey to America* (New York: Simon & Schuster, 2009), 204.

experiences in prison, which had borne such a heavy spiritual and physical toll. Indeed, he could not bear the thought of returning to prison. Nor were his fears of a possible death sentence groundless. Even so, concerns over the effects of his decision gnawed at his conscience for the rest of his life. By choosing to remain in Hungary, he became the embodiment of a disturbing, ever-present protest. This was true even though complete isolation awaited him at the legation, and the silencing of political resistance accelerated the natural "wear and tear" of public memory. Perhaps in the free world he could have done more to make his voice heard.

Why did the Hungarian primate choose the diplomatic mission of a majority-Protestant country, the United States? Why did he not flee to the mission of a Catholic country or of neutral Switzerland? Did his choice simply reflect the proximity of the US Legation to the Hungarian Parliament building, where he spent the night of November 3? In making his decision, he was clearly influenced by his belief that he would be most secure under the protection of a superpower and the defender of democracy. A further hope was that the Americans might be spurred into taking a more active diplomatic role in East Central Europe, whereby his presence at the legation might become highly significant. Finally, no-one – and clearly not even Mindszenty – thought that his request for asylum, a mere "temporary" solution, would result in fifteen years of isolation, during which time he would be prevented from influencing the life of the Catholic Church in Hungary, even while formally remaining the head of his archdiocese.

The Request for Asylum

Based on information received from the cardinal and from legation personnel, US Chargé d'Affaires N. Spencer Barnes summarized the story of Mindszenty's request for protection as follows:

> According to the Cardinal himself, he did not even think of coming to the American Legation until some twenty or thirty minutes before he actually arrived in the early morning of November 4. The Cardinal spent the night of November 3 and the morning of November 4 in the Parliament building, where he had been invited by Zoltán Tildy to receive up-to-the-minute news and apparently to be afforded protection in the case

> of trouble. About seven o'clock in the morning the Cardinal, then in company of his secretary, decided to return to his residence. His car, however, had disappeared. He was also informed that he could not return on foot because the Russians had seized the bridges. At that point he asked his secretary what was the nearest Western legation. The secretary replied that it was the American Legation on Szabadság Square. This, according to the Cardinal, was the first time it had occurred to him to seek refuge with the Americans. At this point the Cardinal and his secretary were standing outside of Parliament. Part of Parliament Square was already occupied by Russians who were in the process of disarming some Hungarian soldiers. A Hungarian army officer, a captain, then approached the Cardinal and said, "Everything is lost. I want to save you at least". The captain summoned two civilians and the group of five (the Cardinal, the secretary, the captain, and the two civilians) walked to the American Legation. When the group reached this destination, the captain said to the Cardinal, "Thank God, I have succeeded at least in this". With that he and the civilians left.[10]

Mindszenty's arrival at the US Legation can be reconstructed in precise detail. From the beginning of the Soviet attack in the early hours of November 4, the legation was in constant contact (save for several technical interruptions) by telex with the State Department in Washington. The State Department requested prompt and precise information about the dramatic agony of the revolution, but the legation staff could only detail events that had been reported to them or which they themselves had witnessed. At 5.35 a.m., the secretary of Minister of State Zoltán Tildy had telephoned to say that the Soviets were on the offensive throughout the country and that the Hungarian government was requesting the assistance of the United States. Such requests were made in vain, as the Americans had already decided that there was no question of their risking a military intervention or even taking a tough diplomatic stand. On October 29, in Moscow, US Ambassador Charles Bohlen had submitted to Khrushchev a message from US

10. NARA RG 84, Records of the Foreign Service Posts of the Department of State, Hungary, Records Relating to Cardinal Mindszenty 1956–72, Box 1, Mindszenty–Classified 1956–June 1957. Report from the American Legation in Hungary to the Department of State, March 8, 1957.

Secretary of State John Foster Dulles. The essence of the message was that the United States viewed neither Hungary nor Poland as a potential military ally.[11] In diplomatic speech, this meant that the United States would not intervene if the Soviet Union chose to take military action against either country. In effect, it gave the green light to a Soviet invasion. President Eisenhower had no desire to alter the status quo established in 1945, and he was not prepared to risk a third world war for the sake of the Hungarian revolution.

Edward T. Wailes, the new US envoy who had arrived in Budapest just two days earlier, pointedly referred to the chaotic conditions prevailing in Hungary when he joked that even if he managed to reach the government buildings by scurrying along the city's bullet-ridden streets, he still would not know to whom he should present his diplomatic credentials. It was while these words were being teletyped to Washington that István Bibó, who had been appointed on November 3 as a minister of state in Imre Nagy's coalition government, appeared at the legation's gate. He was bearing a plea for assistance addressed to President Eisenhower. The new envoy immediately commenced the forwarding of Bibó's message. In the meantime – at around 7.50 a.m. – the United Nations Security Council, which had been convened to discuss the Soviet invasion, issued an urgent request for information concerning Soviet troop movements. "We Americans have actually seen numbers of tanks bearing markings," Wailes responded, and then without any interruption his teletype message continued as follows: "The Cardinal is now at the door and we are now taking him in. I'll speak with him and be right back."[12] At 7.58 a.m. the teletype message posed the following question: "Cardinal accompanied by his secretary, can we also take him in?" Wailes had to wait only a minute for an affirmative reply.

11. István Vida, "Bibó István kibontakozási tervezete, 1956. november 6," *História* 8, no. 16 (1988); László Borhi, *Magyar–amerikai kapcsolatok 1945–1989: Források* (Budapest: MTA Történettudományi Intézet, 2009), 52–70.

12. *Foreign Relations of the United States, 1955–1957*, vol. XXV, part 1, general editor John P. Glennon, editors Edward C. Keefer, Ronald D. Landa, and Stanley Shaloff (Washington D.C.: United States Government Printing Office, 1990), 379. Transcript of a Teletype Conversation Between the legation in Hungary and the Department of State, November 3–4, 1956. On the Internet: https://history.state.gov/historicaldocuments/frus1955-57v25/d162.

The teletype message does not provide further details, but it is evident that Mindszenty's arrival did not come as a surprise to Wailes, albeit he had not expected the cardinal to be accompanied by his secretary. Two hours before Mindszenty's arrival at the legation, the State Department had sent a message approving his being granted refuge at the legation. The only mystery for the legation personnel was how Washington had learned of the cardinal's need for asylum. The telegram containing the State Department's authorization for the granting of refuge was lost in the confusion and never subsequently found.

Who had informed the State Department in Washington of the possibility of an asylum request from Cardinal Mindszenty when he himself was yet to decide upon this course of action? The details of this mystery have never been revealed, and the various memoirs offer no further information in this regard. As far as the daily meetings held by the US president with his closest advisors are concerned, the first mention of the cardinal was made in a memorandum drawn up after a meeting on November 5, 1956: Herman Phleger, a State Department legal advisor, informed that

> Cardinal Mindszenty is in our legation. We will refuse to turn him over. We will try to keep him quiet. Our international position is not too strong on trying to safeguard him. Perhaps we can get the UN into the matter to help him.[13]

The US government promptly informed Amleto Giovanni Cicognani, Apostolic Delegate to the United States, about the granting of refuge to Mindszenty and requested the position of the State Secretariat on the matter. However, following a renewed intervention by Cardinal Spellman of New York, Cicognani chose to remain silent. In contrast, the United States waited some time before notifying the authorities in Budapest that Cardinal Mindszenty was at its legation. (According to the Hungarian side, such notification only took place on October 18, 1958, in a formal note requesting permission for Mindszenty to travel to Rome for the papal

13. Eisenhower Library, Papers as President of the United States, 1953–61, Ann Whitman File, DDE Diary Series, Box 19, Nov. '56.–Staff Memos. Memorandum of Conference with the President. November 5, 1956.

conclave.) At the time of the cardinal's arrival at the legation, this lack of communication was perfectly understandable, as all contact with the Hungarian authorities had been abandoned. Superficial contact was subsequently established between the US Legation and the Hungarian Ministry of Foreign Affairs, but one American diplomat characterized the US tactics as "our policy of lying low."[14] Still, thanks to reports in the Western press, the cardinal's whereabouts soon became public knowledge in the world at large, even while the Hungarian population was left in the dark. On November 16, the State Department reaffirmed the refuge that had been granted on November 4:

> Legation is authorized subject to following considerations, to afford Cardinal Mindszenty continued refuge and protection while period [of] active danger remains. Legation will not surrender him to Soviet occupation Authorities, authorities of Hungarian Puppet Regime, or any mob, and all demands for his surrender should be refused. It should be realized that should forcible means be used to violate Legation premises and seize Cardinal, Legation would not be in a position physically to resist such violence effectively.[15]

The successors to President Eisenhower later renewed Mindszenty's right to refuge. The first to do so was President John F. Kennedy, who expressed his "sympathetic understanding"[16] on February 10, 1961. Finally, in late July 1971, the US envoy to Hungary stated that the cardinal could stay put for so long as he liked.[17] This was essentially how things later transpired, for it was the cardinal himself who ultimately chose to leave the legation fifteen years after his arrival.

14. NARA RG 84, Records of the Foreign Service Posts of the Department of State, Hungary, Records Relating to Cardinal Mindszenty 1956–72, Box 1, Mindszenty–Classified July–Dec 1957. Letter of Garret G. Ackerson, Chargé d'Affaires, to Henry P. Leverich, Deputy Director of Office of Eastern European Affairs, October 10, 1957.

15. Ibid., Mindszenty–Classified 1956–June 1957. Telegram no. 241 of the Department of State, November 16, 1956.

16. Ibid., Mindszenty–Classified 1961. President Kennedy's letter to József Mindszenty, February 10, 1961.

17. Mészáros, *A száműzött bíboros szolgálatában*, 32. Record of July 4, 1972.

When the legation gate closed behind him, Mindszenty was no longer subject to the jurisdiction of the Hungarian state, albeit the legality of his asylum stood on less than firm foundations, as the United States of America does not recognize the institution of diplomatic or political asylum. Nor does it consider the right to asylum to be a part of international law. Historically, when US diplomatic missions or vessels have provided refuge, they have done so on humanitarian grounds or to save human lives. Indeed, the State Department has always drawn a distinction between political asylum on the one hand and temporary refuge on the other. This distinction explains why, in Mindszenty's case, the US authorities referred to the granting of *refuge* rather than *asylum* and proceeded on this basis for the ensuing decade and a half. While, on the one hand, they were protecting the life and personal security of the Hungarian cardinal, their actions nevertheless resulted in the cardinal's isolation from public and ecclesiastical life in Hungary. In this way, they sought to strike a balance between the sovereignty of the Hungarian state and the refuge offered to the cardinal. At the same time, the general public, being uninterested in the finer legal and diplomatic differences between asylum and refuge, usually referred to Mindszenty's situation as political asylum. Mindszenty himself also erroneously used this term.

When József Mindszenty knocked on the legation's door, East-West relations were completely overshadowed by the Cold War. Fifteen years later, at the end of Mindszenty's time of confinement at the US mission, the Cold War had subsided. Indeed, in 1975, just four years later, the Helsinki Accords would be signed. The world had changed greatly in the course of a decade and a half. The period saw the commencement of Western European integration, the independence of many African states, and the blossoming of the Non-Aligned Movement. During these years, man walked for the first time on the Moon, China detonated its first atomic bomb, and the Berlin Wall was erected. Crises, local wars, political assassinations, student riots, and political banditry became constant features of life around the world. US foreign missions were besieged by armies of protestors demanding an end to the Vietnam War. In 1968, the desire for freedom blossomed in Czechoslovakia before it was crushed by Soviet tanks. The Soviet empire seemed unshakeable, while the civil rights movement was still in its infancy. During this fifteen-year period, there were four US presidents, two Soviet party general secretaries, and three popes in Rome. In Hungary, however, János Kádár continued to head the Hungarian Socialist Workers' Party, in line with the wishes and demands of the Soviet Union.

POLITICAL REFUGE – WITH THORNS

The first hours and days of Mindszenty's stay at the US Legation were a time for mutual introductions and relief. The cardinal was alive, in good spirits, and with an unquenchable thirst for work. At last, he could enjoy such things as a daily breakfast and an evening cigar. Legation staff converted the envoy's private study into a bedroom for Mindszenty. On November 5, Wailes permitted CBS and NBC to film the cardinal as he celebrated Mass with an American flag in the background (given the lack of a chalice, the communion wine was served from a simple glass). The envoy even gave permission for a press conference, but the assembled journalists were required to pose questions as if they were being addressed to the cardinal before he took refuge at the legation.[18] Someone asked him to state his opinion of the Russian aggression. "I condemn it, unqualifiedly," he answered. Which government do you recognize as the government of Hungary? Imre Nagy's government or the Kádár government formed in Szolnok? "I consider the government of Imre Nagy to be the sole legal government of Hungary. János Kádár was installed by foreigners. I reject him and his illegal government," he replied, then going on to refer to the Kádár government as the "so-called" government or regime.[19] At the time, no-one was concerned with the time dimension of his asylum and its scope. Did it encompass legal protection and the right to work and communicate with the outside world and protection against authoritarianism?

18. NARA RG 84, Records of the Foreign Service Posts of the Department of State, Hungary, Records Relating to Cardinal Mindszenty 1956–72, Box 1, Mindszenty–Classified 1956–June 1957, 570.3. Telegram no. 242 of Legate E. T. Wailes to the Department of State, November 19, 1956.

19. Mindszenty, *Memoirs*, 214.

Mindszenty immediately set to work on November 4, and he kept working during the ensuing days. Perhaps he was trying to make up for things he had put off doing during the days of the revolution. One of his first tasks was to address several personnel issues relating to church governance. He removed eleven leading peace priests from their offices and made them subject to a suspension order (*suspensio*). He then sentenced them to serving as rural chaplains or parish priests. Finally, he banned two of the most important peace priests – Canon Miklós Beresztóczy and the Cistercian monk Richárd Horváth – from performing any kind of ecclesiastical or public function in the future. In a statement, he emphasized that what he expected was "unconditional loyalty to Rome and to the chief shepherd."[20] Mindszenty then redeployed to Budapest seven parish priests who had earlier been removed from their posts by the State Office for Church Affairs.

Cardinal Mindszenty's instructions were released to the outside world by his secretary. Their implementation, however, was much slower than the expected twenty-four hours. Indeed, it was some weeks before some of the priests received notification of their suspension. By transferring certain priests to rural areas, Mindszenty effectively decapitated the peace priest movement, which had served since 1950 as a means for the communist regime to bring the Catholic priesthood and laity into line with the goals of the regime. Following in Mindszenty's footsteps, several ordinaries took similar measures in their respective dioceses. The removal of priests peaked after the *Sacra Congregatio Concilii* (Sacred Congregation of the Council) – which was responsible for disciplining priests and laymen in moral matters – issued a decree on January 21, 1957, dismissing twenty-one persons who had earlier been appointed as episcopal vicars or heads of office at the express wish of the State Office for Church Affairs. All these men were banned by the Congregation from occupying such posts in the future.[21] The provision hit particularly those whose loyalty to the regime had led to them being appointed to major offices within the church during the preceding years or who had played a leading role in the priest peace movement. The regime's "Catholic personnel policy" seemed to be in a

20. MMAL 026. dosszié, Ecclesiastical measures in 1956–57. MFN 8216, L-3164. Handwritten note, US Legation in Budapest, November 6, 1956.

21. AAS 49 (1957) 38–39. Decree no. 20504/D.

state of collapse. According to an April 1958 report, in total fifty-seven "progressive priests," who had been appointed to their posts under government pressure, were suspended by the Catholic Church.[22]

In the view of the State Office for Church Affairs, all these actions represented violations of the 1950 accord between church and state – even though the scope of that agreement had not extended to the appointment of parish priests. Acting under pressure from the State Office for Church Affairs, Archbishop Grősz requested the cancellation of the papal decrees. The Vatican authorities rejected Grősz's request on June 22, 1957, and then scolded him for supporting the peace movement and the Patriotic People's Front. In a further development, the *Sacra Congregatio Concilii* called on priests who had been serving as members of Parliament since 1953 to resign from their positions within six months or face automatic excommunication under a special mechanism that had been retained by the Apostolic Holy See.[23] In February 1958, the three peace priests who had refused to resign from their parliamentary seats by the designated deadline – Miklós Beresztóczy, János Máté, and Richárd Horváth – were then duly excommunicated.[24] Even though the Hungarian authorities refused to consent to the publication of the Sacred Congregation's decrees, the provisions still entered into force in terms of canon law. Not until 1971 would the excommunication of the three peace priests be lifted – a move linked with Cardinal Mindszenty's departure from the US mission.

All this proves that the Holy See enthusiastically supported Mindszenty's measures in the field of church governance. In other areas, it was far less forthcoming, and it was expressly opposed to the cardinal encouraging resistance to the regime from his refuge in the legation. This, at least, is how one must interpret Pius XII's diplomatic message that the cardinal should focus his energies on prayerful devotion.[25] Here, one should note that Mindszenty's activities had not been limited to administrative matters but had also been directed at maintaining the international community's

22. For Cardinal Mindszenty's instructions and the reactions of the leading peace priests, see Rosdy, *A katolikus egyház 1956-ban*, 135–39.

23. AAS 49 (1957): 637. Decree no. 25446/D.

24. AAS 50 (1958): 116. "Excommunicationis declaratio."

25. AMAE AD Série: Europe, 1956–1960, sous-série: Hongrie, dossier 101, Questions religieuses, janvier 1956–juin 1957, fol. 201. Telegram no. 341–343, March 4, 1957. (The Italian legate delivered the message to Cardinal Mindszenty.)

interest in Hungary. His means of achieving this included various calls to action, which the diplomats at the legation initially encouraged. For instance, in the minutes following his arrival at the legation, he was asked to make such a call to action. He immediately agreed to meet the request:

> Under the pretense of serious negotiations the assembling Soviet troops at dawn occupied the Hungarian capital and the entire country. I protest against this aggression and I ask for forceful and speedy defense of my country from the USA and other powers.[26]

Mindszenty did what his fellow freedom fighters – those whom he had abandoned – expected from him. In the end, however, the Americans decided against publishing his statement. The foreign affairs apparatus recoiled from giving even the remotest impression that the United States was to provide military assistance. Those with experience of international politics knew that the United States would have to pass through Austria before it could offer military assistance to Hungary. This, in turn, might have resulted in World War III. Still, the cardinal was encouraged to compose calls for assistance that could be sent to leading politicians around the world. For instance, in a call to action addressed to Secretary-General Dag Hammarskjöld of the United Nations, an organization Mindszenty refers to in his memoirs as a "salt office" (i.e., an office with a venerable title but no practical function), the Hungarian primate requested the dispatch to Hungary of a UN peacekeeping force.[27] The legation carefully weighed up the pros and cons of publishing this manifesto, deciding in the end to merely forward it to Washington.

Embittered by the absence of foreign intervention, Mindszenty sought to ensure that his messages would reach their destination by taking the matter into his own hands. He entrusted this task to his secretary, who,

26. Glennon et al., *Foreign Relations*, 1955–1957, vol. XXV, 1, 380. https://history.state.gov/historicaldocuments/frus1955-57v25/d162

27. NARA RG 59, GR of the Department of State, CDF 1955–59, Box 4805, 864.413/1–1055 and NARA RG 84, Records of the Foreign Service Posts of the Department of State, Hungary, Subject Files Relating to Cardinal Mindszenty 1956–72, Box 1, Mindszenty–Classified 1956–June 1957, 570.3. Outgoing telegram no. 256 of the US Legation in Budapest. November 9, 1956. (Based on the sources available in the United Nations Archives in New York City, Cardinal Mindszenty's appeal was not forwarded to its addressee.)

on November 8, left the legation in the company of an American journalist named Leslie Balogh Bain. Their automobile, which had a foreign registration number, was soon stopped by the police, whereupon both men were arrested. Two days later, the American journalist was released on account of his US citizenship. Thus, it was he who subsequently smuggled Mindszenty's letter out of the country and delivered it to the White House.[28] Mindszenty's message emphasized the determined struggle of the Hungarian people, their indomitable longing for freedom, and the prelate's profound concern for the fate of his homeland:

> As a shipwreck of Hungarian Liberty, I have been taken aboard by your generosity. I am a refugee in my own country and a guest of Your Legation. Your hospitality surely saved me from immediate death. With deep gratitude I am sending my heartfelt congratulation to Your Excellency on the occasion of your re-election to the Presidency of the United States, an exalted office whose glory is that it serves the highest ambitions of mankind: God, Charity, Wisdom and Human Happiness. Let your abundance in these endeavors reflect a ray of hope on our long-suffering people who at this moment are undergoing the fifth day of bombardment, gunfire, and flaming death in testimony before God and the World of their will to be free; whose sons are even now being dragged into slavery, whose children with their dying breath are crying out for help from their destroyed homes, shelters and hospitals, whose daughters are facing looted stores and certain starvation.
> God bless you, Mr. President and the People of the United States. I am ardently praying to our Heavenly Father to save and lead you and your people toward your common aims of bringing peace and happiness to this sorely tried world. May the Lord grant you and your nation greater strength and richer life. On the threshold of an ever-greater future, I beg of you, do not forget, do not forget, do not forget this small honest nation who is enduring torture and death in service of humanity.
> Budapest, November 8, 1956.
>
> † Joseph Card. Mindszenty
> Cardinal Mindszenty[29]

28. Leslie B. Bain, *The Reluctant Satellites: An Eyewitness Report on East Europe and the Hungarian Revolution* (New York: Macmillan, 1960), 178.

29. Eisenhower Library, Central Files, Official File 154-L War Claims, Box 823. 154-N Revolutions against Russia in Poland and Hungary, Oct 1956. Memo for President Eisenhower,

Several weeks later, Bain arranged for a photocopy of the letter to be published in the magazine *Look* without first receiving permission for its publication from either the US president or Cardinal Mindszenty.[30] This indiscretion proved most embarrassing to the legation in Budapest, which was then required to make a series of explanations to the State Department in Washington. Moreover, Cardinal Mindszenty denied having shown anyone his letter to the president, which he claimed had been no more than a draft message.[31] Whatever the truth may be, there is no denying that it was thanks to Balogh Bain that Mindszenty's letter to President Eisenhower became known not only to the White House but also to the American public and, indeed, to people around the world. The name of the journalist was not recorded by Mindszenty in his memoirs: he deleted it from his manuscript on hearing that Balogh Bain was spreading the false report that the cardinal had spoken exclusively to him about how, among other things, he had been forced to watch naked orgies during his pretrial detention.[32]

Communication Shuttle

On November 16, 1956, at a leadership meeting of the Hungarian Socialist Workers' Party, which had been formed – under Soviet supervision – out of the ruins of the former communist party (the Hungarian Working People's Party), János Kádár, the country's new leader, who would remain an influential figure until 1989, noted how Mindszenty was "demanding [the restoration of] Imre Nagy's government" from the sanctuary of the US Legation.[33] Given the country's instability, this news was weakening Kádár's attempts to shore up his own legitimacy. To counter Mindszenty's

---

with József Mindszenty's message attached, November 11, 1956. For the contents of the memo, which was sent as a telegram, see Somorjai, *Mindszenty bíboros követségi levelei – Letters to the Presidents*, 427–28.

30. *Look* 20, no. 26, special Christmas edition (December 25, 1956): 23.

31. NARA RG 84, Records of the Foreign Service Posts of the Department of State, Hungary, Records Relating to Cardinal Mindszenty 1956–72, Box 1, Mindszenty–Classified 1956–June 1957, 570.3. Outgoing telegram no. 411 from the US mission in Budapest, December 8, 1956; Ibid., Mindszenty's handwritten note and its English translation, December 7, 1956.

32. MMAL 34. d. "Ispánky [!] Béla által átnézett fejezetek"; "Emlékiratok."

33. Sándor Balogh, et al. eds., *A Magyar Szocialista Munkáspárt ideiglenes vezető testületeinek jegyzőkönyvei, 1. 1956. november 11.–1957. január 14.* (Budapest: Intera Rt., 1993), 63. Minutes of the meeting of the Temporary Executive Committee of the HSWP, held on November 16, 1956.

influence, Kádár repeatedly misquoted the cardinal. For instance, on November 22, 1956, he stated the following to a reporter from the Romanian state news agency:

> Mindszenty elaborated the counter-revolutionary program and sought to liquidate the government of Imre Nagy. Mindszenty is the enemy of the democratic and social achievements; he is against land reform and factories owned by the people.[34]

These comments gave rise to the regime's main slander – that József Mindszenty was the principal counter-revolutionary (or at least one of the main counter-revolutionaries). Thereafter, there was no stopping the avalanche of increasingly irrational accusations. Just as in 1948, so too now – and for many subsequent decades – Mindszenty was branded an unrelenting collaborator of the fascists, the Arrow Cross, the imperialists, and the capitalists. In the eyes of the Kádár regime, Cardinal Mindszenty thus became the link between the "treacherous" government of Imre Nagy and capitalist imperialism.

Under such circumstances, the Americans grew justly concerned about the possibility of reprisals and provocations. The situation was aggravated by the fact that the new envoy Wailes had the status of a diplomatic "tourist": although he had received the *agrément* of the Hungarian authorities months earlier, he was refusing to submit his credentials to the country's new authorities in protest at the Soviet invasion.[35] As even an experienced diplomat might have found it difficult to explain away the violations of the neutrality that are a requirement of the status of asylum, the legation's staff members called on the Hungarian primate to exercise caution: he was told that he should not telephone, write or send messages to anyone.

Another consideration was the incompatibility of Mindszenty's "extraterritoriality" with the exercise of his rights and privileges as head of the Catholic Church in Hungary, given the United States' strong tradition of government non-interference in ecclesiastical and religious matters. In

34. Péter Magyar, "Magyar kommunista megnyilatkozások Mindszentyről a forradalom után," *Katolikus Szemle* 17, no. 2 (1965): 179.

35. Tamás Magyarics, "Az Egyesült Államok és Magyarország," *Századok* 130, no. 6 (1996): 573.

view of the separation of church and state, "American taxpayers should not be called upon to maintain a base for the exercise of the episcopal functions of any church."[36] While US public opinion supported the granting of refuge to Cardinal Mindszenty, who was viewed as a victim of communist oppression, the American people would have been very critical of their government if it had been shown to be assisting the cardinal in his personal or ecclesiastical affairs. For all these reasons, Mindszenty's work as head of the Catholic Church in Hungary came to an abrupt halt. Any letters and telegrams sent to him at the legation were returned by legation staff to the sender. Despite this measure, some messages did reach Mindszenty, and it would appear he responded to several of them. Consequently, the State Department issued new administrative restrictions covering his stay at the legation and expressly barring him from receiving visitors and from corresponding with the outside world.[37] This explains why Mindszenty, who had still been praising American hospitality on November 9,[38] wrote some days later that he was feeling the "thorns of asylum law."[39] Wailes felt something similar: "Our house guest is a most interesting and delightful person, but since having taken him on board, I now realize why the Department is most chary in granting asylum."[40] Evidently, the initial enthusiasm had given way to an awareness of the difficulties of confinement.

From then onwards, Mindszenty could only correspond with Washington and with the Vatican, albeit he could also undertake – subject to his letters being checked by legation personnel – private correspondence with family members. Concerning the letters to the Vatican, in early 1957 the US envoy in Budapest assured other diplomats that Cardinal Mindszenty

36. NARA RG 84, Department of State, Hungary, Subject Files Relating to Cardinal Mindszenty 1956–72, Box 1, Mindszenty–Classified 1956–June 1957. Letter of Robert M. McKisson, Office of Eastern Europeans Affairs, Department of State, to Chargé d'Affaires N. Spencer Barnes, April 26, 1957. Enclosure: *The Christian Century*, April 24, 1957.

37. Ibid., Incoming/outgoing telegrams nos. 350 and 411, December 7/8, 1956.

38. Ibid., Letter of József Mindszenty to Legate E. T. Wailes. Budapest, November 9, 1956.

39. Mindszenty, *Memoirs*, 218.

40. NARA RG 84, Records of the Foreign Service Posts of the Department of State, Hungary, Subject Files Relating to Cardinal Mindszenty 1956–72, Box 1, Mindszenty–Classified 1956–June 1957. Letter of Legate E. T. Wailes to Elim O'Shaughnessy, Acting Chargé d'Affaires in Bonn, January 17, 1957.

continued to correspond in the usual manner with the Holy See and the clergy, even though this was contrary to the conditions of his refuge at the legation.[41] Wailes also stated that Mindszenty was still seeking to raise an independent voice, for which reason his letters in Hungarian were being checked by legation personnel, while those in Latin – in the absence of the required language knowledge at the legation – were being examined by the State Department.[42] Meanwhile, the Vatican authorities denied once more that they were in receipt of letters or messages from Mindszenty.[43] Wailes, it seems, was not telling – or could not tell – the full truth. Although Mindszenty's letters in Latin were being sent to Washington, he failed to point out that they were not then being forwarded to Rome. Thus, although Mindszenty wrote several letters to Pius XII, none of them actually reached the pope.[44]

The letters in question caused no small headache for the US foreign affairs apparatus. Mindszenty had always been a fervent letter-writer. And now, given his incapacity to act in any other manner, how better could he serve his church and his nation? For his part, Wailes dutifully sent the letters to the State Department in Washington. He suggested that they be translated and then – if found to be "innocuous" – forwarded to the Vatican. If, however, "the letters contain matters of business, you may want to return them to me [...] and direct me to tell the Cardinal that we just can't send them to Rome."[45] The envoy classified as "harmless" any information relating to the personal fate of the cardinal, but he marked as "important" anything that was political in nature or related to his tasks as head of the Catholic Church in Hungary.

41. AMAE AD Série: Europe, 1956–1960, sous-série: Hongrie, dossier 101, Questions religieuses, janvier 1956–juin 1957, fol. 166. Incoming telegram no. 19, Budapest, January 5, 1957.

42. Ibid., fol. 167. Incoming telegram no. 78, Budapest, January 18, 1957.

43. Ibid., fol. 155. Report no. 894/EU of Roland de Margerie, December 21, 1956; Ibid., fol. 165. Incoming telegram no. 179–181, Vatican City, December 27, 1956. (They informed the American diplomats in Paris about the information acquired by the French diplomat.)

44. The original manuscripts of the letters – at least thirteen copies or rough drafts – can be found at the Archives of the Mindszenty Foundation in Hungary, in File 24: MFN 8162–8163, 8168–8170, 8174, 8176–8180, 8187, 8189. L-3110–3111, 3116–3118, 3122, 3214–3128, 3135, 3137.

45. Glennon et al., *Foreign Relations*, 1955–1957, vol. XXV, 1, 555. Document 227. Memorandum from the Deputy Assistant Secretary of State for European Affairs to the Deputy Under Secretary of State for Political Affairs. Washington, January 24, 1957. On the Internet: https://history.state.gov/historicaldocuments/frus1955-57v25/d227.

The State Department apparatus reviewed the situation and drew three conclusions:

> 1. If these six letters are transmitted they will probably be followed by more and thus the Department's pouch facilities would tend to become a regular channel of covert communication between the Vatican and the Cardinal. Written records of this nature, if inadvertently revealed or "leaked" to the press or to the church hierarchy, would cause us embarrassment and might compromise our Legation and prejudice the Cardinal's safety. 2. Whether the current letters or any which may follow constitute "conduct of business" cannot be determined until they are translated and read. If they are read, the Department is immediately placed in the position of censoring the Cardinal's correspondence on the basis of criteria which will be difficult to define clearly and equally difficult to justify to the Cardinal and the Vatican. 3. It must also be anticipated that if letters from the Cardinal are sent to the Pope, the Vatican will logically expect the privilege of replying via the same channel. The Department might then be faced with the necessity of scanning and possibly rejecting messages from the Pope.[46]

The State Department's dilemma well illustrates the difficulties typically faced by diplomats – who must give attention to every detail and consider all potential pitfalls. In the end, the decision was taken not to forward Cardinal Mindszenty's letters to the Vatican. Still, the State Department had no wish to prevent all contact between the Hungarian primate and the pope. It therefore offered to forward short oral messages of a personal nature, thereby hoping to limit the volume and frequency of communication. As the messages were to be oral ones, the State Department could discover their content without evoking the unpleasantness of formal censorship. In effect, the State Department's decision ended Mindszenty's contact with the outside world. During the following decade and a half, the US administration's consistent position was that Cardinal Mindszenty could not use the Legation as an ecclesiastical or political operational base, as neither field of activity fell under humanitarian assistance.

46. Ibid.

In consequence of these developments, during his long sojourn at the legation, the Hungarian primate had barely any contact with Pius XII or John XXIII. A refreshing exception was a letter he received in 1962 from Egidio Vagnozzi, Apostolic Delegate in Washington, in which Vagnozzi forwarded the blessing and greeting of John XXIII on the occasion of Mindszenty's seventieth birthday. Despite its strict controls, the State Department classified the letter, which was inadvertently dated a day later than the actual birthday, as deliverable.[47] A favorable advance – in terms of opportunities for contact between Mindszenty and the Holy See – came in the spring of 1963, when the Americans concluded that their guest's situation could not be resolved without input from the Holy See.

A similar decision was taken in the matter of Mindszenty's letters to the US president, the secretary of state and other members of the administration. With a view to preventing regular correspondence, Cardinal Mindszenty was to be given short oral responses (mostly acknowledgements of receipt). The aim in Washington was to prevent the opening of even the narrowest channel of communication and the generation of further correspondence. Despite such limits, Mindszenty relentlessly wrote to all the presidents and secretaries of state. Indeed, from the legation he sent twenty-four letters to Dwight D. Eisenhower, twenty letters to John F. Kennedy, twenty-four letters to Lyndon B. Johnson, and four letters to Richard Nixon.[48] The correspondence was almost completely one-way, as he received no more than two written replies: one from Kennedy after his inauguration as president in 1961 and one from Nixon in 1971. In the latter, Nixon sought to persuade Mindszenty to consider leaving the legation. For

47. NARA RG 59, GR of the Department of State, Bureau of European Affairs, Office of Eastern European Affairs, Records Relating to Hungary 1941–77, Box 11, Refuge Part Four, 1962. Letter of Harold C. Vedeler to Chargé d'Affaires Horace G. Torbert, Jr., April 4, 1962. Enclosure: Letter no. 293/49 of E. Vagnozzi, Apostolic Delegate, of March 30, 1962.

48. For these letters, see Ádám Somorjai and Tibor Zinner, *Do Not Forget This Small Honest Nation: Cardinal Mindszenty to 4 US Presidents and State Secretaries 1956–1971 as conserved in American Archives and commented by American diplomats* (Bloomington, IN: Xlibris Corporation, 2013). – Having left the US diplomatic mission, Mindszenty wrote further letters to President Nixon, and he received from Nixon at least two letters, one marking his 80th birthday in 1972 and the other at the time of his first visit to the United States in 1973. See Richard Nixon Presidential Library and Museum (Yorba Linda, California) (hereafter: Nixon Library), National Security Council (NSC) Files, Name Files, Box 828, Mindszenty, Cardinal (April 70–May 74) 3613. and NSC Files, Presidential Correspondence 1969–74, Box 755.

his part, President Eisenhower chose not to reply in writing to any of Mindszenty's letters, not even to the first one, in which the Hungarian primate had expressed sincere gratitude for American hospitality. As the then head of the State Department's Bureau of European Affairs later recalled, "The interesting part of it is that Eisenhower was angry because Mindszenty wrote him a letter every week."[49] Eisenhower's irritation is understandable: while he may not have been receiving a letter every week, the following is an extract from the third letter Mindszenty sent him within a six-month period requesting US assistance for his country:

> I beseech you to hasten the liberation of Hungary, and until this takes place, to find some means for alleviating our unbearable lot.[50] On another occasion he wrote: I beg of you, Mr. President, before our country is destroyed, that after an exhaustive inquiry, something be done about this valley of blood and misery. Do not permit the Hungarian land to become an inheritance of some Marxist concept as the result of a solution suspended in mid-air – a land which you, Mr. President, and the world have called a glorious land of freedom.[51]

When Mindszenty wrote of his refuge status or of his personal well-being, the US bureaucrats seem at least to have noted his concerns. They refused, however, to react to his political conclusions or to his conflict with the Hungarian communist regime, which was a recurrent issue throughout the fifteen-year stay at the legation. Whereas in 1957 they had been willing to inform him about developments at the United Nations relating to the "Hungarian question," in subsequent years even this topic was off limits. The barrier to correspondence meant that Mindszenty could not expect a reply from the US president or from the secretary of state and his staff. The task of explaining the various arguments to Mindszenty was left to the

49. Oral History Interview with Jacob D. Beam by Niel M. Johnson. Washington D. C. June 20, 1989. On the Internet: www.trumanlibrary.org/oralhist/beamjw.htm.

50. NARA RG 84, Department of State. Hungary, Records Relating to Cardinal Mindszenty 1956–72, Box 1, Mindszenty–Classified 1956–June 1957. Letter of József Mindszenty to President Eisenhower, May 4, 1957.

51. Ibid., Mindszenty–Classified July–Dec 1957. Letter of József Mindszenty to President Eisenhower, December 19, 1957.

diplomats in Budapest. Although they made countless attempts, the Hungarian primate stubbornly refused to accept what he considered to be purely bureaucratic considerations. As time passed, it seems he concluded that fear of the Soviets explained why the Americans were treating him so "poorly." As one diplomat noted,

> He will, of course, never understand (and I cannot explain to him) that we are not 'afraid of the Soviets,' but we have many in the US who would be extremely critical if there were the slightest suspicion he might be exercising either political or ecclesiastical functions from this Legation.[52]

The ban on visits applied to everyone, including the Hungarian Catholic prelates. Dulles himself noted the instruction that was given to the head of the diplomatic mission in Budapest: "Visits or communication by Hungarian ecclesiastical representatives cannot be permitted in present circumstances."[53] When Robert F. Kennedy, the younger brother of the man who was later to become president, expressed a wish to travel to Hungary as a journalist working for the *Boston Globe*, the legation received a special instruction: "In our view, he should under no circumstances be allowed access to the Cardinal for any purpose."[54]

Naturally, over the years, many exceptions were made. Thus, Mindszenty could receive his confessor priest, his sisters, several relatives, a barber (the main source of gossip), an American physician from Belgrade, and one or two diplomats. One of the first visitors was a member of staff from the French diplomatic mission, who saw him on November 26, 1956. The French diplomat concluded that although Mindszenty was clearly saddened by the turn of events, he was in good physical and mental health.[55] Every

52. Ibid., Mindszenty–Classified 1960. Letter of Chargé D'Affaires Garret G. Ackerson to Robert M. McKisson, Office of Eastern European Affairs, Department of State, July 6, 1960.

53. Ibid., Mindszenty–Classified 1956–June 1957. 570.3. Incoming telegram no. 782 from the State Department to the US mission in Budapest, April 26, 1957.

54. Ibid., Mindszenty–Classified 1959. Letter of Robert M. McKisson to Garret G. Ackerson, December 17, 1959.

55. AMAE AD Série: Europe, 1956–1960, sous-série: Hongrie, dossier 101, Questions religieuses, janvier 1956–juin 1957, fol. 107. Incoming telegram no. 825/826 from Legate Jean Paul-Boncour, Budapest, November 26, 1956.

three months or so, Mindszenty's mother was permitted to stay for a few days at the legation. The first such visit took place between Christmas and New Year's Eve in 1956.

ASYLUM PROSPECTS

The first seven years of Mindszenty's stay at the legation (1956–63) marked a low-point in Hungarian–US relations. Despite the prohibition on Mindszenty's contacting the outside world and even though the legation was protected under international law from intrusions and searches by the Hungarian authorities, the State Department was fearful – at least until the late spring or summer of 1957 – that violence or other provocations might be employed against its diplomatic mission. A specific fear was that Hungary's communist regime might stage a mass demonstration outside the legation, during which the crowd would initially demand the peaceful surrender of Mindszenty and then forcibly enter the mission and drag the Hungarian primate away.[56]

To Stay Put or to Leave?

At 10.30 a.m. on November 6, 1956, the legation received a telegram from Washington stating that, according to radio news reports, Russian soldiers had removed Cardinal Mindszenty from the building. The State Department inquired "What is situation?"[57] Denying the veracity of the report, Wailes stated that there had been no attempt to remove the Hungarian primate from his legation. Everyone at the legation simply could not imagine voluntarily surrendering Mindszenty, who would then suffer further years in prison or even death. In the event of coercion, "we have prepared in English and Russian a note of protest signed by both Barnes and myself.

56. NARA RG 59, GR of the Department of State, Bureau of European Affairs, Office of Eastern European Affairs, Records Relating to Hungary 1941–77, Box 10, Refuge Part I, 1956–57 (1971). Memorandum, Asylum for Cardinal Mindszenty, November 7, 1956.

57. NARA RG 84, Records of the Foreign Service Posts of the Department of State, Hungary, Records Relating to Cardinal Mindszenty 1956–72, Box 1, Mindszenty–Classified 1956–June 1957, 570.3. Telegram no. 207 from Herbert C. Hoover, under-secretary of state, to the US mission in Budapest, November 6, 1956.

We shall insist upon presence of senior Sov[iet] officer."[58] Wailes gave no further details about how the legation might react if such a statement of protest were to be ignored. Evidently, staff at the legation would have had little option but to be passive onlookers. The means available to diplomats do not include physical resistance.

As well as fearing an anti-Mindszenty protest, the legation's staff also anticipated an official extradition request from Hungary. The American side well understood that, from the Hungarian perspective, Mindszenty's being granted refuge at the legation was unlawful. Even an internal US review had concluded that the granting of refuge to Cardinal Mindszenty constituted an unusual exception (the same gesture had been denied to Béla Kovács, former general-secretary of the Independent Smallholders' Party). A statement issued by the State Department on November 21, contained a short official explanation of the US position:

> The Government of the United States has instructed this Legation to refuse any demand to surrender Cardinal Mindszenty. Any question relating to the refuge afforded to Cardinal Mindszenty should be the subject of communication between the United States Legation and the Ministry of Foreign Affairs.[59]

The timing of the statement was barely coincidental. It was around this time that the Hungarian leadership gave a secret written assurance of its earlier oral pledge to refrain from taking any measures against Imre Nagy and his associates (who had fled to the Yugoslav Embassy) and, indeed, to guarantee their safety. This reassurance, however, did not even mention Mindszenty. To resolve the difficulty, Wailes – who still gave credence to the Hungarian assurances concerning Imre Nagy – proposed that Mindszenty be treated in a similar manner.[60] Evidently, he would not have made this proposal if he had known that despite their assurances the Hungarian authorities would subsequently seize Imre Nagy and his associates as they made their way home from the Yugoslav Embassy. We know that smooth-

58. Ibid., Telegram no. 241 from Legate E. T. Wailes to the State Department, November 6, 1956.

59. Ibid., Telegram no. 265 from the US State Department, November 21, 1956.

60. Ibid., Outgoing telegram no. 336, Budapest, November 23, 1956.

talking their way into apprehending the Hungarian primate would not have been alien to the Soviet secret services. Indeed, the sources reveal that an unidentified Soviet agent had been given the task of persuading Mindszenty to flee the legation. Were Mindszenty to accept this offer, he was to be arrested once outside the diplomatic mission. The plan was elaborated by none other than General Ivan A. Serov, the infamous chief of the Soviet security agency, the KGB. From Budapest, he reported on the plan to Nikita Khrushchev on November 27, 1956.[61]

It is possible that the US Embassy in Austria encountered the story of this Soviet agent. One of the embassy reports mentions how an individual named Lajos Nagy drew attention to himself at the Stockerau refugee camp by claiming to be a representative of Soviet intelligence. The man asserted that he had long been a confidant of Mindszenty. When the Soviets had arrested Lajos Nagy and threatened him with deportation to Siberia, he had accepted their fiendish offer: to persuade Cardinal Mindszenty into signing up as a Soviet agent in return for a promise of freedom. On November 27, Nagy had indeed gone to the legation and had spoken with the envoy, who, however, had refused him access to Mindszenty, while permitting him to write in a letter what the Soviets were requesting. Having read Nagy's letter, Cardinal Mindszenty had allegedly asked him to deliver a message to the Vatican, whereupon Nagy had left the country.[62] The man's story seems more than comical, if we are to imagine Mindszenty as a recruited Soviet agent. Yet, in view of the many unscrupulous means employed by the Soviet security agency, perhaps the story is not so comical after all. The image of Mindszenty would have been irrevocably destroyed if a document outing him as a Russian agent had been published in the world press. Still, those who believed in the plan's successful implementation were obviously ignorant of Mindszenty's personality and character. Indeed, even the most

61. Hoover Institution Archives, fond 89, finding aids 45, delo (file) 53. Mikrofilm. Telegram message from Ivan Serov to Nikita Khrushchev. November 27, 1956. (Serov also informed three other members of the CPSU CC.) For a transcript of the telegram, see T. Sereda and S. Stikalin, eds., *Sovetskiy Soyuz i vengerskiy krizis 1956 goda: Dokumenty* (Moscow: ROSSPEN, 2008), 704.

62. NARA RG 84, Records of the Foreign Service Posts of the Department of State, Hungary, Subject Files Relating to Cardinal Mindszenty 1956–72, Box 1, Mindszenty–Classified 1956–June 1957. Alleged Soviet Attempt to Implicate Cardinal Mindszenty (Alfred Puhan, first secretary of American Embassy), Vienna, April 5, 1957.

cunning of secret agents would have failed to persuade him to sign up. Some aspects of the story were confirmed by the legation in Budapest. A staff member reported that the man had indeed visited the legation, but that he had met with neither Mindszenty nor Wailes. And while the staff member acknowledged that the man had given him a greeting card for Cardinal Mindszenty, he also stated that the card had been destroyed in the presence of this provocateur. When the staff member had subsequently mentioned the visitor to Mindszenty, the Hungarian cardinal had struggled to identify the man – who had claimed to be his ex-butler. In the staff member's view, the Hungarian primate had certainly not entrusted the man with any specific information.[63]

Mindszenty's departure from the US Legation or his staying put were both possible scenarios from the day one. In fact, theoretically speaking, there were three possible options: 1) to remain at the legation; 2) to leave the building and surrender himself to the Hungarian authorities – which implied a renewed prison term; and 3) to leave the country with a letter of safe conduct, which would have required the consent of the Kádár government. In early 1957, citing a reliable informer, Wailes, the US envoy, reported to Washington that in the event of Mindszenty's departure abroad, the Hungarian security service would agree not to harm him. If, on the other hand, Mindszenty were to leave the legation but remain in the country, he would immediately be detained. Wailes expressed doubt that the Hungarian primate could be persuaded to leave the country voluntarily.[64] Among the various options, the idea of Mindszenty's secret evacuation was also raised. Evidently, the Americans would have welcomed his departure from the legation. Although they considered an evacuation to be feasible, they nevertheless recognized the extent of the risks: the success of the plan would depend on the full cooperation of the main actor, which, however, could not be guaranteed. This was the plan's key weakness.[65] In

63. Ibid., Memorandum from Geza Katona, a US Legation employee, to Chargé d'Affaires N. Spencer Barnes, May 3, 1957.

64. Ibid., Outgoing telegram no. 525 from Legate E. T. Wailes to the State Department, January 10, 1957.

65. NARA RG 59, GR of the Department of State. CDF 1960–63, Box 2681, 864.413/11–1760, Doc. no. 3–3161. Letter of H. G. Torbert, Jr. Chargé d'Affaires in Budapest, to H. C. Vedeler, Director of the Office of Eastern European Affairs, Department of State, March 31, 1961; Somorjai and Zinner, *Do Not Forget*, 126–30.

Wailes's view, the best policy was to continue the chosen strategy until the coming to power of a government that could credibly guarantee Mindszenty's freedom. If, however, the Hungarian primate chose to "simply" leave the legation, then "We would, of course, seek to obtain a written statement that he was leaving of his own will and that the right of asylum had not been withdrawn by the legation."[66] The possibility of Mindszenty leaving the legation was a matter of interest even in East Asia. At a reception, the Japanese journalist Joneo Sakai – one of the most influential Asian journalists accredited to the White House – inquired of the Hungarian ambassador to the United States whether his government would object to Mindszenty leaving the country for Japan. The ambassador then told the journalist "once he has left the country, it would be indifferent to us on which continent he settles."[67]

Naturally, Mindszenty himself was concerned what might happen to him if Soviet soldiers were to storm the legation and kidnap him. He feared for his life. Such concerns appear to have inspired him to formulate his intellectual testament – a testamentary will – to the Hungarian nation.[68] Albeit full of pathos, the thoughts and ideas in the document were clearly sincere, as they were expressed in the shadow of the nation's tragedy and amid the sound of canon fire. Figuratively, Mindszenty bowed his head to the revolutionaries who had sacrificed their lives for the cause and idea of an independent and sovereign Hungary. His wish was to leave a legacy of loyalty, faith, and love of liberty. He condemned the Soviet Union's aggression and its "servants with Hungarian names," while calling for passive national resistance rather than violence. As executors of his will, he named Pius XII and US President Eisenhower, the two men who – in his view – were "the most suited" to this task.

The Vatican made no response to the "stay or go" question. Some voiced the opinion that "Cardinal Mindszenty's presence at the US Legation is so

66. NARA RG 84, Foreign Service Posts of the Department of State, Hungary, Records Relating to Cardinal Mindszenty 1956–1972, Box 1, Mindszenty–Classified July–Dec 1957. Report of Garret G. Ackerson, Chargé d'Affaires, to James S. Sutterlin, Hungarian Desk Officer at the Office of Eastern European Affairs, Department of State, August 21, 1957.

67. MNL OL XIX–J–29–a–KÜM, Washington, TÜK-documents 1945–64, 11. d. Report of Tibor Zádor, Acting Chargé d'Affaires, Hungarian Legation in Washington, D.C. May 30, 1957.

68. MMAL 026. dosszié, Testamentary will. Budapest (US Legation), November 6, 1956. For an English translation of the document, see Somorjai and Zinner, *Do Not Forget*, XV–XVI.

regrettable that it would be better if the prelate would leave Hungary," while others argued that from the perspective of canon law and public expectations of a prelate, rather than in terms of Hungarian constitutional or public legal requirements, Mindszenty's departure from Hungary would be a devastating blow.[69] This latter position was the majority view at the Vatican until 1962 when preparations were made for the Second Vatican Council. The dominant view was one of *wait and see.* Indeed, for a decade and a half, whether Mindszenty should stay or go was considered his own personal decision. For reasons of security and principle, the Hungarian primate decided to remain in Hungary.

Conserving His Refugee Status

Even while it clearly disliked the situation, the Kádár government made few real efforts to change it. Ultimately, the regime did not regret that Mindszenty was held "captive" at the legation, for the situation meant that it was freed from having to initiate legal proceedings against him, which inevitably would have added to his reputation as a martyr. Although some in the regime might have been inclined towards taking a more forceful stand, the majority position was that – in place of vengeance – an effort should be made to utilize Mindszenty's captivity. Moreover, the Hungarian primate's presence at the legation doubtless helped ensure that despite undeniable tensions, US–Hungarian relations were not broken off entirely, but were "merely" reduced to chargé d'affaires level until 1966.

In the meantime, the regime pursued a hybrid policy of ambitious pledges coupled with retribution. On November 15, 1956, János Kádár was still promising to hold free elections. Merely a week and a half later, however, a wave of arrests took place. It rapidly became clear that the ecclesiastical policy strategy of the old-new political establishment remained unchanged: It aimed to steadily diminish the role of religion in society and of its organizational framework – the churches. Still, even the government recognized the benefit of temporarily suppressing the role

69. AMAE AD Série: Europe, 1956–1960, sous-série: Hongrie, dossier 101, Questions religieuses, janvier 1956–juin 1957. fol. 150. Telegram no. 386/EU from Étienne Manac'h, head of the Eastern European Department of the French Ministry of Foreign Affairs, to the ambassador of the Holy See, December 10, 1956.

of the unpopular State Office for Church Affairs. As a first step, the Presidential Council abolished – as of December 31, 1956 – the autonomy of the State Office for Church Affairs, which until early 1959 operated as a department of the Ministry of Culture and Education. True though, there were no personnel changes and the competences remained roughly the same. On January 6, 1957, János Kádár, Chairman of the Council of Ministers, announced a new program: complete loyalty to the Soviet Union in foreign policy, freedom of worship and of religious education in domestic policy, and collectivization in agriculture. The gloss soon wore off. And it was not long before the ministerial commissioners – referred to as "moustached bishops" – returned to the episcopal offices, where they once again checked up and reported on everything. On March 20, 1957, a law-decree (No. 22 of 1957) on state approval for the filling of certain ecclesiastical posts came into force. The new piece of legislation essentially replaced a similar provision from 1951, which, however, had been less strict. Under the new provisions, the approval of the state was required not only for appointments to the posts of archbishop, bishop, abbot, or provincial but also for the appointment of theological professors or principals of church secondary schools. Even transfers and dismissals were made subject to the state's approval. Subsequently, for a period of many years, no new bishops were appointed. The absence of new bishops resulted in grave operational problems. This explains why the appointment of bishops became such a key issue in negotiations between the Vatican and Hungary, which were commenced in 1963. The issue was "settled" in a fashion by the partial agreement of 1964. The stringent provisions of the 1957 decree were diluted only in 1971, a development that was linked with the departure of Mindszenty from the US Embassy in that year.

The fate of Cardinal Mindszenty was unfavorably influenced by the decision (February 21, 1957) of the 11th session of the UN General Assembly to take no action on Hungarian credentials (thus refusing either to reject or approve them). In response, on the following day, the government in Budapest called upon Wailes to submit his credentials (which would have amounted to a quasi-official recognition of the Hungarian government). As Wailes was still unwilling to take this step, he had no option but to leave Hungary. As a further consequence of these developments, on March 9 the Hungarian regime officially announced that the earlier judgment against

Mindszenty was still in force. In other words, if he were to leave the legation building, he would then be required to resume his prison sentence. For this reason, Mindszenty "could no longer perform an ecclesiastical function" and the execution of any of his decrees would count as a criminal offense against the laws of the state.[70] By means of this declaration, the regime wished to annul the legal force of the decisions made by Mindszenty in his capacity as archbishop of Esztergom in November 1956. Those decisions had been aimed at removing peace priests who collaborated with the regime. The announcement was a landmark decision in terms of Cardinal Mindszenty's subsequent status and fate. From then onwards, in the regime's view, he was no more than a fugitive prisoner residing on foreign territory. We shall never know whether the threat to make the Hungarian primate resume his prison term was an empty one. What was clear, however, was that the Hungarian government had no intention of taking proactive measures in the matter.

After this decision, the Americans had no choice but to arrange for a lengthy period of giving hospitality to Mindszenty. During the six months since his arrival at the legation, Mindszenty had received assistance from a member of the legation staff. In the aftermath of the Hungarian government's statement, the member of staff summarized his experiences and proposals, noting which issues and subject matters would require attention in the future. This summary report offers rare insights into the everyday work of staff members at a diplomatic mission. For this reason, Geza Katona's report is cited at length in the following:

> 1. Purchase, or requisition of sufficient bed linen (sheets and pillowcases), bath towels, and small tablecloths to provide a weekly change and laundry. (At the present time, these materials are being furnished from my own household, but if I should leave the local scene, some other arrangement would have to be made.) This function is logically an administrative matter.
> 2. Supervising the cleaning of the Cardinal's bedroom, change in bed linen, condition of toilet supplies, laundry of clothing. (The Legation charwomen usually come in once a week to do the cleaning, but they require someone to be on hand for physical security reasons.)

70. MNL OL XIX–A–21–d–0013/1957, and MNL OL XIX–A–21–e–107/1957/Eln. 2. ő. e. Statement on József Mindszenty's condition.

3. Checking on stock of other items used by the Cardinal, such as candles, wafers, and wine for ecclesiastical ceremonies – and seeing that sufficient supply of vitamin pills, fresh fruit, cigars, etc. are always on hand. (Since this requires a closer contact and a daily check, I can continue to look after these items.)
4. Demands placed on me for numerous research in books and for secretarial type jobs usually keep me occupied for varying periods each day. I have tried to point out by hints to the Cardinal that I have other duties to perform also, but this tactic has not worked too effectively. I have finally resorted to postponing some of his work until he asks for it two or three times, hoping to give him the impression that his work is only a side issue with me. This, too, has not been entirely effective. I try to stay out of his sight and out of his room as much as possible, going in once each during morning and afternoon hours to deliver the daily newspapers or set his radio for him. Since he maintains a small storage space in an extra desk in my office, he feels free to come in to see me frequently. Lacking others to converse with, he naturally takes such opportunities to express his thoughts or to make a request for some additional information or favor. (I am at a loss in coping with this situation, for the Cardinal has the impression that I am on hand to act as his 'handy man' or private secretary during his stay here. I suppose we'll just have to become adjusted to these extra demands on my time, unless we can get another Hungarian-speaking officer on board to share such work.)
5. Items which will be given attention in the near future:
a) Storing of his winter garb. This requires cleaning, moth-proofing, etc.
b) In order to keep a fresh supply of fruit on hand for the Cardinal's consumption, I believe we can circulate a note among staff officers, asking them to bring back a small amount of bananas, oranges, lemons, etc., any time any of them go to Vienna. I'll make arrangements to reimburse them for such expenses from our special fund.[71]

The report shows that everyday problems had to be addressed and sometimes individual requests had to be met, alongside the usual requirements

71. NARA RG 59, GR of the Department of State, Bureau of European Affairs, Office of Eastern European Affairs, Records Relating to Hungary 1941–77, Box 10, Refuge Part I, 1956–57 (1971). Memo on the discussions, May 16, 1957.

of the daily routine. And, of course, everything cost money. On average, the cost of looking after the cardinal was two dollars and fifty cents per day. Although the Americans living in Hungary would doubtless have agreed to cover these costs, the bill was met initially by the State Department and then by the National Catholic Welfare Council (a body established by American bishops in 1919) and by private US citizens.[72] The sum covered the cost of three meals served in Mindszenty's room, two cigars daily, wine for the weekly mass, laundry expenses, and utilities. The Hungarian primate regularly took a multivitamin tablet and, in the fall and winter months, he often used a sun lamp. A daily bottle of beer or, during cooler weather, a glass of wine counted as an extra. Another challenge was arranging for Mindszenty to be seen by a physician. His teeth also required attention, as he had been denied a toothbrush during his prison years. While the legation had access to aspirin and clove oil, the proper technical equipment was unavailable. The legation staff made efforts to find a portable dental drill that could be plugged into an electric socket, for the cardinal could not simply be taken to a local dental surgery. The necessary equipment had to be brought in and assembled on site.[73] Mindszenty's other expenses (clothing and medicines) amounted to an average annual sum of a thousand dollars. This sum was covered by the NCWC using a special confidential fund. Cardinal Mindszenty also had a small amount of personal spending money, coming from the United States for Mass intentions. He gave the money to his sisters or to his confessor.[74] Making these gifts made him feel useful. Indeed, helping people by offering them a modest donation gave him strength.

72. NARA RG 84, Records of the Foreign Service Posts of the Department of State, Hungary, Records Relating to Cardinal Mindszenty 1956–1972, Box 1, Mindszenty–Classified 1956–June 1957. Letter to the envoy "Paul," November 4, 1956; Ibid., letter of Legate E. T. Wailes to Jacob D. Beam, Deputy Director of the Bureau of European Affairs, December 12, 1956. (According to information revealed some time later, the cost of accommodating Cardinal Mindszenty at the US mission was USD 160,000 per year. The figure seems an exaggerated one. Perhaps the informer mistook an amount in Hungarian forints for a sum in US dollars. See MNL OL XIX–J–1–j–IV–14/1960–63/k. n. 1963. Vatikán TÜK-documents, 2. d. Memo of the Press Department of the Hungarian Ministry of Foreign Affairs on a conversation with István Swift Somlyó, chairman of the University Lectures Series, April 30, 1963.)

73. Ibid., Mindszenty–Classified July–Dec 1957. Letter of Geza A. Katona to Joseph B. Johnston, an American physician in Bucharest, October 11, 1957.

74. Ibid., Box 2. Cardinal File – Limited Distribution 1962–64. Memorandum of the retiring chargé d'affaires, H. G. Torbert, Jr., December 4, 1962.

Other than on days when Mindszenty received a rare visitor, his time spent on the third floor of the legation building was rather monotonous. In his room, he would read books or write letters to presidents, government ministers, state secretaries, and the pope. The head of the US mission characterized his mood and circumstances as follows:

> The fact of the matter is, of course, that he leads a very circumscribed and frustrated life. He cannot be expected to be always in the best of humor. In point of fact, he is remarkably patient and even tempered. He does, however, have a misconception of his position as a 'guest' in the Legation and of his relations with the Department, the Secretary, and the President. No useful purpose would be served by trying (any more than has already been done) to change his understanding of the situation. He is a pretty determined old man and does not easily change his ideas.[75]

Self-Sacrifice

In his letters, Mindszenty focused on the aftermath of the revolution, on the historical injustices suffered by the country, on the peace treaties concluding the two world wars, on the circumstances of the Hungarian minorities in the ceded territories, on the Soviet invasion, on the failure of the United Nations to send a peace-keeping force, on the retribution practiced by the illegitimate Kádár regime, on the fate of youths deported to the Soviet Union, on the abuses of the system of martial law, and on the increasing number of death sentences and subsequent executions. In almost every letter, he touched upon an issue that was of concern to the entire Hungarian nation or to the Hungarian minorities in the neighboring countries. Some of the problems were limited to Hungary, while others pertained to the entire East Central European region. He detailed the human rights violations and the various forms of abuse and demanded the practical application of humanitarian principles, the abolition of the forced labor camps, and the return to Hungary of the prisoners-of-war. His style

75. Ibid., Box 1. Mindszenty–Classified July–Dec 1957. Letter of Garret G. Ackerson, Acting Chargé d'Affaires, to James S. Sutterlin, Hungarian Desk Officer, Office of Eastern European Affairs, November 21, 1957.

of writing was pompous and excessively emotional. His view of events had not changed: he continued to blame the godless Soviets and communists for Hungary's problems.

His inexperience of diplomacy meant that he brusquely listed his demands: an end to foreign (Soviet) aggression and a "correction" of the terms of the Treaty of Trianon (1920) and the Paris Peace Treaty (1947). In his conversations, he explained several times how the Treaty of Trianon had so weakened Hungary in the interwar period that the country had been incapable of resisting Nazi Germany's demands. There is no denying that if the country's natural borders had been upheld in 1920, Hungary, as a more resistant economic and political power, might have played a far more important role in the region as a bulwark against both Bolshevism and Nazism. This, in turn, might have completely altered the course of European history in the 1930s.

The cardinal did not temper his criticism of the neighboring countries. Over time, therefore, even the more patient of the American diplomats came to regard him as chauvinistic and irredentist.[76] In view of Mindszenty's revisionist ideas concerning the peace treaties, the diplomats became increasingly convinced that the decision to severely restrict Mindszenty's communication with the outside world had been correct. As Jordan T. Rogers, first secretary of the US Legation, concluded,

> Unless his views were to modify, in my opinion, his influence in a free Hungary would be more ultra-nationalist rather than internationalist. His mind, however, is by no means set as it has sometimes been pictured.[77]

At the same time, Rogers acknowledged that Mindszenty's mind had doubtless been affected by the eight years he had spent in prison.

Cardinal Mindszenty repeatedly returned to the fate of the revolutionaries of 1956. He was profoundly upset to learn of the execution, on December 10, 1957, of Antal Pálinkás (Pallavicini), the army officer who had accompanied him to Budapest. Pálinkás, it seemed, had been executed

76. Ibid., Mindszenty–Classified 1960. Memorandum for Brig. Gen. A. J. Goodpaster, July 20, 1960.

77. Ibid., Mindszenty–Classified July–Dec 1957. Memo on the discussion between Cardinal Mindszenty and Jordan Thomas Rogers, first secretary at the Legation, May 1957.

as a symbolic figure of the counter-revolutionary aristocracy. Mindszenty was so affected by the dramatic news that he offered to bear any accusation and punishment in political cases where a defendant, whether priest or layman, was accused of having obeyed him or having shown loyalty to him. This, he made clear, would not signal his recognition of the lawfulness of the proceedings.[78] Evidently, his offer was an attempt to make amends for having abandoned the revolutionaries. In this way, the dilemma of whether to stay or leave was raised to the moral level, in view of his willingness to sacrifice himself for the sake of rescuing the innocents – an action Mindszenty hoped would shake up the world. As a legation staff member observed, Mindszenty supplemented all this with an appeal to public law: "He is the constitutionally legal agent of government at this time" as the continuity of law in Hungary was broken with the German invasion of 1944, and "he cannot stand by."[79]

This was one of the first occasions during his stay at the US Legation when Mindszenty referred to his public legal role as primate. Embassy staff were baffled by his arguments. Previously, Mindszenty had spoken in mere general terms of the future tasks. Now, however, he cited his constitutional role, his historical rights and his duty to lead the country as knight banneret. The Americans were completely thrown by this latter element. Such a course might have been open to a political asylum seeker, but it was not a possibility for Mindszenty, who had sought refuge because his life was at risk – which is how the Americans were treating him. Meanwhile, Mindszenty requested that his offer be forwarded to the Hungarian Ministry of Foreign Affairs, but the US side categorically dismissed this possibility, arguing that it would not help the defendants but would cause harm both to the legation and to the cardinal. Mindszenty sadly acknowledged the rejection of his offer. Having received no counsel as to whether it would be more beneficial for him to surrender to the Hungarian authorities and resume his prison sentence or to continue to live in solitude at the embassy, he fell into apathy and indifference. For a long time, he wavered between the two options.

78. Ibid., Mindszenty–Classified 1958, 570.3. Telegram no. 365 from G. G. Ackerson, acting chargé d'affaires, to Secretary of State Dulles, January 10, 1958.

79. Ibid., Memo from Louis Toplosky, second secretary at the legation, to Chargé d'Affaires G. G. Ackerson. January 10, 1958.

With a view to obtaining international recognition and to improving domestic political stability and the chances of realizing its new economic policy, the Kádár regime replaced its overtly anticlerical stance with a people's front policy that prioritized "national unity." This new policy was announced in a decree of the HSWP CC, issued on July 22, 1958. A month earlier (on June 17, 1958), world public opinion had been shocked to learn of the execution – on June 16 – of both Imre Nagy, the man who had been prime minister at the time of the revolution, and his associates. At the time, the Vatican authorities began to have serious concerns about the fate of Mindszenty. Consultations about a possible rescue mission were held with the governments of the United States, West Germany, and Austria, with the latter pledging to grant the Hungarian cardinal political asylum. Experts on Eastern Europe were agreed, however, that Mindszenty would not be sentenced to death, as death sentences were given exclusively to former communist "turn-coats" as a means of intimidating the internal party opposition.

These were the circumstances prevailing when news broke of the death of Pope Pius XII on October 9, 1958. The election of Pius XII's successor represented the first real opportunity for a speedy and painless resolution of Mindszenty's situation, as he was required by canon law to take part in the papal conclave. The opportunity presented by the conclave was recognized by staff at the US diplomatic mission in the Vatican. They began conciliating with Vatican officials without first obtaining the prior consent of the State Department. The College of Cardinals debated the matter on October 13, 1958. The next day a written invitation to Cardinal Mindszenty was issued and dispatched to the US Legation in Budapest. This form of invitation is not stipulated by canon law and perhaps it should have been avoided on this occasion too, as a hurtful error was made: Mindszenty's first name was written as István rather than as József... Irrespective of this error, the College of Cardinals evidently viewed the conclave as an excellent opportunity to resolve the question of Cardinal Mindszenty's asylum. Moreover, the cardinals seem also to have accepted that the United States was uniquely able to initiate talks on Mindszenty's departure from Hungary. It mentioned two conditions that would cause it to welcome Mindszenty's traveling to Rome: "1. That he be given absolute personal security in leaving

Hungary; and 2. that he do so of his own free will."[80] Evidently, therefore, the Vatican did not instruct Mindszenty to leave his native land. Still, it was also clear that if he were to receive a passport from the Hungarian authorities, then he would be expected to attend the conclave, which was to begin on October 25. Any refusal to do so would be considered a grave moral transgression. It was thought that the obligation to attend the conclave would reduce any possible resistance on Mindszenty's part.

Mindszenty was informed about the procedure and the contents of this "conversation" were then written down as a precaution. Cardinal Mindszenty emphasized the following:

> I will obey the order. I do not recognize the government. And only on Rome's order am I willing to ask for safe conduct. Kádár will let me out, but on my return will have me arrested.[81]

His biggest fear was that he would be forced to choose between obedience to the Church (travelling to Rome) and service to his country (remaining at the legation). Chargé d'Affaires Ackerson saw the situation as follows: "Cardinal is fearful Sacred College does not understand his position as last remaining representative of 'legitimate' government in Hungary."[82] Staff at the legation were used to hearing such claims from Mindszenty, but they had little idea what it all meant. The cardinal, meanwhile, now regarded this as his life mission, and so for him his departure from the legation would also mean abandoning this noble cause. The Americans wished to avoid any doubts, and so they asked once again for Rome's position. A new message promptly arrived for Cardinal Mindszenty from the Vatican:

> The Sacred College has carefully considered all points made in your message. The College repeats its original insistence in the formal message in Latin which was recently sent to you. If the Hungarian authorities agree to permit your departure, the Sacred College strongly enjoins you not to

80. Ibid., Telegram from James David Zellerbach, US ambassador to Italy, to the US Legation in Budapest. October 13, 1958.

81. Ibid., Typed "conversation." October 15, 1958.

82. Ibid., Telegrams nos. 133 and 7 from Acting Chargé d'Affaires G. G. Ackerson to the State Department and to the US Embassy in Rome, October 15, 1958.

lose this golden opportunity to comply with your responsibility – an opportunity which may not come again.[83]

After these statements, there was no place for hesitation or excuse; the provisions of canon law took precedence over Mindszenty's anticommunist mission and the public legal duties that he regarded as his constitutional prerogative. With reluctance but in obedience to canon law, he prepared for the journey, with it being his firm intention to return.

After clarification of these issues, in an official note dated October 18, 1958, Garret G. Ackerson, the US chargé d'affaires requested the Hungarian Ministry of Foreign Affairs to guarantee Cardinal Mindszenty's free departure from the legation. Diplomats at the legation were confident that the guarantee would be issued, even though Minister of Foreign Affairs Endre Sík had cynically stated some months previously that the only place to which the cardinal would be permitted to depart was "heaven itself."[84] Optimism at the legation seems to have been derived mainly from the Hungarian government's statements concerning the improved relations between church and state. Another positive signal was that the Hungarian government – uniquely among the regimes of the Eastern Bloc countries – had expressed its condolences at the time of Pius XII's death. It was thought that the Hungarian government might utilize this event, demonstrating its generosity in the face of the "vis maior" and thus without loss of prestige. The Americans even hoped that after the conclave the Vatican authorities would ask Mindszenty to stay in Rome. According to French diplomatic information, Mindszenty would have been strongly advised (ordered) in Rome to refrain from returning to Budapest, regardless of whether or not his passport had been stamped with a re-entry visa.[85] The general view was that his return would not solve anything; rather, the legation would face the same situation as before.

83. Ibid., Typed "conversation," October 18, 1958.

84. The statement was made on April 7, 1958, when French Legate Jean Paul-Boncour suggested to Minister of Foreign Affairs Endre Sík that it would be a wise gesture to let Cardinal Mindszenty leave Hungary. See ibid., Incoming telegram no. A–117. May 6, 1958.

85. AMAE AD Série: Europe, 1956–1960, sous-série: Hongrie, dossier 103, Questions religieuses, juillet 1958–décembre 1960. fol. 87. Report no. 631/EU of Legate Jean Paul-Boncour, Budapest, December 9, 1958.

The US initiative was prematurely leaked to the press, and a large number of ravenous journalists gathered at the Hungarian–Austrian border stations in the hope of witnessing Mindszenty's sensational departure from Hungary. The leak was detrimental to the cause, for the intransigence of the Hungarian politicians now morphed into stone-hard stubbornness: On October 22 (the eve of the second anniversary of the revolution), the Hungarian authorities rejected the US proposal, referring to it as grave interference in Hungarian domestic affairs.[86] The official Hungarian response to the proposal noted that Mindszenty's being given refuge at the legation was contrary to both international law and American practice. The status of Cardinal Mindszenty was a domestic matter for Hungary, whereby it could not be the subject of negotiations between Hungary and the United States. An even more important statement was made in point 4 of the diplomatic note, which was not made public. It referred to the cardinal's stay at the legation as absurd and intolerable, and it claimed that Hungarian public opinion was rightly outraged about the situation, which needed to be followed with "particular attention." The need for such attention was underlined by a "spontaneous" demonstration in the evening of the same day: a small group of protestors gathered outside the US Legation to condemn Mindszenty's possible departure. According to a report submitted by the Austrian legate, armed civilians surrounded the legation building, in front of which stood eight trucks full of men and with their engines running.[87] The holding of the protest, the presence of the vehicles and the armed civilians and policemen who were patrolling the building signaled vigilance and alertness on the part of the authorities. They were clearly prepared to use all means to prevent a US attempt to remove Mindszenty from the building and bring him to safety or an attempt by his supporters to liberate him by force. Despite the Hungarian government's note, the US reaction came only through the press: The legation would continue to guarantee refuge for Mindszenty. The oppor-

86. NARA RG 84, Records of the Foreign Service Posts of the Department of State, Hungary, Subject Files Relating to Cardinal Mindszenty 1956–72, Box 1, Mindszenty–Classified 1958. Record no. 005726/1958 of the Ministry of Foreign Affairs of the People's Republic of Hungary, October 22, 1958. See Borhi, *Magyar–amerikai kapcsolatok 1945–1989*, 332–33.

87. ÖStA, AdR, BMfAA, Sektion II-pol. Zl. 21.–POL/58. Kardinal Mindszenty, zu Telegrammerlass Zl. 58029 3-fach. Report of Austrian Legate Walther Peinsipp, Budapest, October 27, 1958.

tunity presented by the conclave had been lost, and there had been no change in Mindszenty's personal fate.

In truth, no-one could have sincerely believed that the Hungarian authorities would decide to conclude the matter and permit Cardinal Mindszenty's departure from the country, as the regime had no interest at all in Mindszenty becoming a leader of the Hungarian émigré community. It was the Austrian legate who detailed the more profound reasons for the regime's rejection of the proposal:

> At present, he is one of the regime's most significant assets and trump cards in its conflict with the Americans. The regime can commit any act of insolence or provocation against the Americans or their legation here for so long as the cardinal is with them, for it knows well that the Americans cannot draw the final consequences, having regard to their high-ranking protégé. The regime exploits this situation to the full.[88]

Indeed, even though, in the fall of 1958, the American side considered – with unprecedented seriousness – the possibility of breaking off diplomatic relations with Hungary, the United States never closed its legation. Rather than yield to illusions and romanticism, it weighed up the situation by focusing on the political utility of relations against the backdrop of the Cold War. Thus, the United States decided that it would rather place the Hungarian question (i.e., an inquiry into the 1956 revolution and the war for independence) on the agenda of the United Nations.

At the papal conclave that began on October 25, 1958, there were just two absentees who had been prevented from attending by political authorities: Archbishop Mindszenty of Esztergom and Archbishop Stepinac of Zagreb. The conclave was not merely concerned with choosing a successor to sit on the throne of Saint Peter; another issue was the Catholic Church's mission in the modern world. Several cardinals opined that with the easing of the Cold War, a continuation of the aristocratic conservatism of Pope Pius XII might lead to isolation from the real world. In their view, the need was for a pope capable of bringing about change and of applying the thaw in international politics to the Church. In the end, the cardinals

88. ÖStA, AdR, BMfAA, Sektion II-pol. Zl. 21.–POL/58. Kardinal Mindszenty, zu Telegrammerlass Zl. 58029 3-fach.

agreed upon Cardinal Angelo Giuseppe Roncalli, a Venetian patriarch known for his tolerant views and his ability to work with the left wing. Roncalli was already rather aged, and so it was expected that he would be a transitional pope. The new pope, who took the name John XXIII, appointed as his cardinal secretary of state *(segretario)* Domenico Tardini, who had been Pius XII's pro-secretary of state *(pro-segretario)*, and was known for his conservative views. Conservative cardinals hoped that Tardini would limit the actions of John XXIII.[89] Indeed, for as long as Tardini lived (he died in 1961), there were no fundamental changes in ecclesiastical organization and government. Thus, it was some years before the breath of fresh air could be felt at the Vatican.

John XXIII took the view that an "ecumenical council of the Universal Church" would be the best forum in which to elaborate a policy against socialism and communism. He wanted bishops from around the world to reinterpret the role of the Church in a secularized world. On January 25, 1959, John XXIII announced his intention to call this ecumenical council, as well as a diocesan synod for Rome. He also revealed plans to update the Code of Canon Law. In place of the "debating Church," John XXIII's ambition was for a "loving and serving Church" that would engage in dialogue with non-Catholics, non-Christians, and non-believers. The former struggle was to be replaced by something rather different that one might call peaceful neighborliness or coexistence. Of course, this did not mean that the Vatican was abandoning its anticommunist stance. Even so, the shift in Vatican policy led Mindszenty to conclude that the world would not rush to Hungary's aid; and truth would not be victorious. "Some sort of negotiation could begin. But this certainly would have no results for either side, for the current softening and thaw did not come for the good either of my country or of my course."[90] In his notes, Mindszenty wrote

89. The election of John XXIII strengthened the position of Tardini. On November 17, 1958, he was appointed cardinal secretary of state *(segretario)* and, on December 15, he was created a cardinal of the Catholic Church. Though these acts, John XXIII abandoned his predecessor's practice of directing foreign and domestic policy. The new pope entrusted policy-making in these fields to Tardini, granting him membership of the most important congregations.

90. *Foreign Relations of the United States*, 1958–60, vol. X, part 1, general editor Glenn W. LaFantasie, editors Ronald D. Landa, James E. Miller, David S. Patterson, and Charles S. Sampson (Washington, D.C.: United States Government Printing Office, 1993), 103. Document

even more frankly of his dissatisfaction: "What I missed most among the [Council's] decrees was condemnation of militant atheism and communism, as the continuation of [the encyclicals] *Rerum Novarum* and *Quadragesimo Anno*."[91]

In a telegram, the new pope, John XXIII, regretted that Cardinal Mindszenty had been prevented from attending the conclave.[92] For his part, however, Mindszenty was troubled less by his failure to attend the conclave than by his portrayal – in a note issued by the Hungarian Ministry of Foreign Affairs – as a "fugitive." He had never regarded himself as a man who had fled justice, for the government of Imre Nagy had rehabilitated him. Moreover, his flight to the legation had been made in response to historical circumstances.

The extent of his mental wounds became clear when he made a further reckless decision. On learning of the arrest of the young revolutionaries who, at the time of the revolution, had come from Újpest to Felsőpetény with a view to liberating him, he once again offered – on November 27, 1959 – to sacrifice his own freedom (and, indeed, his life) in return for the release of the defendants. On this occasion, he addressed his appeal to US Secretary of State Christian A. Herter:

> So that these innocent young people should not die for him or because of him, the cardinal primate offers to surrender himself in their stead in exchange for their liberation and a safe conduct. This latter, however, has to be more acceptable than that given to Premier Imre Nagy. If the local government cannot grant this, then let it be granted by that one of the great powers which is here illegally and actually controls matters, to the heads of state of the Western powers. With a serious guarantee in his possession, the cardinal will give himself over to the hands of the regime, whether sentenced or not, and will assume the execution meted out to the youths.[93]

---

23. Letter from Joseph Mindszenty to President Eisenhower. Budapest, November 13, 1959; On the Internet: https://history.state.gov/historicaldocuments/frus1958-60v10p1/d23.

91. MMAL 041. dosszié: "Mindszenty Rómában" [Mindszenty in Rome].

92. Acta Iohanis PP XXIII Telegraphici Nuntii. AAS 50 (1958): 904.

93. NARA RG 59, GR of the Department of State, Bureau of European Affairs, Records Relating to Hungary 1941–77, Box 10, Refuge Part III, 1960–61. Letter of József Mindszenty to Secretary of State Christian A. Herter, November 27, 1959. See Adam Somorjai and Tibor Zinner, *Do Not Forget*, 75.

In the case brought against the young revolutionaries, the action to liberate cardinal Mindszenty of October 30, 1956, was just one of a whole series of indictments. Even so, the Hungarian cardinal felt responsible for their fate. His stance seems to have been rooted in several factors: concern for the youngsters' welfare, a self-accusatory nature, and a degree of theatricality. Did he really believe that the Hungarian government would expose itself to international consternation and ridicule by accepting his heroic offer of self-sacrifice (which would lead perhaps to his subsequent execution)? In any event, his offer came too late: two of the Újpest revolutionaries had already been executed – Pál Kósa on August 5, 1959, and László Gábor on September 23.

Chargé d'Affaires Garret G. Ackerson considered Mindszenty's offer both unrealistic and unrealizable. In his reply letter of December 11, 1959, Secretary of State Christian A. Herter merely reaffirmed the hospitality of the US Legation and extended the cardinal warm Christmas greetings.[94] In response to a subsequent attempt by Mindszenty to have his voice heard, Ackerson told him that the Americans were unwilling to perform the function of intermediary and that he and his staff could not, in good conscience, be party to his proposal of self-sacrifice.[95] Thereafter, the US State Department considered the matter closed.

Mindszenty's disappointment was then overridden by some sad news: At 10.30 a.m. on February 5, 1960, he was informed by telegram that his mother – who had visited him at the legation as recently as Christmas – had passed away in the early hours of the day and that her funeral was to be held at 2 p.m. on February 7. The entire village – essentially, Mindszenty's relatives and acquaintances – hoped that the cardinal would be able to attend. Of course, they were to be disappointed: Mindszenty could not go to the funeral; he bid farewell to his mother by sending a wreath. His goddaughter, by way of consolation, brought him a handful of earth from the site of the grave.

94. Ibid., Central Decimal Files 1955–59, Box 4806, 864.413/12–959. Letter of Secretary of State C. A. Herter to József Mindszenty, December 11, 1959. See Adam Somorjai and Tibor Zinner, *Do Not Forget*, 77–78.

95. Ibid., Bureau of European Affairs Office of Eastern European Affairs Records Relating to Hungary 1941–77, Box 10. Refuge Part III, 1960–61, 570.3. Letter of Under-Secretary of State Foy D. Kohler to Acting Chargé d'Affaires Garret G. Ackerson, Jr., January 20, 1960.

By the end of the third year of Mindszenty's stay at the legation, a stalemate had arisen. Neither the United States, nor the Vatican, nor the Hungarian government sought a rapid solution to the problem. The position of the communist regime remained what it had outlined in its statement of March 9, 1957 and its note of October 22, 1958: If Mindszenty were to leave the legation, he would be required to resume his prison sentence. As time passed, however, this stated position sounded less threatening. Despite the regime's supercilious indifference to Cardinal Mindszenty's fate, the unresolved nature of his status cast a shadow over the domestic and foreign policy objectives of the Hungarian Socialist Workers' Party and over its efforts to implement a popular front policy in its relations with the country's various religious denominations.

Actions in the Political Field – Illusions and Realities

The Hungarian government gradually became interested in resolving the matter in some way. Following Khrushchev's measures towards achieving a thaw in international relations, on August 15, 1959, the Hungarian leader János Kádár informed Terentii Shtykov, Soviet ambassador to Hungary, that

> We want to negotiate with the pope and sign an agreement that we shall release [Mindszenty] to them, so that they do not use him as a means of attacking the system and order in Hungary. If we simply release him to them, he could take a stand, and undertake propaganda, against Hungary.[96]

Evidently, Kádár wished to gain acceptance for his regime in the international community and neutralize the criticism made against him and the country at the United Nations. At the time, the United Nations was not only refusing to accept the credentials of the Hungarian delegation; it had also established a committee of five countries (Australia, Ceylon, Denmark, Tunisia, and Uruguay) to inquire into the events of 1956, and the commit-

96. AVP RF f. 077 op. 40. papka (paper folder) 204. delo (file) 4. l. 82. T. F. Shtykov's memo on the discussion with János Kádár. August 15, 1959. See Magdolna Baráth, *Szovjet diplomáciai jelentések Magyarországról a Hruscsov-korszakban* (Budapest: Napvilág Kiadó–Politikatörténeti Intézet, 2012), 174.

tee's report had been detrimental to international perceptions of Kádár's government.

Kádár recognized that the Mindszenty affair could be an opportunity to accomplish his objectives. In this way, the cardinal became a pawn in the government's game plan. At a meeting of the Political Committee of the HSWP on March 1, 1960, General Secretary János Kádár stated, during a discussion of US–Hungarian relations, that a change in Mindszenty's status would only serve the Hungarian government's interest if it were part of a political deal.

> "How can this [Mindszenty's departure from the legation] be achieved without there being a loss of prestige on our side?" he asked. "Perhaps as follows: Mindszenty reports to the Hungarian authorities; the Hungarian authorities guarantee to hand him over at the Austrian border within twenty-four hours, if the pope undertakes to deploy [Mindszenty] at the court and to isolate him from public political life. Roughly speaking, this would be the basis for a possible deal."[97]

However, the execution of Imre Nagy and his associates had occurred just eighteen months previously. In view of people's distrust of the Hungarian government, no-one would have accepted the offer. Even so, for the first time, a leading Hungarian politician was suggesting that Mindszenty would not be detained immediately if he were to leave the US Legation!

As an intermediary, Kádár suggested none other than Austrian Minister of Foreign Affairs Bruno Kreisky. As early as October 1959, during bilateral talks between Austria and Hungary, Kreisky had offered to mediate on the Mindszenty issue, and his Hungarian counterpart had expressed interest in the offer.[98] Indeed, Hungarian Minister of Foreign Affairs Endre Sík had stated that if Kreisky were to make a specific proposal concerning Mindszenty's release, then the Hungarian government "would give it serious consideration." Indeed, Sík had even "stated that the government would

97. Ólmosi, *Mindszenty és a hatalom*, 71. János Kádár's speech at the meeting of the HSWP PC on March 1, 1960.

98. MNL OL XIX–J–1–j–0059541/16/1959. KÜM, Ausztria 5/a. Report of István Sebes, Hungarian legate to Austria, on the discussions between the ministers of foreign affairs of Austria and Hungary. October 21, 1959. See Lajos Gecsényi, ed., *Iratok Magyarország és Ausztria kapcsolatainak történetéhez 1956–1964* (Budapest: MNL OL, 2000), 153–54.

guarantee the cardinal free movement across Hungary to Austria." Sík's sole condition had been that the initiative should not stem from the Americans.[99]

Kreisky informed the apostolic nuncio in Vienna, who doubted, however, that Mindszenty would be willing to leave Hungary, as this would mean separating himself from his flock. The US Embassy in Vienna then reported that the attempt had failed:

> Vatican has given its reply through papal nuncio here. Reply was negative indicating Vatican is not interested in any initiative re: cardinal.[100]

At this point, however, Kreisky was not willing to give up. He asked the Vatican how it would react to an initiative and a guarantee from the Hungarian government concerning Mindszenty's release. The Vatican's reply was rather diplomatic: due consideration would be given to this new situation if and when it arose.

The new situation was not long in coming: In February 1960, staff at the Hungarian Ministry of Foreign Affairs began formulating a draft political deal that may be regarded as a corollary of Kreisky's action. The basic principles of the deal were hammered out at a meeting in Moscow on February 5 between Endre Sík and Soviet Deputy Minister of Foreign Affairs Nikolay P. Firyubin, who suggested that the correct position should be one that did not damage the prestige of Hungary or, by extension, that of "the socialist camp." Thus, the solution would have to be one in which Mindszenty exited the legation and surrendered to the Hungarian authorities, whereupon representatives of the Kádár regime would make a positive decision on his fate. In Firyubin's view, in return for suitable concessions from the US (e.g., the removal of the "Hungarian question" from the UN's agenda), Mindszenty might then be allowed to leave the country.[101]

99. NARA RG 84, Records of the Foreign Service Posts of the Department of State, Hungary, Subject Files Relating to Cardinal Mindszenty 1956–72, Box 1, Mindszenty–Classified 1959. Telegram no. 1118 from the US Embassy in Vienna to the diplomatic mission in Budapest, October 21, 1959.

100. Ibid., Telegram no. 1550 from Freeman H. Matthews, US ambassador to Austria, to the secretary of state, December 21, 1959.

101. MNL OL XIX–J–1–j–SZU TÜK–IV–138/1–1960. Cited in Baráth, *Szovjet diplomáciai jelentések*, 194.

The first internal Hungarian government report on Mindszenty's situation was issued on March 25, 1960. Essentially, it contained a solution resembling the one agreed upon with the Soviet minister of foreign affairs.[102] The analysis in the report, however, mentioned more arguments in favor of the status quo than against it, and there was little support for the "silent diplomacy" envisaged by Kádár. Three main arguments were made against altering the status quo: 1. It would reignite the myth of martyrdom; 2. Mindszenty would become the principal leader of the émigré community; 3. the Hungarian Catholic Church would be placed once again at the focus of interest both in Hungary and abroad, while in the meantime a new church leadership had evolved in the absence of Mindszenty and – partially – in contradiction to him. The arguments in favor of change were centered upon confidence in a political deal: The United States would assist Hungary in bringing the UN inquiry to a conclusion and in obtaining diplomatic recognition for the Hungarian delegation. In return, it "would rid itself" of its guest. The Hungarian government would, for its part, ignore the fact that Mindszenty was a "convicted felon." For the Hungarian communist regime, it was self-evident that limitations on Mindszenty's role as head of the church and in public life would need to be guaranteed in any deal.

While it was sensible to link the matter of Cardinal Mindszenty with the Hungarian question, the demand that the UN inquiry be terminated was unrealistic. It soon became evident that the regime would have to act more convincingly if it wished to gain "forgiveness" for the consequences of the 1956 revolution. For its part, the US government was insisting on the retention of the Hungarian question on the UN agenda and on the release of all political detainees – not only Mindszenty – charged with offences committed during the revolution.[103] Meanwhile, the Vatican had no wish to order Mindszenty to leave the country. From the outset, its view had been that the cardinal should leave the country of his own accord if at all.

102. MNL OL M–KS 288. f. 32/1960/11. ő. e. 161. fol. Proposal of the Department of Foreign Affairs of the HSWP CC and the Ministry of Foreign Affairs to the Political Committee of the HSWP CC on the matter of resolving the situation of Prince Primate József Mindszenty, March 25, 1960. For the contents of the proposal, see, for instance, Borhi, *Magyar–amerikai kapcsolatok 1945–1989*, 354–61.

103. Borhi, *Magyar–amerikai kapcsolatok 1945–1989*, 93–96; János Radványi, *Hungary and the Superpowers: The 1956 Revolution and Realpolitik* (Stanford, CA: Hoover Press, 1972), 92–97.

Accordingly, the Hungarian question remained on the agenda of the UN General Assembly and Mindszenty continued to reside at the US Legation in Budapest. Even so, the year 1960 saw the unfolding – albeit at a snail's pace – of a scenario for Cardinal Mindszenty's release that would be acceptable to all parties. More than ten years would have to pass before a final consensus could be reached. During this period, however, the process itself never ground to a complete halt, despite several hitches and setbacks.

Renewed hope appeared on the election of John F. Kennedy, the thirty-fifth president of the United States. As the first Catholic ever to be elected president, Kennedy took office in January 1961. It soon became clear that he favored building relationships rather than a retreat into isolation. Recognizing that there was now a nuclear balance between the two superpowers, he called for talks between the two sides on arms control and disarmament. This, in turn, presented an opportunity for the Hungarian question to be brought to a conclusion. On January 12, 1961, Mindszenty requested the new US president to extend his refuge at the legation, expressing to him his views – already well-known to the State Department – concerning the subjection of his nation to atheism and the indifference of the international community to the fate of his country.[104] Against the advice of his counselors, President Kennedy replied in writing to Cardinal Mindszenty; he was the first president to do so. In a short letter dated February 10, 1961, Kennedy assured the Hungarian cardinal of his sympathies and of the continued provision of refuge,[105] a response that was of great comfort to the Hungarian cardinal's troubled soul. Then, however, the fears of the State Department apparatus came true. Having been emboldened by the receipt of a written reply, on March 13 Cardinal Mindszenty wrote a further letter to President Kennedy. He then wrote six more letters to him in that year alone, followed by four in 1962 and nine in 1963. Thus, President Kennedy received in total twenty-one letters from Cardinal Mindszenty, who seemed to view himself as Kennedy's foreign policy consultant. If, however, Mindszenty's expectation had been one

104. NARA RG 59, GR of the Department of State, CDF 1960–63, Box 2861, 864.413/2–361. Letter of József Mindszenty to President J. F. Kennedy, January 12, 1961. Published in Somorjai and Zinner, *Do Not Forget*, 117–20.

105. Ibid., 864.413/2–1061. Letter of President Kennedy to József Mindszenty, February 10, 1961. Published in Somorjai and Zinner, *Do Not Forget*, 121.

of regular correspondence with the president, then he was soon to be disappointed, for the White House returned to its earlier practice of non-response, which it then maintained for a decade.

Owing to the policies of the new president, rumors appeared linking Mindszenty with various dramatic meetings and secret deals. When, in late 1961, Cardinal Cicognani, Vatican secretary of state, made a short visit to the United States (where he had served as apostolic delegate between 1933 and 1958, before becoming, in 1961 after Tardini's death, state secretary to John XXIII at the age of seventy-eight), the press naturally assumed that he was also holding talks about Mindszenty's possible departure from the Budapest legation.[106] The Austrian envoy to the Holy See sought information on the veracity of the press reports, but all he got was a rebuttal:

> ...far-reaching speculations and assumptions have appeared in the press. The Hungarian government truly seems to be engaged with such considerations, but Cardinal Cicognani did not raise this subject while in America. Moreover, in the view of the Vatican, it is fully and solely Cardinal Mindszenty's decision as to whether or not he wants to end his refuge at the US mission and leave Hungary. It is not the Curia's decision to make...[107]

Yet, something had in fact happened. While many of the details remain unclear, we do know that, on February 13, 1962, Egidio Vagnozzi, the apostolic delegate, met in Washington with Harold C. Vedeler, Director of the State Department's Office of Eastern European Affairs, and with August Velletri, head of the State Department's Western European division. At this meeting, the three men discussed Mindszenty's fate, each of them concluding that it would be best for Mindszenty to remain at the legation.[108] A few months later, a second meeting was held – on May 2. On this occasion, Vagnozzi, the apostolic delegate, said that both Pope John XXIII and Car-

106. MNL OL XIX–A–21–d–0022–7/1962. The Vatican's Policy and the Ecumenical Council. Information report, June 26, 1962.

107. ÖStA, AdR, BMfAA, Sektion II-pol. Zl.59-Pol/61. Report of the Austrian Embassy at the Vatican to Federal Minister of Foreign Affairs Bruno Kreisky, December 7, 1961. (Underlining in the original text – the author.)

108. NARA RG 59, GR of the Department of State, Bureau of European Affairs, Office of Eastern European Affairs, Records Relating to Hungary 1941–77, Box 11, Refuge Part Four, 1962. Memorandum of Conversation, Washington, February 13, 1962.

dinal Cicognani were of the view that "the existing conditions were not suitable for undertaking efforts to solve the problem of the cardinal's refuge."[109] Around this time, however, communist party leaders in Hungary were informed by a reliable source (probably the Pontifical Hungarian Ecclesiastical Institute in Rome) that the Vatican would be prepared to urge Mindszenty to leave the legation subject to the fulfillment of four conditions: 1. The Hungarian government's consent to the filling of the vacant episcopal sees; 2. its approval for a reorganization of the Hungarian Catholic hierarchy; 3. its acceptance of the appointment of a prince primate; and 4. its consent to the Church sanctioning the peace priests. If all these matters were indeed raised, it would mean that Mindszenty's deposition as archbishop was already being envisaged in Rome (too). Thus, by the opening of the Second Vatican Council, two positions existed in parallel, with the first regarding any change as untimely and premature and with the second being in favor of a shift. The latter stance was given momentum by the Vatican's resolve to invite to the Council those bishops and archbishops – among them Mindszenty – who were being prevented from carrying out their duties in their home countries.

Adjusting to the Vatican's "Eastern Policy"

Against the backdrop of the thaw in international politics, John XXIII no longer insisted on the detained and imprisoned prelates remaining with their flocks at any price. He invited to the Council both free and detained bishops from behind the Iron Curtain. He did so with a view to resolving the situation of several leading churchmen: Josyf Slipyj, metropolitan of Galicia and archbishop of Lviv, who had been held at a labor camp in the Mordovian ASSR since 1945; Cardinal Beran, archbishop of Prague, who was being held under house arrest; and Cardinal Mindszenty, archbishop of Esztergom, who had taken refuge at the US Legation in Budapest.

Among these three men, it was Slipyj who experienced the first radical turn of fate. Nothing happened of course at one blow; still, the result came as a surprise: having spent years in prison, the greatly respected archbishop, who had been the head of the Ukrainian Greek Catholic Church, was

109. Ibid., Memorandum of Conversation, Washington, May 2, 1962.

released at the age of seventy-one years and permitted to leave the Soviet Union. It seems Khrushchev could afford this unique gesture because Slipyj's departure no longer incurred any great risk. The Ukrainian Greek Catholic Church had officially ceased to exist in 1946. In exchange for his freedom after eighteen years of imprisonment and hard labor, Slipyj pledged to remain silent, for which the Italian government and the Vatican authorities vouched.[110] The pope announced his arrival in Rome to the Council Fathers on February 10, 1963. Metropolitan Slipyj – soon to be known as Major-Archbishop and then, from 1965, as Cardinal Slipyj – could travel to Rome bearing a Soviet diplomatic passport and, as a Soviet citizen, with the right to return to the Soviet Union. All of this signaled the altered international political atmosphere.[111]

Slipyj's case was simpler than that of Mindszenty in the sense that he was permitted to travel to Rome "merely" from a gulag rather than from the diplomatic mission of a third country. Further, at the time of his release, Slipyj had not yet been created a cardinal. Hungarian diplomats in Rome drew the impression that the Vatican would have welcomed a similar procedure and agreement for Mindszenty.[112] It was clearly unrealistic, however, to believe that Mindszenty might passively remain in Rome under a pledge of silence resembling that made by Slipyj. Such a belief took no account of Mindszenty's very different personality or his sense of Christian mission, which was now stronger than ever.

Despite the difficulties, conditions were ripening for direct talks between the Hungarian government and the Vatican. An issue to decide was whether the Mindszenty affair should be treated as a problem existing between the Hungarian government and the Catholic Church or as a part of the process of normalization in Hungarian–US intergovernmental relations. In the former case, the matter could be linked with the annulment/cancellation of all Vatican measures directed against the peace priests (e.g., their excommunication in 1957). In the latter case, however, an improvement could

110. Stehle, *Geheimdiplomatie im Vatikan*, 291.

111. NARA RG 84, Records of the Foreign Service Posts of the Department of State, Hungary, Subject Files Relating to Cardinal Mindszenty 1956–72, Box 2, Mindszenty–Classified Jan–April 1963. Telegram no. 1937 from the US Embassy in Rome to the legation in Budapest, March 23, 1963.

112. MNL OL XIX–A–21–e–004–4/d/1963. 7. ő. e. Memo of József Száll, Hungarian legate in Rome, March 9, 1963.

be made in Hungary's international reputation. For the regime's apparatus, the importance of Hungarian–US relations took precedence. It concluded that the tables had been turned and that the Americans now seriously wished to get rid of Mindszenty, for which a price could be exacted.[113]

On August 11, 1962, the Political Committee of the HSWP CC issued a decree containing the principles of negotiation.[114] They continued to anticipate assistance from the Americans in arranging for the dropping of the Hungarian question from the agenda of the UN General Assembly and for the acceptance of the Hungarian diplomats' credentials. To increase the chances of success, they also consulted with Anatoly Dobrynin, Soviet ambassador to the United States, who expressed his agreement with the "theoretical position and methods."[115] In the talks with the Vatican, the aim was to gain acceptance, in a bilateral agreement, of three conditions, whose fulfilment would be followed – after the conclusion of the Council – by Mindszenty's release: 1. (The Vatican) should respect the Hungarian government's traditional rights of patronage (i.e., *ius supremi patronatus*[116] which allowed it to interfere in the appointment of prelates); 2. after Mindszenty's release, he should be stood aside and prohibited from undertaking any activities against the People's Republic of Hungary; 3. Mindszenty should request the Hungarian government in writing for an exemption concerning his prison sentence (for clemency).

113. Ibid., M–KS 288. f. 5/274. ő. e. 95. fol. Proposal to the HSWP PC on the matter of Mindszenty, August 4, 1962.

114. Ibid., 5/275. ő. e. 2. fol. Minutes of the extraordinary meeting of the HSWP PC on August 11, 1962. See Ólmosi, *Mindszenty és a hatalom*, 88–90 and Csaba Szabó, *A Szentszék és a Magyar Népköztársaság kapcsolatai a hatvanas években* (Budapest: Szent István Társulat, 2005), 57–58.

115. Borhi, *Magyar–amerikai kapcsolatok 1945–1989*, 94.

116. Until 1918 the crowned monarch – more broadly, whoever was the head of state – had the right to appoint prelates in Hungary. As of 1918, the patronage rights of the monarch were suspended under Hungarian public law but they were terminated in the view of the Vatican. After the adoption of the Constitution of 1949, a consequence of the separation of Church and State was that the People's Republic of Hungary could not demand to exercise the rights held by Hungarian heads of state for centuries. The principle of the separation of Church and State, however, did not mean that the State was indifferent to ecclesiastical appointments. Soon, the communist regime began insisting that it was entitled to exercise the rights previously exercised by the heads of state. This was then stipulated in Law Decree no. 20 of 1951 and, even more forcefully, in Law Decree no. 22 of 1957. Until the issue was "settled" by virtue of the partial agreement of 1964, it was impossible to fill vacant episcopal sees of the Hungarian Catholic Church in line with the provisions of Canon Law.

At the opening of the Second Vatican Council on October 11, 1962, all the world's prelates were present, apart from the Hungarian and Cuban cardinals. Although their empty seats were not marked with a sign saying "prevented from attending" as Cardinal Spellman had proposed, their absence was nevertheless striking. The Hungarian delegation comprised no more than three prelates, all of whom were known for their proximity to the Kádár regime: Bishop Hamvas of Csanád (who had been chairman of the Bishops' Conference since the death of Archbishop Grősz of Kalocsa on October 3, 1961); Bishop Kovács of Szombathely; and Pál Brezanóczy, apostolic administrator of Eger. An invitation has been sent to Cardinal Mindszenty by way of the nunciatura in Vienna, but the Americans, fearing complications, had not forwarded it to the addressee.

Mindszenty's situation was discussed at the pope's first meeting with the Hungarian prelates on October 9, 1962. At the meeting, John XXIII underlined the importance of a settlement, stating that "the Mindszenty affair is a situation that must and can be resolved" as soon as possible.[117] The pope gave no further details, as he wished to consider thoroughly the consequences. He acknowledged that Mindszenty's departure from Hungary would mean the removal of the Catholic Church's final symbol of resistance to communism. Still, he was unsure whether this would risk subordinating the Hungarian Church to the wishes of the regime or whether, conversely, it would enable the Church to meet such important challenges as the appointment of new bishops, the release of detained priests, and the proper operation of the religious orders. The right way forward could only be to seek a resolution of Cardinal Mindszenty's situation, while concurrently – or even anticipatorily – consolidating the situation of the Hungarian Catholic Church and guaranteeing its operability.

The pope's stance heartened those who sought a prompt resolution. Thus, on November 11, 1962, Bishop Hamvas submitted to Monsignor Antonio Samorè, secretary of the Congregation for Extraordinary Ecclesiastical Affairs, a pamphlet entitled *Quaestio Mindszentyana* summarizing the position of the Hungarian government. The essence of that position:

117. MNL OL M–KS 288. f. 22/5. ő. e. 1962. 148. fol. Information report on the main developments at the first session of the Second Vatican Council. See Szabó, *A Szentszék és a Magyar Népköztársaság*, 70–73.

If the Vatican were to guarantee that Mindszenty would not undertake activities hostile to the People's Republic of Hungary, he would be free to leave the country.[118] This meant, in effect, that the Hungarians wished to resolve the Mindszenty affair by proceeding in the same way as the Soviets had done in the matter of Metropolitan Slipyj. This proposal – made by way of Bishop Hamvas – can be considered the first official formal offer made by the Hungarian regime to the Vatican authorities.

Further progress was stymied when, shortly after the opening of the Council, the world experienced the most fraught period in the Cold War: the Cuban Missile Crisis. Amid the crisis, Pope John XXIII acted firmly, assisting in its resolution. It was during the ensuing abatement of tensions that the Hungarian communist regime's long-awaited hope was realized: On December 20, 1962, the UN General Assembly settled the "Hungarian question." The regime was not completely let off the hook, however, for in its decision the General Assembly confirmed the objectives of its earlier resolutions (the holding of free elections, the withdrawal of Soviet forces, the restoration of national sovereignty, etc.). Yet, even without releasing Cardinal Mindszenty, the Hungarian regime had successfully ended its international isolation – a change signaled by the upgrading of relations to ambassadorial level by Great Britain, France, and Belgium in 1963, and by Sweden, Italy, Switzerland, and Canada in 1964. In the light of the UN decision, in March 1963 the Hungarian government announced a general amnesty. Subsequently, the credentials of the Hungarian delegation to the UN were accepted. Mindszenty commented upon these developments with bitterness:

> In a Constitutional function of the historical Hungary I protest against every bargain and the oversimplification of the case of a heroic nation with an amnesty when – according to the bolshevik usage only with a reversal – amnestied prisoners would receive only a greater more extensive prison in the captive remaining, already two times – in 1956 and 1962 – defeated Hungary.[119]

118. Ólmosi, *Mindszenty és a hatalom*, 101; Szabó, *A Szentszék és a Magyar Népköztársaság*, 78–81.

119. Somorjai and Zinner: *Do Not Forget*, 201. Message from Cardinal Mindszenty to Secretary of State D. Dean Rusk, February 6, 1963.

The thaw in world politics brought success and consolidation for the Kádár regime, but in the eyes of Cardinal Mindszenty the changes amounted to a further betrayal of the Hungarian nation. In his view, the dropping of the "Hungarian question" from the agenda of the UN General Assembly further undermined Hungary.

THE VISITORS

When the Hungarian question was removed from the agenda of the UN General Assembly, Hungary's communist politicians initially concluded that "Mindszenty is not wanted by anyone now." At the same time, they recognized that the Mindszenty issue needed to be addressed, because the normalization of Hungarian–US relations was in the interest of both sides.[120] The US government did indeed show a willingness to initiate bilateral talks with Hungary on problems affecting relations between the two countries. One of the items in the negotiation "package" was the situation of Cardinal Mindszenty, who had now spent nearly seven years at the US Legation in Budapest.

During these years of "cohabitation" with Mindszenty, US diplomats had come to the realization that without the Vatican's assistance they would be incapable of resolving the Mindszenty affair. They began urging the Vatican to send a representative to Budapest, who would discuss matters with Cardinal Mindszenty. With this aim in mind, they took steps to facilitate contact between the Vatican and Mindszenty. The first sign of this came in January 1963 when Mindszenty was permitted to receive gifts that had been sent by John XXIII. Meanwhile, the Vatican also abandoned its previous passive stance and cautiously began assessing the opportunities. This change in the US stance coupled with the engagement of the Vatican represented a further landmark in the development of Mindszenty's situation.

Did Pope John XXIII really have an interest in bringing Mindszenty – who would tread in Slipyj's footsteps – to Rome? The question itself reflects the differences of view that separated the pope and the Hungarian primate. John XXIII had convened the Second Vatican Council in the spirit

120. AVP RF f. 077 op. 46. papka (paper folder) 226. delo (file) 9. l. 57. Report of Soviet Ambassador G. A. Denisov on his discussions with Hungarian Minister of Justice Ferenc Nezvál, February 25, 1963. See Baráth, *Szovjet diplomáciai jelentések*, 307.

of modernization, whereas Mindszenty's image of the church remained that of the period before its staging. The differences between the two men are exemplified by the encyclical *Pacem in terris*, published on April 11, 1963, in which the pope, having emerged from the Cuban Missile Crisis with a greater sense of the threat of nuclear war, did not rule out a dialogue between Christians and communists. In contrast, Mindszenty regarded such a dialogue as unimaginable; it was something that he had been arguing against for years and his resistance had been consistently firm. The encyclical emphasized the importance of distinguishing between "false teachings" (atheism and Marxism) and the "misled" (atheists and Marxists). Cooperation and dialogue with the misled was thus possible, and "something good" might even be found in undertakings spawned from false philosophy.

Several analysts have argued that in view of the polemics at the Council (the position on the "silent churches" of Eastern Europe and on the condemnation of communism), John XXIII had no interest in Mindszenty coming to Rome immediately and did not necessarily wish to bring in a "stubborn and intransigent man ... who had a nimbus of heroic fame" and who would strengthen the domestic opposition.[121] It would seem, however, that John XXIII's stance was defined more by his sympathy for Mindszenty than by political craftiness. Despite the differences of approach, the pope sincerely believed in the ongoing success of the Vatican's burgeoning Eastern policy. And yet, if an appropriate communication strategy had been elaborated, then it might have been possible to portray Cardinal Mindszenty's possible attendance at the Council as a victory of modernist forces. What is certain is that the Vatican had still not reached a final position on Mindszenty's fate.

Cardinal König's Mission

Mindszenty's own position on resolving his situation was known to the Vatican only through the American filter. Pope John XXIII, however, sought

121. ÁBTL 3.2.3. Mt–772/4. 168–169. fol. Information report of the agent codenamed "Urbán" [= the journalist Endre László Lóránt, Vienna correspondent of MTI, the Hungarian news agency], April 17, 1963; MNL OL MNL OL XIX–A–21–e–004–4/b/1963. Report of József Száll, Hungarian legate in Rome, February 4, 1963.

direct and up-to-date information. To this end, he sent a personal representative to Budapest. Several potential candidates were floated. Soon, however, it became an open secret that Cardinal Franz König was the chosen intermediary. Although some expressed doubts about his suitability, Cardinal König did at least have the advantage of speaking a little Hungarian.[122] Several other factors influenced the pope's choice, the main ones being König's prominent role in representing the new Vatican policy and his specialist knowledge of the sensitive eastern mission.

On hearing of the idea of a journey to Hungary, König was initially unimpressed: How could the Holy Father expect him to cross the Iron Curtain! Still, John XXIII saw no great difficulty in the plan: "Just go to the train station in Vienna, buy a ticket for the Budapest Express, travel to the Hungarian capital, and seek out Mindszenty at the US Legation!"[123] Of course, Cardinal König's journey, which was framed as a strictly private visit, would not be that easy.

The actual journey, however, was delayed for months, owing to the whirl of events at the Council. Meanwhile, further parties became engaged in seeking a solution to the Mindszenty affair. One of the most important of these was Giorgio La Pira, the Christian Democratic mayor of Florence (Italy), who had been promoting a thaw in international politics since 1952. On March 6, 1963, while paying a visit to József Száll, the Hungarian envoy in Rome, La Pira told the Hungarian diplomat that the Vatican would shortly be making public its formal ideas concerning Mindszenty – as a response, in effect, to Bishop Hamvas's paper that had been submitted in November – and that it would do so by way of Ettore Bernabei, the chairman of RAI, the Italian public broadcasting company, who would be acting under the authorization and instruction of Angelo Dell'Acqua, substitute for general affairs to the secretariat of state.[124] Meanwhile, the international press was reporting on a spectacular rapprochement between the Soviet Union and the Vatican: On March 7, 1963, the pope received Aleksei I. Adzhubei, the

122. ÁBTL 3.2.3. Mt–764/7. 308. fol. Report of the agent codenamed "Arnold" about the visit of Mons. Filippo Giobbe, Apostolic Pronotary, April 18, 1963.

123. László Lukács, "A Vigilia beszélgetése Franz König bíborossal," *Vigilia* 57, no. 11 (1992): 851.

124. MNL OL XIX–A–21–e–004–4/d/1963. 7. ő. e. Memo of József Száll, the Hungarian legate in Rome. March 9, 1963; ÁBTL 3.2.4. K–318. 10. fol. Report, March 10, 1963.

editor-in-chief of *Izvestia*, at a private audience. Adzhubei was Khrushchev's son-in-law.

Ettore Bernabei did indeed visit the legate just days later – on March 9. The conversation between the two men, which was secretly recorded using a hidden tape recorder, reveals how both sides were seeking a resolution, but such could not be said of Mindszenty.[125] As Mindszenty was a cardinal, the pope had to proceed with special care. He did not want to give the impression that he was instructing Mindszenty or imposing his will upon the Hungarian prelate. Rather, he presented his expectations as a wish. In view of the importance to the Vatican of the principle of the freedom of the church (*libertas ecclesiae*), it also sought to avoid giving the impression that the Church was reacting to pressure from a secular power. What preconditions did the Vatican wish to establish by way of Bernabei? Two wishes were expressed: 1. that Mindszenty should leave Hungary with his status as primate of Hungary intact; 2. that Mindszenty should be permitted, prior to his departure, to conduct a religious rite in Budapest, which would not have to be open to the public. The purpose of this would be to prevent Mindszenty's departure from appearing like the desperate act of a fugitive and to serve as proof to the Hungarian cardinal that he had not been removed from office and had retained his status. In return, the Vatican – as in the case of Metropolitan Slipyj –would vouch for Mindszenty's refraining from making further public statements. According to the secret plan, on his arrival in Rome, Mindszenty was to receive an assignment, relating either to the Council or to the festivities marking the anniversary of Saints Cyril and Methodius or some other event.

These attempts by the Vatican to circumvent normal direct relations seem somewhat odd. At any rate, the offer was taken seriously by the authorities in Budapest. The State Office for Church Affairs suggested that the government should agree to Mindszenty's departure (perhaps in time for him to attend the second stage of the Council to be held in the fall of 1963), subject to the following conditions: 1. Mindszenty would leave the country for good; 2. he would refrain from engaging in Hungarian affairs; 3. he would not undertake hostile activities against the regime; and 4. he would maintain no contact with churchmen in Hungary. The Hun-

125. Ibid.

garian authorities were also opposed to the idea of Mindszenty conducting a religious ritual (e.g., hold a Mass or preside at a closed meeting of the Bishops' Conference) prior to his final departure from the country. They further rejected – and this represented a shift from their previous position – that Mindszenty would leave Hungary as primate of Hungary.[126] Such a condition had never been expressed before. Indeed, the Hungarian conditions had mentioned nothing more than Mindszenty's removal. It had never been clarified whether under removal the Hungarian authorities were thinking of resignation, deposition, or ostracization.

The Political Committee of the HSWP CC debated the proposal at a meeting on April 3, 1963. A consensus could not be reached on several points. Indeed, acting as though they were encountering the problem for the first time, some members of the Political Committee refused to give ground. For instance, the hardliner Béla Biszku, secretary of the Central Committee of the HSWP, queried the meaning of Mindszenty's being "free to leave" the country. Biszku was not satisfied with the government's answer – that Cardinal Mindszenty would simply depart the country without having been rehabilitated. For him, the question was whether Mindszenty should formally request clemency or not. Someone else then stated that the Vatican should request clemency on behalf of the cardinal. For his part, the Hungarian premier, János Kádár, spoke in a more concessionary fashion in the debate. The important point according to him was whether Mindszenty should stay or leave; everything else was secondary and would follow from there. Consequently, the question that needed to be answered was as follows: "Should we seek to solve this, or should we not do so?" In Kádár's view, the correct course was, in fact, to strive for this objective, doing so, however, without any loss of prestige. Therefore, it was of secondary importance whether Mindszenty should be regarded as "Prince Primate or not, for time itself would answer the question. What they – the Vatican etc. – are doing in terms of ecclesiastical law is up to them. If they deploy him to internal service, this would mean that they were refraining from insisting

126. Ibid., M–KS 288. f. 22/7. ő. e. 88–89. fol. Proposal on resolving some issues between the Vatican and the Hungarian state. March 22, 1963; Szabó, *A Szentszék és a Magyar Népköztársaság*, 78–81.

forcefully on: Mindszenty is the Prince Primate of Hungary."[127] In view of the prestige considerations, however, Kádár also considered clemency to be an important issue. This meant, however, that a humiliating and irresolvable element had been placed among the conditions, thereby placing at risk a possible future agreement, which was just beginning to germinate.

The clemency petition was inspired in part by the government's previous announcement, made on March 21, 1963, of a general amnesty. During the amnesty, most prisoners who had been sentenced for crimes committed at the time of the revolution in 1956 were released, as were also those war criminals who had already served two-thirds of their sentences. Political prisoners, including fifty-four priests and monks, were also released under the amnesty.[128] The question arose: Did the amnesty also apply to Mindszenty? János Kádár gave a "yes and no" answer to this question:

> This provision of amnesty applies to Mindszenthy [sic]. In fact, it applies to every criminal. If you had read the text, you might have noticed a series of disqualifying clauses, but also a section that provides for the making of individual petitions – where there have been exclusions – to the Presidential Council. In this sense, it [the amnesty] applies to everyone. The amnesty provision does not apply automatically to Mindszenthy, because he is disqualified in two regards. First, because he is a repeat offender. His actions during the 1956 counter-revolution constituted a repeat offence, in which a trial has not been held, but the fact, that is the crime, is there. Thus, it [the amnesty] does not apply to him automatically, but the point about being able to request it in an individual petition does apply to him. Legally, this is how the matter stands.[129]

The general amnesty did not, therefore, apply to Mindszenty because he was considered a repeat offender, but he could seek clemency on an individual basis. The fact that the communist regime turned the issue

127. Ibid., 5/296. ő. e. 40–44. fol. Minutes of the meeting of the HSWP PC on April 3, 1963; Szabó, *A Szentszék és a Magyar Népköztársaság*, 84–87.

128. Konrád Szántó, *A kommunizmusnak sem sikerült: A magyar katolikus egyház 1945–1991* (Miskolc: Új Misszió Alapítvány, 1992), 59.

129. Ólmosi, *Mindszenty és a hatalom*, 96. Speech of János Kádár to the HSWP CC at its meeting of March 8, 1963.

of clemency into a matter of prestige slowed down a resolution of the Mindszenty affair. At the same time, the Hungarian authorities squandered what would have been an ideal opportunity to release Mindszenty, a victim of the earlier Rákosi regime, which the post-1956 communist government had itself condemned. Kádár and his associates were clearly ambivalent about reaching a solution. They tried to appraise which course would be of greater benefit to them: Mindszenty's departure or his remaining at the legation? They evidently feared that if Mindszenty left the country, he might then become a political leader in the émigré community. For the regime, therefore, it was crucial to obtain a guarantee from the Vatican, ruling out a possible leadership role for Mindszenty. Another consideration was the possibility that Mindszenty's departure from the country would herald a spectacular improvement in Hungarian–US relations.

Kádár's reference to Mindszenty's "repeat offender status" was linked with an indictment launched against the cardinal by the Supreme Public Prosecutor's Office on December 28, 1962. In the indictment, Mindszenty was accused of treason and of having conspired to overthrow the state.[130] It was no coincidence that the Supreme Public Prosecutor's Office opened this investigation at a point in time when the entire justice apparatus was preparing for the general amnesty. One may justifiably assume that the indictment was made with a view to preventing Mindszenty (as a "repeat offender") from benefiting automatically from the general amnesty. The regime's intent was evidently to force him to submit a clemency petition, which would be seen by many as an admission of "guilt." Still, the authorities did not bother to launch a proper investigation or court proceeding, which suggests that the ultimate political goal of the regime was in fact a solution of the Mindszenty affair.

The authorities were deluding themselves, however, if they believed that Mindszenty would ever request clemency from what he regarded as an illegitimate communist regime. His sense of justice and his pride precluded such action. Mindszenty wrote about this in a letter to President Kennedy:

> As in the convict prison I did not ask for this so-called grace of the bloody cruelty in a similar situation, so today I will not ask for it which would be

130. MNL OL LÜ TÜK-documents. Decision ordering an investigation no. 00-755/1963.

> a condemnation of myself and the rehabilitation of Kádár, the minister of interior, the first instrument of the Rákosi regime against the Church, the fatherland and me.[131]

Concerning Cardinal König's journey to Hungary, Mindszenty was upset on hearing the news because he feared that he would be required to give up his refuge status and that his fellow bishops would portray him in a negative light, perhaps even making him into a "scapegoat" and blaming him for the restrictions on religious freedom in Hungary.[132] This became the subject of almost every conversation Mindszenty had at the time. For the first time since his arrival at the legation, he now asked to consult with Bishop Shvoy of Székesfehérvár, one of his confidants. His justification for doing so was that his role as "prince primate" of Hungary was a very special one, which Cardinal König did not understand. Indeed, even at the Vatican, there were few people who understood the importance of his status, because its unique nature was unknown to them, namely that "by Hungarian law as prince primate he is political head of [the] country in [the] absence of [a] king."[133] The US chargé d'affaires in Budapest concluded that Cardinal Mindszenty's hostility towards the regime and the sense of responsibility that he felt as prince primate might impel him "to give more weight to his political responsibilities to the Hungarian people than to his religious connections to the Vatican."[134] The conclusions made by the chargé d'affaires, an outsider, were on the mark: rather than travel to Rome, Cardinal Mindszenty was more inclined to stay put at the US Legation, even if this meant missing such an important event as the Council.

131. John F. Kennedy Presidential Library and Museum, Boston, Papers of President Kennedy, National Security Files, Countries, Box 105A, Hungary General 1963. Letter of József Mindszenty to President Kennedy, April 1, 1963; See Somorjai and Zinner, *Do Not Forget*, 206.

132. NARA RG 84, Records of the Foreign Service Posts of the Department of State, Hungary, Subject Files Relating to Cardinal Mindszenty 1956–72, Box 2, Mindszenty–Classified Jan–April 1963, 570.3. Telegram no. 461 from Chargé d'Affaires Owen T. Jones, April 2, 1963.

133. Ibid., Telegram no. 416 from Chargé d'Affaires Owen T. Jones, March 11, 1963.

134. Ibid., Telegram no. 429 from Chargé d'Affaires Owen T. Jones to the secretary of state, March 19, 1963.

The Vatican authorities seem to have been aware that the title and the accompanying public legal status of "Prince Primate" had not always been awarded by a papal appointment, but had arisen as part of the development of ecclesiastical and public law in Hungary over seven centuries. Indeed, in the early 18th century (1714), the title had become a hereditary one, on the pattern of the chief shepherds in the Holy Roman Empire. To become Primate of Hungary, however, one had to be appointed by the pope as archbishop of Esztergom. By the mid-20th century, the Vatican had come to regard the politico-legal role of the Prince Primate as an outdated relic. As early as 1951, Pope Pius XII – a more conservative pope than his successor, John XXIII – had prohibited the use, in the Catholic Church, of secular ranks and titles that were rooted in feudal privilege. As of 1951, therefore, the title "prince primate" had become, in a formal sense, "merely" primate. (Meanwhile, the laws in Hungary had abolished feudal titles in 1947.)[135] As Mindszenty had had no access to the Holy See's official gazette in prison, he remained ignorant of this change. Thus, prior to June 1964, he always signed his letters as Prince Primate. Thereafter, however, he dropped the prefix of "Prince" and referred to himself merely as "Primate." We may conclude, therefore, that he became aware of the 1951 papal provision in 1964.[136] Mindszenty's absence from the Vatican Council meant that he lacked firsthand knowledge of the new positions taken there. At best, he could learn of the changes from the newspapers. It is widely recognized that the Second Vatican Council was imbued with the spirit of a modern dialogue with the world, whereby the Church could no longer accept the mixing of ecclesiastical and public legal functions.

135. The state provision was contained in Act IV of 1947 on the abolition of various ranks and titles, while the abolition of the rank under Canon Law was contained in the Decree of May 12, 1951 of the *Sacra Congregatio Consistorialis* (Sacred Consistorial Congregation). See "Decretum de vetito civilium nobiliarium titulorum usu in Episcoporum inscriptionibus et armis." AAS 43 (1951): 480.

136. See Ádám Somorjai, *Sancta Sedes Apostolica et Cardinalis Ioseph Mindszenty III/2. Documenta* 1967–1971. (Budapest: METEM, 2012), 373–74 and 395 (Note no. 32). – Author's note: In contemporary sources and even in communist party documents, Mindszenty was referred to as prince primate. Since Mindszenty was the last archbishop of Esztergom to bear this secular title, he is referred to – out of respect or custom – as the prince primate even today. In practice, it was Archbishop Lékai of Esztergom (1976–86) who stopped using the title.

The basis, however, for Mindszenty's insistence on his public legal status and political role as prince primate was not canon law, but rather a traditional legitimist consideration, namely the prince primate's role as "the country's first knight banneret." It was this conviction that compelled him to remain at the US Legation despite all the inconveniences. As we shall see, however, it was this same intransigence that resulted in the pope's ominous decision of 1974 to depose Mindszenty from the archiepiscopal see of Esztergom.

The Americans refused to permit Mindszenty to hold consultations with András Zakar, his former secretary, or with Bishop Shvoy of Székesfehérvár. They considered Zakar to be "[a] marked man in [the] eyes [of the] Hungarian authorities,"[137] and they believed that Shvoy was perceived by Mindszenty more as a tool to influence Hungarian ecclesiastical policy than as someone who might assist in resolving his situation of refuge.

> Indeed, he is in no hurry to leave the legation and might be disposed to continue his asylum indefinitely and seek more such consultations. He does not want to leave Hungary. It would be out of character for him to seek from the Kadar regime an amnesty under the recent decree. Thus there are risks in allowing the cardinal to broaden his present base of authorized contacts with the outside beyond his sisters for humanitarian-family reasons and his old confessor for personal-religious reasons. These are risks it would be unwise for us to take at a time when the Hungarian government is consciously and publicly attempting to provide a base for improving US–Hungarian relations. Thus we do not believe the US Government should be directly involved in attempting to arrange such consultations.[138]

137. NARA RG 84, Records of the Foreign Service Posts of the Department of State, Hungary, Subject Files Relating to Cardinal Mindszenty 1956–72, Box 2, Mindszenty–Classified Jan–April 1963. Telegram no. 393 from Secretary of State D. Dean Rusk to the US Legation in Budapest, April 17, 1963.

138. NARA RG 59, GR of the Department of State. Bureau of European Affairs, Office of Eastern European Affairs, Records Relating to Hungary 1941–77, Box 11, I, Nov 1, 1962–April 30, 1963. Letter of Chargé d'Affaires Owen T. Jones to Harold C. Vedeler, Director of the Office of Eastern European Affairs, Department of State, April 8, 1963.

If Cardinal König were to inquire whether he wanted to stay or leave, Mindszenty would himself have to decide how to answer this question...

At 11 a.m. on Thursday, April 18, 1963, Cardinal König arrived at the US Legation in Budapest in the Austrian envoy's car.[139] He spent four hours at the legation, conversing with Cardinal Mindszenty in private for more than three hours. Here, it is worth noting that Cardinal König's visit to Budapest was remarkably short; indeed, there was not even time for the meeting with Bishop Hamvas, which had been the objective cited in the visa application. While Cardinal König repeatedly stressed the private nature of his visit, there were many who expected him to play the role of "battering ram" for the Vatican and to persuade Mindszenty to leave the legation and thus close the Mindszenty affair. At least, this seems to have been the expectation of the US chargé d'affaires, who stated in anticipation of König's visit: "We, as well as the Vatican, will be the losers if it fails."[140]

Acknowledging that the room was likely to be "bugged," the two cardinals turned the radio on loud and conversed in a mixture of Hungarian, Latin, German, and English. Mindszenty spoke of the situation of the Hungarian Church, as he viewed it from the legation. He then criticized the peace priests and the submissive stance of the bishops. Thereafter Cardinal König brought up the object of his mission: the pope's desire was for Mindszenty to leave the country and travel to Rome for the Council. Mindszenty's diplomatic response was simply that if there was no need for him to demonstrate his obedience (that is if it was not an instruction from the pope), he was indifferent as to whether he should stay or leave. Although, three weeks later, he would state something rather different to the Vatican's representative, nevertheless on this occasion he told König that he was

139. For more information about Cardinal König's visits, see Mária Pallagi, "Ein unerwünschter Gast – Kardinal Mindszenty in der Amerikanischen Botschaft und die Besuche von Kardinal König (1956–1971) – Die Ostpolitik des Vatikans gegenüber Ungarn und der Fall Mindszenty," in *Österreich und Ungarn im Kalten Krieg*, ed. István Majoros, Zoltán Maruzsa, and Oliver Rathkolb (Budapest and Vienna: ELTE BTK Új- és Jelenkori Egyetemes Történeti Tanszék and Universität Wien, Institut für Zeitgeschichte, 2010), 373–405; Somorjai, *Sancta Sedes Apostolica et Cardinalis Ioseph Mindszenty II. Documenta 1956–1963 (Budapest: METEM, 2009)*, 67–69, 151.

140. NARA RG 59, GR of the Department of State, Bureau of European Affairs, Office of Eastern European Affairs, Records Relating to Hungary 1941–77, Box 11, I, Nov 1, 1962–April 30, 1963. Letter of Chargé d'Affaires Owen T. Jones to Harold C. Vedeler, Director of the Office of Eastern European Affairs, Department of State, April 8, 1963.

prepared to leave Hungary "but only as the primate of Hungary, for under these circumstances I owe it to my people to remain loyal [to them]. But I cannot request anything at all from Kádár and his circle."[141] Mindszenty knew that the regime would offer him neither a retrial nor rehabilitation.

After the meeting, Cardinal Mindszenty wrote to Cardinal König thanking him for the visit. In the letter, he laid out his conditions for leaving the legation, many of which were repeated subsequently: 1. A review of the issue of the hindered bishops; 2. the release of detained priests and members of the laity; 3. the return of the prisoners-of-war and deportees to their families; 4. the redeployment of parish priests in their own dioceses; 5. the construction of a new parish church at the site of the demolished Regnum Marianum Church in Budapest.[142]

Having traveled to Rome, Cardinal König relayed Mindszenty's reply to the Vatican authorities. Nothing of importance from what he said was leaked to the press. Even so, reporters did manage to squeeze out of König that he was skeptical of there being a quick solution to the Mindszenty affair.[143] It was now clear to everyone that Mindszenty's position would not be changed through a private visit of an individual – even if that individual were a cardinal and archbishop of the same rank. It was therefore unrealistic to expect an immediate and simple resolution of the matter. Meanwhile, the Hungarian authorities also made it plain that negotiations on the Mindszenty problem would have to be conducted by officials.

Another event further undermined Cardinal König's mission. In 1963, the Hungarian premier, János Kádár, and his wife were invited to attend the International Balzan Prize Foundation's awards ceremony, at which Pope John XXIII and Andrey Kolomgorov, the Soviet mathematician, were to receive prizes. There was nothing odd in the invitation itself. It was strange however, that on April 10, the Balzan Foundation sent a letter to

141. Mindszenty, *Napi jegyzetek*, 269. Entry of April 18, 1962 [The correct date is 1963].

142. NARA RG 59, GR of the Department of State, Bureau of European Affairs, Office of Eastern European Affairs, Records Relating to Hungary 1941–77, Box 11, I, Nov 1, 1962–April 30, 1963. Letter of József Mindszenty to Cardinal König, April 18, 1963. Author's note: The letter was – exceptionally – forwarded to the addressee, after State Secretary D. Dean Rusk issued a special authorization. See Somorjai, *Sancta Sedes Apostolica et Cardinalis Ioseph Mindszenty* II, 136–37.

143. "König: Fall Mindszenty ungelöst," *Süddeutsche Zeitung*, May 18, 1963. Cited in Mária Pallagi, "Ein unerwünschter Gast," 382.

János Kádár proposing that Cardinal Mindszenty also attend the ceremony as his presence would greatly enhance the occasion.[144] Ulisse Mazzolini, the deputy chairman of the Balzan Foundation, even suggested that the Hungarian government let Mindszenty attend. The sources do not reveal whether the proposal was made with Vatican approval or whether it was simply an act of benign dilettantism. In all likelihood, it was the latter. Nevertheless, both the Political Committee of the HSWP CC, as well as Hungarian government officials, took the view that the proposal had come originally from the Vatican, which was using the Balzan Foundation as its pawn with the aim of securing Mindszenty's release. They based this view on the inconsistent nature of the invitation: other than Khrushchev and Brezhnev, Kádár was the only communist leader to have been invited. In view of the list of illustrious invitees, Hungarian Minister of Foreign Affairs János Péter opted to consult with the Soviet ambassador to Hungary, telling him that "the Hungarian side is willing to hold talks with official Vatican representatives on the Mindszenty affair."[145] The response of the CPSU CC came a week later: "[We] share fully the opinion of the HSWP CC."[146] As far as the Hungarian government was concerned, the emphasis was clearly on the word "official," whereby it regarded the proposal made by the deputy chairman of the Balzan Foundation as a private (unofficial) initiative. The Soviets agreed with this stance, while also lauding the Hungarian government's willingness to negotiate. As an outcome of these consultations with the Soviet comrades, Hungarian premier János Kádár stayed away from the awards ceremony. We see, however, that in 1963 there was a broad agreement in Washington and Moscow, as well as in Budapest and at the Vatican, that Cardinal Mindszenty should leave Hungary for Rome in a prompt and quiet fashion. A solution to the situation depended primarily upon Mindszenty.

144. MNL OL XIX–J–1–j–1945–64, Olaszország, 14/h. Letter of Ulisse Mazzolini, Deputy Chairman, to János Kádár, Milan, April 10, 1963.

145. AVP RF f. 077. op. 46. papka (paper folder) 226. delo (file) 9. Memo of Soviet Ambassador G. A. Denisov to Hungarian Minister of Foreign Affairs János Péter on the discussions held on April 17, 1963. April 24, 1963; See Baráth, *Szovjet diplomáciai jelentések*, 325.

146. Ibid., delo (file) 10. Memo of Soviet Ambassador G. A. Denisov to Hungarian Minister of Foreign Affairs János Péter on the discussions held on April 25, 1963. April 27, 1963; See Baráth, *Szovjet diplomáciai jelentések*, 330.

On April 20, 1963, Bishop Hamvas of Csanád, the chairman of the Hungarian Catholic Bishops' Conference, informed the Secretariat of State in Rome that he wished to submit a report on the situation in Hungary.[147] The pope then authorized Monsignor Agostino Casaroli, who at the time was in Vienna for the UN Conference on Consular Relations, to meet discreetly with Bishop Hamvas and hear his report. If required, Casaroli should then travel to Hungary.

And so it happened that on April 27, Casaroli made an unexpected call on István Sebes, the Hungarian legate in Vienna. Casaroli assured Sebes that the Vatican now had a sincere desire to settle ecclesiastical issues not only in Hungary but also in the other communist countries.[148] This marked a turning point in Vatican policy: Instead of using an intermediary (La Pira, Bernabei, König, or the deputy chairman of the Balzan Foundation), the Vatican was now deploying a high-ranking member of its own staff – Agostino Casaroli – in an effort to resolve its relations with the Hungarian government. For Monsignor Casaroli, who was 49 years old at the time, this marked the beginning of several decades of work in the role of Vatican troubleshooter in matters of relations with the Eastern Bloc countries. Although Casaroli had been in the service of the Vatican Secretariat of State for almost a quarter-century (since 1940), dealing mostly with Latin American affairs, it was only in 1961, on his being appointed by Pope John XXIII as under-secretary (*sottosegretario*) of the Congregation for Extraordinary Ecclesiastical Affairs, that he had become known to the broader public. It was a fortuitous coincidence that he was given this new role in the east, for by nature he was both courteous and diplomatic. Indeed, those who knew him called him "God's Chinaman."

Two days later, on April 29, Casaroli met with Bishop Hamvas, who was accompanied by Pál Brezanóczy, apostolic administrator of Eger. (In 1958,

147. Giovanni Barberini, ed., *La politica del dialogo: Le carte Casaroli sull'Ostpolitik vaticana* (Bologna: Il Mulino, 2008), 78. Petition to the Sacred Congreation for Extraordinary Ecclesisatical Affairs. July 16, 1963.

148. MNL OL XIX–J–1–j–IV–14/1960–63. Vatikán TÜK-documents, 2. d. "Magyarország és a Vatikán kapcsolata, 1963" [Relations between Hungary and the Vatican, 1963] and MNL OL XIX–A–21–e–004–4/f/1963. 9. ő. e. Appendix to the report no. 001/98 of the legate in Vienna, April 29, 1963.

Brezanóczy had worked for the Hungarian Ministry of the Interior as an agent codenamed "Pál Kékes.") Bishop Hamvas reported frankly to Casaroli on the Hungarian regime's systematic oppression of Catholic religious life, on the measures employed by the police which gave the lie to government propaganda, and the ageing of bishops in Hungary, which posed an increasing danger to the Church's hierarchical structure. A tired and elderly Bishop Hamvas requested the assistance of the Vatican, as he was struggling to meet the demands of maintaining contact with the government in his position as chairman of the Bishops' Conference: "Let him not depart from us when it seems there is a faint ray of hope and the government is showing an inclination for negotiations."[149] In the end, he submitted a ten-point memorandum on the Church's grievances. It was evident that any talks would have to cover in full the Catholic Church's relationship with the Hungarian state, whereby the Mindszenty affair would be a single detail. For his part, Casaroli had no wish to state his position on Cardinal Mindszenty at this point. He wished first to meet with Mindszenty. Still, he did let it be known that the pope made a strict distinction between the "ecclesiastical and political functions" of Mindszenty. "Regarding the former, he has no wish to force Mindszenty onto his knees, but regarding the latter, his position is one of a firm prohibition. (He should not view himself as the country's first knight banneret, as its prince primate, or as a political leader, and so forth.)"[150] In other words, the pope wished to avoid any problems that might arise from what Mindszenty believed were his public legal obligations as primate of Hungary.

On May 7, 1963, Agostino Casaroli traveled incognito to Budapest, having been officially instructed to do so by John XXIII. This was an historic moment, because eighteen years had passed since Hungary severed diplomatic relations with the Holy See. During his three-day stay in Hungary, Casaroli held talks with József Prantner, the "ideologically committed, dogmatic and intransigent" head of the State Office for Church Affairs, with Imre Miklós, Prantner's "less zealous but more bureaucratic" deputy, and with Frigyes Puja, Hungary's "clever-looking" deputy minister of

149. Barberini, *La politica del dialogo*, 53. Report of Agostino Casaroli on the talks held with Hungarian government officials, Vatican City, May 18, 1963.

150. ÁBTL 3.1.5. O–14.963/3–a. 368. fol.; MNL OL M–KS 288. f. 5/299. ő. e. 74–77. fol. Report on Agostino Casaroli's discussions in Vienna, April 30, 1963.

foreign affairs.[151] By entering these talks, the Hungarian government in effect recognized the Vatican's competence (jurisdiction) in religious matters. This marked a break from its previous position, according to which freedom of conscience and religion were matters for the police.

For the time being, the pope authorized Casaroli merely to obtain information on the situation and establish direct relations with the Hungarian government. Casaroli's task was to ascertain

> if and until it would be possible to negotiate for some honest agreement, though making sacrifices perhaps, even onerous, to save the presence and the Ministry of the Church in his country, alleviating, in the meantime, its greatest difficulties.[152]

For its part, the Hungarian delegation had received authorization – as of May 6 – to sign an agreement relating to Mindszenty alone.[153] Indeed, they even elaborated a draft document that was to become an essential element of the 1971 agreement, namely a silence clause guaranteed by the Vatican. The draft agreement was not universally welcomed by the regime's apparatus. For instance, Deputy Prime Minister Jenő Fock called the mere mention of the Mindszenty issue a "blunder."[154] The majority view, however, was that Cardinal Mindszenty's departure from Hungary would be a relatively simple solution to the problem. Their expectations of the talks were greater than warranted by the situation.

It then became clear that Casaroli had no authorization to sign an agreement. Still, it was recognized that his visit might lead to a new round of formal negotiations. Thus, both sides drew up lists of the problems that needed to be resolved. Of course, each of the two lists contained different subject-matters and points of emphasis. A confidential Hungarian government summary of the discussions condensed into seven points the

151. Barberini, *La politica del dialogo*, 54.

152. Agostino Casaroli, *The Martyrdom of Patience: The Holy See and the Communist Countries (1963–1989)* (Toronto: Ave Maria Centre of Peace, 2007), 57.

153. MNL OL XIX–J–1–j–IV–14/1960–63/00140/26/1963. Vatikán TÜK-documents, 2. d. Proposal of Minister of Foreign Affairs János Péter to the government, May 6, 1963.

154. Ibid., XIX–A–21–e–0022–14/1963/Eln. Handwritten note on the reverse side of a document entitled: Guidelines for negotiations between the Hungarian government representatives and the Vatican representatives.

questions that needed to be reviewed, including the Mindszenty affair. Thus, it was the Hungarian side rather than Casaroli, who suggested a debate on this issue! The government's action turned out to be a grave tactical mistake, because it revealed the extent to which Hungarian politicians – who had been feigning indifference – were, in fact, mesmerized by the fate of the cardinal.[155]

In his report on the talks, Casaroli summarized the various topics under discussion in fourteen points. He placed the issue of Cardinal Mindszenty at the top of the list, even though it had not been the first item on the agenda and had been broached by the other side. It was Casaroli's impression that the Hungarian delegation had been strikingly indifferent to the issue. This caused him to doubt their sincerity. As an experienced diplomat, he sensed that a conclusion to the Mindszenty affair would be the prerequisite to a debate of the other issues. If the Hungarians regarded this issue as important, then with his assistance a solution to the various other grievances might be found.

The following procedure was outlined for resolving the Mindszenty affair: the head of the Presidential Council would grant clemency without a petition, and then the cardinal, who could, under the law, even stay in Hungary, would, in fact, leave the country immediately. This procedure had been elaborated on April 3, 1963 as a temporary solution, having regard to Mindszenty's rejection of the idea of having to apply for clemency, while at the same time justifying the earlier communication declaring the cardinal's guilt.[156] (When Mindszenty did in fact leave the legation in 1971, this model was followed.) The government's conditions were already known: Cardinal Mindszenty should refrain from making statements against the People's Republic of Hungary and from seeking to direct the Archdiocese of Esztergom or influence Hungarian ecclesiastical affairs in general. With this objective in mind, the Vatican should vouch for his conduct, thereby preventing him from becoming a Cold War figure hostile to the regime in Hungary. Casaroli considered the conditions to be accept-

155. Ibid., M–KS 288. f. 5/300. ő. e. 25–34. fol. Report on the discussions between representatives of the Hungarian government and the Vatican's representative, May 10, 1963. See Szabó, *A Szentszék és a Magyar Népköztársaság*, 112–17.

156. Ibid., 5/296. ő. e. 42. fol. Minutes of the meeting of the HSWP PC on April 3, 1963.

able overall, but he emphasized his desire to hold discussions with Mindszenty in advance of any agreement.

An opportunity for such discussions arose on May 8, 1963, during an interval in the talks with the government. Casaroli passed to Mindszenty the kind and courteous letter from John XXIII. The Hungarian cardinal was pleased to read in the letter that the Holy See did not blame him for anything. Still, Mindszenty was disappointed that the Vatican wished to commence formal talks with a communist regime. In his memoirs, he criticized Casaroli for having ignored the credible voice of the Hungarian Church, which had been silenced by the communist authorities, and for initiating negotiations based on superficial knowledge – which would benefit the communist regime but disadvantage the Hungarian Catholic Church.[157] Mindszenty could not know that Casaroli was in fact very well informed and that his reports to his superior, Secretary of State Cicognani, were providing a very accurate picture of the situation of Hungarian Catholicism. Here, it should also be noted that Casaroli's reports were far from being the sole source of information available to the Vatican Secretariat of State.

Casaroli also concluded in his reports that Mindszenty's thinking was determined in large part by events in the past, particularly his conviction in 1949 and his rehabilitation in 1956. In Casaroli's view, this explained why Mindszenty was insisting on his innocence and on the need for justice rather than on an act of clemency that would leave both the accusations and the sentence intact. Mindszenty tried hard to persuade Casaroli that the Hungarian primate was the central and main actor not only of religious life but also of Hungarian national life – both in Hungary and in the ceded areas. And "if he also abandons the struggle or departs from Hungarian soil, the hope of resistance and of a new beginning will be ended."[158] In his reply, Casaroli placed the focus on the Church's mission and its duty to make sacrifices with a view to spreading the Good News. He stated plainly that while the pope recognized the concerns relating to Hungarian national problems, he had no wish to address the political and public legal issues, since religious issues were his main priority: How could the difficulties facing the Hungarian Catholic Church be mitigated? How could

157. Mindszenty, *Memoirs*, 226.
158. Barberini, *La politica del dialogo*, 74.

the Church be helped to survive until the situation turned more positive? He asked Mindszenty the following question: Would not the objective justify certain sacrifices? He was not thinking of Mindszenty's resignation as archbishop and primate of Hungary, and Mindszenty himself did not mention it either.[159]

When it came to the question of whether to stay or leave, the answer given by Mindszenty to Casaroli differed completely from his response to König a few weeks earlier. He explained his weakness – his being willing to leave – in terms of the torment that had overcome him in view of the perceived uncertainty of his situation of refuge.[160] Between the two visits, he had often wondered about the validity of his refuge. He wanted to be told whether his long-term residence at the legation was a source of embarrassment for his hosts or for the US government.[161] After he had been reassured that this was not the case, he already felt regret for what he had told Cardinal König, whereupon he insisted on staying, in view of the absence of a papal instruction to do otherwise. It was embarrassing for him to admit to this, so he sought to explain it in terms of factors that were beyond his control. On May 6, 1963, that is, two days before Casaroli's visit, the military doctor of the US Legation in Belgrade, Dr. James Lynsky, examined Cardinal Mindszenty. Mindszenty told the physician that he feared suffering a heart attack and then spoke of the old problem with his thyroid gland. Like a school pupil who tries to avoid writing a test, he asked for a doctor's certificate stating that the hot summers of Rome would be fatal for him, whereas the moderately warm summers of Budapest would be better for his health.[162] In other words, he would go to Rome, but in view of his health problems it would be unwise for him to move his place of residence. After being told by the physician that he was not suffering

159. Ibid., 76.

160. Ibid., 74.

161. NARA RG 84, Records of the Foreign Service Posts of the Department of State, Hungary, Subject Files Relating to Cardinal Mindszenty 1956–72, Box 2, Cardinal File–Limited Distribution 1962–64. Memorandum of Conversation, April 22, 1963. See also the diary entries of József Mindszenty in *Napi jegyzetek*, 288–99 and 311.

162. NARA RG 59, GR of the Department of State, Bureau of European Affairs, Office of Eastern European Affairs, Records Relating to Hungary 1941–77, Box 11, Refuge Part Five, 1963. Memorandum of Harold O. Beeson, Health Division, Department of State, June 6, 1963; Letter of Chargé d'Affaires Owen T. Jones to Harold C. Vedeler, director of the Office for Eastern European Affairs, Department of State, June 13, 1963.

from thyrotoxicosis, Mindszenty sent him a message the next day saying that he no longer needed the doctor's certificate.[163] Even so he told Casaroli about the possible negative effect of Rome's unfavorable climate; with a degree of wonderment Casaroli then forwarded Mindszenty's letter to Cardinal Cicognani, the state secretary.[164]

For Mindszenty it was evident throughout this period that the best way to help the Hungarian Church and the Hungarian nation was to destroy the country's communist regime. He criticized the West, especially the United States, for having allowed the Soviet Union to extend its political, military and ideological influence over a large part of the European continent. His intransigence made him insensitive to the fact that, in the meantime, the world had learned something from its past; the US government and politics were also seeking to avoid a conflict with the Soviets and their allies, for such a conflict would pose an immediate threat of nuclear war (as had been soberly demonstrated during the Cuban Missile Crisis, several months earlier).

What impression did the two men make on each other? Mindszenty quickly formed a rather negative opinion of Casaroli, who arrived at the legation in ordinary clothing rather than in a cassock and who opted to stay at a state-owned mansion in the Rózsadomb district of Budapest rather than at the Central Seminary. The Hungarian cardinal was also aggrieved by the fact that a "monsignore" had been sent to visit him, instead of a bishop or an archbishop – the ones ordinarily tasked with addressing "important affairs" at the Vatican.[165] The notes made by Casaroli, who was a meticulous man, indicate a degree of consternation on his part: for instance, when he remarks – having summarized Mindszenty's main ideas – that, in the cardinal's view, the Hungarian government could be threatened by mobilizing international public opinion and by making an appeal at the United Nations.[166] In fact, the United Nations – similarly to

163. Ibid., Report of Harold O. Beeson on the visit to Budapest of Dr. Lynsky, June 6, 1963.

164. Barberini, *La politica del dialogo*, 75.

165. NARA RG 84, Records of the Foreign Service Posts of the Department of State, Hungary, Subject Files Relating to Cardinal Mindszenty 1956–72, Box 2, Mindszenty–Classified May–August 1963. Telegram no. 525 sent by Chargé d'Affaires Owen T. Jones. May 2, 1963.

166. Casaroli noted that he was only writing all this down with a view to providing a full account (as he considered Mindszenty's views on the matter to be fully impractical). See Barberini, *La politica del dialogo*, 76.

the United States – resisted attempts to link the broader Hungarian problem with the matter of Mindszenty. In this context, it should be noted that the Mindszenty affair had been thoroughly examined by the UN in advance of Secretary-General Sithu U Thant's visit to Hungary, scheduled for the summer of 1963. An internal UN report – which recommended no action by the UN – appraised the matter of Mindszenty as follows,

> The recent visits by Vatican representatives to Cardinal Mindszenty were for the purpose of learning his state of mind and exploring possible solutions of the problem. Thus far there is no indication that the Vatican has made up its mind on the question or has formulated any proposals regarding it. The United States takes the position that the question involves only the three parties, namely Mindszenty, the Vatican and the Hungarian Government and that the United States would concur in any solution on which these three parties agreed. In this context the US role is to facilitate contact between Mindszenty and the Vatican.[167]

Casaroli then left Hungary for Czechoslovakia where, on May 13, he called on Archbishop Beran of Prague, who had also been prevented from traveling to Rome for the Council. In Casaroli's subjective view, Beran was "more amicable" than Mindszenty:

> None of the Hungarian prince primate's arrogance could be found in him [in Beran]; nor did he exhibit those expressly and characteristically 'national' sentiments that were so apparent in the case of His Exc. the Archbishop of Esztergom. Still, one could feel the determination that led him not to concede anything of what a Catholic bishop senses to be his duty, who belongs solely to the Holy See and depends solely on the Holy See. Meanwhile, the devotion he felt towards Christ's vicar on earth was touching.[168]

167. United Nations Archives and Records Management Section, Series 0878, Box 1, File 16, Peace-Keeping Operations Files of the Secretary-General: U Thant: other Countries, Hungary–Cardinal Mindszenty. Memo of U.N. High Commissioner Ralph J. Bunche to Secretary-General U Thant, June 13, 1963.

168. Barberini, *La politica del dialogo*, 235. Report of Agostino Casaroli on his discussions with Archbishop Beran. Vatican City, May 20, 1963.

In Prague, Casaroli strove to employ tactics resembling those utilized in Budapest. His position, therefore, was that the matter of Archbishop Beran should be settled in combination with other church policy issues. Incidentally, this strategy – the handling of problems relating to the Catholic Church in combination – explains why Casaroli did not insist on the immediate resolution of the Mindszenty affair, which, judging by the preparations made by the Hungarian government apparatus, might have been a possibility.

The visits to Budapest of Cardinal König and Monsignor Casaroli constituted a milestone in the Mindszenty affair. The two visits were followed by a fundamental shift in the Vatican's stance on the issue. Here it is worth noting the different roles played by the two men: Whereas König's visit was a pastoral and personal one, Casaroli took a more official, formal and detached position. Initially, it seemed that both men had left Hungary without having achieved tangible results. In fact, however, there had been a significant change. Based on König and Casaroli's direct contact with Mindszenty, the Vatican authorities began to think of the Hungarian primate as a real person rather than as some kind of mythical figure. It had also become evident that the longer Mindszenty remained at the US Legation, the less value he would have for the Church and for the anticommunist cause. Thus, even the Vatican now took the view that the best solution to the whole affair might well be Mindszenty's departure from the legation. The question was how this might be achieved and what conditions might be set. Answering this question would take up much time over the ensuing eight years.

The United States strove to maintain the impression of being in the background. For instance, when the future US president, Senator Richard Nixon, who was already known as a hardliner, visited Hungary in July 1963, he chose not to meet with Mindszenty, the living symbol of anticommunism, even though the Hungarian primate was in the very next room. For political reasons, it seems the Americans were no longer interested in Mindszenty. On the contrary, as US Secretary of State Dean Rusk revealed to his Hungarian counterpart, János Péter, at a private meeting in New York in December 1964, "we have to get rid of that old bone stuck in our throat."[169]

169. László Borhi, "Távozási napló," *Heti Világgazdaság*, October 6, 2001, 99.

Evidently, Mindszenty's presence at the US Legation was increasingly perceived as a burden. Even Mindszenty sensed this, despite the efforts of the diplomatic staff to disguise their real feelings. Regarding the cardinal's perception of his own situation, one of the diplomats noted the following: "when he had appeared at the legation in 1956 seeking asylum he had been received as the representative of Hungary and that now he was 'nothing.'"[170]

The visits of König and Casaroli served temporarily to calm the Hungarian cardinal down. Soon, however, his old stubbornness returned. In a further letter to Secretary of State Rusk, dated May 13, 1963, he expressed a desire to stay at the legation for as long as possible. His main argument for doing so was his obligation to fulfill his duties as primate of Hungary:

> The Primate is today the first initiating constitutional factor for Hungary when a possibility appears. This character cannot be realized in Rome, in Vienna or on every point of the world, neither in Hungary, nor in the birth village according to the experience of Cardinal Stepinac. Only in a such frame where I was fleeing in 1956 and official reception received: on the US Legation. Here the Primate can be and really is a representative of the mutilated Hungary but also of 5 million Hungarians in the vicinity and far on the whole globe.[171]

The increasing frequency with which he emphasized his status as a symbol of the Hungarian nation and national freedom was indicative of his growing doubts. His aching conscience and his sense of having abandoned his people at the time of the 1956 revolution could only be soothed through penance. His duty, therefore, was to stay at the legation, despite all the inconveniences of his confinement there.

170. NARA RG 59, GR of the Department of State, Bureau of European Affairs, Office of Eastern European Affairs, Records Relating to Hungary 1941–77, Box 11, June 19, 1963–Dec 4, 1963. Letter of Counselor Turner B. Shelton to Robert M. McKisson, director of the Office of Eastern European Affairs, Department of State, September 10, 1963.

171. NARA RG 84, Records of the Foreign Service Posts of the Department of State, Hungary, Subject Files Relating to Cardinal Mindszenty 1956–72, Box 2. Mindszenty–Classified May–August 1963, Letter of József Mindszenty to Secretary of State D. Dean Rusk, May 13, 1963; Somorjai and Zinner, *Do Not Forget*, 221.

Pope John XXIII passed away on June 3, 1963, having only recently opened the way to improved relations with the East. After his death, the Vatican suspended its negotiations with the Hungarian government, which had begun only a month before. This decision reflected the fact that after the death of a pope the papal dicasteries (i.e., the Secretariat of State, Congregations, Tribunals, Councils and Offices) do not operate until the election of a new pope. There was no doubt, however, that the policies set in motion by John XXIII could not (easily) be reversed. At the same time, there was a general realization that the Vatican's most urgent task was not to address the "Hungarian question," still less the personal fate of József Mindszenty.

For Mindszenty, the question that now arose was the same as the one he had faced in 1958: Could he travel to the conclave? Although the details of the situation differed, the answer was similar: Cardinal Mindszenty did not attend the conclave of 1963. However, his absence on this occasion was not due to the Hungarian regime's rejection of his request to travel, for such a request was not even made. Having learned the lessons of what happened in 1958, the US State Department took no steps to arrange for Cardinal Mindszenty's travel to Rome. Nor, moreover, did the Vatican request the Hungarian authorities to guarantee Mindszenty's safe passage to the conclave.[172] The reason for the Vatican's "omission of duty" will doubtless become known once its archives are opened. For the time being, however, one can only suppose that the Hungarian Legation in Rome somehow managed to influence the Curia into not inviting Cardinal Mindszenty. The Hungarian authorities knew that without a formal Vatican invitation Mindszenty was very unlikely to want to travel. The Hungarian communist authorities prepared to use any means to diminish Mindszenty's nimbus. It was clearly in their interest to create a situation in which the Hungarian cardinal stayed away from the conclave for personal reasons rather than due to political pressure.[173]

172. Ibid., Box 6, Cardinal Mindszenty–Austrian Embassy 75F164–POL 30. Telegram no. 8063 of the Department of State to the US Legation in Vienna, for forwarding to Budapest. June 14, 1963.

173. MNL OL XIX–A–21–e–004–4/h/1963. 11. ő. e. 001/129. Appendix to daily report. Subject: Possible request concerning Mindszenty being permitted to leave for Conclave.

Irrespective of whether or not the regime was manipulating things from behind the scenes, it is a fact that Mindszenty decided in the end to stay in Budapest and miss the conclave. He made no request to the Americans that they arrange for a passport, even though Cardinal Tisserant, deacon of the College of Cardinals, did, in the end, send him a written invitation. The French ambassador to the Holy See noted in his report that Cardinal Mindszenty was to be absent from the conclave because he was unwilling to leave Budapest without an assurance that his departure would not be construed as his having renounced his rights as primate of Hungary.[174] The world soon learned of Mindszenty's decision from the reports submitted by the news agencies. One interpretation was that he was prioritizing his position over church discipline. In American public opinion the view was gaining traction that a settlement of the Catholic Church's relations with the Hungarian government was being impeded not by the regime's intransigence but – in the words of János Radványi, the Hungarian chargé d'affaires in Washington, D.C. – by "Mindszenty's silly strategy and far-fetched ideas."[175] His absence from the conclave seemed to prove that a resolution of the Mindszenty question (and the speed of such a resolution) depended, or would depend, primarily on the Hungarian cardinal himself.

The Resumption of Talks: Rome, October 1–5, 1963

On June 21, 1963, Giovanni Battista Montini, a moderate progressive and passionate theorist with a talent for diplomacy, was elected as the new pope, taking the name Paul VI. The aims of his manifesto – in addition to bringing the Council to a successful conclusion – were to broaden ecumenicism, to advance the dialogue between Christians and Marxists, and to settle relations with the communist countries. His focus on "dialogue" within his papal service influenced the history of the entire East Central European region. With a view to achieving peace, he did not rule out

174. AMAE AD Série: Europe, 1961–1970, sous-série: Saint-Siège, dossier 69, 11 juin 1963–octobre 1965, fol. 4–5. Report no. 137/EU of Guy de la Tournelle, French ambassador to the Holy See, June 12, 1963.

175. MNL OL XIX–A–21–e–004–4/i/1963. 12. ő. e. Report of Chargé d'Affaires János Radványi, June 24, 1963. Author's note: The chargé d'affaires requested US diplomatic asylum on May 17, 1967.

cooperation with such countries as Hungary that had imposed tough restrictions on the work of the Catholic Church.

On July 16, 1963, less than a month after the new pope's election to the throne of St. Peter, an important confidential meeting of the members of the Congregation of Extraordinary Ecclesiastical Affairs was held. At the meeting, the future of negotiations with the Hungarian and Czechoslovak governments was discussed. This specific Congregation was responsible for matters involving diplomacy. It was headed at the time by Cardinal Amleto Giovanni Cicognani, who had served as apostolic delegate to the United States until 1958. Cardinal Cicognani was assisted in his work by the Congregation's secretary, who at the time was Antonio Samorè, the titular archbishop of Tirnovo. Samorè's deputy was Casaroli in his position as under-secretary. The meeting was held at Casaroli's apartment, from 6 p.m. until 7.20 p.m.

When asked to decide whether, despite the complex and grave difficulties that had already been encountered, the confidential talks should be resumed, those in attendance at the meeting gave their unanimous backing for a resumption. Cardinal Fernando Cento, who, as apostolic nuncio in Brussels, had done so much for the cause of Hungarians seeking to emigrate to the New World, argued that "the initiative that has arisen so far was made in the spirit of Vatican policy as it evolved over several centuries; it is worthy of recognition and has brought benefits [...], it is worthy continuing by any measure."[176] There were differences of emphasis, however, when it came to deciding which conditions should be the cardinal ones in order to achieve at least some kind of tangible results in the negotiations. In some fashion or other, the company of assembled cardinals wished to lessen the burden placed on the Czech and Hungarian archbishops, Beran and Mindszenty. Two opinions were formulated about this modality. Some of the cardinals (Agagianian, Ottaviani, Pizzardo, and Tisserant) regarded such personnel questions as inseparable from the more general questions that faced the Church. The other group of cardinals (Cento, Confalonieri, and Testa), argued in favor of Mindszenty's prompt departure for Rome. In the end, the body identified each of the following as *conditio sine qua non: a)* The

176. Barberini, *La politica del dialogo*, 83. Sacred Congregation for Extraordinary Ecclesiastical Affairs. Confidential discussions, July 16, 1963. Negotiations with the governments of Hungary and Czechoslovakia.

appointment of bishops and their free contact with the Vatican; *b)* the recall of government commissioners assigned to dioceses; *c)* the freedom to spread the Good News, at least in religious instruction at church; *d)* the release of clergy detained for political reasons. At the end of the debate, State Secretary Cicognani pointed out that a basic requirement for both the Hungarian and the Czechoslovak governments was a favorable resolution of the Mindszenty and Beran affairs. In Mindszenty's case, "the task will be to find appropriate means of persuading them of the necessity of the step."[177] In the summer of 1963, therefore, the Vatican's cardinals voted for Mindszenty's departure from Hungary, expecting, in return, greater freedom of action for the Church. At the same time, they were aware of the sensitivity with which the plan would have to be implemented. Evidently, negotiations with the Hungarian communist regime would have to be undertaken in such a way that Cardinal Mindszenty, who was loyal to the pope but hostile to the regime, continued to be shown the deepest respect.

On July 20, 1963, that is, almost concurrently with the cardinals' discussions in Rome on the Vatican's Eastern policy, an interesting meeting took place in Moscow when a Hungarian and an American delegation happened to be in the Soviet capital at the same time. At a dinner hosted by Khrushchev, the Hungarian premier János Kádár (who was both chairman of the Council of Ministers and first secretary of the HSWP) found himself at the same table as William Averell Harriman, US ambassador-at-large. After the umpteenth toast, Harriman suddenly turned to the host, Khrushchev, and bluntly asked him to use his influence to facilitate the normalization of US–Hungarian relations, which had been plagued by the Mindszenty affair. As Kádár late recalled,

> As soon as he mentioned Mindszenty, I jumped into the conversation, remarking that the Mindszenty question was not such a big issue, because for us just two questions had remained open and unresolved since 1956. And, rather than being major theoretical issues, these problems were small ones involving [two] individuals: one of whom was Mindszenty, the other Rákosi. Well, I said, look, the Hungarians are clever people, and they have resolved [these issues] in a crafty manner, giving one of the individuals to the

177. Ibid., 86.

Americans and the other to the Soviets, and they themselves are living happily. Well, even Khrushchev was startled by this, because the two questions are not the same, I was saying it just for the slam-dunk effect. The two men looked at each other, but it was Khrushchev who responded first, telling him [Harriman] that they should swap. One can say that a rather amicable and normal atmosphere was established. We toasted once to the friendship of peoples, then to agreement, and then to normal relations between the three countries present, and so, in this way, the meeting took place in a fully tolerable fashion. Well, this is pertinent here by way of Mindszenty, with the Americans thinking hard about the issue, and with the pope and us having been given a lesson. We do not know what will happen. Experience has shown we should not take fright, because as soon as we take a proactive step, they immediately conclude that the matter is urgent for us. And so, we must always explain that [the matter] is not at all urgent for us, and that we will somehow find a solution at some point in time.[178]

In the subsequent period, this tactic – "it is not urgent for us" – was adhered to by Hungarian politicians in their negotiations with Vatican representatives.

Mindszenty read of this meeting between Kádár and Harriman in the press. The report unsettled him. He lingered on the fact that an influential US diplomat had been publicly photographed with Kádár, whom he referred to simply as "the butcher." The Hungarian primate then

pounded on his chair, saying "I am not only the spiritual leader of Hungary but I am the political leader – this is provided for in the constitution and has been provided for in every Hungarian constitution until the new Communist constitution was drawn up." He repeated on several occasions his statement that he was the political leader.[179]

178. Excerpt from János Kádár's speech at the meeting of the HSWP CC on August 2, 1963. Published in István Feitl and Karola Némethné Vágyi. *Eszmélet* [Awakening] 5, no. 18–19 (1993): 15.

179. NARA RG 59, GR of the Department of State, Bureau of European Affairs, Office of Eastern European Affairs, Records relating to Hungary 1941–77, Box 11, June 19, 1963–Dec 4, 1963. Letter of Turner B. Shelton, counselor of the US Legation, to Robert McKisson, September 10, 1963.

Cardinal Mindszenty's outburst reveals his difficulty in accepting how much the world had changed in the intervening years. Although he must have had a coherent impression of the easing of political rivalries and tensions, he nevertheless reacted antagonistically to the growing strength of more pragmatic policies, to the increasing international acceptance of the Kádár regime, and to the Vatican's Eastern policy. The Hungarian cardinal was offended by the fact that even the Americans now regarded his presence at the legation as an obstacle that threatened to undermine an improvement in their relations with the Hungarian people. Mindszenty was fighting for a noble principle, and in this struggle people needed to stand by him rather than offer support to Kádár's side. In the eyes of US diplomacy,

> These feelings were probably intensified by the Cardinal's strongly parochial outlook, his basic orientation toward the past, and his prolonged removal from any direct contact with the realities of current forces and events.[180]

In view of his personality, Mindszenty found it difficult to find his place in the world of détente.

In contrast, the Vatican's "ministry for foreign affairs" gave its clear support to John XXIII's Eastern policy. Once the decision had been taken, Casaroli wasted no time in implementing it: On August 5, 1963, he wrote to the Hungarian envoy in Rome, informing him that the Vatican was "ready to resume the commenced negotiations, once again in the most confidential fashion."[181] After the consent of the Political Committee of the HSWP CC had been received, the talks that had been commenced in Budapest in May were resumed in Rome on October 1, 1963. Held at the Apostolic Nunciature in the city, this round of negotiations lasted five days. Both sides were reluctant, on tactical grounds, to be the first to raise the matter of Mindszenty, as neither wished to give the impression of urgency, as this might imply a greater willingness to make concessions. In the end, the

180. Ibid., Box 10, Mindszenty Mai?–1964. Memorandum of Conversation, January 30, 1964.
181. MNL OL XIX–J–1–j–IV–14/005535/3/1964. Vatikán TÜK-documents, 2. d. Letter of Under-Secretary of State Agostino Casaroli to József Száll, the Hungarian legate in Rome, August 5, 1963.

Mindszenty affair was placed on the agenda as a common problem but as the last of thirteen items.

As far as the methods of negotiation were concerned, the stance taken by the Vatican officials differed from that employed during the spring talks. Thus, rather than seek the resolution of partial issues, they now aimed for a general settlement. Casaroli realized that it would be beneficial to separate the Mindszenty affair from the other issues. He reiterated that the Holy See would not instruct Mindszenty to leave Hungary, but it no longer dared guarantee the cardinal's silence on Hungary, and was still counting on him as archbishop of Esztergom.[182] At all subsequent rounds of negotiations, the Vatican insisted on these three conditions. Still, with a view to achieving a settlement, it also suggested that the true supervision of the archdiocese should be undertaken by a "*sede plena*" apostolic administrator.

The expression *sede plena* means "with an occupied seat/see." It describes the situation when, under canon law, an archbishop occupies the see, but for some reason he is prevented from undertaking (is unable to undertake) the administration of the archdiocese. Meanwhile, the term apostolic administrator indicates that the pope has taken on the administration of the archdiocese but has then delegated the tasks to someone else (i.e., to the apostolic administrator). The rights and obligations of an apostolic administrator are generally narrower in scope than those of a diocesan bishop. If, however, the Vatican does appoint an apostolic administrator with full bishop's rights, then for the length of his term the jurisdiction of the diocesan bishop is suspended, whereby the suspended bishop can no longer interfere – either directly or indirectly – in the administration of the diocese. In the Archdiocese of Esztergom, the apostolic administrator during the period under discussion was Artúr Schwarz-Eggenhofer, who was not a consecrated bishop and had not been equipped with full rights. In 1969, Schwarz-Eggenhofer passed the "baton" to the titular bishop Imre Szabó, who governed the archdiocese until Mindszenty's departure from Hungary in the autumn of 1971. This means that Mindszenty could have exercised his rights, if he had been physically capable of doing so.

182. MNL OL XIX–A–21–e–II. dosszié–0022–42/a/1963. Memorandum on the discussions held in Rome between representatives of the Hungarian government and the Holy See (October 1–5, 1963), March 22, 1964.

His confinement at the legation, however, meant that there were no opportunities for him to do so.

The Hungarian delegation made it plain that they were anticipating Mindszenty's resignation as archbishop of Esztergom. The hardening of the Hungarian government's position – from its previous mere suggestion of this condition – seems to have been linked with the negotiations held between the Vatican and Czechoslovakia in late September 1963, during which the Czechoslovak side had insisted on the resignation of Archbishop Beran of Prague. The Hungarians could not go lower than this. In the end, Archbishop Beran resigned 'in his private capacity,' and so, in return, he was permitted to retain his title of archbishop. Thus, in 1965, he could travel to Rome, where the pope created him a cardinal.

Mindszenty, however, was not such a "simple" case. Among the various difficulties, Casaroli identified the Hungarian cardinal's nature and temperament as the most significant problem. "Peculiarly, he is not willing to ask the government for clemency: indeed, it is a great difficulty for him to accept clemency, because this supposes his guilt."[183] For Casaroli, another difficulty was that Mindszenty had drawn a connection between his own fate and that of the future of the imprisoned bishops and priests and the fate of the entire Hungarian nation. Mindszenty had listed his conditions in a letter dated July 17, 1963, which he sent to the newly installed Paul VI. In essence, the conditions listed were the same as those contained in his earlier letter (of May 1963) to the US secretary of state: 1. A ban on birth control and abortion; 2. the abrogation of communist "ceremonies"; 3. the reconstruction of the Regnum Marianum Church in Budapest; 4. the release of political prisoners; 5. the return to Hungary of 35,000 young Hungarians who had been deported to Siberia; 6. an improvement in the situation of the Hungarian minorities in the neighboring countries.[184]

183. Barberini, *La politica del dialogo*, 100. Memorandum on the discussions held in Rome between representatives of the Hungarian government and the Holy See, October 1–5, 1963.

184. NARA RG 84, Records of the Foreign Service Posts of the Department of State, Hungary, Subject Files Relating to Cardinal Mindszenty 1956–72, Box 2, Mindszenty Classified May–August 1963. Letter of Cardinal Mindszenty to Paul VI., July 17, 1963. See Ádám Somorjai, *Sancta Sedes Apostolica et Cardinalis Ioseph Mindszenty III/1. Documenta 1963–1966* (Budapest: METEM, 2010), 341–46.

For the Vatican, however, none of Mindszenty's points constituted problems that needed to be resolved. Its main priority was the filling of vacant episcopal sees. Since the adoption of Law Decree No. 22 of 1957 on prior state approval for the filling of ecclesiastical posts, there had been no means of appointing bishops or apostolic administrators to vacant sees. Indeed, by this time, only five of Hungary's eleven dioceses were headed by a bishop (the dioceses of Csanád, Győr, Hajdúdorog, Székesfehérvár, and Szombathely). The other episcopal sees were either vacant – in which case the diocese was headed by a capitular vicar (Pécs, Kalocsa) – or they were headed by an apostolic administrator (Eger), or the appointed bishops were "being prevented" from carrying out their duties (Esztergom, Vác, and Veszprém). Meanwhile, without bishops, there are no priests; and without priests, there are no sacraments; and without sacraments – in as much as there is any validity to their being dispensed by the unworthy – there is no spiritual salvation. The fundamental task of the Church could fail due to a lack of basic infrastructure. The correct solution ruled out a position of firm intransigence, because this threatened to result in a catacomb church and in a shrunken role for pastoral work. The difference of opinion was far more serious than it might have seemed at first sight. Paradoxically, the Vatican's Eastern policy had to be realized in Hungary in opposition to Mindszenty, a figure who symbolized resistance to atheistic communism. It became increasingly obvious that resolving the Mindszenty problem would be a much lengthier process than had been anticipated.

Due to the setbacks in the Hungarian–Vatican talks, the US State Department decided that it was time to undertake a review of Mindszenty's refuge status. In the meantime, following President Kennedy's assassination, Lyndon Johnson, the former vice president, was installed as US president for the period until the holding of elections in the fall of 1964. For the American side, it was annoying that although Cardinal Mindszenty had always been treated with the utmost courtesy, it seemed as if US policy towards Hungary was destined to be forever dependent on his status. In their internal reports, the US diplomats frankly stated that

> our most serious concern arises over the policy implications of his rigidly negative attitude toward the idea of resolving the problem of his refuge and his persistent efforts to hamper and foreclose any practicable moves

> in that direction. The danger is obvious that his intransigence in this regard will both impair and indefinitely delay any effective execution of U.S policy towards Hungary.[185]

On January 30, 1964, State Department personnel sat down at the negotiating table with Vatican representatives with the aim of getting the Holy See to send a further high-ranking envoy to Budapest. The task of such an envoy would be to persuade Cardinal Mindszenty to accept a prompt and sensible solution to his situation.[186] A year earlier, the Americans had recognized that without the Vatican's input they would be incapable of resolving the Mindszenty affair. Now, however, they also admitted that it was not enough for the Vatican and Cardinal Mindszenty to be in written communication alone. Progress could only be made in the event of direct contact and conciliation between the Vatican authorities and the Hungarian cardinal.

The Shift in Policy of March 1964

Two Vatican representatives (Agostino Casaroli and Luigi Bongianino) and two representatives of the Hungarian government (József Prantner and Imre Miklós) held a further round of negotiations (eight discussions) in Budapest from March 14–23, 1964. This was in the spring following the second session of the Second Vatican Council. As on previous occasions, the press began speculating about what was being discussed. The journalists were expecting a positive scenario, with Mindszenty soon receiving permission to leave Hungary.

In fact, however, the Hungarian–Vatican talks examined various topics other than József Mindszenty's stay at the US Legation. For the Holy See, crucial issues included the general situation of the dioceses in Hungary, the new procedure for appointing bishops (Amendment No. 22 of 1957), and overcoming the contradictions between canon law and Hungarian civil law. The two parties also discussed all the other questions that had arisen in

185. Ibid., Sept–Dec 1963. Memorandum: Problem of Cardinal Mindszenty's refuge in the American Legation at Budapest, December 18, 1963.

186. Ibid., SOC 12–Mindszenty 1964. Telegram no. A-61 of the US State Department to the US Legation in Budapest, January 14, 1964.

1963: the freedom to administer the dioceses (i.e., without the intervention/supervision of ministerial commissioners), the oath of allegiance that church figures were required to make to the People's Republic of Hungary, free contact between bishops and the Vatican, the operation of the seminaries, operating licenses for religious orders, opportunities for religious instruction, the imprisoned or dismissed priests, freedom of the clergy to give the sacraments, activities in civil and public life, the peace priest movement, and the work of émigré priests. The discussions also addressed the matter of two diocesan bishops – Bishop Pétery of Vác and Bishop Badalik of Veszprém – whose work was being hindered, as well as the unresolved situation of four auxiliary bishops – the auxiliary bishops of Eger (János Bárd), Kalocsa (Mihály Endrey), Szombathely (József Winkler) and Pécs (Gellért Belon) – whom the Hungarian government had refused to recognize. There followed a general discussion of the problems affecting relations between the Hungarian state and the Catholic Church. The discussions were as frank and sincere as they could possibly be among diplomats. In this respect, they were unprecedented in postwar Hungary.

Once again, the Mindszenty affair featured as the last item on the agenda. Both sides were agreed that although a continuation of the situation was a possibility, they would nevertheless seek a compromise solution. This, in turn, required them to elaborate the conditions for Mindszenty's departure from Hungary. At the center of such efforts lay clemency, a full assurance of silence (silencium), and the title of archbishop of Esztergom. The distance between the respective positions was considerable, and so efforts aimed at reaching a consensus took more time than had been anticipated. Casaroli emphasized Mindszenty's innocence, while the Hungarian side stressed the legitimacy of the criminal proceedings brought against the Hungarian cardinal in 1949. The government insisted upon an act of clemency (amnesty), but it did concede that it might be prepared to offer clemency without having been requested to do so by Mindszenty or the Holy See. As was to be expected, the Hungarian side would not countenance Mindszenty's rehabilitation or his making a statement demonstrating his innocence (and possibly his rejection of clemency).[187]

187. According to Casaroli, the Hungarian side initially agreed to this, but later refused to accept it because, in their view, it would serve to rekindle the Cold War. This would be so,

In addition to clemency, the Hungarian government set two further conditions for Mindszenty's release: his renunciation of political and ecclesiastical-administrative activities and a "fully-fledged" guarantee for his silence (*silencium*). As before, the Hungarian government understood this to mean that, after his release, Cardinal Mindszenty would not undertake any political activities and would not say anything – publicly or privately – against the People's Republic of Hungary or against the communist countries in general. Here, the Hungarian government's evident aim was to prevent Mindszenty from becoming a leading émigré figure.[188] Casaroli admitted that while making such a guarantee would not be impossible, it would certainly be extremely difficult. When József Prantner, head of the State Office for Church Affairs, perplexedly asked why the pope did not simply issue a command of silence – which Mindszenty would have been obliged to honor –Casaroli soberly explained that while the Holy See could certainly take such action, it would be a sheer demonstration of power which would cause great consternation and would make a victim out of Mindszenty. Moreover, an attempt by the Vatican to silence Mindszenty would "elicit the sharpest response against the Holy See, especially from the émigré communities."[189] Casaroli identified this issue as the greatest difficulty. Knowing Mindszenty's attitudes, he stated

> His Eminence apparently does not even understand that under certain circumstances the good of the Church and the nation requires that the two be kept apart in dignity and that heroic silence be practiced.[190]

A further thorny issue was whether Mindszenty should be permitted to retain the title of archbishop of Esztergom. In this regard, the Hungarian

---

even if the Vatican were to make the statement in lieu of Cardinal Mindszenty. Barberini, *La politica del dialogo*, 119. Report of Agostino Casaroli on the resumption of contacts with the Hungarian government [March 14–24, 1964], April 10, 1964.

188. MNL OL XIX–A–21–e–III. dosszié–0022–6/h/1964, and MNL OL XIX–J–1–j–IV–14/005535/3/1964, Vatikán TÜK-documents. Memorandum on the sixth day of talks between the representatives of the Hungarian government and the Vatican, March 19, 1964.

189. Ibid., Memorandum on the fifth day of talks between representatives of the Hungarian government and the Vatican, March 18, 1964.

190. Barberini, *La politica del dialogo*, 129–45. Report of Agostino Casaroli to Cardinal A. G. Cicognani, secretary of state, April 18, 1964.

government seems to have been rather inconsistent: whereas in the spring of 1963 it had been indifferent to Mindszenty's resignation, by the fall it was strongly in favor of compelling him to resign. This, at any rate, was the point of departure at this time, too. However,

> in response to the real threat of His Excellency remaining in the country, members of the government moderated their position and announced that if Cardinal Mindszenty were to leave the country, the government would not insist on his renouncing the use of the title of Prince Primate, as long as he were to refrain from interfering, either legally or practically, in the country's affairs either as archbishop or as Primate,

Casaroli told State Secretary Cicognani.[191] The summary drafted by the Hungarian side also mentions two possibilities: 1. Mindszenty receives clemency and leaves the country, in return for a full-fledged guarantee; 2. Mindszenty receives clemency, he remains in Hungary and resigns from his post as archbishop.[192] The aim of both these variants was evidently to neutralize Mindszenty. The difference between the two was that if Cardinal Mindszenty agreed to leave Hungary, the Hungarian government – as Casaroli had reported – would not insist on his renunciation of the title of primate of Hungary. Hungary's communist regime evidently viewed Mindszenty's moving abroad as the better option. This would remove the cardinal, who was capable of provoking domestic unrest, from the country. At the same time, the regime was evidently quite content to see him remain at the legation, for his silence was assured.

Casaroli also argued for Mindszenty's departure from Hungary and for his retaining the title of archbishop of Esztergom. He explained that, under canon law, it was possible to uphold the formal situation (the unchanged nature of the office of archbishop) while also changing the

191. Barberini, *La politica del dialogo*, 120. Report of Agostino Casaroli on the resumption of contacts with the Hungarian government [March 14–24, 1964], April 10, 1964; MNL OL XIX–A–21–e–III. dosszié–0022–6/h/1964, and MNL OL XIX–J–1–j–IV–14/005535/3/1964, Vatikán TÜK-documents. Memorandum on the sixth day of talks between representatives of the Hungarian government and the Vatican, March 19, 1964.

192. MNL OL XIX–A–21–e–III. dosszié–0022–6/j/1964, and MNL OL XIX–J–1–j–IV–14/005535/3/1964. Vatikán TÜK-documents. Memorandum on the eighth day of talks between representatives of the Hungarian government and the Vatican, March 21, 1964.

situation on the ground: The Vatican would appoint an apostolic administrator *sede plena* to head the Archdiocese of Esztergom. (The apostolic administrator would have full rights, while Mindszenty's jurisdiction as archbishop would be suspended but he would retain the title of archbishop.) Casaroli's proposal was not entirely new; indeed, it had already been mentioned during the round of negotiations in the fall of 1963. What made it qualitatively different, however, was that the apostolic administrator would exercise full rights. Generally, the Holy See refrains from making such appointments, only making an exception where higher interests prevail. This is because where an episcopal see is already occupied (*sede plena*), the granting of full episcopal rights to an apostolic administrator means, in effect, the suspension of the jurisdiction of the diocesan bishop, who cannot subsequently intervene in the governing of the diocese or influence (or prevent) the work of the apostolic administrator. At the same time, regarding his governing of the diocese, the apostolic administrator with full episcopal rights is accountable, not to the diocesan bishop who is unable to perform the functions of his office, but solely to the Apostolic Holy See. Despite these drawbacks, in Mindszenty's case it was this proposal and setup that permitted, finally, progress to be made.

During his stay in Hungary, Agostino Casaroli, who was accompanied by the counselor, Luigi Bongianino, made three visits to Mindszenty at the legation: on March 14, 15 and 22, 1964. On each occasion, the meeting lasted several hours. Cardinal Mindszenty reiterated his view that abandoning his refuge would only be worthwhile if the Hungarian government were to make broad concessions to the benefit of the Catholic Church. This was, of course, the subject of the Hungarian–Vatican talks, but it was obvious that the Hungarian government was not inclined to make major concessions. Once again Casaroli encountered Mindszenty's known views on the prince primate's public legal role. At the same time, the Hungarian cardinal's Spartan way of life and his willingness to make sacrifices persuaded Casaroli that Mindszenty's priority was the fate of his Church and his people rather than his own personal destiny. Casaroli was nevertheless critical of how Mindszenty viewed himself first and foremost as primate of Hungary rather than as archbishop of Esztergom. The importance Mindszenty attributed to his status as primate "blurs his vision and dominates his activities." Casaroli's report faithfully recorded Mindszenty's words: he viewed himself as a "*vices praesidentiales gerens*" (a man with presidential competences, who deputizes for the head of state), whereby he was the one with the right to select a prime minister and install a government.[193] The ambiguous nature of the ecclesiastical and public legal functions that were (or rather had been) tied to the office of primate, form the backdrop to the Mindszenty drama: one of these functions was bound to the Mother Church, and the other to the Hungarian nation.

Mindszenty's references to his historical and constitutional duties, his insistence on his political role under the laws of the kingdom, and his having sought refuge at the legation, beg the question: What was his purpose? The answer is to be found in a letter written by the chargé d'affaires at the US diplomatic mission. In the letter, the issue of constitutional responsibility is raised once again. The cardinal is quoted as having admitted that his constitutional responsibilities were "now largely theoretical" and that this would remain the case, provided that there was no change in Hungary. The chargé d'affaires then wrote:

> As long as there was a 'half percent possibility' [of such change] he [Mindszenty] felt he should preserve the role of Prince Primate. A revolution in Hungary now appeared impossible. None, however, was expected in 1956. It appeared impossible then too. As long as there was such a 'minimum possibility' he felt he should stand ready. Should it materialize, he indicated he would feel called upon to assert his constitutional authority and appoint a government.[194]

In other words, Mindszenty was still hoping for a fundamental shift (or reversal) in politics that would lead to the end of Hungary's Sovietization. Seen from this perspective, the Hungarian cardinal's acceptance of confinement and solitude at the legation was not a renunciation or a sacrifice on his part, but the reflection of an expectation and a hope. Was the possibility of Mindszenty occupying his archiepiscopal seat after a political reversal a realistic one? Yes, it was, but only for so long as the

193. Barberini, *La politica del dialogo*, 133.

194. NARA RG 84, Records of the Foreign Service Posts of the Department of State, Hungary, Subject Files Relating to Cardinal Mindszenty 1956–72, Box 2, Cardinal File–Limited Distribution 1962–64. Letter of Chargé d'Affaires Owen T. Jones to the Department of State, February 17, 1964.

cardinal remained on Hungarian soil. This implied, however, that the overriding interest of the Kádár regime was not to condemn the cardinal but to ensure his departure from the country.

As the two sides still disagreed upon the conditions for Mindszenty's release, at the height of the negotiations József Prantner made an unexpected announcement: the Hungarian government was prepared to settle the other issues without having first resolved the Mindszenty issue. In this way, Casaroli's earlier proposal – made in October 1963 – was realized and, by common consent, the entire Mindszenty issue was separated from the other problems.[195] With this decision, Mindszenty's refuge at the legation reached a further milestone. Indeed, Casaroli suspected American influence behind the unexpected Hungarian motion. By this time, all the Western countries – apart from the United States – had raised their diplomatic relations with Hungary to the ambassadorial level. Casaroli was essentially right in his suspicions, even though the Mindszenty affair had been discreetly avoided in bilateral discussions between the United States and Hungary. The domestic political consolidation seen in Hungary during the 1960s (including the ecclesiastical policy of the Popular Front) was a far more important factor than settling the personal fate of an already isolated political opponent. This explains why the mere fact of an agreement with the Holy See took on greater value. By making its announcement, the Hungarian government in effect removed the obstacles to progress in the drafting of a Hungarian–Vatican agreement – without, however, having first resolved the matter of Cardinal Mindszenty, who – in the regime's view – had chosen for himself pseudo-imprisonment.

A Partial Agreement Without the Cardinal's Involvement

Mindszenty read with disappointment in a Viennese newspaper about the impending agreement between the Hungarian government and the Holy See. On May 29, 1963, he requested, in a telegram sent to Cardinal Cicognani, Vatican state secretary, the text of the "signed or proposed" agreement. At the time, however, none such existed, and so the Vatican

195. MNL OL XIX–A–21–e–III. dosszié–0022–6/h/1964, and MNL OL XIX–J–1–j–IV–14/005535/3/1964, Vatikán TÜK-documents. Memorandum on the sixth day of talks between representatives of the Hungarian government and the Vatican, March 19, 1964.

could not send him anything.[196] Mindszenty expected to be involved in the drafting of the agreement. This took place in a rather superficial fashion when Casaroli visited him three times in the spring of 1964.

In the end, Mindszenty received the final written text of the impending agreement on September 8, 1964, barely a week before it was signed. Casaroli blamed the Americans for the fact that Mindszenty had been ignored, as he could only be contacted via them, whereby it was impossible to rule out an indiscretion. Mindszenty read the draft agreement from start to finish. Although he had previously opposed talks, regarding them as premature and mistaken, he now approved the signing of the agreement. He even acknowledged that the Holy See had not abandoned any of its principles.[197] The text of the agreement also persuaded him that the negotiations had not been conducted against his person. The Vatican had not divulged, to the bishops in Hungary, the part of the agreement that related to him. For this, Mindszenty expressed special gratitude to the pope, as it meant he had not been humiliated.

The partial agreement between Hungary and the Apostolic Holy See was signed on September 15, 1964. This happened to be the second day of the third session of the Second Vatican Council. It was reported by the foreign press as a major news story, since this was the first time a country within the Soviet sphere of influence had signed a formal agreement with the Vatican. Some reports mentioned how the negotiating parties had put aside the matter of Mindszenty. Yet, prior to the agreement, media expectations had been great. Indeed, more than one press report had stated – based on a "high-ranking Vatican source" – that Mindszenty was certain to leave his refuge and then celebrate Mass at St. Stephen's Basilica on August 20, commemorating the foundation of the Hungarian state.[198] Meanwhile, however, in conversation with the Soviet ambassador, János

196. MMAL 030. dosszié, MFN 8509, L-3444. Typed transcript of the telegram. May 29, 1963. See Somorjai, *Sancta Sedes Apostolica et Cardinalis Ioseph Mindszenty, II. Documenta 1956–1963*, 220.

197. Mindszenty, *Napi jegyzetek*, 358–60; Szabó, *A Szentszék és a Magyar Népköztársaság*, 242. Draft speech of József Zágon at the Main Pastoral Conference (for Hungarian clergy in Western Europe), Munich, February 24, 1965; József Zágon, "A magyar egyház helyzete az 1964-es megállapodás után," *Távlatok* 73, no. 3 (2006): 314–33.

198. NARA RG 84, Records of the Foreign Service Posts of the Department of State, Hungary, Subject Files Relating to Cardinal Mindszenty 1956–72, Box 2. Cardinal File–Limited Distribution 1962–64. Press cutting: *Herald Tribune*, August 3, 1964.

Kádár mentioned that "the issue of Mindszenty and the progressive priests whom the Vatican had excommunicated was taken off the agenda because of the improper conduct of the Vatican representatives."[199] It is no coincidence that the two problems had got stuck together in Kádár's memory: As we shall see, even in 1971 the status of Mindszenty and the situation of the excommunicated priests were addressed in conjunction.

Concerning the signing of the agreement, communiques were issued concurrently in Budapest and at the Vatican. Aside from the willingness of two parties to continue negotiations, the only other "revelation" was that an instrument *(atto)*, a protocol *(protocollo)*, and two annexes *(allegati)* had been signed at the Hungarian Ministry of Foreign Affairs.[200] These three constituent parts made up the agreement, which is usually referred to as a partial agreement because it did not comprehensively resolve the problems. Indeed, a consensus had been reached on just three of the sixteen issues under discussion. Thus, the agreement addressed those three issues: the appointment of bishops, the oath of allegiance (to the People's Republic of Hungary), and the status of the Pontificio Istituto Ecclesiastico Ungherese (the Hungarian Papal Institute). The protocol listed the remaining unresolved problems. The first annex concerned the agreement on episcopal appointments, while the second related to the Pontificio Istituto Ecclesiastico Ungherese.

Here, it is worth summarizing the three issues governed by the agreement. Under the terms of the agreement, prior to the appointment of bishops, the Vatican was required to contact the Hungarian government with the names of the various candidates. Appointments were only to be made after the appropriate body of the Hungarian state (the Presidential Council) had granted its approval. In other words, the strict law on ecclesiastical appointments (Law Decree No. 22 of 1957) remained in effect, and the Holy See was still unable to freely appoint bishops. Even so, the agreement marked a shift away from what had become an untenable situation towards greater consensus. (The executive order of 1959 governing

199. AVP RF f. 077. op. 47. papka (paper folder) 230. delo (file) 8. l. 260. Memo of G. A. Denisov, Soviet ambassador in Budapest, on his conversation with János Kádár on September 19, 1964. See Baráth, *Szovjet diplomáciai jelentések*, 461.

200. For the text of the agreement, see Margit Balogh, András Fejérdy and Csaba Szabó, "Az 1964-es magyar–szentszéki részleges megállapodás," *ArchívNet* 18, no. 6. (2018), on the Internet: http://www.archivnet.hu/az-1964-es-magyar-szentszeki-reszleges-megallapodas.

the implementation of the decree was amended only in 1971 in connection with Mindszenty's departure from Hungary in the fall of that year. Despite the 1971 amendment, until as late as 1990, the paralyzing effect of the decree on episcopal jurisdiction and the influence of communist party considerations on diocesan administration remained.) The compromise, however, facilitated progress in terms of the administration of dioceses with vacant sees. Indeed, on the day the agreement was signed, the Vatican announced the appointment of five new Hungarian bishops – the first episcopal appointments in Hungary since 1951.

The second issue governed by the agreement had theoretical rather than practical significance: The Vatican recognized the oath of allegiance of Catholic clergymen to the Constitution with the following proviso: "Inasmuch as it befits a bishop or priest." Finally, on the matter of the Pontificio Istituto Ecclesiastico Ungherese, the agreement provided for the Hungarian Catholic Bishops' Conference to take possession of the Institute for the further training of Hungarian priests.[201] Since both the directors and the students of the Institute were required to be Hungarian citizens, this ruled out the possibility of émigré priests taking a role in the Institute's management in the future. After the transfer of control to the Bishops' Conference, the Pontificio Istituto Ecclesiastico Ungherese became an important center for intelligence gathering at the very heart of Rome.[202] The agreement did not cover such other issues as religious instruction in schools, the Catholic seminaries, and political activity by priests. In these fields, the existing regulations remained in force. The matter of Mindszenty was addressed only to the extent that both parties reiterated their diametrically different positions.[203]

The Hungarian government considered the agreement to have been a victory, while the Catholic Church seemed to have drawn scant benefit.

201. MNL OL XIX–J–1–j–IV–14/005535/2/1964, Vatikán TÜK-documents; MNL OL XIX–A–21–d–0022–23/2/1964. Information report on the agreement signed with the Vatican, October 7 and 12, 1964.

202. István Bandi, "Adalékok a Pápai Magyar Intézet történetéhez, állambiztonsági módszertani megközelítésben," and Stefano Bottoni, "Egy különleges kapcsolat története: A magyar titkosszolgálat és a Szentszék, 1961–1978," in *Csapdában: Tanulmányok a katolikus egyház történetéből, 1945–1989*, ed. Gábor Bánkuti and György Gyarmati (Budapest: ÁBTL, 2010), 189–205, 264–65.

203. MNL OL XIX–A–21–e–0022–20/a/1964. Minutes, September 15, 1964.

Of course, a success for the Church at the time of the agreement was the preservation of its hierarchy, which served as a guarantee for the Hungarian Catholic Church's future survival. This was true even though the hierarchy was to comprise bishops loyal to the government. Criticism of the agreement intensified when it became apparent that it had not brought immediate relief to ecclesiastical life in Hungary and when even the long-term benefits proved to be less substantial than anticipated. Indeed, the Hungarian Catholic Church soon faced a series of new hurdles to its pastoral work, additional restrictions on religious instruction in schools, and a further wave of arrests and criminal convictions based on accusations of conspiring against the state. The Vatican even failed to persuade the Hungarian government to establish formal diplomatic relations through the exchange of envoys. The fundamental problem remained: Hungary's communist party state and the Catholic Church did not share a common way of thinking or – even more importantly – a common morality. Despite this obstacle to achieving a common understanding, the two parties embarked on a series of negotiations with a view to establishing a common vocabulary.

As far as Mindszenty's refuge status was concerned, Casaroli continued to make gloomy statements. He doubted that rapid progress could be made. He identified as a principal obstacle to progress the intransigence of the Hungarian cardinal. At the same time, his attention was caught by one of Mindszenty's casual remarks, namely his expression of a desire to visit the Hungarians residing in the United States and other foreign countries.[204] The year 1964 marked the first occasion that Mindszenty deviated from his much-repeated line that it was his duty to remain in Hungary! Yet, regardless of how he approached his situation, he would always reach the conclusion that his constitutional role as primate of Hungary and his physical presence in "the lands of St. Stephen" were indispensable. When, from June 14–21, 1965, a further round of talks was held in Rome, Casaroli assessed a resolution of the Mindszenty issue as more unlikely than ever before.[205]

204. NARA RG 84, Records of the Foreign Service Posts of the Department of State, Hungary, Subject Files Relating to Cardinal Mindszenty 1956–72, Box 2, SOC 12–Mindszenty 1964. Telegram from Acting Chargé d'Affaires Richard W. Tims to the Department of State, September 11, 1964. See Somorjai, *Sancta Sedes Apostolica et Cardinalis Ioseph Mindszenty III/1*, 192.

205. MNL OL M–KS 288. f. 5/370. ő. e. 116. fol. Report on the Hungarian–Vatican talks, July 9, 1965.

The American diplomats at the legation tried to improve conditions for their guest, without partaking in his theorizing and politicizing or becoming involved in his ecclesiastical functions. Visitors from the Vatican brought some variety to Mindszenty's routine, but everyday life at the legation was generally rather monotonous. A report made at the time notes that "one of the best things that have happened to the cardinal in a long time was the dentist's visit here last week."[206] When his quarters were being painted and Cardinal Mindszenty was required to spend ten days in the room normally used by the chargé d'affaires, the interlude was ironically referred to as "his longest trip" in recent years.[207]

Although the Hungarian cardinal was in safety in the building on Liberty Square (Szabadság tér), long-term confinement took its toll. As a way of passing the time and overcoming his agonizing loneliness, Mindszenty kept a diary of his impressions and observations. The first entry is dated December 22, 1956, while the final one dates to August 29, 1971. His notes reveal many interesting details and a lesser-known image of Mindszenty emerges, namely that of a brooding man who yearned for freedom but also reckoned with death. The Hungarian cardinal had never been the hermit type, always surrounding himself, for better or worse, with advisors. Since November 4, 1956, however, no one had been beside him.

It was during his time at the US Legation that Mindszenty celebrated the fiftieth anniversary of his ordination on June 20, 1965. He had wished to invite eighteen people to his "Golden Mass," but this number had shocked the Americans, and so the service was ultimately attended by a small number of legation staff, Mindszenty's confessor, his two sisters and a nephew. He gave the sermon in English rather than in Hungarian. Cardinal König, who was visiting Budapest for a second time, passed on Pope Paul VI's good wishes and presented Mindszenty with a personal gift.

206. NARA RG 59, GR of the Department of State, Bureau of European Affairs, Office of Eastern European Affairs, Records Relating to Hungary 1941–71. Box 12, IX. Oct 1, 1966–Aug 31, 1967. Report of Acting Chargé d'Affaires Richard W. Tims, November 16, 1966.

207. NARA RG 59, GR of the Department of State, Bureau of European Affairs, Office of Eastern European Affairs, Records Relating to Hungary 1941–77, Box 11, Refuge Part Four, 1962. Letter of Chargé d'Affaires H. G. Torbert, Jr. to Harold C. Vedeler, Director of the Office of Eastern European Affairs, Department of State, March 15, 1962.

Mindszenty, however, was offended by the fact that the golden jubilee of his ordination was effectively ignored by the College of Cardinals, the US Legation diplomatic corps, and the official Hungarian Catholic Church. Still, he received personally twenty-three letters of good wishes, sixteen of which came from abroad and seven from inside Hungary.

Cardinal Mindszenty celebrated holy Mass every day in his room. On Sundays, his Mass was attended by the Catholics working at the legation and by several Catholic diplomats from other diplomatic missions, including the British, Belgian, Danish, French, Italian, Dutch, and Swiss embassies/legations. These occasions served to lighten the Hungarian cardinal's mood and to reassure those diplomats who were interested in his situation but would otherwise have been dependent on rumor and speculation. Often, however, Mindszenty celebrated Mass alone, even occasionally on feast days. He assumed that the Americans were preventing foreign diplomats from attending on security grounds. In fact, however, as noted in one of the reports, interest waned because it was difficult to understand his sermons, which he gave in broken English.[208] Another expectation was that his sermons should be apolitical. Yet, in one of his draft sermons, Cardinal Mindszenty noted, in the context of the shockingly high number of martyrs in early Christianity, that "Only during the Soviet Empire of the twentieth century has the number of the church martyrs been appreciably greater."[209] To the great annoyance of the cardinal, the legation requested that this reference be omitted from the final version of the sermon.

Remedies for Loneliness

Mindszenty read and wrote profusely. He was attentive to events in Hungary and elsewhere in the world throughout his time at the legation. Each morning, he received the Hungarian dailies (published in Budapest and the county seats), and he also was a regular reader of such periodicals as *Pártélet* (Party Life), the HSWP's propaganda magazine. After shorter or

208. NARA RG 84, Records of the Foreign Service Posts of the Department of State, Hungary, Subject Files Relating to Cardinal Mindszenty, 1956–72, Box 1, Mindszenty–Classified, 1961. Letter of H. G. Torbert to Harold C. Vedeler, May 25, 1961.

209. Ibid., Mindszenty–Classified 1958. Memo of Louis Toplosky, second secretary at the legation, for Chargé d'Affaires Ackerson, January 24, 1958.

longer delays, he also received foreign newspapers and the émigré publications. Soon after his arrival at the legation, he began writing his *Memoirs*, and he also spent time writing several historical works.

One of these works was an economic and political analysis of contemporary Hungary, during the writing of which he examined press articles and official government statistics. He focused on the period 1948–1959, addressing in greatest detail the three years of Kádár's government (1957–1959).[210] Under the title *Arcképek materialista talajon, avagy bolsevik arcképek* (Portraits on Materialist Soil, or Bolshevik Portraits), he evaluated and analyzed biographical works on Marx, Engels, Lenin, Stalin, Malenkov, Khrushchev, and eighteen other figures in the workers' movement; this work remains unpublished.[211] He told Cardinal König in confidence that he had studied Marxism in such great depth that he might well have been able to teach it at university.[212] A particular feature of Mindszenty's *Portraits* was the exposure of the responsibility borne by the protagonists for the rise of atheistic bolshevism, a movement which, in Mindszenty's view, had been born in blood and nurtured in terror.

A historical work by Mindszenty entitled *Egy különös sorsú nemzet* (A Nation with a Special Fate) was initially expected to consist of twelve parts, but it remains in manuscript form to this day.[213] His aim in authoring this work was to familiarize the world at large with a thousand years of Hungarian history. In the work, Mindszenty ponders the past from the Magyar conquest until his own era. Some historical periods were intentionally omitted or addressed in no more than summarial form. At the focus of his account were Hungary's struggles to defend western Christianity, including the sacrifices made by the Church. The entire work is written in a pessimistic vein. Other than on a few occasions, the emphasis is laid on the tragedies that have befallen Hungary, whereby three events in the thousand years of Hungarian history are identified as fateful national

210. NARA RG 59, GR of the Department of State, Bureau of European Affairs, Office of Eastern European Affairs, Records Relating to Hungary 1941–77, Box 10, Refuge Part III, 1960–61. Letter of József Mindszenty to US Secretary of State Christian A. Herter, February 5, 1960; Somorjai and Zinner, *Do Not Forget*, 84.

211. MMAL Typed manuscript entitled "01 Arcképek materialista talajon."

212. Ibid., 061/b. dosszié, "Írások a depositióval kapcsolatban 1." [Writings on the deposition] 2. ő. e.

213. Ibid., 50. d. Manuscript of the work entitled "Egy különös sorsú nemzet."

tragedies: the Mongol invasion, the lengthy period of Ottoman rule, and the "Russian" invasion(s). A key idea in the work is that the country survived each of these periods of devastation by virtue of the Christian faith and the adulation of Mary. Consequently, this would be the only way out of the country's current occupation.

The postman brought many letters and greeting cards to the legation. The majority were rejected or immediately destroyed. Only simple postcards that did not contain political or otherwise contentious matters were passed on to Cardinal Mindszenty. From time to time, Mindszenty asked to reply to one or another of the received messages, but the procedure employed at the legation was as follows:

> His own reply is never sent but on occasion the Chargé may wish to authorize one of the officers to write a careful letter to one of the correspondents explaining the circumstances of the cardinal's refuge.[214]

Many times Mindszenty requested the consent of the US State Department to the publication of his works – even under a pseudonym. Such requests were always rejected. The writing of such works never completely satisfied the cardinal's appetite for action, and there was no sense of creative catharsis. This, too, was a price Mindszenty had to pay for his refuge.

As time passed, Cardinal Mindszenty's English language skills improved to the point of being tolerable. He learned the language from records. He practiced small talk with legation personnel, and he wrote countless sermons in English. His mind never rested, but his enterprising spirit sometimes waned. At such times, he would question listlessly: "Why work? It serves no purpose." During the day, Mindszenty was plagued by the dullness of his situation, by his confinement, and by the endless waiting and hoping. At night, he was tortured by his dreams. It seems he feared going to sleep; instead of retiring to his bed, he would often fall asleep fully clothed on the couch or in an armchair. He shaved regularly, but otherwise he tended to abstain from ablutions, doing so perhaps out

214. NARA RG 84, Records of the Foreign Service Posts of the Department of State, Hungary, Subject Files Relating to Cardinal Mindszenty 1956–72, Box 2, Cardinal File – Limited Distribution 1962–64. Memorandum of Chargé d'Affaires H. G. Torbert Jr. on procedures relating to the cardinal, December 4, 1962.

of penitence or in line with the example set by the hermits of old.[215] It was as if he wished in this way to atone for the past and pray for the future. In his dreams, he experienced a strange mixing of the past with the present. He would often find himself in a struggle with Stalin, Kádár or even Khrushchev. In such dreams he would talk to them using the informal form of you – which made him feel very ashamed when he woke up. He was haunted during the night by the specter of detention, interrogation, flight, guards, judges and so forth.

He often mused on the past, as names and faces flashed before him. Thinking about the decades he had spent in Zalaegerszeg brought him relief. On hearing of the death of an old colleague, he more than once wrote self-critically of his excessive strictness and that only now did he truly appreciate the person. He lovingly remembered those who had given him valuable advice or simply their attention. But he recalled even those who had caused him injury. An enduring characteristic of Mindszenty was his reserve when dealing with someone he did not know well. Indeed, his distrust of strangers was slow to dissipate. Yet he even said a quiet prayer for his great adversary, Mátyás Rákosi, on hearing of his death. Later, after his release, he stated that he was not an enemy of the communists but would always remain an enemy of communism.[216] While he could learn of events from the press and from conversations with legation staff and his visitors, he could not shape them at all.

Mindszenty liked to have his room heated even in the summer months. He grew anxious when changes were made to his routine. During his time at the legation, many staff came and went. At times, therefore, it was unclear who was responsible for cleaning and ironing his vestments and the altar-cloth. He was reluctant to burden the wife of a diplomat with such tasks, and yet he did not wish to ask a non-Catholic.[217] There were moments when he felt

215. One of the diplomats stated that Cardinal Mindszenty's "underwear was incinerated after a month, because it was not worth washing it, and his overwear was incinerated from time to time. He ate onions and quite often garlic too, and so the smell became overpowering." ÁBTL 3.2.3. Mt–975/3. 266. fol. Report, February 27, 1976. The information on Mindszenty was provided by the US cultural attaché (Stephen Dachy).

216. Emil Csonka, "A kor és a bíboros," in Mindszenty, *Napi jegyzetek*, 141.

217. NARA RG 84, Records of the Foreign Service Posts of the Department of State, Hungary, Subject Files Relating to Cardinal Mindszenty 1956–72, Box 2, Cardinal File–Limited Distribution 1962–64. Memo on the conversation, April 22, 1963.

his situation was unbearable. There was no-one in whom he could confide at the legation. Thus, he had to be his own counselor, whereby he was sometimes overcome by doubts, hesitation and uncertainty. Work was the only recourse, if he was to free himself from tormenting thoughts. Yet his confinement dampened his desire for accomplishing objectives. On several occasions he wrote in his diary: "I should go outside and get involved."[218]

In the evening hours, after he had finished his work, he would take his daily stroll in the legation's tiny courtyard, accompanied by one of the diplomats or by the officer on duty who spoke Hungarian. One of his dearest companions was J. Theodore Papendorp, who served at the US diplomatic mission from 1961 until 1968, initially as consul and then as first secretary at the embassy. Papendorp assisted the cardinal by acting as a kind of altar attendant, butler and secretary. When staff at the legation wrote or spoke of Mindszenty, they always referred to him as "the Guest." The notes made by legation staff reveal what was of concern to the cardinal when he was not agonizing over his own fate or that of the Hungarian nation. Such records also show how he was perceived by his American hosts. As one diplomat wrote,

> I would describe Cardinal Mindszenty as a courteous elderly gentleman who has certain distinct idiosyncracies [!], but whose predominant characteristic is his single-mindedness about Hungary. [...] He is extremely courteous and formal, but jokes and enjoys light conversation as well as serious. He does not seem disturbed by the sometimes casual treatment he receives in the Legation. [...] He is definitely interested in the operation of the Legation (who does what) and has even accosted visiting Americans to ask their functions. On one [!] occasion he showed a great deal of interest in the development of Israel during the past ten years. He was not aware that a significant feature of Israeli agricultural growth has been the formation of agricultural cooperatives to till new land, and at first assumed that these meant strong Communistic elements. As a Protestant, I have never raised religious questions with the cardinal. He is aware of my church membership and has discussed acquaintances of his in my church, but has gone no further than that. He gives the impression of respecting the

218. Mindszenty, *Napi jegyzetek*, 286. Entry for October 30, 1962.

religious convictions of others. One attendance at mass, and one comment on family religious practices drew no particular response. His major interest, from my experience, has been Hungary. He is more interested in political and historical questions, but also in day-to-day developments, events outside of the Legation, our daily association with Hungarians, and the like. [...] He often concentrates so thoroughly on a topic that he is not aware of his surroundings, and does not hesitate to continue a conversation while standing in heavy rain. As often as not, when this is in Hungarian, I will completely lose his train of thought, and although this must become plain, it does not seem to bother him and little or no comment from me is called for other than nods of agreement. Such conversations, however, are almost always anecdotal or historical in the personal sense.[219]

The cardinal could not complain about his accommodation. He was given a two-room apartment with a bathroom on the third floor of the building. In 1959, *Die Furche*, a Catholic newspaper in Vienna, published a report on Cardinal Mindszenty and his apartment in the legation, claiming that a group of journalists had visited him there. It later transpired that the visit of the journalists was a fabrication. Yet, the description of Mindszenty's apartment was subsequently deemed accurate by the chargé d'affaires:

The correspondents of Die Furche were taken up to the 3rd floor in an elevator. A steel door fitted with electric alarm bells gives access to the wing of the 3rd storey destined for the residence of the Primate and his bodyguard. [...] Over the couch where the cardinal sleeps there hangs a crucifix and a portrait of Pope John XXIII. In front of two half-closed windows there is a round table with a few chairs. In a corner a writing-desk can be seen, and on a nearby table, an improvised altar and a chalice, missals, two candles and a wooden cross. [...] He leads a severe life, eats sparingly, on two days of the week he partakes only of bread and water, often keeps vigils, gets up very early in the morning, celebrates the morning mass, and spends the rest of the day in prayer or studies. During the night,

219. NARA RG 59, GR of the Department of State, Bureau of European Affairs, Office of Eastern European Affairs, Records Relating to Hungary 1941–77, Box 10, Refuge Part I, 1956–57 (1971). Memorandum, May 2, 1957.

> he is hermetically locked within the wing of the building reserved for him, while during daytime – and the office hours – he is allowed to walk to other parts of the Legation as well. Twice or three times a day, accompanied by a guard, he may walk down to the small square courtyard where he can walk a few steps, meanwhile being watched by an impotent Communist guard from the neighbouring building which is higher than the Legation.[220]

Mindszenty declined the offer of a television, but he did listen to the radio, albeit he usually switched it on to confound potential eavesdroppers. In this inner exile, he became isolated from the world, which undoubtedly left its mark on his spirit. Although conditions at the legation were far better than they had been in prison, Mindszenty was still cut off from the outside world, from the faithful, and from the Church. From 1963 he was no longer denied contact with the Vatican, but he still could not correspond with his bishops and priests. Other than his confessor, the first clergyman with whom he could speak – since the departure of his secretary on November 8, 1956 – was Cardinal König, who came to the legation on April 18, 1963. The interval had lasted six and a half years. The route and method of contact remained the same as it had been before: he submitted any letter he wrote in an unsealed envelope, which the legation then forwarded to the State Department. From time to time, Mindszenty attempted to evade the ground rules of his refuge. For instance, on one occasion, he was caught making a telephone call. A security officer noticed that someone was telephoning from an extension on the third floor. Listening in to the conversation, he realized that Hungarian was being spoken and that the "culprit" must be the cardinal.[221] It could not be ascertained whether Mindszenty had done this before, but even this single occasion was enough for the Americans, who concluded that

220. NARA RG 84, Records of the Foreign Service Posts of the Department of State, Hungary, Records Relating to Cardinal Mindszenty 1956–72, Box 1, Mindszenty–Classified 1959, 570.3. The original article, published in *Die Furche* on October 10, 1959 and entitled "Besuch bei Kardinal Mindszenty," was republished in Italian in the newspaper *La Stampa*. It was this article in Italian that the legation received from the Press Service of the Italian Ministry of Foreign Affairs.

221. NARA RG 59, GR of the Department of State, Bureau of European Affairs, Office of Eastern European Affairs, Records Relating to Hungary 1941–77, Box 11, IV, January–June 1964. Letter of Acting Chargé d'Affaires Turner B. Shelton to Harold C. Vedeler, June 4, 1964.

> the guest is not strongly impelled by conscience to abide by the established ground rules of his refuge and is neither sensitive nor concerned (he certainly cannot be unaware of the risk) about possible embarrassment of the Legation or impairment of its position.[222]

On another occasion, he was caught trying to smuggle out money and a letter, when returning a borrowed book:

> "The week before last, Joe Sherman (one of the political officers you met while you were here) was on duty one evening and noted that a package wrapped in newspaper had apparently surreptitiously been placed by the cardinal so that it could be picked up in his room by one of the char force during their nightly cleaning. While this particular member of the char force was busy doing something else, Joe removed the package and, keeping it overnight, showed it to me the next morning," the chargé d'affaires, Turner B. Shelton, reported to Washington. "It was a book published a number of years ago listing the principal members of the Catholic hierarchy. [...] Enclosed in the book was a note thanking the outside individual for sending him the book. [...] There was also an envelope containing some money with a notation requesting that it be used for the poor."[223]

While the cardinal was permitted to receive books, the purpose of doing so could not be to disguise covert messages. The chargé d'affaires had no choice but to admit to the State Department in Washington that "the cardinal's channel with the outside is more effective than had been realized and may be of long standing."[224] After this incident, strict precautions were introduced, and any contact between Mindszenty and the cleaning staff was watched with eagle eyes. Trash was subject to checks before its disposal, with a view to preventing the exchange of written messages.

222. Ibid., Letter of Harold C. Vedeler to Chargé d'Affaires Turner B. Shelton (Budapest), June 10, 1964.

223. Ibid., Refuge Part Five, 1963. Letter of Chargé d'Affaires Turner B. Shelton to Harold C. Vedeler, December 27, 1962.

224. Ibid., Letter of Chargé D'Affaires Owen T. Jones to Harold C. Vedeler, January 10, 1963.

Mindszenty still had access to a few covert channels, and occasionally he would use them to send or receive messages. Cardinal König could pass on messages the most easily, for he was exempted from body searches. When the émigré Hungarian clergy learned that König was to make his first visit to Budapest in April 1963, they arranged for him to take a message to Mindszenty, telling the Hungarian cardinal that, even if requested to do so by the pope himself, he should not travel to Rome, for this would be detrimental to the cause of the Hungarian Catholic Church.[225] Similarly, it was König who, in May 1969, forwarded Mindszenty's letter to John Sabo, a parish priest in South Bend, Indiana. In the letter, the Hungarian cardinal asked Sabo to arrange for the publication of his memoirs after his death.[226] The "conspiring" of the two prelates, who had no experience in such activities, was soon revealed. Although the Americans then expressed their indignation, they nevertheless pledged to ensure that the memoirs – which, as the correspondence had made plain, already extended to between four and six volumes – would not fall into the hands of the Hungarian regime.[227]

"I Do Not Want to Die Here..."

As time passed, Mindszenty's health problems became an increasingly serious issue for his hosts. The possibility of a grave illness or even death was mentioned with growing frequency. The cardinal's health began to decline in the spring of 1964. His respiratory problems gave rise to fears of a recurrence of the tuberculosis he had caught in prison. He suffered a pulmonary hemorrhage and a painful hip. While in prison, he had been beaten on the foot, whereby the blood vessels had become painfully swollen and inflamed. Legation staff feared they would get infected, so the physician ordered that Mindszenty's movements be restricted and he barred contact with other persons, including the giving of communion.

225. András Máthé-Tóth, *A II. vatikáni zsinat és a magyar elhárítás: A Történeti Hivatalban fellelhető levéltári anyag alapján*, www.vallastudomany.hu/Members/matetoth/vtmtadocs/m-ta_II_vatikani_zsinat.

226. NARA RG 84, Records of the Foreign Service Posts of the Department of State, Hungary, Subject Files Relating to Cardinal Mindszenty 1956–72, Box 4, H. E. File, July–December 1970. Letter of József Mindszenty to Fr. John Sabo, May 13, 1969.

227. Ibid., Letter of Ambassador Alfred Puhan to Secretary of State Richard T. Davies, October 20, 1970.

An emergency plan was made for the cardinal's possible evacuation by air to the US military hospital in Wiesbaden, and several emergency scenarios were elaborated. The Americans were prepared for the worst. They drafted detailed instructions on who should be contacted in the event of illness or death, on providing medical care until the last rites had been performed, and on the identification of the corpse (which was to be viewed by the contact persons). A shocking but obvious conclusion was drawn: Refuge would end on the cardinal's death. The corpse was only to be released to whoever had been approved by the Hungarian government to receive it. The destination of the cardinal's earthly remains thus remained an open question. It was acknowledged that the Hungarian authorities might prevent the release of the corpse to Mindszenty's sisters or to representatives of the Church.[228] Later, the instructions were revised, and it was decided that if the cardinal were to pass away under circumstances that made the reason for death a political issue, then an autopsy would have to be performed. Such an autopsy would best then be conducted by an American military doctor in the presence of a Hungarian pathologist.[229]

On August 28, 1965, the US chargé d'affaires in Budapest formally informed the Hungarian Ministry of Foreign Affairs that Mindszenty's life was in danger. At his request, the Hungarian authorities permitted four US physicians to enter Hungary and examine the cardinal at the legation.[230] Minister of Foreign Affairs János Péter even addressed the details of a possible funeral: "He should be buried with a minimum of ceremony in Csehimindszent [his native village]."[231] Thus, regarding the site of his possible burial, American fears of the desecration of the cardinal's memory were unfounded. Meanwhile, however, the Hungarian side remained firmly

228. NARA RG 59, GR of the Department of State, Bureau of European Affairs, Office of Eastern European Affairs, Records Relating to Hungary 1941–77, Box 11, V, July 1, 1964–July 31, 1965. Guidance for use when Cardinal Mindszenty is at point of death or dies in American Legation at Budapest, September 25, 1964.

229. NARA RG 84, Records of the Foreign Service Posts of the Department of State, Hungary, Records Relating to Cardinal Mindszenty 1956–72, Box 4, H. E. File, July–December 1968. Addendum concerning performance of an autopsy, December 26, 1968.

230. MNL OL XIX–A–21–e–0022–5/b/1965. 4. ő. e. The proposal of the State Office for Church Affairs concerning the Mindszenty issue, September 10, 1965.

231. Ibid., XIX–A–21–e–0022–5/c/1965. 5. ő. e. and MNL OL M–KS 288. f. 5/373. ő. e. 120. fol. Proposal of Minister of Foreign Affairs János Péter, August 28, 1965. See Ólmosi, *Mindszenty és a hatalom*, 111.

opposed – if the need arose – to Mindszenty receiving medical treatment abroad. The authorities made it plain that they would insist, under such circumstances, on the fulfillment of their earlier conditions – a guarantee for his silence and the renunciation of the title of archbishop of Esztergom. It seemed they failed to appreciate that a man's life or death was at stake.[232]

For its part, the Vatican showed a better appreciation of the human aspects of the issue and a greater willingness to push for a prompt resolution of Mindszenty's situation. Accordingly, on September 13, 1965, Casaroli made a renewed visit to Hungary – this time accompanied by the young counselor Gabriele Montalvo. The aim of the visit was to persuade Mindszenty of the necessity of his departure from Hungary. This was the first and last time that Mindszenty was at the focus of a visit by Casaroli. In a meeting with Casaroli, the new US chargé d'affaires in Budapest, the Catholic Elim O'Shaughnessy, made no secret of his concerns for Mindszenty's health. He pointed out the inconvenience that Mindszenty's death at the legation would cause. The medical opinion stated beyond any doubt that József Mindszenty had tuberculosis, a condition for which he had already received treatment when under house arrest. This grave disease was a cause for concern. Still, Casaroli found Mindszenty to be in far better health than he had anticipated. Moreover, he noted how the Hungarian cardinal had retained his customary "fighting" spirit. After his departure from the legation, Casaroli even concluded – in contradiction to the physicians' opinion – that "the cardinal's illness is not serious, and the situation is not urgent."[233] In effect, therefore, he declined to insist on further talks on the Mindszenty issue. Of course, he also told Mindszenty that in the pope's view the illness provided an opportunity – without violating principles – for a dignified and just solution to his situation, whereby his treatment abroad would be the best course of action.[234]

232. Ibid., M–KS 288. f. 5/374. ő. e. 56. fol. Joint proposal of the State Office for Church Affairs and the Agitation and Propaganda Department of the HSWP CC concerning the Mindszenty issue, September 10, 1965. For the text of the proposal, see Szabó, *A Szentszék és a Magyar Népköztársaság*, 286.

233. Ibid., XIX–A–21–e–VII. dosszié–0022–5/f/1965. Memorandum on the second day of talks between representatives of the Hungarian government and the Vatican. September 15, 1965.

234. Casaroli, *The Martyrdom of Patience*, 105.

While Mindszenty accepted that his disease presented an opportunity, he attributed little importance to his illness and to the difficulties faced by his hosts. He was, at most, uneasy about the additional costs that had arisen. Once again, he firmly stated that he would not leave the legation until his conditions were met. Even though he often felt too weak for the battle, he was determined to deny the Hungarian communist regime even the slightest satisfaction.

> I should be outside, getting involved. But I am already a dead and buried man. Remorsus sum mundo, praeprimis superioribus [I have drawn away from the world, especially from hauteur]. I do not want to die here, but I have my conditions,

he lamented.[235] It is no wonder that progress in the negotiations was so slow. Further, perhaps to the irritation of those who were preparing for his funeral, Mindszenty recovered from his life-threatening illness. Indeed, despite having been so ill, the Hungarian cardinal made a relatively quick recovery. By the beginning of the following year, his health had returned. In the records of the two governments the disappointment is palpable as their hopes that the matter might be "resolved" were dashed.

THE EXCHANGE OF ENVOYS

After the health scare was over, Mindszenty wrote once more to President Johnson. In his letter, dated July 22, 1966, the Hungarian cardinal inquired about the best solution to his situation. He began by reiterating "I cannot accept exile to my birthplace." He then stated that

> I cannot go in a cloister. 99% of these have been eliminated by deportation of the religious and confiscation of the property. [...] And, without fulfillment of the my and the Vatican's condition for departure, could I leave Hungary? Such a step would make worthless and ridiculous the witness I have sought to give during eighteen years of imprisonment and asylum and signify a victory of Kádár and his illegal regime. What is still

235. Mindszenty, *Napi jegyzetek*, 403. Entry for March 6, 1966.

> more: neither in Hungary nor in the West I can be "as free" a living protest as I was until now in prison and asylum. Further, I would be irreverently forgetting the noble standpoint of the Holy Father concerning me. I cannot ask for mercy from the regime, from the lethal enemy of my Fatherland. My justification is the same today: I can be a persecuted captive of the regime, but I will not be obligated to it.[236]

His words constituted a statement of belief in the necessity of remaining at the legation.

International Détente versus Confrontation

The partial agreement of 1964 had not diminished the difficulties presented by efforts to resolve the Mindszenty affair. Although the conditions set by the Hungarian regime and the Vatican's possibilities had become more transparent, the differences between the two sides nevertheless seemed unbridgeable even now, especially in relation to the need for the cardinal to remain silent and refrain from political activity. True, the Hungarian government's demand that the cardinal abstain from fighting a "war" against the country's communist regime may have seemed sensible. However, the Vatican, lacking Mindszenty's prior consent, was unwilling to guarantee this. At the same time, the Vatican was similarly eager that Mindszenty refrain from any political (or even ecclesiastical) activity that might then provide the regime with a pretext for introducing further repressive measures. As Cardinal Mindszenty grew older, he became a less dangerous foe. Signs of his intellectual decline were noticed by the Americans, with one diplomat even noting that "the letters of the cardinal are becoming more unintelligible."[237]

Yet, in fact, his letters were still very easy to understand. All Mindszenty's writings and statements are steeped in a profound sense of duty

236. NARA RG 59, GR of the Department of State, Central Foreign Policy Files 1964–66, Box 3222, SOC 12–1. 1/1/65. HUNG. Letter of Cardinal Mindszenty to President Johnson, July 22, 1966. See Somorjai and Zinner, *Do Not Forget*, 312–13.

237. Ibid., Bureau of European Affairs, Office of Eastern European Affairs, Records Relating to Hungary 1941–77, Box 11, July 1, 1964–July 31, 1965. Written by hand onto the letter of Chargé d'Affaires Elim O'Shaughnessy of May 22, 1965.

– as primate of Hungary – towards his nation. They reveal a man who was determined to fight for the principles of freedom and justice and against the enemies of his country. It was this sense of mission that nurtured his patriotic commitment and the sense of responsibility he felt towards the Hungarian people. It cannot be denied that, on occasion, this sense of mission led him to write unconsidered lines that are shocking in themselves. For instance, he wrote the following:

> Not a U Thant guest and shameful comedy in Budapest and Western support is necessary, but on moral basis because of the crass genocide and open breach of treaties a Vietnam punishing action would be convenient and justified.[238]

Mindszenty's statement can barely be understood as anything other than acceptance of war as a means to defeat communism, which, in his view, could legitimately be employed against the Soviets and their mercenaries who were occupying Hungary. Is it morally acceptable to confront communism by arguing for a war? Was the historical situation such that there remained no option but to countenance death in the fight for liberty? Such extreme modes of thought have usually been the preserve of revolutionary utopists or millenarian heretics – or of elderly deranged minds who were living in confinement and lacked knowledge of the situation on the ground. Evidently, Mindszenty's appeal was for liberty rather than for war, and yet he failed to consider the possible consequences. He was not a smart or shrewd politician; rather, he was driven by the mission-like cause of defeating godless communism. Indeed, a hatred of communist ideology and a loyalty to the Hungarian nation became forged in his heart.

The time had clearly come for a reconsideration of the various factors and opportunities. If there had been sanguine hopes that the meeting of Paul VI and President Johnson on October 4, 1965 might lead to

238. Accessible in several places, including NARA RG 84, Records of the Foreign Service Posts of the Department of State, Hungary, Subject Files Relating to Cardinal Mindszenty 1956–72, Box 3, SOC 12 Cardinal File, Jan–Sept 1965. Letter of Cardinal Mindszenty to President Johnson, Budapest, March 21, 1965; Published in Somorjai and Zinner, *Do Not Forget*, 296–97.

Mindszenty's departure from the US Legation,[239] such hopes were soon overridden by reality and the seeming impossibility of a solution. In truth, no-one had a strong interest in a prompt solution. The Hungarian side had perhaps the least interest, but even Casaroli's activities began to wane when the realization was made at the Vatican that Mindszenty's presence in Rome would be "detrimental and even a source of conflict."[240] Mindszenty kept savoring the thought of his departure from the legation, but he showed no great determination in this respect. He lingered on Paul VI's earlier message that he could leave at the time of his choosing. But this moment never came.

Perhaps the greatest threat to Cardinal Mindszenty's remaining at the legation was international détente. As the Cold War between East and West began to wind down, so the normalization of Hungarian–US relations took place. A major indication of this shift was the decision of the United States – implemented on November 28, 1966 – to upgrade bilateral relations to the ambassadorial level. Hungary, alongside Bulgaria, was the last country in Eastern Europe to receive this recognition. Mindszenty nearly succeeded in sabotaging the bilateral exchange of ambassadors, for on hearing of the news, he told the legation staff that he had decided to surrender himself to the Hungarian authorities. This was no sudden decision on his part, as he had already mentioned the possibility of taking this step as early as May 1964, during Casaroli's visit. Mindszenty was firmly convinced of the fully mistaken nature of détente, viewing any assistance that was proffered to the Kádár regime as a betrayal of the Hungarian nation. According to the State Department's summary report, Mindszenty was literally depressed as he made preparations for his departure. He gave the gift he had received from the pope to his sister, with the request that it be placed in the church at Csehimindszent. He arranged for his sister to take his personal belongings from the embassy, and then he called in his confessor and revised his testamentary will.[241]

239. US Chargé D'Affaires Elim O'Shaughnessy informed staff at the Hungarian Ministry of Foreign Affairs that the agenda of the meeting would include the refuge status of Cardinal Mindszenty, but in the end the issue was omitted from the proceedings. See Borhi, *Magyar–amerikai kapcsolatok 1945–1989*, 449.

240. Somorjai, *Sancta Sedes Apostolica et Cardinalis Ioseph Mindszenty III/1*, 102. Report of Agostino Casaroli, April 18, 1964.

241. NARA RG 84, Records of the Foreign Service Posts of the Department of State, Hungary, Subject Files Relating to Cardinal Mindszenty 1956–72, Box 3, Cardinal File, Oct

Through such a demonstrative action as leaving the embassy, Mindszenty clearly wished to regain the world's attention, for the official Hungarian position had not changed, whereby Mindszenty would be put on trial if he left the legation. In this sense, the stance of the Hungarian authorities supported, in effect, the argument for providing continued refuge at the embassy.

Mindszenty's audacious plan threatened to turn into a sensational scandal, which, however, everyone – other than the Hungarian cardinal himself – wished to avoid. As Cardinal Mindszenty was a guest rather than a prisoner, the Americans had no powers to prevent him from leaving the building. To avoid a scandal and shore up the decision to exchange ambassadors, Vatican, American and Hungarian diplomats had to work together as a group. For observers of Hungarian affairs, it was amusing to watch the regime's politicians "conspiring" to avoid having to arrest Mindszenty, as his detention had long been their stated aim. It was just as amusing to watch how they then sought to explain the shift in policy to the public – without suffering a loss of prestige. In the end, they decided to inform the Vatican that instead of insisting on Mindszenty's resignation as archbishop, they would be satisfied if the Vatican merely appointed an apostolic administrator of episcopal or archiepiscopal rank to head the diocese. At the same time, however, they continued to insist on the fulfillment of their other conditions, including a Vatican guarantee for the gagging of Mindszenty.[242]

Cardinal Casaroli, who in the meantime had been promoted to the position of secretary of the Congregation for Extraordinary Ecclesiastical Affairs (as of January 1, 1968, this body was renamed the Council for the Public Affairs of the Church), proposed to the pope that he send Cardinal König to Budapest once again. The role of the archbishop of Vienna was now more significant than it had been at the time of his "private" visit of 1963. Whereas Casaroli did not visit Mindszenty again after his journey

1967; Lyndon Baines Johnson Library and Museum (Austin, Texas), NSF, Countries, Hungary, Box 195, Folder 1. Telegram no. 449 from Chargé d'Affaires Richard W. Tims to the State Department in Washington and to the appointed US ambassador to Hungary, Martin J. Hillenbrand, in Bonn, October 5, 1967.

242. Ólmosi, *Mindszenty és a hatalom*, 120–22. Proposal to the Political Committee, September 25, 1967.

to Hungary of September 1965 (returning to Hungary only in May 1973), Cardinal König had become a regular visitor to Budapest. Thus, on October 5, 1967, König made his seventh journey to the Hungarian capital, which included a courtesy visit to the US Legation. His stance – and the enormous distance between Mindszenty and the Vatican's ideas – became clear when he stated that

> the churches will do better if they seek means of existing and operating under the communist governments than if they waste their time on seeking opportunities to attack them.[243]

During this visit, Cardinal König made the following unequivocal statements to Cardinal Mindszenty: The Vatican 1) strongly opposed his departure from the legation and his surrender to the Hungarian authorities; 2) was seeking an acceptable agreement that would permit his departure; 3) the arrival of the ambassador would not influence his refuge, whereby the Vatican's firm wish was that he remain at the diplomatic mission until its efforts came to fruition.[244] König also mentioned the two main conditions set by the Hungarian government: After his departure for abroad, Mindszenty should abstain from criticizing the Hungarian government and from intervening in the life of the Archdiocese of Esztergom and the Hungarian Catholic Church. Concerning the issue of amnesty/clemency, König stated that the Vatican would not be requesting clemency for Mindszenty, but that in his view the Hungarian government would unilaterally grant clemency (it did then do so in 1971).

The negotiations, which lasted two hours, were rather unfruitful. König succeeded in persuading Mindszenty to remain at the US mission *for the time being*, but he failed to secure a pledge from him that he would stay there even *after* the arrival of the ambassador. The determination of the

243. *Amerikai Magyar Élet* [American Hungarian Life], January 20, 1968. Cardinal König's statement in Montreal.

244. NARA RG 84, Records of the Foreign Service Posts of the Department of State, Hungary, Subject Files Relating to Cardinal Mindszenty 1956–72, Box 3, Cardinal File, Oct 1967. Telegram no. 449 from Chargé d'Affaires Richard W. Tims in Budapest to the State Department in Washington and to the appointed US ambassador to Hungary, Martin J. Hillenbrand, in Bonn, October 5, 1967.

Americans to resolve the situation is shown by their willingness to keep the designated ambassador, Martin Hillenbrand, in Vienna, lest his arrival provoke the cardinal into making a sudden move. Still, it was acknowledged that the ambassador's accreditation could not be delayed indefinitely. (Originally, he had been due to arrive in Budapest on October 10, but in the end his arrival was delayed until October 20.) As the US diplomatic papers show, an important – if not the most important – aspect of König's conversation with Mindszenty was that the latter "did not raise objections to a possible pledge of 'silence'."[245] The fact that Mindszenty did not categorically reject this provision heralded a possible break in the deadlock. Yet the cardinal also indicated that he would not agree to this provision until he had met with the pope.[246] At the same time, he announced that he would not renounce the ecclesiastical rights that he exercised over the archdiocese; in other words, he expected his jurisdiction to remain intact.

The US Legation declared this brief respite, which lasted only a few days, a success. Casaroli, however, was of a very different opinion:

> König's visit was fruitless, because, although he told Mindszenty about the pope's proposal, which accorded in full with the Hungarian demands for a guarantee, Mindszenty refused to fulfill any of the conditions set.[247]

It was this difficult situation that gave rise to the memorandum that Casaroli submitted to the Hungarian ambassador in Rome on October 14, 1967 and which had the prior approval of the pope. The memorandum stated the pope's wish that Cardinal Mindszenty be granted an opportunity to leave Hungary. In return, the Vatican would be prepared to appoint one of Hungary's active bishops as the apostolic administrator of the Archdiocese of Esztergom, and this apostolic administrator would have *full rights*. In other words, Mindszenty would be stripped of his rights as archbishop, but he would not be divested of his title.

245. Ibid.

246. Ibid., Telegram no. 512 from Chargé d'Affaires Richard W. Tims to the State Department in Washington and to the appointed US ambassador to Hungary, Martin J. Hillenbrand, at the US Embassy in Vienna, October 17, 1967.

247. MNL OL XIX–A–21–e–0022–7/f/1967. 9. ő. e. Summary of the reports of the ambassador in Rome, October 7, 1967.

Still, the novelty in the memorandum was not the fact that it proposed granting full rights to the apostolic administrator, as this possibility had been in the air since 1963. Rather, it was the statement that

> the chief shepherd of the Roman Catholic Church endeavors – with responsibility, goodwill, and understanding – to ensure that Joseph Cardinal Mindszenty will not, after his departure from the country, cause any harm to the People's Republic of Hungary, to the Catholic Church operating inside the country, or to the bishops and leading personages of the Catholic Church.[248]

This amounted to a statement of will on behalf of the pope and the Vatican; it was a pledge to keep Mindszenty's statements under wraps. The decision by Mindszenty – mentioned above – to acquiesce to the command to silence, acquires greater significance in the light of the following: Pope Paul VI mentioned a guarantee for Mindszenty's silence only after the Hungarian cardinal had himself shown a willingness to accept this condition. In doing so, the pope adhered to the oft-cited principle that a commitment should only be made when the person involved has already expressed a willingness to cooperate and when coercion is not at play. Although the Hungarian side was expecting specific measures to restrict Mindszenty's activities, it nevertheless considered the offer to be suitable for further consultation. Consequently, the talks continued. During this time, however, Cardinal Mindszenty decided that he would leave the legation prior to the arrival of the new ambassador.

This news required an immediate reaction, and so – for the second time in two weeks – the pope sent Cardinal König to Hungary with the task of dissuading Mindszenty from executing his plan. On October 17, 1967, König, dressed in disguise and carrying a passport issued in the name of "Monsignore Fink" (Fink had been his mother's maiden name), traveled to Budapest.[249] König spoke with Mindszenty for almost four hours. He informed him of the main points of the October 14 memorandum: The

248. Ibid.

249. László Imre Németh, *Zágon-leveleskönyv: Iratgyűjtemény-töredék Mindszenty József bíborosról 1967–1975* (Budapest: Szent István Társulat, 2011), 24; MNL OL M–KS 288. f.

Vatican wished for Mindszenty to leave Hungary, but it wanted him to do so not in protest but as the outcome of negotiations. With this in view, the Vatican intended to appoint one of the present bishops as apostolic administrator, *sede plena*, of the Archdiocese of Esztergom. Meanwhile, Mindszenty would be permitted to retain his title. Another matter covered at the meeting was the Hungarian government's condition concerning the cardinal's silence. In the end, owing in large part to König's ingenuity, Cardinal Mindszenty pledged to refrain from causing scandals and to remain in the legation building on Liberty Square. It was König's impression that papal pressure to make him stay had made a major impact on the Hungarian cardinal and had even rather pleased him, for

> it satisfies his ambition, it places the responsibility on the pope, and it gives him a motive to change the plan (which had secretly scared him), without having to abandon his principles or suffer humiliation.[250]

Indeed, only after he received the pope's personal request did Mindszenty agree to change his plan, which he described in his letter to President Johnson:

> I did not expect the Holy Father's request, and I did not agree with his views on the deterioration of relations. I could not give a negative response to the Holy Father, but I did ask that the Vatican's discussions with the regime should be brought to a positive or negative resolution in a short time. I excluded every unreasonable attempt of blackmail by the illegal regime against me or against my Archdiocese. Cardinal König undertook to report my conditions to the Vatican.[251]

7/290. ő. e. 11. and 15. fol. Minutes of the meeting of the HSWP CC Secretariat on October 16, 1967. See Szabó, *A Szentszék és a Magyar Népköztársaság*, 333.

250. NARA RG 84, Department of State. Hungary, Subject Files Relating to Cardinal Mindszenty 1956–72, Box 3, Cardinal File, Oct 1967. Telegram no. 513 from Chargé d'Affaires Richard W. Tims to the State Department in Washington and to the appointed ambassador to Hungary, Hillenbrand, at the US Embassy in Vienna, October 18, 1967.

251. NARA RG 59, GR of the Department of State, Bureau of European Affairs, Office of Eastern European Affairs, Records Relating to Hungary 1941–71, Box 12, Nov 8, 1956–Dec 15, 1967. Letter of József Mindszenty to the US President, November 13, 1967; See Somorjai and Zinner, *Do Not Forget*, 334.

It shall never be known whether, in the absence of the pope's intervention, Mindszenty would indeed have walked out of the legation. It is certain though that he had mainly political considerations in mind when he wished to leave the legation, as in his view, the United States had switched its support from the Hungarian nation to the Kádár regime. At the same time, the unknown consequences of leaving the embassy were a force for the status quo (in this sense, he thought of König's arguments).

Mindszenty's possible actions were pondered over even by the Political Committee (or Politburo) of the HSWP CC. János Kádár expressed his opinion using just three words: "He won't leave!"[252] Either Kádár had heard of König's efficiency and effectiveness or, as an experienced politician, he had a gut sense of what would be the outcome. Yet, no-one could be sure of the Hungarian cardinal's actions. It is certain that if Mindszenty had simply walked out of the legation, the Hungarian authorities – despite their apparent toughness – would have refrained from arresting him, as the politicians of the regime were aware of the negative consequences of such action. They had understood the essence of the Vatican proposal of October 14: The pope would appoint an apostolic administrator as head of the Archdiocese of Esztergom and would simultaneously suspend Mindszenty's archiepiscopal jurisdiction. This minimized the significance of whether Mindszenty would retain or lose his formal title.[253] Meanwhile the Hungarian government had two favorites for the position of apostolic administrator: The first was Pál Brezanóczy, apostolic administrator of Eger, while the second was József Ijjas, apostolic administrator of Csanád. Both men had been consecrated as bishops in consequence of the partial agreement of 1964, and both of them were cooperating with the regime's security apparatus (the State Protection Authority)... Still, no matter that the two sides – Hungary and the Vatican – were essentially in agreement on the resolution of the Mindszenty affair, the affected party refused even to countenance the appointment of an apostolic administrator with full rights, because, in his view, this would simply strengthen the

252. MNL OL M–KS 288. f. 5/437. ő. e. Minutes of the meeting of the Political Committee of the HSWP CC on October 20, 1967. See Szabó, *A Szentszék és a Magyar Népköztársaság*, 349.

253. Ólmosi, *Mindszenty és a hatalom*, 128–29. Proposal to the Political Committee on guidelines for the talks to be held in the matter of Mindszenty, October 19, 1967. (The following quotation is from the same place, 133. fol.)

status of the regime.[254] Hungary's communist politicians now wondered whether Mindszenty might soon be pensioned off. Under the provisions of canon law, Mindszenty, who celebrated his seventy-fifth birthday on March 29, 1967, could have been sent into retirement by the Vatican, but Casaroli objected, saying that the Vatican did not approve of such action where a prelate was being prevented from performing his duties.

"Persuasion and dialogue have come into vogue"

When, on October 20, 1967, Martin Hillenbrand, the first US ambassador to Hungary, finally took up his post, everything went back to normal. At their first meeting, János Kádár, the Hungarian premier, "assured" the new ambassador that the Mindszenty issue was neither urgent nor important, albeit "prior to [Hillenbrand's] arrival some scary incidents had occurred."[255] Yet, owing to these "scary incidents," by the fall of 1967 a scenario was in place for Mindszenty's departure from the legation. And it was this scenario that would be employed four years later.

Why did resolving the issue take so long? Although all three sides had an apparent interest in solving the problem, it was still the case that the bilateral Hungarian–US talks were never limited to the Mindszenty issue. Rather, the issue tended to be viewed as a coincidental matter that could be discussed at a reception or at a formal diplomatic dinner. Meanwhile, trilateral – US–Vatican–Hungarian – discussions were never held on the issue. In view of its situation, the Vatican had the most information at hand, as Vatican representatives held discussions both with the Hungarians and with the Americans. In terms of inconvenience and urgency, the issue affected the United States more than it did Hungary and the Vatican. Perhaps Mindszenty was the least affected in this respect. Both for the Vatican and for Hungary, the status quo was acceptable for the same reason: As long as

254. MNL OL XIX–A–21–e–0022–7/Z/1967. 22. ő. e. Summary of Deputy Minister of Foreign Affairs Béla Szilágyi based on the report submitted by the ambassador in Rome, October 23, 1967; NARA RG 84, Records of the Foreign Service Posts of the Department of State, Hungary, Subject Files Relating to Cardinal Mindszenty 1956–72, Box 3, Cardinal File, Nov–Dec 1967. Letter of Cardinal Cicognani to József Mindszenty, Vatican City, November 29, 1967, and Mindszenty's reply of December 15, 1967.

255. Borhi, *Magyar–amerikai kapcsolatok 1945–1989*, 502.

Mindszenty remained at the US Legation, he was effectively "muzzled" and could not harm either the authority of the Church or Hungarian domestic politics. For the Americans, however, their role as hosts to Mindszenty had become rather inconvenient. When the foreign policy objective of the United States in Eastern Europe became consolidation rather than destabilization, Mindszenty was no longer perceived as a potential tool to be used against communism. It seems that with the advent of détente in the late 1960s, no-one had much time in a political sense for the "Cold War" figure of Mindszenty. Another factor hindering a possible agreement was Mindszenty's multiple redefinition of his conditions for leaving the country, as he struggled with the dilemma of whether to stay or leave. Still, a growing life ambition for Mindszenty was the pastoral care and leadership of the émigré Hungarian communities. This ambition was further strengthened by Paul VI's Apostolic Letter *Pastoralis migratorum cura* of August 15, 1969, in which the pope addressed the problems of migration, emphasizing the Christian duty to care for refugees and migrants and the importance of preserving their faith, language and cultural heritage.

Meanwhile, representatives of the Vatican and the Kádár regime began to discuss the resolution of various side issues, doing so irrespective of Mindszenty and without even informing him of what soon became regular negotiations. While there was no real breakthrough, this was the period when the communist regime embarked on the path of détente in the field of ecclesiastical policy. There were two main reasons for this shift. The first was related to domestic policy; the regime concluded that a steady drip of concessions in the field of freedom of conscience and religion would be less dangerous than ideological and social experimentation, which could lead to the kind of social explosions seen in Budapest in 1956 and in Prague in 1968. The other reason was tied to foreign policy: As far as the West was concerned, the language of negotiation showed Budapest in a better light. This was of clear benefit to the Kádár regime, particularly in view of its collaboration in the invasion of Czechoslovakia (1968). The restoration of diplomatic relations between Hungary and the Vatican would have been a high point in the process of détente, but – as various sources reveal – the domestic policy drawbacks of such a development would have outweighed the assumed foreign policy benefits. The principal fear in this respect was that normalization of diplomatic relations would strengthen clerical resistance, for even news of the bilateral negotiations had led to uncertainty among the peace priests who were loyal to the state. A rumor had spread that before Mindszenty would leave the country, he would return for twenty-four hours to Esztergom "to restore order." An internal report concluded that Mindszenty should not be given the chance "to return to the archiepiscopal see of Esztergom whether for twenty-four hours or even a minute."[256] It is apparent, therefore, that the issue was not simply about authorizing or rejecting a possible farewell event. The mere mentioning of the cardinal's possible release sufficed to cause consternation among the peace priests, who were essentially a prop for the communist regime.

The internal papers of the HSWP on preparations for the Hungarian–Vatican negotiations of 1967–1968 contained no new information about the fate of Cardinal Mindszenty. They did, however, reiterate that the Hungarian government had no wish to initiate a deal but would be willing – while adhering to its previous conditions – to consent to the closure of the Mindszenty affair. The Vatican hesitated to fill the other two vacant episcopal sees in Hungary, despite the Hungarian government's forceful efforts to impose its own candidates. Evidently, there was no purpose in delaying the appointments unduly. Accordingly, in October 1968, the two sides – after some "wrestling in the mud" – agreed upon a lengthier list of candidates. Subsequently, on January 10, 1969, ten new bishops or apostolic administrators were appointed.

It was during this period of Vatican hesitation that Cardinal Mindszenty began to conceive of the ideas that he would then cite in 1971 as grounds for his departure from the US embassy and from his native land. In November 1967, József Zágon, a leading figure among the émigré Hungarian Catholic clergy, wrote to Mindszenty telling him that if he were ever to leave the legation, he should do so, not for political reasons (for example because of the arrival of a new ambassador), but with a view to furthering the interests of Hungary and in a manner worthy of his past. Zágon wrote:

> The departure from the Embassy and from the country – if it comes to that – should conform to the policy line followed by Your Eminence heretofore:

256. MNL OL XIX–A–21–e–0022–7/U/1967. 20. ő. e. "Feljegyzés Prantner elvtárs részére" [Note for Comrade Prantner], November 14, 1967.

> [Your Eminence] has suffered not for himself, not from a political point of view, but in the interest of the Church, and if [Your Eminence] were now to step on free soil, he should wish to do so on the basis of neither personal nor political, but of religious, interests (for example, in obedience to the Holy Father, in order to serve the shaping of the future of the Church, etc). Bowing in humility before the plans of Providence and in indivisible community of destiny with the Hungarian Church, [Your Eminence] undertakes the greatest sacrifice of his life, even departure from the country, in the conviction that the obsession of atheism may be vanquished only by "prayer and fasting," through resignation and sacrifice. A motivation in this sense appears to be suitable also for calling the attention of the world to the situation of the country and of the Church. [...] Since the Council the Church leaders have cast aside the sword; instead of battle, persuasion and dialogue have come into vogue. It is virtually impossible to change this mood today, and even a mere attempt would meet with opposition in ecclesiastical circles.[257]

With these thoughts, Zágon outlined a worthy future for Mindszenty after his possible departure from the legation: the task would be to awaken and activate the Hungarian émigré communities. Still, it took some time for Mindszenty to become amicably disposed towards this image of his future self.

BEARING THE "HEAVIEST CROSS"

Despite the ominous start, Martin Hillenbrand, the first US ambassador to Hungary, soon formed a cordial relationship with Cardinal Mindszenty. Hillenbrand spent just two years in Budapest. He returned to the United States on February 15, 1969, having been appointed as assistant secretary of state for European affairs. With this appointment, the State Department acquired an expert on Hungary with first-hand knowledge of the situation in the country.

257. NARA RG 59, GR of the Department of State, Bureau of European Affairs, Office of Eastern European Affairs, Records Relating to Hungary 1941–71, Box 12, Nov 8, 1956–Dec 15, 1967. Letter of József Zágon to József Mindszenty, n. d. [November 10, 1967]; Somorjai, *Sancta Sedes Apostolica et Cardinalis Ioseph Mindszenty III/2*, 78–82.

Hillenbrand's successor as ambassador, Alfred Puhan, considered resolving the stalemate in the Mindszenty affair to be his special task, whereby he was mindful of the great age (77 years) of the Hungarian cardinal and his failing health.[258] On the first suitable occasion, the ambitious ambassador mentioned to the Hungarian side the fate of the "stubborn and inflexible old man who is impossible to deal with."[259] It was after his initial conversations with Mindszenty that Puhan began to use such adjectives to describe the cardinal. Puhan would later write in his memoirs the following:

> Mindszenty's world, as disclosed in these conversations, consisted largely of his own impressions of Rakocsi's [!] Hungary plus an avid reading of the Hungarian refugee press, which he received regularly from the United States. To be sure, he scanned the *Neue Zuercher Zeitung* and *Die Presse* as well as the Paris edition of the *Herald Tribune*. However, from the articles he called to my attention or that of other embassy officers, it was clear that he read what he wanted to read, and read only those articles that did not change his conception of the world in which we live.[260]

Puhan soon realized that Mindszenty would only leave the embassy if he were to be instructed to do so by the Vatican, to which he was unconditionally obedient.

Puhan's strategy addressed all three of the affected parties. His aims were *a)* to persuade the Hungarian authorities that Mindszenty's departure would serve their interests; *b)* to effect a change in the State Department's position towards greater detachment; and *c)* to persuade the Holy See to abandon its position of "non-commitment" and assist in resolving the issue. A priority task for Puhan was to bring about a softening of the Hungarian regime's position. In his conversations with Hungarian politi-

258. AMAE AD Série: Europe 1961–70, Saint-Siège, dossier 77, "Cardinal Mindszenty 1966 a 1970." Report no. 485/EU of Raymond Gastambide, French ambassador in Budapest, July 10, 1969.

259. Zoltán Szatucsek, "Makacs öregúr vagy nemzetmentő vátesz? Diplomáciai egyeztetések Mindszenty sorsáról 1970–1971-ben," in *Közel-Múlt: Húsz történet a 20. századból*, eds. György Majtényi and Orsolya Ring (Budapest: Magyar Országos Levéltár, 2002), 20–35.

260. Alfred Puhan, *The Cardinal in the Chancery and Other Recollections* (New York: Vantage Press, 1990), 188.

cians, he would often portray the cardinal in poor health. The possibility that he might die at the US embassy visibly unsettled them. How would they approach the burial of this symbol of anti-bolshevism? Puhan decided to employ a larger "bait," telling the Hungarian side that a settlement of the Mindszenty issue might even lead the American public to give its approval to the return of the crown jewels to Hungary.[261] In early 1971, Puhan – in apparent ignorance of the positions adopted in 1947–1949 – proposed to advisors of President Nixon the possible transfer of the Holy Crown to the Vatican, where it could be kept for a temporary period until its ultimate return to the Hungarian nation. In the end, the Americans decided not to burden bilateral talks with the issue of the crown jewels, but the possibility of their return to Hungary immediately drew the attention of Hungarian politicians, for the Holy Crown symbolized the (constitutional) continuity of the state. Indeed, its return to Hungary would have signified full moral recognition of the Kádár regime, an act of far greater symbolic meaning than the release of an elderly cardinal. For this very reason, a new milestone was reached in the story of Mindszenty. Although it cannot be argued that the Hungarian cardinal was exchanged for the Holy Crown, his release did become an unwritten, yet expected and fulfillable prerequisite for its return to Hungary.

Puhan's endeavors in this field drew the interest of Robert F. Illing, an assistant to Henry Cabot Lodge, who served as the personal representative of the president to the Holy See in the period 1970–1976. Since, at the time (and until as late as 1984), the United States did not enjoy full diplomatic relations with the Holy See, Illing was not an accredited diplomat to the Holy See. Rather, he and his boss were responsible for Vatican affairs at the US embassy to Italy. Their position led them to forge a close working relationship with staff members at the Vatican's "top ministry," the Secretariat of State, including Agostino Cardinal Casaroli, who was now an archbishop and was serving as the secretary of the Council for the Public Affairs of the Church, and Giovanni Cheli, an expert on Eastern European

261. MNL OL XIX–J–1–j–1–00361/31/1969. USA TÜK-documents. Memo of János Nagy, Hungarian Ambassador in Washington, on the discussions with Alfred Puhan, August 14, 1969. Published in Borhi, *Magyar–amerikai kapcsolatok 1945–1989*, 535–37; MNL OL XIX–A–21–e–0022–3/c/1970. 4. ő. e. Information report by János Bartha for József Prantner, July 29, 1970.

affairs. The three US diplomats –Puhan in Budapest, Illing in Rome, and Hillenbrand in Washington – had a good understanding of the issues and cooperated towards achieving the common objective, namely the resolution of the Mindszenty issue.

In the final rounds of the Hungarian–Vatican negotiations, the main subjects were the annulment of the papal decrees of 1957 (on the excommunication of priests serving as parliamentary representatives), the abrogation of Law-decree No. 22 of 1957, and various personnel issues. Discussions in the latter field continued to ignore Cardinal Mindszenty, whose fate had not been mentioned in the bilateral talks since the fall of 1967. The cancellation of the excommunication of the three priests who were serving as parliamentary representatives had been a principal demand of the Hungarian side for some years, but no progress had been made on the matter. A breakthrough on this issue came during the talks held from October 6–11, 1970: Vatican State Secretary Jean Villot consented, in a provision adopted on October 8, to the cancellation of the excommunication order. Thirteen years after the announcement of the excommunication order, the Vatican took this step even though the affected priests did not resign as parliamentary representatives or do penance. The Vatican did, however, retain some ammunition, for a *clause* in the provisions prohibited their publication "until the Holy See gives its express consent."[262] Consequently, neither the Bishops' Conference nor the excommunicated priests themselves were informed of the lifting of the excommunication order, whereas a narrow circle of politicians did promptly receive a Hungarian translation of the letter submitted by Secretary of State Villot.

In the short term, the regime focused on the abrogation of the clause by making its cancellation a prerequisite for further talks on the appointment of bishops and auxiliary bishops, a matter that was of great importance to the Vatican. Even if direct linkage was not made between the cancellation of the non-publication clause, the amendment of Law-decree no. 22 of 1957, and Mindszenty's departure from Hungary, there is no denying a palpable sense of "give and take" in the bilateral negotiations.

262. MNL OL XIX–J–1–j KÜM/Vatikán 160. 00505/14/1970. Report no. 0022–7/h/1970 of the State Office for Church Affairs on the negotiations with the Vatican, October 22, 1970.

Breaking the Deadlock: The Hungarian Minister of Foreign Affairs Visits the Pope

Reflecting the thaw in relations between the two superpowers and the spirit of coexistence, at 11 a.m. on April 16, 1971, Paul VI gave a private audience to Hungarian Minister of Foreign Affairs János Péter, who was not regarded as a typical party activist within the political apparatus, as he had once been a Calvinist minister and even a bishop. Moreover, the Vatican was pleased to receive, in his person, Hungary's top diplomat rather than merely the head of the State Office for Church Affairs, a body with a purely executive role in Hungarian political life.

The private, off-the-record discussion between the two men was held in French. After some polite conversation, the pope mentioned, as the first and most far-reaching matter, the situation of Cardinal Mindszenty. He stated that this had been "one of his greatest concerns for years,"[263] as it had been, he believed, for the Hungarian government too. The pope then called Mindszenty a "victim of history," referring to him as "a very difficult man, many of whose actions were hard to understand." Paul VI then unexpectedly announced that he would agree to fulfil the conditions that the Hungarian government had been requesting for years: He stated that, regardless of Mindszenty's wish to remain in Hungary, the Vatican would rather remove him from the country and "place him in some monastery, while barring him – by means of appropriate ecclesiastical rules, applied with sufficient force – from making public appearances." Never had the pope made such an unambiguous statement! In the absence of Vatican sources, it is impossible to be sure that the Hungarian foreign minister's account of the conversation was both accurate and complete – the significance of which will become apparent later. Still, as far as the essence of the pope's offer is concerned, János Péter was clearly not mistaken: The pope had lifted an invisible barrier, with the aim of securing – finally – a solution that would be acceptable to both parties, even at the price of suppressing the personal wishes of the man at center stage, Cardinal Mindszenty. From this point in time, Mindszenty's impending departure from the embassy seemed certain.

263. MNL OL M–KS 288. f. 5/552. ő. e. 45–46. fol. Report to the Political Committee of the HSWP. Budapest, April 19, 1971. (The next three quotations are from the same place.)

Indeed, events did subsequently accelerate. On May 5, 1971, the Vatican counselors Giovanni Cheli and Gabriele Montalvo presented, on a visit to Budapest, the principles of an agreement, but their draft agreement – which resembled the Vatican's proposal of 1967 – did not win the approval of the Hungarian side. In the latter's view, the main deficiency of the draft was the lack of clarity and comprehensiveness of the Vatican's assurances, which were considered a crucial part of any agreement. The Hungarian government insisted that the Holy See – and the pope in person – should guarantee the fulfillment of the conditions, which should not be dependent on Mindszenty's conduct. In other words, the responsibility for fulfilling the terms of an agreement should not be shared between the Vatican and Cardinal Mindszenty. Evidently, the Hungarian authorities were mistrustful of the Hungarian cardinal and unwilling to place confidence in any pledge that might be squeezed out of him. They adamantly rejected a proposal that Mindszenty be permitted to bid farewell to the clergy and laity of the archdiocese. For the Vatican representatives, all this called for some further reflection: Regarding the guarantees that were so important to the Hungarian side, the two counselors stated that the pope could not go beyond what he had already pledged in terms of assurances. They underlined, further, that the pope could not compel Mindszenty to leave his current residence.

An apparent deadlock had been reached. A memorandum drawn up at the time of the negotiations contains the following words (albeit they are crossed out): "There is nothing for us to talk about." That the two sides did not then leave the negotiating table was due primarily to Cheli's flexibility. The Vatican counselor emphasized to the Hungarian side that the draft agreement was not a final one; rather, it should be viewed as a starting point for further negotiations. A small detail indicates the growing sense of uncertainty felt by the head of the Hungarian delegation, Imre Miklós. In the minutes of the meeting he noted and then crossed out the eventuality that "our minister of foreign affairs has not fully understood Pope Paul VI's position."[264] In the end, both sides left the negotiating table, pledging to resume talks in the future. When Hungarian Minister of Foreign Affairs

264. MNL OL XIX–A–21–e–XIII. dosszié–0022–1/L/2/1971. 10. fol. Memorandum on the second day of the talks held in Budapest with representatives of the Vatican, May 5, 1971.

János Péter met with Ambassador Puhan on May 13 he acknowledged, in confidence (inasmuch as there can ever be confidence between two diplomats) something that Hungarian leaders had never previously admitted, namely that "the cardinal was a problem for the Hungarian government and the Vatican as well as to us. In the past the Hungarian view had been he was a problem only to the American Embassy."[265]

The Mission of Monsignor József Zágon – June 25–27, 1971.

While negotiating in Budapest, Giovanni Cheli came up with a means of changing Mindszenty's mind: Instead of dispatching König to Budapest, a Hungarian church leader would have to be chosen and then sent to talk to Mindszenty. Evidently, the selectee would have to be someone who enjoyed Mindszenty's trust. Moreover, he would have to be equipped with the skills required to meet this sensitive task. The choice fell on the papal prelate, József Zágon, who was the canon of St. Maria Maggiore Basilica and who had been living in Rome since 1949. Zágon counted as a leader of the Hungarian émigré clergy.

On June 23, 1971, at Paul VI's behest, Cardinal Franz König traveled to Budapest for a day. The next day two other delegates arrived in Budapest from Rome: Giovanni Cheli, a Vatican diplomat, and Monsignor József Zágon, a papal prelate. König represented (or symbolized) high office, Cheli expertise, and Zágon the body of Hungarian priests. König's role was protocol-related: he tactfully prepared the ground and let Mindszenty know about the mission of Cheli and Zágon. Mindszenty's starting position was unchanged: his preference would have been to stay at the embassy until his death.

It was Zágon who then met with Mindszenty on three occasions – on June 25, 26, and 27, 1971. It transpired that Zágon was a clever and skillful envoy. He proceeded tactfully but firmly. His aim was to use persuasive arguments

265. Nixon Library, NSC Files, Box 693, Country Files – Europe, Hungary, vol. I. Telegram From the embassy in Hungary to the Department of State. Bp., May 14, 1971, 0700Z. See *Foreign Relations of the United States*, 1969–1976, vol. XXIX, 1. General editor Edward C. Keefer, editors James E. Miller, Douglas E. Selvage, and Laurie Van Hook. (Washington D.C.: United States Government Printing Office, 2007), 275–77. Document 114. On the Internet: https://history.state.gov/historicaldocuments/frus1969-76v29/d114.

so that Cardinal Mindszenty himself would make the final decision on his departure from Hungary. Zágon described the Holy Father's concern and the difficulties posed by advanced age. He commended Mindszenty for his heroic stand, while also reminding him that his martyrdom might become a little threadbare if he were to remain at the embassy.

> The world is apt to forget and it can only with difficulty judge the sojourn in the Embassy as a necessary sacrifice for the Church. The Holy Father on the other hand is considering such a solution which would place Your Eminence's sacrifice in a new light and which would raise it all the more, in its moral significance, in world public opinion, would in no way detract from its merits, and would serve as an example for the entire Church.[266]

On one side of the scales, Zágon placed "the forgotten man," while on the other he put the martyr prelate who had borne the burden of the cross for his principles and for the Church. In doing so, Zágon aimed to show the reality of the situation, whereby Mindszenty might himself come to see the significance and advantages of his departure.

When Cardinal Mindszenty inquired about the price of his leaving the embassy, he was told that four stipulations had been made over the years. The *first stipulation* was that Mindszenty would retain his titles as archbishop of Esztergom and primate of Hungary, but that the rights and obligations stemming from these offices would be suspended. Moreover, he would not, in the future, be permitted to engage himself in the affairs of the country or in those of the Archdiocese of Esztergom, whereby his place would be taken by an apostolic administrator "*sede plena*." Mindszenty agreed to the suspension of his jurisdiction in the archdiocese, but he did so only "orally." Further, he demanded that his consent should not be given in writing to anyone, including the new apostolic administrator, and that the Pazmaneum in Vienna should be returned to his nominal jurisdiction. The Hungarian cardinal was opposed to the "*sede plena*" ("occupied see") solution, and continued to insist on his status as an "*impeditus*" ("hindered")

266. NARA RG 84, Records of the Foreign Service Posts of the Department of State, Hungary, Subject Files Relating to Cardinal Mindszenty 1956–72, Box 5, Cardinal Mindszenty July–Dec 1971. Pro memoria. Subject: Visit with Jozsef Cardinal Mindszenty, primate of Hungary and archbishop of Esztergom, at the American Embassy in Budapest, June 25–26–27, 1971.

prelate. Since 1949, this Latin word had been placed beside his name in the volumes of the *Annuario Pontificio* (Papal Yearbook). The *second stipulation* was his departure from Hungary, concerning which he would not be permitted to make any statement or send a circular letter. Mindszenty wished to consider this very thoroughly, but he could already state that if he were to decide in favor of departing Hungary, his preference would be to settle at the Pazmaneum. He had no wish to make a statement on this, but Zágon saw no obstacle to Mindszenty expressing his considerations in a letter to the pope. The *third stipulation* was that, after his departure from Hungary, Mindszenty should refrain from making any oral or written statements that would disturb relations between the Holy See and the Hungarian government or which would offend the Hungarian government or the People's Republic. Mindszenty's reaction to this point reveals his irritation. He demanded his full rehabilitation and rejected the Hungarian communist regime and any conditions it might set. Regarding the silence that he was to maintain, he stated that he would only accept the Holy See's jurisdiction when it came to judging whether a possible statement by him had harmed Hungarian–Holy See relations or not. More than a few commentators have questioned whether Mindszenty even knew about the requirement for him to be silent. According to the documents available, he clearly did know about this requirement, albeit its scope may have been unclear to him. The Vatican diplomat Cheli's words are the sole indication that Mindszenty would be required to maintain complete silence on political issues: "Cardinal has already given word that he will maintain silence on [the] Hungarian political situation."[267] Later, Mindszenty would express his great discontent with the gag order. In a letter to the pope, he explained that it would be a mistake to conclude that he was willing to accommodate the wishes of the communists and make his publications and statements subject to advance censorship.[268]

267. Ibid., Telegram no. 4337 from the US Embassy in Rome to the State Department in Washington and to the embassy in Budapest, July 9, 1971. See Ádám Somorjai and Tibor Zinner, "Washingtonból jelentjük: A budapesti amerikai nagykövetség Mindszenty bíboros tevékenységére vonatkozó, 1971-ben keletkezett iratai," *Századok* 144, no. 1 (2010): 153–54.

268. MMAL 060. dosszié, MNF 7919, L-2870. Letter of József Mindszenty to Pope Paul VI. Vienna, March 10, 1972. Published in German in Gabriel Adriányi, *Die Ostpolitik des Vatikans 1958–1978 gegenüber Ungarn. Der Fall Kardinal Mindszenty* (Herne: Schäfer, 2003), 162–65.

At this stage, Zágon could not have spoken to Mindszenty about the Vatican guaranteeing his silence on political affairs, because a month would pass before the Vatican issued such an assurance in writing. Yet, Cardinal Mindszenty must have been informed about the Vatican's guarantee in October at the latest, during his sojourn in Rome. Evidence for this is a letter sent by Paul VI to Mindszenty on December 14, 1971:

> You are familiar with the condition that demands not only much wisdom but also the responsible conduct that we have agreed to [...] you can easily understand how difficult it is for Us to reiterate those admonitions and recommendations which we already gave you when, to our great delight, we met.[269]

The occasion to which the pope's letter refers was the moment of Mindszenty's departure from Rome for Vienna. On October 23, 1971, after he and Cardinal Mindszenty had concelebrated holy Mass, the pope had received the Hungarian cardinal in a private farewell. During their conversation, the pope had requested that Mindszenty "bear with patience the difficulties of his situation and the limitations desired by the circumstances."[270] It is doubtful that Cardinal Mindszenty would have left the US Embassy in Budapest if he had been fully aware at that time of the extent of the requirement for silence.

The *fourth and final condition* was aimed at preventing Mindszenty from publishing his memoirs, which would instead be bequeathed, in his testamentary will, to the Holy See. The restriction on the publication of his memoirs was far more irritating to Mindszenty than the requirement (accepted by or imposed on him) to be silent. The Americans had long realized that the publication of his memoirs was an issue that could be used to persuade or motivate Mindszenty to leave the embassy and depart from Hungary. Their realization was shown to be true by subsequent developments. On the one hand, it was true that Monsignor Zágon had been provided those chapters of the memoirs that dealt with the history

269. MMAL 060. dosszié, MFN 7910, L-2861. Letter of Pope Paul VI to József Mindszenty. Vatican City, December 14, 1971. See Somorjai and Zinner, *Washingtonból jelentjük*, 154 and 172.

270. MMAL 020/a. sz. dosszié, I. 14. ő. e. Pro memoria, Rome, October 23, 1971. Typed transcript signed by József Zágon.

of Hungary and had seen no obstacle to the publication of a major part of the contents during Cardinal Mindszenty's lifetime. Yet the explanation for this concessionary stance was a misperception: At the time, Cardinal Mindszenty had understood his memoirs to mean his entire life's work, including his historical works, rather than merely his personal life story. (It was only in the fall of 1971 that Mindszenty began to divide his work into two parts: his historical writings and his memoirs.)

A discussion of these four conditions or stipulations took up the entire first day of Zágon's visit. Indeed, a thorough reading of the memorandum reveals how the question of "rehabilitation versus clemency" was not even raised at this stage. It seems that a fatigued Mindszenty was now prepared to bow his head and leave Hungary – primarily with the aim of safekeeping his memoirs. When the two men resumed their discussions on the second day of Zágon's visit, the Vatican representative sought in vain to have Mindszenty agree to a specific date for his departure. The Hungarian cardinal requested time to consider his options, but he did promise the following: "I will not prolong the decision for a year."[271]

The memorandum of the discussions, which was ready by the third day of the visit,[272] detailed in full Mindszenty's remarks. After some hesitation, the Hungarian cardinal signed it. While he subsequently acknowledged having done so to those in his narrow circle,[273] he omitted this fact from his memoirs.[274]

Subsequently, Cheli met several times with staff from the State Office for Church Affairs. He gave them a short account of what had been achieved:

271. NARA RG 84, Records of the Foreign Service Posts of the Department of State, Hungary, Subject Files Relating to Cardinal Mindszenty 1956–72, Box 5, Cardinal Mindszenty July–December 1971. Pro memoria, June 25–26–27, 1971.

272. To date, only the parts for June 25 and June 26 have been published. See Gábor Adriányi, "Miért és hogyan hagyta el Mindszenty József a budapesti amerikai nagykövetséget," in Török, *Mindszenty József emlékezete*, 81–85. See also for a facsimile in Mészáros, *A száműzött bíboros szolgálatában*, 181–84. The part covering July 27 is published in Italian in Ádám Somorjai, *Sancta Sedes Apostolica et Cardinalis Ioseph Mindszenty. Documenta 1971–1975* (Rome: Pro manuscripto, 2007), 163–64.

273. "When the matter was first mentioned, he told Zágon that he accepted it but would not sign it. Two days later, however, he did then sign it." Mészáros, *A száműzött bíboros szolgálatában*, 166 and 169 – entries for January 10 and 11, 1974; MMAL 020/a dosszié, I.15. ő. e. Memo on the talks held with József Zágon.

274. Mindszenty, *Memoirs*, 234.

the discussions had been fruitful, but Mindszenty was requesting to receive word about the pope's wishes in writing before making a final decision. Cheli also informed them of a shift in Vatican policy on the 1957 papal decrees: The Holy See was now ready to cancel the clause barring the publication of the abrogation of the provisions. Lest Mindszenty change his mind, however, publication would take place after his departure from Hungary. It seemed that the Mindszenty affair was drawing to a close.

The Decision

Cardinal Mindszenty knew that there was only one way for him to ensure the publication – at least in his lifetime – of his memoirs: his leaving the embassy and Hungary. Nonetheless it was only after considerable inner conflict and anguish that Mindszenty determined to take this step. In advance of this, however, in broken English, he complained in a letter to President Nixon, dated June 27, 1971,[275] that the Vatican was seeking to change his refuge situation. Having thanked the president, the legislature, the government and the American people for their attention to his situation, he requested Nixon's assistance in resolving this nagging and unspoken issue: Could/should he remain at the embassy? He noted that his departure might undermine the hope which his presence at the embassy instilled in the many Hungarian émigrés and "slaves" (the Hungarian population).[276] In expressing such sentiments, he effectively revealed that he was hoping for a response that would encourage him to stay.

The very next day – that is, before he received President Nixon's reply – he wrote to the pope informing him of his decision. In the letter, dated June 28, he stated that although he would like to remain in Hungary, he was nevertheless willing to depart the country, if his departure would best serve the interests of the Church. He would be willing to take upon himself perhaps the "heaviest cross" in his life and make the atonement

275. Presidential Advisor Henry Kissinger noted that "*the actual text is rather difficult to understand, since the Cardinal wrote in English*," which sometimes gave rise to problems of interpretation. Nixon Library, NSC Files, Box 828, Name Files, Mindszenty, Cardinal (Apr 70–May 74). Memorandum for the president from Henry A. Kissinger, July 12, 1971.

276. Ibid., Letter of József Mindszenty to President Richard Nixon, Budapest, June 27, 1971. Published in Somorjai and Zinner, *Do Not Forget*, 372.

of exile for the Church and his nation.[277] After so many trials and tribulations, Mindszenty now abandoned his dream of living and dying in his native land as a symbol of staunch resistance. Obedience to the Church took precedence. His soul, however, was wracked by doubts. Indeed, he believed that his sacrifice would go to waste and that he would be forced to leave Hungary like a man who had been "shipwrecked." The letters and telegrams sent and received in the ensuing weeks tell of the Hungarian cardinal's hesitation to go through with his decision and of the consequent anxious anticipation among embassy personnel, who feared that an unexpected turn of events would prevent the cardinal's departure.

While – in view of Mindszenty's obedience to the pope – the outcome was never in doubt, the concerns expressed by embassy staff were far from groundless. Indeed, during the two-week wait for President Nixon's reply to his letter, Mindszenty theorized about how he might still remain at the embassy despite having consented to his departure in his letter to the pope. Ambassador Puhan feared that if Mindszenty received no reply from President Nixon, he might feel entitled to state that the Americans had not told him to leave and thus he could not give a certain reply to the Vatican. A very delicate situation arose. Mindszenty continued to cause delay, either by claiming that he needed time to finish his memoirs or by demanding a further guarantee for his safe departure from Hungary. He still refused to say when exactly he would leave. Evidently, he was more inclined to stay than to leave despite the fact that the Hungarian authorities had even agreed to forward the books he needed when writing his memoirs.[278] The US Embassy informed the Hungarian government that the cardinal's departure was touch and go. During this period, each day received its own special significance. In the evening of July 14, 1971, Cheli and Zágon arrived once again in Budapest. That day also saw – thanks to the coordinated efforts of various parties – the arrival of two "fateful" documents that

277. MMAL 060. dosszié, MFN 7903, L-2854. Letter of József Mindszenty to Pope Paul VI, June 28, 1971. A detailed contemporary account is given in *L'Osservatore Romano*. September 29, 1971.

278. Ádám Somorjai, "*His Eminence Files.*" *American Embassy, Budapest: From Embassy Archives*, 15 (1971) – *Mindszenty bíboros az amerikai nagykövetségen. Követségi Levéltár*, 15 (1971). (Budapest: METEM, 2008), 244. Telegram of Ambassador Puhan to the State Department in Washington,September 9, 1971.

would determine the outcome of the "game": the letters of reply sent by Pope Paul VI and President Nixon. Mindszenty received both letters within the space of a few hours.

The pope's letter, which was dated July 10, 1971 and began with the words *Animo penitus commoto tuas obsequii plenas litteras accepimus*, was delivered to Mindszenty in the evening of July 14 by the Vatican's representatives, who went straight to the US Embassy after their arrival at Budapest Airport. In the letter, the pope expressed his approval for Mindszenty's decision as well as his eager anticipation of the cardinal's arrival in Rome. Yet he set no deadline and indicated that it would be up to Mindszenty to decide where he wished to reside in the future.[279] Still, the pope's letter left the Hungarian cardinal with little room for maneuver. Mindszenty's hope now was that President Nixon's reply might negate the strength of the Vatican's urging. Owing to the time zone differences, Nixon's letter, also dated July 14, reached the US Embassy in Budapest at 2.55 a.m. on July 15. The contents of the letter were then made known to Cardinal Mindszenty at 9.25 a.m. The cardinal's succinct reaction was: "Thank you. Why so late?"[280] President Nixon's letter was not a harsh rejection of the Hungarian cardinal's request. On the contrary, it was written in a tactful manner. Still, as the letter contained no words of consolation nor an invitation to stay at the embassy, it was clear that the presence of Cardinal Mindszenty at the embassy was no longer desirable. In fact, the original draft of the letter had been less tactful:

> As you prepare to leave the Embassy in Budapest, I should like you to know that I fully understand the reasons that have prompted you to make this difficult and unselfish decision.[281]

279. MMAL 060. dosszié, MFN 7906, L-2857. Letter of Pope Paul VI to József Mindszenty, July 10, 1971.

280. NARA RG 84, Records of the Foreign Service Posts of the Department of State, Hungary, Subject Files Relating to Cardinal Mindszenty 1956–72, Box 5, Cardinal Mindszenty July–Dec 1971. Memorandum; The ambassador's handwritten notes in the margin of the president's letter, which had been received by telegram: "Conveyes to Cardinal Mindsz. 0925, 7/15/71. A[lfred] P[uhan]", "Briefed Zagon (Cheli delayed) at 10:00 AP", "Briefed Cheli at 11:00 am AP."

281. Nixon Library, NSC Files, Box 828. Name Files, Mindszenty, Cardinal (Apr 70–May 74) 30123. Letter of President Richard Nixon to József Mindszenty July 14, 1971. Suggested message.

In lieu of these words, the version received by Mindszenty contained the following:

> Your decisions about the future are, of course, ones between yourself and the Vatican. I know that in reaching them you and His Holiness will be guided by your faith, by the interests of the Church, and by your concern for its ministry to the people of Hungary. I fully understand the difficulties involved in making your decision.[282]

The explanation for this change is revealed in a memorandum drafted by Helmut Sonnenfeldt, an experienced national security advisor: Mindszenty had written about his possible departure from the embassy only in his letter to the pope, whereas he had not specifically mentioned it in his (rather "opaque") letter to President Nixon.[283] Thus, had President Nixon's reply contained a clear reference to the cardinal's departure as a decision that he had already taken, it would have been evident to all that Mindszenty's sealed letter to the pope had in fact been opened by the Americans and its contents duly recorded.

Evidently, Mindszenty had no option but to leave the embassy. Even so, during a fourth discussion lasting more than ninety minutes, he repeatedly tried to alter his earlier decision. Indeed, he mentioned new conditions that would have to be met before his departure, including the complete revision of the ecclesiastical policy of the Kádár government. Zágon had no choice but to rebut Mindszenty's ideas. As the US Embassy's report stated,

> he [Zágon] finally took the bull by the horns and said that Wyszinski (sic) had followed the right path; that every day which Cardinal Mindszenty spent in this Embassy would lessen his value to the church and diminish his prospects for presenting to history the image of a constructive Prelate

282. Ibid., Copy of letter sent by President Nixon.

283. "In any case his decision was conveyed in a private letter to the pope and not to the President." Nixon Library, NSC Files, Box 828. Name Files, Mindszenty, Cardinal (Apr 70–May 74). Memorandum from Helmut Sonnenfeldt (National Security Council) to Gen. Alexander Haig, July 9, 1971. (Underlining in the original – the author.)

> of the church. He said that if he died in this Embassy, history would show him as a thick-headed (Dickshaegel) (sic, Dickschädel).[284]

Zágon then suggested that, instead of setting new conditions, Mindszenty should write an account of the unresolved issues affecting Hungarian Catholicism, requesting their prompt settlement and stating that his own departure from Hungary would not in itself signify the resolution of the Church's problems. To Zágon's surprise and relief, Mindszenty accepted this suggestion – which had been a risky one for Zágon to make. Thereafter, Mindszenty had little other option than to state his intention to leave the US Embassy in September or October and take up residence in Vienna.[285]

The Departure

As the departure date drew near, Cardinal Mindszenty grew increasingly agitated. Suddenly, there were so many things he still needed to do, and he also wanted to finish writing his memoirs as soon as possible. A US diplomat was assigned to Mindszenty with the task of assisting him. In his report to the ambassador, the diplomat wrote the following:

> I have gotten the impression rather rapidly that being an aide to H.[is] E.[minence] is a rather difficult and annoying job when a person has other things also on his mind. He keeps popping in and out and up with all kinds of requests that are penny ante at times and frequently most confusing. But, I'm keeping him bemused. [...] His removal from reality is evidenced in great measure to me by what happened this morning: when I informed him that one set of folios could not be taken out of the Szechenyi Library, he asked if I would go over and photograph them. I could not let that one pass. I told him I would not and that it would look pretty suspicious for anyone to do so. Also, I said we had no such camera. He is presently

284. NARA RG 84, Records of the Foreign Service Posts of the Department of State, Hungary, Subject Files Relating to Cardinal Mindszenty 1956–72, Box 5, Cardinal Mindszenty July–Dec 1971. Submission of Ambassador Puhan on a conversation with József Zágon, July 15, 1971.

285. Nixon Library, NSC Files, Box 693, Country Files – Europe, Hungary, vol. I, telegram no. 1450Z. from the embassy in Hungary to the State Department in Washington, July 16, 1971.

> collecting books on the societies for the blind, deaf, and also insane asylums. I suspect he is writing about Catholic aid to these.[286]

The series of excuses made by Mindszenty and the delay in fixing the date of departure irritated the embassy staff. In a report, the French ambassador noted how the US chargé d'affaires – a Catholic with Irish roots – had told him of his regret that Mindszenty had failed to go through with his earlier plan to surrender himself to the Hungarian authorities.[287] Meanwhile, Mindszenty's greatest concern was that his memoirs be safely delivered abroad. Indeed, he told embassy staff that if his memoirs were to be lost, his entire life would have been in vain.[288]

In the summer heat, the impending Hungarian–Vatican agreement began to shape up, with Vatican representatives setting a mutually acceptable frame on July 21. Thereafter a draft of the agreement was elaborated in Budapest. Concerning the finalization of the agreement, Giovanni Cheli and Angelo Sodano of the Vatican Secretariat of State held talks with representatives of the Hungarian government from September 6–8, 1971. The outcome of these negotiations was awaited with great anticipation. On September 7, officials in Budapest and at the Vatican approved the main body of the agreement as well as its annexes. Finally, at 10 a.m. on September 9, the agreement on Mindszenty's departure from Hungary was signed by Giovanni Cheli (the Vatican diplomat) on behalf of the Vatican and by Imre Miklós (head of the State Office for Church Affairs) on behalf of the Hungarian government. The two parties to the agreement undertook the following:

286. NARA RG 84, Records of the Foreign Service Posts of the Department of State, Hungary, Subject Files Relating to Cardinal Mindszenty 1956–72, Box 5, Cardinal Mindszenty July–Dec 1971. Memo from Clement G. Scerback to Ambassador Puhan, July 20, 1971. For the contents of the memo, see Somorjai, "*His Eminence Files*," 184–85.

287. AMAE AD Série: Europe, Hongrie, versement aux Archives (1971–juin 1976), boîte 3330, dossier Questions religieuses (1 janvier 1971–30 juin 1976), sous-dossier "Cardinal Mindzenty." Incoming telegram no. 800–813, Budapest, October 4, 1971.

288. NARA RG 84, Records of the Foreign Service Posts of the Department of State, Hungary, Subject Files Relating to Cardinal Mindszenty 1956–72, Box 5, Cardinal Mindszenty July–Dec 1971. Memo from Clement G. Scerback to Ambassador Puhan, July 28, 1971. For the contents of the memo, see Somorjai, "*His Eminence Files*," 198–99.

1.) The Holy See assures the Government of the People's Republic of Hungary that Joseph Cardinal Mindszenty shall, after his departure from Hungary, refrain from interfering – directly or indirectly – in the life and affairs of the Catholic Church in Hungary and from making statements or actions that are hostile to the People's Republic of Hungary or to its Government.
2.) The Government of the People's Republic of Hungary accedes to Joseph Cardinal Mindszenty leaving the territory of Hungary once the Presidential Council of the People's Republic of Hungary has taken the necessary measures. These measures shall be communicated in a Memorandum.
3.) After Joseph Cardinal Mindszenty has left the territory of Hungary, both parties to the agreement shall publish the official announcement contained in the Annexe.
4.) In the expectation of a final resolution to the issue of the archiepiscopal see of Esztergom, the Vatican shall appoint from among the currently active bishops an apostolic administrator 'sede plena' for this archdiocese, who shall have the same rights and obligations as those possessed by a diocesan bishop. (This appointment shall be made in the usual way.)
5.) Joseph Cardinal Mindszenty shall leave the territory of Hungary at a time to be determined later and in the company of those persons whom the Vatican shall designate, doing so either in the automobile of the Apostolic Nunciature in Vienna or on an airplane and bearing a Vatican passport. The journey shall be made from the United States' mission in Budapest without interruptions to Rome or to the seat of the Apostolic Nunciature in Vienna.[289]

Cardinal Mindszenty accepted none of the demands made on multiple occasions down the years: his silence on Hungarian affairs, his resignation as archbishop, and his submission of a written request for clemency. The demands placed upon him had recently been softened by the Hungarian government but toughened by the Vatican. The wording of the stipulations, especially on the matter of the "condition for the conditions," namely the guarantees relating to Mindszenty's conduct, reflect the shifting positions of the two sides. In the end, the Vatican did finally make assurances to the

289. MNL OL XIX–J–1–j KÜM/Vatikán 160. 28. tétel (item), 002428/10/1971. Original watermarked and signed document. For the official text of the agreement in Hungarian and Italian, see Margit Balogh, "Az 1971. szeptember 9-ei magyar–szentszéki megállapodás," *Századok* 147, no. 4 (2014): 911–14.

Hungarian government concerning Mindszenty's future statements. The other differences between the two sides, which had appeared to be unresolvable, were also settled. Another change – in relation to the original positions taken in the Hungarian–Vatican negotiations (1963) – concerned the title and office of archbishop. The apostolic administrator *sede plena* was to have the same rights and obligations as a diocesan bishop. Since August 16, 1950, apostolic administrators had presided over the Archdiocese of Esztergom, other than during a few short interludes. Their status had been variously listed in the papal yearbooks: in the period 1950–1956, as *sede plena* ("occupied see," whereby Mindszenty's jurisdiction had been suspended), and in the period 1959–1971, as *ad nutum Sanctae Sedis* ("with the approval of the Holy See," whereby Mindszenty's jurisdiction had not been suspended). When the hour of departure came, no changes were made to his commissions and offices, and the Hungarian side acknowledged that Mindszenty would retain the title of archbishop for the time being at least. The Vatican made no written undertaking to arrange for Mindszenty's resignation or deposition! The agreement merely refers to an expectation of a "final solution." Perhaps – in view of Mindszenty's advanced age – they were counting on the passage of time to resolve the issue. Owing to the firm stance taken by the Vatican representatives, the agreement did not state that the Presidential Council of the People's Republic of Hungary would grant clemency to József Mindszenty, even though such a provision had featured in the first draft of the agreement.[290]

The amnesty (or clemency) issue was only mentioned in the Hungarian government's memorandum. In accordance with this, the Presidential Council, acting on its own accord, granted clemency to József Mindszenty and cancelled the criminal proceedings that had been launched against him in 1962. Another expectation that was only formulated at the memorandum level was a Vatican undertaking to take action "when the occasion arises" (for instance, on his 80th birthday in March 1972) to have Mindszenty formally resign from the archiepiscopal see of Esztergom.[291]

290. Ibid., M–KS 288. f. 5/563. ő. e. 40. fol. Draft agreement between the Hungarian People's Republic and the Apostolic Holy See on the matter of József Cardinal Mindszenty, September 1971.

291. Ibid., XIX–A–21–e–0022–6/b/1971 and XIX–A–21–e–0022–6/c/1971. Memoranda of the representative of the Hungarian government and the representative of the Vatican. Published in Ólmosi, *Mindszenty és a hatalom*, 172–73.

Although the Vatican gave no written assurance of Mindszenty's resignation as archbishop, the Hungarian authorities treated it as a fait accompli. At a meeting of the Presidential Council on September 23, János Kádár summarized the essence of the agreement as follows:

> The Vatican will later terminate [Mindszenty's] commission under ecclesiastical law, whereupon the matter will be settled, as the interested parties have mutually granted guarantees for this.[292]

In making this statement, Kádár added something to the agreement which – although it had been mentioned by the two parties – had not been fixed in writing. Nevertheless, this "clause" became a part of public consciousness, which is rather insensitive to subtle differences. Rumors then began to spread that the Vatican had signed a top secret agreement with the Hungarian government, laying out, well in advance, not only Mindszenty's departure from Hungary but also a ban on the publication of his memoirs and his forced resignation. In fact, however, Mindszenty was able to leave Hungary without asking for clemency, without admitting to his guilt, and without resigning from his post as archbishop of Esztergom. In Hungarian politics, the departure of Mindszenty led to a fundamental reappraisal of the events of 1956. Whereas their initial hope – at the time of the first round of talks – had been the removal of the Hungarian question from the UN agenda (a matter of significance for both domestic and foreign policy), by 1971 the Hungarian side was expressing its satisfaction with the return of the excommunicated priests to the ecclesiastical flock.

Monsignor József Zágon returned to Budapest on September 13, 1971 with the aim of preparing for Mindszenty's journey to Rome. The original departure date was to have been September 27, but once again Mindszenty began frantically to haggle, citing a need to prepare spiritually and technically and then his swollen foot (he could not put his shoes on). He now stated that his preferred time for leaving the embassy was around October 10 (i.e., two weeks later).[293] Zágon attempted to persuade him to

292. Ibid., XVIII–2–b–61. d. Minutes of the meeting of the Presidential Council of the People's Republic of Hungary on September 23, 1971.

293. Ibid., XIX–A–21–e–0022–7/1971. 22. ő. e. Memo of Imre Miklós, president of the State Office for Church Affairs, September 14, 1971; MNL OL M–KS 288. f. 5/564. ő. e. 20–21.

adhere to the first date, arguing that his delaying tactics might elicit the disapproval of the pope. Zágon failed to budge him, and so, on September 16, he traveled to Vienna and requested further instructions from Casaroli by phone.[294] Zágon, who had been rather overwhelmed by his desperate mission and by the superficiality of Vatican diplomacy, finally made his return to Budapest with a message from the pope that he would await Mindszenty at the opening of the Holy Synod in Rome. The report even received the attention of the National Security Council in the United States:

> This past weekend, the Pope finally sent the cardinal a personal telegram warmly but firmly informing the cardinal that he expected to see him in Rome before the September 30 opening of the Synod of Bishops.[295]

The Synod of Bishops *(synodus episcoporum)* comprised selected bishops from around the world. After the Second Vatican Council, the Synod became one of the major ecclesiastical bodies. Its tasks included fostering relations between the pope and the bishops and arranging for the bishops to assist the Pope by providing him with advice. The first Synod of Bishops was held in 1967, and it was followed by four further synods during the reign of Paul VI. Mindszenty rightly felt honored to have received an invitation to the Synod. Since the invitation was a personal one from the pope, Mindszenty could no longer keep making excuses and delaying his departure.

József Mindszenty stepped out of the US Embassy in Budapest at 8.28 a.m. on September 28, 1971. His journey by car to Vienna began eight minutes

---

fol. Report for the Political Committee of the HSWP on the status of the Mindszenty affair and about the procedure for familiarization with the agreement between the government of the People's Republic of Hungary and the Vatican, September 18, 1971.

294. Nixon Library, NSC Files, Box 693, Country Files – Europe, Hungary, vol. I, telegram no. 1783 from Ambassador Puhan in Budapest to the State Department in Washington, September 16, 1971. See Somorjai, "*His Eminence Files*," 252.

295. Keefer et al., *Foreign Relations*, 1969–1976, vol. XXIX, 1, 291. Document 124. Memorandum from Arthur Downey of the National Security Council Staff to the president's assistant for national Security affairs (Kissinger), September 23, 1971. On the Internet: https://history.state.gov/historicaldocuments/frus1969-76v29/d124. – Author's note: although several sources mention a papal telegram, it was in fact a letter sent by Secretary of State Villot.

later.[296] The few passers-by who happened to be in the vicinity of the embassy building, showed no signs of having recognized the historical significance of the moment. Cardinal Mindszenty left the building quietly and without causing a stir. He had little baggage with him, as his personal belongings and his memoirs were to be sent after him by diplomatic courier. At 4 p.m. on the preceding day he had formally thanked the government of the United States and the American people for their hospitality.[297] Hungary's last prince primate left his native land in a Buick, accompanied by Opilio Rossi, nuncio of Vienna and titular archbishop of Ancira, and Monsignor József Zágon. The car was permitted to make a stop on the journey, but Mindszenty declined to make use of this opportunity, as he wished to avoid accepting even the smallest favor from the Hungarian authorities.[298] True, by this time, none of his close relatives were alive (his sister Teréz had died on February 8, 1966, while Anna had passed away barely two months earlier, on July 28, 1971). The car thus took Cardinal Mindszenty and his two companions directly to Vienna International Airport at Schwechat, a few miles east of Vienna, where Archbishop Casaroli awaited them. On the same day, Mindszenty traveled on an Alitalia flight to Rome that was scheduled to leave Schwechat at 1.25 p.m. After Archbishop-Major Slipyj of Lviv and Archbishop Beran of Prague (the latter had passed away two years earlier), Mindszenty became the third Eastern European prelate to arrive in Rome, having suffered multiple trials and drama.

After the arrival of Cardinal Mindszenty at Rome Airport, the Hungarian and Italian media reported briefly on the events of the day. The Hungarian government duly informed its "allies" – whom János Kádár considered to be the peace priests affected by the 1957 decree, the Bishops'

296. Nixon Library, NSC Files, Box 693, Country Files – Europe, Hungary, vol. I, telegram no. 1851 from the US Embassy in Budapest to the State Department in Washington, September 28, 1971.

297. NARA RG 84, Records of the Foreign Service Posts of the Department of State, Hungary, Subject Files Relating to Cardinal Mindszenty 1956–72, Box 5, Cardinal Mindszenty July–Dec 1971. Telegram from Ambassador Puhan to the State Department in Washington, September 30, 1971.

298. Nixon Library, NSC Files, Box 693, Country Files – Europe, Hungary, vol. I, telegram from Ambassador Puhan to the State Department in Washington, Budapest, September 27, 1971; Robert F. Illing, *America and the Vatican: Trading Information After World War II* (Palisades, NY: History Publishing Company, 2011), 197–98.

Conference, and the Czechoslovak and Polish fraternal parties, ("the topic is only of political interest to the Soviet comrades").[299] Local communist party organs, the National Council of the Patriotic People's Front, and representatives of the various religious denominations were informed of what was to happen just hours in advance of Mindszenty's actual departure. In Rome, Pope Paul VI's decision concerning ecclesiastical administration in Hungary was announced: the auxiliary bishop Imre Szabó, who had been serving as the apostolic administrator of the Archdiocese of Esztergom and who was now old and infirm, was removed from his office due to his failing health and replaced by the titular bishop Imre Kisberk, who had thitherto been the apostolic administrator of the Diocese of Székesfehérvár. On September 29, the approval of the Presidential Council of the People's Republic for Kisberk's appointment was published in the *Magyar Közlöny* (Hungarian Gazette). Doubtless this appointment was disputed within the communist regime, for Kisberk had long featured on the HSWP's black list. This explains why his appointment was hailed by Western commentators as a success for the Vatican. They could not even imagine that Kisberk's role was in fact far more contradictory and that the Hungarian secret services had managed, with varying success, to recruit him.[300] The path trodden by Kisberk, which is now public knowledge, well illustrates the dramatic tensions of loyalty and opposition that characterized the Hungarian Catholic Church during these decades.

In a courteous letter dated November 5, 1971, Pope Paul VI thanked President Nixon for the refuge provided to József Mindszenty over so many years by the US diplomatic mission in Budapest.[301] The entire foreign affairs apparatus had learned from the experience of offering humanitarian refuge. While the Americans had, in the end, actively cooperated in bringing about Mindszenty's departure from the embassy, this had only been possible

299. MNL OL M–KS 288. f. 5/560. ő. e. 158. fol. Minutes of the meeting of the Political Committee of the HSWP on July 27, 1971.

300. An attempt had been made to recruit him in 1951. Revealingly, the file on him was named "Traitor." The only surviving covert reports written by him are from the period 1968–71. See Gergely Mózessy, "Az 1956-ot követő megtorlás hatása Kisberk Imre püspök életútjára," in *Magyar Katolikus Egyház 1956: A Lénárd Ödön Közhasznú Alapítvány évkönyve 2007*, ed. Csaba Szabó (Budapest: Új Ember, 2006), 123–42.

301. Nixon Library, NSC Files, Box 732, Country Files – Europe, Vatican, Vol II. June 1970–31 Dec 1971 [2] Letter of Pope Paul VI to President Nixon, November 5, 1971.

because of the new and deeper relations forged by President Nixon with the Vatican, and by the tacit agreement of both parties in the US–Hungarian negotiations not to let the Mindszenty affair burden bilateral relations, which were already complicated by so many other factors.

Was it worth insisting on Mindszenty's departure? Archbishop Casaroli did not hide his doubts even when conversing with the Soviet ambassador in Rome: "It is hard to decide whether bringing Mindszenty out or leaving him there would have been the better course; perhaps future events will determine this."[302] We can surely concur, as even now the question cannot be answered with a simple yes or no. In my view, among the three "actors," it was the Hungarian government that drew the greatest benefit from Mindszenty's departure for Rome, for it ruled out even the slightest possibility of his death eliciting a wave of protests among the Hungarian populace. Whether the Catholic Church lost out is disputed by commentators. Perhaps the issue needs to be addressed as part of an overall assessment of the Vatican's Eastern policy. It is my conviction that the Holy See did not expect a quid pro quo in return for Mindszenty's departure from Hungary. After his arrival in Rome, the Hungarian–Vatican talks could return to some of the old issues (raised in 1971), while also addressing new questions: a careful sifting of the prelates, issues affecting religious life, and the cautious relaxation of the repressive measures affecting the life of the Catholic Church. The calm in Hungarian domestic politics – which, of course, was accompanied by repressive communist party control – spurred the forces of modernization within the Hungarian Catholic Church to adopt the spirit of the Second Vatican Council and make it their own (leading to liturgical changes and the adoption of the community church model). What can be said in terms of how Cardinal Mindszenty came out of the events? It seems that the cardinal exited his enduring struggle against the passage of time as the defeated party and to the relief of all other actors involved, including the Vatican. Evidently, instead of defeat, one might well speak of the sacrifices made by the imprisoned and persecuted prelate for his Church and for the future of Christian faith. His departure, however, was primarily a means to an end, namely the

302. MNL OL M–KS 288. f. 32/1971/18. ő. e. 197. fol. Document no. 002428/14: Duplicate copy of the report issued by the embassy in Rome on October 27, 1971.

publication of his memoirs, on which his role and position in history would be based. The single means of achieving this goal was for him to exit the US Embassy and leave Hungary.

It took a while for Ambassador Puhan and his staff to grow accustomed to Mindszenty's absence from the embassy. Two years later, he weighed up his work in Budapest:

> Well, when I arrived here I found relations between the United States and Hungary nonexistent but I did have a Cardinal of the Roman Catholic Church in my office. Today, four years later, relations between our two countries, given the fact that the United States is the Western factor in the West-East equation, the biggest power in NATO, and this is a small country occupied by 50,000 Soviet troops, are quite normal. The Cardinal no longer lives here. I have quite normal contacts with the Hungarian Government.[303]

The "Mindszenty affair" had still to be brought to a conclusion, but the main protagonist had been forced – at the age of 79 – into exile.

303. Nixon Library, White House Central Files (WHCF) Subject Files Countries (CO) Box 35, [Ex] CO 64 Hungary 1/1/73. Letter of Ambassador Alfred Puhan to Secretary of State Henry Kissinger, January 30, 1973.

CHAPTER 9

CARDINAL MINDSZENTY,
THE SPIRITUAL PASTOR OF HUNGARIANS THROUGHOUT THE WORLD

CHAPTER 9

In Exile

IN THE GOLDEN CAGE

In the Western world, news of Cardinal Mindszenty's departure from Hungary spread like wildfire. The primate of Hungary left the country for Rome on September 28, 1971. Some parts of the press acclaimed him as a martyr in the deathly struggle against communism, while others viewed his departure as a reasonable solution to an acute "problem" and as marking the conclusion of an outmoded version of Christianity. All this seemed to confirm Monsignor József Zágon's view of the forgetfulness of the world community. Soon, press outlets – both in the Eastern Bloc and in Western countries – were calling Mindszenty a relic of the past. Even the semi-official Vatican newspaper, *L'Osservatore Romano,* saw in Mindszenty's departure from Hungary and his arrival in Rome an opportunity for improved relations between the Holy See and the People's Republic of Hungary. At the same time, many newspaper commentators wrote respectfully about Mindszenty. His "stubbornness" was portrayed as both a character virtue and a political impediment. Regardless of what they thought about Mindszenty, all media outlets welcomed the departure agreement and the resolution of the asylum issue, which had become a chronic international problem.

Mindszenty left Hungary in silence, but arrived in Rome greeted by fanfare and celebration. Cardinal Villot, secretary of state, accompanied the Hungarian primate from Rome airport to the Vatican, where Pope Paul VI awaited him. The Sistine Chapel bustled with prelates from around the world. This was the venue for the second regular assembly of the Synod of Bishops, which commenced on the morning of September 30, 1971. In recognition of his steadfastness, the pope invited Mindszenty to celebrate Mass with him. It was a historic scene at a historical site. On the ceiling was a depiction of the divine act of creation, with the drama of the fall into sin and the coming atonement. At the altar, Christ's sacrifice proclaimed man's salvation. Stood alongside the pope, Cardinal Mindszenty, who was dressed in festive parament with a white miter on his head, caught the attention of all. Finally, after so many years, Mindszenty could stand once again at the altar as the head of his flock. He doubtless contemplated his enormous sacrifice that he had made and which had been borne out of his loyalty and faithfulness. Everyone was overcome with awe when they considered how Mindszenty had been liberated just days earlier. They marveled at how this man from behind the Iron Curtain could now be standing among them and giving thanks to God. In his sermon after the Gospel, the pope spoke warmly of Cardinal Mindszenty's unshakable faith and his supreme effort and sacrifice as head of the Hungarian Church. When the pope had said his final words, those assembled applauded the long-suffering Hungarian primate. Still, as he had not been appointed by the pope as a member of the Synod, Mindszenty could not officially attend or speak at the meeting. Nor could he hold a public Holy Mass or give a sermon.

The Vatican provided Mindszenty with a comfortable apartment in La Torre San Giovanni (Saint John's Tower). The Hungarian primate, however, never felt comfortable at the Vatican. His first stroll took him to the Vatican Grottoes and the tomb of Pius XII, a pope with whom he felt a close spiritual and philosophical bond. He prayed in front of the tomb for the salvation of Pius's soul. On a trip outside the Vatican, he visited Rome's four great cathedrals. The Hungarian primate also visited the Casa di Santo Stefano, the reconstruction of which in 1967 had been funded by donations. It had been an old dream of Mindszenty to revive the pilgrims' hostel that had been established by King Stephen I of Hungary and which had been demolished in 1776. Cardinal Mindszenty then visited his titular church, Santo Stefano Rotondo. (Mindszenty had sought in vain to secure the status of Hungarian national church for this church.) For the Hungarian primate, both the Casa di Santo Stefano and his titular church constituted a little bit of Hungary at the heart of Rome. Meanwhile, however, Mindszenty experienced a series of disappointments at the hands of the Vatican authorities and individual Vatican officials. Indeed, he soon came to regret having left Hungary. Robert F. Illing, an assistant to the US president's personal envoy to the Holy See, gave the following account to Ambassador Puhan:

> The day after his arrival in Rome, he became very depressed, lamented having departed your Embassy and sharply attacked the Vatican authorities, particularly Casaroli for making him a pawn in their 'unwise' dealings with the Hungarian government. At first the cardinal refused to consider celebrating mass with the Pope in the Sistine Chapel the following day. He even announced his intention to hold a press conference in Rome. He said he wished to consult with a group of prominent Hungarian emigres in Rome before taking a final decision. Five or so Hungarians visited him that same afternoon and fortunately they all advised against holding any press conference and, perhaps more important, freely assured him that his decision to leave Hungary had been right. A number of staunchly conservative Cardinals like Ottaviani and Antoniutti also called on Mindszenty and expressed agreement with his decision to depart Hungary. Much to everyone's relief, Mindszenty has subsequently settled down and now seems firmly convinced that he took the right decision. Cheli told me he has never seen such a hard-headed, difficult man in his life. He feels sure the cardinal would have difficulty getting along with any kind of government, including one run by his own Church.[1]

The comfortable but formalized life of Rome was alien to Mindszenty's nature. He wished to free himself of Vatican supervision as soon as possible. He expressed a wish to move to the Collegium Pazmanianum in

1. NARA RG 84, Records of the Foreign Service Posts of the Department of State, Hungary, Subject Files Relating to Cardinal Mindszenty 1956–72, Box 5, Cardinal Mindszenty July–Dec 1971. Letter of Robert F. Illing to Ambassador A. Puhan, October 29, 1971. Cf. Illing, *America and the Vatican*, 197–98.

Vienna, a plan politely opposed by the Vatican authorities. Still, his decision became final when he suffered a further disappointment: In mid-October, the Hungarian press reported on the revoking of the earlier papal decree that had excommunicated the peace priests.[2] Even if there was no direct cause and effect relationship between the cancellation of the excommunication order and the Hungarian government's decision to permit Mindszenty's departure from Hungary, the proximity in timing of the two events inevitably led the press and the public to suspect that a deal had been done. Mindszenty viewed this development as confirmation of his belief that his freedom had been obtained in exchange for the absolution of the excommunicated priests. State Secretary Villot had no option but to go to Mindszenty and explain to him what had happened,[3] namely that the sealed letter had been written a year earlier and that it had inadvertently been published now. For Mindszenty, the turn of events was particularly humiliating because whereas the peace priests – men who had collaborated with the communist regime – were being absolved, he, the head of the Hungarian Catholic Church, who had even endured a prison sentence, had been left without moral recompense and was now living in exile thanks to an act of mercy that had been "thrown after" him, so to speak. This explains why Mindszenty then wrote a letter to the Hungarian minister of justice, in which he rejected amnesty, because the injustice he had suffered could only be put right through rehabilitation. The Hungarian government minister sent him a matter-of-fact reply: under the country's laws, the procedure had been the only way for the cardinal to leave the country.[4]

The Move to Vienna

When Imre Miklós, head of the State Office for Church Affairs, inquired about Mindszenty's plans during a renewed round of talks between the Vatican and Hungary (held in Rome on October 14–16, 1971), nearly everyone knew that Mindszenty was intending to move to Vienna and make the city

2. "Az Apostoli Szentszék rendelkezése" [Papal decree], *Új Ember* 22, no. 42 (October 17, 1971), 4.

3. ÁBTL 3.1.2. M–38.914. 170. fol. Report of the agent codenamed "Maróti," August 15, 1972.

4. MNL OL XIX-A-21-e-0022-9/e/1971. Letter of József Mindszenty to Minister of Justice Mihály Korom, Vienna, October 31, 1971. Also, Korom's response, December 27, 1971.

his final place of residence. In Miklós's view, this change conflicted with the established game rules. Indeed, the move might even affect relations between the Holy See and the Hungarian government. Vatican officials insisted, however, that they were handling Mindszenty's fate in accordance with two principles: "They shall adhere to the terms of agreement, but they shall view Mindszenty as a free man."[5] Moreover, during the talks in Budapest, no-one had raised objections to the Pazmaneum as a possible place of residence.

Vatican diplomats failed to organize Mindszenty's move to Vienna in time, and the Austrian authorities were caught unaware. In response to questions from journalists concerning the position of the Austrian government, Chancellor Bruno Kreisky asserted merely that no residence application had been made and that, under the laws in force, any foreign citizen – including Mindszenty – who wished to stay in the country for more than three months would be required to submit such an application.[6] Evidently, the Austrian government was seeking to avoid controversy or a dispute with the Hungarian authorities. It was clearly fearful that Cardinal Mindszenty's presence in the country would damage bilateral relations.

In view of the sensitive nature of the situation, when interviewed by Austrian Radio on October 4, Mindszenty chose to sidestep questions about his possibly residing in Vienna. Yet his plan was to leave Rome for Austria as soon as possible. The initial date of his departure – October 10 – proved unsuitable, as elections were being held in Austria on that day. Another reason for his silence was that, in addition to the Pope's approval for his plan, he also needed a formal invitation from Archbishop König, which would only be issued after the conclusion of consultations between König and Paul VI. Archbishop König, who had worked for years on a solution to Mindszenty's predicament but who had largely been ignored during the final act of the drama, was initially averse to the idea of Mindszenty settling in Vienna. He wished first to clarify who was going to direct the

5. Ibid., XIX–A–21–e–XVII. dosszié–0022–8/e/1971. 3. fol. Report on the talks held with representatives of the Vatican, October 25, 1971.

6. AMAE AD Série: Europe, Hongrie, versement aux Archives (1971–juin 1976), boîte 3330, dossier Questions religieuses (1 janvier 1971–30 juin 1976), sous-dossier "Cardinal Mindzenty." Report no. 661–664 of François Leduc, French ambassador to Austria, October 12, 1971.

Pazmaneum and which rights and competences would be granted to Mindszenty.[7] In a papal instruction, the Vatican then let it be known that Mindszenty would not be permitted to hold Mass in the Archdiocese of Vienna, apart from in the chapel at the Pazmaneum. This left König with no choice but to inform Mindszenty that he would be "pleased" to see him.[8] Mindszenty was not appointed as ordinary of the Hungarians in Austria. Rather, the post continued to be held by István László, diocesan bishop of Eisenstadt. Consequently, Cardinal Mindszenty was thus not entitled, under canon law, to speak to "his priests" or "his faithful" in Austria. The final hurdle to his moving to Vienna fell when the Austrian government's consent arrived in Rome on October 22. The Austrian government set just one condition, namely that Mindszenty abstain, like any other émigré, from political activity.[9] Having received the Austrian government's consent, Mindszenty expressed a desire to travel the very next day to Vienna. No-one in Rome encouraged him to stay.

On October 23, Paul VI bid farewell to Mindszenty, after the two men had jointly celebrated Mass at 7.30 a.m. in the Matilda Chapel, the pope's private chapel. After the Mass, the pope, who stood alone with Cardinal Mindszenty in the vestry, said the following words in Latin: "Tu es Archiepiscopus Strigoniensis, Primas Hungariae. Labora! Inter difficultates veni ad me, adjuvabo" (You are the archbishop of Esztergom, the primate of Hungary. Set to work! When confronted with difficulties, turn to me, and I shall help).[10] At least, these were the pope's words according to a note made by Mindszenty at the time, which he subsequently cited in his letters and threw back at Paul VI when the latter later demanded that Mindszenty resign as Hungarian primate. The same sentence, with a minor but significant difference, can also be read in Mindszenty's Memoirs as follows: "You are and remain archbishop of Esztergom and primate of Hungary,"

7. ÁBTL 3.2.9.˙R–8–009/1. 65. fol. Memorandum, October 7, 1971.

8. Ibid., 138. fol. Memorandum, November 16, 1971.

9. Ibid., 125. and 136. fol. Memorandum, January 10 and January 11, 1972.

10. MMAL 061/a. dosszié, "Írások a depositióval kapcsolatban, 2." [Writings on the deposition], 1. ő. e. MFN 8824, L-3717. Letter of József Mindszenty to Cardinal John Heenan, February 23, 1974; MMAL 060. dosszié, MFN 7948, L-2899 (in German: MFN 7949, L-2900). Letter of József Mindszenty of January 6 to Pope Paul VI. Published in Ádám Somorjai, *Ami az emlékiratokból kimaradt: VI. Pál és Mindszenty József 1971–1975* (Pannonhalma: Bencés Kiadó, 2008), 43.

These words, however, were jotted down by Monsignor József Zágon, who was also present at the time, and in his memoirs Mindszenty was referring to him.[11] The essential difference between the two variants is that the first refers to the ecclesiastical office in the present, whereas the second implies – by virtue of the word "remain" – a pledge that it would last for a lifetime.

Serious controversy came to surround the interpretation of the statement and the issue of what really had been said. The question was not whether the pope considered Mindszenty to be archbishop of Esztergom and primate of Hungary, but for how long he would do so in the future: *permanently* or *only for some time?* A philological analysis of the sources[12] has shown that Mindszenty himself wrote down different variants of the ominous sentence, but that he never once, in his letters, mentioned the word "remain." The sources also reveal that the pope was never inclined to make Mindszenty's departure conditional on his resignation (the issue was not even mentioned in the agreement). Moreover, the pope made no commitment to such effect, despite the Hungarian government's firm intent to achieve linkage. This, however, did not mean that the pope would never review the status of Cardinal Mindszenty, a man for whom he had profound respect.

It is important to note that at the farewell, the pope spoke about "the limitations that are required by the circumstances."[13] Did Cardinal Mindszenty understand the pope's words uttered in Italian? It seems he may not have done so. Yet, those words clearly reveal that Mindszenty's own conduct would determine – at least in part – whether he could formally retain the title of archbishop of Esztergom, which he had held for twenty-three years. In the end, during the rest of Mindszenty's life, the pope chose merely to appoint an apostolic governor to head the Archdiocese of Esztergom. He opted for this course of action despite criticism from various influential individuals within the Vatican, who would have favored Mindszenty's being cast aside. Allegedly, even Cardinal Villot, state secretary, suggested to the pope that a second Hungarian cardinal be created. "If the Holy Father were to take this action, the Mindszenty affair

11. Mindszenty, *Memoirs*, 239.

12. László Németh, "VI. Pál és Mindszenty József 1971. október 23-án," *Vigilia* 63, no. 4 (1998): 247–52; Gábor Adriányi, "A prímási szék megüresedetté nyilvánítása 1974-ben," *Vigilia* 63, no. 6 (1998): 425–28; Somorjai and Zinner, *Washingtonból jelentjük*, 159–61.

13. MMAL 020/a. sz. dosszié, I. 14. ő. e. Pro memoria. Rome, October 23, 1971. A facsimile is published in Mészáros, *A száműzött bíboros szolgálatában*, 675.

could be considered closed."[14] For his part, however, the pope had no wish to add to the Hungarian primate's bitterness. Indeed, when he finally did take a decision on his status, other factors were motivating him.

Accompanied by Monsignor József Zágon, Cardinal Mindszenty arrived in Vienna, the one-time capital of the Austro-Hungarian Monarchy, at 11 p.m. on October 23, 1971. He was given no special welcome, as both Archbishop König and the nuncio, Rossi, were away from Vienna at the time. The excuse given for the two men's absence was a transparent one (their being oblivious to his arrival due to the lack of a telephone connection), which leads one to conclude that neither the archbishop nor the nuncio wished officially to receive Mindszenty. On the evening of his arrival, the Hungarians living in Vienna were commemorating the fifteenth anniversary of the 1956 revolution. The rector of the Pazmaneum, Egon Gianone, was attending this commemorative event. It was here that he received the unexpected news of Mindszenty's arrival in Vienna. He returned to the Pazmaneum, reaching the building minutes in advance of Cardinal Mindszenty's arrival from the airport.

The Pazmaneum (in Latin: Collegium Pazmanianum), a seminary in Vienna, had been established by Cardinal Péter Pázmány, one of Mindszenty's predecessors as archbishop of Esztergom, in 1623. Between 1953 and 2002, in view of the isolation of the Hungarian Catholic Church and the resulting risk to the institution's maintenance, the Pazmaneum was subject to the oversight of the archbishop of Vienna. This arrangement was based on a decree of the Holy See issued on February 14, 1953.[15] Notwithstanding this legal status, Mindszenty was of the view that the Pazmaneum belonged to the Archdiocese of Esztergom and should therefore be run by him, in view of his status. This emotional link with the Pazmaneum renewed his zest for life. He no longer felt like an exile, for he experienced his time at the Pazmaneum as the realization of his wish to live out his final years on "Hungarian" soil. Indeed, he perceived the Pazmaneum as the single part of his archdiocese that remained

14. ÁBTL 3.1.2. M–40.530/2. 45. fol. Report of the agent codenamed "Igaz Sándor," November 10, 1971.

15. Margit Beke, *"Fejezetek az új- és legújabbkori elitképzéshez: A katolikus egyház szerepe a modern magyar értelmiségi elit nevelésében a bécsi Pázmáneumban"*, Doctoral Thesis, Budapest, 2010, 106–12. http://real-d.mtak.hu/13/3/Beke.pdf.

accessible to him. Such emotions were reflected in what he wrote in the guestbook on his arrival: "I have arrived at this place as if it were my home."[16] It was a mere coincidence that the building lay in the immediate vicinity of the US Embassy in Vienna...

Cardinal Mindszenty introduced himself to the Hungarians living in Vienna at a Holy Mass celebrated in the Capuchin Church on November 19, 1971. He did so to Austrian Catholics at a Holy Mass held two days later in the city's St. Stephen's Cathedral (Stephansdom). It was the first time since 1948 that Mindszenty could celebrate a Pontifical High Mass. In a short greeting, Archbishop König of Vienna referred to Mindszenty as "the symbol of faith." Within a short time, even Austria's politicians had moderated their position. Chancellor Kreisky emphasized that Austria was not embarrassed by Mindszenty's presence in the country. The Hungarian primate was now, finally, a free man, and no-one in Austria wished for him to suffer the confinement he had endured for so many years at the US Embassy in Budapest.

A new stage in Mindszenty's life had begun, but his lifestyle altered little. He continued to practice self-denial, in relation to food, drink, and homely comforts. His schedule included little time for rest or relaxation. Whenever he could, he adhered to his daily routine: office work, modest meals with his seminarians, a short after-lunch rest, a half-hour stroll in the garden in the company of one of the priests. Then, work at his desk until midnight at least. He held Mass in the house chapel on weekdays and in the main chapel of the Pazmaneum on Sundays. It took months for his initial distrust of the people around him to subside.[17] In terms of mental health, he was balanced and felt at peace. He remained in this state, despite a series of subsequent disappointments.

The three and a half years that remained to Mindszenty in his life were spent on carrying out pastoral work among the one and a half million Hungarian exiles and émigrés and on compiling his memoirs, which pointed to the dangers of bolshevism. The authorities in Budapest watched him with eagle eyes, hoping to spot some deed that might constitute a vi-

16. "A rektor visszaemlékezése: Mindszenty utolsó évei" [Recollections of the rector: The final years of Mindszenty], *Népszabadság* 49, no. 99, April 29, 1991, 6.

17. SzTTTI 1192/110a. Witness statement of Natália Palágyi, Sister of Social Service, on the matter of the beatification of József Cardinal Mindszenty, Buffalo, May 17, 1985.

olation of the terms of the Hungarian–Vatican agreement of September 9, 1971 (which had set out the conditions for Mindszenty's departure from Hungary). News of the publication of his memoirs elicited strong and recurrent protests from the Hungarian government, as did several of his statements. From Hungary's perspective, it seemed that Cardinal Mindszenty's departure from the country had reignited the whole affair rather than conclude the matter.

During a new round of Hungarian–Vatican talks, held in Rome from October 14–16, 1971, the implementation of the agreement was assessed for the first time. With a sense of relief, the two parties concluded that "both parties have mutually adhered to the terms of the agreement."[18] Utilizing the sense of satisfaction felt by both parties, the Holy See managed to effect seven personnel changes (acceptance of the resignation of the bishop of Szombathely and the appointment of six new bishops, including that of the parish priest of Badacsonytomaj, László Lékai, who became, as of February 8, 1972, apostolic administrator of Veszprém). Still, with a view to keeping the Hungarian authorities happy in the longer term, a few weeks later the Holy See had to call the Hungarian primate to order.

What happened was that on the first Sunday in Advent (November 28, 1971), Cardinal Mindszenty – having been influenced by some people who were close to him, especially by József Vecsey – wrote a pastoral letter to the Hungarian émigrés on five continents, signing the letter as "József Mindszenty, archbishop of Esztergom and primate of Hungary." This was the first pastoral letter to be drafted since his move to Vienna. The letter drew public attention because it contained a poorly formulated sentence that could easily be misinterpreted as being irredentist in intent: "It was faith and hope in God that we passed the prison threshold and the temporary but life-destroying national border."[19] The governor of Burgenland issued an immediate protest. In his view, Cardinal Mindszenty

18. MNL OL 288. f. 5/567. ő. e. 27. fol. Report on the talks held with representatives of the Vatican, October 25, 1971.

19. MMAL 060. dosszié, 507/1971; Ibid., 040/b dosszié, Articles and memos from 197]; MNL OL XIX–A–21–c ÁEH Adattár, 17.1. Mindszenty József hercegprímás 1–101. 1966–71. 50. tétel (item). Published in József Mindszenty, *Hirdettem az igét: Válogatott szentbeszédek és körlevelek, 1944–1975*, comp. József Közi Horváth (Vaduz: Mindszenty Alapítvány, 1982), 188–91.

had "placed a question-mark over Austria's territorial integrity."[20] Various parts of the Austrian media likewise interpreted the text as indicating that Mindszenty regarded the Hungarian–Austrian border as temporary. In fact, however, the Hungarian primate – as he pointed out in a hurriedly published clarification – had been referring exclusively to the temporary nature of the "Iron Curtain," an obstacle that had even taken people's lives. He then let the BBC's Hungarian correspondent know his real thoughts: to the outside world "he explained himself by saying that he had been thinking of the Iron Curtain, while everyone could know (and at this point he gave a wink!) 'that we were thinking of Trianon'."[21]

The matter was debated by the Austrian Council of Ministers. Mindszenty's claim that he had been thinking of ideological rather than physical boundaries, was viewed with skepticism, but in the end the Austrian authorities accepted the "clarification." The information received by the authorities in Hungary, which accorded with the reports of US diplomats, pointed to a tougher stand having been taken by the Austrian government: Minister of Foreign Affairs Rudolf Kirchschläger informed the Vatican that if Cardinal Mindszenty were to take any further action that might undermine the good neighborly relations between Austria and Hungary, the Austrian government would promptly review his Austrian residence permit.[22] Thereafter Mindszenty refrained from writing any further pastoral letters to Hungarian Catholics living outside Hungary. (It was only in 1973 that he wrote a message – in the form of a kind of testamentary will – to Hungarians living in Canada and the United States.) In the light of these events, Paul VI requested Mindszenty in the future to submit for prior approval any statement he wished to make, including sermons.[23]

20. AMAE AD Série: Europe, Hongrie, versement aux Archives (1971–juin 1976), boîte 3330, dossier Questions religieuses (1 janvier 1971–30 juin 1976), sous-dossier "Cardinal Mindzenty." Report no. 772/EU of François Leduc, French ambassador to Austria, December 10, 1971.

21. ÁBTL 3.2.3. Mt–975/3. 10. fol. Report of the agent codenamed "Kőműves Sándor" [= the former Jesuit, Töhötöm Nagy], October 19, 1972.

22. NARA RG 84, Records of the Foreign Service Posts of the Department of State, Hungary, Subject Files Relating to Cardinal Mindszenty 1956–72, Box 5, Cardinal Mindszenty July–Dec 1971. Telegram no. 7793 of the US Embassy in Vienna on the reception in Austria of Mindszenty's Advent pastoral letter, December 7, 1971. Published in Somorjai, "*His Eminence Files*", 309.

23. MMAL 060. dosszié, MFN 7910, L-2861. Letter of Pope Paul VI to Mindszenty, December 14, 1971. For the text of the letter in Latin, see Adriányi, *Die Ostpolitik des Vatikans*, 160–61.

The Hungarian primate, however, was oblivious to the trouble he had caused. Based on the pope's request, his sole conclusion was that he should place the manuscript for his memoirs, fifteen years of work,

> ...in unpublished form, in a locked cupboard. And this shall be my lot, so that the Holy See can gain the goodwill of the communists for the Church in Hungary. [...] Do the leaders of the State Secretariat – having submitted to the will of the communists – wish to prevent me from publishing my Memoirs by means of this advance censure?[24]

Mindszenty failed to perceive that the pope's instruction was directed not only at the hated Hungarian communists but also at political life in Austria, for, according to diplomatic reports, Paul VI had given an assurance to the Austrian government that Mindszenty was residing in Vienna "exclusively in a private capacity" and would not be undertaking any official activities.[25] Mindszenty's blunt reply was not even read by the pope, as Monsignor József Zágon returned it to Vienna, saying that "...I cannot give the letter, in its present form, to His Holiness. The Holy Father would rightly be offended by its contents and tone, and it would damage the great goodwill and esteem that His Holiness feels towards him."[26] Zágon's dismissive approach led to a breach of confidence between him and the Hungarian primate. Indeed, Mindszenty began to have doubts that Zágon was wholeheartedly representing his cause at the Vatican.[27] His suspicions were unjustified, however, as Zágon was making all efforts to fulfill a task of the utmost difficulty. Even in withholding the letter, his main aim had been to protect Cardinal Mindszenty's best interests. In his reply – which Zágon

24. Ibid., MFN 7917, L-2868. Letter of József Mindszenty to Pope Paul VI. Vienna, January 25, 1972. For its text, see Somorjai, *Sancta Sedes Apostolica et Cardinalis Ioseph Mindszenty. Documenta 1971–1975*, 126.

25. AMAE AD Série: Europe, Hongrie, versement aux Archives (1971–juin 1976), boîte 3330, dossier Questions religieuses (1 janvier 1971–30 juin 1976), sous-dossier "Cardinal Mindzenty." Telegram no. 699–700 of the French Embassy in Vienna, October 25, 1971.

26. MMAL 060. dosszié, MFN 7918, L-2869. Letter of József Zágon to József Vecsey, January 31, 1972. Its text is published in Somorjai, *Sancta Sedes Apostolica et Cardinalis Ioseph Mindszenty. Documenta 1971–1975*, 129.

27. Németh, *Zágon-leveleskönyv*, 87–88. Letter of József Zágon to Károly Fábián, February 8, 1974.

did now pass on to the pope – Mindszenty reiterated his concerns regarding his memoirs and requested the cancellation of the prescribed censure in Rome.[28] The pope's response was concessionary: "This is not about censorship, but about the necessary organizing of affairs and mutual cooperation." He then assured Mindszenty that he could contact him directly at any time.[29] This marked the conclusion of the matter for the time being. The Vatican's apparent aim was to fulfill the terms of its agreement with the Hungarian government without having to discipline Mindszenty in a humiliating fashion. As regards the prior approval necessary for his statements, by way of a solution Mindszenty requested that he be required to "subjugate himself only to the Holy Father."[30] The style of Cardinal Mindszenty's subsequent sermons was, indeed, more reserved – at least until mid-1973. The papal admonition sufficed to persuade the aged Hungarian primate to exercise self-restraint. Still, his pent-up bitterness was such that he imperiously rejected the financial allowance granted to cardinals, the so-called *piatto*.[31] This action was reminiscent of his rejection – in 1945 – of his archbishop's salary. At that time, he had been protesting the policies of the secular authorities; now, however, he was clashing with the highest body of his Church.

Slowly, Vienna and the rest of Austria grew accustomed to the Hungarian cardinal's presence at the Pazmaneum. The Hungarian secret services did not lose sight of him either. Meanwhile, the Austrian Catholic elite – although it acknowledged Mindszenty's presence – did not encourage him to take an active role.

> I am convinced that not only our professors [...] are mature enough, in a political sense, to ascertain the anachronistic nature of Cardinal Mindszenty's person, his attitudes, and his actions. He simply lags behind by two centuries. For these matters, it may be that he can win applause and

28. MMAL 060. dosszié, MFN 7919, L-2870. Letter of József Mindszenty to Pope Paul VI, March 10, 1972. For its text, see Adriányi, *Die Ostpolitik des Vatikans*, 162–65.

29. Ibid., MFN 7921, L-2872. Letter of Pope Paul VI to József Mindszenty, April 18, 1972. For its text, see Adriányi, *Die Ostpolitik des Vatikans*, 166–67.

30. MMAL 802/3. dosszié, Bamberg. Letter of Sándor Csertő to József Vecsey, May 19, 1972.

31. Letter of József Mindszenty to Cardinal Villot, state secretary. December 31, 1971. See Somorjai, *Sancta Sedes Apostolica et Cardinalis Ioseph Mindszenty. Documenta 1971–1975*, 180–81.

> encouragement from a small fanatical group, but he cannot count on supporters among ordinary citizens or among the faithful. His views are past their sell-by date,

stated Rudolf Weiler, a professor at Vienna University's Faculty of Theology.[32] Others feared that the setting aside of historical facts would be ridiculed and that the otherwise venerable Hungarian ideas would be the subject of scorn and contempt in Austria.[33]

Life at the Pazmaneum changed fundamentally. While some avoided the institution for this or that reason, others were now even more keen to gain entry. The rector of the seminary, Egon Gianone, complained that although he took lunch with Cardinal Mindszenty "he dared talk with him about little more than the weather, and [Mindszenty] also shrouded himself in silence and said nothing about either the present or the future."[34] In addition to several nuns, Mindszenty was assisted in his work by his secretaries – Monsignor Ferenc Harangozó, Father László Ikvay, and Father József Vecsey – and, from the summer of 1972, by a deputy secretary, Tibor Mészáros. The most influential of these men was József Vecsey, who had earlier served as clergyman to the Hungarian community in Paris. The impression of Vecsey gained from the sources is a particularly negative one. Indeed, many regarded him as Mindszenty's "bad angel." Vain efforts were made to remove Vecsey from his post.[35]

Pastoral Ways

In the final years of his life, one of Cardinal Mindszenty's main aims was to promote the preservation of faith and national identity among his fellow Hungarians around the world. Indeed, the Hungarian primate spent the ensuing years making journeys that were driven by the Hungarian national

32. ÁBTL 3.2.3. Mt–988/1. 262. fol. Information report, February 24, 1972.

33. Ibid., 265. fol.

34. Ibid., 3.1.2. M–38.914 44. fol. Report of the agent codenamed "Maróth" on Mindszenty's situation, November 17, 1971.

35. Ibid., 3.2.5. O–8–552/12. 79. fol. Report of "Dér" [i.e., the intelligence officer Oszkár Kiss] on his meeting with Archbishop Casaroli, January 9, 1973; Mészáros, *A száműzött bíboros szolgálatában*, 28. Record of June 26, 1972.

idea. He would go wherever he was called. Other than during some shorter or longer breaks, he traveled the world, seeking out members of the Hungarian diaspora from Toronto to Cape Town and from San Francisco to New Zealand.

His first journey (in May 1972) took him to Germany, where he attended the Pentecost festivities in Bamberg commemorating the reign of King Stephen. His hosts welcomed him as the symbolic constitutional representative of St. Stephen's Hungary, as the first knight banneret of the nation. Parts of Mindszenty's sermon were removed by the censor: for example, his critique of Marxism and a section in which he drew an analogy between the Soviet occupation of Hungary and the journey to the east made by Father Julianus in the 13th century in search of the ancient Hungarian homeland.[36] On Whit Monday, Mindszenty celebrated Mass at Frankfurt Cathedral, whence he traveled to Regensburg. Everywhere he experienced the joyful love of the émigré Hungarians, who, by listening to and watching the living "apostle of anti-communism," drew confirmation and vision for their own experiences of exile. Even if his sermons were censored, he became the embodiment of national independence, a symbol for a Hungary that hoped for its liberation from Soviet occupation. The stay in Germany was followed by a brief, two-day visit to Belgium. Thereafter, Mindszenty returned to Austria, giving a sermon at Mariazell on September 17. His words on this occasion were interesting because he gave his support to the long-held desire of the émigrés for "national unity" and extended a fraternal hand to Protestant Hungarians, as "we welcome them into the great united camp of Hungarians."[37] Having relinquished the prejudices of his youth, the older Mindszenty looked to the Hungarian identity of his compatriots rather than to their religious affiliations.

The significance of these initial journeys is dwarfed by Mindszenty's trip to Portugal, where he stayed from October 11–18, 1972. An old dream of the Hungarian primate was fulfilled when Bishop João Pereira of Leiria invited him – at the behest of the Hungarian émigrés in Portugal – to

36. MMAL 802/3. dosszié, Bamberg. "Pro memoria Őeminenciája bambergi beszédével kapcsolatban" [Pro memoria regarding His Eminence's speech in Bamberg], May 18, 1972.

37. MNL OL XIX–A–21–e–0022–14/b/1972. 21. ő. e. Summary of József Mindszenty's statements, 4. fol.

preside over the Fatima festivities, the annual celebration of the apparition of Our Lady of Fatima. His travel schedule in Portugal included two important highlights: a journey to Madeira, where he prayed over the tomb of Charles IV, the last emperor of Austria and king of Hungary, whose beatification was already in progress; and a trip to the British military cemetery in Lisbon, where he laid a wreath at the grave of Regent Horthy. Something that would have been unimaginable during his stint as parish priest of Zalaegerszeg or during his term as bishop of Veszprém now – amid the bitterness of exile – took place: Mindszenty bowed his head to Hungary's Calvinist former head-of-state, a man whom he had once regarded as an usurper. Both these men – Charles IV and Miklós Horthy – were symbols of a world that no longer existed. In communist Hungary, they were disparaged figures. Indeed, Mindszenty's show of reverence at their graves was regarded in Budapest as a provocation and as sending a hostile message to the People's Republic of Hungary. Meanwhile, however, these events were barely registered by international public opinion, being mentioned in the reports of no more than a few diplomats. Mindszenty's planned trip to Spain, which would have followed his stay in Portugal, was thwarted by the Spanish government authorities, which wished to avoid jeopardizing Spanish–Hungarian economic relations.[38]

The major events of the following year – aside from short trips to Germany and Great Britain – were Cardinal Mindszenty's journeys to North America and to Africa: in late September 1973, Mindszenty visited Canada, whence he went on a three-day trip to the United States (a longer stay in the United States took place in May 1974), and then, a month and a half later, he traveled to South Africa. Hungarian state security diligently observed all these journeys, but they could do nothing, because Mindszenty always received a visa and the Vatican had no wish to restrict his movements.

Now aged eighty-two years, Mindszenty prepared for his journey to Canada with a degree of nostalgia. The warm reception exceeded his expectations. This journey differed from the others, because it came in the form of a "visitation" to the "Hungarian flock" rather than being made to mark a church festival or as a pilgrimage. The Hungarian community in Canada linked Mindszenty's visit with a celebration to mark the millennium

38. ÁBTL 3.2.9. R–8–009/3. 62. fol. Summary report, September 15, 1973.

of the Hungarian people's Christian faith; they welcomed him as the "exiled primate." The festivities were memorialized in a brochure in English entitled "973–1973," which was decorated with images of the Hungarian double cross and the Holy Crown. In addition, a memorial coin with an image of Cardinal Mindszenty was issued. The venues on the trip were: Montreal, Toronto, Winnipeg, Calgary, and Vancouver. At each venue, the program took on a similar form: arrival, welcome greeting, bouquet, press conference, photographs, comment in the guestbook. Prayers, blessings and greetings for the assembled Catholics. The official events were also rather monotonous: Holy Mass, a series of audiences and greetings, consecration of the flag, and a reception. Wherever he gave an appearance, Mindszenty would begin his sermon by expressing his sincere gratitude for the welcome received by the Hungarian exiles and émigrés. He would then request his compatriots to prove themselves useful and loyal citizens to their new homelands, while never forgetting the old country. Crowds of people came to hear his words. Mindszenty's presence poured a spirit of faith, confidence and enthusiasm into what was a factious and fractious émigré community. The Canadian Hungarian press recognized a new Savonarola in the aged Hungarian primate, whose fighting spirit and unshakeable determination had earned him respect.

Still, the problems lying behind these protocol events should not be ignored. The assimilation of the Hungarian immigrants was unstoppable, and materialism was spreading among the people. Patriotic spirit was no longer a driving force. Indeed, many of the priests were not even Hungarians. Even when a priest was Hungarian, it was often he who was undermining the unity of the community. The Hungarian community's churches had many empty pews and the ceilings were on the verge of collapse.[39] There was nothing exaggerated about this devastating picture. The comfortable and wealthy Canadian Catholic Church viewed with distrust the priests who had arrived from distant Eastern Europe. Many of these men started drinking, suffered from depression, or left the priesthood and got married.[40] Moreover, Mindszenty's visit was an

39. MMAL 808. dosszié, Kanada, 1973. 10. ő. e. Péter Noel's summary, Calgary-Edmonton, September 26, 1973.

40. MMAL 808. dosszié, Kanada, 1973. MFN 10211, L-5056. Letter of the physician János Mahig to József Mindszenty, Montreal, March 15, 1973.

opportunity for a range of political groupings to hold gatherings. Some of these groups even handed out revisionist leaflets.

Mindszenty's visit cast a long shadow over diplomatic relations between Hungary and Canada. Although Prime Minister Pierre Trudeau, a free-thinking liberal, sidestepped a personal meeting with Mindszenty, he sent State Secretary for External Affairs Mitchell Sharp to greet Cardinal Mindszenty. Sharp did so in somewhat exaggerated terms:

> This is not the first time that I have addressed a large audience. This is not the first time that I have addressed an audience that included distinguished personages. Never before, however, have I ever addressed an audience that included such a distinguished personage as our guest of honor Cardinal Mindszenty. Never has this man abandoned his faith. Never has he bowed to the oppressor.[41]

Sharp's greeting elicited disapproval from the Hungarian foreign affairs apparatus, followed by a clarification from the Canadian state secretary: his last sentence had related to Mindszenty's defiance against the Nazi German occupiers, he claimed. The clarification eased tensions. Both sides were determined not to sacrifice the accomplishments of Hungarian–Canadian relations.

The highlight of the three-day trip to the United States was the consecration of the newly rebuilt St. Ladislaus Church in New Brunswick (NJ). Mindszenty was asked to perform this task by Julián Füzér and Vazul Végvári, the two parish priests. The dedication, which took place on September 30, was attended by around five thousand people, most of whom were Hungarian émigrés. Regarding the attitudes shown towards him by America's top clerics, Mindszenty was disappointed to find that Spellman's successor as archbishop of New York, Cardinal Terence Cooke – whose beatification is now in progress, just like that of Mindszenty – received him with far less sympathy and goodwill. Although Cooke was present at the airport to welcome Mindszenty, he failed to organize a representative program in his honor. Mindszenty, in festive attire, sat through the Holy Mass celebrated by his host. The two men were

41. MNL OL XIX–A–21–e–0022–3/N/1973. 22. ő. e. Report of Károly Szabó, Hungarian ambassador to the United States, November 17, 1973. (Please note: the spelling mistake in the original has been corrected here.)

then photographed together, but it became apparent that for the native-born Cooke, the world-famous Hungarian primate was merely a piece of scenery on the stage. Evidently, it was not easy to have a casual conversation with a living legend, a man who had sacrificed his entire life for the defense of his principles. Mindszenty was given barely a quarter of an hour by Archbishop Cooke, who then rushed off to a football game. Cooke showed little enthusiasm for discussing the matter of a Hungarian parish in New York, which had been an issue since 1929. Nor was he interested in welcoming a Hungarian auxiliary priest, whose appointment might have served to offer spiritual guidance to the Hungarian diaspora in North and South America.[42] Mindszenty wanted to see the appointment of a Hungarian auxiliary bishop, who would not be tied to a single territory. The Vatican, however, was averse to the idea of a separate Hungarian émigré church, which might have been headed by Mindszenty himself.

Apart from his brief conversation with Cardinal Cooke, Mindszenty did not meet with any leading Catholic churchmen in the United States. Nor was he met by any senior government figures, albeit President Nixon did welcome him to the United States in a telegram sent on September 29 and Senator Edward Kennedy mentioned him in the Senate.[43] The major newspapers and magazines reported Mindszenty's arrival in the United States, but the greatest interest in his schedule was shown by the Hungarian émigré press outlets. Cardinal Mindszenty's "newsworthiness" grew when he chose not to evade the political questions of journalists. Indeed, he even took the opportunity to announce that he would not be prevented by

> the agreement between the Hungarian government and the Vatican [the agreement concerning his departure from Hungary, signed on September 9, 1971] from publishing his memoirs (expected in the spring of 1974), from visiting the Hungarians on five continents, or from making statements, and so forth.[44]

42. For the relevant papers, see MMAL 054. dosszié, Correspondence concerning the appointment of a Hungarian émigré bishop.

43. Nixon Library, NSC Files, Presidential Correspondence 1969–74, Box 755. President Nixon's telegram to József Mindszenty, September 29, 1973.

44. ÁBTL 3.2.9. R–8–009/3. 69. fol. Copy of the report of the Hungarian Embassy in Ottawa dated October 4, 1973. (The Memoirs were published in the fall of 1974 rather than in the spring.)

It seemed, therefore, that he had abandoned the reserve shown on earlier journeys. What caused this change? The answer is to be found in a key word uttered at the press conference: *Memoirs*. Shortly before his journey to Canada, Mindszenty had received a letter from Paul VI, dated August 30, 1973, requesting that he delay publication of his memoirs. Mindszenty's response to the pope's request was one of defiance: If the Vatican were to violate its pledge (made in the summer of 1971) concerning the right to publish his memoirs, then he would no longer be bound by the game rules imposed upon him.

On All Saints' Day, Mindszenty gave a spiritual testamentary will to the Hungarians living in Canada and the United States:

> Before my eyes close for the last time, neither man, nor pathos, but God and our ancestors have entrusted to me, and I should like to place this beneath the pillow of every Hungarian, wherever he or she might be in the world, not to rest until the hour of his death: from the little that remains we must reconstruct our Hungarian motherland. This is our purpose in this world. [...] Put aside rivalries, and inordinate ambitions. The belief that no-one else can do it but me. Looking neither to the right nor to the left, everyone must do his part, where life has placed him. Let us create a church community based on the Christian faith. Let there be children in a family, for that remains a blessing and means the future, whatever the world may say. Let children receive the Hungarian language and a Hungarian identity in the family, and at the weekend school – if there is no possibility of this on an everyday basis.[45]

He expounded, in a clearly understandable way, on the tasks of the Hungarian émigré community: even if a communist regime is dictating developments in the ancient homeland, that time would eventually pass, and then would come the time of the Hungarians living in foreign lands; a great mission of salvation for the homeland would await them. Until that day, the Hungarian community abroad should preserve its language, its culture, and its traditions. The only problem was that the émigré community changed

45. MMAL 808. dosszié, Kanada, 1973. 8. ő. e. "Kedves Magyarok Kanadában és Amerikában!" [Dear Hungarians in Canada and America] Message of József Mindszenty, Vienna, All Saints' Day [November 1], 1973.

during the ensuing following decades. The first generation of émigrés grew old, and members of the next generation struggled to speak the language of their ancestors. The third generation could barely speak even broken Hungarian.

Mindszenty's energetic pastoral journeys had an invigorating effect on the Hungarian émigré communities. His mere presence thrilled all parts of the diaspora, including non-Catholics. He missed no opportunity to urge Hungarians around the world to fulfil their Christian and patriotic duties and to foster their mother tongue. Another leitmotiv was the need to counter population decline among the Hungarian communities and the unacceptable practice of abortion. Cardinal Mindszenty's legendary struggle for the Church and for the Christian faith and his undeserved persecution gave him unmatched prestige and honor among the Hungarian émigrés of the 20th century. As a man who had suffered and endured many trials, the Hungarian primate was held in high esteem by all. Yet, while the Hungarian émigré community accepted him as its spiritual leader, as a political leader he provoked differences of opinion and tended to further divide an already fractious community. For a time, however, he was able to stand at the head of the Hungarian community abroad.

Mindszenty barely had to say a word before he was received and celebrated as the figure his audience wished him to be. His pastoral journeys easily turned into political demonstrations, not so much because of what he did as because of the actions of émigré circles that were inclined to invite him and then celebrate his presence. All this inevitably irritated the political elite in Hungary. The Hungarian Catholic Bishops' Conference – very possibly at the behest of the communist authorities – informed Pope Paul VI that Mindszenty's travels "are always linked to attacks against the Hungarian state and against the situation of the churches in Hungary."[46] After his return from North America, rather than being able to devote his attention to preparations for his upcoming journey to South Africa, Mindszenty had to confront what for him was an unexpected turn of events but one that the Vatican authorities had been planning for many months: his deposition as primate of Hungary.

46. ÁBTL 3.2.9. R–8–009/3. 77. fol. Letter of the Hungarian Catholic Bishops' Conference to Pope Paul VI, November 2, 1973. For the letter's text in Latin, see KFL I.1.a. 1111/1974.

"IF I RESIGNED,
I WOULD BECOME AN ACCOMPLICE TO THE CRIME..."

On March 29, 1972, József Mindszenty celebrated his eightieth birthday. He received a flood of congratulations, and Paul VI's salutation was published on the first page of *L'Osservatore Romano*. Even President Nixon sent a message to the Pazmaneum, expressing his best wishes to Cardinal Mindszenty.[47] The Hungarian primate's eightieth birthday constituted a fitting opportunity for his dignified and uncontroversial resignation.

In Breach of the Agreement?

The resignation of bishops at the age of 75 and their subsequent retirement from public life had been "earnestly requested" (but not made binding) by Paul VI in *Ecclesiae Sanctae* an apostolic letter issued *motu proprio* on August 6, 1966. The recommendation had come into force on October 11, 1966. At the time, Mindszenty had indicated to the Vatican authorities that he was soon to celebrate his seventy-fifth birthday in a letter dated November 14, 1966, which was sent to the pope from the US Legation in Budapest. However, rather than petition for his own retirement, Mindszenty had requested that, for the sake of the Church and his country, he might be permitted to remain in his post as archbishop of Esztergom.[48] Paul VI had acquiesced to this request, as he was unwilling to force retirement on a primate who was being prevented from exercising his duties.

Now, having reached the age of eighty, he was expected – both by the Vatican and by the government in Budapest – to retire voluntarily. This expectation shows, however, that they did not know Mindszenty well. There was only one option: a decision by his superiors. Mindszenty had provided the Vatican authorities with several pretexts for his accelerated removal. Several weeks after the appearance of his controversial Advent letter of 1971, he gave – for the first time since his departure from Hungary – an

47. Nixon Library NSC Files, Name Files, Box 828. Mindszenty, Cardinal (April 70–May 74) 3613. Birthday Greeting for Cardinal Mindszenty, March 28, 1972.

48. MMAL 061/a. dosszié. MFN 8816, L-3709. Letter of József Mindszenty to Pope Paul VI, November 14, 1966. Its text is published in Somorjai, *Sancta Sedes Apostolica et Cardinalis Ioseph Mindszenty, III/1. Documenta 1963–1966*, 514–17.

interview with the Hamburg newspaper, *Welt am Sonntag*.[49] The Hungarian authorities protested both against the interview itself and against certain statements made by Mindszenty on this occasion. Yet Mindszenty's words had been said dispassionately. The Hungarian primate had merely denied the accusations made against him in 1949. It was during this interview that, for the first time, he drew a distinction between his historical works and his memoirs in the classical sense. In response, Imre Miklós, head of the State Office for Church Affairs, requested information from the Vatican about "the measures it was planning to take with a view to ensuring the agreement was adhered to."[50] The pope, however, was ahead of Imre Miklós. He had already instructed Mindszenty – in the note of December 14, 1971 – to submit his statements to the Vatican for prior approval. Casaroli acknowledged that both the pastoral letter and the interview were in breach of the agreement, but that this was not his view of the other newspaper articles that had been published. He refused to confirm a press leak concerning a letter written by Mindszenty to President Nixon, in which the Hungarian primate had stated his opposition to the Holy Crown being returned to Hungary. For the time being, the Hungarian government had to be satisfied with Casaroli's reply. In fact, Mindszenty had indeed contacted President Nixon in this matter, who, however, had assured him that there were "no plans to relinquish the crown."[51] Rumors about the crown's impending dispatch to Hungary were so strong that Mindszenty had then written a further letter to President Nixon, arguing for the crown to be sent to the Vatican for safekeeping. This second letter caused consternation even among the more fanatical of Mindszenty's émigré supporters, as – fifty years after the death of the last Hungarian king – the Hungarian primate justified his own efforts as follows: "The undersigned primate of Hungary representing the absent king has to act on behalf of it as a

49. The interview was published in the Christmas edition of *Welt am Sonntag*, December 25–26, 1971.

50. MNL OL XIX–A–21–e–0022–1/1972. 20. ő. e. Message of Imre Miklós to Agostino Casaroli. Rome, January 5, 1972. Cf. ÖStA, AdR, BMfAA, Sektion II-pol. Zl. 2032-GS/1972. Official memo of Austrian Minister of Foreign Affairs Rudolf Kirchschläger, January 18, 1972.

51. Ibid., XIX–A–21–e–0022–1/j/1972. 20. ő. e. Letter of Deputy Minister of Foreign Affairs János Nagy to Imre Miklós concerning Casaroli's reply, February 8, 1972; *Katolikus Magyarok Vasárnapja*, February 20, 1972, cover page: Letter of Harry S. Dent, special counsel to President Nixon, to Tibor Eckhardt, January 19, 1972.

national property."[52] It seemed, therefore, that Mindszenty did not regard Otto von Habsburg as effective in this role. President Nixon's response to Cardinal Mindszenty's insensitive letter was less than reassuring from the latter's perspective: The imminent relinquishing of the Holy Crown was mere speculation; it was the property of the Hungarian nation, but its placement at the Vatican could not be an option, as "it should eventually be returned to that nation."[53] The answer tactfully ignored the issue of the king's representation...

At subsequent rounds of the Hungarian–Vatican talks, which had now been underway for a decade and continued to be monitored by Hungarian intelligence officers and covert informers, the Hungarian side made every effort to bring about Mindszenty's dismissal or his compulsory retirement. From April 25–28, 1972, the Vatican diplomats Giovanni Cheli and Angelo Sodano participated in talks in Budapest. They first came to an arrangement on the appointments that were required in various dioceses. Subsequently, the two parties spoke at length about József Mindszenty. It was Imre Miklós who broached the subject:

> ...was not the situation now ripe for the seat of Archbishop of Esztergom to be filled and for a final conclusion to the Mindszenty affair? [Mindszenty] ... is a free man, he is aged over 75, or even 80, mentally and physically he is no longer quite with it, the Vatican had arranged for the retirement even of men who were younger and healthier than him.[54]

By way of reply, Cheli said the following words:

> Our wish is that Mindszenty resign, saying that he is doing so mainly for pastoral reasons. No-one approves of the current situation in Esztergom. It is a matter of concern to the Holy See, too. However, we cannot force

52. Nixon Library, NSC Files, Name Files, Box 828. Mindszenty, Cardinal (April 70–May 74). Letter of József Mindszenty to President Nixon, October 26, 1972.

53. Ibid., Letter of Russel Fessenden, assistant secretary of state, to József Mindszenty, December 6, 1972.

54. MNL OL XIX–A–21–e–XVIII. dosszié–0022–7/i/1/1972. 8. fol. Memorandum on negotiations with Vatican representatives Giovanni Cheli and Angelo Sodano. April 25, 1972. (The following quotations are from the same source, 10–11. fol.)

> Mindszenty to resign. [...] If we make a solution to the matter of Esztergom a prerequisite for resolving the other personnel issues, I frankly do not know when we will be able to move forward.

This "sidestepping" of the matter irritated Miklós. His next question had a threatening edge: "What was the bigger issue – Mindszenty's 'freedom' or an improvement in relations between the Holy See and the communist countries?" At this point, Cheli took a more conciliatory approach. While emphasizing the need for caution and circumspection, he stated that the Holy See was "determined to adhere to the agreement" and "would intervene not only when Mindszenty made statements but also when the intent to do so was being shaped." This implied the censure of Cardinal Mindszenty's speeches and sermons.

When, from October 3–8, 1972, Imre Miklós, head of the State Office for Church Affairs, traveled to Rome for renewed talks, he made the removal of the archbishop's title from Mindszenty the priority personnel issue. He then stated that if the Holy See were unable to fulfil its pledge to prevent Cardinal Mindszenty from making statements against the People's Republic of Hungary, then it should have him resign. In Miklós's view, "putting a brake" on Mindszenty was a shared interest, for his statements were not only putting at risk a "satisfactory" relationship between Hungary and the Catholic Church (including the peace priest movement), they were also "devaluing" the Holy See. Archbishop Casaroli promised to reconsider the issue, but in one particular matter he made an immediate clarification: "The Holy See is a complex organization; Mindszenty it seems, is only criticizing the Office for Foreign Affairs and seeking to avoid a clash with the pope."[55] (The Apostolic Holy See can be understood as the pope himself or as the pope in conjunction with the Roman Curia, the administrative unit.) At the same time, Casaroli acknowledged that the Holy See was indeed unable to adhere to all parts of the agreement. Still, it could not force Mindszenty to resign, as there were no canonical grounds to do so. The most it could do was request and encourage him to step down.

55. Ibid., XIX–A–21–e–XIX. dosszié–0022–13/j/1972. fol. 10. fol. Report on the talks held with Vatican representatives, October 3–8, 1972.

According to the memorandum describing these discussions, "the frank debate on the fate of the archiepiscopal see of Esztergom took two-thirds of the time spent in talks, during which time Casaroli consulted with the pope on two occasions."[56] Having consulted with the pope, Casaroli spoke exclusively about Mindszenty's statements; he did not include, as a matter governed by the agreement, either his dismissal or the withdrawal of his title of archbishop. He sought to explain that there was no possibility under canon law of dismissing Mindszenty. Casaroli also emphasized that the pope wished to avoid a coercive solution, for this would simply add to the gravity of the problem. Although Cardinal Mindszenty's political positions were outdated, they would receive greater and undue significance and strengthen criticism of the Ostpolitik. Casaroli's attempts to describe the difficulties of a forced resignation were met with consternation. Imre Miklós cited the history of the Catholic Church, which showed that the Holy See had always succeeded – "without issuing commands or resorting to the law" – in resolving its sensitive personnel issues. In the end, Miklós left the negotiating table, saying: "I acknowledge that you will not be able to get rid of Mindszenty in the near future."[57] These debates serve to refute the common myth according to which the two sides had agreed on the removal of Mindszenty from his post at the time of the 1971 agreement governing his departure from Hungary. Even now, Vatican officials made no official pledge to arrange for his dismissal. They merely indicated – outside the official talks – that they were aware of the pressing nature of the issue and were seeking its resolution.

A further round of talks took place in Budapest on May 14–16, 1973. On this occasion, it was agreed that "the unresolved nature of the Mindszenty question constitutes an objective obstacle to the settlement of other issues."[58] By means of this stance, the Hungarian side succeeded in limiting the scope of talks to episcopal appointments, thereby further postponing a discussion of such issues as religious instruction, the internal autonomy

56. Ibid., XIX–A–21–e–XIX. dosszié–0022–13/g/1972. 5. fol. Report on the talks held with Vatican representatives, October 3–8, 1972.

57. Ibid., XIX–A–21–e–XIX. dosszié–0022–13/j/1972. 34. fol.

58. Ibid., XIX–A–21–e–XXI. dosszié–0022–7/b/1973. 4. fol. Memorandum on the discussions held with Vatican representatives on May 14–16, 1973. (The following two quotations are from the same source, 5. and 15. fol.)

of the dioceses, the unhindered instruction of seminarians, and the granting of operational licenses to the religious orders. Casaroli reiterated what he had tried to make clear in the fall: the Vatican could not force Cardinal Mindszenty to resign. In response, Imre Miklós stated his view that Mindszenty would never voluntarily resign, and so acts of persuasion were not the way forward. This was the fundamental difference in view between the two sides. In the light of subsequent events, it seems that the Hungarian government official may have better understood Mindszenty's character than did the Vatican's representatives. Regardless of its different view concerning the means of a possible solution, the Vatican nevertheless began looking for a successor to Cardinal Mindszenty as archbishop of Esztergom. This implied that the impasse might soon be overcome. Cheli noted the criteria that had to be met: "There is a need for a person who is in good physical shape, who enjoys the confidence of the bishops, and who can get a good rating in all aspects." Casaroli then added the following:

> A person who correctly appraises reality, regarding church and state, and who is able to sustain a proper relationship with the state. He should not seek merely agreement; rather, he should choose well the means of cooperation. The primate's tasks are historical in nature. There exists a relationship between the Bishops' Conference and the state, in which the significance of the primate is no longer so great; his significance is on the decline. The primate's role and significance in public life are also on the decline. The primate's prestige is grounded in historical traditions, and so it is not negligible. Who might be the person who best personifies all this?

Based on these criteria, various possible candidates were excluded – bishops who were too old, too young, or infirm. The remaining candidates were the bishop of Vác (József Bánk), the bishop of Pécs (József Cserháti), and the ordinary of Veszprém (László Lékai). Imre Miklós then "smuggled" a fourth candidate onto the list: the aged archbishop of Kalocsa, József Ijjas. During their stay in Hungary, the Vatican representatives sought out the opinion of the Bishops' Conference concerning its preference among the four candidates. From then onwards, it was no secret that something was about to happen. The findings of the consultations were summarized by Cheli and Sodano on June 19, 1973. In effect, the Vatican had decided that the archiepiscopal see would soon become vacant. The only question was when exactly this would happen. The cogwheels had been set in motion, and no-one, apart from the pope, had the means to halt them.

On their return to Rome, the two Vatican envoys found themselves at the center of some personnel changes that also affected the diplomats responsible for the Eastern policy. Although Archbishop Casaroli remained in his post, his right-hand man, Giovanni Cheli, was replaced, having been promoted to the post of permanent observer of the Holy See to the United Nations. Cheli had been the best-informed of all the Vatican counselors when it came to the Mindszenty affair. Although he had been moved up on the career ladder, his removal was linked with the errors he had made during negotiations with the authorities of the communist countries. Priests with close ties to Mindszenty or to Radio Free Europe had even called Cheli a communist agent, who – they alleged – was being bribed by the Hungarian government to represent Hungarian interests in the matter of Mindszenty.[59] Cheli's successor, Archbishop Luigi Poggi, was the former nuncio in Lima. It soon became evident that the personnel changes would not lead to any real change in the Vatican's policy towards the communist countries.

Meanwhile, Mindszenty's journey in the summer of 1973 to Great Britain and his journey in the fall to North America were viewed by the Hungarian government as having overstepped the ecclesiastical bounds. In London, for instance, Mindszenty had received a hearty welcome not only from Cardinal John Carmel Heenan but also from conservative political circles. While the British government did not officially receive Mindszenty, he was nevertheless welcomed at the House of Commons by the secretary for education and by a group of MPs headed by Winston Churchill, grandson of the wartime leader. In his speeches, Mindszenty emphasized that he felt no anger towards the communist regime in Hungary and did not want to take revenge for the grievances he had suffered. He also refused to answer any questions that related to his imprisonment under the regime or relations between Hungary and the Vatican. But what Mindszenty could not say was then said by Cardinal Heenan. The result, therefore, was the same: a sharp critique of the communist regimes. Visits to cities outside London failed to live up to expectations. For instance, despite major prepa-

59. ÁBTL 3.2.5. O–8–552/11. 142. fol. Report on Giovanni Cheli's dismissal, July 19, 1973.

rations, the crowd in Manchester was remarkably small – barely a hundred Hungarians turned out, far fewer than the anticipated five hundred. In Salford, however, at least 1,500 people attended a Holy Mass celebrated by Cardinal Mindszenty, even though the church service was held on a weekday. Mindszenty again addressed the dangers of bolshevism, telling Hungarians living in Great Britain to refrain from visiting the old homeland, as such visits might help to sustain the Kádár regime.

On hearing the news from Great Britain, the Hungarian government reiterated its demand that the terms of the agreement be upheld. In his response, Casaroli let it be known – at least this is what is alleged in a summary report of the Hungarian Ministry of Foreign Affairs – that in his view Cheli, whom he otherwise held in high esteem, was responsible for the problems that had arisen out of the talks held in Budapest in the summer of 1971. This was because it was only subsequently that he realized that Mindszenty had not been precisely informed about everything. And yet Cheli had assured him that the Hungarian primate would fulfil the conditions that had been agreed upon. Obviously, the discussions had been accompanied by many differences of interpretation or even conscious efforts to mislead. Despite all this, Casaroli promised to continue the Ostpolitik. He reiterated that the Holy See would do everything to ensure that the terms of the agreement were upheld. At the same time, he noted the "difficulty of putting a brake on the 82-year-old cardinal."[60]

The Vatican authorities needed no reminding of the need to resolve the Mindszenty question. Ultimately, the outcome would have to be the vacating of the archiepiscopal see of Esztergom. The only question concerned the means to achieve this aim: Should it be done through Mindszenty's *resignation* or through his *dismissal*? The final turn of events – Mindszenty's humiliating loss of his title as archbishop of Esztergom – was linked not so much with Mindszenty's journeys abroad and his anticommunist comments as with reports of the impending publication of his memoirs. Indeed, by now, their upcoming publication was already being treated as a fait accompli in Canada and the United States. Mindszenty's firm intent in this regard was ruffling feathers not only in Budapest but also in Rome. Indeed, he had

60. MNL OL XIX–A–21–e–0022–3/b/1973. 23. ő. e. Information provided by Deputy Minister of Foreign Affairs János Nagy to Imre Miklós based on a report submitted by the Hungarian Embassy in Rome, October 1, 1973.

crossed the Rubicon. Subsequently, even Paul VI accepted the opinion of his advisors: Cardinal Mindszenty posed a major threat to the continued development of the Vatican's Eastern policy.

Attempts to Have Him Resign

In the summer of 1973, the Italian transcript of Mindszenty's memoirs was forwarded, by way of Archbishop König of Vienna, to Pope Paul VI, who tactfully but forcefully questioned the timeliness of their publication.[61] Mindszenty, however, was not receptive to the refined language of Rome or simply had no wish to heed the pope's advice. Indeed, Mindszenty was so committed to the publication of his memoirs that he inadvertently started the process leading to his removal from the archiepiscopal see. As a Vatican monsignor explained to the Hungarian primate's secretary, "Rome cannot allow an archbishop or primate in office to make such a serious indictment against a current regime, no matter how wicked it may be, when it itself [Rome] has recognized it [the regime]."[62] In other words, József Mindszenty could not publish his memoirs while he remained archbishop of Esztergom and primate of Hungary. The Vatican could simply not agree to this, in view of its ongoing negotiations with the Hungarian government. This was the essence of the difference of view that existed between Mindszenty and Paul VI: The Hungarian primate refused out of principle to accept the Kádár regime as the lawful government of Hungary, whereas the pope, for practical and political reasons, did recognize it as such. The Vatican authorities seem to have initially believed that Cardinal Mindszenty might be dissuaded from publishing his memoirs. If this scenario had unfolded, the pope would probably have supported Mindszenty against those who were "calling for his head," seeking to calm down the Hungarian government.[63] But all such attempts merely poured oil onto the fire.

61. MMAL 060. dosszié, MFN 7934, L-2885. Letter of Pope Paul VI to Archbishop König of Vienna, August 30, 1973. For the letter's text in Italian, see Somorjai, *Sancta Sedes Apostolica et Cardinalis Ioseph Mindszenty. Documenta 1971–1975*, 204–05.

62. Mészáros, *A száműzött bíboros szolgálatában*, 166. Record for January 10, 1974.

63. AMAE AD Série: Europe, Hongrie, versement aux Archives (1971–juin 1976), boîte 3330, dossier Questions religieuses (1 janvier 1971–30 juin 1976). Telegram no. 44–49 of the French Embassy to the Holy See, February 11, 1974.

The Hungarian prelates also sought to think of incisive arguments for Mindszenty's dismissal. In a letter written in Latin and dated September 27, 1973, the archbishop of Kalocsa, József Ijjas, summarized for the pope the situation of the Catholic hierarchy in Hungary:

> One cannot deny the scale of the damage caused by the more than 20-year absence of a prelate of bishop's rank from the head of the Archdiocese of Esztergom, to which the world city of Budapest belongs. Experience has shown us that statements from the apostolic administrators cannot serve as a substitute for the pastoral care of archbishops, whose charismatic nature stems from their consecration – and this is especially so in historical times. The salvation of souls comes before legal considerations![64]

This main argument – the demand for stability in ecclesiastical governance – became even more powerful when Archbishop Ijjas explained that, in addition to Esztergom, the question of leadership was a pressing issue in the other dioceses, too, as at the time – in 1973 – only three of Hungary's eleven dioceses (Kalocsa, Vác, and Pécs) were headed by a diocesan bishop. Six of the dioceses were headed by apostolic administrators, while two were administered by capitular vicars. The Hungarian government, meanwhile, had made it plain that it would not give its approval to any other personnel questions until Mindszenty had been dismissed as archbishop of Esztergom. Other than Mindszenty, everyone now looked to the pope for a solution. Archbishop Ijjas advised him that if Mindszenty refused to resign and could not be persuaded to do so, then his dismissal would have to be considered.[65] Did Archbishop Ijjas offer these words of advice voluntarily or had he been influenced by the State Office for Church Affairs? Whatever may have been the truth of the matter, the Hungarian government must have been happy with the outcome.

During the fall, József Cserháti, bishop of Pécs, was also staying in Rome. On October 18, 1973, during a private audience with Paul VI, he highlighted the discontent of the Hungarian clergy and their need for a

64. KFL I.1.a. 2652/1973. *Relatio de actuali statu hierarchiae in Hungaria*. Report of Archbishop Ijjas of Kalocsa to Pope Paul VI, September 27, 1973.

65. ÁBTL 3.2.9. R–8–009/3. 60. fol. Memorandum on cipher telegram no. 314 (dispatched from Rome), October 10, 1973.

bishop. His message sought first and foremost to promote the interests of the Hungarian communist regime. We know this because, several days before his meeting with the pope, Cserháti had consulted with the State Office for Church Affairs about what he should tell the Holy Father.

> The factor that makes our situation particularly serious is the matter of Cardinal József Mindszenty, archbishop of Esztergom. His archdiocese has been governed for twenty years by various persons, infirm individuals and those unsuited to [ecclesiastical] administration. [...] It seems to us that a 'solution to the Mindszenty affair' would represent progress.[66]

By "solution" Cserháti clearly meant Mindszenty's removal from post.

Having been influenced by the weight of advice coming from many quarters, Pope Paul VI decided upon action. To signal his esteem and respect, the pope sent Cardinal Mindszenty a handwritten letter in Italian. Dated November 1, 1973, the letter contained a papal request that Hungary's last prince primate resign from the post of archbishop of Esztergom. After his resignation, "he could freely and better decide whether now was the right time to publish his memoirs, with a view to revealing the truth and defending his own good reputation."[67] Without a doubt, the fate of the memoirs was a critical issue. Indeed, Paul VI's decision to remove Mindszenty was taken only after the Hungarian primate had made it clear that he would not renounce their publication. Here it is worth noting that Paul VI's patient efforts to bring Mindszenty into line would not have been countenanced by Pius XI or Pius XII, neither of whom would have bothered to plead with the insubordinate prelate, who would simply have been silenced by the power of words.

A day later (November 2, 1973), the pope's request was affirmed by the Hungarian Bishops' Conference in a petition that was signed by every bishop: The Holy Father should not permit this impossible situation to continue.[68]

66. KFL I.1.a. 2652/1973. Transcript of the speech made in French by Bishop Cserháti of Pécs during his audience with Pope Paul VI, October 14, 1973.

67. MMAL 060. dosszié, MFN 7935, L-2886. Letter of Pope Paul VI to József Mindszenty, November 1, 1973.

68. MNL OL XIX–A–21–e–0022–3/l/1973. 24. ő. e. and ÁBTL 3.2.9. R–8–009/3. 77. fol. Letter of the Hungarian Catholic Bishops' Conference to Pope Paul VI, November 2, 1973; KFL I.1.a. 1111/1974. Copy in Latin.

Concerning the circumstances surrounding the drafting and adoption of this etition, we know that, while Archbishop Ijjas was on a trip to Moscow, Bishop Cserháti submitted the draft document to an extraordinary meeting of the Bishops' Conference on October 30. It is telling that the Hungarian text of the draft petition has been preserved among the state security documents. The Latin translation of the original Hungarian document was very poor; the grammatical mistakes contained therein would surely not have been made by a prelate. Moreover, in the valediction the bishops are referred to as "*fratres*" (the brothers of the pope), whereas in fact they called themselves "*filii*" (his sons). There is a strong suspicion, therefore, that the State Office for Church Affairs influenced the contents of the petition and then undertook its translation. In retrospect, it is difficult to excuse the conduct of the bishops in this matter. Still, their actions did have some positive outcomes: for instance, the state funding granted to the Church under the 1950 agreement was extended for five more years.

The new "Mindszenty affair" dominated the agenda at the talks held between Hungary and the Holy See in the fall of 1973. These talks marked the 24th round of bilateral negotiations in a ten-year period. This time, State Secretary Imre Miklós held talks in Rome from November 13–17. The Political Committee of the Hungarian Socialist Workers' Party had set him the task of arranging for Mindszenty "to go into retirement this year." In return, he was to assure the Holy See that the Hungarian government would show flexibility regarding Mindszenty's successor.[69] At the talks, Miklós diligently adhered to this stance, insisting on Mindszenty's resignation as a prerequisite for resolving any other problems and personnel issues. In response, Casaroli felt inclined to emphasize that the Vatican had never agreed to remove Mindszenty from his post. Even though Miklós conceded that this was so, he refused to back down.[70] Casaroli opted not to reveal to Miklós that two weeks earlier Paul VI had sent a letter to Mindszenty urging him to resign. He did, however, hint at a shift in policy, telling Miklós that "we are now on the verge of an outcome." Casaroli and Miklós then debated

69. Ibid., M–KS 288. f. 5/621. ő. e. 5., 97–99. fol. Minutes of the meeting of the HSWP PC held on October 9, 1973, Point 7.

70. Ibid., XIX–A–21–e–XXIV. dosszié–0022–11/e/1973. 13. fol. Memorandum on the talks held with Vatican representatives, November 13–17, 1973. (The following quotations are from the same source, 8., 11. and 16. fol.)

how these words should be interpreted. What did "now" or "verge" mean? "Perhaps, it means tomorrow," said Miklós. In response, Casaroli revealed merely that "the Holy See has reached its final position." Imre Miklós, however, wanted to be told a more exact date. He requested that the Holy See agree to a deadline for the legal vacating of the archiepiscopal see of Esztergom. In return, he promised the Hungarian government's approval for personnel changes in the Church. In other words, either Mindszenty's dismissal would be speeded up or talks between the Vatican and the Hungarian government would be broken off.

In effect, the rounds of Hungarian–Vatican talks, which had been underway for a quarter-century, had reached a grave juncture. Further delays or vacillations were no longer feasible. Casaroli did not make any decisions on his own, and so it was only the next day that an affirmative reply was made: "We accept a deadline for before Christmas, let's say, at some point between December 15–20." The guarantee was an oral pledge, a kind of "Vatican word of honor." In addition, however, a short memorandum was drawn up in Italian and signed by Casaroli. A Hungarian translation of the document was then signed by Imre Miklós. According to the memorandum, the Holy See "having examined the issue in depth and listened to the opinion of the Hungarian Bishops' Conference, reached the conviction that the archiepiscopal see of Esztergom must be vacated in line with canon law."[71] Even a deadline was set: the Hungarian government would receive confidential notification on developments by December 20, 1973. With this deal, Casaroli and his staff made the careless mistake of scheduling the papal decision for a period marking the twenty-fifth anniversary of Mindszenty's original arrest (December 26, 1948) and his subsequent show trial (February 3–8, 1949). The talks also saw a decision on who should be appointed ordinary. As Kisberk had fallen sick, the Vatican chose Lékai. The Hungarian side had no objection to this choice. Indeed, Imre Miklós made sure that, if a "proper solution" could be found, the Hungarian government would give its approval to several episcopal appointments. This was the reward given to the Catholic Church for having pushed Mindszenty aside.

71. Ibid., XIX–A–21–e–sz. n. 24. ő. e. Memorandum, November 17, 1973. Signed by Imre Miklós, original; Pro memoria, 17 November 1973. Signed by Agostino Casaroli, duplicate copy.

Cardinal Mindszenty was profoundly shaken by the pope's request that he resign as archbishop of Esztergom. He sent three replies to the pope's handwritten letter – on November 15, November 21, and December 8. In each of these replies he rejected the pope's request.[72] Only the latter two letters verifiably reached the addressee. In the final letter, composed after his return from South Africa, Mindszenty listed his reasons for not resigning: 1. Distrust of the communists and their promises; 2. The exclusively negative impact of the ten-year relationship between the Holy See and Hungary; 3. Future appointments in the Hungarian Church would be dependent on the regime; 4. A detrimental effect on Hungarian Catholics abroad; 5. Grave impact on his memoirs – and on the cause represented by his life; and 6. "If I resigned, I would become an accomplice to the crime."[73] In essence, his argument was that his resignation would serve to legitimize the communist regime. Thus, whereas in earlier decades he had had no qualms about resigning from a post to serve a certain cause, he now felt a sense of historical responsibility to remain in office, thereby upholding the unwritten constitution and showing his allegiance to the Holy Crown and the 1000-year-old Christian Hungarian state, of which the Catholic Church was a part. Rather than view the matter as one of ecclesiastical discipline, Mindszenty approached the consequences of his possible resignation from a secular (power-political) angle.

The pope took some time to respond to Mindszenty's rejection of his offer. Ultimately, he had no other option but to make use of his papal authority, even if he did so reluctantly. In an official letter, composed at the Secretariat of State and dated December 18, 1973, he let it be known to Mindszenty – using formal legal language – that he intended to declare the archiepiscopal see of Esztergom vacant:

> ...having regard for the good of the Church, we have determined – and we will actually be announcing this – that henceforth the archiepiscopal see

72. MMAL 060. dosszié, MFN 7939, L-2890. Draft letter (and its typed fair copy) of József Mindszenty József to Pope Paul VI, November 21, 1973.; Ibid., MFN 7940, L-2891. Letter of József Mindszenty to Pope Paul VI, December 8, 1973. The letter of November 15, 1973, is not to be found among the letters preserved in the archive. However, the text of that letter was published with those of the other two letters in Somorjai, *Ami az emlékiratokból kimaradt*, 36–40.

73. MMAL 060. dosszié, MFN 7937, L-2888.

> shall be declared vacant. This vacancy and all its canonical effects shall become known when we announce officially the appointment of an archbishop to this see or – "sede vacante" – an apostolic administrator.[74]

The pope thus refrained from forcing Mindszenty to act against his own conviction and resign. Rather, he took on the burden and responsibility of the decision. Instead of stating that he was to remove the title of archbishop from Mindszenty, he merely informed the Hungarian cardinal that, with the see having been declared vacant, it was an automatic outcome that the Archdiocese of Esztergom would in future be headed by someone else. The letter is ambiguous with respect to the date on which the decision would come into force: the *accusativus cum infinitivo* of the subordinate clause in the Latin text does not distinguish between what is concurrent and what is subsequent. In other words, the sentence can be understood as meaning that the archiepiscopal see "shall be declared vacant in the future" or "henceforth is declared vacant." This ambiguity can be dispelled if we accept that the pope dismissed Mindszenty *de jure* on December 18, 1973, and that the canonical effects of the decision were felt in practice *(de facto)* only with the public declaration of his successor's name on February 5, 1974.[75] Obviously, the decision on the archiepiscopal see did not affect Mindszenty's status as cardinal. It is worth noting, however, that he was an octogenarian and therefore no longer entitled to take part in the work of a conclave.

Mindszenty had yet to receive Paul VI's letter when, on December 19, 1973 (i.e., a day before the deadline), Casaroli passed on the pope's "affirmative answer" to the Hungarian ambassador in Rome.[76] The Hungarian diplomat naturally inquired as to the exact meaning of this "affirmative" response, whether it meant the decision would come into force immediately,

74. "...Ecclesiae bonum spectantes, archiepiscopalem Strigoniensem Sedem declarare decrevimus, quemadmodum in facto declaramus, posthac esse vacantem. Quae vacatio, cum omnibus effectibus canonicis, tunc innotescet, ex quo nominatio novi eiusdem Sedia Archiepiscopi, vel eius Apostolici Administratoris 'sede vacante' publici iuris facta sit." MMAL 060. dosszié, MFN 7942, L-2893. Letter of Pope Paul VI to József Mindszenty, dated December 18, 1973.

75. For more on this issue, see Somorjai, *Ami az emlékiratokból kimaradt*, 19–31.

76. ÁBTL 3.2.9. R–8–009/3. 99. fol. Cipher telegram no. 23745, Rome, December 20, 1973, 2.15 p.m.

and whether Mindszenty knew about it and other similar matters. The Vatican's response was that their aim had been to avoid creating a disturbance during the festive period and that the pope wished to make known his decree relating to Mindszenty in a gradual fashion. At the time, it was still not known for certain whether Mindszenty would resign or be dismissed. In his reply letter of January 6, 1974, Cardinal Mindszenty refused to accept the papal decision, which had been made "under extortion."[77] In making this accusation of extortion, however, he crossed an important line. The accusation was not only offensive but also unjust. Although it was true that Cardinal Mindszenty had withstood many trials during his lengthy struggle for freedom and for the faith, this did not mean that he was no longer bound by the unspoken rules. No other bishop in the 20th century would have dared state that the pope had let himself be blackmailed. And no other bishop would have included this accusation in a letter sent to the Vatican! Mindszenty's main objection to his deposition as archbishop was that through its engagement with the Hungarian authorities, the Vatican was placing both the Church and the people at the mercy of a hostile and "godless" communist regime. He, for one, was not prepared to facilitate the Vatican's endeavor. In his bitterness, Mindszenty – for the second time in his life – threatened to resign as cardinal unless the pope altered his course. However, as in 1947, Mindszenty's brinkmanship once again failed to bring about the desired result. Perhaps he knew that the only effect of his resignation would be to render even more difficult (if not impossible) his pastoral journeys to the Hungarian communities abroad. The letter was taken to Rome by Tibor Mészáros, who personally delivered it to Paul VI on January 9. In his meeting with the pope, Mészáros vainly tried to persuade him to change his mind.

In the meantime, Archbishop Luigi Poggi and the Vatican diplomat, Angelo Sodano, had arrived in Hungary. On January 10, 1974, they made it known officially that "the Holy See announced the vacancy, under canon law, of the archiepiscopal see of Esztergom as of December 18, 1973."[78]

77. MMAL 060. dosszié, MFN 7948, L-2899. Letter of József Mindszenty to Pope Paul VI, dated January 6, 1974. For the text of the letter in German, see Adriányi, *Die Ostpolitik des Vatikans*, 115–17.

78. MNL OL XIX–A–21–e–XXV. dosszié–0022–1/N/1974. 3. fol. "Emlékeztető Louigi (sic) Poggi érsek és Angelo Sodano tanácsossal 1974. I. 10–17. között folytatott tárgyalásról.

They also confidentially informed Archbishop Ijjas of Kalocsa of this decision. Archbishop Ijjas, acting in accordance with Hungarian laws, made a written request to the State Office for Church Affairs, seeking its approval for personnel changes arising out of the decision of the Holy See. Such approval was then promptly received,[79] removing the final obstacle to the proclamation of the papal decision.

After these developments, Paul VI chose not to delay in taking the final step. His decision was final, but on January 14, he wrote the following words to Mindszenty: "With the greatest respect, we ask you again to place your trust in the Apostolic Holy See."[80] The pope's letter, which was written in response to Mindszenty's rebuff of January 6, was handed to Cardinal Mindszenty on January 22 by Monsignor Sándor Csertő and Cardinal König, in whose presence he then read the letter. These were doubtless bitter moments for Mindszenty, even though it was made known to him that for the time being the Holy See intended to appoint an apostolic administrator rather than an archbishop to the see. The apostolic administrator, he was told, would be Bishop Lékai. Mindszenty declined to express an opinion about the candidate. It was he who, as Apostolic Administrator of Veszprém, had made László Lékai his private secretary, partly in recognition of the fact that Lékai had loyally followed him into imprisonment at Sopronkőhida. Mindszenty had even referred to Lékai as "my man" and had evidently noticed his practical abilities and negotiating skills, which now, three decades later, had resulted in his being appointed to administer the Archdiocese of Esztergom. Still, much had happened in the meantime: for instance, Lékai had attended a meeting of the peace priests, which had been enough to shatter Mindszenty's trust in him. "God does not, however, permit us to so easily alter what we have once said. "'If' he is your man, then he is

[Memorandum on negotiations with Archbishop Louigi (sic) Poggi and Counsel Angelo Sodano, Januar 10–17, 1974]"

79. KFL I.1.a. 147/1974. Typed memo of Archbishop Ijjas beginning with the words "Mindszenty ügyében megoldás van" [There is a solution in the Mindszenty affair], January 10, 1974; Ibid., 151/1974. Proposal of Archbishop Ijjas of Kalocsa, Chairman of the Hungarian Catholic Bishops' Conference, to State Secretary Imre Miklós, head of the State Office for Church Affairs, January 16, 1974.

80. MMAL 060. dosszié, MFN 7950, L-2901. Letter of Pope Paul VI to József Mindszenty, dated January 14, 1974. For its text, see Adriányi, *Die Ostpolitik des Vatikans*, 168–71.

your man, whether you like it or not! – This is God's policy" a confidant of the cardinal said about Mindszenty and the party's human policy.[81]

Mindszenty wrote four draft replies to the pope's letter of January 14, 1974, but he ended up sending none of them.[82] He remained confident that the pope might alter his decision once he had considered the Hungarian cardinal's past, his life and his sacrifice. His hopes were boosted by the uncertainty surrounding the date on which the see was to be vacated. Soon, however, both his doubts and his hopes were dispelled when, on January 30, 1974, the pope wrote him another cordial and courteous letter, which was subsequently published in several major languages, in which he bid farewell to Mindszenty, archbishop of Esztergom. Regarding the future, the pope said merely that publication of his decision was impending, but that he could not yet give the exact date.[83] Nevertheless, it rapidly became public knowledge that the news agencies would receive the news on February 5.

Mindszenty's Removal

On February 5, 1974, the papal decision declaring the archiepiscopal see of Esztergom vacant was made public, as was also László Lékai's appointment (made three days earlier, on February 2) as the apostolic administrator of the archdiocese.[84] The news was announced by Vatican Radio in its midday news broadcast. MTI, the Hungarian news agency, then published the information, as did all the world's major news agencies within a few hours. In appointing an apostolic administrator rather than an archbishop to head the Archdiocese of Esztergom, the pope's intention had been to

81. Arquivo do Colégio Santo Américo, Sao Paulo (Brazil), 02-007 Dom Severino Kögl (Jean Severin Kögl) Pasta 3. Letter of Tibor Mészáros (in Washington) to the Benedictine monk Severin Kögl (Nova Santa Rosa, Paraná, Brazil), December 30, 1977. My gratitude to Ádám Somorjai – the author.

82. For an analysis of the unsent letters, see Somorjai, *Ami az emlékiratokból kimaradt*, 56–69.

83. MMAL 060. dosszié, MFN 7954, L-2904. Letter of Pope Paul VI to József Mindszenty, dated January 30, 1974. First published in Latin in "Epistula E.mo. P. D. Iosepho S. R. E. Cardinali Mindszenty." AAS 66 (1974): 63; for the same in Italian, see "Lettera del Santo Padre al Card. Jozsef Mindszenty," *L'Osservatore Romano* 114, no. 30, February 6, 1974; and in German, see *L'Osservatore Romano* 114, no. 37, February 15, 1974.

84. *Magyar Kurír* 64, no. 30, February 5, 1974, 2nd edition, 10 a. m.; "Nostre informazioni. Nomina di Amministratori Apostolici," *L'Osservatore Romano* 114, no. 30, February 6, 1974, cover page.

mitigate Mindszenty's bitterness at the loss of his office. In truth, the method was nothing unusual, as this was how the archdiocese had been governed since 1950. Lékai received his appointment "*ad nutum Sanctae Sedis*" ("with the approval of the Holy See"), just as the apostolic administrators had done in the period 1959–1971. The difference lay in the fact that Lékai's predecessors had been appointed *sede plena* ("the see is occupied," that is, the see is not vacant), whereas Lékai was appointed *sede vacante* ("the see is vacant"). In 1971, Mindszenty had been able to leave his post with a new ordinary governing the archdiocese "*sede plena*." Now, however, the vacating of the see was beyond doubt, and so László Lékai could not have become apostolic administrator unless as *sede vacante et ad nutum Sanctae Sedis*. The contemporary news reports made no mention of such details.

The removal of Mindszenty elicited a heated debate. According to *Lumen gentium* (i.e., the Dogmatic Constitution on the Church and one of the principal documents of the Second Vatican Council; adopted on November 21, 1964), bishops are, by divine purpose, successors to the Apostles. They acquire their apostolic authority through their consecration as bishops. They may only exercise their authority (their office) in community with the head of the Church. Since the pope has universal sovereignty over the entire Church (and thus over the national churches, too), he is the one who accepts the resignation of a bishop, transfers him to another diocese or dismisses him from office (*privatio*). The latter normally occurs as part of a legal proceeding, but the pope can also dismiss a bishop without giving grounds.[85] The 1917 Code of Canon Law, which was still valid in 1974, did not mention the dismissal of a bishop; it merely determined that the responsibility of making judgments and decisions about bishops belonged only to the pope (Canon 1557). Even so, many commentators still dispute the pope's decision. Such critics argue, based on the Council of Trent, that a bishop can only be removed from his post in the event of grave deficiencies and that this condition had not been met in Mindszenty's case.[86] While not unprecedented, the pope's action was extremely unusual. Indeed, in the history of the

85. Péter Erdő, *Egyházjog* (Budapest: Szent István Társulat, 1992), 152, 254.

86. MMAL 062. dosszié: "Támadások a Vatikán ellen a depositio után" [Criticisms of the Vatican after the deposition], 6. ő. e. Cf. Franz Xavier Wernz and Petri Vidal, *Jus canonicum, 2: De personis* (Rome: Apud Aedes Universitatis Gregorianae, 1943), 763; Emil Friedberg, *Lehrbuch des katholischen und evangelischen Kirchenrechts* (Leipzig: 1909). Unchanged reprint of the original (Frankfurt am Main: 1965), 384.

Catholic Church, a similar decision had been taken no more than once or twice in each century. In most cases, the backdrop had been political: for example, in 1803 under Napoleon, when Pope Pius VII had dismissed thirty-seven French bishops, or, in 1924, when Pope Pius XI had dismissed the archbishop of Bucharest in connection with negotiations on a concordat between Romania and the Holy See. Such a course of action had never affected the archiepiscopal see of Esztergom, in nearly a thousand years of history. The only similar development had been when the ruler had exerted pressure – by means of his right of patronage – on the prince primate: for instance, for financial reasons, Emperor Franz Joseph had exerted pressure on Kolos Vaszary and had then arranged for his dismissal in 1912.

Was it necessary to deprive Mindszenty of his office? On this issue, there is disagreement among the experts even today. As described above, the Roman Curia cited grave pastoral needs as justification for the decision. It was not accurate, however, to argue that the Archdiocese of Esztergom had been without leadership for a quarter-century, for in fact it had been administered by five successive apostolic administrators – four of whom had been consecrated bishops – in the period 1950–1974. Moreover, throughout this period, Mindszenty had remained archbishop. Thus, the administration of the archdiocese had been met, albeit the temporary nature of the situation must have had a detrimental effect on pastoral care. Why was it that the Vatican chose not to appoint a sixth apostolic administrator, who might have then administered the archdiocese until Mindszenty's death? Could the Vatican authorities really have believed that Mindszenty's removal might save even a single soul in this secularized world? Perhaps it did. Yet, the pope's decision caused disappointment among some Catholics. When, after lengthy consideration, Paul VI chose to shoulder the spiritual burden and sacrifice Mindszenty, he was also signaling to politicians in Hungary that for the Vatican the goal was to safeguard Catholics in Hungary rather than to secure a political advantage or popularity for the Church. The pope did not expect Catholics in Hungary to go underground, and he was fully aware that a modern state disposes of far more effective means to control and influence the population than did government authorities in earlier periods of persecution.

Opinions also diverge on the issue of whether Mindszenty was being disobedient to the pope. Fervent arguments have been made by both sides

– those who think he was obedient and those who think he was disobedient. On the one hand, contrary to the pope's clear instruction, Mindszenty insisted on publishing his memoirs, and he continued to make politically loaded statements. Moreover, ignoring the pope's request, he refused to resign, albeit here one should note that it is every bishop's right and duty to present his own opinion to the pope. It would seem Mindszenty never even considered the issue of obedience and disobedience. For him, the emphasis was on his commitment to the nation and on his struggle for the freedom of the Hungarian people. He insisted on retaining his status as primate of Hungary, because he could utilize it in his struggle for the liberty of Hungary and the Church. His point of departure was always a criterion of a higher order, namely the battle against atheism. In effect, he perceived his sidelining or even his silencing as an act that would assist the communist regime. Although he could see no reason for the pope's decision, he accepted it out of obedience. The Vatican never mentioned any accusations of disobedience. Any internal debates concerning Mindszenty's conduct will only become public after the opening of sealed documents in the Vatican archives. What is certain, however, is that since only the pope had the right to decide, it was he who ultimately determined the course of action. Any argument against his decision would have been in vain.

An inquiry into the possible explanations for Mindszenty's removal should not ignore the fact that he disagreed with the Vatican's Eastern policy and prioritized his principles over any perceived need to secure the Catholic hierarchy. In the meantime, however, the world had set off on a radically new path – the path of dialogue – with a view to avoiding a nuclear confrontation. For its part, the Holy See was not indifferent to political initiatives aimed at establishing peace and security in Europe; indeed, it was guided by a desire for consultation and negotiation. It hoped that the Helsinki process would facilitate the success of its own Eastern policy and of the dialogue with the central and eastern European countries, whereby promises and expectations could be realized. Held several years later, the Helsinki Conference would be the first multilateral political conference to be attended by the Vatican since 1815. The Vatican would attend the conference even though its mission was primarily of a spiritual kind.[87]

87. For a review of the literature on this issue, see Stehle, *Die Ostpolitik des Vatikans 1917–1975*; Stehle, *Geheimdiplomatie im Vatikan*; Chenaux, *L'Église catholique et communisme en*

The Vatican's Eastern policy sought first and foremost to secure the structure of the hierarchy and the operation of the Church. It also addressed the issue of the freedom of lay Catholics, which was to be based on cooperation with the communist regimes – with the more civilized form of "socialism with a human face" rather than with its Stalinist variant. How could it have made any other response to the historical and political circumstances and to the challenges posed by state atheism in the communist countries? The Holy See did not have the means to pursue power politics, so its pastoral goals were the priority. In his memoirs, Casaroli acknowledged that the Holy See's position had been much criticized, but that the Vatican authorities were adhering to it because, in the long term, a lack of bishops would evidently weaken the Church. As it elaborated its foreign policy, the Vatican based its position on what was in the interest of the universal church rather than what benefits it might bring to the existing form of government in a certain country. The Church's efforts were designed to persuade the communist countries to offer assurances for the proper functioning of the Church. Such efforts, however, did not mean conceding to atheism. Although the accomplishments of the Eastern policy were slight and the negotiations kept on stalling, the Church benefitted because the deterioration in its position was halted. Of course, freedom of religion was still subject to many limitations, but over time the ideological battles were replaced by diplomatic and scholarly debates and an invisible protective shield was formed over the Catholic communities.

Mindszenty's worldview and character stood in stark opposition to the essence of the Vatican's Eastern policy. Consequently, therefore, the Hungarian cardinal was perceived as a major obstacle to the politics of dialogue. Indeed, if the Vatican had simply let him do as he liked, this would have placed a question-mark over the seriousness of its contribution to a deepening of the processes of détente and cooperation in Europe. And just as the Vatican had successfully hindered the Ukrainian Greek Catholic

---

Europe; Adriányi, *Die Ostpolitik des Vatikans*; Alberto Melloni, ed., *Il filo sottile: L'Ostpolitik vaticana di Agostino Casaroli* (Bologna: Il Mulino, 2006); Barberini, *La politica del dialogo*; András Fejérdy, ed., *The Vatican "Ostpolitik" 1958–1978: Responsibility and Witness during John XXIII and Paul VI.* (Rome: Bibliotheca Academiae Hungariae, 2015); András Fejérdy, *Pressed by a Double Loyalty. Hungarian Attendance at the Second Vatican Council, 1959–1965* (Budapest and New York: Central European University Press, 2016).

archbishop, Josyf Slipyj, from proclaiming himself patriarch, so also it sought, in Mindszenty's case, to remove the baton from his hand. Both these men had aimed to hamper the Vatican's policy of seeking a compromise with the Soviet Union and the other communist countries. Even so, it may well be that it was more painful for the pope to take these fateful decisions than it was for Mindszenty or Slipyj to accept them.[88]

A further consideration is that Mindszenty's criticism of the Vatican's Eastern policy would not have led, by itself, to his removal, since other cardinals clearly shared his opinion. For instance, in 1974, Cardinal Wyszyński (Poland) expressed his reservations at the Council, calling the Vatican's foreign policy towards the communist countries mistaken (*sbagliato*).[89] The goal of strengthening the Hungarian ecclesiastical administrative hierarchy effectively ruled out, however, the possibility of Mindszenty remaining in his post, for the Hungarian government had made his removal a prerequisite for its pledge to approve ecclesiastical appointments. Albeit plagued by cognitive dissonance, the Vatican was prepared to pay this price, trusting in the communists' pledge.

Another issue concerns the impact of the restoration of the ecclesiastical hierarchy on religious life in Hungary. Did the Catholic faithful view their bishops with respect or with scorn? In other words, did they regard them as true spiritual leaders or simply as puppets of the regime? For the time being, our answer can only be a sketchy one: whereas in the 1950s the policy of cooperation was aimed specifically at securing the survival of the Church (thus it divided both the laity and the clergy into anticommunists and cooperators), from the mid-1960s some ordinary Catholics and sections of the clergy adapted to the more comfortable and normal framework that was offered by the Kádár regime. They received encouragement in doing so from the many active Western supporters of peace.

An important contributory factor was the Vatican's new conviction that ecclesiastical and state constitutional functions should not be mingled. This position was most adamantly expressed after the Second Vatican Council, but it had been evolving ever since the end of World War II. Had

88. Achille Silvestrini, ed., *L'Ostpolitik di Agostino Casaroli 1963–1989* (Bologna: Edizioni Dehoniane, 2009), 33.

89. ÁBTL 3.2.5. O–8–552/12. 267. fol. 11/3/4/1974. Report, November 14, 1974.

Mindszenty accepted that his status as "primate of Hungary" was, in a public legal sense, a merely decorative one *(epitheton ornans)*, then his title would have been politically harmless. However, as has been documented, Mindszenty considered himself – in his position as primate and in the absence of the king – to be the legal representative of the Hungarian state. He had been impelled to think in such terms by, among others, the Hungarian right-wing émigré community. As several diplomatic reports concluded, this circumstance was becoming increasingly unpalatable for the Vatican. The authorities in Rome did not believe that it was the Church's task to engage in a constitutional dispute. Still, the impression could easily arise that the Vatican supported Mindszenty's interpretation of the functions of the archbishop of Esztergom.[90]

In summary, therefore, it can be stated that Mindszenty's removal was accomplished for political reasons, with pastoral considerations providing merely a pretext for action. The measure served as clear indication that the Catholic Church was embarking on a very different policy towards the communist countries. In this process, Mindszenty was perceived as an awkward figure. His way of thinking and his support for a Habsburg restoration were considered outmoded in the corridors of the Vatican. The world had moved on, and détente was now at the top of the agenda.

DENIED HIS TITLE AND STATUS

"Mindszenty has resigned!" – This was the erroneous headline of several press releases. In response, on February 6, 1974, Cardinal Mindszenty published his final statement on the matter: he had not resigned from the post of archbishop of Esztergom; the decision had been made by the Holy See alone.[91] He made no mention of his status as cardinal, and yet he was the one who had threatened to resign as cardinal if he were to be removed from the post of archbishop. At the same time, he did not miss the

90. ÖStA, AdR, BMfAA, Sektion II-pol. Zl.18-Res/74. Report of Hans Reichmann, Austrian ambassador to the Holy See, on Vatican–Hungarian relations, February 14, 1974.

91. MNL OL XIX–A–21–e–4–3/b/1974. 26. ő. e. Statement; MMAL 062. dosszié: "Támadások a Vatikán ellen a depositio után" [Criticisms of the Vatican after the deposition], 6. ő. e. Mindszenty's paper on the deposition. Typed script with handwritten corrections, February 5, 1974.

opportunity to criticize the Hungarian government's policy towards the churches and what he regarded as the servile attitude of the Catholic Church in Hungary. Having made his statement, Mindszenty regarded the matter as closed. He never again used the title of archbishop or primate, either in word or in writing. In fact, he really had no other choice, as he was bound by the pope's decision.

After the Dismissal

The reaction to Mindszenty's dismissal was not as had been anticipated by the Vatican. This, however, was denied by Casaroli, who stated that the pope had expected strong criticism:

> The Holy See seeks to explain that it has not paid a price for something or signed an agreement with specific and two-way commitments; rather, it has acted in the interests of the Hungarian Church, as is stated in the papal decree removing Mindszenty from his post. They hold in high esteem the conduct of the Hungarian government since the [issuing of the] decree.[92]

Yet, these rationalizing explanations suggest that the pope's staff had not been expecting such vehement criticism of the Vatican's Eastern policy. Perhaps they had given insufficient attention to Mindszenty's reputation – established over long decades – among those who opposed East–West détente. They had also underestimated the influence of such people within the media and had failed to anticipate the otherwise unusual lack of discipline that characterized not only Mindszenty but also (and even more so) his circle in Vienna.

The affront felt was even greater when it became apparent that the pope had made – concurrently with the dismissal – appointments that would have been possible even without Mindszenty's removal from office. The impression arose that "the Hungarian government's demand for Mindszenty's removal had played an important role in the making of the

92. Ibid., XIX–J–1–j–Vatikán 160. 00759/13/1974. Report of the Hungarian Embassy in Rome on Casaroli's communications concerning the Vatican's relations with Hungary and with Czechoslovakia, April 24, 1974.

decision."[93] The Hungarian émigré communities fell into a state of shock, openly declaring that Mindszenty was the victim of the pope's Eastern policy. There followed signature protests, banner demonstrations, and various events held in support of Mindszenty. The reaction in Canada, where people still had vivid memories of Cardinal Mindszenty's visit a year earlier, was particularly intense. Even the country's minister of foreign affairs publicly condemned the pope's decision. In several European cities, Hungarian émigrés organized events protesting the pope's decision. They did so – according to the Hungarian secret services – with Mindszenty's knowledge and consent. A scandalous "epigraph" was painted onto a wall of the Vatican: "Pope Paul VI is Mindszenty's traitor. Mindszenty for pope!"[94] In the religious broadcasts of Radio Free Europe, it was even asserted that in 1971 the pope had invited Mindszenty to leave Hungary with the express intention of "dealing with him here, abroad."[95] Between March 20 and March 30, 1974, 1,792 people signed group messages. Further, at least 596 letters and 124 telegrams arrived in Vienna addressed to Mindszenty.[96] In Hungary, people were understandably more cautious in their statements. In reaction to László Lékai's appointment many people breathed a huge sigh of relief; they were pleased that, finally, there was someone who would lead and restore order. The appointment of an ordinary who had once been a colleague of Mindszenty was regarded as a gesture made to the Vatican.[97] Meanwhile the pope's decision was heralded as a great success by the Hungarian political leadership.

The waves caused by his dismissal had yet to subside when Mindszenty travelled to the United States, having been invited there some time before. As he was no longer an archbishop, he could travel freely. His grand tour of the United States lasted from May 6 until June 29, 1974. He travelled

93. Ibid., 00759/10/1974. Compiled report of György Misur, acting chargé d'affaires at the Hungarian Embassy in Rome, on the Vatican's perceptions of the Mindszenty affair, March 28, 1974.

94. Mészáros, *A száműzött bíboros szolgálatában*, 218. Record for February 7, 1974.

95. Németh, *Zágon-levelesköny*, 88. Letter of József Zágon to Károly Fábián, Rome, February 8, 1974.

96. MMAL Other materials, I. sz. d. Typed statement on work carried out between March 20 and March 30, 1974.

97. ÁBTL 3.1.2. M–38642/1. 255. fol. Report of the agent codenamed "Kiss János" and dated March 22, 1974.

throughout whole country, from east to west. Preparations had been underway for some months and people awaited him with excitement, albeit the news of his dismissal as archbishop had somewhat cooled passions. Mindszenty spent the first two weeks in the New York area and in cities in Connecticut and New Jersey. According to a piece of information that Monsignor József Zágon, living in Rome and no longer in close contact with Mindszenty, but still showing interest in his activities, received from New York,

> the organization was better in some places and not so good in others, but everywhere there were crowds of Hungarians. This time we even managed to get clerical and sometimes even secular dignitaries to appear. But the schedule was very rushed... [...] To mitigate the previous storms, there were attempts in several Hungarian newspapers and on the radio to explain the age limit and the resignation. There was even one radio presenter who apologized publicly on air for his previous indignation.[98]

In many places on the journey, Mindszenty was greeted in English by those who had forgotten their mother tongue and by second-generation Hungarians.

Mindszenty arrived in Washington D.C. on May 20, 1974. During the two-day lightning visit, he was the guest of Archbishop Baum of Washington (William Wakefield Baum). Few Hungarians were living in the American capital; the small community did not even have its own parish church. Evidently, Cardinal Mindszenty traveled there in the hope of a possible meeting with President Nixon, whose staff, however, advised against a meeting with the "retired" archbishop. They argued that such a meeting would elicit a protest from the Hungarian government, while Mindszenty might seek to persuade the president to alter his stance on Hungary and/or argue for the return of Saint Stephen's crown.[99] For some years already, the United States had been pursuing a different policy

98. Németh, *Zágon-leveleskönyv*, 92. Letter of Sister Irma to József Zágon, New York, July 4, 1974.

99. Nixon Library, WHCF Subject Files Religious Matters (RM) Box 19. RM3-1 Catholic 1/1/73–[6/74] II. A. Report of Denis Clift (National Security Council) for Secretary of State Henry Kissinger, March 21, 1974.

towards the People's Republic of Hungary, and so, even at the risk of alienating voters of Hungarian ancestry, President Nixon chose not to receive Mindszenty.[100] Even in the absence of this meeting, Mindszenty had a full schedule: he met with dozens of Hungarians and visited both the Congress and the Kossuth House. The main event was a Holy Mass held in Hungarian at the National Shrine of the Immaculate Conception, the largest Marian church in the United States. An estimated 2,500 people attended the service, including Hungarians in folk costume and even some Cuban refugees. At a reception given the next day, the Hungarian Calvinist bishop, Zoltán Béky, called Cardinal Mindszenty "the greatest living Christian martyr." In his response, Mindszenty mentioned several "objectionable" topics: he referred to the Trianon Peace Treaty as a nation's murder and expressed gratitude to the US Congress for having refused to ratify the treaty. He then made an appeal to the consciences of statesmen and their duty to uphold human rights. Finally, he raised the question of the Holy Crown, which for Hungarians "represents a thousand-year-old constitution and a thousand years of statehood, and for us this will not be a cheap toy for so long as a single Hungarian is living in the world."[101] His speech was met with a roar of applause. On May 21, Mindszenty traveled from Washington D.C. to Buffalo, where the Sisters of Social Service had made their base. Sadly, Margit Slachta, Mindszenty's loyal "accomplice," had died several months earlier (on January 6, 1974). Cardinal Mindszenty then made a brief, two-day visit to Detroit on May 23–24.

His trip to Cleveland, the city in Ohio with more than 100,000 Hungarian inhabitants, took place from May 25–30. The city welcomed the Hungarian cardinal with all the honors befitting a head of state. Mayor Ralph J. Perk even awarded him the golden key of the city. The most important event was held at the city's St. John's Cathedral. Mindszenty entered the building between two rows of scouts. After the Holy Mass, Cardinal Mindszenty blessed the Captive Nations Monument on the city's main public square, where he also lit the Eternal Flame of the monument. During his time in

100. Ibid., NSC Files, Name Files, Box 19. RM3-1 Catholic 1/1/73–[6/74] I. Letter of Tom C. Korologos, deputy assistant to the president, to Senator Hugh Scott. May 4, 1973.

101. MMAL 086. d. Amerikai út [Journey to the USA], 1974. 5. dosszié, Washington. Gizella Róna, *Mindszenty bíboros Washingtonban* [Cardinal Mindszenty in Washington], manuscript, Washington, May 22, 1974.

Cleveland, one event followed the other, and there were many different venues. Mindszenty was interviewed on television, and he gave blessings on the radio to the sick and the lonely. He visited the city's Greek Catholic (Uniate) and Protestant churches, and then went on to the local school, the printing facility and several other Hungarian institutions that were still in operation. On June 1, he traveled to the Shrine of Our Lady of Mariapoch (Ohio), the most important Greek Catholic place of pilgrimage in the United States. He presided over Holy Mass in the cathedral and was met by a large crowd of well-wishers. By the evening, however, he was in Youngstown, where he dined with the city leaders. The next day he inaugurated a library, paid a visit to the "Iron Curtain Stations of the Cross," and then went on the Pentecost Procession. On June 3, he gave an interview on television and visited the local cemetery and printing facility. He then attended a luncheon organized by the city's Protestant clergymen.[102]

On June 5, he left Youngstown for San Francisco. At the invitation of Archbishop McGucken, he spent a whole week there. The plan was for him to receive an honorary doctorate at the Jesuit Santa Clara University, an event that would be televised. The event was canceled, however, because Mindszenty, who had been told that the university's management were failing to adhere to the Catholic Church's stance on abortion, chose not to accept the honorary degree.[103] From June 12–25, Mindszenty spent time in Los Angeles, Dallas, St. Louis, and Chicago. On June 18, in recognition of his heroic and self-sacrificing battle for justice, the University of Dallas (Texas) awarded Cardinal Mindszenty an honorary doctorate in law. The final days of the tour (June 26–28) were spent in Pittsburgh, where once again he had a very full schedule. The Mayor of Pittsburgh even proclaimed a "Joseph Cardinal Mindszenty Day" on June 26, 1974.[104] On his arrival in the city, Mindszenty held a press conference at the airport. He was asked by a reporter whether he wished to return home to Hungary. He answered: "I shall go back to Hungary when the communists convert to Christianity!"[105]

102. Ibid., 1. dosszié, Máriapócs.

103. For more on this issue, see József Jaszovszky, *Mindszenty, a főpásztor Észak-Kaliforniában* (Menlo Park, CA: Published by the author, 1980), 30–112.

104. MMAL 086. d. Amerikai út [Journey to the USA], 1974. 3. dosszié, Pittsburgh. Press cuttings from *Magyarság* [Hungarians], editions of June 14 and June 21, 1974.

105. Ibid., Press cutting from *Magyarság*, edition of June 28, 1974.

In the evening, at St. Paul's Cathedral, the city's largest church, he celebrated the liturgy with four bishops. Thousands of people attended the service. Not all of them were Hungarians; at the time, around two hundred families kept up the Hungarian church and parsonage. To what extent did Mindszenty obtain a clear view of the situation of the Hungarian parishes in the US and the difficulties they faced? He must have learned a good deal, as many of the letters he received tell of grievances, disputes, ageing congregations, the loss of Hungarian language skills, the changing ethnic and racial character of urban districts, and a thousand other problems. For Mindszenty, however, the efforts of the émigré communities to preserve and pass on Hungarian culture and identity would never be in vain.

Soon after his return to Europe, Mindszenty embarked on another tour – this time to West Germany. In Cologne, he symbolically opened the Hungarian House, which had been named after him. A most distinguished guest at the events was Cardinal Frings, archbishop of Cologne. Originally, it was planned that Mindszenty would also visit South America, but the trip had to be postponed to the following year. A journey to Paris, which Mindszenty had planned after having received an invitation from Hungarian priests in France, was cancelled. Cardinal Marty, archbishop of Paris, decided that he could only invite him if the government gave its approval for the visit.[106]

The first reaction to Mindszenty's journeys and statements came on October 14, 1974, when, at the Third General Assembly of the Synod of Bishops and in the presence of 198 delegates 21 invitees, Archbishop Ijjas of Kalocsa, chairman of the Hungarian Catholic Bishops' Conference, called "unjust criticism" of Hungary an impediment to evangelization and an act that called into question the competence of Hungarian church leaders. Even though no names were mentioned, it was clear to everybody whom Archbishop Ijjas was referring to:

> He who is not obedient in spirit to the pope (non est in oboedienti animo) but turns against him, becomes a stumbling block for those to whom the

106. AMAE AD Série: Europe, Hongrie, versement aux Archives (1971–juin 1976), boîte 3330, dossier Questions religieuses (1 janvier 1971–30 juin 1976), sous-dossier "Cardinal Mindzenty." Memo of Jean Guéguinou, chief of staff to the French minister of foreign affairs, March 18, 1974.

> Gospel speaks. In our country, there are grave obstacles to spreading the Good News. Thus, it is even more important not to undermine the credibility of the Church.[107]

Then, in an attempt to highlight the merits of the Hungarian regime's policy towards the churches, Archbishop Ijjas announced that a few days earlier the government in Budapest had finally given its permission for school pupils to attend religious instruction classes at church twice a week; this represented progress on an issue dating back many years.[108] Archbishop Poggi responded by saying that it was risible for Ijjas to boast about school pupils' freedom to attend classes in religious instruction. Such boasts could be made "by an atheist communist, but not by a bishop," he stated.[109]

In fact, the regime's acceptance of twice-weekly religious instruction at church was its first concession for ten years (since the start of Casaroli's negotiations). Moreover, for several months after Mindszenty's dismissal the regime in Budapest had apparently been unwilling to offer anything in return for the primate's removal from office. Indeed, the Hungarian authorities seemed to be utilizing the publication of Mindszenty's memoirs as a pretext for their refusal to offer the anticipated concessions. Nevertheless, the Kádár government recognized that without sound proof of freedom of worship in Hungary, it would be difficult for the regime to rid itself of its Stalinist image. Hence, a year after Mindszenty's dismissal and following further rounds of bilateral talks in November 1974 and January 1975, the regime agreed to additional personnel changes. Accordingly, on January 10, 1975, the pope made five apostolic administrators into diocesan bishops and four priests into titular bishops. For the first time since the partial agreement of 1964, bishops stood at the head of nine of Hungary's eleven dioceses. In addition, Imre Miklós, head of the State Office for Church Affairs, announced the authorization of the printing of catechisms and bible translations. In 1974, seventy-nine theology

107. Stehle, *Geheimdiplomatie im Vatikan*, 295; ÁBTL 3.2.5. O–8–552/12. 262. Report of Department no. III/I-4 of the Interior Ministry, October 26, 1974.

108. MNL OL XIX–J–1–j–Vatikán 160. 005752/1974. Memo on the Third General Synod of Bishops. Department no. XI of the Ministry of Foreign Affairs, Italian desk, November 23, 1974.

109. ÁBTL 3.2.3. Mt–975/3. 142. fol. Information report, January 20, 1975.

students enrolled at the five seminaries in Hungary (in 1973, there had been only thirty-eight). On November 13, 1975, Paul VI received Prime Minister György Lázár at a private audience in the Vatican. In the same year, the peace movement of Catholic priests celebrated its twenty-fifth anniversary. Roughly speaking, this was, therefore, the state of the Catholic Church in Hungary a decade after the signing of the partial agreement, about which Cardinal Mindszenty had said that "barely nothing essential in it can be further ravaged."[110]

The Memoirs

The major happening of 1974 was the publication of Mindszenty's memoirs, an event that had been announced and then repeatedly postponed. The delay was not the result of political intrigue. The truth of the matter was revealed by József Vecsey as early as the summer of 1972: "The cardinal has lost so much time on the Tatars and Turks [i.e. studying Hungarian historical topics] that he has got nowhere with his memoirs covering the recent past."[111] Moreover, at the outset, Mindszenty had been very insistent that the trials of the Hungarian Church and of the nation should be published alongside his own experiences in a work comprising at least ten volumes. His advisors had struggled to persuade him that it would be impossible to find a publisher – or indeed a readership – for such a lengthy work.[112] In the end, a publishing house in Canada (Vörösváry Publishers) oversaw the publication of five thousand copies of his memoirs. In Hungary, the only available copies of the book were those that had been smuggled into the country. The book soon became highly sought after; it was recognized as one of the few works that successfully challenged and undermined the monolithic ideology of the communist regime.

Cardinal Mindszenty attended the launch of his memoir at the Frankfurt Book Fair on October 11. He was asked by a reporter whether he had squabbled with the pope, who had allegedly placed a ban on the publication of his memoirs. Mindszenty responded as follows:

110. Stehle, *Geheimdiplomatie im Vatikan*, 297.

111. Mészáros, *A száműzött bíboros szolgálatában*, 28. Record for June 26, 1972.

112. Emil Csonka, *A száműzött bíboros: Mindszenty az emigrációban* (San Francisco–Munich, Új Európa, 1976), 74.

> I would not regard it as a ban, rather merely as an expression of concern [...] that the perpetrators mentioned in my book will attack me. He thought that the group of perpetrators was larger. Then it became clear that their number is negligible today, because the same thing has happened to them as what Bolshevism did to us. It has gobbled up its own people. And anyway, having experienced this for thirty years, one more attack will not really hurt me, because I have grown accustomed to such attacks, like a dog [grows accustomed] to being beaten.[113]

Mindszenty described the state of the Hungarian Church as extremely dire, mentioning three explanatory factors: fear, food and comfort.

The memoir itself has the strengths and weaknesses of many such works: subjectivity, selectivity, and bias. As we know, memoirs invariably contain accounts of events that do not match the facts or get the dates wrong. Mindszenty's memoirs are not free of these "symptoms" either. In his case, however, his status as an anticommunist national hero and the martyr of a political show trial has meant that his memoirs are treated by some as a kind of inviolable icon. Yet, when a historian casts doubt on one or more statements made in a memoir, s/he is not questioning the life's work of the author of the memoir. In his memoirs, Mindszenty showed no indication whatsoever of having understood or accepted the social and political changes that had occurred in Hungary. His socio-political ideas stemmed from the pre-1949 period and were of scant use to the true opponents of communism in later periods.

The memoirs took on the role of a kind of discussion paper: Mindszenty could finally give his version of events, doing so while his adversaries were still alive. He achieved his goal: his memoirs largely dispelled the communist propaganda image of a politicizing priest and outmoded figure who was demanding the return of the Church's estates. That negative image was replaced by a far more positive profile of a good pastor who had risen from lowly beginnings as a young catechist in Zalaegerszeg to the rank of a cardinal, and who had then been wrongly deprived of his ecclesiastical titles. The image was of a man who would not hesitate to

113. *Mindszenty breviárium* (3rd edition, Budapest: Magyarok Mindszenty Mozgalma, 1998), 21.

give his life for his flock. It is striking that the memoirs fail to give an account of the fifteen years Mindszenty spent at the US diplomatic mission. One might think that this was because his primary objective was to reveal the awful deeds of the communists, whereby his refuge at the legation/embassy was of mere secondary importance. In fact, however, he was driven by a desire to avoid a false sense of politeness. If he had been honest about his time at the legation, his criticism of the Americans might have been interpreted as ingratitude. In private conversations with Hungarian émigrés, however, Mindszenty revealed his true opinions. He even called the Americans "stupid," for having – in his view – forfeited their position as the leading world power, thereby risking Europe's future.[114] To his close confidants, he even stated that the Americans had sought, in 1956 "to disguise their shame at their betrayal by making him their guest." He then accused the United States and Freemasonry of being responsible for the existence of the Soviet Union and of communism.[115]

In his memoir, he briefly touches upon the dispute with Paul VI over his removal from the archiepiscopal see of Esztergom. In doing so, he proceeds in such a way that his own image of reality is not lost (due to his obedience or discretion) and that the authority of the highest representative of faith and morality – the Holy See – is not undermined. Ultimately, his portrayal of events seems to indicate that, in his view, the Holy See sacrificed him on the altar of its Eastern policy. Even now, the prevailing image of Mindszenty is that of an anticommunist hero who was sacrificed by the Vatican. This reflects the fact that the other side of the story (i.e., the account of the Vatican apparatus) has never been heard.

Mindszenty's memoirs were successfully published in Hungarian, German, French and Italian. Problems arose, however, with the English version, published in the United States. Media outlets – both liberal and conservative – ignored the book's publication, as did also the religious press. Why was so little interest shown in North America for Mindszenty's memoirs? A conspiracy theory quickly emerged among the émigré community: it was alleged that the Macmillan publishing house had been bribed by the Soviets. The accusation was as follows: in return for the

114. ÁBTL 3.2.9. R–8–009/2. 37. fol. Relations between Mindszenty and the Hungarian émigré communities.

115. Mészáros, *A száműzött bíboros szolgálatában*, 33. Record for July 4, 1972.

publishing rights of the works of all the Russian composers, Macmillan had pledged to halt the distribution of Mindszenty's memoirs. Even Mindszenty knew that the accusation was false. If someone had poked the Russians in the eye, it was not him but Solzhenitsyn with his work *The Gulag Archipelago*. Yet that work was freely available in US bookstores. Several factors were at play, the most important being Macmillan's business difficulties. It was during this period that the company was forced to dismiss four hundred staff members, including the editor of the memoirs.[116]

Just as controversy surrounded Mindszenty's public image, so too his memoirs elicited a mixed reception. Progressive Catholics opined that such publications were detrimental to the peaceful coexistence of East and West. A review published in the Dutch Catholic newspaper, *De Tijd* (November 15, 1974), stated the following: "This is none other than a portrait of a limited and somewhat vain man, who was opposed to coercive social change in the late 1940s."[117] In contrast, Cardinal Mindszenty received a flood of congratulatory and praising letters, including one from a fellow victim of communism, Cardinal Slipyj, major archbishop of the Ukrainian Greek Catholic Church, and another from Cardinal Ottaviani, a prominent conservative in the Catholic Church. If Mindszenty had been an ordinary public figure, an analysis of his life – or even of his memoirs – would not have given rise to so much controversy. Cardinal Mindszenty, however, lived on the boundary between two historical eras, becoming a legendary figure of public life. For this reason, a discussion of his ideas inevitably morphs into an evaluation of 20th-century European history in its entirety and an appraisal of both the past and the present.

The Final Journey

In late October 1974, Cardinal Mindszenty traveled to Australia, having been invited there by the bishops of Sydney and Melbourne. He returned to Vienna in mid-December. People's recollections of these journeys are consistent: Mindszenty thought in terms of a single Hungarian nation,

116. MMAL MFN 9776–10108. L-4239, Box with a label "Correspondence on the publication and dissemination of the *Memoirs abroad*."

117. MMAL 15/3. dosszié, material from period of exile, correspondence with the book publishers.

wherever individual Hungarians might be living. He no longer drew a distinction between Catholics and Protestants; for him, the important thing was that the person was Hungarian. At the Hungarian House in Perth (Western Australia), he lauded the efforts of local Catholics and Protestants to outdo each other in terms of their contribution to preserve the national identity of the Hungarian émigrés. He asked both Catholic and Protestant clergymen to give their support to weekend Hungarian schools and to religious instruction conducted in Hungarian. He repeatedly stated how the legacy of the Hungarian language could only be upheld if families taught their children about the Christian faith in Hungarian.

Mindszenty's final foreign journey took him to South America from April 9–26, 1975. He first visited Caracas, Venezuela, where his host was Cardinal Quintero, the retired archbishop. It was here that Mindszenty wrote his last pastoral letter to Hungarians around the world. In the letter, he reiterated the need to preserve Hungarian identity – an obligation that had to be met by the émigré communities.[118] Between April 21 and April 26, he visited the Colombian capital of Bogota. Several aspects of the trip to Colombia were familiar to Mindszenty from his earlier journeys: for instance, although he was welcomed by parts of the Catholic hierarchy, some leading Catholic churchmen – for example, Cardinal Aníbal Muñoz Duque, archbishop of Bogota, and Nuncio Angelo Palmas – were initially cautious and avoided contact with him. In the end, however, both men welcomed him, and Mindszenty could celebrate High Mass at the main cathedral. Cardinal Mindszenty worked indefatigably, presiding at confirmations, celebrating Mass, and giving sermons. Every night, hundreds of members of the local Hungarian community went to the place he was staying at, where he would meet them and talk to them often well until after midnight. He was happy to spend time talking with his compatriots and ministering to them.

The press in Venezuela reported on his visit with some reticence. In contrast, in Colombia there was a lively response in the media to his visit. Many photographs, articles and commentaries appeared in the press, and the Hungarian cardinal gave a televised interview. Cardinal Mindszenty

118. See Julián Füzér, comp., *Szentnek kiáltjuk!* (Youngstown, OH: Katolikus Magyarok Vasárnapja, 1987), 74–76.

spoke in subdued terms to the public. It was only in his narrow circle that he would criticize conditions in Hungary and speak of the peace priests, the imprisoned clergy, the difficulties surrounding the import of ecclesiastical literature from abroad, the lack of new, young priests, and the challenges facing religious education. Even in such conversations, however, he tended to avoid such topics as his dismissal from the post of archbishop or his disagreements with the Holy See. In such instances, his response would often be: "Ask the Vatican..."[119]

The South American climate and the full work schedule overburdened Mindszenty's elderly body. He felt so unwell on the flight back to Europe that his traveling companions wanted the aircraft to make a stop in Morocco with a view to his being admitted to a hospital in Casablanca. In the end, this did not happen. The initial plan was for him to travel to Nuremberg to receive an award. From there he was to travel to Paris, where he had a longstanding invitation. A medical examination, however, revealed the need for surgery. There was general optimism that the operation (a routine urological procedure) could be accomplished without complications. However, the heart of the 83-year-old cardinal proved too weak for the surgery. Shortly after the operation, at 2.15 p.m. on May 6, 1975, József Mindszenty passed away at the Hospital of the Brothers of Mercy. The official cause of death was calcification of the coronary artery. Cardinal Franz König published the obituary, and the funeral bier was placed in the nave of St. Stephen's Cathedral in Vienna. Before the coffin was closed, a photograph of Mindszenty's mother and a handful of earth from her grave were placed inside, as were also a copy of Mindszenty's memoirs and a stone from his titular church in Rome (Santo Stefano Rotondo). A Requiem Mass took place on May 9.

The funeral was scheduled for May 15, 1975. On the same day, the 20th anniversary of the Austrian State Treaty was being celebrated in Austria. Citing their attendance at the celebrations, many Austrian bishops and the apostolic nuncio, Archbishop Opilio Rossi, chose not to attend Cardinal Mindszenty's funeral. Evidently, their absence was motivated in part by the Holy See's reservations towards the Hungarian cardinal. Austrian

119. ÖStA, AdR, BMfAA, Sektion II-pol. Zl. 82-Res/75 222.04.02/1-II. 3/75. Report of Herbert Grubmayr, Austrian ambassador to Colombia, on József Mindszenty's visit to Bogota.

Chancellor Bruno Kreisky was represented at the funeral by a ministerial counselor. There were also notable absentees at the funeral from among the diplomatic corps. Members of the European and Hungarian aristocracy, however, were present, among them Regina von Habsburg (wife of Otto von Habsburg), Albrecht, Duke of Bavaria, and members of the Esterházy family and the Bourbons of Parma. The Austrian broadcasting company broadcast the funeral live on TV. The funeral Mass in Mariazell was jointly celebrated by Archbishop Döpfner of Munich, Archbishop König of Vienna, Bishop László of Burgenland, and Bishop Weber of Graz. On behalf of Hungarians around the world, György Ádám, head pastor to the Hungarian community in Munich, bid farewell to Mindszenty. At the funeral, Father Werenfried van Straaten, the Dutch monk, also said some words, calling the pope, in view of his decision, "a means of the Divine will that is unfathomable at the present moment."[120] None of the Hungarian bishops dared even ask for permission to travel to the funeral. Sadly, no-one among the Hungarian community in Austria was prepared to hold the flag, lest such an act diminish their chance of receiving a travel visa to Hungary (which was only granted to émigrés exhibiting "impeccable conduct") In the end, the flag was placed up against one of the church pillars.[121] Archbishop König spoke of Mindszenty as

> a martyr, who with wonderful steadfastness had borne his physical and spiritual sufferings, while remaining loyal throughout to his Church and to his people. He was a martyr of our era, of an era in which a new type of martyr had been created by religious persecution on ideological and political grounds... We bow in respect and with great esteem to this martyr of the modern era.[122]

It was Mindszenty's wish that he be buried at Mariazell, the famous Marian pilgrimage site in Styria (Austria). In his will, however, he stated that if/when "the star of Muscovite atheism" fell from the Hungarian sky, his earthly remains should be taken from Mariazell to Esztergom and

120. See Füzér, *Szentnek kiáltjuk*, 160.

121. Borbándi, *A magyar emigráció életrajza*, 1945–1985, vol. 2: 24.

122. MNL OL XIX–J–1–j–Vatikán 160. 003594/2/1975. Report of Lajos Nagy, Hungarian ambassador to Austria, May 29, 1975.

buried at the final resting place of the Hungarian primates.[123] This did then happen sixteen years later: on May 3, 1991, Cardinal Mindszenty's ashes were brought to Hungary in a veritable march of triumph. By that time, the country had already undergone its political transition. The communist regime had been abolished and a democratic, pluralist European state had been founded through peaceful means. Some voices criticized the Church for its delay in bringing Mindszenty's earthly remains back to Hungary, as the event occurred almost two years after the reburial (on June 16, 1989) of former Hungarian Prime Minister Imre Nagy, who had been executed in 1958. Others, however, believed the Church had acted all too quickly: while it was true that the withdrawal of Soviet troops had begun in the spring of 1990, it was not until June 19, 1991 that the last Soviet soldier departed from Hungary. In their view, therefore, Mindszenty's ashes had been returned to Hungary prematurely. Mindszenty's former secretary, Tibor Mészáros, protested the exhumation in graphic fashion, chaining himself to Mindszenty's tomb in Mariazell. He had to be removed by the Austrian police. According to Mészáros, Cardinal Mindszenty's final wish – albeit not stated in the written will – had been that his remains should remain in Austria until the last Russian soldier had left Hungary. Mészáros's crude act caught the world's attention, but it achieved nothing: On May 4, at a ceremonial funeral, the last prince primate of Hungary was laid to final rest in the archiepiscopal crypt of the Primatial Basilica of Esztergom. The service was conducted by Cardinal Opilio Rossi, who had served as apostolic nuncio in Vienna from 1971 until 1976.

The criminal proceedings that had been launched against József Mindszenty in 1949 were declared null and void by the Municipal Court of Budapest on May 11, 1990.[124] As the Municipal Court did not order his rehabilitation, the impression of a tainted reputation remained. Finally, following a request from Péter Cardinal Erdő, primate of Hungary, in March 2012 the Supreme Court of Hungary issued a decree pronouncing the official termination of the reopened investigation of 1989–1990. Concurrently,

123. Füzér, *Szentnek kiáltjuk*, 78–79.

124. BFL XXV. 1. a. 254/1949. Municipal Court of Budapest, Certificate no. 10.B.714/1990/2. May 11, 1990.

the Supreme Court proclaimed Cardinal Mindszenty's full legal, moral and political rehabilitation.

Preparations for the beatification of Cardinal Mindszenty began when, on May 6, 1985 (the tenth anniversary of his death), Franciscan Father Julián Füzér and Salesian Father János Szőke started collecting witness statements. Three years later, the Archdiocese of Vienna, which had competence in view of the place of death, commenced the official process, but little progress was made for some years. For this reason, in 1993, Cardinal László Paskai requested the transfer of the matter to Esztergom, where the first stage of the beatification process (the Diocesan Inquiry) was relaunched on March 14, 1994. The Diocesan Inquiry was concluded within two years and the documentation was passed – on October 17, 1996 – to the Congregation for the Causes of Saints (*Congregatio de Causis Sanctorum*).[125] Those who hold Cardinal Mindszenty in high esteem eagerly await the Congregation's positive decision on this "Servant of God."

There is no denying that Mindszenty left a vacuum behind him. At a new round of talks, held in Rome from November 26–29, 1975, the Hungarian government and the Holy See agreed upon the appointment of a new archbishop of Esztergom, in accordance with the procedure that had been accepted by both parties in 1973 and 1974.[126] On February 12, 1976, nearly a year after Mindszenty's death, the Holy See appointed László Lékai, who had been serving as apostolic administrator of the archdiocese, as archbishop of Esztergom. Two days earlier, the Political Committee of the HSWP had approved the appointment. The inauguration ceremony took place on February 24, whereby László Lékai became archbishop of Esztergom and primate of Hungary. Concurrently, Lékai became chairman of the Hungarian Catholic Bishops' Conference. Lékai was chosen to head the Hungarian Catholic Church in part because, having avoided excessively close relations with the regime, he was regarded as the country's least

125. László Imre Németh, "Mindszenty József a boldoggá avatás útján," in *Hogy jobban értsük a huszadik századot* [József Mindszenty on the path to beatification, in To better understand the 20th century], eds. György Markó and Mária Schmidt (Budapest: Közép- és Kelet-európai Történelem és Társadalom Kutatásáért Közalapítvány – XX. Századi Intézet, 2014), 92–101.

126. MNL OL XIX–A–21–e–XXX. dosszié–0022–7/e/1975. 2. fol. Report on the talks held with Vatican representatives, December 8, 1975.

compromised bishop. Archbishop Ijjas of Kalocsa, who had been chairing the Bishops' Conference, was awarded the title of Assistant to the Pontifical Throne in recognition of his services, but he was not subsequently elevated to the rank of cardinal. In March 1976, two further bishops were appointed. Thus, after a thirty-year interval, the Hungarian Catholic ecclesiastical hierarchy was complete once more. The authority of the new primate of Hungary grew when, soon after his appointment as archbishop of Esztergom, Pope Paul VI created him a cardinal on May 24, 1976. In the ensuing period, the Hungarian Catholic Church – now with a full leadership – had to seek opportunities for its own recovery and for a redefinition of its relationship with the Hungarian state, doing so in the absence of Cardinal Mindszenty, who may have symbolized the past but whose stature as a legendary Catholic figure was steadily increasing.

"It is in accordance with their dignity as persons – that is, beings endowed with reason and free will and therefore privileged to bear personal responsibility – that all men should be at once impelled by nature and also bound by a moral obligation to seek the truth, especially religious truth. They are also bound to adhere to the truth, once it is known, and to order their whole lives in accord with the demands of truth."

(Dignitatis Humanae, the Second Vatican Council's Declaration on Religious Freedom)

CONCLUSION

In compiling this portrait of Mindszenty, my intent has been to avoid simplifying his life story into one of perpetrators and victims or giving a distorted – hagiographic or slanderous – account. It is my conviction that one cannot (should not) reduce a person to his or her roles, thereby reinforcing the clichés. Attempts to do so necessarily diminish the richness of the personality. Accordingly, my aim has been to give a balanced account. Let the reader decide whether I have succeeded in this endeavor. This conclusion seeks to summarize the historical mission of József Mindszenty.

The Parish Priest

As befits a parish priest, József Pehm/Mindszenty always gave priority to his pastoral work. After his ordination he opted not to attend university either in Hungary or abroad, and so he never acquired a doctorate in philosophy or theology. Instead, he became a practicing priest and pastor, renowned for fostering social causes. Even in this early part of his life we already encounter Mindszenty's legendary verve and enthusiasm. His work amounted to more than mere pastoral activities, for, in addition to revitalizing Catholic religious life and social work, he also made an impact on the administration of an entire municipality, where no important decisions could be taken without his input.

As time passed, he took a growing interest in the work of the Catholic movements, becoming an active figure in political Catholicism. In Hungary, political Catholicism – similarly to the movements linked with the

Protestant Christian denominations – developed as a highly conservative movement and as a response to the advance of liberalism, social democracy, and democratic ideals based on broad suffrage – all of which were regarded, in view of their anticlericalism, as a threat to the Church and to the faith. Throughout his life, Pehm combined his loyalty to Catholicism with his loyalty to the king. His actions in public life were largely determined by his conservative royalism (legitimism). He sought the restoration of the House of Habsburg to the Hungarian throne and believed in the accompanying principles of state autocracy. It was in this political context that Pehm/Mindszenty served as parish priest in Zalaegerszeg for a quarter of a century. During that time, Catholic life in the town developed at a rate otherwise only seen in the diocesan seats. When the Vatican authorities began to look for a candidate for the episcopal see of Veszprém, they found in József Mindszenty a man with twenty-five years of solid pastoral experience, a bishop who had already played an active part in political and public life. Moreover, his influence was felt throughout western Hungary, a predominantly Catholic region.

The Prelate Shows Resistance

József Mindszenty's rejection of Hitler and Stalin's totalitarianism was elicited by the "justice" he experienced under the Arrow Cross and then under the communists. After World War II and following the attrition of all democratic forces, the Hungarian communists came to view the Catholic Church as the country's last independent institution. Indeed, Cardinal Mindszenty, archbishop of Esztergom, was now the only person with the influence and authority to launch a rearguard action, even at the risk of bringing about his own martyrdom.

As primate of Hungary, Mindszenty faced the immense challenge of sustaining both the free operation of the Church (coupled with freedom of worship) and the social influence and authority of the Catholic Church in Hungary. Essentially, the cardinal had two options: he could either join those who believed that the future lay in accepting the political situation in Hungary with all its imperfections, or he could reject everything put forward by the government in power. In the former case, he would have urged his flock to support a strategy of compromise and negotiation with the government. The other route – which soon became his preference – meant adhering to one's principles while ignoring the advice received from the internal church opposition and disregarding the negative consequences for the Church.

Issues and controversies which the Catholic Church had – in other countries – worked through during the culture wars of the 19th century, were still pertinent to the Hungarian Church even in 1945. This was more a consequence of history than a result of the Church's insistence upon its many rights, privileges and landed estates. What was needed was a process of internal renewal, a great "clean-out." The harbingers of such change were visible for a time, but then subsided. After 1945 the broom was seized by others, who, however, swept away not only what was superfluous to the Church but also structures that were vital to the Church's future. The critical juncture for the two potential scenarios – resistance or accommodation – was the proclamation of a republican form of government in Hungary (the final abolition of the monarchy), as this development rendered the public legal role of ecclesiastical figures defunct. Throughout the rest of his life, however, Mindszenty believed – based on the historical constitution – that in the absence of a monarch the archbishop of Esztergom, as prince primate of Hungary, should protect and represent the constitutional rights of the Hungarian nation. This role became part and parcel of his psychological makeup. Perhaps he identified with it too closely. Posterity must move on to a more spacious historical horizon.

Cardinal Mindszenty blamed Soviet influence for the switch to a republican form of government in Hungary. The Soviet Union had not merely occupied the country; it had also turned the political system upside down, leading to the advent of people's democracy and of communism. He believed it was incumbent upon him to reject any deal with the "Devil." Hence, whenever there was good reason to do so, he fought against the government's measures. His actions reflected a principled stance: the rejection of decisions taken by, or attributed to, the communists.

Why did Mindszenty opt for this route? It seems he did so because he was hoping for a reversal in world politics and because he was acting in the firm belief that his actions would receive the support of the Holy See. Pope Pius XII, however, was averse to prescribing a specific course of action under a specific set of circumstances. Nevertheless, he generally expected the faithful to resist atheistic communism. At the time of Mindszenty's creation as cardinal, Pope Pius XII gave him the task of averting the communist threat. Yet, until the end of 1946, Pius was also offering encouragement and support to those clerics who supported a *modus vivendi*. The pope evidently had confidence that Mindszenty – like other prelates working under communism – would prove able to decide whether to accommodate or resist the regime. Though Mindszenty's actions were not always to the liking of Vatican officials, it appeared to outside observers that he had their firm support.

Has history vindicated Mindszenty's intransigence? The principle of "all or nothing" rarely leads to success and acclaim in public life. Rather, it often results in martyrdom or public disdain. Mindszenty correctly saw the direction of change (bolshevization). One might even say that he had great political foresight. What he could not accept was being incapable of altering the course of events. Moreover, he failed to spot the limited opportunities that were available to him. Yet such opportunities could have helped him extend his influence. Believing in the superiority of his status as primate, he misappraised the various options and their consequences: the refusal of the Vatican and of the United States to defend him or to intervene on his behalf. His chosen course inevitably brought him into conflict with the nascent communist dictatorship.

Mindszenty's uncompromising stance has customarily been referred to as the *loyalist* position (faithful to the Church), while supporters of the other option – a compromise with the regime – are usually called *survivalists*. This distinction implies that loyalty was the unique prerogative of the first group. In fact, however, many among the survivalists were equally faithful Catholics. In my view, Max Weber's distinction – between the *ethics of principle* and the *ethics of responsibility* – is more helpful. On this basis, we can state that the two approaches had a common element, namely a shared perception of the temporariness of the situation. However, there was discord on its duration. Supporters of the ethics of principle were driven – regardless of the circumstances and the costs incurred – by a desire to remain faithful to Gospel values. They accepted several rules and sought to adhere to them.

Supporters of the other approach – the ethics of responsibility – had no wish to be unfaithful to the fundamental religious-ethic tenets. They too had principles; yet, while seeking to survive what they viewed as a temporary period, they were also minded to achieve the best result. This applied especially to the period of the coalition government, when the survivalists argued that one must be patient with any government (even with the most awful one). Even under the most difficult circumstances, it would be possible to find a minimum level of mutual understanding. Survival would thus be possible until the circumstances changed. There were some who argued that the concessions made in return for survival constituted an unprincipled retreat. Others, however, thought that it was simply being realistic to seek the maximum that could be realized – in terms of the fulfillment of principles – under the given conditions. In making this assessment, mistakes would often be made, but this amounted to an error rather than a full-blown transgression. Even if they did sometimes make mistakes, they were not acting unethically by assessing the situation and searching for a way forward. And the same was true of the other side: even if errors or excesses were made, the defense of values and the making of self-sacrifices did not constitute a reckless and callous gamble with their own lives and with the lives of others.

Mindszenty's contemporaries rightly saw in him a man whose very constitution and strong faith were such that he would be prepared to give his life for the "cause." His "stubbornness" can also be viewed as "spiritual fortitude." But it was this unassailable consistency on matters of principle that lay at the root of his political weakness. Mindszenty had to pay a high price for all of this. For his heroic stand, he did win a martyr's wreath, but this brought no advantage at the time to him or to the Catholic clergy and laity. Compromise came to symbolize the post-WWII era. In the shadow of nuclear weapons, survival was made subject to the new rules of the game. However, Mindszenty's stance of opposition and resistance enabled his opponents to reshape (and recalibrate) public opinion: Mindszenty and his supporters were portrayed, not as democrats seeking to protect the country from dictatorship, but as supporters of the Horthy regime fighting a rearguard action.

When Pope Pius XII welcomed the new cardinals – among them József Mindszenty – on February 20, 1946, he raised an age-old question: What is the task or function of the Church in human society? The answer has been known for a thousand years: The Church continues the mission of its divine founder when it carries the Gospel to the entire world. In view of the postwar reconstruction work – and the enmity between nations – the Church gave emphasis to its supranational nature and the fact that its *modus operandi* differed entirely from that of a state or an empire. The message was simple: The Church does not seek power for its own sake; at the same time, it does not wish to renounce its own vocation. Under the specific circumstances prevailing in Hungary, the question could be altered to: What is the task of the Church in a hostile society? Is it to exercise spiritual care or to show political resistance? Or are these two factors intertwined when the "struggle for souls" is being waged in the political field or – as under Rákosi – within the confines of a police state? If the answer is an affirmative one, then does a prelate have the right to lead the Catholic laity into existential ruin? Rather than insist on his own ethical principles, should not a pastor try to save for his flock what can be saved under the circumstances? Mindszenty clung to his principles even when this risked dividing his own supporters and weakening the long-term effectiveness of the Church. He did not reckon with the fact that he stood in opposition to a political force that had the backing of the entire Soviet Empire. Or, even if he did so, he believed it to be a temporary circumstance. Hence, rather than save what could be saved, he commenced a solitary battle against it. His peasant-farmer background, his lengthy imprisonment, and his many sufferings transformed Mindszenty into an almost mythical hero. He became a legendary figure, a modern David, and a hero of the anticommunist struggle. Mindszenty was the man who dared confront the far more powerful Goliath. The people saw their own feelings, passions, and prejudices reflected in Mindszenty. It is this picture of the Hungarian cardinal that was immortalized in his memoirs, published in 1974. The picture has been carefully fostered by historians and hagiographers ever since.

Mindszenty's unbending and principled way of thinking prevented him from discovering nuances in his ideological and political adversaries. He simply did not notice potential allies when they arose. Meanwhile, he often saw enemies in people who were seeking the same ends. He lacked the sophistication of a politician, the flexibility of a diplomat, and the wisdom of a ruler. Even so, despite the many contradictions, at a given historical juncture, it was József Mindszenty, a conservative and royalist prelate, who actively defended the values of democracy, doing so against those who loudly proclaimed their support for such values but who then built a dictatorship.

The unmatched accomplishment of Cardinal Mindszenty was his success – in respect of most Hungarians – in bringing religious feelings and traditional national sentiment to a common denominator that was based on Catholic grounds. In doing so, he ended the antagonism between these two "irrational forces." He achieved this even though Hungarians had tended to view the prince primates as the principal exponents of Habsburg rule (with a paralyzing effect on Hungarian independence efforts). In contrast, József Mindszenty became the high priest of the Hungarian nation. Indeed, the nation, Hungarian identity and religion became inextricably intertwined in his person.

From a historical perspective, what rescued the Church and assured its survival? Was it submission or martyrdom? There is evidence for both. For a time, the moral significance of their joint presence (or "co-existence") was that the Hungarian Church could not be broken – at least not until 1964 and the signing of the partial agreement between Hungary and the Holy See. Even after this date, it could not be destroyed entirely, for history, in my view, does not justify the actions of knights tilting at windmills or people who bend their backs. Rather, it shows that the Church was a wise institution that provided a common space for both the barricade fighters and the collaborators, for the peace priests and an underground, oppositional, and spiritually free church. Of course, everyone reacts in accordance with his or her own conscience to the ambivalence concealed in these matters or arising out of these circumstances. Just as a hilltop can be reached by following different trails, so too a variety of approaches may lead us to the same goal. The wisdom or folly of our choices becomes apparent only after the event.

The Spiritual Pastor of Hungarians Throughout the World

The image of Mindszenty as victim and martyr became an indelible one, based on his show trial and the long years he spent in prison. In contrast, an image of Mindszenty as the high priest of the 1956 revolution never became a part of people's consciousness. For decades, the generations affected by the revolution could not even hear his name. Escaping from the Soviet invasion, Mindszenty requested and received refuge at the US Legation in Budapest. During the fifteen years spent at the legation, he was prevented from carrying out his duties as Hungarian primate. It was only a decade and a half later, as his life drew to its close, that he could begin a new and more active stage. Psychologically, he needed to undergo much contemplation to prepare himself for the departure from his native land. The seeming defeat did not discourage Mindszenty. He had devoted the decade and a half of his confinement to the writing of his memoirs. Now, having been released from captivity, he began to arrange for their publication, while also devoting himself to efforts aimed at preserving the faith and Hungarian identity of his compatriots around the world.

On his pastoral visits abroad, Mindszenty – the representative of tradition and of the unchanging nature of old-school Catholicism – addressed the Hungarian émigrés who viewed everything through the lens of nostalgia. The cardinal was not only unfamiliar with the pro-détente Western world, the rebellious younger generation, and the sexual revolution, he also had no knowledge or experience of the new ideas and liturgical forms, with which the Catholic Church had been experimenting ever since the Second Vatican Council (1962–65). In his church, the holding of Beat and Blues masses with the help of rock bands would have been unimaginable. Thanks to his traditional view of the Church, Mindszenty became a paragon not only for the anticommunists but also for the conservatives who were resisting social (and ecclesiastical) changes. In a world of peaceful coexistence, however, there was broad acceptance in every country that the international political divisions were lasting ones that had to be coped with. The tragedy of Hungary's last prince primate was that the post-détente world had less and less need for his historical task – unwavering opposition to communism.

Mindszenty wished to build a future by adhering to the past. He proved incapable of moving on from his own reality into the real world. His static approach to history became especially visible in his attitude towards his public legal role as prince primate – a role that even the Vatican considered an outdated relic. The Second Vatican Council advocated – in its entire spirit – a modern dialogue, in which a mixing of ecclesiastical and public constitutional functions could no longer be countenanced. When, in 1971,

Paul VI called Mindszenty a "victim of history," he was condensing this change into a metaphor.

His removal, in 1974, from the post of archbishop deeply shocked Cardinal Mindszenty, as it did millions of Catholics who sympathized with him. While referring to the need for a pastor, Paul VI clearly withdrew his support for the line represented by the Hungarian cardinal and seemed even to be devaluing Mindszenty's earlier heroic stand. On the other hand, the pope's actions facilitated a renewal of the Hungarian Catholic hierarchy. In retrospect, it may seem that the Vatican was attributing excessive importance to its episcopal appointments and living under the false impression that the Hungarian Catholic Church could not survive without a restored hierarchy. In fact, however, the long-term goal was a much broader one: the normalization of the status of the Hungarian and other oppressed churches. Thus, József Mindszenty fell victim to the Vatican's new Eastern policy. We should recognize, however, that from the perspective of Rome there was no real dilemma when it came to choosing between the viability/operability of the Hungarian Catholic Church and the position of Cardinal Mindszenty, a man who had undergone the spiritual sufferings of his voluntary captivity.

Even today, appraisals of the Vatican's Eastern policy often question whether it eased the fate of the Catholic Churches in Central and Eastern Europe. Undeniably, there was hope of this happening, for this was the era of a "thaw" in international relations. The Second Vatican Council and the Helsinki process had established an atmosphere in which people could have confidence in the fulfillment of religious freedom. Today, however, few deny that the results of the Eastern policy were less favorable than anticipated. Negotiations were slow to proceed, and the regimes fulfilled only in part (or not at all) the provisions in the agreements. Still, several archbishops were appointed and a small number of imprisoned churchmen were released. This was still a long way from proper religious freedom, but the rate of "deterioration" of the churches was slowed. Other than faith and hope, the only "munitions" at the Holy See's disposal were diplomacy and law.

*

Many commentators have given emphasis to Mindszenty's obstinate and stubborn nature, while others have portrayed his every step as the embodiment of perfection. His life amounts to a whole series of contradictions – Mindszenty was both tough and gentle, austere and serene, close-minded and far-sighted, and many other opposite pairs (contradictions) could be listed. The historian – without crossing the boundaries of the profession – may find the "solution" in the response given by those with "more wisdom" in the documents issued by the Second Vatican Council, among which *Dignitatis humanae* addressed religious freedom, touching upon the issue of conscience. As Point Three of the document's first chapter states:

> Truth, however, is to be sought after in a manner proper to the dignity of the human person and his social nature. The inquiry is to be free, carried on with the aid of teaching or instruction, communication and dialogue, in the course of which men explain to one another the truth they have discovered, or think they have discovered, in order thus to assist one another in the quest for truth.
> Moreover, as the truth is discovered, it is by a personal assent that men are to adhere to it.
> On his part, man perceives and acknowledges the imperatives of the divine law through the mediation of conscience. In all his activity a man is bound to follow his conscience in order that he may come to God, the end and purpose of life. It follows that he is not to be forced to act in a manner contrary to his conscience. Nor, on the other hand, is he to be restrained from acting in accordance with his conscience, especially in matters religious.[1]

If we carefully read these lines about the search for truth, then it becomes clear that this truly modern Council is the one – no matter how shocking it seems, for the ideas expressed appear to be contradictory ones – which vindicates the intransigent Mindszenty. Indeed, unless our aim is

1. Declaration on Religious Freedom *Dignitatis humanae* on the Right of the Person and of Communities to Social and Civil Freedom in Matters Religious. Promulgated by His Holiness Pope Paul VI on December 7, 1965. On the Internet: http://www.vatican.va/archive/hist_councils/ii_vatican_council/documents/vat-ii_decl_19651207_dignitatis-humanae_en.html.

to interpret and evaluate his life on a single plane, we can see that, at a more profound level, his actions, decisions, subsequent pensiveness, and his perceived "constitutional rights" were rooted in a search for truth and the demands of his conscience. As the Second Vatican Council had stated: "All men should be at once impelled by nature and also bound by a moral obligation to seek the truth." The sincerity of Mindszenty's intentions cannot be denied. At the same time, the path taken in a search for truth and the decisions made in all conscience can be wrong – as the historian should point out. But one must not judge either the intransigent or the accommodating – if the search for truth was their guide.

József Mindszenty stuck to his convictions until – quite literally – his final breath. He is a unique figure in Hungarian – and, indeed, universal – history, a man who exhibited a rare personal authority and a superior moral force. His life is rightly exalted as a symbol of resistance to dictatorship and as an example of loyalty and faithfulness; he was a man who remained true to his God, his Church, his nation, and his people. This is so, even if he sought to carry a greater cross on his shoulders than that which mortals can bear...

SOURCES AND BIBLIOGRAPHY

I. ARCHIVAL SOURCES

Állambiztonsági Szolgálatok Történeti Levéltára (Budapest)
(ÁBTL, Historical Archives of the Hungarian State Security)

1.2. Magyar Államrendőrség Államvédelmi Osztályának iratai (ÁVO)
2.1. A volt Zárt Irattár levéltári anyaga
2.2.2. Hálózati nyilvántartások
3.1.2. Központi operatív nyilvántartást végző szervezeti egységek által kezelt munka dossziék (M-dossziék)
M–38.642, M–38.642/1. "Kiss János"
M–40530, M–40530/2. "Igaz Sándor"
3.1.5. Központi operatív nyilvántartást végző szervezeti egységek által kezelt operatív dossziék (O-dossziék)
O–11.701 Legitimista pártok
O–12.547/1. Badalik Bertalan
O–13.405/1–3a. Magyar Római Katolikus Püspöki Kar
O–14.759/7. Kovács Sándor
O–14.963/1–9a. "Canale"
3.1.8. Régi archív számon kezelt operatív dossziék
Sz–222, Sz–222/2–18. Mindszenthy József
3.1.9. Központi operatív nyilvántartást végző szervezeti egységek által kezelt vizsgálati dossziék (V-dossziék)
V–700/1–59. Mindszenthy József és társai ügy

V–19.441 P. Mócsy Imre

V–82.897/1. Endrédy Vendel és társai

V–103.458/1–13. Bozsik Pál és társai

V–142.947/1–3. Kósa Pál és társai

V–150.019/1, 5. Farkas Mihály és társai

V–150.393/4. Tánczos Gábor, Tildy Zoltán, Tóbiás Áron és Turcsányi Albert anyaga

V–105.752/1–14a. Grősz József és társai

3.2.3. A III/I. Csoportfőnökség és jogelődjei által kezelt munkadossziék (Mt-dossziék)

Mt–764/1–8. "Amadeo ("Ligeti Béla" és "Arnold")

Mt–772/1–4. "Urbán"

Mt–807/1–3. "Ludwig Beron"

Mt–975/1–3. "Kőműves Sándor", "Franc Kirchenbauer"

3.2.4. A III/I. Csoportfőnökség és jogelődjei által kezelt kutatódossziék (K-dossziék)

K–318 Mindszenty-ügy

K–384/1–2. Kovrig Béla ["Bihari"]

4.1. Állambiztonsági munkához készült háttéranyagok

A–3240 Magyar–amerikai kapcsolatok, 1945–1965

Archives du Ministères des Affaires étrangères (Paris) (AMAE)

Europe 1944–1949, Hongrie, dossier 16–17. Politique intérieure

Europe 1944–1949, Hongrie, dossier 18. Questions religieuses

Europe 1944–1949, Hongrie, dossier 29. Culture

Europe 1944–1949, Saint-Siège, dossier 6, 8–10.

Europe 1949–1955, Hongrie, dossier 51–53. Questions religieuses

Europe 1949–1955, Saint-Siège, dossier 15, 26–29.

Europe 1956–1960, Hongrie, dossier 101–103, 153–154. Questions religieuses

Europe 1956–1960, Saint-Siège, dossier 45, 49, 69.

Europe 1961–1970, Saint-Siège, dossier 69, 77, 135.

Europe, Hongrie, versement aux Archives (1971–juin 1976), boîte 3330, dossier Questions religieuses

Archives of the Archdiocese of New York (New York, Yonkers) (AANY)

Collection 007 Francis Cardinal Spellman Collection

Arkhiv Vneshney Politiki Rossiyskoy Federatsii (Moscow) (AVP RF)
(Archive of Foreign Policy of the Russian Federation)

Fond 077 Referatura po Vengrii

Fond 77 Referatura po Vengrii

Fond 56b Otdel pechati, Vatikan 1945–1948

Fond 0453 Soyuz Kontrolnoi Komissii, Vengria 1945–1947

Budapest Főváros Levéltára (Budapest) (BFL, Budapest City Archives)

XXV. 1. a. A jogszolgáltatás területi szervei (1945–2003). Budapesti Népbíróság iratai (1945–1949). Büntetőperes iratok (1945–1949)
 293/1946. IV. Szálasi Ferenc és társai
 254/1949. Mindszenty József és társai

XXV. 4. f. Fővárosi Bíróság (1951–1953 Budapesti Megyei Bíróság) iratai (1958–2000). Titkos ügykezelés [TÜK] alól kivont perek iratai (1951–1980)
 105.752/2-a. Grősz-per
 1003/1949/3. Matheovits Ferenc és társai
 4016/I./1957. Turcsányi Albert Egon és társai
 8017/VIII./1958. Kósa Pál és társai

Budapesti Fegyház és Börtön Irattára (Budapest) (Archives of Budapest Prison)

Fogoly-gyűjtőkönyv, 1949

Csornai Premontrei Prépostság Szombathelyi Rendház Könyvtára (Szombathely)
(Library of the Szombathely Monastery of the Premonstratensian Provostship of Csorna)

Dwight D. Eisenhower Presidential Library (Abilene, Kansas) (Eisenhower Library)

Central Files, Official File, Of 154-L War Claims, Box 823, 874.

Herter Christian A., Papers, 1957–61, Box 1–2, 4, 6, 10, 18.

Papers as President of the United States, 1953–61. [Ann Whitman File] DDE Diary Series, Box 17–20, 23, 27.

Papers of John Foster Dulles, White House Memoranda Series. Box 6.

Republican National Committee News Clippings, Box 274.

Staff Secretary Records, 1952–1961 Subject Series, State Department Subseries, Box 1–4.

Egyházmegyei Levéltár, Győr (GyPL, Diocesan Archive, Győr: Episcopal Archive)
Egyházkormányzati iratok, 1944–1949

Gosudarstvennyi Arkhiv Rossiyskoy Federatsii (Moscow) (GARF)
(State Archives of the Russian Federation)

Fond 6991 op. 1–6.
Fond 9401 op. 2. delo (file) 240. Osobaya papka (paper folder) 1–2.

Harry S. Truman Library (Independence, Missouri) (Truman Library)
(A collection formed by Szabina Bognár as part of her own research)

Of 226 Hungary Misc. Mindszenty Folder to Of 227 Farm Matters Misc. (1950–53) Box 970.
Records Group 46. Record of US Senate. Senate Committee on Foreign Relations. Selected Documents, January 25–April 5, 1949. Box 5.

Hoover Institution Archives (Stanford, California)

Florian, Tibor Box 6.

John F. Kennedy Presidential Library and Museum (Boston, Massachusetts)
(Kennedy Library)

Papers of President Kennedy
Departments and Agencies, Box 284, 284A, 285, 285A, 286, 287, 286A, 287A, 288,
National Security Files, Countries – Hungary General, 1961–1962; 1963. Box 105, 105A,
President's Office Files, Countries – Hungary, Box 65, 65A, 118, 118A.

Kalocsai Főegyházmegyei Levéltár (Kalocsa)
(KFL, The Archives of the Archdiocese of Kalocsa)

I.1.a. Egyházkormányzati iratok
Püspökkari iratok 1945–1975
I.1.c. Perszonális iratok
Grősz József iratai, a Grősz-per visszaszolgáltatott dokumentumai

Lyndon Baines Johnson Library and Museum (Austin, Texas) (Johnson Library)

National Security Files, Country Files, Hungary, Cardinal Mindszenty Correspondence, Box 195.

Magyar Rádió Hangarchívuma (Budapest) (Hungarian Radio's Voice Archive)
Mindszenty József és társai pere, 1–12. magnószalag-tekercs

Magyar Nemzeti Levéltár Országos Levéltára (Budapest)
(MNL OL, The National Archives of Hungary)

K Államfői hivatali levéltár. Kormányzói kabinetiroda
K Miniszterelnökségi levéltár. Miniszterelnökség
  K 27 Minisztertanácsi jegyzőkönyvek, 1919–1944
K Belügyminisztériumi levéltár. Belügyminisztérium
  K 148 Elnöki iratok
  K 149 Reservált iratok
M–KS 276. f. Magyar Dolgozók Pártja központi szervei
M–KS 288. f. MSZMP központi szervei
  5. Politikai Bizottság (Intéző Bizottság), 1956–1975
  7. Titkárság, 1957–1975
  9. Központi Bizottság Irodája, 1956–1971
  22. Agitációs és Propaganda Osztály (Társadalompolitikai Osztály), 1956–1971
  32. Külügyi Osztály (Nemzetközi Pártkapcsolatok Osztálya), 1957–1971
XVIII Az államhatalom felsőbb szervei
  XVIII–1–b Nemzetgyűlés általános iratai
  XVIII–2–b Népköztársaság Elnöki Tanácsa jegyzőkönyvei
  XVIII–4 Nemzeti Főtanács
  XVIII–5 Nemzetgyűlés Politikai Bizottsága
XIX–A Az államigazgatás felsőbb szervei. Központi (nem miniszteriális) kormányzati szervek iratai.
  XIX–A–1 Miniszterelnökség. Minisztertanács elnökének hivatala (1944–1949)
    XIX–A–1–e Nagy Ferenc miniszterelnök, 1946–1947
    XIX–A–1–j Nemzeti Kormány Miniszterelnökségének általános iratai (1944) 1945–1949
  XIX–A–2 Minisztertanács Titkársága
    XIX–A–2–ab Dobi István miniszterelnök
  XIX–A–21 Állami Egyházügyi Hivatal
    XIX–A–21–a Elnöki iratok
    XIX–A–21–c Adattár
    XIX–A–21–d Visszaminősített TÜK iratok, 1957–1975
    XIX–A–21–e Tematikusan rendezett iratok, 28–34. d.

XIX–A–83 Minisztertanács (Testület)

XIX–A–83–a Jegyzőkönyvek és mellékleteik

XIX–I Kultúra

XIX–I–1 Vallás- és Közoktatásügyi Minisztérium

XIX–I–1–v Ortutay Gyula miniszter, 1947–1950

XIX–J Külügy

XIX–J–1 Külügyminisztérium

XIX–J–1–c Magyar békedelegáció

XIX–J–1–d Mindszenty-gyűjtemény, 1945–1960

XIX–J–1–j TÜK iratok

1945–1964; 1964–1975: Amerikai Egyesült Államok; Ausztrália; Ausztria; Jugoszlávia; Kanada; Kolumbia; Olaszország, Szovjetunió; Vatikán; Venezuela

XIX–J–29–a Washingtoni nagykövetség, TÜK iratok, 1–12. d.

XIX–J–30–a Párizsi nagykövetség, TÜK iratok, 1948–1949

XIX–J–42–a Moszkvai nagykövetség, TÜK iratok, 2, 8. d.

XX A jogszolgáltatás felsőbb szervei

XX–5–h Legfelsőbb Bíróság. Visszaminősített büntető TÜK iratok (korábbi elnevezése: 1956 utáni koncepciós perek iratai), Nagy Imre és társai

P233 Ferences Szűz Mária Rendtartománya/Ferences Rendtartomány Levéltára, 4–16. csomó

Magyar Nemzeti Levéltár Zala Megyei Levéltára (Zalaegerszeg)
(MNL ZML, National Archives of Hungary Zala County Archives)

IV.401. Zala vármegye főispánjának iratai

IV.402. Zala vármegye Törvényhatósági Bizottságának iratai, 1918–1944

IV.404. Zala vármegye alispánjának iratai, 1919–1944

V.1606. Zalaegerszeg város képviselőtestületének jegyzőkönyvei, 1918–1944

V.1607 Zalaegerszeg város polgármesterének iratai

VII.2. Zalaegerszegi Kir. Törvényszék iratai, Bűnügyek (politikai) kiemelt csomók, 1920–1944

XIV.23. Gr. Teleki Béla főispán személyi iratai (1906–1969), 4, 6. doboz

Magyar Tudományos Akadémia Kézirattára (Budapest)
(Manuscript Collection of the Hungarian Academy of Sciences)

Mihályfi Ernő hagyatéka

Magyarországi Mindszenty Alapítvány Levéltára, Mindszenty Archívum (Budapest) (MMAL) (Archives of the Hungarian Mindszenty Foundation, Mindszenty Archives)

Tematikus dossziék rendezés utáni besorolásban: 010–017, 020/a–e, 024, 026, 030/a–b, 031–032, 040, 040/a–b, 041–042, 044–045, 054, 060, 061/a–b, 062, 086.

Tematikus dossziék rendezés előtti besorolásban: 801–803, 805–806, 808, 810–813.

Tematikus gyűjtők: 45–46, 50.

Ministero degli Affari Esteri, Archivio Storico-Diplomatico (Rome) (ASDMAE)

Affari Politici 1931–1945 Ungheria, Busta 37.

Affari Politici 1946–1950 Ungheria, Busta 2, 5–6, 8, 10–11, 14.

Affari Politici 1950–1957 Ungheria, Busta 1152, 1177, 1218, 1250, 1286, 1342, 1376–1380.

Affari Politici 1946–1950 Santa Sede, Busta 2–3, 6, 10, 13, 19.

Ambasciata d'Italia presso la Santa Sede 1946–1954, Busta 229.

Direzione generale affari politici raccolta generale 1947–1960, Busta 23.

National Archives and Records Administration (College Park, Maryland) (NARA)

Records Group (RG) 59. General Records of the Department of State. Central Decimal File 1945–49, Box 6887, 6888.

RG 59. General Records of the Department of State. Central Decimal File, 1955–1959 Box 4805, 4806.

RG 59. General Records of the Department of State. Central Decimal File 1960–1963, Box 2681.

RG 59. General Records of the Department of State. Central Decimal File 1963–1971, Box 3067, 3068, 3229, 4209.

RG 59. General Records of the Department of State. Central Foreign Policy Files 1967–69. Box 3071.

RG 59. General Records of the Department of State. Bureau of European Affairs, Office of Eastern European Affairs. Records Relating to Hungary 1941–1977, Box 1–12.

RG 59. General Records of the Department of State. Central Foreign Policy Files 1964–66, Box 3222.

RG 59. General Records of the Department of State. Bureau of Intelligence and Research Office of Soviet and East European Analysis, Intelligence Reports on the USSR and Eastern Europe 1942–1960, Box 3, 15.

RG 84. Foreign Service Posts of the Department of State, Hungary, Budapest Mission, General Records 1945, Box 64–66.

RG 84. Foreign Service Posts of the Department of State. Hungary, Budapest Legation, General Records 1946, Box 103.
RG 84. Foreign Service Posts of the Department of State. Hungary, Budapest Legation, General Records 1948, Box 13, 145, 147, 156, 161–163, 167, 172, 174, 176.
RG 84. Foreign Service Posts of the Department of State. Hungary, Budapest Legation, General Records 1953–55, Box 179.
RG 84. Records of the Foreign Service Posts of the Department of State. Hungary, General Records 1946–1963, Box 4.
RG 84. Foreign Service Posts of the Department of State. Hungary, Budapest, Subject Files Relating to Cardinal Mindszenty, 1956–1972 Box 1–6.

Országos Széchényi Könyvtár (Budapest) (OSZK, National Széchényi Library)

Kézirattár

107/83. fond Udvardy Jenőné iratai
177. fond Keresztury Dezső iratanyaga
216. fond Nagy Töhötöm iratanyaga
514. fond Gereben István iratanyaga

Österreichisches Staatsarchiv (Wien) (ÖStA)

Archiv der Republik, Bundesministerium für Auswärtige Angelegenheiten, 1945–1975

Pécsi Püspöki Levéltár (Pécs) (PPL) (Episcopal Archives of Pécs)

Egyházkormányzati iratok, 1944–1948
Cserháti József irathagyatéka, 9, 12. mappa
Rogács Ferenc püspök irathagyatéka, 1944–1961, 44–45, 87. iratköteg

Piarista Rend Magyar Tartományának Központi Levéltára (Budapest) (PMKL, Central Archive of the Hungarian Province of the Piarist Order)

Tartományfőnöki levelezés
IV. 198. Tomek Vince hagyatéka
IV. 213. Albert István hagyatéka

Politikatörténeti és Szakszervezeti Levéltár (Budapest) (PIL, The Archives of Political History and of Trade Unions)

I. Pártok

274. f. Magyar Kommunista Párt (MKP)

VI. Személyi gyűjtemények
704. f. Károlyi Mihály és Károlyi Mihályné Andrássy Katinka
867. f. Visszaemlékezések
VIII. Külföldi levéltárakból származó magyar vonatkozású iratmásolatok
508. f. Nyugat-Európa és az Amerikai Egyesült Államok levéltárai
1. állag Nagy-Britannia, National Archives, London

Praha Ministerstvo Zahraničných Vecí (Prague) (Ministry of Foreign Affairs)

Teritorialni odbory – obyčejné (TO-O) 1945–1959. Maďarsko
Teritorialni odbory – obyčejné (TO-O) 1945–1959. Vatikán

Prímási Levéltár (Esztergom) (PL, Primatial Archives)

Cat. D/c (until 1939)
Egyházkormányzati iratok, 1939–1955
Fotótár – Mindszenty
Mindszenty magánlevéltár, 1–47. doboz
Processus Josephi Card. Mindszenty – Mindszenty periratok V–700, 1–21. doboz

Richard Nixon Presidential Library and Museum (Yorba Linda, California)

Wilderness Years Collection, Series II: Trip File, 1963. Box 3. Budapest, Hungary
Nixon Presidential Materials Staff, National Security Council (NSC) Files, POW/MIA President's Daily Briefs, Box 1.
Nixon Presidential Materials Staff, National Security Council (NSC) Files, President's Trip Files, Box 463.
Nixon Presidential Materials Staff, National Security Council (NSC) Files, Country Files – Europe, Box 693, 732.
Nixon Presidential Materials Staff, National Security Council (NSC) Files, Presidential Correspondence 1969–1974. Box 755.
Nixon Presidential Materials Staff, National Security Council (NSC) Files, Name Files, Box 828.
White House Central Files (WHCF) Staff Member and Office Files Michael P. Balzano, JR.
White House Special Files (WHSF), Subject Files: Confidential Files, 1969–1974, Box 35.
White House Subject Files, Religious Matters (RM), Box 19.

Rossiiskii Gosudarstvennyi Arkhiv Noveishei Istorii (Moscow)
(RGANI) (Russian State Archive of Contemporary History)

Fond 2. op. 1. delo (file) 635.
Fond 5. op. 16. delo (file) 689–690.
Fond 5. op. 30. delo (file) 10, 53, 126, 146, 162, 190.
Fond 5. op. 28. delo (file) 476.
Fond 5. op. 33. delo (file) 162, 190.
Fond 5. op. 34. delo (file) 57.
Fond 5. op. 55. delo (file) 10, 72.

Rossiiskii Gosudarstvennyi Arkhiv Sotsial'no-Politicheskoi Istorii (Moscow)
(RGASPI) (Russian State Archive of Socio-Political History)

Fond 17 Tsentralnyi Komitet VK(b)P
op. 128. Otdel vneshney politiki
Fond 74 K. J. The Voroshilov papers
Fond 82 The Molotov papers
Fond 588 Stalin's personal archive

Szeged-Csanádi Püspökség Levéltára (Szeged) (SzCsPL)
(Archives of the Episcopate of Szeged-Csanád)

I.1.a. Egyházkormányzati iratok 1944–1949
IV. Hagyatékok

Székesfehérvári Püspöki és Székeskáptalani Levéltár (Székesfehérvár)
(Episcopal and Cathedral Chapter Archives of Székesfehérvár)

Egyházkormányzati iratok
ÁEH iratok, 74/70. csomó

Szent István Társulat Irattára (Budapest) (Archive of the Saint Stephen's Association)

Esty Miklós irathagyatéka

Szombathelyi Egyházmegyei Könyvtár (Szombathely)
(SZEK, Szombathely Diocesan Library)

Ős. XXVIII/alsó I–II.

Szombathelyi Egyházmegyei Levéltár (Szombathely)
(SZEL, Szombathely Diocesan Archive)

I. 1. Acta Cancellariae (AC) 1912–1945
Géfin Gyula hagyatéka
Pehm József iratai, 1–6. d.
Mikes János püspök iratai, Missilis

Szociális Testvérek Társasága Történeti Irattára (Budapest)
(SZTTTI, Historical Archives of the Sisters of Social Service)

The National Archives of the UK (London)

Foreign Office (FO)
Religious affairs: proposal to accredit Vatican representative to Hungary: position of Prince Primate, Cardinal Mindszenty, archbishop of Esztergom: Soviet reactions. Code 21 File 436
Legation, Vatican: General Correspondence, FO 380/128: Hungary 1948
Political Departments: General Correspondence from 1906–1966. NORTHERN (N): Hungary (NH), FO 371/171776: Roman Catholic Church, 1960, 1961, 1963
Political Departments, General Correspondence from 1906–1966. SOUTHERN (R): Hungary (RH). FO 371/95231
Foreign Office and Commonwealth Office (FCO)
Northern Department and East European and Soviet Department: Registered Files (N and EN Series). HUNGARY. Social. Religious affairs: Cardinal Mindszenty, 1967–1968

United Nations Archives and Records Management Section (New York)

Peace-Keeping Operations Files of the Secretary-General, U Thant. Other Countries Series 0878, Box 1, File 16.

Veszprémi Érseki és Főkáptalani Levéltár (Veszprém)
(VÉL, Archives of the Archdiocese and Cathedral Chapter of Veszprém)

Egyházmegyei Hatóság iratai
I.1.2. Litterae Circulares
I.1.41. Bullae
I.1.43. Archivum Kollerianum
I.1.44.a. Acta dioecesana, Iktatott iratok

Hagyatékok

VIII.25. Mindszenty József hagyatéka [Legacy of József Mindszenty]

Zalaegerszegi Mária Magdolna Plébánia Irattára (Zalaegerszeg)
(ZMMPI, Archive of the Parish Church of Mária Magdolna, Zalaegerszeg)

Egyházközség 1. (Vegyes iratok.)

Egyházközség képviselő-testületi jegyzőkönyvek

1930–1940; 1940–1970

Esperesi iratok

1919–1929; 1930–1932; 1935–1937; 1935–1940; 1942–1957

II. PRINTED SOURCES

II.1. József Mindszenty's Works in Chronological Order

Pehm, József. *Az édesanya* [Mother]. 2nd ed. Budapest: Stephaneum Nyomda, 1916.

———. *Vigyázzatok az újsággal!* [Beware of the newspaper!] Zalaegerszeg: Zalaegerszegi Sajtóbizottság, n. d. [1920].

———. "Egy sajtóstatisztika" [A Press Statistic]. *Egyházi Lapok – Papok Közlönye* 46, no. 12 (1923): 128.

———. *Zala segélykiáltása* [Zala's cry for help]. Zalaegerszeg: [s. n.], 1927.

———. *Padányi Biró Márton veszprémi püspök élete és kora* [The life and times of Márton Padányi Biró, the bishop of Veszprém]. A veszprémi egyházmegye múltjából, no. 2. Zalaegerszeg: Zrínyi Nyomdaipari Rt., 1934. Reprinted in Miskolc: Mindszenty József Emlékmúzeum Alapítvány, 2012.

———. *Az édesanya* [Mother]. 2 vols. 3rd ext. ed. Zalaegerszeg: Zrínyi Nyomdaipari Rt., 1940–42.

Mindszenty, József. *Die Mutter*. Luzern: Rex, 1949. Fifth edition published in 1951.

———. *Moeder: Ein Loflied op het moederschap*. 2nd ed. Utrecht: Fontein Utrecht, 1949. Third edition published in 1950.

———, Cardinal. *The Mother*. Dublin: Clonmore and Reynolds, 1949. Reprinted in Post Falls, ID, 2008.

[———.] *Weissbuch: Vier Jahre Kirchenkampf in Ungarn*. Zürich: Thomas Verlag, 1949. Simoultaneously published in Hamburg: Drei Türme Verlag, 1949.

———. *Mutter in Gottes Augen*. Luzern: Rex, 1950.

———. *La Madre*. Milano, Edizioni Paoline, 1950. Reprinted in Alba, 1950; Milano, 1957, 1960; Catania, 1968.

———. *The Face of the Heavenly Mother*. New York: Philosophical Library, 1951.

———. *A mãe*. Lisbon–Coimbra: Editorial Aster, 1951.

———. *La mère, miroir de Dieu*. Tours: Mame, 1953. Reprinted in Paris: Mame, 1996.

———, Cardenal. *La madre*. Madrid: Patmos, 1951. Reprinted in Madrid: Rialp, 1958.

[———.] *Mindszenty-Dokumentation, I–III. Reden, Hirtenbriefe, Presseerklärungen*. Edited with notes and an introduction by Josef Vecsey and Johann Schwendemann. St. Pölten, 1956–1959.

Vecsey, József, comp. *Mindszenty okmánytár: Pásztorlevelek, beszédek, nyilatkozatok* [The Mindszenty Papers. Pastoral Letters, Sermons, and Statements]. Vol. 1. *Mindszenty tanítása* [Mindszenty's Teachings]. Munich: [s. n.], 1957.

———. *Mindszenty okmánytár: Pásztorlevelek, beszédek, nyilatkozatok*. Vol. 2. *Mindszenty harca* [Mindszenty's Struggle]. [s. n.] München, 1957.

———. *Mindszenty okmánytár: Pásztorlevelek, beszédek, nyilatkozatok*. Vol. 3. *Mindszenty áldozata* [Mindszenty's Sacrifice]. [s. n.] München, 1957.

Mindszenty, József. "Egy különös sorsú nemzet" [A Nation with a Special Fate]. I–XII.fejezet. Unpublished manuscript. Magyarországi Mindszenty Alapítvány Levéltára, Mindszenty Archívum, [1957–1971]

———. *La madre agli a los ojos de Dios*. Bilbao: Ediciones Paulinas, 1961.

———. *"...the World's Most Orphaned Nation."* New York: Publisher Julius Tarlo, 1962.

———. *Emlékirataim* [My Memoirs]. Toronto: Vörösváry, 1974.

———. *Erinnerungen*. Translated by József Vecsey and Felix. Eisenring. Frankfurt a.M.–Berlin–Vienna: Verlag Ullstein–Propyläen Verlag, 1974.

———. *Memoirs*. Translated by Richard Winston and Clara Winston. New York: Macmillan, London: Weidenfeld and Nicolson, 1974.

———. *Mémoires: Des prisons d'Hitler et de Staline ...à l'exil*. Paris: Table Ronde, 1974.

———. *Emlékirataim* [My Memoirs]. 2nd ed. Vaduz: Mindszenty Alapítvány, 1975.

———. *Memorie*. Translated from German by Biagio Marenco. Milano, 1975.

———. *Napi jegyzetek: Budapest, Amerikai Követség 1956–1971* [Daily Notes: The US Embassy, Budapest, 1956–1971]. Compiled by Iván Batthyány, M. J. Hillenbrand, and Emil Csonka. Vaduz: Mindszenty Alapítvány, 1979.

———. *Hirdettem az igét: Válogatott szentbeszédek és körlevelek, 1944–1975* [I preached the Word: Selected sermons and pastoral letters, 1944–1975]. Compiled by József Közi Horváth. Vaduz: Mindszenty Alapítvány, 1982.

———. *Emlékirataim* [My Memoirs]. 3rd ed. Kardinal-Mindszenty-Stiftung, Vaduz, 1988.

———. *Emlékirataim* [My Memoirs]. 4th ed. Budapest: Szent István Társulat, 1989.
———. *Emlékirataim* [My Memoirs]. 5th ed. Budapest: Magyarországi Mindszenty Alapítvány–Don Bosco Kiadó, 2002.
———. *Az édesanya*. Budapest: Hunikum–Zrínyi, 1990.
———. *Emlékirataim*. Edited and redacted by Viktor Soós and Attila Zoltán Kovács. Budapest: Helikon Kiadó, 2015.

II.2. Periodicals

Acta Apostolicae Sedis. Commentarium Officiale. Città del Vaticano: Typis Polyglottis Vaticanis, 1945–1976
Életünk. Sankt Gallen, 1969–1977
Esti Szabad Szó. Budapest: Sarló Lapkiadó, 1945–1948
Északmagyarország. Miskolc: [s. n.], 1945–1946
Haladás. Budapest: Hungária, 1945–1947
Katolikus Szemle. Rome, 1949–1979
Katolikus Magyarok Vasárnapja. Cleveland [s. n.], 1949
Kommentár. Budapest, 2006–
L'Osservatore Romano. Giornale quotidiano politico religioso. Città del Vaticano, 1945–
Magyar Egyháztörténeti Vázlatok. Budapest, 1989–
Magyar Szemle. Budapest, 1992–
Magyar Hírlap. Budapest, 1945–1948
Magyar Kurír. Budapest [Actio Catholica], 1945–
Népszava. Budapest, 1945–1948
Népszabadság. Budapest, Hírlapkiadó, MSZMP, 1957–1975
Szabad Nép. Budapest, Szabadság Lapkiadó, 1945–1950
Tartós Békéért, Népi Demokráciáért. Belgrade (Budapest: Szabadság Lapkiadó), 1948–1949
Új Ember. Katolikus hetilap. Budapest, 1945–1975
Veszprémi Hírlap. Veszprém, 1944
Veszprémi Népújság. Veszprém [s. n.], 1944
Veszprémvármegye. Veszprém [s. n.], 1944
Vigilia. Budapest, 1935–
Zalai Hírlap. Zalaegerszeg, 1935–1940
Zalai Magyar Élet. Zalaegerszeg, 1940–1944
Zalai Napló. Zalaegerszeg, 1933–1935
Zalavármegye. Zalaegerszeg, 1922–1933
Zalamegyei Ujság. Zalaegerszeg, [1918]–1944

III. Literature

A Mindszenty bűnügy okmányai [The Mindszenty criminal papers]. Budapest: Athenaeum, 1949.

Adibekov, G. M., A. Di B'yadzho, L. Ya. Gibianskiy, F. Gori, and S. Pons., eds., *Soveshchaniya Kominforma 1947, 1948, 1949. Dokumenty i materialy*. Moscow: ROSSPEN, 1998.

Adriányi, Gábor. "A prímási szék megüresedetté nyilvánítása 1974-ben" [The announcement of the vacation of the Primatial See in 1974]. *Vigilia* 63, no. 6 (1998): 425–28.

———. *Die Ostpolitik des Vatikans 1958–1978 gegenüber Ungarn: Der Fall Kardinal Mindszenty*. Studien zur Geschichte Ost- und Ostmitteleuropas, 3. Herne: Schäfer, 2003.

———. "Miért és hogyan hagyta el Mindszenty József a budapesti amerikai követséget?" [Why and how did József Mindszenty leave the US Embassy in Budapest]. In *Mindszenty József emlékezete*, edited by József Török, 73–89. Budapest: Márton Áron Kiadó, 1995.

András, Imre, ed. *Kerkai Jenő emlékezete* [Remembering Jenő Kerkai]. Budapest: Kerkai Jenő Egyházszociológiai Intézet, 1995.

Artner, Tivadar. "A bíborosról, gyerekszemmel" [On the Cardinal through a child's eyes: In Memoriam József Mindszenty]. *Vigilia* 58, no. 8 (1993): 582–89.

Bain, Leslie Balogh. *The Reluctant Satellites: An Eyewitness Report on East Europe and the Hungarian Revolution*. New York: Macmillan, 1960.

Balogh, Margit, ed. *A Magyar Katolikus Püspöki Kar tanácskozásai 1949–1965 között: Dokumentumok* [Meetings of the Hungarian Catholic Bishops' Conference, 1949–1965: Documents]. 2 vols. Budapest: METEM, 2008.

———. "Az 1971. szeptember 9-ei magyar–szentszéki megállapodás" [The Hungarian–Vatican agreement of September 9, 1971]. *Századok* 147, no. 4 (2014): 875–930.

———. "Die Erinnerungen. Gedanken und Tatsachen zur Erinnerungen von József Kardinal Mindszenty." In Szabó, *József Kardinal Mindszenty in Wien*, 144–62.

———. "'...do not forget this small honest nation': József Mindszenty, the archbishop of Esztergom in the Documents of the National Archives and Records Administration (USA). Part II. 1956–1971." *Prague Papers on the History of International Relations* 18, no. 2 (2013): 173–83.

———. "'...I beg Your Excellency, that you take steps': József Mindszenty the archbishop of Esztergom in the Documents of the National Archives and Records Administration (USA). Part I. 1945–1948." *Prague Papers on the History of International Relations* 18, no. 1 (2013): 170–79.

———. "Two Visits – Two Eras: The Canadian Tours of Cardinal Joseph Mindszenty, 1947 and 1973." *Hungarian Studies Review* 40, no. 2 (2013): 123–46.

———. "József Kardinal Mindszenty und der Schutz der Menschenrechte am Ende des Zweiten Weltkrieges." *Ungarn Jahrbuch* 31 (2014): 363–412.

———. *Kardinal József Mindszenty. Ein Leben zwischen kommunistisher Diktatur und Kaltem Krieg*. Berlin: Osteuropa Zentrum, 2014.

———. *Mindszenty József (1892–1975)* I–II. Budapest: MTA Bölcsészettudományi Kutatóközpont, 2015.

Balogh, Margit, András Fejérdy, and Csaba Szabó. "Az 1964-es magyar–szentszéki részleges megállapodás" [The Hungarian–Vatican partial agreement of 1964], *ArchívNet* 18, no. 6. (2018), on the Internet: http://www.archivnet.hu/az-1964-es-magyar-szentszeki-reszleges-megallapodas

Balogh, Sándor and Lajos Izsák, eds. *Magyarországi pártprogramok 1944–1988* [Party programs in Hungary, 1944–1988]. Budapest: ELTE Eötvös Kiadó, 2004.

Balogh, Sándor, Karola Némethné Vágyi, and Levente Sipos, eds. *A Magyar Szocialista Munkáspárt ideiglenes vezető testületeinek jegyzőkönyvei. I. 1956. november 11.–1957. január 14* [Minutes of the provisory leading body of the HSWP. Vol. 1, November 11, 1956 – January 14, 1957]. Budapest: Intera Rt., 1993.

Bandi, István. "Adalékok a Pápai Magyar Intézet történetéhez, állambiztonsági módszertani megközelítésben" [Information on the history of the Hungarian Papal Institute, using a state security methodological approach]. In *Csapdában: Tanulmányok a katolikus egyház történetéből, 1945–1989* [Trapped: Studies on the history of the Catholic Church, 1945–1989], edited by Gábor Bánkuti and György Gyarmati, 189–205. Budapest: ÁBTL, 2010.

Bánkuti, Gábor. "Mócsy Imre jezsuita szerzetes római küldetése, és ami utána következett" [The mission to Rome of the Jesuit monk Imre Mócsy, and subsequent events]. In *Megértő történelem: Tanulmányok a hatvanéves Gyarmati György tiszteletére* [A History that shows understanding: Studies in honor of György Gyarmati at sixty], edited by Magdolna Baráth, Gábor Bánkuti, and János Rainer M., 173–81. Budapest: L'Harmattan Kiadó, 2011.

Barankovics, István. *A katolikus hit és az egyház helyzete Magyarországon* [The Catholic faith and the situation of the Church in Hungary]. New York: Hungarian Quarterly, 1963.

Baráth, Magdolna. "Soviet Counsellors at the Hungarian State Security Organs." In *NKVD/KGB Activities and Cooperation with other Secret Services in Central and Eastern Europe 1945–1989*, edited by A. Grúňová, 87–99. Bratislava: Ústav Pamati Naroda, 2008.

———. *Szovjet diplomáciai jelentések Magyarországról a Hruscsov-korszakban* [Soviet diplomatic reports from Hungary during the Khurshchev era]. Budapest: Napvilág Kiadó–Politikatörténeti Intézet, 2012.

Baráth, Magdolna and István Feitl, eds. *Lehallgatott kihallgatások: Rákosi és Gerő pártvizsgálatának titkos hangszalagjai, 1962* [Bugged interrogations. The secret voice tapes of Rákosi and Gerő's Party inquiry, 1962]. Budapest: Napvilág Kiadó–ÁBTL, 2013.

Barberini, Giovanni. *L'Ostpolitik della Santa Sede. Un dialogo lungo e faticoso.* Santa Sede e politica nel novecento vol. 6. Bologna: Il Mulino, 2007.

Barberini, Giovanni, ed. *La Politica del dialogo: Le carte Casaroli sull'Ostpolitik Vaticana.* Santa Sede e politica nel novecento 7. Bologna: Il Mulino, 2008.

Beke, Margit, ed. *A magyar katolikus püspökkari tanácskozások története és jegyzőkönyvei 1919–1944 között* [The history and minutes of the meetings of the Hungarian Catholic Bishops' Conference, 1919–1944]. 2 vols. Munich–Budapest: Auróra, 1992.

———, ed. *A magyar katolikus püspökkari tanácskozások története és jegyzőkönyvei 1945–1948 között* [The history and minutes of the meetings of the Hungarian Catholic Bishops' Conference, 1945–1948]. Dissertationes Hungaricae ex historia Ecclesiae XIV. Cologne–Budapest: Argumentum, 1996. Republished in Budapest: MTA Bölcsészettudományi Kutatóközpont, 2015.

———. "Fejezetek az új- és legújabbkori elitképzéshez: A katolikus egyház szerepe a modern magyar értelmiségi elit nevelésében a bécsi Pázmáneumban" [Chapters on the training of the elite in modern and contemporary history: The role of the Catholic Church in the education of the Hungarian intellectual elite at the Collegium Pazmanianum in Vienna]. Doctoral Thesis, Budapest, 2010. real-d.mtak.hu/13/3/Beke.pdf

Békés, Csaba and Ágnes Tóth. "'Ha csak a bűnösöket büntetnék, hallgatnánk...' Mindszenty József levelei a hazai németség ügyében" [If the transgressors alone were to be punished, we would remain silent: József Mindszenty's letters on the matter of the German minority in Hungary]. *Forrás* 23, no. 7 (1991): 56–59.

Bibó, István. "1956. október 23–november 6.: Huszár Tibor interjúja" [October 23 – November 6, 1956. Interview by Tibor Huszár]. *Valóság* 32, no. 2 (1989): 52–67.

Borbándi, Gyula. *A magyar emigráció életrajza 1945–1985* [A biography of the Hungarian exiles, 1945–1985]. 2 vols. Budapest: Európa Kiadó, 1989.

Borhi, László. *A vasfüggöny mögött: Magyarország nagyhatalmi erőtérben 1945–1968* [Behind the Iron Curtain: Hungary in the space between the Great Powers]. Budapest: Ister, 2000.

———. *Magyar–amerikai kapcsolatok 1945–1989: Források* [Hungarian–US relations, 1945–1989: Sources]. Budapest: MTA Történettudományi Intézet, 2009.

———. "Távozási napló" [Departure diary]. *Heti Világgazdaság*, October 6, 2001, 98–100.

Bottoni, Stefano. "Egy különleges kapcsolat története: A magyar titkosszolgálat és a Szentszék, 1961–1978" [The history of a special relationship: The Hungarian secret service and the Holy See, 1961–1978]. In *Csapdában: Tanulmányok a katolikus egyház történetéből, 1945–1989* [Trapped: Studies on the history of the Catholic Church, 1945–1989], edited by Gábor Bánkuti and György Gyarmati, 261–89. Budapest. ÁBTL, 2010.

Braham, Randolph L., ed. *The Destruction of Hungarian Jewry: A documentary account.* 2 vols. New York: Pro Arte for the World Federation of Hungarian Jews, 1963.

Casaroli, Agostino. *The Martyrdom of Patience: The Holy See and the Communist Countries (1963–1989).* Toronto: Ave Maria Centre of Peace, 2007.

Chenaux, Philippe. *L'Église catholique et communisme en Europe (1917–1989): De Lénine à Jean-Paul II.* Paris: Les Éditions du Cerf, 2009.

Chernobaev, A. A., ed. *Na prieme u Stalina: Tetradi (zhurnaly) zapisei lits, priniatykh I. V. Stalinym (1924–1953 gg.)* Moscow: Noviy Hronograf, 2008.

Choma, Ivan. *Josyf Slipyj.* Milan: La Casa di Matriona, 2001.

Cseszka, Éva. *Gazdasági típusú perek, különös tekintettel az FM-perre (1945–1953)* [Trials of an economic kind, with the focus on the case involving the Ministry of Agriculture trial]. Budapest: Gondolat, 2012.

Csonka, Emil. "A kor és a bíboros" [The era and the Cardinal]. In József Mindszenty, *Napi jegyzetek: Budapest, Amerikai Követség 1956–1971*, 21–148. Vaduz: Mindszenty Alapítvány, 1979.

———. *A száműzött bíboros: Mindszenty az emigrációban* [The exiled cardinal: Mindszenty in exile]. San Francisco–Munich, Új Európa, 1976. (Second edition published in Szekszárd: Babits Kiadó, 1993.)

Cúthné Gyóni, Eszter, ed. *Egy fogoly apát feljegyzései: Endrédy Vendel zirci apát feljegyzései az ÁVH börtönében* [The notes of an imprisoned abbot: The notes of Vendel Endrédy, abbot of Zirc, written in the State Protection Authority's prison]. Budapest: METEM–ÁBTL, 2013.

Dobri, Mária. "'...szívélyesen üdvözöl barátod és híved...' (Pehm [Mindszenty] József és Géfin Gyula barátságáról)" ['...warm greetings from your friend and supporter...' About the friendship between József (Mindszenty) Pehm and Gyula Géfin]. *Vasi Szemle* 49, no. 2 (1995): 273–85.

Eckhart, Ferenc. *A Szentkorona-eszme története* [The history of the concept of the Holy Crown]. Budapest: MTA, 1941.

Erdő, Péter. *Egyházjog* [Canon Law]. Budapest: Szent István Társulat, 1992.

Farkas, Vladimir. *Nincs mentség: Az ÁVH alezredese voltam* [There's no excuse: I was a State Protection Authority Lieutenant-Colonel]. Budapest: Interart, 1990.

Feiszt, György, ed. *Géfin Gyula emlékezete* [In memory of Gyula Géfin]. Acta Savariensia, vol. 20. Szombathely: Szombathely önkormányzata, 2008.

———. "Mindszenty a direktórium túsza" [Mindszenty, hostage of the Directory]. *Vasi Honismereti Közlemények* 19, no. 1 (1992): 17–18.

Feitl, István, ed. *A magyarországi Szövetséges Ellenőrző Bizottság jegyzőkönyvei 1945–1947* [The minutes of the Allied Control Commission in Hungary, 1945–1947]. Budapest: Napvilág Kiadó, 2003.

Fejérdy, András. "József Kardinal Mindszenty und die ungarischen Priester im Exil: Einfluss und Beirat." In Szabó, *József Kardinal Mindszenty in Wien*, 144–62.

———. "Mindszenty József szellemi portréja" [A spiritual portrait of József Mindszenty]. *Kommentár* 1, no. 4 (2006): 43–54. kommentar.info.hu/attachment/0001/423_kommentar0604.pdf

———, ed. *The Vatican "Ostpolitik" 1958–1978: Responsibility and Witness during John XXIII and Paul VI*. Rome: Bibliotheca Academiae Hungariae, 2015.

———. *Pressed by a Double Loyalty: Hungarian Attendance at the Second Vatican Council, 1959–1965*. Budapest and New York: Central European University Press, 2016.

Fenzl, Annemarie. "Kardinal König und Kardinal Mindszenty – die Ostpolitik des Vatikans." In Szabó, *József Kardinal Mindszenty in Wien*, 59–79.

Föglein, Gizella. *Államforma és államfői jogkör Magyarországon 1944–1949* [The form of government and the powers of the head of state in Hungary, 1944–1949]. Budapest: Osiris Kiadó, 2001.

Foreign Relations of the United States, 1955–1957. General editor: John P. Glennon. Vol. XXV, part 1, *Eastern Europe*, edited by Edward C. Keefer, Ronald D. Landa, and Stanley Shaloff. Washington D.C.: United States Government Printing Office, 1990.

Foreign Relations of the United States, 1958–1960. General editor: Glenn W. LaFantasie. Vol. X, part 1, *Eastern Europe Region, Soviet Union, Cyprus*, edited by Ronald D. Landa, James E. Miller, David S. Patterson, and Charles S. Sampson. Washington, D.C.: United States Government Printing Office, 1993.

Foreign Relations of the United States, 1969–1976. General editor: Edward C. Keefer. Vol. XXIX, part 1, *Eastern Europe; Eastern Mediterranean, 1969–1972*, edited by James

E. Miller, Douglas E. Selvage, and Laurie Van Hook. Washington D.C.: United States Government Printing Office, 2007.

Füzér, Julián, ed. *Szentnek kiáltjuk! Emigrációs magyarok Mindszenty bíborosról, halálának 10. évfordulóján* [We proclaim him a Saint!: Hungarians in exile on Cardinal Mindszenty, on the tenth anniversary of his death]. Youngstown, OH: Katolikus Magyarok Vasárnapja, 1987.

Gannon, Robert I. *The Cardinal Spellman Story*. Garden City, NY: Doubleday & Company, 1962.

Gárdonyi, Máté. "Mindszenty József somogyi plébánia-alapításai" [Parishes established by József Mindszenty in Somogy County]. In *Somogy megye múltjából: Levéltári évkönyv, 33*. [From the past of Somogy County: Archival Yearbook, 33], edited by László Szántó, 165–80. Kaposvár: Somogy Megyei Levéltár, 2002.

Gecsényi, Lajos, ed. *Iratok Magyarország és Ausztria kapcsolatainak történetéhez 1956–1964* [Documents on the history of relations between Hungary and Austria]. Budapest: MNL OL, 2000.

———. "A Demokrata Néppárt 'igazoló jelentése' a Mindszenty József bíboros hercegprímással keletkezett konfliktusáról" [The "verification report" of the Democratic People's Party on the conflict with Cardinal József Mindszenty, Hungarian Primate]. *Századok* 127, nos. 5–6 (1993): 761–80.

———. "Fürst Pál Esterházy im Mindszenty-Prozess." In *Paul Esterházy, 1901–1989: Ein Leben im Zeitalter der Extreme*, edited by Stefan August Lütgenau, 85–131. Innsbruck–Vienna–Bozen, 2005.

———. "Mindszenty (Pehm) József politikai tevékenysége az 1930-as években" [The political activity of József Mindszenty (Pehm) in the 1930s]. In *Mindszenty József veszprémi püspök 1944–1945* [József Mindszenty, bishop of Veszprém, 1944–1945], edited by Lajos T. Horváth, 6–16. Veszprém: Veszprémi érsekség–Veszprém Megyei Jogú Város Önkormányzata–Laczkó Dezső Múzeum, 1996.

———. *Gömbös Gyula: Vázlat egy politikai életrajzhoz* [Gyula Gömbös: Outline for a political biography]. Budapest: Elektra Kiadóház, 1999.

Gergely, Jenő and Lajos Izsák, comps. *A Mindszenty-per* [The Mindszenty trial]. Budapest: Reform Rt., 1989.

Göncz, László. *A muravidéki magyarság 1918–1941* [The Hungarians of the Mura Region, 1918–1941]. Lendva: Magyar Nemzetiségi Művelődési Intézet, 2001.

———. "'Álmaink álma Alsólendva és a Muraköz.' Mindszenty (Pehm) József erőfeszítései a Mura mente visszacsatolásáért" [The dream of our dreams, Lendava and the Međimurje: The efforts of József (Pehm) Mindszenty aimed at the re-annexation of the Mura area]. In *Zalai Múzeum*, vol. 21. Zalaegerszeg: Göcseji Múzeum, 2013. 45–58.

———. *Felszabadulás vagy megszállás? A Mura mente 1941–1945* [Liberation or Occupation? Aside the Mura, 1941–1945]. Lendva: Magyar Nemzetiségi Művelődési Intézet, 2006.

Gori, Francesca and Silvio Pons, eds. *Dagli archivi di Mosca: L'Urss, il Cominform e il PCI (1943–1951)*. Rome: Carrocci, 1998.

Hajdu, Tibor, ed. *Károlyi Mihály levelezése V. 1945–1949* [Mihály Károlyi's correspondence V. 1945–1949]. Budapest: Napvilág Kiadó, 2003.

Hanebrink, Paul A. *In defense of Christian Hungary: religion, nationalism, and antisemitism, 1890–1944*. Cornell University Press, 2006.

Hatos, Pál. "József Kardinal Mindszenty (1892–1975): Divergierende Erinnerungen und die Perspektiven der vergleichenden Forschung." In Szabó, *József Kardinal Mindszenty in Wien*, 9–27.

Horváth, M. Ferenc. *Vác '56 – Vác 1956-ban és a megtorlás időszakában* [Vác '56: Vác in 1956 and during the period of retribution]. Vác: Váci Levéltár, 2006.

Hubai, László. "Viták és álláspontok a II. Magyar Köztársaságról" [Debates and positions on the Second Hungarian Republic]. *Múltunk* 50, no. 2 (2005): 203–20.

Huszár, Tibor, ed. *Bibó István (1911–1979): Életút dokumentumokban* [István Bibó (1911–1979): His life's journey in documents]. Budapest: 1956-os Intézet–Osiris–Századvég, 1995.

Illing, Robert F. *America and the Vatican: Trading Information After World War II*. Palisades, NY: History Publishing Company, 2011.

Ispánki, Béla. *Az évszázad pere: Megszólal a tanú. A Mindszenty-kirakatper ismeretlen adatai* [Trial of the century: The witness talks; Unknown data on the Mindszenty show trial]. With an epilogue by Hetényi Varga, Károly. Abaliget: Lámpás Kiadó, 1995. (1st ed. Toronto: Vörösváry, 1987.)

Izsák, Lajos and Miklós Kun, eds. *Moszkvának jelentjük: Titkos dokumentumok 1944–1948* [We report to Moscow: Secret documents, 1944–1948]. Budapest: Századvég, 1994.

Jakovina, Tvrtko. *Američki komunistički saveznik: Hrvati, Titova Jugoslavija i SAD 1945–1955* [America's Communist ally: Tito's Yugoslavia and the United States, 1945–1955]. Zagreb: Profil International, 2003.

Janek, István. "Mindszenty József tevékenysége a felvidéki magyarok megmentéséért 1945–1947 között" [József Mindszenty's efforts to save the Hungarians in Slovakia, 1945–1947]. *Századok* 142, no. 1 (2008): 153–81.

Jaszovszky, József. *Mindszenty, a főpásztor Észak-Kaliforniában* [Mindszenty, the chief pastor in Northern California]. Menlo Park, CA: Published by the author, 1980.

Judt, Tony. *Postwar: A History of Europe Since 1945*. New York: Penguin Press, 2005.

Kálmán, Peregrin. *Dokumentumok Grősz József kalocsai érsek hagyatékából 1956–1957* [Documents from the legacy of Archbishop Grősz of Kalocsa, 1956–1957]. Budapest: Szent István Társulat–Hamvas Béla Kultúrakutató Intézet, 2011.

Kaplan, Karel. *Stát a církev v Československu 1948–1953* [State and Church in Czechoslovakia, 1948–1953]. Brno: Doplněk, 1993.

Károlyi, Mihály. *Hit, illúziók nélkül* [Faith without illusions]. Budapest: Magvető Könyvkiadó, 1977.

Klestenitz, Tibor. *A katolikus sajtómozgalom Magyarországon 1896–1932* [The Catholic press movement in Hungary, 1896–1932]. Budapest: CompLex Kiadó, 2013.

Klimo, Arpad von. "Catholic identity in Hungary: The Mindszenty Case." *Hungarian Studies* 24, no. 2 (2010): 189–213.

———. "Kardinal Mindszentys Reisen 1971–1975: Die Reformulierung des Antikommunismus in Westdeutschland und in den USA in neuen Perspektiven." In Szabó, *József Kardinal Mindszenty in Wien*, 133–43.

Kókai, Károly. "Kardinal Mindszenty und die Wiener Emigration." In Szabó, *József Kardinal Mindszenty in Wien*, 81–90.

Konasov, B. and Tereshchuk, A. V. "Berija és a *malenkij robot*: Dokumentumok Ausztria, Bulgária, Magyarország, Németország, Románia, Csehszlovákia és Jugoszlávia polgári lakossága 1944–1945-ös internálásának történetéről" [Beria and the *malenkiy robot*: Documents on the history of the internment in 1944–1945 of the civilian population in Austria, Bulgaria, Hungary, Germany, Romania, Czechoslovakia, and Yugoslavia]. *Történelmi Szemle* 46, nos. 3–4 (2004): 345–402.

Körmendy, József. "Mindszenty József veszprémi püspök plébánia- és iskolaszervező munkája 1944–45-ben" [The work of József Mindszenty, bishop of Veszprém, in organizing parishes and schools, in 1944–45]. In *Ministerio: Nemzetközi történész konferencia előadásai 1995. május 24–26* [Ministerio: Papers of the International Conference of Historians, May 24–26, 1995], edited by István Bárdos and Margit Beke, 81–88. Esztergom: Esztergom-Budapesti Érsekség, Komárom-Esztergom Megye Önkormányzata, Kultsár István Társadalomtudományi és Kiadói Alapítvány, 1998.

———. "Mindszenty József veszprémi püspöki tevékenysége" [The work of József Mindszenty, bishop of Veszprém]. In *Mindszenty József emlékezete* [In Memory of József Mindszenty], ed. József Török. Budapest: Márton Áron Kiadó, 1995. 9–18.

Kothen, R., ed. *Documents Pontificaux de Sa Sainteté Pie XII 1948*. Paris: Éditions Labergerie, Louvain: Éditions Warny, 1950.

———. *Documents Pontificaux de Sa Sainteté Pie XII 1949*. Paris: Éditions Labergerie, Louvain: Éditions Warny, 1951.

Kovács, Éva. "A magyar közoktatásügy története 1945 és 1956 között (A magyar közoktatás-politika ideológiai változásai)" [History of Hungarian education in the period 1945–1956: Ideological changes in Hungarian education policy]. PhD dissertation, ELTE BTK, Budapest, 2003.

Kovács, Gergely. "Das Erbe des Pazmaneum: Das sachliche Vermächtnis des Kardinal Mindszenty." In Szabó, *József Kardinal Mindszenty in Wien*, 177–84.

———. "Isten szolgája, Mindszenty József tárgyi hagyatéka" [God's Servant, József Mindszenty's material legacy]. In *"Szenteltessék meg a Te neved..."* [Hallowed Be Thy Name...], edited by Viktor Attila Soós, 95–103. Lakitelek: Antológia Kiadó, 2012.

Kovács, Zoltán. "Hetyey Sámuel pécsi püspök (1897–1903)" [Sámuel Hetyey, bishop of Pécs (1897–1903)]. In *Egyházi arcélek a pécsi egyházmegyéből* [Ecclesiastical Profiles from the Diocese of Pécs], edited by Tamás Fedeles, Zoltán Kovács, and József Sümegi, 145–51. Pécs: Fény Kft., 2009.

Kuntár, Lajos. "Mindszenty József szombathelyi diákévei" [József Mindszenty's student years in Szombathely]. *Vasi Honismereti Közlemények* 19, no. 1 (1992): 7–16.

Lehnert, Sr. M. Pascalina. *Ich durfte Ihm dienen: Erinnerungen an Papst Pius XII*. 3rd ed. Würzburg: Verlag Naumann, 1983.

Lombardi, Lapo. *La Santa Sede e i cattolici dell'Europa Orientale agli albori della guerra fredda*. Roma–Budapest: Editrice Pontificia Università Gregoriana–METEM, 1997.

Lukács, László. "A Vigilia beszélgetése Franz König bíborossal" [*Vigilia*'s Interview with Cardinal Franz König]. *Vigilia* 57, no. 11 (1992): 849–54.

Magyar, Péter. "Magyar kommunista megnyilatkozások Mindszentyről a forradalom után" [Statements made after the revolution by the Hungarian Communists about Mindszenty]. *Katolikus Szemle* 17, no. 2 (1965): 179–84.

Magyarics, Tamás. "Az Egyesült Államok és Magyarország" [The United States and Hungary] *Századok* 130, no. 6 (1996): 571–608.

Major, Ákos. *Népbíráskodás – forradalmi törvényesség: Egy népbíró visszaemlékezései* [People's justice – Revolutionary legality: Recollections of a People's Judge]. Budapest: Minerva Kiadó, 1988.

Maróthy-Meizler, Károly. *Az ismeretlen Mindszenty: Életrajz és korrajz* [The unknown Mindszenty]. Buenos Aires: Editorial Pannonia, 1958.

Marton, Kati. *Enemies of the People: My Family's Journey to America*. New York: Simon & Schuster, 2009.

Máthé-Tóth, András. *A II. vatikáni zsinat és a magyar elhárítás: A Történeti Hivatalban fellelhető levéltári anyag alapján* [The Second Vatican Council and Hungarian counter-espionage: On the basis of archival sources available at the Historical Office]. www.vallastudomany.hu/Members/matetoth/vtmtadocs/m-ta_II_vatikani_zsinat

Melloni, Alberto, ed. *Il filo sottile: L'Ostpolitik vaticana di Agostino Casaroli*. Bologna: Il Mulino, 2006.

Mészáros, István. "Az 'első zászlósúr'-cím" [The Title of 'Knight Banneret']. In *"Állok Istenért, Egyházért, Hazáért": Írások Mindszenty bíborosról* [I stand for God, for the Church, and for the Country: Writings on Cardinal Mindszenty], 73–84. Budapest: METEM, 2000.

———. *Boldogasszony éve 1947/48: Mindszenty bíboros evangelizációs programja* [Year of the Virgin Mary, 1947/1948: Cardinal Mindszenty's evangelization program]. Budapest: Ecclesia, 1994.

———. "Juramentum non – Nincs eskü! Mindszenty veszprémi püspök írása 1944. november elejéről" [Juramentum non – No oath of allegiance! An article by Mindszenty, bishop of Veszprém, from early November 1944]. In *Mindszenty-mozaik: Írások a bíborosról*, 53–56. Budapest: Ecclesia, 2002.

———. "Mindszenty és Vas megye" [Mindszenty and Vas County]. *Vasi Szemle* 49, no. 3 (1995): 321–35.

———. *Mindszenty-mozaik: Írások a bíborosról* [Mindszenty mosaics: Writings about the Cardinal]. Budapest: Ecclesia, 2002.

———. *Prímások, pártok, politikusok: Adalékok a magyar katolikus egyház XX. századi történetéhez* [Primates, parties, and politicians, 1944–1945: Contributions to the 20th-Century history of the Hungarian Catholic Church]. Budapest: Szent István Társulat, 2005.

———. "Választás 1945 őszén" [The elections in the Fall of 1945]. In *Mindszenty-mozaik*: Írások a bíborosról, 69–126. Budapest: Ecclesia, 2002.

Mészáros, Tibor. *A száműzött bíboros szolgálatában: Mindszenty József titkárának napi jegyzetei (1972–1975)* [In the service of the exiled Cardinal: The daily notes of József Mindszenty's secretary, 1972–1975]. Abaliget: Lámpás Kiadó, 2000.

Mindszenty breviárium: A bíboros hercegprímás megnyilatkozásaival [Mindszenty breviary: With the views of the cardinal]. 3rd edition, Budapest: Magyarok Mindszenty

Mozgalma, 1998. On the Internet: http://www.ppek.hu/konyvek/Mindszenty_breviarium_1.pdf.

Mindszenty József a népbíróság előtt [József Mindszenty at the People's Court]. Budapest: Állami Lapkiadó, 1949. (Budapest: Pannon Kiadó, 1989.)

Mócsy, Imre S.J. *Hagytam magam szerettetni* [I let myself be loved]. Biblikus írások 8. Budapest: Szent Jeromos Katolikus Bibliatársulat, 2007.

Mózessy, Gergely. "Az 1956-ot követő megtorlás hatása Kisberk Imre püspök életútjára" [The impact of the retribution in the aftermath of 1956 on the life path of Bishop Imre Kisberk]. In *Magyar Katolikus Egyház 1956: A Lénárd Ödön Közhasznú Alapítvány évkönyve 2007*, edited by Csaba Szabó, 123–42. Budapest: Új Ember, 2006.

———. "Noteszlapok Shvoy Lajos fogságából" [Notes from Lajos Shvoy's captivity]. *Soproni Szemle* 60, no. 1 (2006): 26–32.

Nagy, Töhötöm. *Jezsuiták és szabadkőművesek* [Jesuits and Freemasons]. Buenos Aires: Danubio, 1965. Republished in Szeged: Szent Gellért Kiadó, 1990.

Németh, László. "VI. Pál és Mindszenty József 1971. október 23-án" [Paul VI and József Mindszenty on October 23, 1971]. *Vigilia* 63, no. 4 (1998): 247–52.

Németh, László Imre. *Mindszenty megvalósult álma: A Santo Stefano Rotondo és a Szent István Ház* [Mindszenty's realized dream: The Santo Stefano Rotondo and the House of Saint Stephen]. Budapest: Szent István Társulat, 2009.

———. *Zágon-leveleskönyv: Iratgyűjtemény-töredék Mindszenty József bíborosról, 1967–1975* [Zágon leaf-book: A fragmentary collection of documents on Cardinal József Mindszenty, 1967–1975]. Budapest: Szent István Társulat, 2011.

Nyisztor, Zoltán. *Vallomás magamról és kortársaimról* [A confession about myself and my contemporaries]. Rome: Magyar Ny. St. Gallen, 1969.

Olasz, Lajos. "A kormányzói jogkör" [The legal competences of the Regent]. In *A magyar jobboldali hagyomány, 1900–1948* [The Hungarian right-wing tradition, 1900–1948], edited by Ignác Romsics, 102–37. Budapest: Osiris Kiadó, 2009.

Ólmosi, Zoltán, ed. *Mindszenty és a hatalom: Tizenöt év az USA-követségen* [Mindszenty and the regime: Fifteen years at the US Embassy]. Budapest: Lex Kft., 1991.

Paksy, Zoltán. "Kisvárosi elit: Zalaegerszeg város virilisei 1873–1939" [Small town elite: The strongmen of Zalaegerszeg, 1873–1939]. In *Végvárból megyeszékhely: Tanulmányok Zalaegerszeg történetéből* [From a border fortress to a county seat: Studies on the history of Zalaegerszeg], edited by András Molnár, 169–94. Zalaegerszeg: Zala Megyei Levéltár, 2006.

———. *Zalaegerszeg társadalma és politikai élete 1919–1939* [Society and political life in Zalegerszeg, 1919–1939]. Zalaegerszeg: Millecentenáriumi Közalapítvány, 2011.

Pálffy, Géza. *A Magyar Királyság és a Habsburg Monarchia a 16. században* [The Kingdom of Hungary and the Habsburg Monarchy in the 16th century]. História Könyvtár, Monográfiák 27. Budapest: MTA Történettudományi Intézete, 2010.

Pallagi, Mária. "'Die Causa Mindszenty' in der Ostpolitik des Vatikans mit besonderer Berücksichtigung der Vermittlerrolle von Kardinal Franz König." In *Mediterrán tanulmányok: Études sur la région méditerranéenne*, XVII., 87–104. Szeged: Szegedi Tudományegyetem, 2008.

———. "Ein unerwünschter Gast" – Kardinal Mindszenty in der Amerikanischen Botschaft und die Besuche von Kardinal König (1956–1971) – Die Ostpolitik des Vatikans gegenüber Ungarn und der Fall Mindszenty." In *Österreich und Ungarn im Kalten Krieg*, edited by István Majoros, Zoltán Maruzsa, and Oliver Rathkolb, 373–405. Wien–Budapest: Institut für Zeitgeschichte–ELTE BTK Új- és Jelenkori Egyetemes Történeti Tanszék, 2010.

Perger, Gyula. "Mindszenty (Pehm) József tevékenysége a szombathelyi egyházmegyében, különös tekintettel a zalai kuráciák megszervezésére" [The activities of József Mindszenty (Pehm) in the Szombathely Diocese with particular focus on the establishment of the curacies in Zala]. PhD dissertation, Pázmány Péter Katolikus Egyetem, Budapest, 2007.

Perneki, Mihály, ed. *Shvoy Kálmán titkos naplója és emlékirata, 1918–1945* [The secret diary of Kálmán Shvoy, 1918–1945]. Budapest: Kossuth Kiadó, 1983.

Petrás, Éva. "'Álarcok mögött': Nagy Töhötöm élete" ['Behind masks': The life of Töhötöm Nagy] *Századok* 149, no. 1 (2015): 203–12.

Petróczi, Sándor. *Emlékek Pétery József püspökről [Memories of Bishop József Pétery]*. Compiled by József Török. Budapest: Szent István Társulat, 1997.

Pritz, Pál. *A Bárdossy-per* [The Bárdossy trial]. Budapest: Kossuth, 2001.

Puhan, Alfred. *The Cardinal in the Chancery and Other Recollections*. New York: Vantage Press, 1990.

Pünkösti, Árpád. *Rákosi a csúcson: 1948–1953* [Rákosi at the zenith of power: 1948–1953]. Budapest: Európa, 1996.

Rácz, Piusz. *Ferencesek az ország nyugati részén* [Franciscans in the western part of the country]. Zalaegerszeg: A Szűz Máriáról nevezett Ferences Rendtartomány kiadása, 2004.

Radelić, Zdenko. *Hrvatska u Jugoslaviji 1945. – 1991: Od zajedništva do razlaza* [Croatia in Yugoslavia, 1945–1991: From unity to split]. Zagreb: Hrvatski institut za povijest, Školska knjiga, 2006.

Radványi, János. *Hungary and the Superpowers: The 1956 Revolution and Realpolitik.* Stanford, CA: Hoover Press, 1972.

Rákosi, Mátyás. "A kievi borzalmak. 1944. március 2" [The Kiev atrocities, March 2, 1944]. In *A magyar jövőért* [For the Hungarian future]. Budapest: Szikra, 1945.

———. Építjük a nép országát [We are building the people's country]. Budapest: Szikra, 1949.

———. *Válogatott beszédek és cikkek* [Selected speeches and articles]. Budapest: Szikra, 1951.

———. *Visszaemlékezések 1940–1956* [Memoirs, 1940–1956]. Vol 2. Edited by István Feitl. Budapest: Napvilág Kiadó, 1997.

Rétfalvi, Balázs. "Czapik Gyula 1948-as római útja és az apostoli vizitáció ügye" [Gyula Czapik's journey to Rome in 1948 and the matter of the Apostolic Visitation]. *Egyháztörténeti Szemle* 12, no. 2 (2009): 3–38. www.uni-miskolc.hu/~egyhtort/cikkek/retfalvibalazs.htm

Rosdy, Pál, ed. *A katolikus Egyház 1956-ban* [The Catholic Church in 1956]. Budapest: Új Ember, 2006.

Saád, Béla. *Tíz arckép* [Ten portraits]. Budapest: Ecclesia, 1983.

Sági, György. "Egy katolikus főpap vívódásai: Hamvas Endre csanádi püspök és az államhatalom, 1961–1964" [Struggles of a Catholic Prelate: Bishop Hamvas of Csanád and the regime, 1961–1964]. *Egyháztörténeti Szemle* 14, no. 2 (2013): 63–82.

Salacz, Gábor. *A magyar katolikus egyház tizenhét esztendeje (1948–1964)* [Seventeen years of the Hungarian Catholic Church, 1948–1964]. Dissertationes Hungaricae ex historia Ecclesiae 9. München: Görres Gesellschaft, 1988.

Schreiber, Thomas. Életmorzsák [Crumbs of life]. Budapest: I.A.T., 2009.

Semjén, Zsolt. *Két pogány közt* [Between two heathens]. Budapest: Barankovics Alapítvány, 2013.

Sereda, T. and S. Stikalin, eds. *Sovetskiy Soyuz i vengerskiy krizis 1956 goda: Dokumenty* [The Soviet Union and the Hungarian crisis in 1956: Documents]. Moscow: ROSSPEN, 2008.

Sík, Endre. *Egy diplomata feljegyzései* [Notes recorded by a diplomat]. Budapest: Kossuth Könyvkiadó, 1966.

Silvestrini, Achille, ed. *L'Ostpolitik di Agostino Casaroli 1963–1989*. Bologna: Edizioni Dehoniane, 2009.

Sipos, Péter. *Imrédy Béla.* Budapest: Elektra Kiadóház, 2001.

Sipos, Péter and Vida, István. "Az 1945. augusztus 27-én megkötött szovjet–magyar egyezmény és a nyugati diplomácia" [The Soviet-Hungarian economic agreement of August 27, 1945 and Western diplomacy]. *Külpolitika* 12, no. 4 (1985): 102–18.

———. "Mindszenty József és az amerikai követség" [József Mindszenty and the US Embassy]. *História* 5, nos. 5–6 (1983): 42.

Somorjai, Ádám. *Ami az emlékiratokból kimaradt: VI. Pál és Mindszenty József, 1971–1975* [Omissions from the Memoirs: Paul VI and József Mindszenty, 1971–1975]. Pannonhalma: Bencés Kiadó, 2008.

———, ed. *"His Eminence Files." American Embassy Budapest: From Embassy Archives, 15 (1971) – Mindszenty bíboros az Amerikai Nagykövetségen. Követségi Levéltár 15 (1971).* Budapest: METEM, 2008. Second improved edition published in 2012.

———. "Il pensiero del cardinale Giuseppe Mindszenty circa il suo ruolo costituzionale e politico." *Rivista di Studi Ungheresi* (Roma) XXVI, N. S. 11 (2012): 69–95.

———, ed. *Mindszenty bíboros követségi levelei az Egyesült Államok elnökeihez, 1956–1971 – Letters to the Presidents: Cardinal Mindszenty to the Political Leaders of the United States, 1956–1971.* METEM, Budapest, 2011.

———. *Sancta Sedes Apostolica et Cardinalis Ioseph Mindszenty, II. Documenta 1956–1963. Az Apostoli Szentszék és Mindszenty József kapcsolattartása, II. Tanulmányok és szövegközlések.* Budapest: METEM, 2009.

———. *Sancta Sedes Apostolica et Cardinalis Ioseph Mindszenty, III/1. Documenta 1963–1966 – Az Apostoli Szentszék és Mindszenty József kapcsolattartása, III/1. Tanulmányok és szövegközlések.* Budapest: METEM, 2010.

———. *Sancta Sedes Apostolica et Cardinalis Ioseph Mindszenty, III/2. Documenta 1967–1971 – Az Apostoli Szentszék és Mindszenty József kapcsolattartása, III/2. Tanulmányok és szövegközlések.* Budapest: METEM, 2012.

———. *Sancta Sedes Apostolica et Cardinalis Ioseph Mindszenty. Documenta 1971–1975. – Az Apostoli Szentszék és Mindszenty József kapcsolattartása 1971–1975. Tanulmányok és szövegközlések.* Rome: Pro manuscripto, 2007.

———, ed. *The Cardinal Mindszenty Documents in American Archives: A Repertory of the six Budapest Mindszenty Boxes – Mindszenty bíboros budapesti amerikai követségi tartózkodásának dokumentumai: Repetórium.* The Cardinal Joseph Mindszenty Papers, Subsidia 1. Pannonhalma: Pannonhalmi Főapátság, 2012.

Somorjai, Ádám and Tibor Zinner. *Do Not Forget This Small Honest Nation: Cardinal Mindszenty to 4 US Presidents and State Secretaries 1956–1971 as conserved in American Archives and commented by American diplomats: A dokumentary overview.* Bloomington IN: Xlibris, 2013.

———. *Majd' halálra ítélve: Dokumentumok Mindszenty József élettörténetéhez* [Almost sentenced to death: Documents to the life of József Mindszenty]. Budapest: Magyar Közlöny Lap- és Könyvkiadó, 2008.
———. "Washingtonból jelentjük: A budapesti amerikai nagykövetség Mindszenty bíboros tevékenységére vonatkozó, 1971-ben keletkezett iratai" [We report from Washington: Papers from the US Embassy in Budapest on the activity of Cardinal Mindszenty in 1971]. *Századok* 144, no. 1 (2010): 143–96.
Soós, Viktor Attila. "Apor Vilmos és Mindszenty kapcsolata" [Vilmos Apor and József Mindszenty's relationship]. In *In labore fructus: Jubileumi tanulmányok Győregyházmegye történetéből* [In labore fructus: jubilee studies on the history of the Győr diocese], edited by Gábor Nemes and Ádám Vajk, 375–87. Győr: Egyházmegyei Levéltár, 2011.
———. "Mindszenty József a forradalom idején" [József Mindszenty at the time of the revolution]. In *A katolikus egyház 1956-ban*, edited by Pál Rosdy, 129–39. Budapest: Új Ember, 2006.
Stark, Tamás. *Magyar foglyok a Szovjetunióban* [Hungarian prisoners in the Soviet Union]. Budapest: Lucidus Kiadó, 2006.
———. "Magyarország háborús emberveszteségе" [Hungary's wartime human losses], II *Rubicon* 11, no. 9 (2000): 44–48.
———. *Magyarország második világháborús emberveszteségе* [Hungary's human losses in World War II]. Budapest: MTA Történettudományi Intézete, 1989.
Stehle, Hansjakob. *Die Ostpolitik des Vatikans 1917–1975*. Munich and Zurich: R. Piper und Co. Verlag, 1975.
———. *Geheimdiplomatie des Vatikans: Die Päpste und die Kommunisten*. Zürich: Benziger, 1993.
Stern, Samu. *Emlékirataim. Versenyfutás az idővel: A "zsidótanács" működése a német megszállás és a nyilas uralom idején* [My memoirs. Racing against time: The operations of the "Jewish Council" at the time of the German occupation and the rule of the Arrow Cross]. Hungarica Judaica 3. Edited by Gábor Ács. Budapest: Bábel Kiadó, 2004.
Šutaj, Štefan. *Maďarská menšina na Slovensku v rokoch 1945–1948 (Východiská a prax politiky k maďarskej menšine na Slovensku)* [The Hungarian minority in Slovakia, 1945–1948: The basis of practice and policy concerning the Hungarian minority in Slovakia]. Bratislava: Veda, 1993.

Szabó, Csaba. *A Szentszék és a Magyar Népköztársaság kapcsolatai a hatvanas években* [Relations between the Holy See and the People's Republic of Hungary in the 1960s]. Budapest: Szent István Társulat–Magyar Országos Levéltár, 2005.

———. Die katholische Kirche Ungarns bis zum Prozeß gegen József Kardinal Mindszenty. In *Im Räderwerk des "real existierenden Sozialismus": Kirchen in Ostmittel- und Osteuropa von Stalin bis Gorbatschow*, edited by Hartmut Lehmann and Jens Holger Schjørring, 41–64. Göttingen: Wallstein Verlag, 2003.

———, ed. *József Kardinal Mindszenty in Wien (1971–197)*. Publikationen der ungarischen Geschichtsforschung in Wien, vol. 4. Vienna: Institut für Ungarische Geschichtsforschung in Wien, 2012.

———, ed. *Magyar katolikus egyház 1956: A Lénárd Ödön Közhasznú Alapítvány évkönyve, 2007* [Hungarian Catholic Church 1956: The Yearbook for 2007 of the Lénárd Ödön Public Benefit Foundation]. Lénárd Ödön Közhasznú Alapítvány, Budapest: Új Ember, 2007.

Szakolczai, György and Róbert Szabó. *Két kísérlet a proletárdiktatúra elhárítására: Barankovics és a DNP 1945–1949, Bibó és a DNP 1956* [Two attempts to prevent a proletarian dictatorship]. Budapest: Gondolat, 2011.

Szántó, Konrád. *A kommunizmusnak sem sikerült: A magyar katolikus egyház 1945–1991* [Even Communism failed to do it: The Hungarian Catholic Church, 1945–1991]. Miskolc: Új Misszió Alapítvány, 1992.

———. *Az 1956-os forradalom és a katolikus egyház* [The 1956 Revolution and the Catholic Church]. Miskolc: Szt. Maximilian Kiadó, 1993.

Szathmáry, Béla. "Keresztény értékek az alkotmányozásban" [Christian values in constitutional Law]. In *Történelmi tradíciók és az új Alkotmány* [Historical traditions and the new Constitution], edited by András Téglás, 18–24. Budapest: Országgyűlés Alkotmányügyi, igazságügyi és ügyrendi bizottsága, 2011.

Szatucsek, Zoltán. "Makacs öregúr vagy nemzetmentő vátesz? Diplomáciai egyeztetések Mindszenty sorsáról 1970–1971-ben" [A stubborn old man or a national savior and soothsayer: Diplomatic negotiations on Mindszenty's fate in 1970–1971]. In *Közel-Múlt: Húsz történet a 20. századból* [Recent past: Twenty stories from the 20th century], edited by György Majtényi and Orsolya Ring, 20–35. Budapest: Magyar Országos Levéltár, 2002.

Szekeres, Márton. *Egy ujságiró kálváriája* [A journalist's calvary]. Budapest: Published by the author, n.d. [1927]

Szijártó, M. István. *A diéta: A magyar rendek és az országgyűlés 1708–1792* [The Diet: The Hungarian estates and the Diet, 1708–1792]. Keszthely: Balaton Akadémiai Kiadó, 2010.

Szűcs, László, ed. *Dálnoki Miklós Béla kormányának (Ideiglenes Nemzeti Kormány) minisztertanácsi jegyzőkönyvei 1944. december 23. – 1945. november 15* [Minutes of the Council of Ministers of the government of Béla Dálnoki Miklós (Provisional National Government), December 23, 1944 – November 16, 1945]. Budapest: Magyar Országos Levéltár, 1997.

———, ed. *Dinnyés Lajos első kormányának minisztertanácsi jegyzőkönyvei 1947, június 2. – szeptember 19* [Minutes of the Council of Ministers of Lajos Dinnyés's first government]. Edited with notes and an introduction by László Szűcs. Budapest: Magyar Országos Levéltár, 2000.

T. Horváth, Lajos, ed. *Mindszenty József veszprémi püspök 1944–1945* [József Mindszenty, bishop of Veszprém, 1944–1945]. Felolvasóülések Veszprém történetéből, 4. Veszprém: Veszprémi érsekség–Veszprém Megyei Jogú Város Önkormányzata–Laczkó Dezső Múzeum, 1996.

Tarján, Gábor. "Mindszenty József 1917–1945." PhD dissertation, Budapest: ELTE BTK, 1981.

Török, József, ed. *Grősz József kalocsai érsek naplója 1944–1946* [Diary of József Grősz, archbishop of Kalocsa, 1944–1946]. Budapest: Szent István Társulat, n. d.

———, ed. *Mindszenty József emlékezete* [In Memory of József Mindszenty]. Studia Theologica Budapestinensia, vol. 13. Budapest: Márton Áron Kiadó, 1995.

Tóth, Ágnes. *Telepítések Magyarországon 1945–1948 között* [Resettlement actions in Hungary, 1945–1948]. Kecskemét: Bács-Kiskun Megyei Önkormányzat Levéltára, 1993.

Tyekvicska, Árpád. "A bíboros útja: Mindszenty József kiszabadításának története" [The Cardinal's journey: The story of József Mindszenty's liberation]. In *Írások a forradalomról*, 105–156. Balassagyarmat: Stúdium Libra Bt.–Nógrád Megyei Levéltár, 2006. www.nogradarchiv.hu/data/files/206414719.pdf

———. *Írások a forradalomról* [Writings on the Revolution]. Balassagyarmat: Stúdium Libra Bt.–Nógrád Megyei Levéltár, 2006.

United Nations. *Official Records of the Third Session of the General Assembly. Part II. Plenary Meetings of the General Assembly. Summary Records of Meetings 5. April – 18. May 1949*. Lake Success, New York, n. d. [1949].

United Nations. *Official Records of the fourth session of the General Assembly. Plenary Meeting of the General Assembly. Summary Records of Meetings, 20 September – 10 December 1949.* Lake Success, New York, n. d. [1949].

Vadkerty, Katalin. *A kitelepítéstől a reszlovakizációig 1945–1948* [From resettlement to Re-Slovakization, 1945–1948]. Pozsony: Kalligram, 2007.

Vámos, György. "Itt a Szabad Európa Rádiója, a szabad Magyarország hangja" [This is Radio Free Europe, the voice of Free Hungary]. *Századok* 140, no. 5 (2006): 1163–233

Varga, Éva Mária. *Magyarok szovjet hadifogságban (1941–1956) az oroszországi levéltári források tükrében* [Hungarians in Soviet captivity as reflected in Russian archival sources]. Budapest: Russica Pannonica, 2009.

Varga, József. "Magyar Függetlenségi Párt" [The Hungarian Independence Party]. In *Jelenkori magyar történelmi dokumentumok IV.* [Contemporary Hungarian historical documents, 4], 44–68. Washington D.C.: Amerikai Magyar Kultúrközpont, 1988.

Varga, László, ed. *Kádár János bírái előtt: Egyszer fent, egyszer lent 1949–1956* [János Kádár before his judges: Up and then down, 1949–1956]. Budapest: Osiris Kiadó–Budapest Főváros Levéltára, 2001.

Vida, István. *A Független Kisgazdapárt politikája 1944–1947* [The policies of the Independent Smallholders' Party, 1944–1947]. Budapest: Akadémiai Kiadó, 1976.

———. "Bibó István kibontakozási tervezete, 1956. november 6." [István Bibó's plan of disentaglement, November 6, 1956]. *História* 8, no. 16 (1988): 15–16.

———, ed. *Iratok a magyar–szovjet kapcsolatok történetéhez 1944. október – 1948. június* [Documents on the history of Hungarian–Soviet relations, October 1944 – June 1948]. Budapest: Gondolat Kiadó, 2005.

Volokitina, T. V., G. P. Murashko, A. F. Noskova, and D. H. Nokhotovich, eds. *Vlasty i cherkov v Vostochnoy Evrope 1944–1953: Dokumenti rossiyskih arhivov, Tom 1, 1944–1948. Tom 2. 1949–1953* [Power and the Church in Eastern Europe, 1944–1953. Documents of the Russian Archives, vol. 1, 1944–1948, vol 2. 1949–1953]. Moscow: ROSSPEN, 2009.

Volokitina, T. V. et al., eds. *Vostochnaja Evropa v dokumentah rossiyskih arhivov 1944–1953, Tom 1, 1944–1948, Tom 2, 1949–1953* [Eastern Europe in the documents of the Russian Archives, 1944–1953, vol. 1, 1944–1948, vol 2. 1949–1953]. Moscow and Novosibirsk: Sibirskiy hronograf, 1997, 1998.

Vonyó, József. *Gömbös Gyula és a jobboldali radikalizmus: Tanulmányok* [Gyula Gömbös and right-wing radicalism: Studies]. Pécs: Pro Pannónia Kiadói Alapítvány, 2001.

———. *Gömbös Gyula.* Budapest: Napvilág Kiadó, 2014.
Vörös, Géza. "Die Beobachtung von József Mindszenty und die Methoden des Staatssicherheitsdienstes." In Szabó, *József Kardinal Mindszenty in Wien*, 101–13.
Wernz, P. Francisco Xavier, and P. Petri Vidal. *Jus canonicum, 2: De personis.* Rome: Apud Aedes Universitatis Gregorianae, 1943.
Zágon, József. "A magyar egyház helyzete az 1964-es megállapodás után" [The situation of the Hungarian Church after the 1964 Agreement]. *Távlatok* 73, no. 3 (2006): 314–33.
Zinner, Tibor. "Háborús bűnösök perei: Internálások, kitelepítések és igazoló eljárások 1945–1948" [The trials of war criminals: Internments, expulsions and screening procedures, 1945–1948]. *Történelmi Szemle* 28, no. 1 (1985): 119–40.

LIST OF PLATES

INDEX